Digital Illusion

Entertaining the Future
with High Technology

Clark Dodsworth Jr.
Contributing Editor

ACM Press • SIGGRAPH Series
New York, New York

ADDISON-WESLEY

An Imprint of Addison Wesley Longman, Inc.

Reading, Massachusetts • Harlow, England • Menlo Park, California
Berkeley, California • Don Mills, Ontario • Sydney • Bonn • Amsterdam
Tokyo • Mexico City

Library of Congress Cataloging-in-Publication Data

Digital illusion : entertaining the future with high technology /
    Clark Dodsworth Jr., contributing editor.
        p.   cm.—(SIGGRAPH series)
    Includes index.
    ISBN 0-201-84780-9
    1. Interactive multimedia.   2. Computer games—Programming.
    I. Dodsworth Jr., Clark.   II. Series.
    QA76.76.I59D55   1998
    794.8'16—DC20   96–5713
                                                                          CIP

ISBN 0-201-84780-9
Text printed on recycled acid-free paper.
1 2 3 4 5 6 7 8 9—MA—0100999897
First printing, July 1997

This copyright page continues on page 545.

For Janet Kelly Dodsworth, who taught me to pay attention.

Chapter 6   Networked Synthetic Environments: From DARPA to Your Virtual Neighborhood   115
Warren Katz

Chapter 7   VRML: Low-Tech Illusion for the World Wide Web   129
Tony Parisi

Chapter 8   You Are Hear: Positional 3D Audio   137
Scott Foster and Toni Schneider

PART 6 Trends in the Business of Entertainment Technology   439

Chapter 30 Coin-Op: The Life (Arcade Videogames)   443
Mark Stephen Pierce

Chapter 31 The Stories We Played: Building BattleTech and Virtual World   463
Jordan Weisman

Preface

Digital Illusion refers to the ancient art of crafting an experience in the listener's mind—but with new tools. My professional life, and that of the authors, involves the development and use of increasingly programmable tools for entertainment and communication. Every era's best creators take the tools at hand and push them to the limit. Perhaps the most far-reaching push occurred in 1876, when Richard Wagner darkened the audience and devised Bayreuth's hidden orchestra pit and double proscenium, all to enable lighting effects and heighten the illusion of depth on stage. Now we'd say he designed a more expressive user interface for his work, and we'd point to all the advances that built upon his innovations. We'd also say we've left many of our analog tools behind, perhaps having pushed them to their ultimate limits.

But the goal remains the same: to propel the imagination.

It's just the tools and techniques that change—and the audiences' expectations, the context of their lives within which we develop, tune, and deliver our offerings for their diversion. That context is faster-moving, more complex, more dynamic, more distracting, and more mediated by technology than ever. We give them the ageless stories with the technical and pop culture trappings of the moment, but we also have the occasional opportunity to devise something new. Sometimes our constantly evolving tools open up new ways to entertain or new ways for people to participate in their own entertainment. This book is about those ways.

We're in the midst of rapid speciation of both high technologies and ideas—a Jamesian blooming, buzzing confusion as beautiful, dangerous, and compelling in its own way as any equatorial rainforest. We use the variants and mutations to construct ever more nuanced interfaces between our audiences and their pleasure. Some of those interfaces will flourish, beginning a new cycle of speciation with each success. Along the way, we're beginning to custom-tailor the leisure experience for the individual, and all kinds of training and educational benefits are close behind. The tools of illusion allow us to express our unique visions ever more vividly. They will help some of our formerly passive audiences do the same. And, unavoidably, some of those people will dive into the worlds we build and never come back, a problem that grows as the illusions become more real.

This book is written by top practitioners in their respective fields who made time in their schedules to produce 35 chapters, each about a key aspect of the "entertainment beast" and its future. These extraordinary individuals are in position to see where change can occur in high-technology entertainment and to influence much of its course. Just as a stage magician develops new routines, the authors and their peers develop new means and memes of expression and delivery.

The Parts

In Part 1, we begin by establishing a context for the disciplines of high-tech entertainment. The first three chapters present its antecedents, recent history, and the critical fact that, at heart, it's a matter of the *interface*, which shapes both the entertainment experience and our perception. Each of us is in some sense an interface designer, and every facet counts, in all that we design.

Part 2 is about infrastructure—some of the enabling technologies that interactive applications ride upon. Much of it is based on work done for an $11-billion U.S. defense project known as SIMNET, coincidentally conceived about the same time as *Neuromancer*.

Part 3 deals with content design—how the designers put in the magic. Some of their techniques are ancient; others are only now being invented; all the technology is useless without them. This is the *how* of shaping and delivering an experience with the new design affordances we have and the ways they affect (or restrict) the user. There's more of this thinking on a grander scale in the special effects and theme park stories of Part 5.

Hardware can at last mean cost-effective interactive multimodal sensory displays, carefully integrated to more richly present our fictions. They're becoming more powerful and less obvious all the time, just as Arthur C. Clarke foretold. Part 4 describes some of the much-needed ways that the interface is evolving without a keyboard. It's overdue.

Part 5, Serious Fun, is where it seems all the money is spent—the $14-billion theme park industry. A budget of $70 million for the design and construction of a single attraction is not unique. And, when four million people visit it per year, it's money well spent. The most dramatic and effective high-tech illusions of our era are in theme parks. They push the limits of optics and the physiology of perception, using centuries-old theatrical gags folded within one-off implementations of new technology that are impossible to justify in any other context. It's an industry that must always top itself.

Part 6, the business perspective, describes how to operate a creative design facility and relates two seminal efforts at themed high-tech entertainment. It also has an insider's history and explanation of the arcade business—the original high-tech Location-Based Entertainment concept. Another chapter describes the situation and future of museums and cultural institutions; prior to World War II, they were a key part of our entertainment mix and innovators in experience design. There is also an excellent description of the requirements for economically viable online communities; they're coalescing as you read this and will be important transaction centers.

Tacit knowledge is the essence of craftsmanship. Each digital illusion we make is done with tools that are obsolete before we finish, making the refinements of virtuosity a rare pleasure—so much so that most high-tech entertainment experiences fall far short of justifying the resources expended. As interfaces improve for designers and users alike, so will the magic we jointly create. You can combine the elements and processes described here in myriad ways to develop wonderful experiences. Just follow the authors' example: Combine talent, years of practice and sweat, plenty of trial and error, a keen sense of fun, and a good idea. And ideas are cheap.

Clark Dodsworth Jr.
San Francisco

Acknowledgments

I want to thank the extraordinary authors, many of whom didn't have the time to write what they did, much less endure my efforts to make it fit within the context of the book.

I am indebted to the reviewers for their generous donation of time, advice, and reality checks: Brian Blau, Linda Branagan, Don Brutzman, haila darcy, Patricia Glovsky, Michael Harris, Farid Mamaghani, Jody Van Meter, Marney Morris, John Morrison, Judy Rubin, and Christopher Stapleton.

This book would not have happened without my extraordinary editor, Helen Goldstein, and the original impetus of Steve Cunningham. Additionally, several people contributed their expertise and support during the book's development, including Dona Aaron, Louis Brill, Diane Burns, Anthony Christopher, Nick Freeman, John Fujii, Peter Gordon, Kristin Kelleher, Ron Lichty, Jeff Mayer, Molly Morgan, David Pratt, Mary Rasmussen, Maggie Rawlings, John Whitney, Jr., and Michael Whitney.

I am deeply indebted to the following people, who saw where I was going over the years, and helped—by teaching, encouragement, or example: Ellen and Emmett Allen, John S. Banks, Lynne Anne Blom, Beverly Blossom, Mary Brinocar, Pat Brymer, Robert H. Caldwell, James W. Carey, Ray Caton, Coco Conn, Cathi Court, Tom DeFanti, Bill Deutsch, Jr., Terry Disz, Doris and JW Dodsworth, Rod and Putter Dodsworth, Paul Mark Evans, Robbert Flick, Norman Gambill, Linda Garland, Laure van Heijenoort, Roland W. Holmes, Nancy Moctezuma Hynes, Marilyn Johnson, Margaret S. Kelly, Myron Krueger, Mary Helen Leasman, Ruth Lowe, Howard Maclay, Diane Beck MacWilliams, Dan Martin, Manny Mendelson, Mike Miles, Ted Nelson, James Edward Newell III, Randy Nogel, Charles E. Osgood, Nam June Paik, Charles R. Peterson, Joe Pytka, Emil Radok and Josef Svoboda, Millie Riley, Steve Samler, Dan Sandin, Peter Sellars, Dianne and Stuart Selwood, Tim Settimi, Jaap Spek, Sherril Taylor, Bruce Vetter, Nina Vishnevska, Wolfgang Wagner, Dana Walden, Robert Ward, Jr., Jim Weisz, John Whitney, Rita Winters, and Lydia Wozniak.

Picasso with flashlight. An example of a well-designed user-interface system, applied here to gestural communication. Time exposure plus flash, by Gjon Mili, January 30th, 1950, *Life Magazine,* copyright © Time, Inc.

PART 1

Context: Evolution of the Tools

Same as it ever was.

Talking Heads, "Remain in Light"

At its best, interface is indistinguishable from entertainment, a goal that tends to grow more difficult as we add technology. This is not a failure of technology—it's a mark of the human fascination for new tools, with or without the skill to wield them effectively. Picasso's performance with the flashlight took perhaps 5 seconds and communicates immediately in any language; this is partly the result of a good user interface. It's ubiquitous, easy to learn, works in either hand for 2D and 3D, and requires no configuration for the user, the platform, or the medium. It doesn't get in your way, and, most importantly, its expressiveness scales effortlessly with one's skill.

In 30 years we've put thousands of powerful and expensive digital tools into the hands of a growing number of skilled entertainment specialists—designers and artists. In fact, we keep reinventing the same tools every few years, based on newer, more expressive technologies. Each time, powerful functions become easier and more fluid, and new functions become available. For the most part we use these tools to continue doing the same kinds of entertainment but with higher-quality illusions.

The digital tools have evolved sufficiently—and plummeted in price—to enable their diffusion throughout the culture. We're on the brink of putting extremely powerful low-cost tools into the home—for quick online production of graphics, audio, video, and 3D animated extravaganzas. When that happens, we will see the equivalent of dialects and linguistic drift emerge in animation and experience design. Every user can be both creator and distributor; personal multicasting becomes standard, without the requirement of any composition or communication design skills. The result will be twofold: Mountains of bad collage will clog the Internet, and a few magnificently talented individuals will emerge who, like Jimi Hendrix, single-handedly define new genres—

1

multimodal, distributed-context, heteromorphic—and who are indispensable to the future of entertainment.

I'm particularly interested in the tools and techniques that make illusions we couldn't do before, that allow collaboration in the process of creation, or that enable more people to become active in their play. Two of the authors in Part 1 have made careers of this. Dan Sandin has been inventing his own systems since 1969—first, interactive physical environments; then, graphics computers and interfaces for live performance in the 1970s; fully immersive stereoscopic environments in the 1980s; and linking them for collaboration in the late 1990s. Since 1982, David Rokeby has been inventing systems with extraordinary human interfaces that are on display and in collections on four continents. He explains how we evolve *with* our most used interfaces and how they inherently shape our perceptions and our culture, quite apart from the content they convey. The third author, Walt Bransford, is a software developer, historian, and student of architecture. He visits the birthplace of high-technology entertainment, world's fairs, where entrepreneurs made sure the attendees were amazed by the latest illusions. Expensive tricks became pervasive, profitable, culture-shaping tools, just like today.

Chapter 1

Digital Illusion, Virtual Reality, and Cinema

Daniel J. Sandin
Electronic Visualization Laboratory, The University of Illinois at Chicago

Introduction

The earliest publicly released silent films were often short, sensationalistic "special effects," such as a train driving straight toward the audience. That startling effect was produced by introducing a perceptual modality that had not been experienced before in the theatrical context. The experience of the audience depended more on engaging the motion detection apparatus of our perceptual system than on their intellectual understanding of the scene. When any large object approaches the viewer, motion on the retina of the eye flows from the center toward the edges. This is a very direct experience. It requires neither empathy with a character nor narrated descriptions of the context to elicit a quick reaction. In the century that followed, filmmakers invented ways to communicate more subtle emotions through myriad techniques besides visual motion, but this early trick still has considerable power. Virtual reality (VR) technology enables a direct first-person experience to a much greater degree than any previous medium. Merging VR technology with cinematic technique makes available to the creator and consumer new experiences communicated by new perceptual modalities. This chapter addresses some key issues of the merger.

The popular media would have you believe that VR is a new thing, having first appeared in the late 1980s. However, in 1965, Ivan Sutherland published the paper "The Ultimate Display," which outlined the goals of VR. More importantly, D. L. Vickers demonstrated a display device that incorporated most of the properties of modern VR systems in 1970. VR is not new; it represents the growing edge of the field of interactive 3D computer graphics, which has been developing since the invention of the computer. After 30 years of development, 3D computer systems can finally produce images of sufficient complexity and with sufficient speed to enable a broad range of interactive expression.

I first became inspired to pursue electronic visual kinetic experiences when I saw "Off/On," a video-film by Scott Bartlett, in 1968. I began making interactive digital illusions in April of 1969. Jerry Erdman, Myron Krueger, Burt Levy, and I developed a computer-controlled gallery installation called "Glowflow" at the University of Wisconsin at Madison. The gallery was completely dark and had several clear plastic tubes that were filled with phosphorescent fluid and attached to the walls, circling the perimeter. At the corners of the room and the centers of the walls, the tubes briefly entered eight floor-to-ceiling columns containing switchable directional audio sources and hidden lights for "charging" the fluid phosphors. In the floor was an array of pressure-sensitive pads associated with the light columns. A Moog Model 2 audio synthesizer and all the other elements were controlled by a LINC 8 computer made by Digital Equipment Corporation. The LINC 8 was designed to run experiments in laboratories by providing inputs for measurement instruments and supplying outputs to control the test apparatus. The system sensed the positions of people in the room and used that information to synthesize and place sounds and music while it also manipulated the pulsed patterns of phosphorescent light flowing through the space.

We were surprised to see the installation immediately develop long lines and a set of repeating visitors. In designing interactive systems, it's very important that the participants quickly realize they have control and understand what the parameters of that control are. One of our design decisions was to allow only a small number of visitors in at a time so that the effects of their actions would not be randomized by too many footsteps. Upon entering, users learned simple relationships between their actions and the patterns of light and sound in the room. Then, as people tested their theories of control over the environment, we made the patterns and relationships more complex and global. Glowflow and other interactive environments, developed by artists and scientists in the late 1960s, came upon many of the problems and solutions common to contemporary interactive design.

History

In the 1960s and early 1970s, "calligraphic" or vector displays were dominant. They operated by drawing an image on a CRT, scanning an electron beam with the same movements you would do to draw an image on paper with a pencil (Figure 1.1, left). The calligraphic image would fade away and have to be redrawn 20 or 30 times a second. An interesting feature of these systems is that it was almost as easy to draw a different image each time as it was to draw the same image. In other words, interactive graphics was almost as easy as static graphics. Current technology uses raster scan, moving the electron beam in a series of horizontal lines, one below the other, filling the screen with

 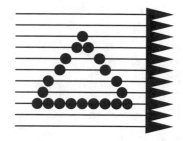

Figure 1.1 *Left:* In a calligraphic display, the computer draws in an order that is the same as a human would draw. *Right:* In a raster display, the scan pattern is independent of image content. The image is made visible by intensifying the drawing beam in the places where there is image content. Standard television uses raster scan.

a motion that is similar to the way your eyes scan this page of text (Figure 1.1, right).

Early in the history of computing (say, the late 1960s and early 1970s), computer graphics was very interactive. Systems were developed that allowed the real-time manipulation of two- and three-dimensional models. Because the display was limited to a small number of line segments, it had a low degree of realism and visual complexity. The images were schematic in nature, lacking the kind of realism associated with cinema and photography. Figure 1.2 shows a calligraphic display with its interactive control devices, including dials and buttons.

By the late 1970s, frame buffers were replacing calligraphic displays, and computer graphics stopped moving. More precisely, computer graphics stopped being interactive. Raster graphics systems have a large amount of memory associated with the frame buffer, which holds the image. If one wants to move an image that covers most of the screen, one has to copy most of the memory in the buffer from one place to another. It's no longer as easy to change the image as it is to leave it static. The appeal of raster (frame buffer) graphics was improved image quality. Single, static computer images could potentially look as good as photographs or television.

In this new raster-based method, motion in computer graphics could only be accomplished via frame-by-frame animation. Each frame of the animation was computed, displayed, and recorded onto film or videotape. This mode of motion computer graphics, which threw away interaction and gained realism, completely dominated computer graphics production and research until the late 1980s. With the development of computer workstations with specialized geometry processors, interactive 3D computer graphics reemerged.

Figure 1.2 A 1976 Vector General calligraphic display with dials, buttons, and force-feedback dials used for interaction.

So there was a period of over ten years when interactive 3D computer graphics was very difficult and expensive. This historical description is a simplification based largely on my experience as an artist trying to do interactive three-dimensional environments. There were notable exceptions. Early video games, such as Gorf, utilizing specialized hardware, allowed interaction by moving small areas of the frame buffer, known as sprites, around the screen. Paint systems such as NYIT PAINT (1974) allowed interaction by rewriting even smaller areas of the screen, that is, with brushes under the control of an artist. Flight simulators accomplished the goal by commandeering massive resources, namely, the defense budget. One means of generating a moving portion of an image, used in high-end flight simulators, was to actually project a second image (like an enemy plane) from a video projector mounted on a motion base.

Computer graphics stopped moving when it got caught up in the search for the holy grail of realism. Computer graphics workers traded off all interactivity for making the display more photo-realistic, that is, simulating the process of a photographic camera. Realism is a seductive goal that painters were pursuing until long after the invention of the camera. Photographers have been seduced by it until very recently. For computer graphics researchers, realism was particularly seductive. One could easily verify progress by comparison with photographs, and physics provided highly reliable models for how light interacts with matter. All one had to do was understand the physics, invent efficient algorithms to simulate the physics, and code those methods into a computer language. Physics also provided guides to the behavior of systems over time, such as water waves, colliding automobiles, wiggling Jell-O, rocket exhaust, fire, clouds, and waving grass. This process continued to incorporate new mathematic techniques, like fractals, to simulate geometric complexity and dynamical systems. Then, physics combined with biology to simulate walking, running, and the movement of living things. These research directions will continue to produce more stunning, more photo-realistic images; the same pursuit of realism is now being applied to the production of 3D environments. One of the major costs of this direction has again been interaction and realtime motion.

In the late 1980s, computer graphics began to actually move again because some of the simplest physical models of light's interaction with matter and basic geometric operations had been built into pipelined hardware. These frame buffer systems had some degree of realism, having cast into silicon the most efficient rendering methods of the previous decade. Most images looked like they were glued together from sheets of cardboard or matte plastic. They didn't cast shadows or have textures or transparency, but they did move! So after more than 15 years of hiatus, we could combine the innovations of interactive calligraphic displays with modest realtime rendering techniques on raster displays. This combination made possible early VR systems that would capture the world's attention.

All the research into static-image photo-realism is modeled on how photographic and video cameras work. This is not the same as trying to make an environment real to the human perceptual system. Interactive 3D computer graphics and VR define realism differently. They essentially rely on the fact that our understanding of the world is very dependent on our activity in the world. We usually determine what something is by interacting with it—looking at it from different viewpoints, picking it up, or kicking it. Whether something seems real or not doesn't just depend on whether it simulates the way light bounces around the room, but whether it simulates correctly how the object and the environment respond to our activities.

Another major difference between camera reality and human reality is that cameras typically don't support many of the perceptual channels of information that a person processes. A good story illustrating how badly our tools support our perceptual capabilities was told by Bill Buxton in 1986.

To paraphrase the story, imagine that in the distant future a group of alien anthropologists have dug up a twentieth-century computer room long buried by a mudslide. They're looking at one of our standard interactive computer graphics systems and are trying to figure out what kind of species could have used it. It's got a mouse; it's got a screen; it's got a keyboard. What would that say about the species that designed the system? First of all, the species must have had only one eye (with maybe a second eye for backup). That is, of course, based on the fact that our computer displays are monoscopic. The second thing they would probably conclude is that this species had no ears or maybe one tin ear, because most of our computer systems have no sound or very low fidelity, monaural sound. The anthropologists would also probably conclude that we have tunnel vision, because our computer displays typically support a 40-degree angle of view. And they would conclude that we have no feet, no legs, no tactile sense, no nose, and maybe 100 fingers. If you look at our computer systems or other media such as TV or cinema that way, you can see how badly matched our tools are to our perceptual and effector systems!

Our visual system has an angle of view larger than 180 degrees without rotating the head and a full sphere with head movement. We have two-eyed vision, and a sizable chunk of our brain is devoted to processing those two viewpoints in order to directly calculate the distance to objects viewed. Our brain knows that if the two images from the two eyes are the same, the world is stuck on a plane. We can hear and feel sounds from below 16 Hz to above 20,000 Hz. We can also accurately sense the direction of a sounding object over the full sphere. In addition, sound gives us information about the space enveloping the listener: how large it is, whether it has hard or soft surfaces, how big a slamming door is and what material it's made of. Touch, smell, and taste are harder to quantify and are not supported well by current media. Mort Heilig's Sensorama Theater, designed in 1960, was the first well-thought-out effort to address most of the senses systematically. Contemporary VR systems attempt to address our visual and aural perceptual systems and sometimes include our vestibular system.

It's quite inaccurate to think of our perceptual systems as passive receivers. To see or hear better, we move around, getting different perspectives on the world. We manipulate objects to best perceive them and to see their relationships to other parts of the environment. A profound example of this phenomenon is that if the eyes are prevented from scanning an image, by paralysis of eye muscles or by a retinal-stabilized image created by mounting a projector on a contact lens, the image *fades out*. Many optical illusions depend on presentations that don't allow viewers to disambiguate the image by changing their viewpoint (Figure 1.3).

An analysis of the technologies employed by VR systems to better match the human perceptual and effector systems can form a definition of VR. One of the important characteristics of our normal perceptual system that is not supported by conventional computer displays is a large angle of view. There are a

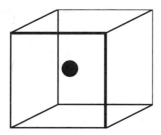

Figure 1.3 Is the darker square in back or in front? Is the dot in the plane of the darker square or the lighter square? In the real world and in VR, the motion of the viewer would disambiguate this optical illusion.

couple of ways to get large angles of view. One is to move closer to the screen (Figure 1.4, left). If you move very close to a screen, a magnifying glass needs to be added so that you can focus on the screen (Figure 1.4, right). There are diminishing returns as one gets very close, as the picture elements near the center get very large and the angle of view does not increase much. The magnifying lens can be replaced by a fish-eye lens to increase the angle to match the eyes' angle of view, and an acceptable but distorted image is typically produced (Figure 1.5).

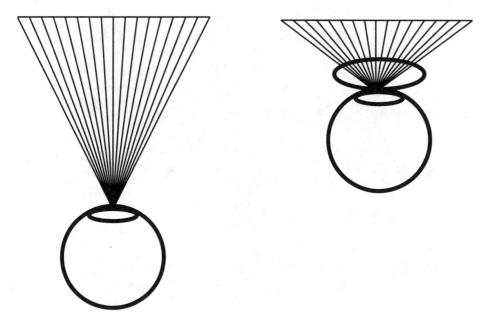

Figure 1.4 *Left and right:* As the viewer approaches the screen, the angle of view increases. If the viewer is very close to a small screen, a magnifying lens is required to focus on the screen.

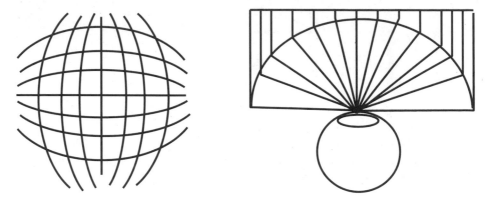

Figure 1.5   Large angles of view can be implemented with a fish-eye lens. The BOOM and many HMDs use this technique. *Left:* A uniform grid distorted by a fish-eye lens. *Right:* A side view of the eye, fish-eye lens, and display screen. (See Figure 1.7 for front view.)

Figure 1.6   Head-Mounted Display (HMD): In the public mind, HMDs are synonymous with VR. In this system, the display screens are carried on the viewer's head. Because of the weight and size restrictions, the resolution and angle of view are among the lowest of VR display systems.

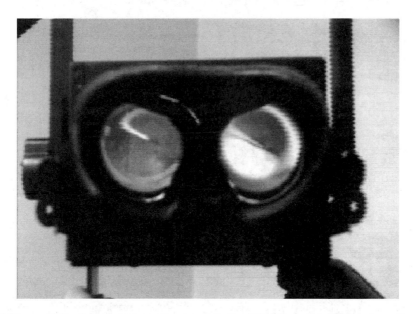

Figure 1.7 Looking down the lenses of a BOOM: In this VR system, the display screens are supported by a boom, allowing for heavier and hence higher resolution and higher angle-of-view displays. The participant uses them like a pair of binoculars to look into the virtual world.

Two VR devices, a head-mounted display (HMD) and a Binocular Omni-Orientation Monitor (BOOM), are shown in Figure 1.6 and Figure 1.7, respectively.

Another approach is used in the CAVE Automatic Virtual Environment (CAVE), where the user is surrounded by multiple screens (Figure 1.8 and Figure 1.9).

The ImmersaDesk (IDESK) achieves large angle of view by placing the viewer close to a large, high-resolution screen (Figure 1.10 and Figure 1.11).

Another important characteristic not supported by conventional computer displays is stereo vision. To do stereo, one has to get a different image to each of two eyes. HMDs or BOOMs use two screens, one in front of each eye (Figure 1.7). In the case of the CAVE, IDESK, or a monitor display, the viewer wears a set of glasses that, by various techniques, allows for time-multiplexing different images into different eyes. The particular system used is LCD shutter glasses (Figure 1.12). These glasses blink transparent and opaque, alternating between eyes. The display is synchronized so that when the left eye's image is being displayed on the screen, the left eye's shutter is clear, and when the right eye's image is being displayed, the right eye's shutter is clear. The switching between views is fast enough that the image appears to be continuous.

Figure 1.8   Diagram of CAVE Automatic Virtual Environment (CAVE) with projectors, screens, and mirrors: The CAVE achieves wide angle of view by surrounding the participant with large projected images. The three walls are rear projected, and the floor is front projected from above. The CAVE was developed at the Electronic Visualization Laboratory (EVL) at the University of Illinois at Chicago (UIC).

Figure 1.9   An artist immersed in a virtual world in the CAVE.

Figure 1.10   The ImmersaDesk (IDESK) is a single-screen, projection-based VR system developed at the Electronic Visualization Laboratory at the University of Illinois at Chicago.

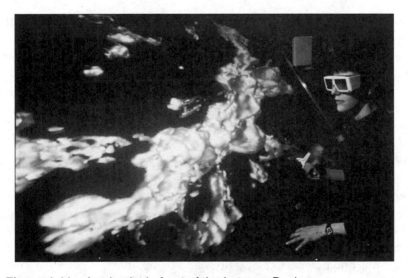

Figure 1.11   A scientist in front of the ImmersaDesk.

Figure 1.12   Dan Sandin wearing LCD shutter glasses: The small white cube above the head is the tracking receiver that tells the computer where the participant is in space.

The most exciting thing about VR is that it redefines perspective. It's the first redefinition of perspective since the Renaissance. It's sometimes called viewer-centered perspective or first-person perspective. Renaissance perspective is well illustrated by Dürer's print "The Designer of the Lying Woman" (Figure 1.13). Here, the draftsman sights through a grid to calculate the position of different parts of the model when projected onto a plane. Figure 1.14 shows a schematic diagram of the process. We tend to forget the obelisk at the eye of the draftsman; Renaissance perspective is correct from only one point of view. To carry out this kind of projection, you need to hold your eye in a particular spot; if you move your eye, the image changes. Photography, film, and conventional computer graphics use this kind of perspective. The only real problem is that you're never at the position for which the projection was calculated, so you're always getting incorrect perspective. We've become very good at reading that incorrect perspective. It's a skill learned by looking at lots of photographs and perspective drawings and being able to infer the correct rela-

Figure 1.13 "The Designer of the Lying Woman" by Albrecht Dürer, illustrating the perspective projection: User-centered perspective or first-person perspective is a defining feature of VR. It is the first redefinition of perspective since the Renaissance.

tionship of objects in the scene. For a photograph, the perspective would be correct if you were squared up with the center of the photograph at exactly the right distance. In order to do that, you would need to know at least the focal length of the camera lens and, combining that with the size of the photograph, calculate your placement. From a practical point of view, you're almost always at the wrong position. This means the perspective used by all of our media (outside of carefully designed VR) is incorrect.

Viewer-centered perspective is calculated the same as Renaissance perspective with the addition of constantly updating the viewpoint based on where the viewer's eyeballs are. To do this, the computer needs to know where you are in the scene. That enables a viewer in the VR system to see the left side of an object when he or she is positioned to the left of the object and the right side of an object when positioned to the right. There are many different tracking methods based on light, sound, mechanical linkages, or

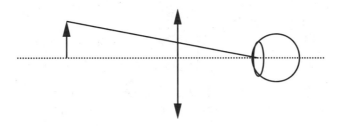

Figure 1.14 A schematic side view of the perspective projection.

electromagnetic radiation. The BOOM pictured in Figure 1.15 uses mechanical tracking by measuring the angles of the BOOM's joints. Another system, used in the CAVE, is pictured in Figure 1.16. The large 12-inch cube is the antenna transmitting an electromagnetic signal; the small cube on the headband is receiving the signal. This system returns the position and orientation of the receiving antenna. Orientation information is also needed to accurately calculate the position of the eyeballs because the receiver is mounted several inches from the eyes.

Good sound can make a profound difference to the illusion of reality or "being there." Hearing is omnidirectional; it operates in all directions, while our sight operates only in the hemisphere where we are looking. We can readily take advantage of this in VR applications using either of two different directional sound techniques: speaker arrays and binaural sound. Stereo is an example of a speaker array system that operates in one dimension, on a line be-

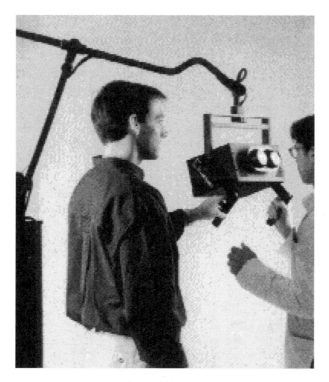

Figure 1.15   Users with a BOOM: The position of the viewpoint is calculated by knowing the length of the boom arms and measuring the angles of the joints.

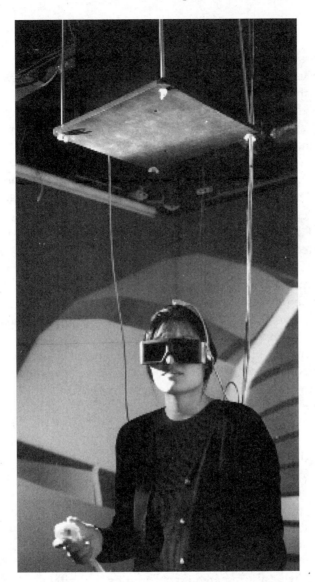

Figure 1.16 CAVE VR apparatus (shutterglasses, two-part head-tracker system, 3D wand, cables, and rear-projection screens): The large 12-inch cube is the antenna transmitting an electromagnetic signal, and the small cube on the headband is receiving the signal. This system returns the position and orientation of the receiving antenna. This information is necessary to calculate viewer-centered perspective.

tween the two speakers. Four speakers arranged in a square surrounding the viewer can support directional sound in two dimensions, right, left, front, and back. Speakers above and below could add another dimension, up and down. The CAVE uses an array of four speakers. Binaural sound is delivered by earphones. One might think that this gives sound along only one dimension like stereo, but if the sound is computed to include the filtering properties of the human head and ears, dramatic directional sound effects are possible. Many people use binaural sound in conjunction with HMDs.

Tactile or force feedback is one of the most difficult and misunderstood areas of VR. It, like many of the "advanced" areas of VR, has a long history. In 1976, Kent Wilson wrote a paper titled "Computing with Feeling," where he outlined a force-feedback ball suspended by four wires. In the same year, Tom DeFanti and I developed force-feedback dials. Although there is nothing nearly as sophisticated as the force-feedback systems of the Star Trek Holodeck, there are some effective limited force-feedback systems. Steering wheels that feed back a sense of the road's interaction with the tires are used in videogames and driving simulators. There are other specialized devices, such as a force-feedback scalpel for medical simulation. One is able to grasp a scalpel handle and feel realistic simulations of cutting skin and running into bone. It has a limited range of motion but can give important feedback clues. Motion platforms are an important element in flight simulators. They are mechanical devices that tip, rotate, move, and shake the pilot to simulate the accelerations encountered in flight. In the entertainment arena, these devices come in a variety of scales, seating from 1 to 60 people. Probably the biggest gap between the Star Trek Holodeck and current VR systems is in the area of force and tactile feedback. There's no indication that there will soon be a good simulation of a contact sport such as football. VR is a great place to design a chair, but you can't sit in it.

VR, as it currently exists, is best at delivering sight and sound. Adding touch, smell, and taste, one has the grade-school list of five human perceptual systems. Smell is being worked on and is used to good effect in a few top theme park attractions, like "Kongfrontation" and T2-3D at Universal Studios. I don't know of any VR work being done on taste. This list provides a basis for thinking about what VR research is contributing to digital illusions.

Interaction is central to the illusion of reality in VR. If your interaction with a modeled object is not similar to the way that object responds in the real world, the model isn't perceived as real. Viewer-centered perspective is one form of interaction. As you move around an object, you see different sides of it; if you walk around a picture of an object, you don't see its different sides. Objects in the world always respond to forces. Models in VR might respond to gravity, bounce when they fall, or get knocked out of the way when you bump into them. They often respond to your activity. For this reason, VR researchers talk about worlds instead of objects or models, implying that the models have

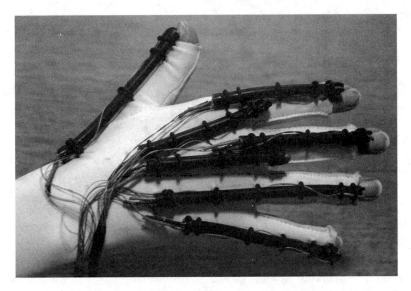

Figure 1.17 The Sayre Glove was developed by Tom DeFanti, Dan Sandin, and Richard Sayre in 1976. The black tubes measure the angle of the joints so that the computer can recreate the hand in a virtual environment.

behaviors in addition to geometry. Behavior doesn't stop with physics. One can imagine simulating pets, people, and societies, as is being done in several online 3D social/recreational experiments now.

Interaction implies input, but in VR, keyboards and mice don't work well. With an HMD, you can't see a keyboard or mouse anyway. The participant, no longer a passive viewer, is often standing up and walking about. Two common input devices are gloves (Figure 1.17) and wands (Figure 1.18). Both use a position and orientation tracker; the glove also measures joint angle. With such input devices, VR allows for more physical interaction than a traditional computer environment, movies, or TV. The participant interacts by moving objects around, picking them up, operating them, pointing in a direction, and flying there.

The ImmersaDesk (IDESK)

The design of the IDESK and its subsystems makes it an effective VR environment that is significantly different from other VR delivery systems. The IDESK is projection-based and supports viewing by small groups (Figure 1.19). The screen is large and close to the participants, producing a large angle of view. If one looks at the center of the screen, one doesn't see the edges; the feeling of immersion is strong. The screen is tilted at 45 degrees, similar to a drafting

Figure 1.18   The wand is a three-dimensional version of the mouse or tablet. It has three buttons and a joystick. A tracking receiver, the same kind that is used for head position, is shown.

table, which allows one to look forward and see things from the side or look down to see things from above. If one looks left or right, the illusion of immersion is lost, but the other people in the group who are sharing the experience can be seen. This feature is extraordinarily important because superimposition of the real and virtual worlds is essential to facilitate human-to-human sharing of information while we experience the virtual world. It's difficult to overemphasize this point; small groups sharing information are central to science, design, education, sales, and many modes of play and entertainment.

Figure 1.19   Sharing the VR experience is a natural part of projection-based VR systems such as the IDESK.

Projection-based systems have several advantages. Most importantly, they don't encumber a participant by covering up the eyes with a typically heavy helmet. In HMD systems, the participant is cut off from the real world; you often need another person to make sure you don't fall or get tangled in cables. You're cut off from other people in the environment and from your own hands and feet. In the IDESK, the participant wears only LCD shutter glasses with an Ascension Technologies Space Pad receiving antenna mounted on a band attached to the glasses (Figure 1.12). The stereo glasses are comparable in size and weight to a good pair of sunglasses.

The glasses have a large angle of view, about 90 degrees per eye, and are synchronized by an infrared signal (similar to your TV remote control) from emitters located near the screen. The emitters can synchronize glasses for several people seeing the same stereo image. When the computer is displaying the left eye's image, the infrared emitter signals the left lens of the glasses to become transparent and the right lens opaque. When the subsequent frame is displayed, this process is repeated for the right eye. The system supplies 96 images per second, 43 per eye per second. This "field-sequential" method has excellent separation between left- and right-eye views. Using viewer-centered perspective, each eye's image is computed for that eye's exact location. The stereo here is personal for the person being tracked. Other participants see stereo, but from the tracked person's perspective.

Head tracking is necessary for calculating viewer-centered perspective. The computer has to know where you are to calculate your personal perspective on the virtual world. For head tracking, an electromagnetic signal emitted by the Space Pad antenna (placed above the projection screen) is received by an antenna mounted on the stereo glasses (Figure 1.12). This electromagnetic system has an advantage over optical and sonic systems in not being blocked by body parts. It's easy and common to put your hand in front of your face when grasping objects in the virtual environment, while doing so can block the signal from optical or sonic tracking systems.

The wand (Figure 1.18) is the primary device for interaction with the IDESK virtual environment. It's the 3D analog of a 2D tablet or mouse. The wand has three buttons and another Space Pad receiver, identical to the one used in head tracking. This receiver reports to the computer the position and orientation of the wand in 3-space. With the wand, it's easy to grab and reposition an object in the virtual world by placing the wand near the object and pushing a button. We've found it easier to use a wand than a data glove for most operations. People are very experienced at using instruments such as a screwdriver or pliers to manipulate the world and less experienced with instrumented gloves. The wand in the virtual world is a generalized version of a hand tool or instrument.

Sound for the IDESK is generated by a Silicon Graphics Indy workstation running the Sound Server program developed by the Virtual Environments group at the National Center for Supercomputer Applications and the Electronic Visualization Laboratory at the University of Illinois at Chicago (UIC). This workstation is networked to the graphics computer to synchronize the visual displays with the audio. Directional sound is supplied by an array of four speakers. Controlling the direction of sound is very important in enveloping the participant in the virtual experience. In addition to playing back samples of sound, the sound server has several synthesis engines controlled by the same program that generates the graphic images, putting sound and image control at the same level. This is particularly important in making the sound as responsive as the imagery. It always amazes me how dead VR environments can be without sound.

The computer graphics system in the IDESK is usually an SGI Onyx computer with a Reality Engine or an SGI Maximum Impact. Although any computer that supports field-sequential stereo could be used, the quality (hence expense) of the computer is the most important component (after content) in determining the quality of the VR experience. To support viewer-centered perspective, the computer must recalculate the scene as the head moves. This calculation must be performed at least 10 times a second, 20 times for stereo. The illusion is more convincing if the frame rate is increased to 40 frames a second, 80 frames for stereo. If the frame rate is too low, viewer-centered perspective is delayed. You move your head and some time later the virtual world responds. This delay destroys the core VR illusion that the world is static and the head is moving. Instead, the world distorts. High frame rates for realtime image generation demand very fast computers. In the cinema context, the audience is used to seeing computer animation that takes 30 minutes or more per frame to render, at hundreds of megabytes per frame, in some cases. This means that computers in realtime interaction would have to be 54,000 times as fast as the computers used in animation to produce similar levels of quality. Even the world's best realtime computer graphics systems have to generate images that are much simpler than audiences are used to seeing in computer-animated films. This is very possible with physically based models but much more difficult and radically more expensive when you include significant live social interactions. In current high-performance VR systems, 80 percent or more of the cost of the complete system is the computer, and few of them attempt to process more than the simplified gestures of a couple of users.

The IDESK is a furniture-sized statement of the CAVE, which is itself an architectural statement. An IDESK trades off being able to look right and left for much lower cost and transportability. It shares with the CAVE the major features of a VR system: large angle of view, stereo, viewer-centered perspective, directional sound, and rich interaction.

Cinema

Recent innovations in cinema share some of the characteristics and problems of VR. IMAX and IMAX *Dome* are film systems that use large screens to increase the angle of view. Contemporary theaters have elaborate multichannel sound systems to envelop the viewer. The new small theaters in cineplexes can have modest screen sizes with large angles of view by seating a small audience close to the screen. A recent innovation is the addition of a motion platform to a small theater. This is, of course, a type of tactile or force-feedback. Such systems are currently being used to simulate airplanes, land vehicles, spaceships, submarines, and rollercoasters, and they constitute a key element of the most elaborate theme park attractions.

There is an interesting set of problems and conflicts in trying to combine the technologies, goals, and traditions of VR and cinema. Cinema typically is done on film, and film is not interactive. Cinema usually assumes passive audiences, seated and unmoving, while one of the central themes of VR is interaction. In cinema, one can present the illusion of interaction by having prefilmed segments that are played back, based on audience participation. The mechanical technology of film makes this technique difficult because of the time needed to load and thread film. Transferring the images from film to videodisc or computer is necessary to support even this minimum interaction. Because film has immense resolution compared to most video or computer systems, this transfer implies a reduction in quality. Unless the audience's options are severely limited, the number of prefilmed segments quickly and necessarily grows very large. In order for participants to have five significant choice points within the film, each choice having two options, the producer needs to create 63 prerecorded segments (Figure 1.20). Ten choices would require 2,047 prerecorded segments. In this case, a single viewer would experience only ten segments, or one-half of 1 percent of the work created. There are, of course, inventive special-case solutions. Consider a story that has choices, but the plot line converges to the same point after each choice, independent of the choice. Then, five choices would require only 11 segments (Figure 1.20).

One reasonable solution to handling the immense variety of experiences that interaction requires is realtime image generation, instead of prerecorded segments. One has to simulate the world and compute the effects of the participants' choices.

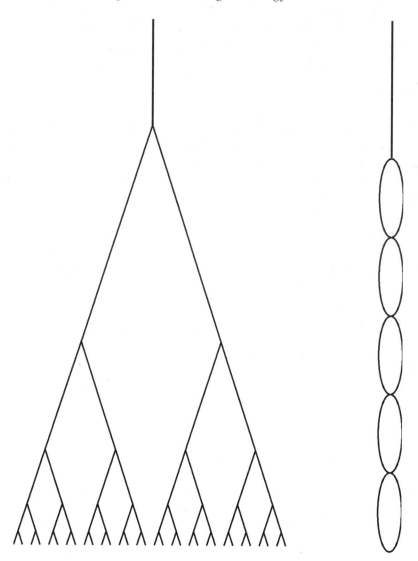

Figure 1.20   Plot choices: A prerecorded story that has five choice points might require 63 different recorded segments; however, an individual experiencing the story will experience only 10 percent of the prepared material. If the story is designed so that the two paths always converge to the same next choice, only 11 segments are required.

Physically based modeling is well understood and allows simulation of simple physical systems such as airplanes, spaceships, projectiles, and wiggling Jell-O. Simulation is now being extended to reproduce behavior that is good enough to portray things like pet animals. Simulation of large political and ecological systems is possible at a level that is reminiscent of the real thing. There are, however, no good simulations of interpersonal interactions. As computer power increases and our ability to simulate the world gets better, options will expand greatly, but simulation systems are currently limited to mechanical, physical, and very simple biological worlds.

Much human interaction is one-on-one. Cinema implies an audience of more than one and is quite successful with all control in the hands of the director. How does one share control? For viewer-centered perspective, whose perspective is it? A common solution is "vehicle-centered perspective," where the images are calculated for the center of the room and the room is moved around. This is particularly appropriate for flight-simulator-style systems. There are also solutions to sharing control. Voting games of various sorts have been applied. At the SIGGRAPH '91 Electronic Theater, a large audience played Pong on one large screen. Each audience member "voted" by rotating a wand that was colored green on one side and red on the other. The right half of the audience controlled the right Pong paddle on the screen, and the left half of the audience controlled the left paddle. An overall red vote made the screen paddle move up; green made it move down. Several energetic interactive sets were played. The system has since been installed in a science museum in Pittsburgh. There are always special-case solutions for carefully constructed experiences.

The IDESK and the CAVE can be thought of as very small theaters, with an optimum audience size of five to ten persons. To share control, we simply pass the wand and head tracker around the group. I believe there is a central conflict between the cinema traditions of large audiences passively viewing a story and the VR requirements of interaction. If interaction is to be maintained and the most important properties of VR exploited, large-scale entertainment systems must become more like video games, moving toward one complete system per participant. The economic issues involve finding solutions that are cost-effective and easy to use, attract long-term repeat use, and appeal to sufficiently wide audiences. The creative issues involve the invention of new artistic devices and strategies that can bring the depth of experience we have come to expect from literature, cinema, art, and music to the VR medium.

Biography

Daniel J. Sandin is a director of the Electronic Visualization Laboratory (EVL), professor in the School of Art and Design at the University of Illinois at Chicago (UIC), and adjunct professor at the National Center for Supercomputing Applications at the University of Illinois at Urbana-Champaign.

In the mid-1960s, Sandin completed an M.S. in physics at the University of Wisconsin, then began developing image transformation techniques with electronic video image processing and digital image generation. In 1969, he developed a computer-controlled light/sound environment that responded to the positions of people in the environment; this installation was part of the Glowflow exhibit at the Smithsonian Institution. By 1973, he developed the Sandin Image Processor, a highly programmable analog computer for processing video images. He and Tom DeFanti combined the image processor with DeFanti's computer graphics system to create "Electronic Visualization Events," a series of live performances in which images were computer generated and color processed in realtime with musical accompaniment. In 1976, along with Rich Sayre, they developed a VR glove (referred to in the literature as the Sayre Glove). They also established the Circle Graphics Habitat, which evolved into the EVL program, a joint effort of UIC's School of Art and Design and College of Engineering—the oldest formal collaboration between engineering and art in the country offering graduate degrees in visualization. There, they conceived and developed the CAVE virtual reality theater, providing a new and functional modality for data immersion, followed by the ImmersaDesk.

Sandin has exhibited his electronic art worldwide and has received grants and fellowships from the Rockefeller and Guggenheim Foundations and the National Endowment for the Arts. His 1975 video "Spiral PTL (Perhaps The Last)," created with DeFanti, is in the inaugural collection of video art at the Museum of Modern Art in New York. Current interests include virtual environments, computer-based interactive systems, computer animation, and mathematical visualization. He can be reached at dan@evl.uic.edu

Chapter 2

The Construction of Experience: Interface as Content

David Rokeby
Toronto, Ontario, Canada

Introduction

I'm an interactive artist; I construct experiences. Since the early 1980s, I've been exhibiting my installations in galleries, trade shows, science museums, and public and private spaces. These exhibitions serve as a public research laboratory where my ideas about interaction and experience are tested, affirmed, or shot down. This is a condensation of the results of my free-form research.

Entertainment has traditionally involved heavily coded communication. It has predominantly been delivered through words, sounds, symbols, and gestures that stimulate the imagination to render an experience. The visual arts and theatre at various times in history, and film and television in the past century, use the direct visual experience of images as a way to make the experience more immediate—to make the audience feel more "there." But these experiences remain things that happen to you. Interactivity's promise is that the experience of culture can be something you *do* rather than something you are given. This complicates our conventional ideas about "content" in the context of this new medium.

Interfaces Are Content

Everyone is talking about content in interactive media these days. Independent artists and the entertainment industry alike now see that these new technologies are relatively flat without significant content. But the rush to stuff content into interactive media has drawn our attention away from the profound and subtle ways that the interface itself, by defining how we perceive and navigate content, shapes our experience of that content. If culture, in the context of interactive media, becomes something we "do," it's the interface that defines how we do it and how the "doing" feels. Word processors change the experience of writing, regardless of the content; they affect the manner in which that content is expressed. Hypermedia provide multiple trajectories through content, but the nature of the links, branches, and interconnections influences our path and inevitably changes our sense of the content. Active agents, either in our software or on the Net, guide us through the information jungle; they're sorting demons, deciding what's relevant and irrelevant, providing us with interpretation and point of view. Marshall McLuhan's phrase "The medium is the message" became a tired cliché long before our media became flexible and intelligent enough to live up to the epithet. Like most clichés, it carries plenty of truth and needs a full reexamination in the context of emerging active and interactive technologies.

The Tricks of the Trade

The creation of interactive interfaces carries a social responsibility. I've come to this conclusion from my experience creating and exhibiting interactive systems. At first glance, it may seem that I'm stretching the point here. It's really just entertainment, right? Indeed, as an artist, it's my traditional right to use every trick in the book to create a magical experience. Fantasy and illusion are key elements of most effective culture, from high-brow theatre to video games. Hollywood has always relied on sets, stunt people, and special effects to get its stories across. Computer game developers are the newest masters of illusion.

One of the clearest examples I can recall is an early videodisc-based video game in which users got the impression that they were flying at great speed over a terrain. The videodisc was made up of video clips that linked together in a branching and merging structure. The image I saw on the screen was the middle portion of the full video frame. If I turned to the left during a linear video segment, the section of the frame that I saw instantly panned in that direction, giving an immediate sense of responsiveness, but I was, in fact, still travelling along the same restricted path. The illusion that I had the freedom to roam the entire terrain was maintained for a surprisingly long time partly because I was moving at a high "virtual" speed without time to reflect on the degree to which my actions were being reflected. That technique was a brilliant and an effective way to get around the inherent limitations of videodisc as a realtime interactive medium. Whether you really had freedom to wander the terrain was beside the point because the game was engaging and exciting.

The line between entertainment and everything else is getting very vague these days (infotainment, edutainment). The Web represents a convergence of the video game industry and commercial transaction systems, and this leads to a potential problem; illusion translated into the commercial world becomes deception. The tricks of today's artists and hackers are the commercial tools of tomorrow. Perhaps more significantly, with the explosive growth of the Internet, these sleights-of-hand are becoming incorporated into communications systems and, by implication, into our social fabric. Whether we intend it or not, we're redesigning the ways that we experience the world and each other.

Virtual Spill

There are two levels of leakage here. On one level, there is the effortless migration of code and hardware from the entertainment world to the "serious" worlds of commerce, justice, and communication. At the second level, artificial experiences subtly change the way we feel, perceive, interpret, and even describe our "real" experiences.

The most graphic and extreme example of virtual spill into the real is probably VR-sickness, an aftereffect of VR. My experience was that I would suddenly lose my orientation in space at apparently random moments for about 24 hours after my virtual immersion. I felt as though I were off the floor and at an unexpected angle. As far as I can tell, the explanation was that when I was immersed, I had desensitized my response to the balancing mechanisms in my inner ears in order to sustain the illusion of motion in a purely visually defined 3D space. Once I was desensitized, I was free to accept the illusion of space that the VR system provided. But on returning to "real" space, my inner ears didn't immediately resume their job. I was taking my sense of orientation in space entirely from visual cues. One attack may have been stimulated by a design of sharply angled lines painted on a wall. My visual system seems to have interpreted this cue as vertical and abruptly changed its mind about my body's orientation, while my ears were certain that I was standing quite straight, bringing on a wave of nausea.

I've also experienced aftereffects from spending extended periods interacting with my most exhibited interactive installation, called "Very Nervous System." In this work, I use video cameras, an artificial perception system, a computer, and a synthesizer to create a space in which body movements are translated into sound or music in realtime. An hour of the continuous, direct feedback in this system strongly reinforces a sense of connection with the surrounding environment. Walking down the street afterward, I feel connected to all things. The sound of a passing car splashing through a puddle seems to be directly related to my movements. I feel implicated in every action around me. On the other hand, if I put on a CD, I quickly feel cheated that the music does not change with my actions.

When I first got a Macintosh computer and spent endless days and nights playing with MacPaint, one of the things that amazed me most was the lasso tool, which allows you to select a part of the image and drag it across the screen to another location. The most intriguing thing was the automatic clipping of the background behind the dragged selection. Walking down the street after an extended MacPaint session, I would find myself marvelling as backgrounds disappeared behind trees, and acutely aware of what was momentarily hidden from view.

Interfaces leave imprints on our perceptual systems that we carry out into the world. The more time we spend using an interface, the stronger this effect gets. These effects can be beneficial or detrimental. Dr. Isaac Szpindel at the Jewish General Hospital in Montréal is experimenting with the use of Very Nervous System as a therapy for Parkinson's disease. People suffering from this disease tend to lose their ability to will their own movement but remain capable of responding quickly in emergencies. While the results are still preliminary, it appears that regular interactions with Very Nervous System can help to reengage Parkinson's suffers' ability to motivate their own movement in their normal day-to-day lives.

Conceptual Spill

Exposure to technologies also changes the ways that we think and talk about our experiences. We use terms borrowed from computers when describing our own mental and social processes. We "access" our memories, we "interface" with each other, we "erase" thoughts, we "input" and "output." In a chillingly insightful comment on the way technologies and ideas interact, Alan Turing, one of the great computer pioneers wrote, "I believe that at the end of the [twentieth] century, the use of words and general educated opinion will be altered so much that one will be able to speak of machines thinking without expecting to be contradicted."[1]

This statement is often taken to mean that Turing believed that machines would be able to think by the turn of the century. In fact, he is saying that our ideas of what thinking is and what computers can do will converge to the point that we cannot express or grasp the difference. This sort of convergence may

---

1. Quoted by O. B. Hardison, Jr., *Disappearing Through the Skylight* (New York: Viking Penguin, page 319).

also soon take place in the realm of experience; we may lose our ability to differentiate between raw and simulated experience.

In 1983, I was invited at the last minute to exhibit my interactive sound installation in an exhibition called "Digicon '83" in Vancouver. This was to be my first public show, and I was very excited, but there was a tremendous amount of work to be done. I worked between 18 and 20 hours a day refining an interactive interface from a barely implemented concept to an actual experiential installation. I spent no time with friends and didn't get out at all. I got the piece done and was extremely pleased with the results. After setting up my installation in Vancouver, I was astonished by the fact that it did not seem to respond properly to other people and sometimes didn't notice people at all. I didn't really understand the problem until I saw videotape of myself moving in the installation. I was moving in a completely unusual and unnatural way, full of jerky, tense motions that I found both humorous and distressing. In my isolation, rather than developing an interface that understood movement, I had evolved *with* the interface, developing a way of moving that the interface understood as I developed the interface itself. I had experienced a physiological version of the very convergence that Turing described.

While we may lose our ability to understand and articulate the differences, we will still have some intuitive sense of them. But many of the differences between virtuality and reality will be subtle and easy to discount, and intuition often loses in the face of hard logic; we may find it as easy to ignore our intuitions as to ignore our inner ears while immersed in VR. I believe there are important reasons, beyond simply romantic nostalgia, to nurture awareness of the distinctions between the real and the virtual.

The Experience of Being

By defining a way of sensing and a way of acting in an interactive system, the interface defines the "experience of being" for that system. Through their design of the interface, the creators have in large part defined the user's "quality of life" while they are interacting with the system. Unfortunately, the design parameters for quality of life are pretty undefined. There seems to be no agreement on what makes for a high quality of life. I suspect it's dependent on a whole range of parameters that we rarely pay attention to.

In order to better understand what those parameters are, we need to look at how our experience of the real world is constructed. In other words, what is our user interface for *reality*? Or, what is the nature of our relationship with the world? I don't intend—and I am not qualified—to plumb the depths of philosophical thinking on this subject. There is a branch of philosophy dedicated to these questions called *phenomenology* for those who want to explore this in greater depth.

The Bandwidth of "Reality"

Our "organic" interface is extraordinarily complex and massively parallel. Our sensing system involves an enormous number of simultaneously active sensors, and we act on the world through an even larger number of individual points of physical contact. In contrast, our artificial interfaces are remarkably narrow and serial even in the multimedia density of sound and moving image. These interfaces are also unbalanced in terms of input and output. At the computer screen, we receive many thousands of pixels at least 60 times a second from our monitors, while we send a few bytes of mouse position or keyboard activity back to the system. We appear to most of our interactive systems as a meagre dribble of extremely restricted data. Even in immersive VR systems, we're commonly represented as a head orientation and a simple hand shape. We may imagine ourselves immersed in the virtual reality, but the virtual reality is not, from its point of view, enveloping us.

It's not simply a question of lack of senses such as touch and smell. It's also a question of the actual number of contact points through which an interaction passes. Our nervous system, senses, and perceptual systems integrate an enormous number of separate inputs in order to construct our sense of being. The "bandwidth" of real experience is almost unimaginable. In order to fit interaction into the available bandwidth of our computers and communications systems, we must decide what narrow aspects of the user's presence and actions will be involved. It's an extreme form of compression, and it's "lossy."

Bottom-Up Versus Top-Down

Through our human interface, we access a pool of content of unimaginable complexity. This content exists at many levels. There is raw sensual content. There are people and things and their complex behaviours and interactions. There are conjunctions of actors and actions that play out in an apparent causality. There are stories, symbols, words, and ideas. While our attention is often focussed at one or another of these levels, our sense of being is constructed by input at all of these levels simultaneously.

The whole system is built from the ground up. Subatomic particles interact to produce atoms and molecules. Atoms and molecules interact to produce organic and inorganic matter. Matter gathers into things with higher-order behaviours like mountains, rivers, plants, and humans. These things interact in the whole complex process of life. Ideas, words, and concepts are things that we use to describe these processes. They're inexact generalizations and simplifications that are necessary for our sanity.

Artificial interfaces may access a pool of information as large as the Internet, but the Internet is tiny compared to reality. And that pool of content generally starts at the level of words and ideas. A digital image is similarly abstracted. It's not self-generated from the interactions among its constituent pixels.

Artificial experiences are built up as a sort of collage of *representations* of things torn out of context. In the virtual realm, context is purely a matter of the taste of the creator. One decides arbitrarily to put these things together. In "reality," the context is not just the ground against which you see something; it represents the set of conditions that makes the presence of the thing possible. The difference is immense, and the more interactive, immersive, or convincing an artificial environment is, the more careful we must be.

Real experience has a fundamental integrity that virtual experience does not. This aspect of virtuality can be a great advantage because it allows you to break the "rules" of reality. Escaping reality is liberating when one spends the greater part of one's time in reality. But this lack of fundamental integrity is potentially quite unsettling to those spending most of their time in virtual spaces.

A Hardened Perceptual Exoskeleton

The input from our senses generally reaches our awareness only after passing through the powerful filters of our perceptual systems, but we can also open ourselves to raw sensuality. There is something profoundly important about the fact that the base of our human/reality interface is raw and uncoded. We can, to some degree, bypass our own perceptual filtering.

I had an experience in art school that brought this home in a very direct way. One of my professors told us one day that we would be looking out a window for the whole three-hour class. I was incensed. I had been willing to go along with most of the unusual activities these classes had entailed, but I felt this was going too far. I stood at my assigned window and glared out through the pane. I saw cars, two buildings, a person on the street. Another person, another car. This was stupid! For 15 minutes, I fumed and muttered to myself. Then, I started to notice things. The flow of traffic down the street was like a river, each car seemingly drawn along by the next, connected. The blinds in the windows of the facing building were each a slightly different colour. The shadow of a maple tree in the wind shifted shape like some giant amoeba. For the remaining hours of the class, I was electrified by the scene outside. After 15 minutes, the "names" had started separating from the objects.

It seems that we stop seeing, hearing, and smelling as soon as we have positively identified something. At that point, we may as well replace the word for the object. Since identification usually happens quickly, we spend most of our time not really sensing our environment, but living in a world of predigested and abstracted memories.

This explains our attraction to optical illusions and mind-altering experiences (chemically induced or not). Those moments of confusion, where identification and resolution aren't immediate, give us a flash of the raw experience of being. Such moments of confusion are also the fulcra of paradigm shifts. It's only when our conventional way of dealing with things breaks down that we can adopt another model, another way of imagining and experiencing a scenario.

The adrenaline rush of a high-speed video game has something in common with this experience of filter-breakdown; the barrage of images and the need to act quickly test the limits of our perceptual and responsive systems. But these systems have then added themselves to our internal filters, and they aren't subject to this same sort of breakdown. Paradigm shifts in the interface can happen only through the software and hardware development cycle, which is burdened with economic considerations and intense industry competition. The interface becomes a hardened and brittle perceptual exoskeleton that we can't easily question or redefine. This becomes increasingly problematic as the interface becomes more "transparent" and "intuitive." At those difficult and confusing moments when our way of viewing the world needs to change, we may not know to examine the interface as a potential contributor to the problem. For this reason, I believe we need to develop an interactive literacy. We need to learn and then teach others to critique and understand the influences of our interfaces as we use them.

Punch and Scream

Our interface with reality is not only multisensory or multimedia but also "multimodal." We can talk, scream, gesture, or punch. We can interpret, analyze, or simply enjoy the raw sensation. It's only a multimodal approach with multiple simultaneous levels of meaning and communication that can properly express that complex experience of reality.

In 1988, I was invited to exhibit Very Nervous System at the SIGGRAPH Art Show. "Interactivity" was just emerging as a buzzword, and there was a lot of skepticism on the floor. Many attendees entered my installation to "test" it using what I've come to call the "First Test of Interactivity." The test involves determining whether the system will consistently respond identically to identical movements. (Note that an intelligent agent will probably fail this test.) They would enter the space, let the sounds created by their entrance fade to silence, and then make a gesture. The gesture was an experiment, a question to the space: "What sound will you make?" The resulting sound was noted. Second and third gestures were made with the same motivation, and the same sound was produced. After the third repetition, interactors decided that the system was indeed interactive, at which point they changed the way they held their body and made a gesture to the space, a sort of command: "Make that sound." The command gesture was significantly different from the early "questioning" gestures particularly in terms of dynamics, and so the system responded with a different sound. I observed a couple of people going through this cycle several times before leaving in confusion. Their body had betrayed their motivation.

Body movement can be read on two different levels. There is the semantic content of the gesture, in which the movement is interpreted symbolically (the OK sign or the raised middle finger), and there is the raw visual experience of the gesture, to which my system was responding. The questioning and commanding gestures were semantically similar but quite different in terms of physical dynamics. More practical interactive interfaces might filter out the involuntary dynamics of the gesture, treating them as unwanted noise, and focus on the semantic content. In interpersonal communications, we're always simultaneously interpreting gestures on many levels. This combination is the basis for richer communication. For this breadth and quality of communication to be carried through interfaces, the designers must be aware of the importance of these multiple modes and then must be able to actually create the code and hardware to support them.

A multimodal interface would be particularly important in engendering trust and intimacy through communications systems. Sweat, smell, nervous gestures, cold or warm hands, tone of voice, and exact direction of gaze are all elements by which we gauge subtle interpersonal conditions like honesty and nervousness. I'm not advocating interfaces involving every possible sense; the literal replication of the whole nervous and sensing systems would be cumbersome. I'm just pointing out the many complex levels that exist in real flesh-to-flesh communication. We need effective ways to accommodate simultaneous layers of communication if our telecommunication is to be satisfying and richly successful.

Human Interfaces as Belief Systems

So, there are very large differences between the human and artificial interfaces. Quite often, the simplified, symbolic nature of the artificial experience is a useful characteristic. This is particularly true for situations that involve abstractions like numbers, words, or ideas. The interface in this case clearly suits the material and can make those abstractions more accessible through simulation and visualization.

But we're spending more and more time amongst our simulations, and we're in danger of losing sight of the fact that our models and ideas of "reality" are drastically simplified representations. If we do lose this awareness, then our experience of being will be significantly diminished. Simulations offer us formerly unimaginable experiences, but the foundations of these simulations are built up from a relatively narrow set of assumptions about the structure and parameters of experience. And the built-in exigencies of product development mean that this narrow set of assumptions and ideas quickly becomes a standard and, soon after, crystallizes into silicon for performance gains. Once there is an inexpensive chip available, these assumptions have become practically unassailable for a considerable length of time.

In an odd way, this parallels medieval Christianity. During the Middle Ages, the church sanctioned a certain set of ideas about the world. This system of beliefs became the standard "browser" for viewing reality. Many of the assumptions built into that system were clearly absurd from our contemporary point of view, but they had a grip on the imagination of the whole Christian world, to the point that brilliant philosophers went through ridiculous contortions to justify officially sanctioned ideas that seem to us ridiculous. The interface designers of this era were the monks, bishops, and popes.

Our user interfaces are also a kind of belief system, carrying and reinforcing our assumptions about the way things are. It's for this reason that we must increase our awareness of the ways that the interface carries these beliefs as hidden content. It may be hard to conceive of the standard GUI as a belief system, but the "holy war" between Macintosh and Windows users on the Internet indicates an almost religious passion about interface. It's also useful to realize that effective interfaces are usually intuitive precisely because they tap into existing stereotypes for their metaphors. An interface designed for racists might tap into racist stereotypes as a source for icons and metaphors that would be immediately understood across the user base. A metaphoric interface borrows clichés from the culture but then reflects them back and reinforces them.

Beyond Literal Simulation

I've argued that virtual experiences don't do justice to the richness of the human experience. I'm not suggesting that the richness of experience cannot be increased through interactive technologies or that the best interface would be one that exactly replicated the full experience of reality. In fact, designers of virtual experiences are often so literal in their attempts to simulate reality that they stifle some of the most exciting potentials that these new media offer.

There is an artist named Tamas Waliczky who has been working with the idea of alternate systems of 3D representation. The conventional binocular, perspectival model that is currently being standardized in software and hardware is useful for normal representations of 3D objects and space. The fact that it has reached the level of silicon represents the kind of crystallization I mentioned previously. Waliczky sees much broader possibilities for the representation of space than this limited Renaissance model. He has been creating alternate perspectival systems, writing code to render other experiences of space. In one of his works, he renders a world from the self-centred point of view of a young child. For another, he has created a program that renders inverted perspective, in which things get larger as they get farther away from you, and vice versa. This is a real mind-bender to see, a rich exploration of the potentials of virtual media to go beyond the restrictions of reality and, indeed, of our own imaginations.

I'm suggesting that there is a sort of middle-of-the-road (MOR) virtuality that does justice to neither our rich experience of reality nor the richness of possible virtual experience. This MOR virtuality diminishes experience in several dimensions without enhancing it in others. If virtual experiences are to add to the dimensions of experience, we must avoid this mushy middle ground when imagining and designing them.

Designing the Experience of Being

How does an interface form the experience of being? How do the decisions of the designer and programmer shape the experience of the user? I'll examine these questions by looking at several general characteristics or "qualities" of the interface.

The Distorting Mirror

An interface inherently constructs a representation of the user. To a computer with a simple graphical user interface, the user is a stream of mouse clicks and key taps. Advanced interfaces involving intelligent agents compile much more detailed representations of the user by interpreting this stream of input and attempting to determine the intentions of these activities so that the interface can help the user be more efficient. How the user is represented internally by the system defines what the user can be and do within the system. Does the system allow the user to be ambiguous? Can the user express or act upon several things at once?

Interactive systems invariably involve feedback loops. The limited representation of the user is inevitably reflected back to the user, modifying his or her own sense of self within the simulation. The interface becomes a distorting mirror, like those fun-house mirrors that make you look fat, or skinny, or like a bizarre combination of the two. A standard GUI is a mirror that reflects back a severely misshapen human being with large hands, huge forefinger, one immense eye, and moderate-sized ears. The rest of the body is simply the location of backaches, neck strain, and repetitive stress injuries. It's generally agreed that the representation of women or visible minorities in magazine and television advertisements affects their self-image. If we accept this, then we must also accept that interface-brokered representations can exert a similar, though more intimate, effect on the reflected computer user.

The Construction of Subjectivity

We are who we are, with a unique character and personal idiosyncrasies, largely because of our individual subjective viewpoint. That viewpoint is formed by our windows out into the world (our senses), in conjunction with our memories and experiences. An interactive interface is a standardized extension that shapes and modifies the user's subjective point of view. By presenting information in a specific manner or medium, the interface designer defines the way this interface shapes this point of view.

There is a paradox in the manner that interactive systems affect our subjectivity. The noninteractive system can be seen as stubborn in refusing to reflect the presence and actions of the spectator *or* as flexible in giving the spectator complete freedom of reflection and interpretation by not intervening in the process. An interactive system can be seen as giving the user the power to affect the course of the system *or* as interfering in the interactor's subjective process of exploration. An extreme example would be an interactive system that detected whether the user was male or female and presented different content or choices to members of each sex. The system would be closing off parts of the system to each person because of gender. Such an interactive system displaces some of the user's freedom to explore the content. Any interactive interface implicitly defines the "permissible" paths of exploration for each user.

This irony gets increasingly pronounced as the technology of interaction becomes more sophisticated. In the introduction to his book, *Artificial Reality II*, Myron Krueger invites us to "Imagine that the computer could completely control your perception and monitor your response to that perception. Then it could make any possible experience available to you."[2] Florian Rötzer responds that a system that gives you this "freedom" of experience must necessarily be a system of infinite surveillance.[3] When a system monitors its users to

2. Myron W. Krueger, *Artificial Reality II* (Reading, Mass.: Addison-Wesley, 1991), xvi.

3. Florian Rötzer, "On Fascination, Reaction, Virtual Worlds, and Others," Virtual Seminar on the BioApparatus (Banff: The Banff Centre, 1991), 102.

this extent, it has effectively taken control of their subjectivity, depriving them of their idiosyncratic identity and replacing it with a highly focussed perspective that is entirely mediated by the system. Subjectivity has been replaced by a synthetic subjective viewpoint. The fact that the system responds to the interactor does not guarantee in any way that the system is responsible to the user; the interactor can fairly easily be pushed beyond reflection to the edge of instinct, capable only of visceral response to the system's stimuli, mirroring the system's actions rather than being mirrored by the system.

The Interface as a Landscape

Interactive interfaces can explicitly define "permissible" paths of exploration for each user, but, in most cases, it's more subtle than that. It's usually not so much a matter of permission as of paths of least resistance. An interface makes certain actions or operations easier, more intuitive, or more accessible. By privileging some activities, it makes the unassisted operations more difficult and therefore less likely to be used. A feature that requires seven layers of dialogue boxes is less likely to be used than one that requires a single keystroke. The interface defines a sort of landscape, creating valleys into which users tend to gather, like rainwater falling on a watershed. Other areas are separated by forbidding mountain ranges and are much less travelled. A good interface designer optimizes the operations that will be most often used. This practise carries the hidden assumption that the designer knows how the interface will actually be used. It also tends to encourage operational clichés—things that are neat, easy to do, and thus get overused. Software assistants add another layer to this landscape. Like a Tibetan Sherpa guiding you up Mount Everest, intelligent assistants make it easier to traverse the more forbidding parts of the landscape, but they themselves create a second landscape. A guide selects and interprets and may just as easily hide possibilities from you as present them.

Drowning in Our Own Clichés

My early interactive sound installations were programmed in 6502 assembly language (the 6502 was the processor in the Apple II). I developed interactions in those days by setting up a simple interactive algorithm, testing the experience for a while, and then modifying the code to implement the resulting new ideas. After the programming, I would have to do some debugging. Finally, after up to several hours of work, I could actually step in and experience the alteration. As a feedback loop, this process was severely flawed. By the time I had implemented the idea, I had often lost track of the idea that sparked the modification. I decided to make the development process as interactive as the experience itself, so I wrote a simple language with which I could modify the behaviours in realtime. I took the basic structures and processes that I had been coding in assembly language and turned them into standard objects and instructions. This language allowed me to create works in hours that would have taken months to realize in assembly code. It also allowed me to build more complex interactions from these standard building blocks, like any higher-level language. However, it took me a few months to realize that the language was having another effect on my installations. They were becoming less interesting; the building blocks of interaction that made up the language had become clichés.

Assembly code itself contains very little in the way of abstraction. I would take my idea and build it, as it were, atom by atom. It presents a relatively level playing field. My higher-level language was more of a terrain, with peaks and valleys. Once I was placed somewhere on that landscape, there were pathways that were easy and pathways that were difficult. My decisions about how and what to implement were inevitably influenced by this terrain. A landscape gives you a fine view in some directions and obscures others.

Everything that builds on abstractions (languages, perception, and user interfaces) creates a biased terrain, even as it makes certain previously impossible things possible. Structural differences between languages like Chinese and English subtly cause native speakers to view the world differently. But whereas a spoken language has evolved over centuries and has had millions of unique codesigners from all walks of life, a user interface or computer language has usually been designed by a small team of people with a lot in common. And they were probably in a big hurry.

Software Publishing as Broadcasting

When the Apple Macintosh first came onto the market, MacPaint sent a shock wave through the creative community. For the first year, MacPaint-produced posters were everywhere, an explosion of the possibility for self-expression. But while the MacPaint medium reflected the user's expressive gestures, it also refracted them through its own idiosyncratic prism. After a while, posters began to blend into an urban wallpaper of MacPaint textures and MacPaint patterns. The similarities overpowered the differences. Since then, graphics programs for computers have become more transparent, flexible, and commonplace, but the initial creative fervour that MacPaint ignited has abated. The restrictions that made MacPaint easy to use were also the characteristics that ultimately limited its usefulness as a medium for personal expression.

Television, radio, and print broadcasting are portrayed as the "bad boys" from which interactivity rescues us. Interaction allows us to access a wider range of information, not just what the networks choose to broadcast. However, interactive systems do their own kinds of broadcasting, transmitting processes and modes of perception, action, and being. When you define how people access and experience content, you have a more abstract form of control over their information intake. It does not matter that every piece of information in the world is on the Internet, if the browsers and search engines, through biases in their design, make it unlikely that certain information will be found. It is not difficult to imagine an Internet search engine provider selling search priority points; you pay your money, and your company's Web pages would automatically get an extra 10 percent rating on each query in which they come up, putting them closer to the top of the list of results and so more likely to be accessed.

I've no desire to demonize interactive technologies. But we need to remind ourselves of the ways they subtly shape our experience, particularly in the face of the wild utopian rhetoric that currently surrounds interactivity. Yes, interactive media can empower and enfranchise. But they simultaneously create new kinds of constraints on abstract and psychological levels—constraints that are more difficult to understand and critique than the familiar biases of the press and broadcast media. Information itself does not create meaning; meaning is created by context and flow, selection and grouping. By guiding us through jungles of content, interfaces are partially responsible for the meanings we discover through them.

Freedom Versus Control

In the early days of Very Nervous System, I tried to reflect the actions of the user in as many parameters of the system's behaviour as possible. I worked out ways to map velocity, gestural quality, acceleration, dynamics, and direction onto as many parameters of sound synthesis as I could. What I found was that people simply got lost. Every movement they made affected several aspects of the sound simultaneously, in different ways. Ironically, the system was interactive on so many levels that the interaction became indigestible. A user's most common response was to decide that the sounds from the system were not interactive at all, but were being played back on a cassette deck.

I found that as I reduced the number of dimensions of interaction, the user's sense of empowerment grew. This struck me as problematic. I had, at the time, very idealistic notions about what interaction meant (and how it would change the world). In retrospect, the problem seems to have been a linguistic one: People were unfamiliar with the language of interaction that I gave them. Simplifying the language of interaction by reducing its variables let people recognize their impact on the system immediately. With repeated exposure, users could handle and appreciate more nuanced levels of interaction. In time, they could appreciate the flexible, expressive power I had been trying to offer in the first place.

This is a comforting notion, but it works only if the interactive system stays the same long enough for users to become expert. At the current rate of technology development, such familiarity may never have a chance to develop. As perpetual new users, we may be drawn inexorably toward simplistic systems, trading real power for an ever-evolving glimpse of some never-to-be-achieved potential.

Through the Feedback Loop

Interactive systems inherently involve feedback. The system responds to your actions, and you respond based on its responses and your desires. In Very Nervous System, I constructed tight real-time feedback loops with complex behaviours that illustrated several interesting characteristics of interactive feedback. The responsive character of Very Nervous System is built up of little virtual instrumentalists, each of which improvises according to its personal style based on what it "sees" through the camera. Some of those virtual players are drummers, who respond to movement with rhythmic patterns. A rhythmic pattern doesn't necessarily have anything to do with an on-camera person's rhythmic motion; it's merely that virtual player's way of responding. People often involuntarily fall into sync with one of those rhythms, then exclaim that the system is so "intelligent" that it synchronized to their movement!

This illustrates an interesting side effect of realtime interactive feedback loops. An action provokes a response, which immediately provokes a shift in action, which likewise immediately changes the system's response, ad infinitum. The issue of who is controlling whom becomes blurred. The intelligence of the human interactors spreads around the whole loop, often coming back in ways they don't recognize, causing them to attribute intelligence to the system.

Consciousness Lags Behind the Body

Another reason for the confusion between what we as interactors do and what the system does is that our consciousness seems to trail our actions by up to one-tenth of a second. It takes that long for us to be fully aware of what we're doing. I once programmed Very Nervous System to respond very clearly as soon as it saw the slightest movement. In every instance, the system responded before I realized that I had started moving. In fact, the system seemed to respond at the moment that I *decided* I would move. This delay in consciousness makes it possible for systems with high sampling rates and response speeds to slip under the user's consciousness. At this point, the system and its responses are experienced in the same way that we experience our own body. The interactive system becomes integrated into our proprioceptive system—the same internal sensing system that defines our sense of being in our body and establishes the relative position of our arms and legs to our "point of consciousness."

This phenomenon, like all the others I describe in this chapter, cuts both ways. Part of the desire that drove me to produce Very Nervous System was a desire to slip out of my own self-consciousness into direct, open experience of the world. In the right circumstances, the feedback loop of Very Nervous System effectively neutralizes consciousness and can occasionally lead to states that could best be described as shamanistic. It can be intoxicating and addictive. I made a real breakthrough in the responsive quality of the system in 1987. I had written a program where powerful drum sounds were produced by very aggressive movements. The result was extremely satisfying. After a week of developing and experiencing this new version, I found that I had seriously damaged my back. I had been throwing my body in the air with abandon, crashing myself against the virtual in search of those most satisfying sounds. This was a classic case of positive feedback.

Most natural and stable feedback systems are negative feedback systems, intended to keep a system in balance. If things get into any extreme state, the feedback mechanisms work against that state to restore balance and maintain the sustainability of the situation. This particular tuning of Very Nervous System worked in reverse, egging me on to greater feats of physical movement until I wore myself out.

Pushing ourselves out of equilibrium is a way of opening to change, but it can also lead to self-destruction or external manipulation. The mechanism that governs the evolution of life involves enormous test periods during which impossible or unsustainable life-forms are weeded out. Humans have evolved over a very long time to be well adapted to the stresses of everyday physical reality, and our species has evolved ways of balancing new pressures. But we now invent new pressures and stresses at an extraordinary rate. While technologies can be developed to counterbalance some of these stresses, the stability of this balance is not guaranteed. I'm not advocating a return to Darwinian rule, but just pointing out the seriousness of the task of "engineering" this balance.

Havens for Safe Interaction

The recent explosion of interest in interactivity surprises me. Interaction is so much a part of our daily life as to be virtually banal. Breathing is a profoundly intimate social and physical interaction: We breathe air into our lungs, extract oxygen, and expel carbon dioxide into the air, to be breathed in by others or transformed by plants back into oxygen. Talking, crossing the street, and driving a car are all interactions significantly more complex than those supported by most interactive computer systems.

The world with which we interact has become increasingly abrasive. We breathe in exhaust fumes. A growing list of foods interact with our bodies to cause cancer. Infectious diseases like AIDS make us squeamish about physical contact (whether justified or not). Under this bombardment, we're turning to ways of reducing our interaction with the world. The condom is, for example, a device intended to prevent interaction (either between sperm and ovum or between sperm and blood).

So perhaps the explosion of interest in interactivity is part of a search for havens of safe interaction—clean, sterile, nonphysical spaces where we can satisfy our natural human desire to engage in things outside of ourselves.

Theoretical Claustrophobia

While the physical sterility of virtual experiences may be the easiest to grasp, the key type of sterility in artificial experience, for me, is that the ideas themselves are hermetically sealed. In "reality," our concepts, models, and abstractions are always projections onto a complicated reality that never fully yields to our logic. Simulated experiences are built up from models that we have ourselves defined or that we already understand. In a contained interactive system, we enter into our own models, into a space of no true ambiguity or contradiction. There is no "unfathomable," which is a way of saying that there is no "God" in this virtual space.

Simulated Complexity

In a similar vein, it's important to understand the difference between "fractal" complexity and the complexity of life experience. Fractals are fascinating because a rich variety of forms are generated by a single, often simple algorithm. The endless and endlessly different structures of the Mandelbrot set are generated by a single equation addressed in an unusual way. This relationship between the infinite detail of the fractal and its terse mathematical representation is an extreme example of compression. The compression of images, sound, and video into much smaller encoded representations is one of the keys of the current multimedia explosion.

Opposed to the incredibly compressible "complexity" of fractals is the complexity of true randomness. Something can be said to be random if it cannot be expressed by anything less than itself, that is to say, it's incompressible. This rather philosophical notion can be observed in our everyday online communication. To move data around quickly and efficiently, we compress it and then send it through a modem that compresses it further. What is left is the incompressible core of the information. As you can hear through your modem when you dial up your Internet service provider, the result sounds close to random noise.

Randomness and noise are usually things we avoid, but in the purely logical space of the computer, randomness and noise have proven to be welcome and necessary to break the deadly predictability. But random number generators, used so often to add "human" spice to computer games and computer-generated graphics, are not "random" at all. They merely repeat over a fairly long period—a sterile simulation of the real thing.

The Power of Randomness

The classic story of the power of randomness is the story of the many monkeys at typewriters typing away for many years. The laws of probability suggest that one of these monkeys will at some point accidentally type the entire works of William Shakespeare. And if you accept evolution, then you could say that this has already occurred. Many subatomic particles working over a long but not infinite amount of time have managed to generate the works of William Shakespeare by gathering quite arbitrarily into molecules, proteins, life-forms, social structures, and ultimately into Shakespeare himself.

On the other hand, neither a fractal nor a pseudorandom number generator is capable of this feat. Those systems are "closed." No matter how far you expand them, Shakespeare's work will not be generated. Shakespeare is actually beside the point here. Replace the work of Shakespeare in the preceding discussion with any extremely unlikely but theoretically possible occurrence (the origin of life, the birth of the first consciousness, or meeting the love of your life). These occurrences are statistically unlikely, but they can have a profound effect on the life of those who run into them. When you think back over your life, which were the really pivotal events: the predictable ones or the ones that seemed the most improbable?

In designing environments for experience, we must remain humble in the face of the power of irresolvable, nonfractal complexity. The computer is an almost pure vacuum, devoid of unpredictability. Computer bugs, while annoying, are never actually unpredictable unless this "vacuum" fails, as when the hardware itself overheats or is otherwise physically damaged. This vacuum is extremely useful, but it's no place to live.

When I started working with interactive systems, I saw the "vacuum" of the computer as the biggest challenge. I developed Very Nervous System as an attempt to draw as much of the universe's complexity into the computer as possible. The result is not very useful in the classical sense, but it creates the possibility of experiences that in themselves are useful and thought-provoking, particularly by making directly tangible that what is lost in oversimplification.

Summary

One of the initial motivations behind interactive interfaces was that they would allow users to apply their accumulated common sense and knowledge of the world to their navigation of the abstract realm of information. Abstract things become sensual and experiential. The use of familiar metaphors to approximate simulations of the real world enables users to make decisions and handle data in familiar, intuitive ways. This has been the reason for the dramatic success of the graphical user interface. In retrospect, however, this may have been merely a transitional strategy. Children now spend enough time interacting through synthetic interfaces that their common sense and knowledge of the "world" will have been formed partly by the interfaces and abstract simulations themselves. The shifting of the experiential base from "reality" to the video game's or educational software's virtual reality has far-reaching implications. Interaction is not a novelty to today's children; it's an integral part of the only reality they have known.

From a purely practical point of view, this is a useful situation. (Imagine a touch of sarcasm here.) Children are adapting from birth to the language of synthetic interfaces. We will no longer have to worry about the real-world behaviours and expectations of our users that make designing intuitive interfaces so difficult. Common *virtual* sense will be widespread.

In the process, however, those of us who design interactions inadvertently step into the realm of theologians and philosophers, perhaps even gods. We're laying the foundations for new ways of seeing and experiencing the world. And, through communications interfaces, we're building new social and political infrastructures. Economic pressure, intense competition, and shrinking product development cycles make it difficult to accept and do justice to this responsibility.

But accepting responsibility is at the heart of interactivity. Responsibility means, literally, the ability to respond. An interaction is possible only when two or more people or systems agree to be sensitive and responsive to each other. The process of designing an interaction should also itself be interactive. We design interfaces, pay close attention to the user's responses, and make modifications as a result of our observations. But we need to expand the terms of this interactive feedback loop from simply measuring functionality and effectiveness to including an awareness of the impressions an interaction leaves on the user and the ways these impressions change the user's experience of the world.

We're always looking for better input devices and better sensors to improve the interactive experience. But we also need to improve our own sensors, perceptions, and conceptual models so that we can be responsive to the broader implications of our work.

Biography

David Rokeby is an artist based in Toronto, Ontario, Canada and has been creating interactive sound and video installations since 1982. Most of his work reflects his strong interests in language, vision systems, and gestural interfaces. His best known work, Very Nervous System, translates human gestures into music. His work has been exhibited in North and South America, Europe, and Asia, including the Venice Biennale, the SIGGRAPH '88 Art Show, Ars Electronica (Linz, Austria), the Triennale di Milano (Milan), the Kwangju Biennale (Korea), and the Biennale di Firenze (Florence). He was awarded the first Petro-Canada Award for Media Arts in 1988 and the Prix Ars Electronica Award of Distinction for Interactive Art (Austria) in 1991.

A modification of Very Nervous System is now being used to enable a paralyzed woman to speak and write. David is currently working on a new installation entitled "The Giver of Names," a system that describes objects presented to it in poetic and metaphoric ways.

Chapter 3

The Past Was No Illusion

Walt Bransford
Thrillistic LLC

Are We Really at the Front of the Line?

There's much to consider in the marriage of digital technology with the art of illusion, which has taken many forms over the ages. In creating fictions—whether through storytelling, writing, live performance, or still or moving images—space and time are elements upon which many illusions depend. Manipulations of either may be subtle or overwhelming, designed-in or an artifact of another goal. Many technologies of the recent past weren't created for the purpose of illusion but enabled new ways to perceive and interact with the world and with people. They were powerful—and often entertaining. These experiences stimulated the imagination, becoming a basis for new forms of entertainment products. One path spawns ten more, and opportunity follows new expectations. Many early attractions sold what we would now call simulation experiences. It's informative to look back at some inventions that blended the concepts of experience, immersion, illusion, interaction, and distribution via the perceived manipulation of space and time. This chapter creates an illusion of its own: a trip back in history. There's adventure back there—keys, secrets, and a character or two—hints we can use today.

Film is one of the developments with prominent illusion and immersion components that were later exploited for entertainment, but thrills were delivered long before that in more mundane forms. Such thrills share certain traits; they provided an experience that many participants perceived as magical, transcendent, or at least very different. Many late nineteenth-century developments in transportation and electricity were practical but amazing for the time. They delivered experiences for diverse audiences, showcased new technologies, or used familiar technologies in new ways. They would soon affect nearly everyone's lives, stimulating our imagination, elevating our perceptions, and transforming our awareness of the world and of ourselves.

Entertainment is a product, just as are its foundation technologies. Its developers usually expect some return for their efforts beyond the satisfaction of creation. That return on the entertainment investment drives much of the evolution of our popular culture. Our step back into a colorful past will show that the art and science of high-tech illusion is a constant. We can anticipate continuous serendipitous discovery of new ways to combine new inventions.

Getting There: Unbounded Immersion

What is now thought of as early mechanized travel—railroad trains—stimulated the imagination of a nation. This immense moving object, propelled by a large, loud locomotive that seemed alive, brought the high-technology steam engine from the factory floor into near-direct contact with everyone in their everyday lives. Trains met practical necessities but were also a form of entertainment (and still are for rail fans of all ages worldwide). Rapid (30 miles per hour was *fast* in 1890) train transportation over yet-unassimilated landscapes was a vividly compelling experience.

In 1893, there were no movies showcasing a culture and its communities, no broadcast cultural norms, few widely available books about great American cities or the Majestic Land, and few travelogues for armchair journeys. This was the year of the Chicago World's Fair, and simply getting to Chicago was an event of unparalleled discovery. The expanding continental American rail network was just over 20 years old, providing for many people their first experience of moving across land faster than they or an animal could walk. This early conjoining of consumer and high technology challenged the imagination in many ways: One was immersed in a moving object with many other people, propelled by machine, and provided the collective experience of seeing the landscape of a huge, developing country in all its natural and man-made splendor. The associated anticipation, experience, and discovery of the trip itself combined to define a sense of place.

Comfortable and secure in these machines, early rail travelers encountered a new kind of territory. Portions of the personality of an emerging nation developed there. It was fertile ground for the imaginations of many, as they encountered shifting boundaries between reality and illusion. From this experience grew new forms of expression in American literature and art. It also helped spawn a technology-based industry of illusion for mass entertainment and education.

The World's Columbian Exposition at Chicago: New Edges of Imagination

By 1893, there had been several world's fairs, each a means of disseminating culture, technology, and architecture. But the World's Columbian Exposition at Chicago that summer was like no other before or since. Located 12 miles south of downtown Chicago on the shore of Lake Michigan and covering 633 acres, it was the largest fair to date and the first event of such magnitude in the Western Hemisphere. The timing of the fair as a punctuation in the establishment of American Culture offered extraordinary opportunities. America was adapting commercial, social, and cultural systems to an infrastructure that was the crowning achievement of the Industrial Era: maturing systems of mechanized farming, production, transportation, and early electrical communication.

The fair at Chicago was a showcase for technology, art, and entertainment. It was the world's introduction to America as a thriving Nation of Vision. It officially changed the perceived geographic center of the county—a sociospatial concept—from the East Coast to its actual location: a booming modern city, the gateway to a newly conquered Wild West frontier.

Just getting to the fair was an experience few could have anticipated (and many were probably ready to walk right back home). The Chicago Fair was a mass experience that packaged the familiar and the bewildering with a furiously developing future. It was palace, mud, and marble, plow and violin—a mind-expanding agitation soothed by the waves of Lake Michigan. It was thousands of tiny experiences found by millions of visitors during two Chicago summers. The scale, diversity, and quantity of attractions and people provided a feast for the imagination.

Immersion in a Technology Showcase

As at all the preceding international expositions, new technologies were abundant. Huge steam-powered machines performed tasks never imagined—part of a parade of technology that was freeing people from relentlessly boring jobs and allowing them time for leisure. But steam power was becoming old news. At the fair, energy was converted from steam by a really new device: the steam-driven AC Electric Generator. Several electrical technologies were showcased at the fair. Extensive electric lighting introduced a spectacular nighttime experience across the immense spread of buildings, ponds, and grand promenades. Until then, night was a slice of time spent in an area no larger than what one sees, usually only several feet. Most people stayed home or slept. Society's concept of day really was over at night! Large-scale lighting at the fair opened new vistas and new shared spatial perceptions of the familiar. It is difficult to appreciate the impact of this now, but it was simultaneously bewildering and enchanting. And this was not electricity's only impact on space and time in its appearance at the Chicago fair.

Transmission of information over long distances was not new; the telegraph was nearly 50 years old. It really shrank time and space; information traveled much faster than it could be carried. But at the Chicago fair, visitors were treated to long-distance telephone calls between Chicago and Boston and between Chicago and New York! Phones were connected to phonographs, concert halls, and opera houses on the East Coast. The great-grandparent of the fax machine made an appearance, too; Gray's Teleautograph transmitted handwriting by electricity. These were just as exciting and revolutionary at that moment as the mechanized transportation of people and goods had been a few decades earlier. What must it have been like to experience for the first time a human voice carried farther than the ear could hear? All these experiences with technology fired the imagination of the day much as the confluence of computers, interactivity, and the Internet does now.

Entertainment at the Fair: Collisions of Cultures, Vistas, and Motion

The Midway Plaisance was critical to the fair's solvency. It was a long, narrow strip of land extending for nearly a mile eastward from the main grounds, with the first separate entertainment area for a world's fair. Familiar forms of entertainment were abundant, along with many installations representing foreign countries. Time and space jumbled and jumped amid a crop of ancient and old-world village recreations, first tried at an earlier Paris world's fair and now alive on an immense scale. A Night in Tunisia, a hot afternoon in Cairo, or a quick stop by The World Congress of Beauty of the International Dress and Costume Company could be had by all. The Panorama of the Bernese Alps was billed as an "electric theater," where light and sound effects combined with landscape paintings to create the illusion of a mountain storm . . . Disneyland, a decade before Walt was born. This artificial fantasyland forever established the idea that leisure time could casually seek destination beyond one's home turf—a respite from the reality of what was still a difficult survival situation for many.

Going Up

One thing didn't escape the view of anyone who came near the fair. At the center of the Midway, spinning in grandeur above the Midwestern plain, was a contraption that is now a fixture of the global language of fairs and theme parks: the world's first Ferris Wheel. It was designed and built (in eight months) by Pittsburgh engineer and bridge builder George W. Ferris. Rising nearly 270 feet in the air, it spun upon a 45-foot axle, the largest single piece of steel yet forged. It had 36 wood-veneered passenger cars, each the size of a bus and carrying 60 passengers—40 of whom sat on plush swivel chairs for the 20-minute ride of two revolutions. One compartment was reserved for a band, which provided full-time music to fair goers and wheel riders. For many, this was their first introduction to a view of mass human activity from a point higher than eye level. The Eiffel Tower at the Paris World's Fair of 1869 did much the same trick, but the Ferris wheel went further; not only was it surrounded by human activity, it *moved*. It offered a vivid experience of an environment just moments before absorbed on foot; it was another machine that called to question the normal arrangement of time and space. But unlike a train trip, this gizmo went up, over, under, and back around, delivering a remarkable view of the fair and nearby neighborhoods of Chicago. Just imagine a family fresh off the Iowa prairie, arriving days earlier on their first train trip, now experiencing the enchanting, surely pleasurable overload of a ride on the Ferris Wheel. Who can know what visions and dreams arose from these friendly and startling experiences with technology? The Ferris Wheel became the memory of the fair for many visitors. It survives today in local fairs everywhere—in an entertainment venue and cash machine called "The Midway."

The Paris Fair of 1900: Changing Context, Rising Expectations

By 1900, leisure time was a reality; people sought ways to spend their new leisure capital. Large-scale sports such as professional baseball and amusement parks on the scale of Coney Island were designed to meet this demand. The Paris World Exposition of 1900 meant to eclipse the popular successes of 1893 Chicago. More people knew about convenient travel and had seen pictures of faraway locales. Electric communications and print media brought news and views of the planet and its peoples to a knowledge-hungry populace. The Trans-Siberian Railway Panorama, the Mareorama, and the Cineorama Air-Balloon Panorama were devised for the Paris fair to capitalize on this new awareness. Milestones in the development of illusion technology, they were a means for relieving the participant of leisure capital as well as capital in its familiar form.

People had become accustomed to stationary dioramas and panoramas—they were common even at county fairs. The mountain storm simulation at the Chicago fair added electric lighting and sound. The Railway Panorama and Mareorama at Paris enlivened panoramas—as the Ferris Wheel enlivened towers—by introducing motion. Further, the attractions were designed such that no two experiences were identical. These "rides" were elaborate, expensive, and, as is common today, developed and funded by corporations dealing in the real thing—a related product to sell. The Trans-Siberian Railway Panorama was built and sponsored by the Compagnie Internationale des Wagons-Lits, a major European railroad company. The designers wanted to deliver magic with the best in technology, but the medium was not just a showcase. It was illusion for illusion's sake, riding on assumptions about the ability of the imagination to transcend the medium.

The Railway Panorama

This 45-minute experience was an essay in detail. It offered a chance to experience the 14-day journey by rail from Moscow to Peking, a 6,300-mile journey over tracks not yet completed at the time of the Paris fair. There were three realistic railway cars, each 70 feet long with saloons, dining rooms, bars, bedrooms, and other elements of a luxury train. Totally detailed and lavishly equipped, the cars were elevated a little above a place for spectators in conventional rows of seats. This gallery faced a stage-like area where the simulated views along the train trip were presented by an inventive contraption. The immediate reality of a vehicular trip is that nearby objects seem to pass by more rapidly than distant ones. So, nearest to the participants was a horizontal belt covered with sand, rocks, and boulders, driven at a speed of 1,000 feet per minute! Behind that was a low vertical screen painted with shrubs and brush, traveling at 400 feet per minute. A second, slightly higher screen, painted to show more distant scenery, scrolled along at 130 feet per minute. The most distant one, 25 feet tall and 350 feet long, painted with mountains, forests, clouds, and cities, moved at 16 feet per minute. Real geographical features along the way were depicted on this screen: Moscow, Omsk, Irkutsk, the shores of great lakes and rivers, the Great Wall of China, and Peking. The screens, moving in one direction only, were implemented as a belt system. Due to the inexact speeds of the scenery, the "journey" never repeated itself exactly, providing an ever-changing combination of scenes and a reason to pay to visit the attraction again.

The Mareorama

The scenery in the Railway Panorama moved, but the spectator's seats and the railway cars didn't provide any motion cues. The Mareorama eliminated that shortcoming. An ingenious system provided movement to a ship-shaped platform, positioned between a pair of moving screens. Each was 2,500 feet long and four stories tall, painted by a team of artists working under Hugo d'Alesi, well-known at the time for his beautiful vistas on the posters of railway and shipping companies. The 215,000 square feet of screen were rendered with scenes based on sketches made by d'Alesi during the real voyage that the Mareorama simulated. The extremely heavy cylinders holding the rolled-up screens were supported by floats in a water basin. A system of jacks, floats, hydraulic pistons, and pumps driven by electric motors moved the cylinders to roll and pitch the panoramas. This same mechanism controlled the motion of the spectator platform. As the platform rocked and the screen moved from one cylinder to another, the participant was treated to a simulated fair-weather, hazard-free voyage from Nice to Constantinople.

What is important about both the Railway Panorama and the Mareorama is that they were high-technology illusions as entertainment product. They were immersive and shared, just like the real things they simulated, and they were expensive, on a scale equivalent to theme park attractions today.

Going Up Again: The Cineorama Air-Balloon Panorama

Similar quality, detail, contemporary high-tech tricks, and expectations were prominent in the final example of attractions at Paris in 1900—the Cineorama Air-Balloon Panorama. This blend of new technology and creativity may have been the first-ever ride-film attraction.

The Air-Balloon Panorama took its cue from a then-novel invention: the hot air balloon. (Remember, this was a few years before the Wright brothers.) The thought of air travel must have strained the mind much more than imagining what it would be like to travel on one's first train trip! The Railway Panorama and the Mareorama delivered a virtual journey on familiar modes of transportation; they were heavily themed earthbound experiences with enhancements of depth and motion. The Air-Balloon Panorama attempted to deliver an experience into territory traveled only by, at that time, a handful of people: straight up into the air and across the land, a Ferris-Wheel car without the axle leash.

Full 360-degree stationary painted panoramas had been displayed before, and wide-angle stationary scenes projected from slides had also been attempted—enough times, in fact, to solve most of the problems of hiding seams and overlaps. But for the Air-Balloon Panorama, the designers decided to use another exciting embryonic technology: the magic medium of film, a panoramic movie to provide the illusion of rising to the clouds! French engineers, led by a Monsieur Grimoin-Sanson, built scaffolding for ten movie cameras, all driven by a system of gears powered by one hand crank. Each camera was positioned to cover a 36-degree field of view. The 1,000-pound panoramic movie camera was suspended from a real hot air balloon, which ascended over Paris to a height of 1,500 feet.

This experience was virtually recreated in a white-walled polygonal room 100 feet in diameter. At the center sat a large concrete structure housing ten projectors, and on this was the platform on which the spectators stood in an extralarge balloonist's wicker basket. From the ceiling hung the bottom portion of a balloon, complete with nets and rigging. The projection system was a feat of engineering. Electric arc lamps, producing intense light and heat, were vented by a system of ducts and fans. Each of the ten strips of film was glued into a 1,300-foot loop, providing nearly six minutes of projection. From their stationary platform, the participants saw a full-surround movie of the earth receding and experienced the sensation of rising in the air. When the balloon reached its highest elevation, the film direction was reversed, and the participants "descended" safely to earth! Film. Flight. Paris from the air. Magic indeed! Lightening of the senses—and the wallet, too.

It's No Fair

There have been many fairs across the planet since the Paris event. There were high points at Chicago, 1933; Brussels, 1958; New York, 1964; and Montreal, 1967. But the fairs and their attractions quickly became less memorable, finally rolling off the collective U.S. memory with a whimper into the Mississippi at New Orleans in 1984. Today's mega-theme parks, regional amusement parks, county fairs, and high-tech arcades now own the territory of the blockbuster (usually licensed properties) thrill rides and the best, imagination-stretching illusions. As an entertaining educational technology showcase, fairs enabled their own demise. They featured, demonstrated, and made accessible technologies that established entire communications industries, ones that compressed space and time as a matter of course. The fairs helped acclimate Western culture to a free-market future of instant information. They gradually ceased being the only place on Earth to learn where the culture is going, firsthand.

Tickets, Please

When I snap my last paragraph, you will be back in the late twentieth century, creating someone else's past. Much has happened since something as mundane as a passenger train changed the way people see their world. What hasn't changed? People. We will always seek entertainment. We still need constant social contact and exchange; we are drawn to wherever people congregate. Now we have many means of creating opportunities to congregate, to be amazed, to learn. This is resulting in an extraordinary diversity of modern illusionary entertainment experiences: online and out of home, homemade and professional.

So we now have some fine new steam engines, pulleys, cables, and rails; computers, interactivity, and the Internet have combined into our very own imagination-busting, wallet-lightening, and revenue-enhancing technosphere. Time and space spin on new first-forged axles. It's a fun bump and grind: to interact with new vistas of information, floods of never-seen names, and, sometimes, faces and places, becoming friends in growing communities, infant economies, and market opportunities. There are now a few million people here, ready to line up and hand over the plastic for a new World's Eye View of something. Where will this take us? Where do we take it? Where's the fair in all its promise? There are now much more cost-effective ways to disseminate experiences. Is there a "headhouse" of these technologies that will carry us in imagination, image, and interaction to a genuine equivalent of a world's fair? Tickets, please—especially when the other side of the transaction involves some escape or a way to experience familiar things in new ways. For the creative and entrepreneurial types among us, the future is no illusion.

Bibliography

Applebaum, Stanley. *The Chicago World's Fair of 1893: A Photographic Record,* with text. New York: Dover Publications, 1980.

Cronon, William. *Nature's Metropolis: Chicago and the Great West.* New York: W. W. Norton, 1991.

De Vries, Leonard. *Victorian Inventions.* New York: American Heritage Press, 1971.

Klein, Maury. "The Coming of the Railroad and the End of the Great West," *American Heritage of Invention and Technology.* New York: American Heritage, a division of Forbes, Inc., 1995.

Svoboda, Josef. *The Secret of Theatrical Space.* New York: Applause Theatre Book Publishers, 1993.

Biography

Walt Bransford has a B. Architecture and owns Thrillistic LLC in North Little Rock, Arkansas. He has been involved in the design and development of state-of-the-art CAD software since 1982, when he was part of the team at Skidmore, Owings, & Merrill (Chicago) that developed the first large-scale full-featured realtime CAD system for architects and engineers. Thrillistic LLC developed an early automated Web publishing environment for a business journal and provides systems and Internet consulting services. He is a member of ACM SIGGRAPH and chair of the SIGGRAPH '98 conference. He is also an active volunteer in his son's public school and his neighborhood's property owners' association.

PART 2

Infrastructure: All Those Lines of Code

Your tax dollars at play: Research and development projects for the U.S. Defense Advanced Research Projects Agency (ARPA/DARPA) and NASA provided much of the physical and digital infrastructure for today's interactive entertainment. ARPAnet grew into the Internet. Work at NASA Ames Research Center and Wright-Patterson Air Force Base advanced Ivan Sutherland's earlier work on head-mounted displays and contributed to the development and integration of spatialized audio displays, tactile, voice, and gesture interfaces. In the universities, ARPA funded virtual environment research at the University of North Carolina (UNC) at Chapel Hill, Brown, the University of Utah, Cornell, Cal Tech, and MIT. In the private sector, ARPA funded the development of SIMNET software at Bolt Beranek and Newman Inc., and Silicon Graphics, Inc.'s original geometry engine, which resulted in the entire SGI product line as we know it today, as well as the Nintendo 64 game console.

Some of the ARPA-funded research and development that contributes to contemporary entertainment (mostly games) includes simulation database design and architecture, semiautomated forces (artificial characters), intelligent automated opposing forces (artificial characters with resourcefulness), rapidly reconfigurable simulator elements, realtime multiplayer voice over simulation networks, and live multivehicle simulation exercises. This work is associated with enabling individuals and groups to do complex tasks well—much like games but with higher stakes. Researchers and developers from each of the preceding organizations have since become involved in various facets of the entertainment business, online and otherwise.

The second generation of SIMNET is called DIS (Distributed Interactive Simulation); it has enabled multiuser virtual war exercises of over 8,000 entities (many not human-directed). Far more efficient nonmilitary implementations are spreading rapidly; several commercial multiplayer games use derivatives of the DIS communications protocols, like Spectrum Holobyte's Falcon, and subsequent applications are fast becoming common. The next (large and profitable) steps involve applying this expertise and technology to nonshooting recreational virtual environments.

In Part 2, Don Brutzman, Farid Mamaghani, and Warren Katz provide an overview of the territory of networked virtual environments, key problems, and likely solutions. All have been deeply involved in SIMNET/DIS and related work. Tony Parisi is coauthor of a simpler civilian standard for online 3D environments, a foundation for multiuser applications, called VRML. And Scott Foster and Toni Schneider describe how to properly create one of the most important aspects of a virtual environment: the sense of acoustic space.

All this extremely expensive groundwork is of direct and indirect benefit to the purveyors of high-tech entertainment today. The only risk is that developers in Silicon Valley, Hollywood, and elsewhere may not take full advantage of the existing wealth of knowledge and experience.

Chapter 4

Graphics Internetworking: Bottlenecks and Breakthroughs

Don Brutzman
Naval Postgraduate School, Monterey

Introduction

Although networking is thought of as "different" from computer graphics, network considerations are integral to large-scale interactive three-dimensional (3D) graphics. Graphics and networks are now two interlocking halves of a greater whole: distributed virtual environments. New capabilities, applications, and ideas abound in this rich intersection of critical technologies. Our ultimate goal is to use networked interactive 3D graphics to take full advantage of all computation, content, and people resources available on the Internet.

Network breakthroughs repeatedly remove bottlenecks and provide new opportunities. A pattern appears as we attempt to scale up in capability and capacity without limit; every bottleneck broken reveals another. Understanding the bottlenecks, the solutions, and the potential upper bounds to growth enables us to develop effective networked graphics. When we overcome current bottlenecks, "effective networked graphics" will mean "applications."

Key perspectives on graphics internetworking are connectivity, content, interaction, economics, applications, and personal impacts. Internetworking refers to the ability to seamlessly interconnect multiple dissimilar networks globally. Connectivity has numerous dimensions including capacity, bandwidth, protocols, and the many-to-many capabilities of multicasting. Content equals the World Wide Web and includes any type of information, dataset, or stream that might be used in the graphics environment. Interaction implies minimal latency, a sense of presence, and the ability to both access and modify content. The economics of networked graphics environments is developing rapidly, and principal forces can be identified. Applications drive infrastructure development and are the most exciting part of networked graphics. Finally, the personal impacts that accompany these developments range from trivial to profound as high-quality interactive internetworked computer graphics become the norm on all computers.

Connectivity

There are many component pieces to the network connectivity puzzle. We will examine physical connectivity, network layers, the Internet Protocol suite, multicast distribution, the Multicast Backbone (MBone), enabling individuals, and vertical integration. An extensive overview of many networking topics is necessary to provide fundamental technical background. An understanding of each of these components is needed if we are to successfully implement highly shared graphics applications.

Physical connectivity to the Internet is a prerequisite to internetworked computer graphics. Other types of connections do not scale. There are several types of Internet access, roughly corresponding to direct providers, online services, and bulletin board systems (BBSs). Foremost is "direct" connectivity, where a user's computer is connected via a phone modem, local-area network (LAN), or other link to an Internet service provider. The native communication protocol used across these direct links and the global Internet is the Internet Protocol (IP). Designed for minimum complexity and maximum capability, IP compatibility and direct Internet connectivity are essential for any cutting-edge application that uses "anybody anywhere anytime any-kind" connectivity. Lesser degrees of connectivity are possible via gateways when indirectly connected through commercial services such as America On-Line (AOL) or CompuServe. Even lower degrees of connectivity like file transfer and store-and-forward e-mail are possible through dial-up BBSs. To achieve the maximum breakthroughs in networked computer graphics, direct Internet connectivity is essential. We assume such connectivity throughout this chapter.

Network Protocols and Layered Models

To integrate networks with large-scale graphical virtual environments, we invoke underlying network functions from within applications. Figure 4.1 shows how the seven layers of the well-known Open Systems Interconnection (OSI) standard network model generally correspond to the effective layers of the Internet Protocol (IP) standard. Functional characteristic definitions of the

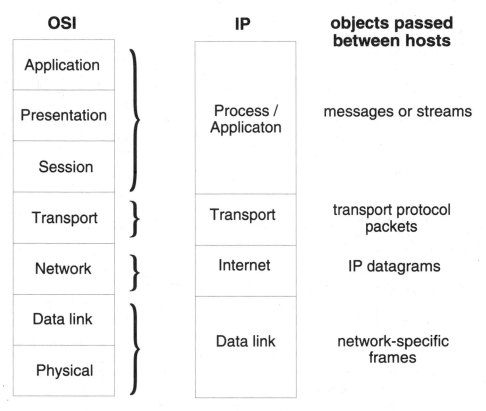

Figure 4.1 Correspondence between OSI and IP protocol layer models and objects passed between corresponding layers on communicating hosts.

IP layers follow later in Figure 4.2. These diagrams and definitions are merely an overview to help illustrate the logical relationship and relative expense of different network interactions. OSI and IP are often viewed as competing approaches to networking. A good overview of relative strengths and weaknesses of OSI versus IP is presented by Malamud (1992). In practice, OSI-related protocols are not of interest due to typically greater overhead and closed standards. For graphics internetworking, IP compatibility is essential for reasons of performance, open specifications, development flexibility, and overwhelmingly strong global deployment trends.

In general, network operations consume proportionately more processor cycles at the higher layers. We must minimize this computational burden to reduce latency and maintain realtime responsiveness. Two protocols are currently available in the transport layer: One ensures reliable delivery; the other makes no guarantees (therefore requiring less overhead).

Information transfer must use either reliable, connection-oriented Transport Control Protocol (TCP) or nonguaranteed-delivery, connectionless User Datagram Protocol (UDP). We choose between the two depending on the criticality, timeliness, and cost of imposing reliable delivery on the particular stream being distributed. Understanding the precise characteristics of TCP, UDP, and related protocols helps the virtual-world designer understand the strengths and weaknesses of each network tool employed. Since internetworking considerations impact all components in a large virtual environment, understanding network protocols and application hooks is essential for virtual-world designers (Internic 1995; Stallings 1994; Comer 1991; Stevens 1990).

Internet Protocol

Although the protocols associated with internetworking are diverse, there are some unifying concepts. Foremost is "Internet Protocol (IP) on everything"— the principle that every protocol coexists compatibly within the Internet Protocol suite. The global reach and collective momentum of IP-related protocols make their use essential. Current IPv.4 and next-generation IPv.6 (Bradner and Mankin 1996) protocols can be run over a complete variety of electrical, radio-frequency, and optical physical media.

Examination of protocol layers (Figure 4.2) helps clarify network issues. The lowest layers (Physical, Data Link) are reasonably stable with a huge installed base of Ethernet and Fiber Distributed Data Interface (FDDI) systems, augmented by the rapid development of wireless and broadband Integrated Services Digital Network (ISDN) solutions such as Asynchronous Transfer Mode (ATM). Compatibility with the Internet Protocol (IP) suite is assumed. The middle transport-related layers (Internet, Transport) are a busy research and development area. Realtime reliability, quality of service, and other capabilities are evolving rapidly due to competing market forces, both academic and commercial. Lower- and middle-layer bottlenecks are mostly solvable using available techniques. The major bottlenecks to large-scale graphics internetworking are at the application layer.

Multicast

Multicast packet distribution is best understood in comparison with two other packet distribution mechanisms: unicast and broadcast. Unicast is point-to-point communication, commonly occurring whenever an e-mail message is sent or a Web browser connects to a home page. Only the recipient host and intermediate routers need to spend computational cycles on a unicast packet.

Process/Application Layer. Invokes TCP/IP services, sending and receiving messages or streams with other hosts. Delivery can be intermittent or continuous.

Transport Layer. Provides host-host packetized communication between applications, using either reliable-delivery connection-oriented TCP or unreliable-delivery connectionless UDP. Exchanges packets end-to-end with other hosts.

Internet/Network Layer. Encapsulates packets with an IP datagram that contains routing information; receives or ignores incoming datagrams as appropriate from other hosts. Checks datagram validity; handles network error and control messages.

Data Link/Physical Layer. Includes physical media signaling and lowest-level hardware functions; exchanges network-specific data frames with other devices. Includes capability to screen multicast packets by port number at the hardware level.

Figure 4.2   Summary of Internet Protocol (IP) suite layer functionality.

One-to-many unicast communications are accomplished by multiple streams corresponding to every recipient. While this is not a problem when sending an e-mail message to multiple recipients, it is clearly an expensive proposition when sending a high-bandwidth stream such as graphics or video.

Broadcasting is at the opposite end of the spectrum from unicast. Broadcast messages reach every host on a local-area network and demand a response from each application or operating system. This is extremely inefficient at high bandwidths. Broadcast is typically prohibited from passing across routers to prevent such packets from propagating everywhere. Figure 4.3 shows typical unicast and broadcast packet stream paths.

Multicast packet functionality lies between unicast and broadcast. A single multicast packet can touch every host on a LAN without duplication. However, each host can subscribe or ignore multicast at the hardware level by informing the network interface card which multicast channels (if any) to monitor. This feature is extremely important since a single high-bandwidth stream can still reach an arbitrary number of hosts, but computational load is seen only on hosts that explicitly subscribe to the multicast channel. Multicast packets are usually prevented from traversing routers to prevent overloading the Internet with arbitrary propagation of such streams. Figure 4.4 illustrates

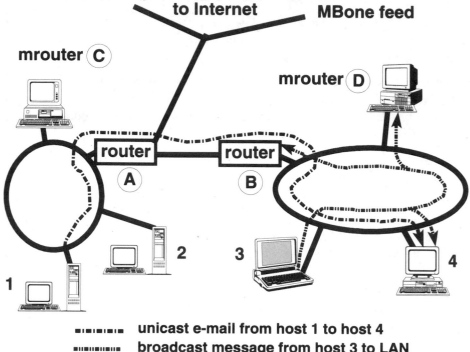

Figure 4.3 Typical unicast and broadcast packet stream paths.

this behavior. To summarize, the key network characteristics that distinguish multicast from unicast and broadcast include the following:

- Individual multicast packets can be read by all host workstations on a LAN.

- Elimination of duplicate streams minimizes bandwidth requirements.

- Workstations can screen unwanted multicast packets at the hardware level, eliminating unnecessary computational burden on applications.

Multicasting has existed for several years on local-area networks such as Ethernet and Fiber Distributed Data Interface (FDDI). Now, with Internet Protocol multicast addressing at the network layer, group communication can be

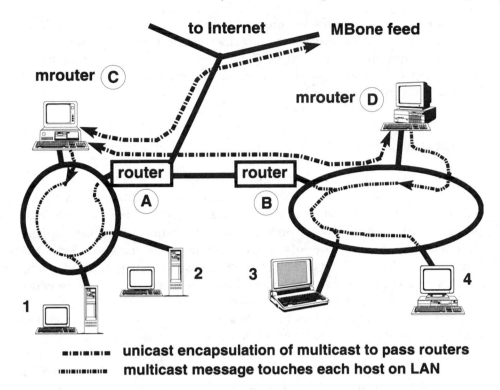

Figure 4.4   Example of multicast routers connecting multicast streams encapsulated by unicast (in order to bypass router prohibitions on multicast). After stripping unicast headers, multicast streams are then available to each host on the LAN. Direct multicast support in routers has recently become available. Such multicast routes between LANs comprise the Multicast Backbone (MBone).

established across the Internet. IP multicast addressing is an Internet standard developed by Steve Deering (1989). Categorized officially as an IP Class D address, an IP multicast address is merely a set of reserved IP addresses in the range (224.0.0.0 through 239.255.255.255). Multicast is supported by numerous workstation vendors including SGI, Sun, DEC, and HP.

Unicast audio/video applications connecting groups of people across the Internet can be harmful because they waste bandwidth and do not scale. Recent examples include PC and Macintosh implementations of CU-SeeMe (Cogger 1995). Multicast applications have long been expected for Intel and Apple processors, but first multitasking must be better implemented in personal computer operating systems. Current audio/video applications for personal computers are typically unicast and need to be modified to support multicast before widespread use of arbitrarily shared data streams can be expected for all computers on the Internet.

Multicast Backbone

The Multicast Backbone (MBone) is one of the Internet's most interesting capabilities and is used for worldwide distribution of live audio and video on a global scale. MBone is a virtual network because it shares the same physical media as the Internet. It uses a network of routers (mrouters) that can support multicast. These mrouters are either upgraded commercial routers or dedicated workstations with modified operating system kernels running in parallel with standard routers. It was named by Steve Casner and originated from an effort in 1992 to multicast audio and video from meetings of the Internet Engineering Task Force (IETF). The fact that the MBone works at all is pretty remarkable since the original multicast backbone code was a student experiment. Encapsulated multicast streams sidestep regular routers through handcrafted tunnels across the Internet. The MBone exemplifies the best of the hacker ethic on a large scale. This pioneer spirit is still visible today as we cooperatively transition to a more carefully engineered backbone service that includes widespread multicast service.

Two things make multicasting feasible on a worldwide scale: installation of high-bandwidth Internet backbone connections and widespread availability of workstations with adequate processing power and built-in audio capability. Today, hundreds of researchers use MBone to develop protocols and applications for group communication. Multicast provides one-to-many, several-to-many, and many-to-many network delivery services. A one-to-many example might be live transmission of an academic conference. A several-to-many event might be a panel interview between different locations attended by many dispersed people. A many-to-many example might be a distributed battlefield exercise with 500 active players. Thus, multicast is useful for a variety of videoconferencing, audio, and multiplayer events where numerous hosts need to communicate simultaneously. Network concepts underlying MBone, bandwidth considerations, application tools, MBone events, interesting MBone uses, and how to connect to the MBone are described in "MBone Provides Audio and Video Across the Internet" (Macedonia and Brutzman 1994).

Lost MBone packets stay lost. Since multicast currently uses only the User Datagram Protocol (UDP) and not the Transport Control Protocol (TCP) of the IP suite, multicast streams are connectionless "unreliable" service. No setup is required, no acknowledgments are used, and no guarantee of delivery exists for this type of "best-effort" service. This is ordinarily a good thing for most real-time information streams (such as audio and video) since it avoids delivery bottlenecks and unwanted overhead. Furthermore, it doesn't matter what kind of data is sent via multicast IP packets. Several researchers are experimenting with "reliable multicast" transport protocols, which try to achieve a different balance by gaining occasional retransmission benefits without unacceptable acknowledgment overheads (Schulzrinne et al. 1996). These considerations are critical when scaling to arbitrarily large numbers of simultaneously interacting users on the network. A breakthrough in this bottleneck will enable new global communication paradigms for widely distributed shared applications.

The keys to understanding MBone constraints are capacity and bandwidth. The reason a multicast stream is bandwidth-efficient is that one packet can touch all workstations on a network. A 64-kilobit per second (Kbps) video stream typically provides 3 to 5 frames per second of quarter-size NTSC video. Each multicast stream uses the same bandwidth whether it is received by 1 workstation or 20. That is good. However, that same multicast packet is ordinarily prevented from crossing network boundaries such as routers. The reasons for this current restriction are religious and obvious from a networking standpoint. If a multicast stream that can touch every workstation jumps from network to network without controls, the entire Internet might quickly become saturated by such streams. That scenario is disastrous, so group controls are necessary. The MBone controls multicast packet distribution across the Internet in several ways. The topological "lifetime" of multicast packets is constrained to limit the number of allowed mrouter hops, and automatic pruning/grafting algorithms adaptively restrict multicast transmission to active participants. Such controls can prevent most (but not all) global MBone problems.

Responsible daily use of the MBone network merely consists of making sure you don't overload your local or regional bandwidth capacity. Appropriate bandwidth values initially seem obscure, but daily practice quickly makes such figures intuitive. MBone protocol developers are successfully experimenting with automatically pruning and grafting subtrees, but, for the most part, MBone uses thresholds to truncate broadcasts to the leaf routers. The truncation is done via setting the "time-to-live" (ttl) field in a packet, decrementing by at least 1 each time the packet passes through an mrouter. A ttl value of 1 prevents a multicast packet from escaping a LAN. An initial ttl value of 16 typically limits multicast to a campus, as opposed to values of 127 or 191, which might send a multicast stream to every subnet on the MBone (currently over 20 countries). Sometimes, we decrement ttl fields by intentionally large predetermined values to limit multicasts to sites and regions.

These issues may sound challenging but are relatively uncomplicated in practice. Some personal technical proficiency is important because use of the

MBone can have a major impact on shared network performance. For example, default video and audio streams consume about 200 Kbps of bandwidth, over 10 percent of a 1.5-Mbps T1 line (a common site-to-site link on the Internet). Several simultaneous high-bandwidth sessions might easily saturate network links and routers. The number of active users on current MBone channels is usually small enough that consensus and planning are able to effectively share this limited global resource. These low numbers will change soon. Planning, consensus, and careful utilization of physical and logical network resources will remain essential components of live large-scale global internetworking.

> *It is not every day that someone says to you, "Here's a multimedia television station that you can use to broadcast from your desktop to the world." These are powerful concepts and powerful tools that extend our ability to communicate and collaborate tremendously. They have already changed the way people work and interact on the net.*
>
> Macedonia and Brutzman 1994

Enabling Individuals

More and more often, the cost of admission for participation in global internetworking is a willingness to learn and participate. The cost of equipment is relatively low, and the price of bandwidth continues to become more affordable in most countries. As physical infrastructure becomes more prevalent, physical connectivity becomes easily available for many people. Public domain software for almost any purpose can be obtained freely over the Internet. Frequently asked question lists (FAQs), mailing lists, and even online books provide amazing depth on almost every subject related to networking and graphics. Individuals are now able to do many things that previously required large groups and large budgets to accomplish. This trend is a tremendous equalizer that lets students, researchers, and companies become effective players in a global arena.

Vertical Integration

For many years, there have been walls separating communities of users corresponding to the computer architecture or operating system used. Supercomputers, mainframes, workstations, and personal computers were so dissimilar that commonality between them was practically nonexistent. Networked applications have changed this situation completely. Once-isolated islands are now complementary, interdependent, and practically seamless.

Initial rudimentary examples of interconnectivity are e-mail, file transfer protocol (ftp), and remote-terminal protocol (telnet). The Internet Protocol suite enables standardized hostnames, host numbers, and Uniform Resource Locators (URLs), which, in turn, convert loosely connected hardware into a shared global address space. Sharable applications such as Mosaic, Netscape, distributed simulation, and the MBone tools show that equivalent functionality can be expected on any computer platform, from supercomputers to PCs. The Hypertext Markup Language (HTML) and the Web now provide a universal interface to any computational process, a fact surprisingly missed by most interface designers. This new interoperability between all computers means that applications designers can think in terms of vertical integration. Thousands of simultaneous users with networked personal computers can now query, drive, and evaluate computationally intensive graphics scenes rendered by powerful computers at arbitrarily distant locations. Such scenarios have been described theoretically for years. While theoretical discussions continue, the practical capability has arrived. Together, all the countless machines interconnected by the Internet are our new supercomputer.

Here are the success metrics for vertical interoperability: "Will the application run on my supercomputer?" Yes. "Will it run on my UNIX workstation?" Yes. "Will it also run on my Macintosh or PC?" Yes. This approach has been shown to be a practical (and even preferable) software requirement. Vertical interoperability approaches are best supported by open nonproprietary specifications developed by responsive standardization groups such as the Internet Engineering Task Force (IETF).

Broad interoperability and Internet compatibility are essential. Closed solutions are dead ends. In order to achieve broad vertical integration, proprietary and vendor-specific hardware need to be avoided. Videoteleconferencing systems are an example of a market fragmented by competing and incompatible proprietary specifications. In the area of new connection-oriented cell-based services such as Asynchronous Transfer Mode (ATM) and Integrated Services Digital Network (ISDN), some disturbing trends are commonplace. Supposedly standardized protocol implementations often do not work as advertised, particularly when run between hardware from different vendors. Effective throughput is often far less than maximum bit rate. Latency performance is highly touted and rarely tested. Working applications that use these services are difficult to find. Corresponding network operating costs are often hidden or ignored. Perhaps worst of all, long-haul services such as ATM may not be fully interoperable with the Internet Protocol, and some core functionality (such as many-to-many multicast) may not be feasible. Application developers are advised to plan and budget for lengthy delays and costly troubleshooting when working with new services.

Connectivity Conclusions

We have seen that connectivity has many facets. A technical overview of these concepts was necessary in order to understand what is feasible. Our technical foundation is now strong enough to consider broader concepts of content, interaction, economics, applications, and personal impacts.

Content and the World Wide Web

Connectivity isn't worth much unless there's information of value (content) to exchange. While human and artificial users have created a wide variety of content for many years, only recently has it been available on a global scale. Many proposals have been made regarding the optimum way to achieve a global database, but only one methodology is a contender: the Web.

If the Internet is our global supercomputer, then the Web is our global database. The Web has been defined as a "wide-area hypermedia information retrieval initiative aiming to give universal access to a large universe of documents" (Hughes 1994). Fundamentally, the Web combines a name space consisting of all visible information stores on the Internet with a broad set of retrieval clients and servers, all of which can be connected by easily defined Hypertext Markup Language (HTML) hypermedia links. This globally accessible combination of media, client programs, servers, and hyperlinks can be conveniently utilized by humans or autonomous entities. The Web continues to fundamentally shift the nature of information storage, access, and retrieval, as best explained by its originator (Berners-Lee et al. 1994). Information content is the crucial component underlying most 3D graphics renderings. Information context is the key quality provided by the universal naming scheme and simplicity of HTML. Anyone can now add any content and any context they might want.

Current Web capabilities are easy to use despite rapid growth and change. An extension mechanism allows new content types and corresponding viewers to be easily integrated into existing browsers. The relative simplicity of HTML has been essential to the rapid growth of the Web. People add their own content because it's easy to do. Convention and common use have standardized many content formats, and ease of use has been the principal engine of success.

The ubiquitous availability of content via the Web has massive implications that we are only beginning to perceive. It's one thing to be vaguely aware that a Library of Congress exists somewhere, with most information sources that might ever be wanted. It's another to have such an information archive close at hand, regardless of your physical location (Library 1995). It's a further step to think such an archive might be rapidly searchable and conveniently retrievable on demand. Until recently, it was unprecedented to think that anyone anywhere might contribute to such a store without formal constraint. Now, such capabilities are common. Future content challenges include easy connections for datasets, databases, and analytic models to the Web.

These ideas are a series of comprehensible steps, but together they imply amazing capabilities. If knowledge is power, then these capabilities are powerful indeed. It is now possible for any question on nearly any subject to quickly provoke more information than is humanly possible to absorb. Eventually, "everybody's everything" can be online. It seems there is now an ocean of information surrounding us. We can swim around the world or drown trying to drink it all in. How we deal with it is our choice.

While the full implications of universal access to massive content are still emerging, it's clear the genie can't be stuffed back into the bottle. We must deal with all this content. Such a challenge is a good match for interactive 3D computer graphics. Since graphics techniques can portray large amounts of information in a meaningful way, realistic rendering and scientific visualization techniques are logical choices for dealing with massive content. Effective 3D user interfaces are also needed for navigating the richness of these worlds. Interfaces must feel intuitive to both novice and expert, particularly if access and interaction are to scale up to match amazingly large volumes of content.

There are two more important points related to networking and the Web: improved interaction and importance of an open standards process. The HyperText Transfer Protocol (http), which is used for most Web-based interactions, typically provides a client-server relationship; a user can push on a Web resource and get a response, but there are no openly standardized mechanisms for a Web application to independently push back at the user. The Netscape Corporation has independently defined and implemented server-push and client-pull techniques that permit repeated queries and replies (Netscape 1995). An example of "push" is when a server can send repeated updates down an open connection to refresh a client display. A "pull" example is automatic repeated queries by a client at intervals matching data refresh cycles on the server. These methods for improving interaction on the Web are steps in the right direction. Better interaction mechanisms will enable new types of Web applications.

Netscape preempted the HTML standards process by unilaterally proposing and incorporating push/pull capabilities. Although server push and client pull are useful concepts likely to be included in forthcoming versions of the HTML specification, unilateral implementations can fragment a common standard into incompatible, inadequate variants. Open standards review means that any specification can be widely scrutinized in detail. Meanwhile (in the IETF at least), two or more independent implementations are needed to validate correct performance prior to acceptance as a standard. Patience and cooperation are essential since coopting standardization through market share creates far more bottlenecks than breakthroughs. Considering this particular technical example, as the demands of interactive client-server queries and replies grow in scale, many of the bandwidth and scaling issues explored in the MBone will reappear. Since cooperative standards development has been essential for the success of the MBone, similar cooperative standards-based efforts will continue to be essential as we scale up the Web.

Virtual Environments

The scope of virtual environment (VE) development is so broad that it can be seen as an inclusive superset of all other global information infrastructure applications. VEs and VR applications are characterized by human operators interacting with dynamic world models of truly realistic sophistication and complexity (Zyda et al. 1993; Durlach and Mavor 1995). Current research in large-scale virtual environments can link hundreds of people and artificial agents with interactive 3D graphics, massive terrain databases, global hypermedia, and scientific datasets. Related work on teleoperation of robots and devices in remote or hazardous locations further extends the capabilities of human-machine interaction in synthetic computer-generated environments. VE construction can include concepts and components from nearly any subject area. The variety of desired connections between people, artificial entities, and information can be summarized by the slogan "connecting everyone to everything." As diversity and detail of virtual environments increase without bound, network requirements become the primary bottleneck.

The most noticeable characteristic of VEs is interactive 3D graphics, which ordinarily involves coordinating a handful of input devices while placing realistic renderings at fast frame rates on a single screen. Networking can connect virtual worlds with realistic distributed models and diverse inputs/outputs on a global scale. Graphics and virtual-world designers interested in large-scale interactions can now consider the worldwide Internet as a direct extension of their computer. A variety of networking techniques can be combined with traditional interactive 3D graphics to provide almost unlimited connectivity. Experience shows that the following services are essential for virtual-world communications: reliable point-to-point communications, behavior interaction protocols such as the IEEE standard Distributed Interactive Simulation (DIS) protocol, World Wide Web (WWW) links, and multicast channels for bandwidth-efficient many-to-many communications. Further examination of behavior-based interaction protocols is next presented using DIS as an example methodology.

Distributed Interactive Simulation

The Distributed Interactive Simulation (DIS) protocol is an IEEE standard for logical communication among entities in distributed simulations (IEEE 1993; DIS 1994). Although initial development was driven by the needs of military users, the protocol formally specifies the communication of physical interactions by any type of physical entity and is adaptable for general use. Information is exchanged via protocol data units (PDUs), which are defined for a large number of interaction types.

The principal PDU type is the Entity State PDU. This PDU encapsulates the position and posture of a given entity at a given time, along with linear and angular velocities and accelerations. Special components of an entity (such as the orientation of movable parts) can also be included in the PDU as articulated parameters. A full set of identifying characteristics uniquely specifies the originating entity. Several complementary dead-reckoning algorithms permit computationally efficient projection of entity posture by listening hosts. Dozens of additional PDU types are defined for simulation management, sensor or weapon interaction, signals, radio communications, collision reporting, and logistics support. Most of these highly specialized "garbage PDUs" are of questionable utility for most VE applications. What is essential is correct (or at least "close-enough") physics, realtime realism, and adequate global consistency.

Here is an example showing how the DIS entity state PDU properly enables networked distribution of realistic physics-based behavior. In 1992, a jet pilot at the Naval Postgraduate School (NPS) developed a real-time model of high-performance aircraft response using parameterized flight coefficients and quaternion mathematics (Cooke et al. 1992). It turns out that tactical aircraft are inherently unstable. Jet pilots require years of training, and onboard computers are continuously making compensatory adjustments to flight surfaces. Qualified fighter pilots are pleased with this quaternion-based model since the simulated jet reacts realistically and "flies" much like a true jet. Unfortunately, naive operators tend to crash when flying this model (and might have similar difficulties in a real jet). Substituting flight coefficients that represent a more benign aircraft like a Piper Cub made operation much easier for casual users. The significant fact related to this substitution is that the underlying DIS model requires no changes. Regardless of whether packet update rates necessary for smooth motion average once per 5 seconds or 20 times per second, the DIS Entity State PDU dead-reckoning algorithms are able to properly track position and orientation. This maximizes precision, maintains proper global consistency, and minimizes network loading.

Of further interest to virtual-world designers is an open-format Message PDU. Message PDUs enable user-defined extensions to the DIS standard. Such flexibility coupled with the efficiency of Internetwide multicast delivery permits extension of the object-oriented message-passing paradigm to a distributed system of essentially unlimited scale. Free-format DIS Message PDUs might provide general message-passing connectivity to any information site on the Internet, extended by use of network pointer mechanisms that already exist for the World Wide Web. This is a promising area for future work.

VE Grand Challenges

The most important "grand challenges" of computing today are not large, static, gridded simulations such as computational fluid dynamics or finite element modeling. Similarly, traditional supercomputers are not necessarily the most powerful or significant platforms because adding hardware and dollars to incrementally improve existing expensive computer designs is a well-understood exercise. What's more challenging and potentially more rewarding is the interconnection of all computers in ways that support global interaction of people and processes. In this respect, the Internet is the ultimate supercomputer, the Web is the ultimate database, and any networked hardware in the world is a potential input/output device. Large-scale virtual environments attempt to simultaneously connect many of these computing resources in order to recreate the functionality of the real world in meaningful ways. Network software is the key to solving VE grand challenges.

Large-Scale Virtual-World Internetworking

Four key communication methods are necessary for large-scale virtual-world internetworking: lightweight messages, network pointers, heavyweight objects, and realtime streams (Figure 4.5). For each of these four methods, bandwidth and latency must be carefully considered. The following networking elements can be combined to implement these four methods:

- Distribution of virtual-world components using point-to-point sockets can be used for tight coupling and realtime response of physics-based models.

- DIS is a well-tested behavior protocol that enables efficient live interaction between multiple entities in multiple virtual worlds.

- A wide variety of alternative behavior protocols are being developed and evaluated for large-scale virtual-world interaction.

- Hypermedia servers and embedded Web browsers provide virtual worlds global access to pertinent archived images, video, graphics, papers, datasets, software, sound clips, text, or any other computer-storable media, both as inputs and outputs.

- Multicast protocols permit moderately large realtime bandwidths to be efficiently shared by an unconstrained number of hosts.

- MBone connectivity permits live distribution of graphics, video, audio, DIS, and other streams worldwide in real time.

Together, these example components provide the core functionality of lightweight messages, network pointers, heavyweight objects, and realtime streams. Integrating these network tools in virtual worlds produces realistic,

---

Lightweight Interactions. Messages composed of state, event, and control information as used in DIS Entity State PDUs. Implemented using multicast. Complete message semantics is included in a single packet encapsulation without fragmentation. Lightweight interactions are received completely or not at all since message size is constrained to moderate lengths to prevent packet fragmentation.

Network Pointers. Lightweight network resource references, multicast to receiving groups. Can be cached so that repeated queries are answered by group members instead of servers. Pointers do not contain a complete object as lightweight interactions do, instead containing only a reference to an object such as a URL.

Heavyweight Objects. Large data objects requiring reliable connection-oriented transmission. Examples include description files for a new entity or world database revisions. Typically provided as an ftp or http response triggered by a network pointer request.

Realtime Streams. Live video, audio, DIS, 3D graphics images, or other continuous stream traffic that requires realtime delivery, sequencing, and synchronization. Implemented using multicast channels.

Figure 4.5 Four key communication components used in virtual environments.

interactive, and interconnected 3D graphics that can be simultaneously available anywhere (Brutzman 1994; Macedonia 1995; Macedonia et al. 1995).

Application-Layer Interactivity

It is application-layer networking that needs the greatest attention in preparing for the information infrastructure of the near future. DIS combined with multicast transport provides solutions for many application-to-application communications requirements. Nevertheless, DIS is insufficiently broad and not adaptable enough to meet general virtual environment requirements. To date, most of the money spent on networked virtual environments has been by, for, and about the military. Most remaining work has been in (poorly) networked games. Neither example is viable across the full spectrum of applications. There is a real danger that specialized high-end military applications and chaotic low-end game hacks will dominate entity interaction models. Such a situation might well prevent networked virtual environments from enjoying the sustainable and compatible exponential growth needed to keep pace with other cornerstones of the information infrastructure.

Next-Generation Behavior Protocols

Successors to DIS are needed that are simpler, open, extensible, and dynamically modifiable. DIS has proven capabilities in dealing with position and posture dead-reckoning updates, physically based modeling, hostile entity interactions, and variable latency over wide-area networks. DIS also has several difficulties: It has awkward extendability, requires nontrivial computations to decipher bit patterns, and is a "big" (complicated) standard. DIS protocol development continues via a large and active standards community. However, the urgent military requirements driving the DIS standard remain narrower than general virtual environment networking requirements. Smaller and more efficient behavior protocols are being investigated by several researchers. The current NPS approach for next-generation behavior communications is to develop a "dial-a-protocol" capability, permitting dynamic modifications to the protocol specification to be transmitted to all hosts during a simulation (Stone 1996). A dynamically adjustable protocol is a necessity for interactively testing global and local efficiency of distributed entity interactions. Our research is motivated by a fundamental networking principle: Realistic testing and evaluation are essential because initial performance of distributed applications never matches expectations or theory. Thus, we're intentionally focusing on mechanisms for finding bottlenecks and demonstrating breakthroughs.

Other Interaction Models

Many other techniques for entity interaction are being investigated, although not always in relation to virtual environments. Several breakthroughs are possible. Just like in the real world, many ways of interacting will be valuable in virtual environments:

- Common Gateway Interface (cgi) scripts are executed on the queried host, often using http (Berners-Lee et al. 1994) query extensions as inputs.

- Java has sparked wide interest as a network-based behavior language. Java enables simple and secure passing of precompiled program object files (applets) for compatible multiplatform execution (Sun 1995).

- Intelligent agent interactions are an active area of research driven by the artificial intelligence and user interface communities. Rule-based agents typically communicate via a message-passing paradigm that is a straightforward extension of object-oriented programming methods.

- Instead of exchanging messages, mobile programs called agents can transport themselves. Telescript is a promising language designed for safe and secure mobile agent interactions (White 1995).

- Ongoing research by the Linda project uses a generalized message-passing construct called "tuples" for logical entity interaction, with emphasis on scaling up to indefinitely large sizes and participants (Gelernter 1992).

- MUDs (multiuser dungeons) and MOOs (MUDs object-oriented) provide a powerful server architecture and text-based interaction paradigm well suited to support a variety of virtual environment scenarios (Curtis and Nichols 1994).

- Passing interpretable scripts over the network in conjunction with predeployed, precompiled source code has been widely demonstrated for the multiplatform 2D graphical user interface (GUI) Tool Control Language (Tcl) (Ousterhout 1994).

Virtual Reality Modeling Language (VRML)

The Web is being extended to three spatial dimensions thanks to VRML, a specification originally based on an extended subset of the SGI OpenInventor scene description language (Wernicke 1994). Key contributions of the initial VRML 1.0 standard were a core set of object-oriented graphics constructs augmented by hypermedia links, all suitable for scene generation by browsers on Intel and Apple personal computers as well as UNIX workstations. The interaction model for 3D VRML browsers remains client-server, similar to most other Web browsers. The 3D browsers are usually embedded in 2D browsers or are launched as helper applications when connecting to a 3D site. VRML specification development has been effectively coordinated by mail list, enabling consensus by a large, active and open membership (Pesce and Behlendorf 1995–1996; Bell, Parisi, and Pesce 1995).

Difficult issues regarding realtime animation in VRML 2.0 (Carey, Marrin, and Bell 1996) include entity behaviors, user-entity interaction, and entity coordination. Currently, animation scripts and experimental servers are used for such functionality. In order to scale to many simultaneous users, peer-to-peer interactions will be necessary in addition to client-server query-response. Although "behaviors" are not formally specified, VRML 2.0 provides local and scripting language hooks—that is, an applications programming interface (API)—to graphical scene descriptions. Thus, dynamic scene changes can then be stimulated by scripted actions, message passing, user commands, or behavior protocols, implemented using either Java or complete VRML scene replacement. A great deal of experimentation is in progress. It appears clear that successful global solutions for VRML behaviors are possible that provide simplicity, security, scalability, generality, and open extensions. The most successful experimental approaches to shared behaviors will likely establish employment conventions and may even inspire behavior specifications.

Finally, as the demanding bandwidth and latency requirements of virtual environments begin to be exercised by VRML, some client-server design assumptions of the http protocol may no longer be valid. Users won't be satisfied with network mechanisms that fail to accommodate high-bandwidth information streams or break down after a few hundred players. A Virtual Reality Transfer Protocol (vrtp) will likely be needed to take advantage of available transport-layer functionality and overcome bottlenecks in http. Experimentation and quantitative evaluation will be essential to develop the next generation of code for diverse interentity virtual environment communications. To achieve these ambitious goals, it's necessary to create a cyberspace backbone (CBone) providing dedicated network resources for a virtual environment testbed.

Note that computer graphics applications now become more flexible than television. From a network perspective, prerendered computer graphics streams are equivalent to video streams. Behavior-based VRML will provide dynamic graphics scene delivery at relatively low bandwidths with viewpoints independently controlled by subscribing users. Effective deployment of globally networked graphics can complement television in fascinating ways.

Economics

Predicting economic developments in new technologies is a risky business. The following points are only a few of many changes, emphasizing major new developments that are likely to produce market impacts. Users and investors can draw their own conclusions.

- Marketplace providers may be far different from traditional companies. Individuals and small groups of people can be economic players, for example. GigaCorp Intergalactic UltraServices Ltd. might be one person working at home producing information products that are as good as (or better than) the products a large multinational corporation produces. Unrestricted access to information, open interest-group efforts, and affordable high-quality software are key. These assets produce the new trump cards in creative product development: imagination, cooperation, and rapid turnaround.

- Value-added becomes a market basis. At first, it might seem that when so much is free, no one needs to buy anything. In practice, people are willing to pay when there's significant value-added relative to what's free. For example, numerous software products are available today in identical free and supported versions. Nevertheless, today's innovative value-added feature is tomorrow's commonplace free feature. Thus, ongoing innovation, responsiveness, and improvement are necessary for software program survival.

- What is "free" in the computer software community is a sliding standard that tracks along with the exponential growth of the computer price/performance technology curve. Historically, companies charging for quality software have been first to market, with quality freeware versions following later. Programmers unwilling or unable to pay fees often create public domain software comparable to commercial versions. Current free availability of quality software development tools and code libraries has accelerated this growth of free software projects. Freeware programmers are often willing to port software to multiple architectures. Mailing lists, news groups, online hyperlinked documentation, and software repositories encourage the growth of diverse and technically proficient user communities. High-quality online experience is usually available to open interest-group members (however informally) at all hours of the day or night. Open cross-platform public domain (free) solutions frequently inspire profitable commercial software products. Both climb the cutting-edge-technology curve in tandem.

- Information dissemination is easier than ever. Content for mass access is no longer solely controlled by television networks, radio broadcasters, and print publishers. As more people put information online and collaborate with groupware, traditional information sources become less necessary. Just as television didn't put radio out of business, expect to see evolutionary changes in information sources rather than elimination of other media. Open access to disparate media over the network fosters both competition and cooperation. These are democratizing and equalizing forces. Everybody will want access to everything, and networking makes it possible. Interactive 3D graphics with independent viewpoint, navigation, and content already provides serious competition to television. New 3D "channels" are creating new businesses, arts, and entertainments.

- It becomes increasingly difficult to preserve original sources as internetworked information grows exponentially. Digital libraries will become essential to provide continuity of access. Context may be supported through ever-more-sophisticated links, browsers, and virtual environments, but secure storage of basic content will remain a fundamental requirement. A forward-looking overview of digital library efforts is given by Garrett and Waters (1995).

- Informal market analysis of an industry that undergoes a complete reorganization every year or two indicates that open methods based on responsive standards survive, while closed proprietary methods struggle and die or get absorbed/killed/subsumed by dominant companies in a market (like Microsoft). Semiopen methods (like ISO OSI) that are overconstrained by standardization or restrictive rules fall behind the pace of the marketplace and become obsolete—in effect, they appear proprietary.

- Security considerations affect all parts of the Internet, including multiuser virtual environments. Encryption, authentication, and nonrepudiation are all feasible using a variety of currently available open and closed cryptographic standards. Public key cryptography, next-generation IPv.6 safeguards, and de facto market standards/solutions used for credit card transactions appear to be the most significant technologies. Next-generation security must safeguard entire networks in addition to individual users, clients, and servers. Security is a moving target that will be solved mostly through independent efforts that eventually gain acceptance on the Internet. Security validation for virtual environments will hinge on the effectiveness of these methods when used together with challenging high-bandwidth fast-response applications.

- Economic problems on both personal and corporate scales often result from misunderstanding or misinformation. This happens everywhere, including the computing and academic communities. Marketing hyperbole takes advantage of the dizzying effects of ceaseless rapid change and the individual's need to stay informed. Rapidly growing bodies of knowledge and information are now part of the intellectual marketplace. Good and bad untested ideas go into the market early to attract resources and influence the development of related work. However, the bottom line is results. Implementation (can it be built?), test (what does it really do?), and evaluation (does it do what we want?) are truer measures of success. Implementation, test, and evaluation are the forcing functions that will produce working large-scale internetworked graphics environments. Visible results cut through the inevitable fog of hype and distorted information that surrounds rapid technical progress.

Applications

Working applications will drive progress, rather than theories and hype. In this section, we present feasible applications that are exciting possibilities or existing works in progress. Many new projects are possible and likely in the near future if virtual environment requirements are adequately supported by the global information infrastructure. Several conjectured scenarios follow.

Sports: Live 3D Stadium with Instrumented Players

Imagine that all of the ballplayers in a sports stadium wear a small device that senses location (through the Global Positioning System and local spread-spectrum radio signal sensing) and transmits behavior packets over a wireless network. Similar sensors are embedded in gloves, balls, bats, and even shoes. A computer server in the stadium feeds player telemetry into a physically based articulated human model that, in turn, extrapolates individual body and limb motions. The server also maintains a scene database for the stadium complete with texture-mapped images of the edifice, current weather, and representative pictures of fans in the stands. Meanwhile, Internet users have 3D browsers that can navigate and view the action from any perspective in the stadium. Users can also tune to multicast channels providing updated player positions and postures (via lightweight behavior interactions) along with live audio and video. Statistics, background information, and multimedia home pages are available for each player. Some remote spectators might even choose to publicly share their own play-by-play commentary. Thus, any number of remote fans might supplement traditional television coverage with a live interactive computer-generated view. Perhaps the most surprising aspect of this scenario

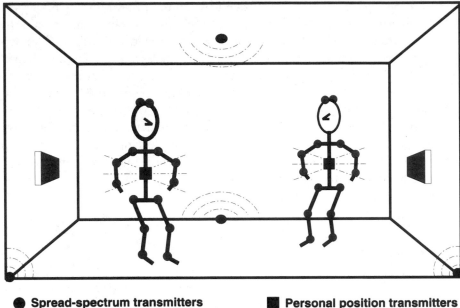

● **Spread-spectrum transmitters**   ■ **Personal position transmitters**

● **Spread-spectrum body joint receivers**   ▨ **Personal position receivers**

Figure 4.6   Example of a Personal Tracking System (PTS) using spread-spectrum radio ranging techniques in a virtual environment (Bible, Zyda, and Brutzman 1995): Fourteen independent joint trackers passively determine body posture using a scheme similar to the Global Positioning System (GPS), and then combined joint signals are multiplexed and transmitted back to the surrounding environment.

is that all component software and hardware technologies exist today. A proposed personal tracking system (PTS) suitable for multiple players in a stadium environment is presented in Figure 4.6 (Bible, Zyda, and Brutzman 1995).

Education

Many people are trying to capitalize on the potential of global content by combining internetworking with education, long-distance teletraining, and lifelong learning. Applying computer graphics to education is also a steadily growing area of activity (Owen 1995). Our approach to learning and research includes grounding all theoretical concepts in real-world applications and events. Networked education efforts in the Monterey Bay region aim at enabling teachers and students of all ages to use all aspects of the Internet (Brutzman June 1995, August 1995; Bigelow 1995). Since students study a great deal of content, regularly produce context, and are excellent evaluators of effectiveness, it's likely that the best new examples combining innovative content with networked graphics will emerge from the educational community. Supporting educational network construction and teacher training is an excellent way to build a collaborative user base for new applications.

Military: The 100,000 Player Problem

"Exploiting Reality with Multicast Groups" describes ground-breaking research on increasing the number of active entities within a virtual environment by several orders of magnitude (Macedonia et al. 1995). Multicast addressing and the DIS protocol are used to logically partition network traffic according to spatial, temporal, and functional entity classes as shown in Figure 4.7. "Exploiting Reality" further explains virtual environment network concepts and includes experimental results. This work has fundamentally changed the distributed simulation community, showing that very large numbers of live and simulated networked players in real-world exercises are feasible. The military origins of this problem will become irrelevant as our abilities to effectively interact socially, scientifically, and educationally scale to the hundreds of thousands. Such growth from military to real-world problems is analogous to the original design of the ARPANET and military predecessors to today's Internet.

Science: Virtual Worlds as Experimental Laboratories for Robots and People

In separate work, we've shown how an underwater virtual world can comprehensively model all salient functional characteristics of the real world for an Autonomous Underwater Vehicle (AUV) in real time (Brutzman 1994). This virtual world is designed from the perspective of the robot, enabling realistic AUV evaluation and testing in the laboratory. In this context, our "Turing test" for the virtual environment is whether the robot behaves identically in the underwater virtual world and in the real world. Realtime 3D computer graphics are our window into that virtual world (Figure 4.8).

Visualization of robot interactions within a virtual world permits sophisticated analyses of robot performance that are otherwise unavailable. Sonar visualization permits researchers to accurately "look over the robot's shoulder" or even "see through the robot's eyes" to intuitively understand sensor-environment interactions. Theoretical derivation of 6-degree-of-freedom hydrodynamics equations has provided a general physics-based model capable of replicating highly nonlinear (yet experimentally verifiable) response in real time. Distribution of underwater virtual-world components enables scalability

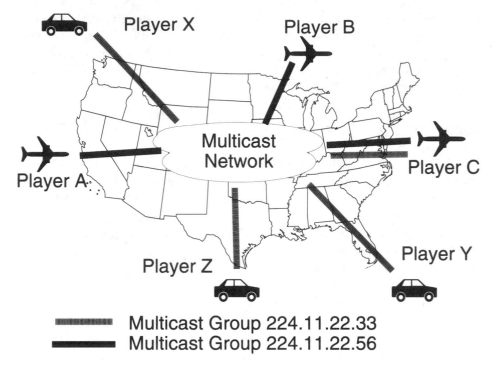

Figure 4.7 Multicast channels can partition network communications into spatial, temporal, and functional classes to minimize traffic and exploit reality (Macedonia et al. 1995).

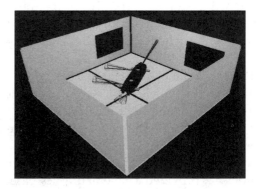

Figure 4.8 An autonomous underwater vehicle (AUV) operating in a virtual test tank: Virtual worlds can incorporate datasets, databases, models, robots, and people (Brutzman 1994).

and rapid response. Networking allows remote access, demonstrated via MBone audio and video collaboration with researchers at distant locations. Integrating the World Wide Web allows rapid access to resources distributed across the Internet. Distributed resources include a text-to-speech sound server that translates robot reports into sound files (Belinfante 1994). Ongoing challenges include scaling up the types of interactions, datasets, models, and live streams that can be coordinated within the virtual world.

Interaction: Multiple CAVEs Using ATM and VRML

A CAVE is a type of walk-in synthetic environment that replaces the four walls of a room with rear-projection screens, all driven by realtime 3D computer graphics (Cruz-Neira et al. 1993). These devices can accommodate 10 to 15 people comfortably and render high-resolution 3D stereo graphics at 15 Hz and higher update rates. The principal costs of a CAVE are in high-performance graphics hardware. We wish to demonstrate affordable linked CAVEs for remote group interaction. The basic idea is to send graphics streams from a master CAVE through a high-speed, low-latency ATM link to a less expensive slave CAVE that contains only rear-projection screens.

Several serious ATM bottlenecks remain that must be resolved experimentally. Automatic generation of VRML scene graphs and simultaneous replication of state information over standard multicast links will permit both CAVEs and networked computers to interactively view results generated in real time by a supercomputer. Our initial application domain is a gridded virtual environment model of the oceanographic and biological characteristics of Chesapeake Bay, as shown in Figure 4.9 (Wheless et al. 1995, 1996; I-WAY 1995). To better incorporate networked sensors and agents into this and other virtual worlds, we are also investigating extensions to IP using underwater acoustics (Brutzman and Reimers, 1995). As a final component, we are helping establish ambitious regional education and research networks that connect scientists, students from kindergartens through universities, libraries, and the general public. Vertically integrated Web and MBone applications and the common theme of live networked environmental science are expected to provide many possible virtual-world connections (Brutzman June 1995, August 1995; Brutzman and Emswiler 1995).

Mobile Global Public Domain Television

Access to the MBone means that anyone can become a global television provider. During SIGGRAPH '95, we experimented with mobile audio/video delivery to demonstrate location-independent multicasting. We loaded a cart with a camera-equipped SGI Indy workstation, a 2-Mbps wireless bridge, wireless microphones, and video gear. Dubbed "MBone Unplugged," we were able

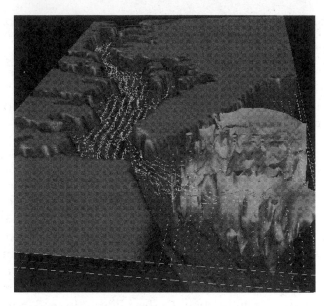

Figure 4.9 The Chesapeake Bay Virtual Environment (CBVE) combines multiple models, datasets, and interaction modes with standard IP and high-bandwidth ATM internetworking (Wheless et al. 1995, 1996).

to roam the convention floor while continuously multicasting exhibits and events worldwide (Figure 4.10) (Brutzman and Emswiler 1995; Clinger 1996). Working under conference auspices provides access to significant content with appropriate release permissions. We now believe that this rig is the workstation of the future: It is totally mobile, has complete graphics and video capabilities, and has no apparent limits. Related work showed that live worldwide multicast of an academic course was possible for an entire quarter (Emswiler 1995). Planned future work includes simultaneous worldwide conference multicasting over ATM and MBone links while directly recording the audio/video at multiple bandwidths to a digital archive. We expect to show that previously transitory content produced by conference events can provide significant long-term value through easy, inexpensive live multicast and storage of high-bandwidth audiovisual streams.

Personal Impacts

Tremendous enthusiasm and deep insights result when people use good interactive 3D graphics applications. Combining graphics and networks looks like a sure win, but the personal impacts of new technology are notoriously hard to

Figure 4.10   "MBone Unplugged" cart used at SIGGRAPH '95 for wireless audio, video, and 3D graphics with worldwide multicast scope (Brutzman and Emswiler 1995).

predict. Here are a few ideas gained during our journey about how people will use large-scale internetworked virtual environments.

Large-scale means everyone and everything. This is a people process just as much as a technical process. Here are some people-related lessons learned from the ongoing growth of the Web: When something is easy, people do it; when something is challenging, people are willing to pay someone else or figure out another way to do it; when something is difficult, people don't do it. Examples of relatively easy things include building personal Web pages and putting information online. Challenging things include professional Web server providers and current Web-server-in-a-box products. Excessively difficult things include early false starts by some commercial online services and overly complex standardization efforts that never reach critical mass.

The personal impact of scaling up virtual environments to arbitrarily large sizes means that connecting and contributing to them can't be harder than setting up your own home page. If the process is not well defined, few people will risk wasting their time. As long as hooking up and authoring virtual worlds remain difficult, the technical solutions aren't yet good enough.

Information overload is the new norm. There's already too much information available. The unexpected will continue to happen, usually right when people think they're caught up with what's current. The possibility of 500 television channels is ridiculously simple; there are already far more content sources on the Internet. With interactive opportunities increasing exponentially, personal impacts will likely have to be experienced to be understood. What does it mean when anyone can create, join, ignore, or compete with any channel of information? No one really knows, but we'll undoubtedly find out. Some individuals look to science fiction for inspiration and models of behavior. Some virtual reality architects on the VRML mailing list appear to go beyond inspiration and use *Snow Crash* (Stephenson 1992) as a design document. Life imitates art; science imitates science fiction.

Projections

Merely by reading the *New York Times*, any individual can get more information about the world than was available to any world leader throughout most of human history. Multiply that single stream by the millions of other sources on the Internet, and it's clear we do not lack content. Mountains of content are accessible. What we need more is context, that is, a way to interactively locate, retrieve, and display related pieces of information in a timely manner. Context establishes the reliability and pedigree of information streams. It also permits selectively culling large volumes of unstructured information that can otherwise overwhelm any single person or process.

Within two lifetimes, we have invented several new technologies for recording and exchanging information. Handwriting gave way to typing, then typing to word processing, and soon afterward came desktop publishing. Now, people can use 3D realtime interactive graphics simulations and dynamic "documents" with multimedia hooks to record and communicate information. Furthermore, such "documents" can be directly distributed on demand to anyone connected to the Internet. In virtual environments, a further paradigm shift becomes possible. The long-term potential of virtual environments is to serve as an archive and interaction medium, combining massive and dissimilar datasets and data streams of every conceivable type. Virtual environments will enable comprehensive and consistent interaction within those massive datasets, data streams, and models that recreate reality. Virtual environments can provide meaningful context to the mountains of content that currently exist in isolation without roads, links, or order.

What about scaling up? Fortunately, there already exists a model for these growing mountains of information content: the real world. Virtual worlds address the context issue by providing information links similar to those in the real world. When our virtual constructs cumulatively approach realistic levels of depth and sophistication, our understanding of the real world will deepen correspondingly. In support of this goal, we have shown how the structure and scope of virtual environment relationships can be dynamically extended using feasible network communications methods. This efficient distribution of information will let any remote user or entity in a virtual environment participate and interact in increasingly meaningful ways.

Open access to any type of live or archived information resource is becoming available for everyday use by individuals, programs, collaborative groups, and even robots. Virtual environments are a natural way to provide order and context to these massive amounts of information. Worldwide collaboration works for both people and machines. Finally, the network is more than a computer and even more than your computer. The Internet becomes our computer as we learn how to share resources and collaborate and interact on a global scale.

Summary

Interactive 3D computer graphics enables people to see things that are otherwise imperceptible, impractical, or impossible. Computer networking can connect everyone to everything, any person to any machine to any information resource. Networks are not "something else" relative to graphics; rather, they are integral as we scale up in every direction. As these interrelated technologies combine, understanding why limits exist will help us break through bottlenecks. Each bottleneck broken reveals another as we consider new-found capabilities and their corresponding limitations.

Large-scale virtual environments are the new grand challenge in computing, a challenge that can include every person and every subject. The best motivation for scaling up can be found in the respective strengths of 3D graphics and networking: perception and bandwidth. Interactive graphics lets us perceive the world in new and familiar ways. Networks provide information bandwidth, broad connectivity, and varied content at rapid rates. Our new challenges are fascinating. Combining graphics and networks now lets us work on perceptual bandwidth, maximizing the depth and breadth and speed we use to interpret the world around us. This achievement may be our biggest breakthrough.

References

Belinfante, Axel, "Say . . ." text to speech sound server, University of Twente, Netherlands, 1994. Available at http://wwwtios.cs.utwente.nl/say/?

Bell, Gavin, Parisi, Anthony, and Pesce, Mark, "The Virtual Reality Modeling Language (VRML) Version 1.0 Specification," May 26, 1995. Available via the VRML Repository at http://www.sdsc.edu/vrml

Berners-Lee, Tim, Cailliau, Luotonen, Ari, Nielsen, Henrik Frystyk, and Secret, Arthur, "The World Wide Web," Communications of the ACM, vol. 37 no. 8, August 1994, pp. 76–82.

Bible, Steven R., Zyda, Michael, and Brutzman, Don, "Using Spread-Spectrum Ranging Techniques for Position Tracking in a Virtual Environment," IEEE Networked Realities Workshop, Boston, Massachusetts, October 26–28 1995. Available at http://www-npsnet.cs.nps.navy.mil/npsnet/publications/NR95-Paper-Bible.ps.Z

Bigelow, Randall J., *Internetworking: Planning and Implementing a Wide-Area Network (WAN) for K-12 Schools,* Master's Thesis, Naval Postgraduate School, Monterey, California, June 1995. Available at http://www.stl.nps.navy.mil/~rjbigelo/thesis.html

Bradner, Scott O., and Mankin, Allison, editors, *IPng: Internet Protocol Next Generation,* Addison-Wesley, Reading, Massachusetts, 1996. Additional information available at http://playground.sun.com/pub/ipng/html/ipng-main.html

Brutzman, Donald P., "A Virtual World for an Autonomous Underwater Vehicle," Ph.D. Dissertation, Naval Postgraduate School, Monterey, California, December 1994. Available at http://www.stl.nps.navy.mil/~brutzman/dissertation/

Brutzman, Don, "Networked Ocean Science Research and Education, Monterey Bay California," Proceedings of International Networking (INET) '95 Conference, Internet Society, Honolulu, Hawaii, June 27–30, 1995. Available at http://inet.nttam.com/HMP/PAPER/039

Brutzman, Don, "Remote Collaboration with Monterey Bay Educators," Visual Proceedings, Association for Computing Machinery (ACM) Special Interest Group on Graphics (SIGGRAPH) '95, Los Angeles, California, August 7–11, 1995, p. 145.

Brutzman, Don, and Emswiler, Tracey, "MBone Unplugged," SIGGRAPH '95 exhibit report, August 1995. Available at http://www.stl.nps.navy.mil/~brutzman/unplugged.html

Brutzman, Don, and Reimers, Stephen, "Internet Protocol over Seawater: Towards Interoperable Underwater Networks," Unmanned Untethered Submersibles Technology 95, Northeastern University, Nahant, Massachusetts, September 25–27, 1995, pp. 444–457.

Brutzman, Don, moderator, "Oceans Web," special interest group for ocean-related datasets/databases/models compatible with the World Wide Web, February 1996. Available at http://www.stl.nps.navy.mil/~brutzman/oceans-web

Carey, Rikk, Marrin, Chris, and Bell, Gavin, editors, "The Virtual Reality Modeling Language (VRML) Version 2.0 Specification, International Standards Organization/International Electrotechnical Commission (ISO/IEC) draft standard 14772, August 4, 1996. Available via the VRML Repository at www.sdsc.edu/vrml

Clinger, Marke, "GraphicsNet '95: Integrated Voice, Video, Graphics, and Data Network Using Asynchronous Transfer Mode (ATM)," *Computer Graphics*, ACM SIGGRAPH, vol. 30. no. 1, February 1996, pp. 10–18. Additional information available at http://www.siggraph.org/conferences/siggraph95/GraphicsNet

Cogger, Dick, CU-SeeMe, desktop videoconferencing software, Cornell University, Ithaca, New York, 1995. Available at ftp://gated.cornell.edu/pub/video/html/Welcome.html

Comer, Douglas E., *Internetworking with TCP/IP Volume I: Principles, Protocols, and Architecture,* second edition, Prentice-Hall, Englewood Cliffs, New Jersey, 1991.

Cooke, J. C., Zyda, M. J., Pratt, D. R., and McGhee, R. B., "NPSNET: Flight Simulation Dynamic Modeling Using Quaternions," *Presence: Teleoperations and Virtual Environments,* vol. 1 no. 4, Fall 1992, pp. 404–420. Available at http://www-npsnet.cs.nps.navy.mil/npsnet/publications/NPSNET.Flight.Simulation.Dynamic.Modeling.Using.Quaternions.ps.Z

Crocker, D., "To Be 'On' the Internet," Request for Comments (RFC) 1775, March 1995. Available at ftp://ds.internic.net/rfc/rfc1775.txt

Cruz-Neira, Carolina, Leigh, Jason, Papka, Michael, Barnes, Craig, Cohen, Steven M., Das, Sumit, Engelmann, Roger, Hudson, Randy, Roy, Trina, Siegel, Lewis, Vasilakis, Christina, DeFanti, Thomas A., and Sandin, Daniel J., "Scientists in Wonderland: A Report on Visualization Applications in the CAVE Virtual Reality Environment," IEEE 1993 Symposium on Research Frontiers in Virtual Reality, San Jose, California, October 25–26, 1993, pp. 59–66 and CP-3.

Curtis, Pavel, and Nichols, David A., "MUDs Grow Up: Social Virtual Reality in the Real World," Proceedings of the IEEE Computer Conference, IEEE Computer Society Press, Los Alamitos, California, 1994, pp. 193–200. Available at ftp://ftp.parc.xerox.com/pub/MOO/papers/MUDsGrowUp.ps

Deering, Steve, "Host Extensions for IP Multicasting," Request for Comments (RFC) 1112, Internet Engineering Task Force (IETF), August 1989. Available at ftp://ds.internic.net/rfc/rfc1112.txt

DIS Steering Committee, "The DIS Vision: A Map to the Future of Distributed Simulation," version 1, May 1994. Available at ftp://sc.ist.ucf.edu/public/STDS/vision.ps

Durlach, Nathaniel I., and Mavor, Anne S., editors, *Virtual Reality: Scientific and Technological Challenges,* National Research Council, National Academy Press, Washington, D.C., 1995.

Emswiler, Tracey, "Internetworking: Using the Multicast Backbone (MBone) for Distance Learning," Master's Thesis, Naval Postgraduate School, Monterey, California, September 1995. Summary video available at http://www.stl.nps.navy.mil/~iirg/emswiler/emswiler.qt.Z

Garrett, John, and Waters, Donald, cochairs, "Preserving Digital Information," Task Force on Archiving of Digital Information, Commission on Preservation and Access and the Research Libraries Group, draft report version 1.0, Yale University, New Haven, Connecticut, August 24, 1995.

Gelernter, David, *Mirror Worlds—or the Day Software Puts the Universe in a Shoebox . . . How It Will Happen and What It Will Mean,* Oxford University Press, New York, 1992.

Hughes, Kevin, "Entering the World Wide Web (WWW): A Guide to Cyberspace," Enterprise Integration Technology, Inc., May 1994. Available at http://www.eit.com/web/www.guide/

IEEE Standard for Information Technology—Protocols for Distributed Interactive Simulation (DIS) Applications, version 2.0, Institute for Simulation and Training report IST-CR-93-15, University of Central Florida, Orlando, Florida, May 28, 1993.

International Wide-Area Year (I-WAY) project, North American ATM network in support of IEEE/ACM Supercomputing '95, San Diego, California, December 3–7, 1995. Information available at http://www.iway.org

Internet Network Information Center (Internic), Request for Comments (RFC) archive, ftp://ds.internic.net, 1995. Hypertext interface and search facilities available at http://www.internic.net

Library of Congress, home page, November 1995. Available at http://www.loc.gov/

Macedonia, Michael R., and Brutzman, Donald P., "MBone Provides Audio and Video Across the Internet," *IEEE Computer,* April 1994, pp. 30–36. Available at ftp://taurus.cs.nps.navy.mil/pub/i3la/mbone.html

Macedonia, Michael R., "A Network Software Architecture for Large-Scale Virtual Environments," Ph.D. Dissertation, Naval Postgraduate School, Monterey, California, June 1995.

Macedonia, Michael R., Zyda, Michael J., Pratt, David R., Brutzman, Donald P., and Barham, Paul T., "Exploiting Reality with Multicast Groups: A Network

Architecture for Large-Scale Virtual Environments," *IEEE Computer Graphics and Applications*, vol. 15 no. 5, September 1995, pp. 38–45.

Malamud, Carl, *Stacks: Interoperability in Today's Computer Networks*, Prentice-Hall, Englewood Cliffs, New Jersey, 1992.

Netscape Corporation, "An Exploration of Dynamic Documents," online documentation page, November 1995. Available at http://www.netscape.com/assist/net_sites/pushpull.html

NRENAISSANCE Committee, *Realizing the Information Future: The Internet and Beyond*, Computer Science and Telecommunications Board, National Research Council, National Academy Press, Washington, D.C., 1994.

Ousterhout, John K., *TCL and the TK Toolkit*, Addison-Wesley, Reading, Massachusetts, 1994.

Owen, Scott, guest editor, focus issue on computer graphics education, *Computer Graphics*, ACM SIGGRAPH, vol. 29 no. 3, August 1995.

Pesce, Mark, and Behlendorf, Brian, moderators, "Virtual Reality Modeling Language (VRML)," working group mail list, 1995-1996. Archived at http://vrml.wired.com/ and http://www.sdsc.edu/vrml

Pesce, Mark, *VRML—Browsing and Building Cyberspace*, New Riders Publishing, Indianapolis, Indiana, 1995.

Schulzrinne, Henning, Casner, Stephen, Frederick, Ron, and Jacobson, Van, "RTP: A Transport Protocol for Real-Time Applications," Request for Comments (RFC) 1889, Internet Engineering Task Force (IETF), January 1996. Available at ftp://ds.internic.net/rfc/rfc1889.txt

Stallings, William, *Data and Computer Communications*, fourth edition, Macmillan Publishing, New York, 1994.

Stephenson, Neal, *Snow Crash*, Bantam Books, New York, 1992.

Stevens, Richard W., *UNIX Network Programming*, Prentice-Hall, Englewood Cliffs, New Jersey, 1990.

Stone, Steven, "NPSNET: A Rapidly Reconfigurable Application-Layer Virtual Environment Network Protocol," Master's Thesis, Naval Postgraduate School, Monterey, California, September 1996.

Sun Microsystems Corporation, Java language home page, November 1995. Available at http://java.sun.com/

Wernicke, Josie, *The Inventor Mentor: Programming Object-Oriented 3D Graphics with OpenInventor, Release 2*, Addison-Wesley, Reading, Massachusetts, 1994.

Summary available at http://www.sgi.com/Technology/Inventor/VRML/TIMSummary.html

Wheless, Glen, LaScara, Cathy, Valle-Levison, Arnaldo, Brutzman, Don, and Sherman, Bill, "Chesapeake Bay Virtual Ecosystem Model (CBVEM): Interacting with a Couple Bio-Physical Simulation," IEEE/ACM.

Wheless, Glen H., LaScara, Cathy M., Valle-Levison, Arnaldo, Brutzman, Donald P., Sherman, William, Hibbard, William L., and Paul, Brian E., "Chesapeake Bay Virtual Ecosystem Model (CBVEM): Initial Results from the Prototypical System," *International Journal of Supercomputer Applications,* to appear. Available at ftp://ftp.ccpo.odu.edu/pub/wheless/wheless_ijsa.tar

Supercomputing '95, San Diego, California, December 3–7, 1995. Information available at http://www.ccpo.odu.edu/~wheless

White, James E., "Telescript Technology: Mobile Agents," white paper, General Magic, Inc., Sunnyvale, California, 1995. To appear in Bradshaw, Jeffrey, editor, *Software Agents,* AAAI Press/MIT Press, Menlo Park, California, 1996.

Zyda, Michael J., Pratt, David R., Falby, John S., Barham, Paul T., Lombardo, Chuck, and Kelleher, Kristen M., "The Software Required for the Computer Generation of Virtual Environments," *Presence: Teleoperators and Virtual Environments,* vol. 2 no. 2, MIT Press, Cambridge, Massachusetts, Spring 1993, pp. 130–140. Available at http://www-npsnet.cs.nps.navy.mil/npsnet/publications/NPSNET.Software.Required.for.the.Computer.Generation.of.Virtual.Environments.ps.Z

All figures and text are available at http://www.stl.nps.navy.mil/~brutzman/vrml/breakthroughs.html

Acknowledgments

I gratefully acknowledge contributions and insights gained from discussions with Mike Macedonia, Mike Zyda, Glen Wheless, Clark Dodsworth, and members of the Virtual Reality Modeling Language (VRML) mail list.

Biography

Don Brutzman is a computer scientist working in the Interdisciplinary Academic Group at the Naval Postgraduate School. His research interests include underwater robotics, realtime 3D computer graphics, artificial intelligence, high-performance networking, and large-scale virtual environments. He is a member of the Institute of Electrical and Electronic Engineers (IEEE), the Association for Computing Machinery (ACM) Special Interest Group on Graphics (SIGGRAPH), the American Association for Artificial Intelligence (AAAI), the Marine Technology Society (MTS), and the Internet Society (ISOC). He serves on the Board of Directors and the VRML Review Board (VRB) for the Virtual Reality Modeling Language Consortium. Collaborative project information is available at http://www.stl.nps.navy.mil/brutzman

Chapter 5

Creation and Use of Synthetic Environments in Realtime Networked Interactive Simulation

Farid Mamaghani
Seattle, Washington

Generating and representing synthetic environments is a key factor in networked simulation systems. It's particularly demanding to create an environment that looks good when traversed at ground level, instead of at 30,000 feet in a flight simulator. Realtime networked simulation places additional constraints on the successful creation of these environments. Because the use of three-dimensional synthetic environments in commercial, educational, and entertainment applications will increase and because these applications will be connected via local and global networks, it is important to understand how synthetic environments can impact networked systems. This chapter describes some of the challenges associated with the creation and use of these synthetic environment databases for ground and near-ground applications in a networked simulation system.

The representation of the information for a particular terrain can be drastically different based on the needs of a simulation platform or the specific application. We touch on these diverse computing needs and how they affect the creation and exchange of a synthetic terrain database in a networked heterogeneous system. For example, creation of electronic or paper maps demands a data representation scheme that may not be suitable for a thermal sight simulator, even though both are intended to depict and operate in the same geographical region.

In this chapter, we review the key steps in creating synthetic databases and highlight the trade-offs in source data selection, geometric representations, and issues such as interchange and interoperability. We also discuss some management considerations in improving the process, quality of simulation, and tool development.

Introduction

Military training simulation systems have been around for decades. Most of these systems have used some derivation of the real environment to represent a slice of the three-dimensional reality. These have ranged from the actual physical environment to detailed analog models of a small region to a completely digital version. In the last three decades, the price-performance benefits of computer technology and the demand for reconfigurable, less expensive, and more realistic representations have driven simulation systems toward realtime digital computing and fully synthesized environments. As a result, capturing and depicting "a slice of the three-dimensional reality" with more precision and fidelity has become more difficult.

Until the early 1980s, simulators were mostly stand-alone systems designed for a specific-task training purpose. Until the introduction of the SIMNET (SIMulator NETworking) program, no one had ever used a multitude of simulators in a combined-forces training environment, interacting over a network in realtime. SIMNET technology allowed crew members in one simulator to interact in realtime in the same synthetic environment with many other manned or unmanned simulators located at the same or other training sites. The interaction takes place within a digitally synthesized environment that represents some region of Earth. Each simulator maintains its own copy of this synthetic region.

In addition to the challenges in building synthetic environments for stand-alone simulators, networking imposed new and stringent demands on the techniques and the process. The initial implementation of SIMNET created a system of homogeneous manned simulators. The idea of using heterogeneous simulators on one network creates even greater challenges in constructing, distributing, and using synthetic environments. These are the key problems the realtime networked simulation community faces today, and, in spite of the rapid acceptance of this technology in the past decade, the techniques for interoperating heterogeneous simulation systems are still being researched, developed, and designed. So, before discussing issues regarding synthetic environments for networked simulation, we should review the more general construction and utilization issues of these environments that apply, in most cases, to both networked and stand-alone systems.

What Constitutes a Synthetic Environment?

In this chapter, the words "terrain database" and "synthetic environment" are used synonymously and interchangeably, although a terrain database is often a subset of a synthetic environment (SE). A synthetic environment is an integrated set of data elements, each describing some aspect of the same geographical region. It often includes additional data describing simulation elements and events expected to take place during the interactions in that environment. For example, data representing trees in a forested region may be found in a database; but, in addition, the geometry of vehicles that might drive through the trees during a simulation would also be found in the SE. The key phrase in the preceding definition is "integrated set of data." It is the integration, infusion, and tailoring of varied data sources that creates a full SE and sets it apart from databases that only use an existing raw data source as is. Here is a list of some of the more important data elements that are integrated into a simulation database.

Terrain Surface

A digital elevation model (DEM) is usually the underlying data that describes the terrain surface and geometry, either as sampled grid posts or after it has been polygonalized. This data is most often from sources such as the Defense Mapping Agency's (DMA) Digital Terrain Elevation Data (DTED). Such data usually represent elevation posts at regular grid intervals and exist at various resolutions and accuracies. Depending on the application, some filtered (or original) version of a DEM eventually becomes the underlying data for describing the surface geometry.

Terrain Features

Features found on the terrain, whether man-made or natural, such as vegetation, hydrology, roads, and obstacles, are brought in from existing digital data sources or by digitizing maps. Feature data sources include Interim Terrain Data (ITD) and Digital Feature Attribute Data (DFAD), both obtainable from the DMA. These feature descriptions do not always match the underlying terrain geometry. In many cases, the original data for the terrain surface and the features are extracted from different source material, are obtained at different points in time, or have been modified after source extraction. This is one of the reasons why data must be "integrated" before it can be used in a simulation. A well-known example of the mismatch between feature and surface data is rivers that flow uphill!

3D Models and Icons

Databases are typically populated with structures, buildings, and other 3D models that are found in the area of interest. The location of objects is sometimes obtained from feature data, but the 3D geometry of the object is constructed from blueprints or CAD data, or extruded from imagery. The orientation of the objects is most often not found in the current feature data and must be entered and integrated from other sources.

Textures, Images, and Colors

When visualizing the terrain surface and its features, color and texture are critical. This information is often extracted from photographs or videos or is synthesized from general geographical characteristics. It's then integrated with the surface information, whether the surface is a grass field, a road, or a structure. When actual data is not available, textures and colors are synthesized and applied to the database. Textures add substantial detail to the visual representation that is not achievable with simple geometry alone.

Object·and Feature Attributes

Most simulation systems require additional attributes needed by either the user or the computational tasks of the simulator. These include such data as infrared signatures of specific objects that allow a user to recognize and detect such objects in the environment. They also include information about surface material or "trafficability" so that the system behavior and vehicle dynamics can respond appropriately to changes in the surface.

Environment Models

These include such phenomena as smoke, rain, and haze. Sometimes, this data is integrated into the synthetic environment; sometimes, it is embedded in the simulation software as a database separate from the SE database.

Other Data

A synthetic environment database may also contain data describing predetermined events that don't need to be fully simulated and are captured in the form of a short animation. These could include explosion effects, water flow in a river, or state transition of specific objects. Other data used in an SE include topological data, system-specific data necessary for platform-specific computational needs (precomputed lines of visibility, occulting planes), and names and labels for producing electronic and paper maps. It is the combination of all these data sources, and more, that is used in the construction of a database and constitutes a Synthetic Environment.

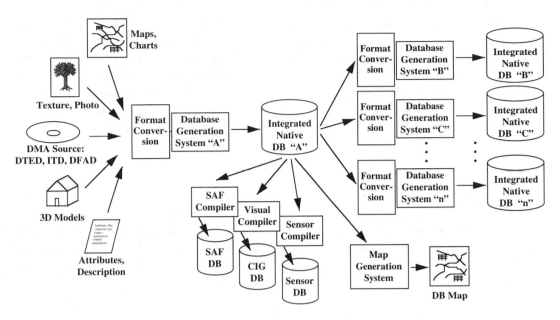

Figure 5.1 Steps in creation and distribution of an integrated synthetic environment.

Integrating this data into a coherent database creates a source database that can be shared by many players. In networked simulation, it is some flavor of this "integrated" database that is viewed as source for input into other simulators' computation system. Figure 5.1 represents the steps in creation and distribution of an integrated synthetic environment.

Applications Using Synthetic Environments

The range of potential players in a networked heterogeneous simulation system is both wide and varied, but predominantly they fall into the five major application categories listed next. The needs of each application for representation of the data of the same exact geographical region can be extremely different, even though the underlying "information" is identical.

Semi-Automated Forces

Semi-Automated Forces (SAF) systems provide additional friendly or opposing elements to augment manned simulators during a training exercise. This allows training of small teams in the context of larger exercises. Depending on the computational platform, the desired fidelity, and the exercise complexity, a single SAF system can produce and control many tens of simulated vehicles.

An effective SAF system can produce tactical behaviors for the vehicles it controls as though they were operated by real crews. This means a SAF system, in addition to other tasks, must be able to navigate and use terrain features under unpredictable conditions. The information in a synthetic environment database must meet the computational needs of SAF systems. This new information was not traditionally included in a simulation database. This stems from the fact that most simulation databases in the past have been built to render realtime images for real crew members.

Sensor Simulation

Sensor simulators form another application category that uses SE data. These include radar, infrared, and night-vision devices. In addition to geometry and feature data, attributes of objects, surface composition, weather, and a host of other information is needed to properly use these simulators.

Computer Image Generators and Visual Systems

Perhaps the most commonly known use of SE data is associated with out-the-window visual systems, or computer image generators (CIGs). These are often used to create 3D images of the environment and display them to crew members at frame rates that create the illusion of animation and continuous motion. Key data elements to CIGs are descriptions of geometry, color, lighting, and texture. Most CIGs use polygonal surface representations.

Constructive Simulation

Constructive simulation traditionally refers to higher-echelon wargaming applications. Aggregations of forces instead of individual vehicles are often the object of these systems. As a result, the terrain data required by these systems is often a macro version of what an individual simulator would need.

Electronic and Paper Maps

The operators of any of these simulation systems, whether manned, semi-automated, or constructive forces, typically deal with paper or electronic maps to orient themselves and interact with the synthetic environment. Therefore, map generation systems must also use the SE database.

The needs of the different applications are diverse, as is the data representation each expects from a synthetic environment. Examples of the different requirements will further highlight this point in the next section.

Same Object, Multiple "Views"

When different simulation applications are operating over the same geographical region, each has a different perspective and "view" of the same object in that region. Multiple representations of the same objects are usually needed to address this difference. Sometimes, the data in an SE doesn't contain the required information, even though it may adhere to the appropriate data format. In these cases, the application must obtain this information by either extracting (often reverse-engineering) the data that is in a synthetic environment database or inserting it from other sources. Sometimes, the information does exist, but not in the optimum format. Both of these data augmentations are most often done when an application downloads the simulation source database and prepares it for its own use. This database conversion process is typically an off-line step prior to any realtime simulation.

Even within the same class of application platforms, the information and data needs may be different. Let's say the same visual system is used to render images for two different simulation purposes: a ground vehicle and an aircraft, both operating in the same geographical region. For proper operation, the ground vehicle requires detailed geometric data describing the surface of the terrain and the 3D objects on the terrain. Surface slopes, location and size of obstacles, and other important detail must be specified with sufficient fidelity so that the vehicle operator can maneuver through the database. The same surface slope, on the other hand, is of no consequence to the pilot of the aircraft simulator flying at 30,000 feet over the same region. In that case, a reasonable 2D image of the area is all that's required to indicate where the ground is.

In one case, 3D polygons are needed; in the other, a texture map representing the same area will suffice. Both applications use the same type of image generator but allocate the computational load differently. The aircraft requires longer viewing ranges at high altitudes, but it doesn't need high-detail geometry. The ground vehicle has a more restricted viewing volume, but it needs more detail in nearby objects. This difference in representations of the same objects and regions can have a significant impact on a synthetic environment database. Such diversity in data representation is largely independent of whether the simulators are networked or not.

The data representation problem becomes more complicated when the same database must be used not only with different fidelity systems but also with different types of systems. A CIG, a SAF, and a map generator require different information to process a road network, for example. The CIG must render the road geometry using 3D surface representation plus color and texture data so that a driver can follow the road. Additional data for transition regions between the road and the surrounding terrain or about surface composition used for vehicle dynamics may also be necessary.

A SAF system, on the other hand, not only requires the 3D surface geometry to properly place its vehicles on the road but also needs topological data so that the vehicles can actually follow the turns and bends of the road. Since there is no human eye to guide a SAF vehicle and avoid obstacles, the system must have sufficient data to "drive" a vehicle reasonably intelligently. This topological data must exist in the SAF version of the SE database, but it is unnecessary for the CIG system's database. Similarly, the SAF system will have no use for the texture and color portion of the surface data.

The map generator can utilize the same topology data a SAF needs but has to process these as 2D line drawings at the appropriate scale. Texture data and 3D geometry are of little significance to the map generator, but it needs road names, road types (freeway or dirt road), and labels to produce a paper or an electronic map.

In these examples, all three systems need access to the same conceptual object, but the types of information and the data formats needed by each are different. To interoperate these different fidelity systems, a complete SE database must accommodate all their needs. Otherwise, the maps may not represent what drivers see in their viewports, or the SAF vehicles may appear to be driving off the road when viewed from a real simulator. Each representation of the data must be taken into account in the creation and use of synthetic environment databases.

Constraints on Making Databases

There are several constraints on the creation of synthetic environment databases. Perhaps the most prominent of these is dictated by the realtime computation requirements. Since processing power is limited, once a platform is chosen for a given cost-performance range, the software, and sometimes the hardware, must be designed for best realtime performance. This means both the data and the data structures stored in a platform-specific version of an SE database play an important role in optimizing the system performance. These optimization concepts are no different from what the computer game industry does in authoring every game; it's just a matter of scale, at least in nonnetworked systems.

Given the fixed computational budget of a system, the database designer must take into account the application-specific requirements, the size and extents of the database, the desired density and fidelity, as well as the type and amount of the available raw data elements that must be incorporated into the database.

If a networked simulation system is the target, then whether it is composed of a homogeneous or heterogeneous set of simulators makes a big difference in the design and distribution mechanism of the database. As the previous examples show, multiple representations of the same object require the designer to take these needs into account during the construction process. In many cases, the needs of all potential participants are not accommodated during the database construction phase. For example, in most SE databases topology data is either nonexistent or lost during the database creation, and the database user who needs this information must attempt to extract this information from the database that has been received.

Other application-specific requirements relate to whether the database will be used for air, ground, sea, near-ground, or any combination of these simulators. The detail needed by a simulator that allows an individual to walk on the terrain is much greater than that expected for a helicopter simulator typically flying several hundred feet in the air. Database density, size and extents, viewing range, field of view, and other important simulation requirements dictate the amount and type of data that can be included in a database without overwhelming the performance requirements.

Often, the intended simulation platform imposes specific constraints. This is most notable in the CIG systems. The specific special-purpose hardware architectures, designed for the sole purpose of realtime image generation, impose vastly different constraints on the database contents. Two database designers building a database of the same region for two different CIGs often arrive at entirely different end results. The polygon or object-processing capacity of a CIG limits the database density to levels that can be processed in realtime. Similarly, image-rendering techniques drive whether a database can contain textures and how many or if the image generator can render all the objects that are potentially viewable in a scene within a fixed frame time. Other architecture-specific features such as caching scheme, occulting calculation, processing of transparent objects, or image enhancement techniques like antialiasing drive how a database must be partitioned, what additional run-time data needs to be added to speed operations, and whether certain data elements can even be included.

Even if networking is not a goal, the preceding examples show that there are many constraints that must be taken into account by a database designer for creating a database. When networking is a goal, the diversity in computation power poses severe problems for interoperability of multifidelity heterogeneous systems. Before discussing these in more detail, let's review a typical database creation process.

Steps in Making a Synthetic Environment Database

There are different approaches to database construction depending on the available tools, intended platforms, system requirements, available data sources, design preferences, and application-specific needs. As a result, there is no standard methodology for creating simulation databases. For the most part, however, some general phases are common to all database construction processes. Sometimes, these phases overlap or are combined; sometimes, one is left out because there is no added benefit; and sometimes, their order of execution is changed or done in parallel. With those caveats, we can break the construction process into the following six phases.

Requirements Definition

As in any project, this is a critical step. It's even more critical for database construction because of the varied levels of knowledge between designers and end users, vastly different construction techniques and system constraints, and the lack of a standard terminology common to the simulation community. Without the involvement of both users and designers throughout the entire construction process, the acceptance or desirability of the resulting database will be left to chance.

Data Collection

Capturing the source data material is a step usually performed early in the process. In some cases, this step is repeated later because insufficient information was collected, requirements became more refined, or the source material did not have the fidelity or quality of data that was expected. Source material can span the range of paper maps, digital elevation products, images and photographs, feature data, 3D models, verbal reports, tabular data, satellite imagery, attributes, environmental data, topological data, existing animation and special effects, and a host of other data sources.

Value-Adding

Often, the source data needs to be further modified or refined before it can be used. For example, a description of the terrain surface obtained from one source may not match the cultural features received from another. In these cases, roads may end up on impossible-to-travel terrain geometry, or rivers may not follow the minimum elevation of the terrain surface. These are often due to data acquisition from varied sources that were never intended to be used in the same application; at other times, the available source data resolution and the point in time when data was acquired may be the cause. In some cases, the value-adding process involves updating the existing data with the latest information reflecting changes in the real environment, like natural disasters (flooding), or human intervention (effects of war), or new data that was simply unavailable previously.

Transforming and Tailoring the Data

Sometimes, the source data, even after value-adding, is not optimal for the computational needs of the target system. In these cases, the data is filtered, tailored, or otherwise transformed to fit the need. For example, a particular grid-post resolution describing sample elevation of the terrain may be greater than the system can process in realtime. In such a case, the data may be resampled to a lower resolution that better matches the available computational power. Sometimes, the same grid posting must be converted to a continuous surface representation by creating polygons between adjacent grid elevations. This typically produces uniform polygons across the entire database. On the other hand, the same grid elevation data can be input to a surface representation scheme that picks optimum elevations based on given criteria and produces triangles of irregular shape and length. This technique is commonly referred to as "TINing" the database, or representing the surface with Triangulated Irregular Networks. Other tailoring techniques involve the partitioning of the data into spatially organized subregions in order to speed up access, retrieval, or processing.

"Assembling" the Database

Once all data sources have been put in an acceptable form, the various data elements are then integrated and assembled into the database one at a time. This may mean combining a surface with a particular texture, color, or attribute or conforming the 2D features, such as roads or rivers, with the underlying 3D terrain surface. There are many other similar steps that take place during this phase; applying realtime performance constraints is one of those. The key, however, is the notion of infusing and integrating inherently varied data sources into a single cohesive database.

Compiling and Transmission of the Database

After sufficient iteration of the previous steps, the synthetic environment database is ready for use and testing by the target platform(s). In this step, the database is compiled from its editable data structures into platform-specific data structures. The database generation facility will either reformat the data for the target platform(s) or provide the data in a known format as input to compilers designed for creating SAF, CIG, or any other special-purpose run-time databases. In a networked simulation system, the ability to interoperate depends on the robustness of the interchange mechanism to ensure whatever data was originally put into the database isn't lost as a result of the data interchange and translation process.

Trade-offs

Realtime processing capacity dictates the need for trade-offs. Given a fixed frame rate, the computational capacity of a simulation platform will be limited to a set number of processing primitives. For most manned simulators using a synthetic environment database, this translates into a fixed number of polygons and pixels that can be processed per second. The database designer, knowing the maximum capacities, makes trade-off decisions in allocating the polygon budget to various objects. For example, representation of the terrain may get a smaller budget in order to allow higher feature density in the database. Similarly, if a specific viewing range is needed for the application, database density may have to be adjusted to permit longer viewing ranges within a constant view volume. In addition, the designer must trade off between the number of polygons allocated to static 3D structures, other features such as roads and forests, and the average expected number of moving models that may congregate within a crew member's view volume when the simulation is running.

The storage volume of the database must also be taken into account. There are times when the realtime processing capacity has not been exceeded, but the database cannot be stored in memory due to its excessive size. The number of texture patterns that can be stored with a database is a good example of this situation. Also, it's possible that the database itself is populated with many simple features, and even though the object/polygon processing capacity of the machine is not exceeded, the online memory cannot hold the description of all the individual objects placed in the database. The construction of a database is often a balancing act between the various competing data objects.

Similar to CIGs, other simulation platforms must adhere to their processing capacity limitations. These include such things as data retrieval rates, collision detection calculations, ballistics calculations, and the time it takes to compute a vehicle's behavior given the surface geometry of a dense database. In any of these cases, if the SE database causes excessive demands on the system's processing capacity, the database must be re-engineered to bring the realtime computation within manageable limits.

Effects of Networking

Additional issues must be considered when systems are networked to operate in a common, fully interactive, synthetic environment. This interactive free-play nature of a networked simulation can lead to unpredictable computational loads. This will be increasingly true in future entertainment applications as the number of multiplayer networked systems increases. Since players can choose to congregate in large numbers, the equivalent database density in these regions during run-time can exceed the processing power of at least some of the simulators. Although some scenarios may be predictable, there is no guarantee a system won't experience overload. To a great extent, this can be helped with proper design of the SE database. The designer takes into account an expected average load due to the processing of moving vehicles. This expected average is based on the anticipated scenarios, the number of objects/vehicles that are expected to participate in an exercise, and the average processing required for handling a single object/vehicle. This average reserve is then subtracted from the total system capacity, and the database is designed based on the remaining budget.

During overload conditions, some simulators employ graceful degradation techniques for managing overload. Although this is a run-time technique, the database designer can facilitate its implementation by incorporating multiple levels of detail (LOD) of an object into the database. LOD is used to reduce computational burden in normal, as well as overload, conditions. When an object is sufficiently far away, a lower level of detail is used instead of the full-fidelity original. Since details at large distances are not viewable by a user, the designer can avoid unnecessary computation of the full-detail object. A database designer may assign and generate multiple LODs per object. Then, during overload conditions, the system processing load can be reduced by switching to lower LODs of objects in the scene. Some systems extend this technique to terrain geometry as well. In networked simulation, this may cause other problems, depending on the viewing range configuration of the systems involved.

Other critical factors in a database that could affect interoperability of networked systems are color, texture, haze, and contrast resolutions and settings. These can vary from system to system and can create unfair advantages for some users. They often lead to differences in speed of detection and recognition of distant objects.

Interoperability and Interchange

Interoperation of multifidelity systems on the same network is highly desirable. The primary reason is to leverage existing hardware investments in legacy stand-alone simulators. The challenge, however, is in determining the "right" type and amount of synthetic environment data that each simulator should use to ensure interoperability. The rules for interoperability of heterogeneous simulators remain unknown for the most part. Some of this is because there are very few multifidelity networked systems in operation today and enough research and experimentation has not been done to arrive at general rules. Most heterogeneous networked exercises to date have been conducted under restricted conditions.

A common misconception is to equate success in the interchange of data with success in interoperability. Interchange of databases does not guarantee interoperability, but it is one necessary condition for achieving it. Since the variables affecting interoperability are many and complex, effective mechanisms for making the database interchange process successful become significantly more difficult and challenging. Examples in previous sections showed the need for multiple representations of the same object, the trade-offs made during the construction and run-time stages, and the processing capacity of different systems. All of these are significant contributors to the type and amount of data each system can use and handle. These demands must be met successfully by the contents of a synthetic environment database, and that is not a trivial problem.

A new effort for addressing the interchange problem is underway. It is the Synthetic Environment Data Representation and Interchange Specification (SEDRIS). The goal of SEDRIS is to provide the means for capturing all the pertinent information in SE databases constructed for networked simulation. Another SEDRIS objective is to allow multiple access paths for getting to the same information while providing polymorphic representation of the same object. The networked simulation community needs a robust interchange mechanism so that it can begin addressing the interoperability issues of heterogeneous simulators.

Tools

A critical factor in constructing and sharing synthetic environments is incorporation and use of good tools. Most existing tools are understandably special-purpose, given the various criteria and techniques employed by different suppliers for constructing and tailoring databases. As the domain of networked simulation expands and commercial applications of this technology in education and entertainment emerge, the need for more common and yet more sophisticated tools will increase. The interest and rapid growth in use of Web sites, the diversity of their content, and the desire to provide 3D interfaces are prime indicators that robust and extensible interchange mechanisms, and tools to support them, are needed. The ability to create databases rapidly, to evaluate trade-off consequences and alternatives, to regenerate "missing" data, and to optimize and inject platform-specific constraints into the database will lead to the need for better database and content generation tools. Efficient toolkits are also needed during the interchange of databases. Intelligent access mechanisms and transparent data retrieval methods are critical for a good interchange process.

For the next three years and in the multiuser networked-based application domains (such as the Internet), tools for interchange and tools for content development will most likely grow in parallel and, to some extent, on common but competing grounds. Interchange formats will try to drive the application content, and application developers will push the interchange envelope. Once the functional and technical differences between run-time and off-line developments take better shape, the relationships between these tools will become more complementary. By contrast, the networked location-based entertainment (LBE) field will likely attend to the growth of content development tools more than interchange toolkits. The perceived competition for stand-alone networked systems will obviate the need for interchange tools. This trend will certainly change once the Internet-based systems begin to solve the problems of interoperation of heterogeneous systems. The market demand for networked LBEs to connect to other sites, as well as home-based systems, will once again push the state of the art in database development and interchange tools.

Summary

This has been an overview of the key issues in construction and use of synthetic environments in realtime networked simulation. We reviewed the general steps in creating databases and highlighted some trade-off examples. An important aspect of database construction is the integration of many sources into one database. Application and performance constraints play key roles in the construction of these databases. The effect of simulator interoperability on the content structure of SE databases is one of the largest challenges we face.

Tools will always play an important role in the construction, tailoring, and distribution process. Increasingly, those managing simulation projects will find themselves demanding better and more intelligent tools for the database generation tasks. They will also see a growing need for teaming designers and users and for increasing the knowledge levels on both sides. In short, capturing, generating, and interchanging the "critical data and information" will become core to the proper use of a synthetic environment in realtime networked interactive simulation.

Biography

Since 1984, Farid Mamaghani has worked in the field of interactive networked simulation. He was one of the original designers of SIMNET's computer image generation system, and he worked as systems engineer and project manager on various components of the SIMNET program. He is currently an independent consultant involved in systems engineering and management of simulation projects. His clients include both military and commercial organizations.

Chapter 6

Networked Synthetic Environments: From DARPA to Your Virtual Neighborhood

Warren Katz
MäK Technologies

Introduction

Over the past 30 years, computer-generated synthetic environments have been developed and used for training people in very complex, dangerous, or financially risky tasks. Because the technology for synthetic environment simulation has always been very expensive, the only jobs for which training devices could be financially justified were those for which the penalty for failed performance was more expensive than the training device itself. Not surprisingly, the pioneers in developing these types of systems have almost always been the military. From the first Link trainer to the most modern dome flight simulators, the price for realism in military training devices has rarely been too high.

This was, of course, before the invention of Distributed Interactive Simulation (DIS) technology, a networking technique for connecting thousands of simulators together on a computer network. Instead of plunking down $50 million for a single flight simulator, demand developed for thousands of simulators to be networked in a synthetic environment for training groups of combatants in collaborative tasks. Even the mighty budget of the U.S. Department of Defense (DoD) could not withstand the purchase of thousands of $50-million simulators. Suddenly, phrases like "selective fidelity" and "part-task trainer" began cropping up to justify the extreme reduction in target price for individual networkable training devices.

This huge paradigm shift on the part of the DoD has been very beneficial to the private sector. The primary benefit comes from the networking technology that enables multiuser video games, transportation simulators, and multiparticipant 3D Web interfaces. With the DoD focused on synthetic environment technology in the same price range as video games, arcade games, and theme park rides, the private sector is also enjoying a historically unprecedented direct benefit from military R&D dollars spent in the areas of computer graphics, microprocessors, simulation software, and human-machine interface technology.

This chapter delves into the history of this cutting-edge technology, some high-level technical discussion of how it works, and its current and future effects on the related commercial markets.

History of Networked Virtual Reality in the Military

Up until about 1983, the commonly perceived notion of a training simulator in the Department of Defense was a stand-alone device designed to train a single individual or single crew in the high-fidelity skills necessary to operate their weapon system, such as flying, shooting, and targeting. The design goal of the engineers who designed and built these devices was to provide the highest degree of realism to the crew, emulating as accurately as possible the real-world cues that the crew would be subjected to in actual combat situations. These lofty goals had a tendency to drive the performance and price of these systems through the roof. Common components of these simulators included the following:

- A full-fidelity mock-up of the vehicle being simulated, including portions of the hull and all controls and displays. This was often the actual hull of the real vehicle.

- 60-Hz, or higher, realtime image generation, typically driven by multimillion-dollar-per-channel image generators.

- 360-degree-by-270-degree fields of view projected onto the inside of a spherical dome. This involved several high-power video projectors, some of which were mounted on gimbals for realtime positioning.

- Head tracking and/or eye tracking for high-resolution insets (up to 1-arc-minute resolution for inset). Each inset would have at least one gimbaled projector associated with it.

- 6-degree-of-freedom hydraulic motion bases. Sometimes, these motion systems would not only move the cockpit within the dome but also move the whole dome itself!

- Integrated computer-generated threat simulation. This subsystem would create automated enemies for the crew to rehearse with.

- 3D sound generation.

Depending on the performance of each of the preceding components, these simulators could cost anywhere from $1 million to $50 million each. Often, the simulator was more expensive than the vehicle it simulated. Since each simulator accommodated only a single crew, which is often one person, and the training facility required several operators to run the simulation, the cost per user-hour of training time was staggering. If a $50-million simulator were operated for 8 hours a day, 200 days per year, for 10 years, it would cost $3,125 per hour to amortize the purchase price, without considering any hourly operating costs or repairs.

For their intended purpose, the rehearsal of individual mission skills, these training devices were well suited, and since they afforded a safe, controlled practice environment, it's likely that lives were spared.

During the heyday of these high-fidelity simulators, the only method available to train teams of soldiers in collaborative tasks, such as practicing tactics, strategies, and procedures, was to transport all the soldiers and their equipment to a real-world exercise site, anywhere from the Sahara to the North Pole, and actually rehearse battle scenarios. There are countless stories of terrible training accidents in these live exercises, including decapitations from rotor blades, soldiers run over by tank treads, soldiers accidentally being left to starve in the middle of a desert after the exercise is over, and other such stupid accidents, mostly due to human error in noncombat-related activities.

In addition to the avoidable loss of human life, there was also collateral damage to property. It's very difficult to rehearse the defense of the Fulda Gap unless you're actually training in the Fulda Gap. Unfortunately, the German farmers who owned land in the Fulda Gap were not too pleased with M1 tanks ripping through their cabbage patches, Apache helicopters flying through their barns, or Dismounted Infantry harassing their livestock. Legends abound of the bespectacled government accountant in flak jacket and helmet following the invasion force, writing checks, and handing them out to local residents in the wake of destruction.

Also, scheduling a live training exercise is almost as daunting a logistical nightmare as scheduling an actual war. For the Gulf War, we had 6 months to get everything prepared. Similarly, major live training exercises are run at most once or twice a year.

Training on live terrain has the additional disadvantage of poor security. In our Fulda Gap scenario, all Ivan had to do was perch up on a tall hill with a cheap pair of binoculars to discover the defensive tactics of the opposition. Even if the training exercises were held on U.S. soil, a second-rate spy satellite could give our adversaries ringside seats.

The frequent loss of life, the horrific expense of live training exercises, the low frequency at which they could be held, and poor security, all begged for a better mousetrap for collaborative training. In 1983, along came a starry-eyed, young Air Force lieutenant colonel named Jack Thorpe, on loan to the Defense Advanced Research Projects Agency (DARPA) as a program manager. DARPA is the venture capitalist of the DoD. Their specific mission is to fund high-risk/high-payoff advanced technologies that can be used by our armed forces to maintain an advantage on the battlefield. The agency was renamed ARPA, its "D" prefix guillotined to signify its additional mission of providing "dual-use" technologies to aid in our economic battles with other global techno-giants. Of course, politics, being a fickle mistress, later caused the "D" to reappear during the first Clinton term of office. All DARPA's current projects must have some potential applicability outside the military to meet funding criteria. Though many of their projects fail, they have a stellar record for innovation. Almost all exotic technologies in the U.S. arsenal, including Stealth radar avoidance, cruise missiles, the Internet, VR, and laser-guided weapons, plus many that won't be known for years, have come out of DARPA projects. Surprisingly, DARPA is one of the leanest, most efficient agencies in the U.S. federal government, with only 150 people or so controlling billions of dollars worth of research projects. DARPA is also a joint agency, meaning that it's staffed by officers on loan from all military branches, as well as some civilians.

Jack Thorpe, along with his ever-faithful consultant, Colonel (retired) Gary Bloedorn (who lost his life in an unfortunate motorcycle accident well before his time), initiated one of the most influential technology revolutions that has ever occurred within the DoD. Jack and Gary envisioned a multiuser computer-generated synthetic environment where collaborative training, weapon concept development, and tactics development could be performed in a very controlled, cost-effective, safe, and secure manner. SIMNET (SIMulator NETworking) was a major paradigm shift for the training community.

Instead of developing a small number of those high-fidelity, multimillion-dollar simulators for part-task training, Jack and Gary contracted Perceptronics, Inc., of Woodland Hills, California, and Bolt Beranek and Newman (BBN), of Cambridge, Massachusetts, to design and build inexpensive $250,000 simulators of lower fidelity than their older cousins. Perceptronics was responsible for designing and manufacturing the fiberglass shells and controls for the simulators, while BBN was responsible for all the software, networking protocols, and image generation. Hundreds of these "selective fidelity" simulators were networked together to provide an electronic world for collaborative tactics development and rehearsal.

"Selective fidelity" was a buzzword coined in the SIMNET program that meant that a simulator need only be good enough to accomplish the training goal at hand. The tank simulators that SIMNET fielded had relatively low resolution (320 x 128 pixels per vision block), a relatively low frame rate (15 Hz), no motion base, an inexpensive fiberglass hull, and a reduced set of controls. For the same 8-hours-a-day, 200-days-a-year, 10-year service life, the amortized cost of a SIMNET simulator is $15.63 per hour. Of course, the proponents of high-fidelity simulators and live training exercises vilified the SIMNET system, claiming that its cartoonish graphics and reduced-fidelity human-machine interface rendered it useless as a training device. For its targeted intention, collaborative training, the SIMNET system ultimately proved an excellent value.

SIMNET training facilities typically consist of several dozen vehicle simulators, data logging systems, after-action review stations, intelligent automated adversary simulators, and off-line data analysis devices. When trainees close the doors of their simulators, they are transported to a time and place where they can rehearse tactics, refight historical battles, test hypothetical weapon systems, become familiar with enemy terrain, and so on. One of the main reasons that SIMNET could so drastically reduce the fidelity of simulators and still maintain "suspension of disbelief" is that, for the first time, manned crews were fighting against other manned crews. Even with cartoonish displays, the fact that both friendly and hostile players were controlled by other humans made the system believable and engrossing.

Over its 10-year life span (now entering its twilight), SIMNET enjoyed widespread success and acclaim for its accomplishments in cost reduction of training, increased quality and quantity of tactical team training, and usefulness as a testbed for new weapon concepts. By today's standards, SIMNET is considered outdated and very low fidelity for its original price point. SIMNET's biggest accomplishment, however, was the spawning of a standard networking protocol for all the training devices the military buys. This standard, called the DIS (Distributed Interactive Simulation) Protocol, is mandatory for all new training devices procured by the DoD. This technology has forever changed the way the Pentagon trains our soldiers.

In addition, the SIMNET system demonstrated that hypothetical weapons could be simulated on a network with simulations of other vehicles that already exist, enabling the value of the new weapon to be assessed long before any prototype was manufactured. The first such experiment was held in 1987 when the Forward Area Air Defense (FAAD) system was mocked up in simulation and placed on the network with dozens of air and ground simulators of vehicles that already existed. The FAAD was a conceptual air defense vehicle that was a follow-on to the ill-fated Sergeant York (an air defense system that the Pentagon spent billions developing before it was finally scrapped). In the course of a few short weeks of testing with the four $250,000 FAAD simulators, the entire combat doctrine for offensive and defensive engagements involving air defense for ground warfare was completely discarded, and new performance requirements for air defense systems were produced.

As a result of FAADs and other early experiments, the entire acquisition strategy of the DoD has changed. Now, if a new system is desired, it must be mocked up and tested in distributed simulation prior to prototyping. This has already saved the DoD billions in wasted development effort for weapons that were either not cost-effective or outright useless.

Even today, there are still decades of research and development to do in the areas of networked simulation for collaborative training. The most notable present-day failing is in the area of simulation of unencapsulated individuals on the battlefield (immersive VR). Even with the mighty budget of the DoD, we still can't field a helmet-mounted display (HMD) with the field of view, resolution, and frame rate necessary to render a usable world. Current HMD offerings, in fact, leave the user legally blind and without necessary visual cues to perform required tasks. Force and tactile feedback are also lagging far behind. State-of-the-art systems currently use exercise bicycles, stair climbers, or linear treadmills to simulate human locomotion.

It's clear, however, that the infrastructure and architecture for a global network of synthetic environment portals for training, entertainment, and education is in place and in constant use at the moment, and it's dragging the more slowly evolving technologies along with it.

Breakthrough Novelties of Distributed Simulation Technology

The DIS Protocol consists of some 29 different types of network packets that are passed between simulation nodes. The application-specific information is encapsulated in UDP/IP Ethernet frames. When using IP multicast, DIS has been used over the Internet with excellent results. The packets can be sent over any network media, from voice-grade phone lines to ATM switches. More bandwidth allows more entities to be supported. The packets describe things like state information of dynamic entities (speed, orientation), combat events (firing, detonation), resupply interactions, and electromagnetic emissions (light, radar, energy weapons). The heritage of the protocol is military in nature and versions up to DIS 2.0.4 have retained many military-specific fields in the packets, but current proposals for DIS 3.0 and beyond remove most of the military content and provide a much more efficient, reconfigurable, and general-purpose packet structure.

One of the unique novelties of this networking technology is the predictive algorithms that allow entities on the network to greatly reduce the frequency of rebroadcasts of state. Each entity broadcasts its type, location, velocity, acceleration, orientation, and angular velocity. All the receiving simulators can then propagate the sending entity into the future, relieving the sending entity of the responsibility to continually rebroadcast. When the error between the exact position of the entity and the predicted position exceeds a certain threshold, the sending entity will update the network with its new kinematic state. The DIS Entity State Packet, which makes up most of the network traffic in DIS 2.0.4, is about 140 bytes long and is broadcast anywhere from once every 30 seconds to four or five times per second. DIS 3.0 and higher will use a much trimmed-down Entity State Packet that will reduce network traffic by a factor of 3 or better.

This architecture provides very flexible trade-offs between computational loading, positional error, and network bandwidth. If highly accurate position is required, such as in some military experiments, the error threshold can be reduced, which will result in more network broadcasts of state. Conversely, if the only network bandwidth available is a 28.8-Kbaud modem and 60 entities are required on the system, the error thresholds can be increased, and more compute-intensive prediction algorithms can be used on the receiving ends. Figure 6.1 shows some sample performance curves for DIS networks. As the figure indicates, currently available bandwidth mechanisms are more than adequate for

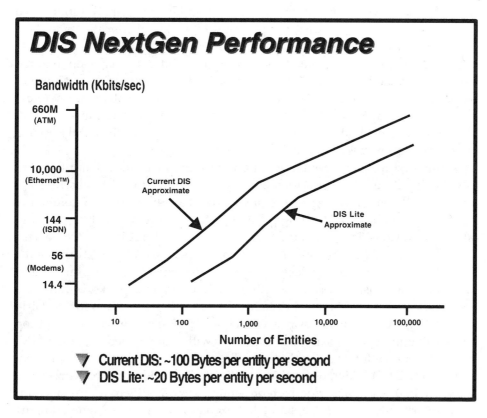

Figure 6.1   Sample performance curves of DIS networks.

significant numbers of players to be networked from geographically dispersed sites. State-of-the-art DIS systems currently in use by the government are running over 10,000 entities on Ethernets, long-haul networked from several locations. As low-cost commercial data services become available (bidirectional cable TV, ISDN), the DIS 3.0 standard goes into effect, and multicast routing for context filtering is implemented, we expect the population of networked worlds to rise an order of magnitude, exceeding the 100,000-player level.

The DIS protocol is self-healing. When a new entity enters the world, it begins to broadcast Entity State Packets. If recipients have never heard from this entity before, they simply add it to their remote entity database. If an entity is not heard from within five seconds, recipients will time it out, removing it from their remote entity databases. Players can enter and leave at will without disturbing other participants (other than their appearance and disappearance), and dropped packets don't cause system failure. In this architecture, there is no central server, thus no single point of failure. Heterogeneous nodes can interact with one another using DIS. The network protocol provides a standard mechanism for communication between simulators that may have radically different architectures. An entity broadcasting an Entity State Packet is simply informing the network of what kind of entity it is and its kinematic information. Two different recipients of the same Entity State Packet may render the remote entity with very different levels of fidelity. For example, a PC may render a remote F-15 with only 10 flat-shaded polygons and may have an internal simulation frame rate of only 5 frames per second. A high-end Silicon Graphics workstation may render the same F-15 with 500 Gouraud-shaded, phototextured polygons at a rate of 60 frames per second. In the entertainment world, this would allow a high-fidelity arcade-based system worth tens of thousands of dollars to interact with a $200 home-based game system.

Compared to the computational power necessary to render out-the-window images in realtime, the DIS prediction algorithms do not represent a significant load. The most expensive prediction algorithm that DIS commonly uses consumes about 100 floating-point operations per remote entity per simulation frame. Considering that the average PC can do about 10 MFLOP per second and a simulation might run at 20 frames per second, a PC can handle several thousand remote entities using the most expensive algorithm. Naturally, this load must be balanced with other computational tasks, but this is a good indication as to the level of hardware necessary to accommodate fairly large DIS entity populations in a virtual world. Emerging cable-TV set-top boxes will undoubtedly be powered by CPUs with more horsepower than a PC.

At the annual Interservice/Industry Training Systems and Education Conference (I/ITSEC), a demonstration of DIS interoperability is orchestrated on the show floor each year. Booths representing over 50 different organizations are networked together for a simulated exercise. DIS node systems, ranging from PCs to high-fidelity flight simulators with multimillion-dollar image generators, are connected for a week of interactive exercises. This (1997) is the third consecutive year such a demo was shown. In addition, at SIGGRAPH '96 in New Orleans, the Bayou Sauvage demo of an entertainment application involved a dozen software and hardware companies, four platforms, and software simulators for two dune buggies, two helicopters, two hovercrafts, a jeep, a Stealth platform, and one alien spaceship, all using the same database. For input devices, we used PC joysticks, PC steering wheels, arcade video-game consoles, a keyboard (for the Stealth platform), and the Fakespace Labs Push-BOOM.

Though there are several commercial-off-the-shelf DIS developer's toolkits available, most of the industry uses a product called VR-Link, by MäK Technologies, of Cambridge, Massachusetts. It was developed by some of the original SIMNET engineers and currently dominates the networked simulation market worldwide. A version of VR-Link that uses MäK's DIS-Lite protocol, a thinned-down, lighter-weight proposal for DIS 3.0, is now being marketed and sold to game companies for Internet-based game worlds.

DIS in the Private Sector

It's no surprise that DIS technology has been slowly finding its way into other industries, such as air traffic control simulation, Intelligent Vehicle Highway Systems research, commercial virtual reality, networked games and entertainment systems, and, most recently, multiuser virtual worlds on the World Wide Web. This section discusses some emerging nonmilitary applications.

FAA Air Traffic Control Trainers

MITRE Corporation of Virginia has used DIS to develop an Air Traffic Control Training system. The student interacts with a display of DIS aircraft (either automated or manned flight simulators) that could be coming from anywhere around the country. Difficult situations can be scripted, repeated, and analyzed for performance. A national dial-in network for pilots in training, as well as air traffic controllers in training, is certainly possible and has been proposed to the FAA.

Intelligent Transportation Systems

The Department of Transportation, Federal Highway Administration has been sponsoring work in the field of Intelligent Vehicle Highway Systems (IVHS), more recently renamed Intelligent Transportation Systems (ITS). The Analytical Sciences Corporation (TASC), of Reading, Massachusetts (www.tasc.com), has developed some experimental automobile simulations to study the effects of increased traffic on pollution. A national network for driver training and city planning is also on the drawing board.

Networked PC Games

Several game companies have adopted DIS as their networking mechanism for multiuser games on the Internet. Among them are Zombie, BMG, Spectrum Holobyte, and Digital Image Design of Great Britain, four of the leading game developers for the new generation of 3D first-person interactive games. Several titles hit the streets in the 1996 Christmas season.

Transition to Theme Parks and Location-Based Entertainment Systems

As the price/performance point of realtime image generation systems decreases, arcades and theme parks will begin to adopt them on a larger scale. Already, many emerging systems such as Magic Edge, Virtuality, and Division are adopting higher-end SGI and Evans and Sutherland image generators for their architectures. Almost all systems being fielded today, including PC-based systems, are capable of DIS networking. It's simply a matter of time before large-scale networked systems begin operation.

DIS and the World Wide Web

There has been great interest generated of late in using DIS for 3D multiuser interaction on the World Wide Web for sales, advertising, and entertainment. Several companies have begun integrating DIS into their Web browsers and servers. DIS is highly complementary to the new VRML standard that is useful for passing around 3D models and databases. Expect to see products adhering to both standards in the very near future.

Interactive Television and DIS

Telephone and cable-TV companies are all gearing up for high-bandwidth, bidirectional data services into the home. They envision such services as movies-on-demand, interactive video games, and home shopping. DIS, or its commercial derivative, is ideally suited to use these services for interactive virtual reality. The bandwidth reduction techniques that allow thousands of entities to exist on LANs will allow people in their living rooms to interact with one another in multiparticipant virtual worlds. Each channel can be associated with a specific activity or experience. Users will be able to select from myriad sporting activities, games of chance, games of skill, fantasy adventure, and even adult themes.

Future Developments

VR Protocol

One major complaint about DIS is that it's difficult to add new behaviors or new players to an ongoing exercise. The VR Protocol research project has demonstrated the ability to transfer the polygonal file for a new entity on a query-response basis when needed. This capability will allow new players to join an exercise and inform the preexisting systems of its appearance. This is different from VRML in that the transaction isn't initiated by a person, but is automatic and transparent to the users of the system.

Another capability of the VR Protocol is the ability to define scripts for newly defined behaviors based on a predefined set of basic primitive behaviors. For example, if there are a hundred virtual people simulated by a single workstation, a very efficient algorithm for wandering around can be defined by that workstation and sent via the VR Protocol to all receivers on the network. This complex behavior can then be regenerated for all 100 entities on each receiving node while using next to no network bandwidth at all. Such scripting capability is similar to Java, and Java will likely be used for this purpose.

Newtonian Protocol

This extension to DIS allows entities to exchange Newtonian forces with one another for tactile and force feedback, towing, combat engineering operations, and other "bumps." It's technologically difficult to maintain a sustained physical contact between entities across a network and also use a small amount of network bandwidth. The Newtonian protocol uses a novel transfer function exchange paradigm to reduce this network traffic.

High-Level Architecture (HLA)

This fairly new effort is concentrating on creating an interoperable architecture for simulations spanning a huge range of scales. The largest scale is Higher-Order Wargaming Models, which are typically simulations that run faster than realtime, simulating objects that are hierarchical aggregates of individual entities (platoons, battalions, swarms, gaggles, tribes, herds). The other end of the scale is high-fidelity engineering models, which run much slower than real time, simulating individual subsystems at very high accuracy (for example, finite element method simulation of the stress within the layers of a cudgel when the damsel clubs a troll over the head).

It's intriguing but currently unclear whether interactions between such a vast range of simulation fidelities and time scales are possible or useful. I guess that's why they call it advanced research.

Multicast Traffic Management

This capability is being implemented as of this writing and will be the means by which very large scale DIS exercises can be run over the Internet. By separating network traffic into groups of interest, whether it be by exercise ID, entity location, or fidelity level, very large numbers of players can selectively send packets to subsets of listeners. On a packet-switched internetwork, traffic will be routed only to those listeners who subscribe to a particular group of interest. Since there is no central server serving as a bottleneck, a pure peer-to-peer DIS network will guarantee minimum latency between sender and receiver and also allow huge numbers of players in the same world.

Summary

There have been several other efforts besides DIS to develop multiparticipant synthetic environments. Though DIS currently has vast technological superiority, several closed, proprietary protocols have cropped up. It's unclear which of the many standards will become dominant, but it's certain to be an open standard, one that will run on the Internet and that will provide the ability to link huge numbers of individual portals into an ever-evolving cyberspace. Combined with the tremendous leaps in real-time rendering, tactile and force feedback devices, and helmet-mounted displays, we're sure to see a revolution in synthetic environment societies in the not-so-distant future. Life online, both real and synthetic, is about to get very interesting.

Biography

Warren Katz cofounded MäK Technologies with John Morrison in 1990, after working for Bolt Beranek and Newman on the SIMNET project. He was the resident drivetrain simulation expert on SIMNET, responsible for mathematical modeling of the physical systems and software development. His current responsibilities include corporate operations, business development, and program management. MäK Technologies provides cutting-edge research and development services to the Department of Defense in the areas of Distributed Interactive Simulation (DIS) and networked VR systems and converts the results of this research into commercial products for the entertainment and industrial markets. MäK's VR-Link developer's toolkit is the most widely used commercial DIS interface in the world, enabling multiple participants to interact in realtime via low-bandwidth network connections.

Chapter 7

VRML: Low-Tech Illusion for the World Wide Web

Tony Parisi
Intervista Software, Inc.

Introduction

The Virtual Reality Modeling Language (VRML) is the standard for describing three-dimensional spaces that are accessible via the World Wide Web. VRML can be thought of as analogous to HTML, but instead of flat pages, it describes user-navigable 3D spaces and structures. This simple definition has grand implications. VRML is a tool for creating worlds—immersive, interactive *places* that anyone with an Internet connection can experience. This makes it a workable foundation for cyberspace, an honest case of reality meeting science fiction. If the many people working to make it ubiquitous are successful, we will soon see fundamental improvements in the way we access information, interact with our environment, and communicate with one another. We will also see profitable extensions of the established entertainment industries and techniques into the constant present of cyberspace.

Much of this book is about the leading edge—specialized systems and equipment that push the envelope. Some of those technologies are young, fragile, and expensive, and may exist in only a few places. Many of them will measure their success largely in terms of the seeds they plant—pieces and parts that over time combine with even newer ideas to push the envelope still more. VRML is distinct from these in that it cannot be held to such limitations and be successful; it will succeed only insofar as its use becomes widespread. When ubiquity is the goal, the leading edge is not the best place to start; we took a pragmatic approach to design, integrating proven 3D graphics technologies with basic networking features. The approach appears to have been successful: Despite its relative youth, VRML is robust, accessible, and affordable—qualities that rarely describe something on the leading edge.

Like any art form, VRML is a medium of illusion—a compelling sense of elsewhere. Its first incarnation was pathetically simple in its functionality, supporting only static 3D geometry and hyperlinks. There was no sound, no video, no rich interaction. Yet VRML 1.0 was promising enough to attract the attention of researchers, hardware and software companies, designers, and developers who were content to build something simple at first and improve upon it later. Mark Pesce and I knew we would draw criticism for specifying such a simple feature set. We did this primarily because we wanted to accelerate the development of the standard. But we also knew that fancy features were not essential to its adoption by designers and content creators. In any art form, illusion is a function of richness, not resolution. Creating compelling content is more a matter of skill than of polygon rendering. Realism has never been a requirement for successful illusion.

3D Plus Hyperlinks

The success of HTML and the World Wide Web can arguably be attributed to the functionality of the hyperlink, which allows users to move seamlessly among documents and databases on the Internet without knowing complicated addresses or commands. In 1993, Mark Pesce and I developed Labyrinth, a simple three-dimensional interface that could describe 3D scenes and support hyperlinks. The ASCII scene description file format that it used was the first incarnation of VRML. We began with a limited feature set; it was clear to us that the huge field of computer graphics offered more than the two of us would be able to implement. When selecting features for inclusion in the language, we knew that there were some limits that content creators and users would tolerate and others that they would not.

For example, we decided up front that VRML would be a data description language, not a programming language. The 3D content is developed by people who are programmers, designers, artists, or some combination of the three; each group is notorious for its strong—perhaps religious—feelings about the tools and technologies they use to express themselves. Developing a language that all of these groups will find useful is an immense and risky enterprise. The history of computing is littered with dozens of programming languages that were as dead as Aramaic a few years after their creation, not because they weren't useful, but because they failed to be more efficient, expressive, or powerful than any of several old standbys. Designing a 3D programming language that thousands of programmers will value enough to learn is a daunting task. Furthermore, a programming language that's enticing for programmers would almost certainly be difficult for artists and designers, who often have little computer science training. By making VRML a data description language, we were able to avoid these pitfalls, though not without sacrificing functionality.

Despite the limitations in the kinds of experiences it could describe, VRML was put to serious use from the beginning. The Smithsonian Institution's United States Holocaust Museum produced "Daniel's Story," which documented the plight of a young Jewish boy through the Nazi occupation. Without a doubt, it was simple, but the illusion it created—the space it put the user in and the story that it told—never suffered from the simplicity of the medium.

Building a Standard

Mark and I presented Labyrinth at the First International Conference on the World Wide Web, in Geneva, Switzerland, in 1994. During a session to discuss virtual reality interfaces to the Web, attendees agreed there was a need for a common language to specify 3D scene description. The term "Virtual Reality Markup Language" (VRML) was coined (the "M" later came to stand for "Modeling"), and a group was formed to begin work on a detailed specification immediately following the conference. A community quickly coalesced and, largely through an electronic mailing list set up at *WIRED* magazine, began to consider the next steps for bringing VRML past the proof-of-concept stage.

The members of the mailing list quickly determined that in order to be successful any future implementations would have to be extensible, platform-independent, and usable over low-bandwidth network connections (like 14.4-Kbaud modems). With these requirements in hand, we began to seek out existing technologies that could be adapted to fit these needs.

Several file formats for three-dimensional scene description had by this time been established. The community examined existing formats and several proposals were put forth. Lead engineers at Silicon Graphics, Inc. offered to donate the OpenInventor file format, which had been proprietary, for consideration. It supports complete descriptions of 3D scenes with polygonally rendered objects, lighting, materials, ambient properties, and realism effects. It has all of the features that professionals need to produce high-quality work, plus an existing tools base with a wide installed presence. By October 1994, a subset of the Inventor file format, with extensions to support networking, had come to form the basis of the specification.

VRML 1.0 provided a platform for authoring limited 3D content. The worlds created with it were static; they were interactive only to the extent that your view changed as you moved through them, and your point of view was the only thing that could move at all. Other than clicking on hyperlinks, you couldn't interact with individual objects within a world—nothing changed as a result of your being there. Furthermore, multimedia features like sounds and video clips that are commonplace in games and other 3D applications were completely missing. However, despite these limitations, professional content creators made an effort to learn VRML and put it to use.

Early Applications

Planet 9 Studios, an architecture and design firm located in San Francisco's SoMa (South of Market) district initiated a project to model SoMa and make it accessible through the Web. As a pilot, they modeled the 10-block area between 1st and 3rd Streets, from Howard to King. This neighborhood is known as Multimedia Gulch. Many of the organizations in the area already had a Web presence; this model was designed to link to their pages. A virtual stroll through the area gave users the opportunity to simultaneously see what the companies there had to offer while learning the lay of the land they occupied—something that neither a cruise through the individual Web sites nor a real walk through the neighborhood would provide.

Also in San Francisco, a team of dedicated volunteers created the VRML Gallery for the First International Interactive Media Festival, an annual competition for innovation and excellence in interactive media. The team made VRML versions of over a dozen physical interactive installations along with the building in which they were displayed. These weren't just descriptions of what the installations did; they were spaces that could be explored nearly as easily as the works themselves. Although the festival occurred in Los Angeles in 1995, it remained accessible online to an international audience for years afterward.

It's important to note that while much of this material was being created and assembled, VRML 1.0 browsers were still being written, and the v1.0 specification (based on OpenInventor) was still technically a draft. Content authors couldn't actually view the results of their work for months, and when they did, it was with unfinished software. The VRML work for the Interactive Media Festival was nearly complete by the time they were able to even test it with a browser, a mere three weeks before the festival launch date!

The Birth of the VRML Industry

In the spring of 1995, before the 1.0 specification was completed, Silicon Graphics announced their first VRML browser product for workstations. At the same time, I founded my own company, Intervista Software, with the goal of bringing high-performance 3D graphics to the mass market. Intervista developed WorldView, a browser that enabled realtime rendered scenes on low-end PCs.

In the summer of 1995, Microsoft licensed WorldView 1.0 for inclusion in its new Internet Explorer browser. The industry was up and running.

The last half of 1995 saw the entry of several browser and tools companies and the emergence of VRML content development companies. It also saw the deployment of the first commercial VRML sites, sponsored by Intel and Ziff-Davis Interactive. These companies realized then what other companies are realizing now: 3D interactive graphics can make an effective marketing tool.

VRML 2.0

Long before the version was complete, it was clear that we needed more functionality. VRML 1.0 was an adequate starting point for content developers, but they wanted to use the medium in more sophisticated ways. They had visions of dynamic, interactive worlds that would respond to users' actions and allow users to make persistent changes to the spaces they visited. The first release was compelling enough to convince everyone that all these things were possible, but not powerful enough to fulfill its promise.

The process of developing the 2.0 specification was better organized. Ten technical experts, all of whom had been involved with the development of version 1.0, formed the VRML Architecture Group (VAG), which endeavored to focus and articulate the sentiments of the VRML community.

The VAG, working with the community, created the process for the next version. They issued a formal Request for Proposals (RFP) and received six submissions. By then, VRML had caught the eye of powerful high-tech companies; proposals came from Apple Computer, IBM, Microsoft, and Sun Microsystems. (The sixth emerged from the German National Research Center for Information Technology.) Sony, Worlds, Inc., and Silicon Graphics submitted a collaborative entry called Moving Worlds.

The VRML mailing list was again used to foster discussion about the relative merits of the six proposals. In the spring of 1996, the community voted (via the mailing list) on the proposals, and Moving Worlds was a clear winner. Its overwhelming success may be due to the fact that it was a collaboration—it had already been thoroughly debated among its creators and stood up well to scrutiny by the larger technical community. Moving Worlds specified features essential to support interactive live venues, integrated with other Web media and data sources. These features include direct manipulation, keyframe animation, sound and video, and integration with the Java and Javascript programming languages. Moving Worlds was also designed to be extensible so that developers could add functionality to a virtual environment in a standard manner.

Just as with the first version, the new round of browser development began in parallel with the specification effort. When the 2.0 standard was published at

SIGGRAPH in August of 1996, several companies, including SGI, Sony, Netscape, and Intervista, had browsers well under way. Beta versions of their efforts began to be available in the early autumn of that year. Stage 2 of market development was under way.

Current Applications

Content developers immediately latched on to the new features that 2.0 provided. Protozoa, a small San Francisco production house, used motion-capture systems to bring realistic animation to VRML characters. Construct Internet Design, formed by some volunteers from the Interactive Media Festival project, combined the talents of artists, designers, and architects to create dozens of compelling spaces. Both these companies are approaching legendary status: Protozoa regularly produces episodic VRML cartoons, much like 3D comic strips, providing proof of concept for interested parties in Hollywood; Construct has a long list of corporate clients, an indication of viability well beyond the high-tech industry.

Planet 9 Studios expanded the Virtual SoMa concept to other cities. Their Web site now sports virtual versions of Chicago, Los Angeles, New York, Boston, Washington, D.C., and New Orleans, to name a few.

Oracle has begun to explore the role that VRML will play in business applications. They are migrating existing proprietary applications, running on Oracle servers and Silicon Graphics workstations, to an open standards framework based on VRML and Java. These systems will combine the power of 3D visualization with the persistence and scalability of industrial-strength database technology. One example of such an application is an oil drilling visualization system for an Australian company.

Perhaps most notably, other companies have begun to work on the last technical obstacles that lie between the today's Web and their vision of cyberspace: multiuser spaces. Thanks to Neal Stephenson's 1992 novel, *Snow Crash,* many people have a shared idea of what cyberspace will be like. In the novel, users are embodied electronically by self-styled avatars and interact with other avatars in realtime. Changes they make in the cyberspace world have permanence, where appropriate. Characters flip between reality and cyberspace easily, using both venues to their advantage. Black Sun Interactive (which takes its name directly from the novel) and Oz Virtual have begun developing applications and network server technology for supporting a cyberspace that is nearly identical to Stephenson's description. While this technology will almost certainly secure its first major profitable foothold as entertainment, much like current text-based chat rooms, it will quickly spread to the business world, which can benefit significantly from dynamic data visualization and from the ability to get people together for certain kinds of work without air travel.

Authoring tools that allow content developers to create worlds via graphical user interfaces rather than text editors are also starting to mature. Artists and designers can now implement their ideas visually, and the content is benefiting predictably.

The State of VRML

The VRML mailing list continues as the primary forum for technical discussions and conversations among developers of authoring tools, browsers, and content. The interactions that take place on this list are undoubtedly unique for the computer industry. The community is no longer a handful of individual visionaries; it's now composed of representatives of large and small companies, partners and competitors alike. Despite competition, there is consensus that authoring tools and browsers should be interoperable—content authored with any tool should work reasonably with any browser. This is a laudable collective goal (however unorthodox), and it's common to see competitors working together to correctly interpret the VRML specification or tackle other factors affecting interoperability.

Version 2.0 has enough extensibility built in to keep it viable for quite some time. Although it's still not a programming language, the specification provides mechanisms for controlling VRML through programming languages. Currently, this may be done with both Java and Javascript (a lightweight scripting language). If other appropriate languages surface in the future, the specification can be easily extended to include them. Unlike the first version, the limitations of VRML 2.0 are less confining; content developers have plenty to work with before they find themselves trapped by its inabilities.

There are several important issues that need to be addressed but that don't require discussion directly in the specification. Speed is arguably the primary concern. As worlds get larger and more complex, navigation speed—and therefore the quality of immersion and illusion—degrades. It simply takes a long time to move through a world with hundreds of objects and textures in it. Fortunately, hardware accelerators for 3D graphics are becoming widely available and dropping significantly in price. Also, the early-stage content developers are beginning to understand how to author efficiently and strive to find ways to avoid placing hundreds of objects in a world in the first place.

The need to minimize download time is a constant struggle. Over a 14.4-Kbps modem, a big world can take several minutes to download, even compressed, and the definition of "big" will always grow. The entertainment companies that are likely to fuel the next stages of this medium all want to convey a richly evocative experience, which tends to mean more polygons and more textures. There are a few viable approaches to this problem currently under way. The first is a hybrid of CD-ROM and online. S3, Inc., the multimedia chip manufacturer, is delivering with its 3D accelerator cards a CD-ROM of common textures and sounds. Content authors can create worlds that use these elements from the user's local computer to reduce download time for many worlds. Content providers will use this technique to distribute entire, detailed worlds with characters, allowing users to launch and run a world from the CD-ROM and download incremental additions to their hard drive. The largest decrease in download time will come from a standard binary format that is currently in development. Once this standard is published and supported by browsers, download times may be reduced by 50 to 70 percent.

As an industry, VRML has jumped its most challenging hurdle—browser distribution. In early 1997, both Intervista and Silicon Graphics announced licensing agreements with several companies, including Microsoft, S3, and Netscape, that will result in tens of millions of browser plugins being distributed through their channels. End users will not have to download a browser to view content; it will already be included with the system. By the fall of 1997, 3D browsing software will be ubiquitous, and useful content will be common.

With continual improvements in technology and breakthroughs in distribution, VRML is poised to become an essential part of the Internet infrastructure and the user experience. Each successive development takes us a step closer to cyberspace, the global stage for creators of digital illusions. But just as in any medium, no matter how capable the platform and no matter how rich the palette, the responsibility of the illusion rests in the hands of the artist.

Biography

Tony Parisi is the president, chief executive officer, and founder of Intervista Software, Inc. He is the coauthor of the VRML standard and is recognized as a leader in the VRML development community. Mr. Parisi was the key developer on WorldView 1.0, the Internet community's first VRML browser, and World-View 2.0, which has received industry acclaim. He is currently spearheading the development of a VRML 2.0-compliant application publishing tool. Prior to founding Intervista, Mr. Parisi worked for ten years developing object-oriented toolkits, client-server software, and desktop productivity applications at Bolt Beranek and Newman, Lotus Development Corporation, and Belmont Research, Inc. He holds an undergraduate degree in computer science from the University of Massachusetts.

Chapter 8

You Are Hear: Positional 3D Audio

Scott Foster and Toni Schneider
Crystal River Engineering/Aureal Semiconductor

Introduction

Manipulation of sound sources and their apparent locations in space is one of the oldest and most powerful of theatrical effects, providing the means to construct more elaborate, convincing sets and characters in the minds of the audience than they could ever see on stage. Since the mid-1980s, we've been developing the tools that allow users to create fully configurable and realtime manipulable three-dimensional acoustic spaces and effects, first for the government and now for a broad range of uses. The technique is binaural acoustic imaging, and it was originally realized as the Convolvotron, the world's first multisource, realtime, digital spatialization system, built by Crystal River Engineering for NASA in 1987. There are currently multiple vendors of this technology.

The goal of a fully accurate binaural 3D sound-rendering system is to present the listener with an audio experience that is indistinguishable from reality. The reason for doing so is to provide the most effective, engaging, and immersive form of audio interface between a computer and a human, or between humans that are communicating via computers, whether or not the humans are aware of the computers. The way to realize this goal is to carefully study how people perceive sound and to efficiently reproduce every physical effect that is found to be a necessary part of the perception process. Today, the technology has matured to a point where it can be incorporated into many areas of computer-based simulation, communication, and entertainment. By closely emulating reality, good 3D sound offers an entirely new level of audio experience: A listener is no longer aware of the audio system, so the application communicates directly with the user, creating levels of awareness, realism, immersion, and engagement previously only possible in real-life situations. This chapter explains the technical workings of binaural (3D) sound-processing methods and relates them to the human perception of sounds in the real world.

Sounds in the Real World

Humans extract a lot of information about their environment acoustically. In order to understand what information can be retrieved from sound and how exactly it's done, we need to look at how sounds are perceived. To do so, we can divide the acoustics of a real-world environment into three components— the sound source, the acoustic environment, and the listener:

- The sound source is any object in the world that emits sound waves. Sound waves get created through a variety of mechanical processes. Once created, the waves usually get radiated in a certain direction. For example, a mouth radiates more sound energy in the direction that the face is pointing than to the left or right of the face.

- In the acoustic environment, once a sound wave has been emitted, several things can happen to it: It gets absorbed by the air (high frequencies more so than low ones—the amount depends on factors like wind and humidity); it can directly travel to a listener (direct path), bounce off an object once before reaching the listener (first-order reflected path), bounce twice (second-order reflected path), and so on. Each time a sound reflects off an object, the composition and surface texture of the object have an effect on how much each frequency component of the sound wave gets absorbed and how much gets reflected. Sounds can also pass through objects such as water or walls. Finally, geometry like corners, edges, and small openings have complex effects on the paths of sound waves (refraction, scattering).

- The listener is a sound-receiving object, typically a set of ears. The listener uses acoustic cues to interpret sound waves that arrive at the ears and extract information about the sound sources and the environment.

How We Perceive Sound

People can be considered sound-receiving objects in an environment. We have an auditory sensing system consisting of two ears and a brain. Additionally, very low frequency sounds can be sensed through the human body. The brain uses several cues that are embedded in the two sound signals it receives from the ears to analyze those sounds and their environment. Most people are unaware that the nuanced acoustic effects around us greatly impact our continuous perception of reality every day of our lives. On the other hand, certain people (for example, nonsighted people) are very much aware of these effects because they heavily rely on their ears for querying and navigating their surroundings.

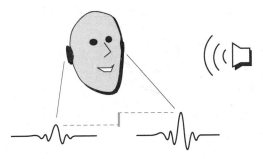

Interaural Intensity Difference (IID)

Figure 8.1   Illustration of IID.

Primary Spatial Localization Cues

The two primary localization cues are called interaural intensity difference (IID) and interaural time difference (ITD). IID refers to the fact that a sound is louder at the nearer ear because the sound's intensity at that ear will be higher than the intensity at the other ear, which is not only farther away but also usually receives a signal that has been "shadowed" by the listener's head (Figure 8.1). ITD means that a sound is likely to arrive earlier at one ear than the other. If it arrives at the left ear first, the brain knows that the sound is somewhere to the left (Figure 8.2).

The combination of these two cues allows the brain to narrow the position of an individual sound source to somewhere on a cone centered on the line drawn between the listener's ears (Figure 8.3).

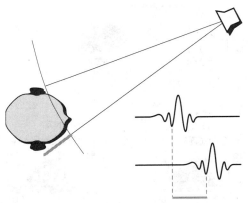

Interaural Time Difference (ITD)

Figure 8.2   Illustration of ITD.

Figure 8.3   IID–ITD cone.

The Outer Ear: Pinna

Before a sound wave gets to the eardrum, it passes through your outer ear structure, called the pinna. The pinna accentuates or suppresses mid- and high-frequency energy (Figure 8.4) of a sound wave to various degrees, depending on the angle at which the sound wave hits the pinna (Figure 8.5). This means that the two pinnae act as variable filters that affect every sound that passes through them. The brain knows how to figure out the exact location of a sound in space by receiving a signal that has been filtered in a way that is unique to the sound source's position relative to the listener.

The pinna plays a key role in the localization process. Since the outer ear and its folds are on the scale of a few centimeters, only sound waves with wavelengths in the centimeter range or smaller can be affected by the pinna. In addition, the two ears are about 15 centimeters apart, so even primary cues are greatly reduced for wavelengths bigger than that. A 3.3-kHz sound signal oscillates 3,300 times per second, while sound travels at about 330 meters per second. The wavelength is therefore about 330/3,300 = 0.1 meters, or 10 centimeters. This means that a sound at 3,300 Hz lies in the area where primary

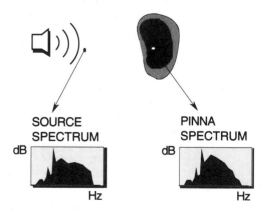

Figure 8.4   Spectrum differences between original and pinna reception at varying elevations.

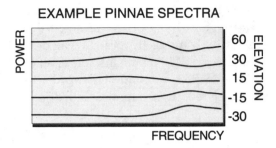

Figure 8.5 Pinnae frequency modulation sound source.

cues are still noticeable, but pinna cues start to be diminished. In general, the higher the frequency of a sound, the shorter its wavelength, and the better it can be localized. This phenomenon can be verified by placing a subwoofer and a tweeter in a room and playing music through them. With closed eyes, you will be able to immediately tell where the tweeter is located; the subwoofer, however, will sound like it is "coming from everywhere."

Propagation Effects, Range Cues, and Reflections

Many things happen to a sound as it travels through an environment before being received by a listener. All these effects allow us to learn more about what we are hearing and what kind of environment we are in; for example, a somewhat muffled, quiet sound is probably off in the distance. If it's heavily muffled, we might be in an enclosed space or listening through glass or other wall materials.

The effect of sound reflections in an environment is crucial because we are able to hear the difference in time of arrival and location between the direct-path signal, first-order reflections, and Nth-order reflections (Figure 8.6). The

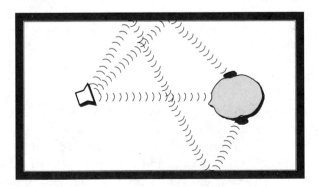

Figure 8.6 Direct-path, first-order, and second-order due to range (listener–source distance) reflections in a typical room.

reflections give us a way to further pinpoint a sound source's location, as well as the size, shape, and type of room or environment that we are in (people with very "good ears" are able to exactly locate a wall or tell the difference between an open or closed door). While humans are capable of individually perceiving first-order reflections, second- and higher-order reflections are harder to distinguish. Those later reflections are also called late-field reflections, or reverb.

Audiovisual Synergy

The eyes and ears often perceive an event at the same time. Seeing a door close and hearing a shutting sound are interpreted as one event if they happen synchronously. If we see a door shut without a sound or we see a door shut in front of us but hear a shutting sound to the left, we get alarmed and confused. In another scenario, we might hear a voice in front of us and see a hallway with a corner; the combination of cues allows us to guess that a person might be standing around the corner. Together, synchronized 3D audio and 3D visual cues provide a very strong immersion experience.

Head Movement

Audio cues change dramatically when a listener tilts or rotates the head. For example, quickly turning the head 90 degrees to look to the side is the equivalent of a sound traveling from the listener's side to the front in a split second. We often use head motion to track sounds or to search for them. The ears alert the brain about an event outside of the area that the eyes are currently focused on, and we automatically turn to redirect our attention. We also use head motion to resolve ambiguities: A faint, low sound could be either in front or in back of us, so we quickly and subconsciously turn our head a small fraction to the left, and we know whether the sound is now off to the right, is in the front, or is in the back.

Interactive Versus Noninteractive

In terms of sound, the distinction between interactive (also called realtime) and noninteractive is important. Noninteractive sound is essentially a soundtrack where every sound action or position is predetermined and can be stored in one recorded sequence. Interactive sound needs to be rendered on-the-fly, at nondeterministic times and positions. In other words, on a soundtrack, a specific explosion of a bridge might always happen 32 minutes and 3 seconds into the movie, off to the left of the screen. In an interactive or realtime experience, the explosion will happen whenever the user blasts the bridge, and it should be positioned wherever the bridge is located relative to the listener at that specific moment.

Perceptual Controllability and Predictability

The goal of digital sound-processing techniques is to provide the listener with the perception of an enhanced audio effect or experience. Aside from providing the technology that creates a perceptual effect, it is also important to provide the interface that allows applications to specify the effect in a clear and simple fashion. To satisfy the requirements of sound engineers or computer programmers, the perceptual outcome of a processing effect needs to be controllable or adjustable for many situations, and it needs to perform in a predictable and smooth fashion throughout its intended range of performance. In terms of a 3D or spatial sound effect, it is not enough to be able to make a sound appear to be coming from a static location. Controls need to move a sound anywhere the user wants it to go and to guarantee that it will react in a smooth, continuous fashion while a sound is placed or moved in 3D space.

Sound-Processing and Playback Techniques

Mono refers to a single channel of audio that can be displayed on a single speaker. Whatever was recorded or is synthesized gets transformed into a zero-dimensional, single-location image. Stereo extends the zero dimensionality of a mono image to one dimension. Sounds can be panned left/right between the two speakers or inside your head between the two earpieces of a headphone set. If the speakers are spread apart widely, a minimal sound field can be created.

By placing multiple speakers around the listener, two-dimensional sound localization can be created by simply panning the sounds among the speakers. While providing minimal (surround sound) to adequate (quadraphonic, six-channel) localization in a circle passing through the speakers, the relatively large distance between speakers makes it difficult to bring sounds in close to the listener. This technique is standard in 70-mm movie theaters and many theme park attractions.

Binaural Audio

Binaural audio is based on replicating the same 3D audio cues that the ears hear in the real world. These cues vary continuously with the relative 3D position of the sound with respect to the listener's head. Because it involves audio rendering, or signal processing, rather than simple audio playback, binaural audio requires sophisticated technology to create satisfactory results.

Like stereo, binaural audio consists of two tracks of audio. However, binaural is based on the principle of providing one psychoacoustically correct track for each ear, whereas stereo is based on providing one track for each speaker. Binaural recordings can be created by using dummy heads (artificial heads with microphones placed at the eardrum locations) or by using HRTF (head-related transfer function, usually based on human subjects) filters and digital signal-processing algorithms to synthetically create the effects. Realtime processed HRTF technology allows sounds to be precisely and interactively located anywhere in the three-dimensional space surrounding a listener. Binaural audio works best over headphones because the two binaural tracks can be fed precisely to the two ears, but it can also be used with traditional stereo speakers. Binaural audio is the only known method that can recreate a natural, immersive, and interactive audio environment that closely approximates a real-life experience.

Positional and Nonpositional 3D Sound

Two different kinds of technologies have been called 3D sound in the past: extended stereo technologies and binaural audio. Although extended stereo does not involve what is usually understood by the term "3D," namely, the three dimensions of X, Y, and Z (or front/back, up/down, and left/right), such techniques have been marketed under that name. Binaural audio has been called 3D sound because it allows placement of a sound source in 3D space. So far, calling two separate technologies by the same name has not been a problem because the two have addressed separate market areas: Extended stereo has been used in multimedia and consumer electronics markets, while binaural audio has been used in virtual reality, simulator, and pro audio. However, since VR-type capabilities (both 3D graphics and audio) are now becoming available to multimedia customers, the term "3D sound" needs to be more closely defined in order to avoid confusion.

The term "positional 3D sound" has been introduced by Microsoft in their Windows 95 DirectSound API to mean 3D sound as delivered by binaural audio. The term "nonpositional 3D sound" then specifies technologies that broaden a stereo image beyond speaker locations but either do not allow placement of sounds at all or only allow placement in a 1D or 2D space. Positional 3D sound describes technologies that allow placement of sound sources in full 3D space.

How to Correctly Model a Sound Field

In order to digitally reproduce a realistic sound field, a system needs to be able to reproduce all of the audio cues humans perceive in the real world. The first step in building such a system is to analyze what happens to a single sound as it arrives at a listener from different angles. Then those same effects need to be synthesized in a computer simulation. Finally, multiple sounds and sound reflections need to be reproduced in realtime to create the entire sound field.

HRTF Analysis and Synthesis

The head-related transfer function (HRTF) of an individual summarizes the physical effects transforming a sound as it propagates from a particular point in space to the two ear canals. The most common method of measuring the HRTF of an individual is to place tiny probe microphones inside a listener's left and right ear canals, place a speaker at a known location relative to the listener, play a known signal through that speaker, and record the microphone signals. By comparing the resulting impulse response with the original signal, a single filter in the HRTF set can be found (Figure 8.7). After moving the speaker to a new location, the process is repeated until an entire, spherical map of filter sets has been devised.

Every individual has a unique set of HRTFs, also called an ear print. However, HRTFs are interchangeable, and the HRTF of a person that can localize well in the real world will let most people localize well in a simulated world. While generic, interchangeable HRTFs are suitable for general applications such as videoconferencing or videogames, individualized HRTFs are useful for certain critical applications of binaural audio, such as military-threat warning systems or air traffic control.

Once an HRTF has been devised, realtime DSP (digital signal processing) software and algorithms need to be designed. This software has to be able to pick out the critical (psychoacoustically relevant) features of a filter and apply them in realtime to an incoming audio signal to spatialize it. The system works correctly if a listener cannot tell the difference between listening to a sound over the speaker setup in Figure 8.8 (the speaker is in a specific position) and

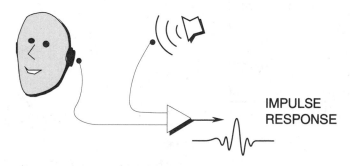

Figure 8.7   Speaker output and microphone input are combined to compute impulse response.

the same sound played back by a computer and filtered by the HRTF impulse response corresponding to the original speaker location.

The Entire Model

Once a single sound can be spatialized, an entire sound field can be synthesized by building software that can process multiple sounds and all their reflected images in a number of ways. Signals and images are

- Attenuated according to their distances from the listener.

- Filtered according to the medium that they pass through (air, water, walls).

- Delayed according to their positions relative to one another and the listener.

- Applied IID, ITD, and HRTF filters according to their positions relative to the listener.

- Filtered according to reflective object materials.

All these signals are computed individually for each ear and added together to left and right outputs to be played back on standard stereo headphones or speakers (Figure 8.8).

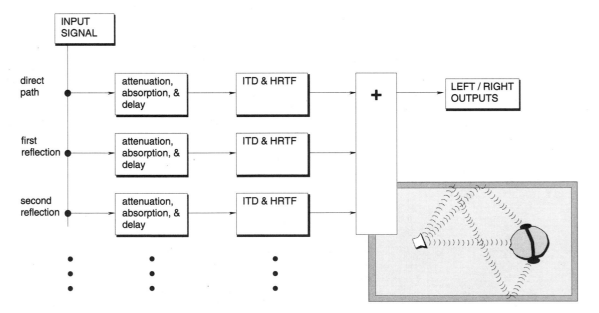

Figure 8.8   Attenuation, absorption, delays, ITD, and HRTFs applied for direct path and reflections.

Realtime Rendering and Control

Being able to run this process allows creation of a sound field that closely resembles sound in the real world. However, unless the process can run in realtime, the system is useless for anything other than research or very tedious creation of prerecorded (noninteractive) sound tracks. Full-functionality binaural systems synthesize entire sound fields in realtime, allowing every object (sound emitter, sound reflector, and listener) to be moved or changed at any time. For example, a system can be combined with a position tracker that is worn on the head and a head-mounted display to facilitate a very immersive and convincing VR experience: A user can hear a roar from behind, whirl around 180 degrees, and see and hear a monster; or, the hum of an airplane can prompt a user to look up and search the sky.

Advantages of Binaural Sound

Binaural Gain

Probably the single most important fact about binaural audio is that if an audio signal is played on top of white noise, it will appear 6 to 8 dB louder if that signal is a binaural signal versus a nonbinaural signal. This means that the exact same audio content is more audible and intelligible in the binaural case because the brain can localize and therefore "pick out" the binaural signal, while the nonbinaural signal gets washed into the noise.

At a cocktail party, a listener is capable of focusing on and understanding a conversation, while there are dozens of other conversations going on all around. If that party were recorded and then played back using a regular mono or stereo procedure, the result would, in most cases, be unintelligible. With a binaural recording of that party, a listener would still be able to tune into and understand individual conversations because they are still spatially separated and "amplified by" binaural gain.

Faster Reaction Time

In an environment such as a jet cockpit or in any combat or competitive situation where a lot of critical information is displayed to a user, reaction time is crucial. In such circumstances, audio information can be processed and reacted to more quickly if presented binaurally because such a signal mirrors the ones received in the real world. In addition, binaural signals can convey synthesized positional information in realtime: A binaural radar warning sound can warn a user about a specific object that is approaching (with a sound that is unique to that object) and transparently indicate where that object is coming from.

Increased Perception and Immersion

Some of the most interesting research into binaural audio shows that a subject will consistently report a more immersive and higher-quality visual ("nicer" colors or "better" graphics) environment when visuals are shown in sync with binaural sound versus stereo sound or no sound at all.

Summary

We are seeing applications of 3D binaural sound and other versions of spatialization in more entertainment applications every day; the virtual worlds on the Internet are just the latest iteration of this process. A screen-based VR's immersive properties can be significantly heightened with the addition of a positional realtime voice channel, for example. As stated in the introduction, the goal of a positional 3D digital audio system is to present the user with an audio experience that's indistinguishable from reality, thereby enhancing the user's ability to perceive and respond to an entire synthetic environment.

Biographies

Scott Foster joined Aureal in June of 1996 through their acquisition of Crystal River Engineering (CRE), where he served as CEO. He currently serves as the chief technical officer. Mr. Foster founded CRE in 1987 to develop digital signal processing (DSP) equipment for three-dimensional rendering of sounds. One of his first clients was NASA/Ames for which he developed the Convolvotron 3D sound systems for applications including audio research, communications, navigation, virtual reality, and telepresence. Before establishing CRE, Mr. Foster was an engineer at Hewlett-Packard Laboratories, a research scientist at Atari, Inc., and a member of the technical staff at Systems Control, Inc., where he collaborated with Stanford's Center for Research in Music and Acoustics on a study of automatic music analysis and transcription. Mr. Foster received a B.S. degree in mathematics from Massachusetts Institute of Technology. He is well known in the field of synthetic generation of three-dimensional audio and has published numerous papers in the field.

Toni Schneider is Vice President, Strategic Alliances at Aureal Semiconductor, also via CRE, where he served as Vice President of Marketing. Prior to CRE, Mr. Schneider worked with some of the early pioneers of VR in various engineering positions at Autodesk's Cyberspace Group and VPL Research. He holds a B.S. degree in computer science from Stanford University.

PART 3

Content Design: Putting in the Magic

Blackstone, the great illusionist, said that the fundamental principle of the magician's art is Misdirection. Subtly forcing an audience's attention away from the momentary mechanics enables suspension of disbelief in a live performance. But Misdirection is little used in the digital realm, since our illusions can be made to persist or repeat in time and we want people to relish the magic we build. The other ageless principles of magic, however, are just as essential as on stage, whether to move the plot along or to speed the traversal of a 3D space. We use software for Creation, Transformation, Obliteration, Restoration, Transposition, Penetration, and Animation every day; we just don't call them "magic" anymore. They're the bread and butter of cinematic special effects and virtual environment construction, as well as in nearly every video game ever designed.

Since magic is based on mystery and digital toolkits for all these fundamentals are now available, audiences' expectations constantly grow more demanding. People know too much. Our work becomes more detailed and articulated; our fictional characters become more articulate. We create better, cunningly nuanced worlds that seem to sense more about the users. In Part 3, Talin, Stephen Clarke-Willson, and Chris Crawford address the design of game environments and the functionality within them. Brenda Laurel, Rachel Strickland, and Rob Tow describe ways to implement play rather than goal-directed games, and Celia Pearce points out how many kinds of play there can be. Athomas Goldberg explains one way to populate our creations with autonomous artificial characters, a critical feature of rich environments. Finally, Michael Harris provides some practical and theoretical groundwork for out-of-home collaborative recreation using technology developed for SIMNET.

If we design these games, environments, and circumstances with the right opportunities and functionality, users will bring in the real magic with them. The best magicians awaken it in their audiences.

149

Chapter 9

Real Interactivity in Interactive Entertainment

Talin
The Dreamers Guild, Inc.

Introduction

This chapter discusses some of the aesthetic and philosophical issues of game design and outlines some of the challenges of the modern interactive entertainment designer. Particular attention is given to the nature of interactivity. Methods are discussed for maximizing the interactivity of entertainment experiences. Comparisons are drawn between nonlinear, interactive entertainment and sequential, story-based entertainment forms.

Interactivity

The task of a computer game designer is to create an experience, using a computer, that is interesting and fun for the player. The designer must create a system of behavior such that the player enjoys interacting with that system and will continue to interact with it.

The key word is "interact." The computer is by nature an active, participatory medium. Players who prefer passive enjoyment can get a far superior experience for less cost through the medium of videotape or laser disc.

The modern computer game is an audiovisual "engine" capable of keeping an internal model of some dynamic system. It can effectively present one or more facets of that model on the player's graphic display while accepting inputs from that player that affect how the system behaves. Unlike a "real" application, however, a game often deliberately hides certain pieces of information about its internal state, working against the user to create a greater challenge.

Game engines tend to evolve over time. Each time the publisher creates a sequel, spin-off, or related product, the designer usually has the opportunity to refine his or her previous work as well as create a foundation for more ambitious future works. Some of these programs are quite sophisticated and borrow algorithms and techniques from many other areas of computer science, all in the service of some particular aesthetic result.

Making the game interesting is the designer's most important task. Part of this involves creating a set of design documents that specify the rules and parameters that determine the behavior of the game's internal model. This specification can come in a variety of forms, depending on the nature of the game and which company you're working for. These forms could include a traditional Hollywood-style "script," source code in either C or a custom game-specific language, equations for a fuzzy logic engine, or even a set of rules for cellular automata.

Degrees of Freedom

From a gaming perspective, the more interactive the system is, the better. However, it is sometimes unclear what the definition of interactivity really is. Let's take that reductio ad absurdum of interactivity, the VCR. Is a VCR interactive? After all, you can stop the tape, rewind it, and such. While these are useful capabilities, they aren't very interesting or fun from the user's point of view. Since we want our experience to be both interesting and fun, it's important to distinguish fundamentally between what our game product does and what a VCR does.

One quality that a VCR lacks is adaptability. While it responds to the user's commands, its memory of those commands is limited to a very simple internal state, and it keeps no record of the "style" in which those commands were invoked. A computer game can potentially adapt to the user's actions, changing its strategy and rules based on what has gone before.

Another distinction is that a VCR gives us control over only one axis—that of time. We have no control over the spatial positions of any of the characters and objects in the movie, or even of our own point of view. Nor do we have any choice in what the characters do or say.

It could safely be said that a product that adapts to the player's behavior and permits as many degrees of freedom as possible is going to be more interesting than a product that lacks these attributes. Now, it is true that there are a number of other important factors in making a game entertaining, such as balancing the amount of nonobvious behavior of the system and controlling the rise of the player's expectations during the course of play. Even more important is the careful omission of "misfeatures" that have been shown to annoy players in previous products. However, this chapter will focus on making an experience that is as interactive as possible since that is one of the primary design challenges for the game creator.

Storytelling

For thousands of years, storytelling has been the basis for most of our entertainment forms. From the classic and colorful storyteller in the marketplace to novels, plays, and motion pictures, the involvement of the listener in the emotional trials of a fictional character is a powerful entertainment process. So, it would be natural to view the computer medium as yet another opportunity for storytelling and to think that the "immortal power of storytelling" will create a great software product. Writer Bruce Sterling calls this the "me an' my good buddy Bill Shakespeare" argument.

I go to conferences and trade shows where I see many talented young authors who want to "break in" to the interactive entertainment medium. They see computers, CD-ROMs, and online games as a medium by which they can express the dramatic situations and interesting characters in their imagination.

Unfortunately, I've found that it can be very difficult for an author to make the transition. Most other media forms are linear—they have a beginning, a middle, and an end. Interactive games represent a multiplicity of paths, each divergently branching to a different experience and ideally a different conclusion. I've worked with some very good novelists who just could not deal with this; their designs had very few interactive choice points, each having very few possible choices, and the choices often led to surrealistically nonsensical outcomes.

I believe that, on a fundamental level, storytelling and interactivity are exclusive to each other. Interactivity puts the player in charge; storytelling puts the author in charge. Interactivity allows the player to go wherever and to do and see whatever he or she wants. Storytelling would dictate that the protagonist be restricted to acting in ways that make sense dramatically. In a novel, it is considered bad for a character to give long-winded explanations; in a computer game, this is perfectly acceptable under some conditions. For example, a player might be interested enough in a particular piece of knowledge that he or she might be unsatisfied with a summary explanation and so would request further detail on the subject. As long as players have the power to control which explanations are given and can interrupt them at any time, they are unlikely to get bored.

Another problem with interactive storytelling is that the emotional reverie of the story is broken whenever the player has to get up and "do something." Making a decision about what the character should do next, which most players approach on a purely intellectual and strategic level, requires a detachment from the mood of the story that most authors would prefer to avoid.

The relationship between the player and the protagonist presents an additional problem for the interactive storyteller. In a story, the character and personality of the protagonist are what make him or her interesting, and we feel a certain sympathy because of our understanding of the character's plight. In most games, however, the protagonist becomes our complete surrogate ego, with no intrinsic personality of its own. As such, we are less interested in the protagonist and more concerned with the external environment in which it is embedded.

This is not to say that a game cannot have elements of both storytelling and interactivity. I would model the relationship between the two attributes as a continuum, with storytelling at one end and interactivity at the other (Figure 9.1).

In general, I feel that, not just storytelling, but all sequences of behavior are the "enemy of interactivity." (By "sequence," I mean a series of events that is preplanned by the designer.) The longer the sequence, the more interactivity it curtails.

For example, "full motion video" (the technique of playing video on a computer screen by spooling video data continuously from a CD-ROM) is, in its current form, a fundamentally sequential medium and, as such, inhibits interactivity. Most games that use video technology stop the game dead while the video is playing. Only when the video completes is the player allowed to make decisions again.

Game designer Chris Crawford believes that, rather than using the model of "story," game designers should be using the model of "conversation." Crawford believes that a conversation requires that both participants must listen, think, and then speak. Ideally, interactive entertainment would be a "conversation in a can" that would not only "speak" eloquently (using multimedia sound and graphics) but also "listen." The player would be given an opportunity to "speak" through a rich, well-designed user interface.

Others have suggested that an amusement park may be a more appropriate model for interactive entertainment. In amusement parks, customers can wander around at will, choosing at any time to participate in various attrac-

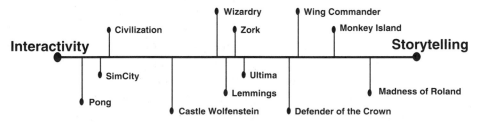

Figure 9.1 Continuum of interactivity: Placement of titles in the illustration is purely subjective. In general, games with a highly scripted, sequential structure are on the right, and games that lack this are on the left.

tions. Some attractions have almost no sequential structure at all (shooting gallery), whereas others are a continuously choreographed multimedia experience (Disneyland "dark" rides).

It's certainly true that the issue of storytelling is one of the more controversial issues being discussed among professional game designers.

Is there a way to combine storytelling and interactivity completely? I believe so; however, the technology for doing so has not yet been developed. Rather than creating a medium for expositing stories to be consumed by a passive audience, this technology would act as a partner to users, allowing them to create their own stories on the fly as they experience them.

The ultimate vision of this is researcher Brenda Laurel's "Artificial Playwright" concept, an expert system that would somehow encode the "laws of drama" into a rule set. This hypothetical system would know about climax and anticlimax, tension and relaxation, and other dramatic principles. As the player moves through the environment, story situations would be generated and developed continuously by the playwright, a sort of software improvisational acting.

Achieving Interactivity with Today's Technology

One form of interactivity is referred to as "branching games," which were first popularized in the "choose your own adventure" novels. In this type of game, the player experiences short, linear story segments. At the end of each segment are a small number of choices (say, two to four), each leading to a new linear segment, which leads to further choices, and so on. Sometimes, the pathways converge; other times, they diverge to different endings. Sometimes, they even loop back on themselves again.

The advantage of the branching game is that it allows an author to write a small (or at least finite) number of alternate story paths. A designer can therefore draw upon the talent developed for existing expository media, and the power of storytelling can be applied.

The disadvantage of this technique, however, is that the full power of interactivity is diminished—the player can choose only those paths that have been anticipated by the designer. The problem is even more acute with modern, high-production-value graphical adventures. These games use CD-ROM technology to store a massive dataset of artwork, music, sound effects, and animation on a single disc. A team of artists, animators, writers, and programmers will work for a year or more, mapping out every possible pathway and choice point that the player will want to take and illustrating every pathway in full cinematic glory.

Of course, since all these graphical data (called "assets" in the trade) are expensive to produce, there is great pressure to cut down on the number of alternative pathways that the player can take. Consequently, there is a strong economic incentive to reduce interactivity to the bare minimum. And since the game can function only on a ROM medium, it means that players are stuck in a mostly "read-only" universe and are extremely limited in the ways they can affect the environment.

In the games industry, we have seen a continuing trend in games that are increasingly awesome to look at and increasingly shallow to play.

Clever Algorithms

The most interactive games, however, do not use the branching technique at all. A typical flight simulator, for example, does not have any discrete choices; the player just goes wherever he or she wants.

Another example of an algorithm-based game with rich interactivity is the highly acclaimed game SimCity. This product simulates the growth and development of an urban metropolis, with the player in the role of city mayor. At each point in the game, the player can perform various operations on the landscape, such as zoning land, demolishing buildings, and laying down roads, water mains, and electric power lines. Since the game map is large (it appears to be a square, 256 grid units on a side) and since the player can perform these operations almost anywhere on the map, the number of possible moves at any given moment in time is clearly immense. Of course, out of that large number of potential moves, probably only several hundred are optimal at any given point. Nevertheless, that is still enough to give the player the feeling of almost complete freedom.

In general, these games use sophisticated algorithms to define behavior of the game rather than preset pathways laid down by a designer. The advantage is clear: The number of possible outcomes is nearly unlimited, given a rich set of inputs.

Algorithms for games don't come just from game theory, but from many application domains. For example, I have used Lee's algorithm (a routing algorithm used in electronic CAD programs to plot the optimum pathway for a copper trace on a printed circuit board) to control the movement of animated characters in a fantasy environment. Especially worthy of attention are systems that exhibit emergent behavior, such as genetic algorithms, neural nets, and cellular automata.

Assuming that the creative spark of the designer can just come up with the right algorithm, a game can be created much less expensively than one that utilizes massive datasets.

The primary difficulty with algorithms, then, is not one of *economy*, but rather one of *technology*. It can be difficult to invent an algorithm that generates a rich set of behavior that is appropriate for a given game concept. It can be especially difficult to craft an artificial opponent to compete against the player—in general, algorithms make much better *environments* than they do *opponents*.

Algorithms are also poor at simulating realistic human behavior. Even the most sophisticated adventures rely heavily on prescripted dialogs for character interaction.

Real People

One of the most interesting and enjoyable interactive systems is the one embodied in the human brain. A real player is often the best choice for an interactive opponent since humans display a larger range of behavior than either massive datasets or algorithms and can engage in complex social relationships. The latter allows for out-of-context social interaction such as telling jokes about the game, chatting, and emotional reactions when one player defeats another, which can significantly enhance the gaming experience.

The problem with multiplayer computer entertainment is *opportunity*: Many game enthusiasts not only don't have two computers, they also don't even have two people. At least, within a given household, it is likely that the number of people interested in playing a particular genre of computer game will be less than two. Nevertheless, many people in the games industry feel that multiplayer games are the most exciting opportunity for the coming decade.

Several technologies have been developed to try to solve the problem of getting players together, some of which work better than others.

- Terminal Sharing. Two players can take turns entering their moves, or each player can choose a different input device and play at the same time. (In some cases, the keyboard is split in half and considered as two input devices.) Unfortunately, since both players are in front of the same screen, it makes games that involve hidden information cumbersome.

- One-on-One Games. A number of successful games now include a "serial-play" or "modem-play" option that allows two users to play against each other, each a dedicated screen. Of course, lugging one's machine over to a friend's house is inconvenient, and playing over the telephone lines ties up the lines and eliminates an important channel of social interplay since the players can't talk to each other over the phone while they are playing the game.

- LAN-Based Games. Many companies have multiplayer games on their local-area networks. Of course, most companies limit the amount of time one can spend playing on company equipment. Also, since the market is limited, such games tend to be primitive compared to popular commercial games.

- Wide-Area Network Games. Most notable are the Multi-User Dungeon games, or "MUD" environments, which are very popular on the Internet, as well as their descendants (MUSH, MUCK, MUSE, and MOO). These text-based games can be incredibly addicting since they have had a long history to build up a rich level of detail as well as a feeling of "aliveness" that single-player adventure games lack. Also, they manage to maintain the social interaction by allowing the players to electronically "chat" at any time during the course of play. However, the text-based interface will probably not appeal to a mass audience, even assuming the average consumer could figure out how to get Internet access in the first place.

- Commercial Network Games. A number of commercial wide-area network services specialize entirely in games, such as the ImagiNation network and MPGNet. These allow players to have a fully graphical, multiplayer experience in their own home, for an hourly fee. High graphical performance is achieved by placing most of the computation in the client program, which runs on the user's home machine. The client communicates with a central server over the telephone line.

- The biggest drawback with this type of game is one of limited bandwidth. Most of these networks use packet-switching technology, which causes a 1-to-3-second delay in returning information to the player and chops the data stream into clumps rather than allowing a continuous flow. The result is that a smooth, responsive interaction is difficult if not impossible. Thus, "turn-based" games tend to be the rule on these systems rather than realtime action. An additional problem is the potential for "cheating" by clever users who modify their client programs. To prevent this from occurring, the amount and type of information sent to the client must be carefully controlled, which often prevents the most effective use of the available bandwidth.

- Location-Based Entertainment. The most ambitious attempts at multiplayer entertainment consist of highly specialized gaming technology clustered into a miniature "theme park" located at a shopping center or mall. Players enter into special "pods" containing a complete audiovisual simulation environment, including wide screens, stereo sound, and mechanical simulation of vibration and acceleration. The advantage is an intense game experience. The disadvantages are that the systems are extremely expensive and (currently) located only in a few areas. Also, the systems tend to be highly customized for a particular game so that when players get tired and want a different game, there is still a large capital investment in the old systems. In addition, many pod-based systems sonically and visually isolate players from one another, which inhibits the social interaction between players.

Summary

While animated graphics and synchronized sound represent significant challenges to the game designer, they are not the primary design problem. Rather, the game design itself—the set of cause-and-effect relationships that determine the behavior of the game—is usually much more difficult to get right.

To create games that the user can enjoy over and over again requires more than traditional storytelling. Techniques for achieving a fully interactive experience, such as sophisticated algorithms or multiplayer technologies, can go much further toward creating a unique experience that does not need to compete with traditional expository media.

Biography

David "Talin" Joiner is an award-winning costumer, programmer, artist, musician, and storyteller. He is best known for single-handedly creating *The Faery Tale Adventure* as well as a number of other games and professional music products. He was creative director on *Inherit the Earth* published by Next World Publishing. He is a founding member of The Dreamers Guild, Inc.

Chapter 10

Avatars and Agents, or Life Among the Indigenous Peoples of Cyberspace

Athomas Goldberg
New York University Media Research Lab

Introduction

> *avatar: 2a. an incarnation in human form. 2b. an embodiment . . . usually in a person. 3. a variant phase or version of a continuing basic entity.*
>
> *agent: 1a. something that is capable of producing an effect: an active or efficient cause. . . . 2. one who acts for or in place of another by authority from him as a representative, emissary, or official . . . or as one engaged in undercover activities. 3. a means or instrument by which a guiding intelligence achieves a result. 4. one that acts or exerts power. 5. a person responsible for his acts.*
>
> Webster's Ninth New Collegiate Dictionary

In cyberspace, the digital landscape of the information superhighway, the term "avatar" generally describes various representations of "real" people in the computer-generated environment. "Agents" are generally thought of as autonomous or semiautonomous pieces of software that may assume some visual embodiment so that we can engage them in a social manner. In addition, I'll be using the term "actor" to refer to any animated figure in the virtual environment, both human and computer-controlled.

The IMPROV Project at New York University's Media Research Lab is building the technologies for producing 3D virtual environments in which avatars and agents interact with one another and with humans in realtime. We use a combination of procedural animation—a toolset for generating realtime interactive animated human and nonhuman figures—and behavioral scripting—a system for creating synthetic personalities with realistic moods, goals, and behaviors and with believable responses to changing situations and stimuli. The system is intended to operate over local- and wide-area networks using standard Internet protocols, enabling anyone with access to the World Wide Web to develop or participate in fully interactive, virtual experiences.

Such experiences may take many forms, from 3D games and other interactive entertainment to graphical Multi-User Domains (MUDs) in which users connect from disparate locations around the globe to meet and socialize in a shared environment. These environments may range from mundane replications of real-world locations to the creation of fantastic and surreal worlds in which none of our natural laws seem to apply.

How are these worlds constructed? What are the necessary elements involved in the creation of complex virtual worlds that grow and change over time, populated by a menagerie of human and computer personalities, worlds that can be entered and traversed from your personal computer?

"The Mind-Body Problem"—Procedural Animation and Behavioral Scripting

Using traditional computer animation techniques, variations in animated motion and the transitions to and from each of these motions must be plotted out ahead of time. This job is generally time-consuming, thereby constraining the animator to an extremely limited set of possible behaviors. Procedurally animated characters are able to automatically generate transitions between animated motions in a smooth and natural fashion in realtime. In addition, motions can be layered and blended to convey an extremely wide range of behavior, mood, and personality. Actors can be given the form of humans, animals, or animate objects, and actors with common components can share sets of animated behaviors.

In IMPROV, an "action" is defined as a single atomic or repetitive activity, one not requiring explicit higher-level awareness or conscious decisions. For example, walking is an action, as is typing, but walking over to the computer and beginning to type constitutes a sequence of several actions.

An actor isn't limited to performing a single action at once, though. In order to appear lifelike and believable, an actor must be able to perform certain activities simultaneously, like walking and chewing gum or typing while talking to someone across the room. Once again, it would be impractical to suggest that the animator should create a separate animated behavior for every combination of activities.

The problem with combining actions automatically is that often there are different ways to combine them. An actor might be instructed to momentarily scratch its head while waving at someone. It wouldn't be very realistic for the actor to perform both these actions at once, making vague scratching gestures toward its head while simultaneously awkwardly waving at another actor. Or, if we wanted the character to wave while walking downstage, it wouldn't make sense to have the actor stop walking each time it waved.

The difference between these two examples is that in the former case we're describing actions that are mutually exclusive, whereas in the latter case the two actions are complementary and can gracefully coexist. What's important here is that there be a clear and powerful structure in which these action relationships can be defined.

We build this structure by dividing actions into "Groups." Actions within a Group are mutually exclusive of one another; activating one causes the action currently active to end. Actions in *different* Groups can operate simultaneously, so activities of certain parts of the body can be layered over those involving others. In general, actions involving a specific body part are layered over those involving a body region, which are, in turn, layered over actions involving the whole body. For example, if one actor is talking to another, one Group may contain the stances the actor assumes, such as shifting from side to side, standing straight, or sitting. At the same time, another Group may contain a set of upper-body motions, like crossing the arms or putting the arms at the sides or behind the back. Still another Group may contain those gestures performed with the right or left hand, like gesturing to make a point or scratching the chin. Using this structure, these few actions can be combined to create dozens of composite animations while minimizing the risk of inadvertently creating behavior that is either unbelievable or not lifelike.

When an actor goes from performing one action to another, it's essential that the body doesn't go through physically impossible transitions. If an actor has the arms crossed in front and then puts them behind the back, what's to prevent the actor from passing the arms through the body? In the "real world," we're bound by the laws of physics, but this isn't the case in the virtual environment. By allowing animators to create "buffer actions," we avoid unbelievable behavior. For example, if we use hands-at-sides as a buffer action for hands-behind-back, we save the actor the embarrassment of accidentally passing the arms through the body by declaring that the arms must always go-to-sides before they go-behind-back. Likewise, when the actor tries to go from hands-behind-back to another action involving the arms, the arms-at-sides action must happen before continuing to the next gesture.

Actions are only useful for defining and blending subtleties of physical motion. Behavioral scripting allows you to describe behavioral "scripts" from which to create more complex sets of actions and behaviors. Scripts may be used to trigger other scripts and/or actions, allowing virtual-world designers to easily construct hierarchies of behavior. These behaviors can range from low-level decisions about the types of gestures and actions to perform to high-level behavior describing an actor's goals and the kinds of social activities an actor will join. Such a wide range of behaviors can be called a "From Life to Picking Your Nose" model of behavior in which there is a continuum from the most abstract descriptions of character activity to the construction of specific motor skills. In this way, long-term goals and activities are made up of component behavior and can be broken down all the way to individual physical activities.

The smallest unit of time in IMPROV is called a "frame," which is approximately one-thirtieth of a second or the length of a single frame of animation. A basic script generally consists of a sequence of steps executed in order, one per frame, though sequencing commands can be used to trigger repeated steps. These sequencing commands include the following:

- "Wait" causes the current step to be repeated for the specified number of seconds. When it appears in a step by itself, it serves as a timed delay between steps.

- "While" causes the current step to be repeated until the specified conditions are met.

- "Loop" causes the current step to be repeated indefinitely or until the current script is deactivated.

- "Do again" causes the current script to repeat from step 1.

Like Actions, scripts are organized into parallel-running Groups. Scripts within a given Group are mutually exclusive of one another: Activating a script within a Group immediately deactivates whatever script is currently active in that Group. Scripts active in different groups operate simultaneously, enabling high-level scripts to continue while the low-level behaviors they trigger are performed. In this way, the actor can address the environment from multiple levels of abstraction, maintaining high-level goals and long-term activities while managing and executing the short-term behaviors necessary to fulfill them.

A simple script might look something like this:

SCRIPT "Greeting"

Steps:

1. Enter room

2. Wait 4 seconds

3. Turn to Camera

4. Wait 1 second

5. Wave to Camera, say hello to Camera

6. Wait 3 seconds

7. Leave room

In this example, the actor first activates the "enter room" script (which instructs the actor to enter the room). The "enter room" script is in a different script-group, so the "Greeting" script continues as the "enter room" script is executed, waiting 4 seconds before activating the "turn," which tells the actor to turn and face the specified target—in this case, the camera. There is another pause of 1 second, giving the "turn" script time to finish, before instructing the actor to begin the "wave" and "say hello" scripts. Another 3 seconds passes as the actor waves and says hello, at which point the "leave room" script is activated, causing the actor to turn and leave.

Two important features of believable human behavior are timing and coordination. While it may be possible to build animated agents with sufficient intelligence to identify and react quickly to rapidly changing events and situations, success along these lines has thus far been limited when applied to complex, coordinated social behavior. In order to create lifelike social scenarios in which multiple actors play out rich interactions, it's important to provide tools that will enable virtual-world designers to design not only the behaviors of an individual actor but also those of groups of actors.

The "cue" command enables actors to cue each other to respond in appropriate ways at the right moments. Here is an example:

SCRIPT "Hello-Hello"

Steps:

1. Turn to my target

2. Wait 1 second

3. Wave to my target

4. Cue my target to Wave to me

5. Wait 1.5 seconds

6. Cue my target to Wave to me

7. Wait 1.5 seconds

8. Turn to Camera, cue my target to Turn to Camera

9. Wait 1 second

10. Wave to Camera, cue my target to Wave to Camera

In this example, the actor turns to face the target (the actor currently of interest), waits 1 second, and then waves. The actor's target turns and, after about a second, waves back. A couple of seconds later, the two turn simultaneously toward the camera and, 1 second later, wave in unison.

"No! Go *that* way!"—Navigating Virtual Worlds

While games like Street Fighter and Mortal Kombat give you pretty direct control over the actions of your avatar, there are times when it may be preferable to direct your animated representative through a more intuitive set of instructions and then let the character play out the scenario in a naturalistic and dramatic fashion. It's not uncommon for new players of games like Doom to make several attempts before successfully passing through a doorway or turning a corner. An example of high-level instruction might involve pointing to a door and telling the character to open it. The character would then cross to the door automatically, avoiding obstacles in the way, and open it.

In the same way that scripts may be triggered from other scripts, they can also be activated by human participants from the user interface. Same behaviors displayed in the "Greeting" example might also have been effected by a human participant directing the avatar to enter the room, waiting a few seconds, and then directing the avatar to turn to the camera. Likewise, the participant might have activated the "Greeting" script as part of a more complex situation in which the exact physical motions of the actor are not what's important but rather that a specific point (saying hello) is made.

The level of the instructions you give the avatar may vary depending on the situation, ensuring the most effective interaction with the environment at all times. The layered structure of IMPROV enables the human participant to direct the actor at whatever level of control is most appropriate from moment to moment.

"The Indigenous Peoples of Cyberspace"— Autonomy for Autonomous Agents

While it may be possible to create virtual worlds entirely populated by human-directed avatars, it's often useful, especially in the case of interactive fiction environments, to have a supporting cast of characters whose purpose is to keep the drama moving forward, provoke conflict, introduce new situations and stimuli, and otherwise maintain the level of excitement in the scenario. In addition to the techniques just described for performing the appropriate animation for any given activity, these actors must also be able to choose an appropriate course of action from the set of myriad possible actions available at any given time. Once again, we could try to envision all the possible situations the agent might be in and write the appropriate action script, but the amount of work involved in ensuring the character always did the right thing without becoming repetitive would rapidly become prohibitive. On the other hand, randomly choosing from the set of possible actions available to an actor isn't particularly believable. The decisions a character makes should somehow reflect that character's role or personality, and certain actions will seem more appropriate to one character than others.

Without going too deeply into a character's deep motivations and the "hard" problems of true humanlike cognition, we can describe a character's personality in terms of the tendency to behave in a certain manner that is consistent from one situation to the next. When confronted with a new situation, reckless characters will tend to choose reckless actions, whereas cautious characters will be likely to choose more cautious behaviors. At the same time, to remain believable, autonomous agents must be able to appear at least as unpredictable as their human-directed counterparts. We can accomplish this through the use of what we call "tunable statistics." Characters make weighted decisions where certain options have a higher chance of being chosen than others.

Take the "Fidget" script for example:

SCRIPT "Fidget"

   Steps:

   1. Choose from (Twiddle thumbs = .7, Scratch head = .3, Pick nose = .2)

   2. Wait 3 seconds

   3. Do again

In this example, we give an actor a choice of three actions to perform: twiddling the thumbs, scratching the head, or picking the nose. To each of these, we assign a weight between 0 and 1: Twiddling is given a weight of .7, scratching is given a weight of .3, and picking is given a weight of .2. In this case, there is a 7 in 12 chance the actor will choose to twiddle, a 3 in 12 (or 1 in 4) chance the actor will choose to scratch, and a 2 in 12 (or 1 in 6) chance the actor will choose to pick.

As we'll discover later, these weights can be determined procedurally, through the combination of one or more actors' personalities with the objects and events in a scenario. For example, agents entering a social situation might be most likely to talk with agents and avatars they are familiar with and have a high sympathy for. This doesn't mean actors will always choose the person they have the highest sympathy for, nor does it mean they will never talk to characters they have a low sympathy for, but, like "real" people, they will generally be drawn to certain characters over others. These techniques allow the agents to always make decisions that are "in character" without ever becoming repetitive or inhumanly predictable. The way these attributes that shape the decision-making process are defined is described in the next section.

"I feel like a number."—Personality Definition for Agents and Avatars

In addition to the scripts an actor can perform, each actor is also assigned a set of behavioral attributes used in giving the impression of a unique personality. Some examples might include the following: strength, coordination, and health (which would govern how a character performed certain physical activities) and intelligence, aggressiveness, and amiability (which would affect how the character interacts with other characters). Attributes can also be used to describe the relationships between actors, objects, and behaviors. A character's behavior toward another character may be influenced by sympathy (or hatred!) for that character. Attributes may be used to describe an actor's knowledge of a given subject or skill at performing certain activities.

Some examples of actor attributes might include the following:

ACTOR "Gregor"

Attribute	Value
Intelligence	.99
Amiability	.5
Strength	.33
Coordination	.3
Sympathy-toward Otto	.15
Sympathy-toward Gabrielle	.9
Knowledge-of ancient Greece	.75
Skill-at public speaking	.9
Skill-at driving cars	.25
. . .	. . .

Attribute values are generally in the range of 0 to 1. Here, we see that Gregor is extremely intelligent, is of average amiability, but is not very strong or coordinated. Gregor dislikes Otto, is extremely fond of Gabrielle, has a pretty good knowledge of ancient Greece, and, while being a fine public speaker, is only a mediocre driver. These attributes are all dynamic and may be assigned and modified at any time, and the animations an actor performs will reflect these changes. For example, when a character encounters a prop for the first time, the actor's attribute list is searched for the relevant skill—in this case, the "skill at driving." If the skill isn't found, it is assigned to the actor at some minimal level. This starting level may be modified based on other characteristics. (A character's Intelligence, Coordination, and/or Skill in driving other types of vehicles may influence how well the character drives a motorcycle for the first time.) As the character spends time riding the bike, the motorcycle driving skill value will increase, and the animation will reflect the increased proficiency. Next time the character comes across a motorcycle, the character's file is again searched for the "Skill-at driving" attribute, and this time the value is found. The character now appears to drive like an experienced biker.

We can also use these mechanisms to simulate the effects of an actor's behavior on the rest of the world. There is an example:

SCRIPT "Oh . . . Excuse me!"

Steps:

1. Belch

2. Wait 1 second

3. Set other-actors' sympathy-toward me to .01

4. . . .

In this crude example, the actor makes an obnoxious noise, which has an almost immediate and profound effect on the other actors' attitudes toward the actor, which will, no doubt, be demonstrated in their future behavior toward the actor.

In addition, attributes can be attached to the scripts a character follows that are used to determine how and when an actor will perform that script. These properties might include the following: the necessary prerequisites for performing the script, the level of difficulty, and the formality/informality of the behavior. Consider this example:

SCRIPT "Ride bicycle"

Attribute	Value
Activity-type	(travel, exercise, fun)
Prerequisites	(have bicycle)
Difficulty	.32
Physicality	.73

Steps:

1. Get on bike

2. . . .

In this example, "Ride bicycle" is a script that may be used for transportation, exercise, and recreation. Executing the script requires the actor to have a bicycle. The difficulty attribute indicates that riding requires a certain amount of skill, though not too much, and the physicality attribute shows us that riding is a somewhat strenuous activity. When the actor executes this script, a comparison between these attributes and the attributes of the actor will be used to determine how the animation for riding a bicycle will be executed.

In addition, scripts can be used to monitor and effect other actor states and properties, allowing the behavior of the actor and the effects of that behavior to influence the actor's personality, which, in turn, may influence the actor's behavior under varying social conditions and changing circumstances. In this way, designers can carefully orchestrate the ways in which actors will appear to grow and change over time due to their actions and the effects of their actions.

"What to do, what to do . . ."—Decision Making in Autonomous Agents

Much of what makes a character believable comes from the choices it makes, and how these choices reflect that character's personality, goals, tendencies, likes and dislikes, and so on. As we described earlier, we can control an actor's tendencies toward certain choices in a decision through the use of weighted lists. For example, in the script "Go to Store," the actor is going shopping and has to decide how to get there. We could write it something like this:

SCRIPT "Go to Store"

Steps:

1. Exit home

2. Choose from (Walk = .1, Take bus = .5, Take cab = .4, Ride bike = .2)

3. Enter store

4. . . .

In this example, the actor executing this script is most likely to take the bus or a cab but will occasionally ride a bike and, on rare occasions, walk. The problem with this is that every actor executing this script is going to have the exact same tendencies toward each of these modes of transportation. Even though in the real world a lazy person might *never* walk or ride a bike, an athletic person might prefer riding or walking, and a person on a strict budget might avoid taking a cab, if at all possible. It would be impractical to try to create a separate "Go to Store" script for every actor just to reflect that individual's personality since there may be thousands of different actors in the virtual world and "Go to store" is only one of hundreds of activities an actor might engage in.

An alternative to this is to specify a set of criteria an actor or set of actors will use in making a decision. These are, in effect, the rules governing how a specific decision gets made, and each actor will interpret them differently based on individual personality. Using criteria-based decision making, our "Go to Store" script might look something like this:

SCRIPT "Go to Store"

Steps:

1. Exit home

2. Choose from (Walk, Take bus, Take cab, Ride bike) using criteria "best way to get there"

3. Enter store

4. . . .

CRITERIA "Ways to get there"

Criteria	Importance
1. my energy compared to its physicality	.7
2. my wealth compared to its cost	.3

In this example, energy and wealth are attributes of the actor, while physicality and cost are attributes assigned to the various options. In this case, each option is assigned a weight based on how close these attributes match. The value under "Importance" represents how much influence each of these criteria has on the final decision—in this case, the amount of energy required by each choice is the most significant factor, but how much it costs also plays a small role. In this example, actors with a high energy attribute will tend toward the more physical activities like walking and cycling, especially if they are low on cash, whereas lazy actors will choose the less physically demanding choices, taking a cab if they've got a lot of money and taking a bus if they don't.

We might also want to be more abstract about the scripts we're choosing from. In this case, the actor might not necessarily be concerned with choosing one of these specific activities, but rather is interested only in finding an appropriate mode of transportation. Here, we accomplish this by choosing from the list of scripts that have some attribute in common (they all have transportation as one of their activity types):

SCRIPT "Go to Store"

Steps:

1. Exit home

2. Choose from (scripts with Activity-type transportation) using criteria "best way to get there"

3. Enter store

4. . . .

CRITERIA "Ways to get there"

Criteria	Importance
1. my energy compared to its physicality	.7
2. my wealth compared to its cost	.3

This way, should we later wish to add an "in-line skate" script, it will automatically be included in the decision as long as we make "transportation" one of its activity-types.

We can already begin to see how we can create a wide variety of interpretations of the "Go to Store" script without greatly increasing the amount of work necessary to accomplish this. Still, in this example, each actor will assign the same importance to physicality and cost, which, while reflecting an actor's current state, doesn't really tell us anything about the actor's values—another important aspect of actor behavior.

Suppose we rewrite the "Ways to get there" criteria as follows:

CRITERIA "Ways to get there"

Criteria	Importance
1. my energy compared to its physicality	my importance-of-physical pleasure
2. my wealth compared to its cost	my importance-of-money

We enable the actor to decide how important each of these factors is. In this case, actors who place a lot of importance on physical enjoyment will tend toward activities that best suit their current level of energy, whereas those who place more importance on money matters will tend toward those activities that meet their current means.

In the same way attributes may be assigned to actors and scripts, attributes can also be assigned to the criteria an actor uses to make a decision, enabling the virtual-world designer to tailor a script to an even wider variety of personalities and interpretations. Perhaps our athlete doesn't care at all about the cost of getting there but just wants the exercise. Meanwhile, a more decadent individual refuses to do anything that doesn't display that individual's wealth or requires too much effort. In this case, our script might look something like this:

SCRIPT "Go to store"

Steps:

1. Exit home

2. Choose from (scripts with Activity-type transportation) using criteria (Choose from (Criteria-type attitude) criteria "Personality")

3. Enter store

4. . . .

CRITERIA "Personality"

Criteria	Importance
1. my decadence compared to its decadence-level	.5
2. my athleticism compared to its athletic-level	.5

CRITERIA "Decadent"

Attribute	Value
Criteria-Type (attitude)	—
decadence-level	.9
athletic-level	.1

Criteria	Importance
1. its physicality is very-low	.7
2. my wealth compared to its cost	.3

CRITERIA "Athletic"

Attribute	Value
Criteria-type (attitude)	—
decadence-level	.2
athletic-level	.99

Criteria	Importance
1. its physicality is high	1

Once again, we've enabled actors with different personalities to play out the same basic activity (going to the store) with their own interpretations. Here, actors at the extremes of Athleticism and Decadence may almost always prefer certain forms of transportation over others, but because the choice of criteria is based on a weighted list as well, actors whose personalities fall somewhere in the middle will occasionally exhibit different reasons for choosing certain scripts over others—perhaps today they are feeling decadent, while tomorrow they will feel more athletic. The frequency with which certain criteria are chosen over others will also fit with an actor's personality.

I've presented a very simple example here, but it's clear that as we add more options and more detailed criteria, we can very quickly develop a rich variety of interpretations of various activities, tailored to each actor's personality, goals, and values.

So far, I've described a broad range of scripted behavior, from linear sequences of scripts and actions to completely personality-based decision making. It's important to note that these are in no way exclusive of each other. Fully autonomous agents may interact freely with avatars following human direction and carefully scripted behavior, while avatars receiving high-level instruction may make these kinds of decisions about their low-level behavior. In addition, there are times when an autonomous agent might be required to perform a predefined set of actions, as in a dance, or when repeating something learned by rote, or when called for to effect certain events in an interactive drama. IMPROV enables the virtual-world designer to freely mix and match these types of behavior and levels of control and autonomy in order to create the desired effect.

"The Tail That Wags the Dog"—Inverse Causality in Animation

Animated actors in dynamic realtime environments are likely to encounter new situations, especially if we allow for worlds that are continuously being developed and characters that persist from one scenario to the next. As circumstances change, it is important that these characters continue to react appropriately, even when confronted with new stimuli. In cases where this means encountering some truly foreign object or situation, it may be OK if the actor doesn't know what to do next. More often though, these are things that the human directing the avatar is familiar with and that are introduced to the world after its creation. In these situations, we want the characters to appear to know what they're doing, even though they have, in fact, never been in the situation before. A traditional AI (artificial intelligence) approach might suggest that we build mechanisms into the characters to allow them to analyze new situations and make judgments as to the appropriate course of action to take (in other words, the right kind of animation to perform). This tends to be pretty compute-intensive, and while the number of trial-and-error iterations that are generally involved in this approach may produce a convincing simulation of learning to do something, we don't want the characters to look like they're learning how to drink a beer, for example—we just want them to drink. Alternately, we could try to take into account everything the characters might possibly encounter and program them to perform the appropriate animations. The problem with this is that eventually we'll want to introduce new props and situations that we hadn't foreseen at the time the characters were created. At this point, it's too late to go back and rewrite every character to account for the new additions.

Take the following example: An actor walks into a bar (no, this is not the start of some obscene VR joke!). The virtual-world designer has just introduced alcohol into the world, and so our actor now encounters beer for the first time. He or she may have already learned the appropriate animations for drinking from a bottle, but suppose not. How do we get the actor to do the right thing? What if, instead of teaching the character how to drink from a beer bottle, we encode the instructions for performing the appropriate animation into the bottle itself? Each item the character encountered would have all the instructions for its use built into it, requiring only that the user direct his or her attention to it in order to enable its use. In one interface scenario, the user points to the bottle with the cursor and is then presented with a number of options for what to do with it (Drink, Throw, Break, and so forth). The user chooses one of these options, and then the animation attached to the bottle drives the character to perform the action. The cause-and-effect relationship is reversed, but, from the user's point of view, the action appears natural.

The advantage to this is that we can continually introduce new elements into the environment because the animations for the elements' uses are included in their design. This method enables us to have an infinitely expandable variety of possible actions/animations available to the character while reducing the character file to a physical description of the character and a set of behavioral modifiers that are used to alter the flavor of the animations, giving each character a unique body language and personality.

In addition to increasing the degree of diversity for animated behavior, the technique also adds a great deal of efficiency by automatically filtering out all the inappropriate animations for any given set of circumstances. While there might be millions of actions possible for a single character, we want to deal only with those that are relevant to the given situation. When the user directs the character into a new environment, a search is performed to determine which objects are available to the character. At this point, the files, which include the animation, as well as the buttons, sliders, and so on used to control the specific activity, are loaded. As the character moves from one environment to another, this information is updated, and the user is presented with a new set of options.

These techniques are useful for actor interactions as well. That beer bottle may also have encoded in it the effects of drinking beer on the actions of the animated actor. After a few beers, the actor may display difficulty walking or standing or whatever other effects the virtual-world designer may have decided should accompany the drinking of alcohol. The human participant, upon seeing this, realizes that it's time to leave but, as he or she attempts to direct the avatar toward the door, accidentally stumbles into another actor, who immediately grows angry and swings a fist at our helpless participant.

In the same way that encoding the appropriate behavior into the bottle enables the actor to perform the act of drinking believably, encoding the appropriate responses to behavior into the actor initiating that behavior allows us to maintain consistent and believable behavior even between actors with completely different sets of abilities. Our human participant may not have the appropriate fighting animations built into the avatar, but the attacker does. These animations contain, in addition to the set of attack animations, a set of possible responses, including those used by actors who don't know how to fight (like getting knocked across the room).

Not that this is limited only to violent situations. If, instead of getting into a fight, our actor was asked to dance, he or she should at least be able to make a clumsy attempt at it, even if the actor has never danced before. Along with the dance animations used by his or her expert partner are those employed by our awkward but earnest hero, allowing the two of them to make a believable (though potentially comic) pair out on the dance floor.

"Lights, cameras, action!"—Behind the Scenes on the Virtual Soundstage

In the production of any movie, from the biggest Hollywood blockbuster to the smallest independent film, there are a number of people whose contributions make the movie possible but who never appear in front of the camera. The director, the cinematographer, the editor, the props and sets and special FX crews, and numerous others all lend their expertise to the creation of the final product, and the quality of their work is largely responsible for the success of the film. What if we could bring this talent and expertise to the creation of virtual worlds?

Unlike the movies, the interactive nature of virtual worlds means that the kinds of decisions that are normally made ahead of time during the making of a film (the choice of camera angles, the editing of shots, and so on) all need to be made on the fly in response to the ever-changing (and unpredictable) actions of the human participants. How can we apply the same autonomous decision-making techniques used for our "actors" to the creation of these offscreen members of the production team?

Interactive Cinematography

In "first-person point of view" (POV) interfaces used in games like Doom, the users have direct control over their movement and actions but are generally limited to one kind of view, greatly diminishing the number of cinematic possibilities. If we instead make the camera an independent actor in the environment, we open up the possibilities enormously. We've also freed up the constraints on the camera. If we treat the camera as another character in the scene, we can then give it its own set of behaviors. The camera can react to the action in the scene and adjust the shot accordingly, giving us a kind of real-time cinematography that isn't possible in POV-type games.

Lighting, Sound, and Special FX

Other elements of the environment can be "embodied" as well. Lighting, Music, Sound, and Special FX agents can be designed to be constantly responding to the changes in mood and tension, in addition to following cues triggered by the accomplishment of goals or the occurrence of key events in the story. The goal in creating these "backstage agents" is not to replace the creative individuals who specialize in these various cinematic art forms, but rather to allow these individuals to construct the aesthetic rules that these agents will follow during the course of the interactive experience.

I want to point out that the use of these agents isn't limited to gaming and interactive fiction environments. In MUDs and other free-form virtual spaces, these agents can be used to maintain a certain visual and aural quality to the experience. These agents might also be custom tailored to the individual. For example, each avatar may have its own sound track, audible only to that participant, that accompanies it and reflects the changing circumstances surrounding that individual. Each person might view the world through an automated camera that tracks the avatar's every move, always presenting the most dramatic or interesting camera angle. Lighting and weather agents can provide interesting and unpredictable atmospheres in reaction to events in the world and their own internal rules. All these can contribute to the creation of compelling experiences even within purely social virtual environments.

"To be or not to be . . ."—The Possibilities for Interactive Drama on the Virtual Stage

Now that we have the actors and production crew ready, how do we bring it all together into the creation of an engaging and a powerful experience? You may be familiar with "branching narratives" in which, at key moments in the story, the player must choose from one of a few options and his or her decision determines how the story proceeds. In these systems, each alternative or "branch" is plotted ahead of time by the author. While we could apply these techniques to systems involving autonomous agents, the restriction of having to know everything in advance negates the advantage we gain from having actors who can continually improvise as they go along under rapidly changing circumstances. At the same time, if we simply allow the characters to go about their business in an unstructured environment, there's no way to guarantee that, as the human-avatar interacts with them in unpredictable ways, the tension will build and the stakes will continue to rise. A participant might fail to provoke the right people, wander around aimlessly for hours, or, worse, get killed right off the bat. In many gaming scenarios, especially those in which combat is the central theme, getting killed is OK; you just start over and keep doing it until you get it right, and wandering around aimlessly is often part of finding your way through some maze.

In games where social scenarios play a much greater role, such complications can hinder, rather than support, the flow of the game. In these cases, we need to introduce one more "invisible" agent, this time in the role of director. This agent is given the task of maintaining the drama and is encoded with rules governing how much time various parts of the story should take and what events need to occur in order to effect this. The point here is not to railroad the participant into following a specific course of action, but rather to ensure that the rest of the world responds to the user's actions in order to keep the story progressing. The drama is continuous, flows seamlessly around the user, and, if done correctly, remains engaging and provocative under almost any circumstance. The ability to create these experiences, once the province of science fiction (the Star Trek Holodeck), is now a matter of creative talent and skill and no longer limited by the technology.

We've now constructed a scenario in which humanlike agents and invisible "backstage" forces work together in the creation of engaging interactive experiences for human-directed avatars. But what does it mean to be an agent in this brave new world? What happens when we take agents out of their roles as actors and technicians for interactive fiction and begin employing them for more mundane and/or practical tasks? How might their unique abilities lend themselves to other aspects of human existence, and what are the implications?

"Reality Bytes"—At Home on the Mean Streets of the Metaverse

It's long been the goal of artificial intelligence (AI) research to create computer programs and systems with the ability to reason and deal with situations requiring the kind of problem-solving ability we normally ascribe only to human beings. Alan Turing, one of the founding fathers of AI, proposed a test, which according to him would determine whether a computer program had achieved consciousness. To pass the "Turing test," as it came to be known, a computer in head-to-head competition with a human being in a blind test, through continuous, sustained conversation, would have to fool a panel of judges that it was, in fact, the human participant. If the program could consistently fool the judges at least half the time, it could be considered to be conscious. The original test was conducted using a text-only interface to make the program and the human subject physically indistinguishable. Though they don't fit the letter of Turing's rules, virtual worlds in which both human and computer-directed agents are represented as computer-animated figures certainly meet the criteria of placing humans and computers on a level playing surface.

The most important feature of Turing's test, and the thing that has brought about some of the most controversy, is that it makes no assumptions about the internal mechanisms that drive the system. In Turing's view, consciousness is attributed to a system based entirely on the observation of its actions. This issue has been a point of contention in AI for many years, but what interests me here is not whether an autonomous agent can be said to have a "mind," but what happens when we begin interacting with an agent as if it does.

What are the social dynamics of cyberspace? How will the social relationships between people and computers evolve on the new frontier? How do the roles of avatars and agents reflect the sociohistorical roles of people and groups in the "real world"?

In our attempts to add humanity and personality to our digital workspaces, will we be opening up new opportunities for interaction and collaboration between artists and audiences, or will we merely be creating a new servant class in which we exert absolute power over our desktop assistants? These questions remain to be answered and will be, no doubt, as the medium matures.

Summary

There is increasing interest in the creation of 3D virtual worlds across many application domains. The development of VRML (Virtual Reality Modeling Language) and of Sun's Java programming language has made it possible to create complex virtual environments that can be experienced on consumer-level personal computers over the Internet. With this, realtime 3D has migrated from the realm of military and aerospace simulation into both entertainment and education. The IMPROV system is being developed to meet the needs of artists and authors interested in creating rich interactive experiences involving lifelike, believable characters.

Biography

Athomas Goldberg is a research scientist currently heading the IMPROV project at the New York University Media Research Lab. He has worked as a filmmaker, a theatrical lighting and set designer, an illustrator, and a performance artist—when he's not sleeping or playing with his cats.

Chapter 11

PLACEHOLDER:
Landscape and Narrative
in Virtual Environments

Brenda Laurel, Rachel Strickland, and Rob Tow
Interval Research Corporation

Virtual Reality as Entertainment

The idea of using virtual reality for entertainment purposes is actually quite recent in the history of the technology. Early VR entertainment applications, appearing in the late 1980s, were extensions of the existing "serious" application of simulation-based training. Flight-sim technologies—motion platforms used in sync with motion video or animation—were much more readily adapted to theme park applications than immersive VR with head-mounted displays. Motion platform rides, of which Star Tours is probably the best-known example, trade off individual viewpoint control and the sense of agency for thrilling, finely calibrated effects and the optimization of "throughput"—that is, getting the most people through the ride in the least time. Networked pods, as used in Virtual World Entertainment systems (previously Battletech), are also derived from flight-sim technology.

"Classic" virtual reality, employing head-mounted displays and various forms of body tracking, presents serious throughput problems in theme park settings. It takes time to get the gear onto the participants. Only a handful of people can experience the attraction simultaneously (though a much larger audience might watch what the people "inside" the VR are doing). A hard-driving plot with distinct beginning, middle, and end is a great way to control how long an experience takes, but "classic" VR is inimical to this type of authorial control—it works best when people can move about and do things in virtual environments in a relatively unconstrained way.

In fact, it may be that the nature of immersive VR makes it inappropriate to think of it as an entertainment medium. Mass entertainment implies the consumption of some performance by a large audience. Generally speaking, the size of the audience is inversely proportional to the degree of influence over the

181

course of events that can be afforded any one person.[1] Nor can we simply turn to human-to-human interaction as the source of engagement and still support a large number of simultaneous participants; virtual spaces seem not to differ from actual ones in terms of social and attentional constraints posed by crowds. There seems to be an upper limit (probably the famous seven plus or minus two) on the number of people who can interact meaningfully or pleasurably with one another (which is why little clusters form at cocktail parties). Even for a small audience, VR is inimical to the kind of passive receptivity that is appropriate in films and amusement park rides. The experience of VR hinges on human action and the environment's response. This is true in both perceptual and emotional terms. In VR, one is not *done unto*, but *doing*.

If, on the other hand, the goal is to create a technologically mediated environment where people can *play*—as opposed to being entertained—then VR is the best game in town. When children play, they typically use their imaginations quite actively and constructively to invent action and assign meaning to materials (or make or find new ones) as the need arises. In VR, as in children's play, there is no sharp distinction between "authoring" and "experiencing." With PLACEHOLDER, we learned that adults can play in the same way—when their imaginations are booted up by a rich virtual environment.

PLACEHOLDER was presented in a public venue with very low throughput (two participants approximately every 15 minutes). A few onlookers were also usually present, watching the participants in the studio and tapping into their experiences through monitors and earphones. It is not likely that people could have a satisfactory experience in a rich VR world in less time or with many more simultaneous participants, but one could imagine working out a way for a much larger audience to look in on the action—by using the virtual camera techniques developed by David Zeltzer's group at the MIT Media Lab, for instance, to automatically synthesize a cinematic presentation of what is going on rather than forcing people to try to construct a coherent mental picture of the action by looking at two individuals' eye views of the world.

We believe that the theme parks of the world—at least some of them—will eventually be virtual. In the end, we think that VR works like PLACEHOLDER will find their natural home on computer networks rather than in public venues. When our version of the Grand Canyon is up on the Net, there won't be several thousand tourists staring over the virtual rim. Instead, there will be a thousand copies of the Grand Canyon running where people can experience

---

1. An interesting exception is the Cinematrix technology developed by Loren Carpenter (and premiered at SIGGRAPH '91), where a very large group interacts on a large video screen via wands with red and green reflective material on them. Each individual controls the color of a logical pixel by turning the wand. Crowds have been observed to learn very quickly to cooperate well enough to play mass games of Pong, make intricate patterns, and even control a flight simulator. This is certainly not virtual reality, but it is a robust technologically enabled form of mass interaction.

a magical place in solitude or in the company of a few good friends—each subtly distinguished by season, weather, historical epoch, critters, voices in the wind and rocks, and the marks of those who have gone before.

About PLACEHOLDER

Experiences are said to take place. One comes to know a place with all one's senses, by virtue of the actions that one performs there, and from an embodied and situated point of view. The mind, observes naturalist Barry Lopez, is a kind of projection within a person of the place that that person inhabits: "Each individual undertakes to order his interior landscape according to the exterior landscape." The environment proceeds to record our presence and actions and the marks that we place there—this is a reciprocal affair.

PLACEHOLDER is the name of a research project that explored a new paradigm for narrative action in virtual environments. The geography of PLACEHOLDER took inspiration from three actual locations near Banff National Park in Alberta, Canada—the Middle Spring (a sulfur hot spring in a natural cave), a waterfall in Johnston Canyon, and a formation of hoodoos overlooking the Bow River. Three-dimensional videographic scene elements, spatialized sounds and words, and simple character animation were employed to construct a composite landscape that could be visited concurrently by two physically remote participants using head-mounted displays. People were able to walk about, speak, and use both hands to touch and move virtual objects.

People's relationships with places and the creatures who inhabit them have formed the basis of many traditions and spiritual practices, as well as ancient stories and myths. The graphic elements in PLACEHOLDER were adapted from iconography that has been inscribed upon the landscape since Paleolithic times. Narrative motifs that revealed the archetypal characters of landscape features and animals were selected from aboriginal tales. Four animated spirit critters—Spider, Snake, Fish, and Crow—inhabited this virtual world. A person visiting the world could assume the character of one of the spirit animals and thereby experience aspects of its unique visual perception, its way of moving about, and its voice. Thus, the critters functioned as "smart costumes" that changed more than the appearance of the person within.

People sometimes leave marks in natural places—pictograms, petroglyphs, graffiti, or trail signs, for example. In PLACEHOLDER, people were able to leave "Voicemarks"—bits of spoken narrative—that could be listened to and rearranged by anyone who passed through. The virtual landscape accumulated definition through messages and story lines that participants left along the way. We hope that the ideas we explored in PLACEHOLDER will foster the emergence of new forms of narrative play.

A Note on Authorship

The following sections of this chapter are authored by different individuals.

The people who worked on PLACEHOLDER shared a core set of goals, but each individual contributor had distinct interests, values, and ways of working. There were neither enough resources nor enough time to accomplish each of everyone's goals; difficult decisions regarding priorities had to be made. In the end, a diverse group of people produced a single artifact—the virtual environment piece that is the subject of this chapter. Each of us reflects on it differently, seeing different shortcomings and strengths in the work and learning different lessons from the process. For these reasons, it seems important to preserve the singularity of each author's voice.

Capturing the Sense of a Place

Rachel Strickland

Most computer graphic virtual environments—and video adventure games in particular—that had heretofore fallen in our paths consist of synthetically generated scenery that comes from nowhere on earth. Even the flight simulator examples with airport runways precisely dimensioned and positioned on geographically correct terrain models most starkly reflect the world of cartoons.

One of our objectives with PLACEHOLDER was to experiment with capturing actual places—in the attitude of landscape painting traditions or documentary cinema, for example—using video and audio recorded on location as the raw material for constructing the virtual environment. It must be emphasized that we weren't concerned with achieving a high degree of sensory realism—something bristling with polygons and mips that might induce a perfect audiovisual delusion of sticking your head in the "real" waterfall. No, it gets more slippery than that. What we really set out to capture or reproduce is just the simplest "sense of place."

Genius Loci

For one thing, there is the "genius loci" (a Latin phrase that refers to the guardian spirit of a place), whose presence accounts for the life of the place and determines its character or essence. Something like this ancient Roman concept is common among indigenous cultures throughout the world. Architectural scholar Christian Norberg-Schulz, who wrote the book entitled *Genius Loci*, proposes two levels of analysis for articulating the structure of place:

1. Spatial Organization, or Knowing Where One Is Here. "Space" denotes the three-dimensional organization of the elements that define a place. This organization may correspond to landscape features. It may reflect early parcel subdivisions or transportation routes. It may be shaped by local building methods, materials, and codes. It may derive from abstract geometric principles. The spatial organization of the place influences how people orient themselves in this environment, how they find their way around, and how they avoid getting lost.

2. Character, or Knowing How One Is Here. Compared with space, which can be mapped, character is too comprehensive to permit succinct specification, and it is also more concrete. It is a condition of atmosphere, weather, lighting, and the passage of time, as well as a function of space-defining form. "Any real *presence* is intimately linked with a character."

Umwelt

Another sense of the sense of place that influenced our designs for PLACE-HOLDER is suggested by the German word "umwelt." The naturalist Jakob von Uexküll tried to imagine the physical world as lived and perceived by different animals. He used "umwelt" to express the organized experience—or point of view—that is unique to any creature and depends on that particular creature's sensory and cognitive apparatus. Employing virtual environment technology to explore alternate "umwelten" has been one of our irrepressible motives. The scheme for PLACEHOLDER included the following:

- Experimenting with approximations of the sensory-motor experiences of nonhuman creatures.

- Experimenting with narrative strategies for supporting transformation, locomotion, and spatial and temporal discontinuities.

- Exploring concepts of space and time that underlie representation systems that have been developed by cultures whose views of the world differ dramatically from our own.

Place Recording and Modeling Techniques

The three locations selected for PLACEHOLDER—cave, waterfall, and river valley—asserted strikingly differentiated characters. By matching capture and representation techniques to the unique qualities of the respective places and by amplifying their contrasts, we hoped to distill distinct environmental caricatures. For example, we determined that the waterfall model should incorporate motion video to render the dynamic flow of the water. The sense of the cave should be auditory rather than visual—a dimly illuminated quick sketch surrounding a lively array of localized sound sources.

Our predilection for sampling and representing actual places rather than synthesizing environments from scratch was reinforced by the collaboration of Michael Naimark. Techniques for constructing 3D computer models out of camera-originated imagery were based on Naimark's previous experiments. One method involved panoramic tiling of multiple video images onto a spherical wireframe. Another used the video picture as a guide for deforming the surface of the wireframe model to approximate the contours of the original.

Extensive location scouting and a series of preliminary trials reminded us that nature affords few landscapes of sufficiently simple form to reveal themselves to a single point of view. Two questions that abided with us throughout the process deserve further pondering:

1. How do we capture a place simultaneously rather than sequentially with a time-based medium like video in order to provide for more than one way of experiencing the representation of the place during a stretch of time?

2. How do we capture a place from multiple camera positions all at once, and how do we join the several vantage points into a spatially coherent representation?

Traditions such as Chinese landscape painting, impressionism, and Cubism experimented with a range of strategies for integrating time and multiple viewpoints into the depiction of places. In the entire history of painting, considering the many achievements made by artists—in the pictorial representation of light, color, and texture, for example—it's curious, observed historian Ernst Gombrich, that the development of linear perspective by Brunelleschi and associates is the sole achievement that has been consistently regarded in the category of true scientific invention.

Placemarks

Several years ago, Brenda Laurel and I found ourselves, along with Michael Naimark, working on a video production in Zion National Park. One of the ingredients that Zion offered for our videotaping was Anasazi petroglyphs. We reverently regarded these evocative figures inscribed on the red sandstone faces of Zion as evidence of their creators' profound spiritual connection with the land. Once taping was finished, we hiked to a particularly spectacular trail that climaxed in the Angels Flight. The steep, tortuous ascent that involved clinging to chains for dear life eventually terminated in a wide ledge that afforded a panoramic view of just about everything. What arrested my attention more than the view was the graffiti. It had spread like a virus over every square inch of stone surface that humans could reach. All the inscriptions were alphabetical, of course—just the rude monograms that a population of Kilroys leave to mark their excursions far and wide.

The question that occurred to me just then was whether the impulse that motivates people to carve unsightly initials on places might have anything at all in common with the impulse that produced those ancient environmental artworks we had been admiring.

Why and how do people mark/erase their marks on places? Had we overlooked some innate human proclivity that deserved to be trained and cultivated rather than discouraged? The phenomenon of place marking—a behavior I've studied carefully since that trip to Zion—yields promising insights about how people might be encouraged to take action in a virtual environment. For PLACEHOLDER, the initial idea was that self-representation of the participants would amount to the marks they leave on things. What would be the virtual equivalent of footprints, graffiti, shadows, planting flags on the moon, or peeing in corners?

Notes on Staging: The Magic Circle

A concept found in fairy tales and traditions of theater, the "magic circle" is the primordial stage—that zone differentiated from darkness by the illumination of the campfire. Consider it this way: We spend most of our lives stumbling around in the dark. Occasionally we wander inside a magic circle here or there where we find our bearings and everything suddenly falls into place. The problem is that we can never stay in such places for long, for they are not the end of the journey.

For the virtual environment of PLACEHOLDER, magic circles yielded a solution to the limited tracking range of the electromagnetic position-sensing devices. We determined the 10-foot diameter of these particular circles by the maximum reliable distance from the Polhemus receivers worn by participants to the transmitters mounted overhead.

However, there's no need to draw a sharp boundary between the physical and the virtual world. Why not do ambient sound with speakers, for instance, or make wind with electric fans, or create physical definition? Rather than restrain people with tethers and railings, perhaps changing the surface underfoot would be a gentler way of letting them know that they were stepping out of tracking range.

Narrative and Interaction in PLACEHOLDER

Brenda Laurel

Notes on Conventions and Constraints

Film began to emerge as an art form distinct from the technology of cinema when conventions began to be established for representing time and space. One is tempted to add to the last sentence, "in other than directly mimetic ways"—but representations are, by definition, distinguishable from actualities, and film could not have achieved absolute verisimilitude by its very nature. Nevertheless, the active use of the camera to orchestrate gaze and define space through attention, for instance, and the use of transitions like cuts, fades, and dissolves to represent spatial and temporal discontinuities are examples of *intentionally* nonrealistic treatments of time and space. Such techniques arose in order to communicate subjective experience and to serve as syntactic elements in the artistic construction of meaning. They became conventions because they were successful in forming the basis of a language of cinema that enabled artists to create works of increasing complexity and power.

Space and Time

In a similar vein, one of the goals of PLACEHOLDER was to experiment with various techniques for representing space, time, and distance. The three environments were separated by several miles of Canadian mountains and forests. We needed a way for participants to move among them without simulating the actual traversal of the intervening landscape. We knew of a few previous experiments in the area, conducted at the NASA Ames Research Laboratory in the mid-1980s, that used various permutations of windowing to allow people to move among unconnected spaces, but we were unsatisfied with the window metaphor, finding it too close to the visual language of computers. Our wanderings through cultural anthropology, mythology, and folklore eventually led us to adopt the idea of active portals that would transport people among the worlds. Our encounters with rock art and aboriginal visual symbols brought us to the spiral as an appropriate sign for the portal (Figure 11.1).

When a person approached, the portal emitted ambient sound from the next environment to which that person might transport. Another person in the same environment might hear the same portal sounds from a distance but, upon approach, might hear the sound of another environment coming through the portal since we determined each person's destination individually by random choice. Within the portal, time was compressed but not absent—the dura-

Figure 11.1   Graphic design of the Portal, defining the connections between the three virtual environments.

tion of a transit was about 10 seconds, in darkness, accompanied by the environmental sounds coming from "ahead." People were able to see two glowing points of light representing the "grip" of each hand (if they happened to raise their hands to within their field of view), and some people seemed to use these points of light to orient themselves and maintain their balance. Many questions remain about the duration of the interval (people might be too disoriented by instant teleportation, but was the transit too long?) and the visual effects of the transit (would a neutral color with the suggestion of a flowfield better represent this metaphorical movement through space?).

Conventions Relating to the Body

In PLACEHOLDER, we reexamined some techniques that were already becoming conventions of the VR medium. For example, as of 1993, it was standard practice to infer both direction of gaze and desired direction of movement from a position sensor mounted on the head. As people would learn this constraint, they would stop moving their heads independent of their torsos, often increasing muscle tension across the neck, shoulders, and upper back. In order to "give people back their necks" without resorting to an expensive and encumbering bodysuit, we resolved to infer direction of gaze from the head-mounted sensor and to make guesses about the desired direction of movement by looking at a sensor mounted on a belt worn just below the waist, on the theory that the pelvis generally gives much more accurate information about the direction in which one intends to move than the head.

Another set of VR traditions involves the treatment of the hands. The assumption is that one needs to gather information as detailed as possible about the movement and position of the hand and that, in general, only the right (or dominant) hand need be tracked. These assumptions stem from typical VR applications involving manipulations of remote or virtual objects in teleoperations and simulation scenarios. We determined that, for people to be able to play in the world of PLACEHOLDER, the system need only know whether a hand was touching or grasping something, so we invented a simple device called a "Grippee." This was a piece of flexible plastic, held in the semicircle defined by thumb and forefinger, which used a sliding variable resistor to measure the distance between the tips of those two fingers, and a Polhemus Fast-Trak position sensor to define the location and orientation of the hand in 3-space. We also reasoned that a person might want to use both hands, alternately or together, and that people would try different things if they had both hands available to them, so we put Grippees on both hands. Since there was no instrumented glove from which one could construct a virtual hand and since participants in the virtual environments would probably spend most of their time in the characters of Critters rather than humans, we decided that the traditional visual representation of a (wireframe or shaded-polygon) human hand would be inappropriate. Instead, each person saw two points of light for each hand as previously described. These points provided unambiguous but minimal feedback about the hand's location in space and whether it was open or closed.

We also questioned certain VR interface conventions using gestural language. It has become customary to move about in virtual environments by "flying," a mode invoked by pointing two fingers in the desired direction of flight (and which must also be explicitly terminated by another gesture). These gestures are formal—that is, not mimetic of any activity one might undertake in order to move or fly—and they demand substantial accuracy for reliable recognition. We did not wish to require people to learn formal gestures in order to use our system, and we did want them to move around fairly naturally in the environment. These desires led us to make two key decisions about movement. First, we resolved to let people walk around by walking around. Since the tracker range was only reliable for a circle of about 10 feet in diameter, we fell upon the notion of the "magic circle"—an ancient theatrical and storytelling convention—as a way to contextualize the technical constraints imposed by the system. Second, we wanted a person to be able to fly like a bird when he or she assumed the character of Crow. We were aware of experiments by Mark Bolas at NASA Ames in the late 1980s with alternative interfaces for flying, including flapping, gliding, and following a virtual paper airplane, but none of these techniques had supplanted "finger-flying" as the convention for movement. We resolved to let Crow fly by flapping his wings.[2]

2. Designing crow flight was a wonderfully interesting problem. At first, we asked everyone we could find to tell us how they fly in their dreams. We were discouraged because so many different methods were reported. But in early tests with the system, we observed that whenever people became embodied as Crow, they inevitably flapped their arms. Voilà! It remained for Rob Tow and Graham Lundgren to figure out what constituted a "flap." Rob designed the strategy for returning the flyer to the position corresponding to the current location of his or her body—an elegant landing that made every Crow feel like an expert flyer—and Graham produced a superb implementation of flight.

In summary, two issues were central to our work with conventions in PLACEHOLDER. One was the definition of the medium—thinking about what it was and could be and how conventions could be used to shape its potential. If VR is to be used as a medium for narrative, dramatic, or playful activity, we should question the appropriateness of conventions derived from computer displays, teleoperations, or training simulators. The other issue was the question of the interface—thinking about how people were being sensed and how they were being constrained to behave. Our motto was "no interface," expressing our desire to maximize naturalness, to enable the body to act directly in the world, and to minimize distraction and cognitive load.

Narrative Elements

We thought of PLACEHOLDER as a set of environments imbued with narrative potential—places that could be experienced and marked through narrative activity. When a person visits a place, the stories that are told about it—by companions, by rock art or graffiti, or even by oneself through memories or fantasies—become part of the character of the place. Stories give us ideas about what can be done or imagined in a place; learning that a particular canyon was an outlaw's hiding place, for instance, or remembering a child saying that a particular rock resembled an old woman's face will certainly influence our experience of that place. It's hard to experience a natural place without remembering or constructing some stories about it.

Motifs

Lucinda deLorimier, a professional storyteller, worked with us to uncover narrative motifs from mythology and folklore that would influence the design and representation of virtual environments. We used many of these motifs as indirect inspirations to design, making decisions about the "feel" of a given environment, for example, and more concretely, determining what the environments said about themselves. We embedded place motifs in the virtual environments as "Placemarks"—fragments of narrative spoken in the "voice of the place" (performed by an actor), emanating from sound sources located within landscape features and triggered by the proximity of a person[3] (Figure 11.2).

A second use of motifs was in the selection of Critters and the creation of their dialogue. We wanted to populate the environments with archetypal critters with which human participants could merge (Figure 11.3). The narrative goal here was to give people character materials to play with. A not-so-obvious

3. Due to time constraints, only a few Placemarks were actually implemented, although many were scripted and recorded.

Figure 11.2   Graphic design of the map of the world shown to visitors as part of their orientation.

Figure 11.3   Graphic design for the Critter bodies.

goal was to make humans aware of being embodied by inducing them to intentionally enter the body of a critter. We did not want the body in the virtual world to be taken for granted, and we did want to explore the idea of how differently places look and feel to different kinds of beings. The experience began in the cave (selected as the starting place for obvious Jungian reasons), where people encountered the Critters as large petroglyphs placed around a pool. Triggered by proximity, the Critters would begin to speak about themselves— their powers, characteristics, and opinions of other Critters. These narratives were typically based on motifs found in stories from widely diverse cultures or on stories improvised by actors who had been exposed to those motifs. As a person moved closer to a Critter, its narrative became more elaborate and persuasive, urging the person to "come closer." Once a person's head intersected the petroglyph, he or she would join that Critter, taking on its appearance, voice, perceptual characteristics, and means of locomotion (see the later section on "smart costumes").

Collaboration with the Precipice Theatre Society

We were fortunate to find and form an alliance with the Precipice Theatre Society, an environmentally oriented improvisational theatre company based in Banff. Under the direction of Colin Funk, the Precipice troupe studies pending legislation or development plans that threaten the natural environment in Canada and then develops scripts on these topics through improvisation. The company gives rollicking, commedia-style performances throughout western Canada, often meeting—and overcoming—vociferous audience disagreement with their point of view. We sought the company's help in developing the characters and interface concepts for PLACEHOLDER. They were ideal collaborators because of their excellent improv and performance skills and because they were generally naive about computers and free of preconceived notions about virtual reality.

By way of preparation, we gave the actors lists of story motifs that Lucinda had found about the kinds of places and Critters we were using. As soon as we had settled on the locations and characters we wanted to use in the piece, we asked members of the troupe to improvise action with the characters in the actual environments. Immediately, we began to see new ways in which people could play in the environments and what kinds of affordances were needed in order to facilitate such play. The actors also improvised vocal and physical characterizations of the environments. We later recreated some of the environmental vocalizations in the studio and mixed them with natural sounds to create an auditory signature for each environment that was played through the portals. The improvs were crucial in shaping the individual Critter characters as well.

After the improvs in the field, we did another series of improvs in the studio, recreating the spaces through mime and vocalization and improvising interface features like "Voiceholders" to see what would seem "natural" to a person who wasn't technologically inclined. When it came time to script the critters' voices and Placemarks, I took much of the dialogue directly from videotapes of these improv sessions. I cast actors from the company in the roles of the various Critters and Places and rerecorded the dialogue digitally. The dialogue was postprocessed in some cases to apply the same Critter voice filter that would be applied in realtime to a participant embodied as that Critter. (Crow always sounded like Crow, whether he was speaking from stored dialogue or with the live voice of a participant.) At performance time, the dialogue was spatialized using the Convolvotrons.

When PLACEHOLDER opened, the Precipice troupe were our first participants. Most of the actors were fascinated with the system and with VR. Their physical fluidity and improvisational skills made their interactions in the environments a joy to watch.

Voiceholders and Voicemarks

Rachel has described our interest in how people leave marks on places. We wanted to give people the ability to "mark" the virtual environments, and we arrived at voice as a convenient modality for doing so. Voice offered several advantages over writing or drawing. Through prosody, voice permits greater expressiveness and personalization than writing; it is also more immediate. Most people are less self-conscious about speaking than about drawing. While drawing would require that we build special virtual drawing tools, capturing voice was relatively easy to implement.

Where and how could voices be stored and replayed? We designed the Voiceholders as virtual record/playback devices. A Voiceholder would capture and store an utterance, or "Voicemark." A "full" Voiceholder (one containing a Voicemark) would play its contents when touched. In order to encourage people to play with relationships among Voicemarks and between Voicemarks and landscape features, we made the Voiceholders moveable, exempt from gravity, and able to be placed anywhere one could reach. Voiceholders could be moved by grabbing them (closing the Grippees while the points of light were "inside" them), dragging them to the desired location (they would stick to your hand), and releasing the grip. We wanted people to think of the Voiceholders more as tools or agents than as devices; machines (including tape recorders) were inconsistent with the fantasy context. We designed them as rocks with faces, using the facial expressions to indicate the state of the Voiceholder (Figure 11.4). This was as close as we came to an iconic or symbolic interface element.

When a Voiceholder was empty, its eyes and mouth were closed, and it was dark. When a person touched an empty Voiceholder, its eyes would open, it would light up from the inside (rather like a jack-o'-lantern), and a voice (emanating from the Voiceholder) would say, "I'm listening." If a person spoke when a Voiceholder was in that state, his or her speech would be recorded.

Figure 11.4   Four facial expressions indicate the states of the Voiceholders. *Left to right:* Empty and asleep; empty and listening; full and asleep; full and speaking.

When the Voiceholder became "full" (ran out of space in the sound file it was creating), the inner light flickered and then went out (rather like a guttering candle), the eyes would close, and the mouth would open to indicate that it was ready to speak. If a person touched a Voiceholder in this state, it would open its eyes, light up, play back its contents, and then would "go to sleep" again.

The Voiceholders turned out to be difficult for many people to use. A major problem was performance speed. The sampling rate for the Grippees' location sensors was constrained by the frame rate of the display (sometimes as low as 5 Hz). That was not fast enough to feel natural; a person's hand could pass through a Voiceholder in less than 0.2 second and therefore not be sensed as a touch. People had to become conscious of and careful with their hand positions in order to activate and grasp the Voiceholders; that distraction made using them more problematic and less natural than it might have been. We hypothesize that these technical difficulties, and not intrinsic design flaws, limited the amount and complexity of narrative activity and other kinds of play with the Voiceholders.

"Smart Costumes"

The sense and status of the body in virtual space have been problematic since VR was invented. As mentioned in the section on conventions and constraints, the body has typically been highly constrained by sensing technologies and strategies as well as by the emphasis on formal gesture. The absence of haptic affordances in VR interfaces has reinforced a sense of incorporality. The now-iconic disembodied hand that floats before one's eyes in most virtual worlds struck us as emblematic of a fundamental difficulty.

We considered two rather oblique approaches in an attempt to create a different sense of the body in VR than we had heretofore experienced. Our original specification included both, but neither was implemented. The first was an extension of the idea of Placemarks—that one knows where one is or has been through evidence in the environment (shadows and footprints, for example). The second approach was based on the idea of having to do something—to take some action—in order to have a body. Mere humans were invisible in the world, to themselves (save for the points of light on the hands) and to one another. They couldn't use the portals or see the Voiceholders. All they could do was talk and explore the immediate environment of the cave. From the moment people entered the world, the Critters were talking to them, bragging about their qualities and enticing people to "come closer." When a person's head intersected one of the critters, he or she became "embodied" as that Critter. The critter, now functioning as a "smart costume," changed how a person looked, sounded, moved, and perceived the world. Thus, the final point of our "body politics" was to draw attention to the sense of body by giving people novel bodies.

The Critters—Crow, Spider, Fish, and Snake—were chosen in large part on the basis of the narrative motifs associated with them. Universality of motifs was also a selection criterion. Complementarity was another, in terms of both pleasing contrasts and potential alliances. The narrative motifs formed the spines of the critter characters, giving rise to both their graphical representations and their voices and dialogue. We hoped that the Critters' traits and the things they said about themselves would give people narrative material to play with after they had become embodied.

We tried to identify characteristics of perception and locomotion for the Critters that were consistent with the narrative motifs. Crow, for instance, has a reputation for admiring and acquiring shiny things; Crow's vision might boost specular reflections in the environment. In myth and lore, Spider is often characterized as being able to "see into all the worlds"—having multiple points of view or levels of reality—hence, representation of Spider's eight eyes (some independently steerable) seemed apt. Snake, renowned for its ability to navigate the dark landscapes of sex and death, could see in the dark, possessing infrared vision as pit vipers do. We also tried to give each Critter physical characteristics that would create unique advantages. Fish, for example, could see clearly underwater, while others' vision was blurred. In the end, "snake vision" was the only perceptual quirk that we had time to implement, and the results were equivocal—people certainly knew when they were Snake, but the implementation was poor in that it simply applied a red filter without increasing apparent luminance, thus effectively reducing rather than enhancing visibility.

Despite these shortcomings, we found that the smart costumes immediately and strongly influenced participants' behaviors. Their voices and body movements became more exaggerated and dramatic. Most people were "in character" the instant they realized that they had become embodied as a Critter.

I suspect that the "masquerade" aspects of the smart costumes—replacing or obscuring one's identity with an exotic persona and amplifying aspects of one's own identity that are obscured by one's ordinary persona—put people in a frame of mind that allowed them to *play*, often quite boldly and imaginatively.

The Goddess

PLACEHOLDER was a performance piece in that one of the characters was improvised live—the character of the Goddess. We originally conceived her as a playmate and trickster, with the goal of enriching dramatic interaction. When people first found themselves in the Cave, the Goddess spoke to them about the world (this bit of the Goddess' dialogue was taped). Unlike the environmental sounds, her voice seemed to reside in the participant's head. We had planned for her to be able to cause many things to happen—change the weather, make rocks fall from the sky, send people through portals, and send her minion, the Mosquito, to pester anyone who displeased her. As with many other narrative elements, the schedule did not permit us to implement these plans. In the end, she simply spoke.

The Goddess workstation consisted of two monitors, each showing the video for one eye of each participant, headphones with corresponding sound channels for each participant, and soundboard controls enabling her to speak to one or both participants or to the audio and computer control rooms. The workstation was located behind glass in a booth facing the two circles so that she could also see the participants' actual bodies. This came in handy because when people got in physical trouble (for instance, one little girl's helmet had slipped down over her nose), the Goddess could provide realtime help; it also gave her additional cues about how people were actually feeling by watching their physical bodies as well as their virtual views.

Most of the time, the role of the Goddess was performed by me or by Jennifer Lewis, a research associate at the Banff Centre. It was also occasionally performed by others, including men. The character of the Goddess changed according to who was performing her and in relation to the participants. With children, she tended to behave (and to be perceived) as a helper and a friend. With adult couples, she was often a cupid and a tease. She answered questions about the worlds and about the interface and coached people who were having difficulties. She often made suggestions about things to do. Occasionally, as with a pair of young men who asked each other, "Can I eat you? Can I shoot you? Well, what can we do here?", the Goddess became downright bitchy. Our interviews with participants after their experiences revealed that people had differing reactions to the Goddess, usually well correlated with the style of her performance in their session.

Some Conclusions

Although our accomplishments with PLACEHOLDER fell far short of our hopes and plans, I believe we achieved proof of concept with many elements of the piece, including the idea of smart costumes, the physical interface strategy, and the various techniques of environmental capture and representation that we employed. In other areas, like the Voiceholders, more work must be done to determine how we can design environments with affordances that induce the kind of collaborative narrative construction we had in mind. A strong measure of our success is the number and quality of new questions that the piece enabled us to ask.

Working on this piece has demonstrated to me that the art of designing in VR is really the art of creating spaces with qualities that call forth active imagination. The VR artist does not bathe the participant in content, but rather invites the participant to produce content by constructing meanings to experience the pleasure of embodied imagination.

Technology and the Senses in PLACEHOLDER

Rob Tow

Technology Overview

PLACEHOLDER was a two-person VR system, with helmets made by Virtual Research that provided both visual and auditory stereo to the participants. We added a small microphone to the helmets to pick up the voices of the users. There were two physical spaces where the participants, wearing display helmets and body sensors, stood, and three virtual worlds through which they could move independently. Position sensors (Polhemus FastTraks) tracked the 3-space position and orientation of the users' heads, both hands, and torsos within a circular stage of about 10 feet.

An additional sensor system was employed—the Grippees, designed by Steve Saunders of Interval. These were placed in each hand and measured the distance between the thumb and forefinger (or middle finger) of the hand, allowing the development of a simple "grasping" interface for virtual objects.

We used a variety of computers in concert in the PLACEHOLDER project. The primary computer used in the project was an SGI Onyx Reality Engine, equipped with 64M of main RAM and 4M of texture memory. It was programmed in C and UNIX, using the Minimal Reality Toolkit (authored by Chris Shaw of the University of Alberta) as the primary VR framework. John

Harrison, the Banff Centre's chief programmer, modified the Minimal Reality Toolkit to provide support for two users and two hands per user from its original one-person, one-dataglove instantiation. Chris Shaw and Lloyd White, also of the University of Alberta, visited to help with code-coordinating support for two users. Glenn Fraser and Graham Lundgren of the Banff Centre and Rob Tow provided additional programming support within the framework of the MR Toolkit.

Rob Tow wrote the C code on the SGI that managed the audio generation and spatialization. This was coordinated with the visual VR code running in the MR Toolkit and controlled sound generation by a NeXT workstation and a Macintosh II equipped with a SampleCell audio-processing card, as well as the spatialization by two PC clones, both equipped with two four-source Crystal River Engineering Convolvotrons. The NeXT, the Macintosh II, and two Yamaha sound processors were programmed by Dorota Blaszczak of the Banff Centre, who was also responsible for the general audio design and integration. Dorota also designed the realtime voice filters that altered participants' voices to match the Critters' "smart costumes." Two SGI VGX computers were used with Alias architectural design tools to lay out the environments' geometries and to apply textures to the resulting wireframes; this effort was accomplished by Rachel Strickland working with Catherine McGinnis, Raonull Conover, Douglas McLeod, Michael Naimark, and Rob Tow. Video capture of environments was accomplished by Rachel Strickland and Michael Naimark; subsequent video digitization using Macintosh-based equipment was done by Catherine McGinnis and Rachel Strickland, with image enhancement in Photoshop done by Catherine McGinnis and Rob Tow. Control of the Grippees was done by C and TCP programming on a Macintosh PowerBook 180 by Sean White of Interval and C and TCP programming on an SGI by Glenn Fraser.

The effort was greatly hampered by the tools used. Due to budget constraints, an old C compiler for an earlier SGI model was used instead of the proper optimized compiler for the Reality Engine. Debugging was largely accomplished by "printf" statements and required a minimum of three people in realtime to do: one in the VR helmet, one running the Onyx Reality Engine, and one running the sound processors. The design of the worlds was done nonimmersively, on workstation screens; the projective geometry of the Alias design software differed greatly from the immersive experience in the VR helmet, which led to tedious difficulties in the world construction. The MR Toolkit itself suffered from memory leaks, which would lead to a sudden slowing down of the worlds during performance from a frame rate of 8 to 12 frames a second to 2 frames a second. This was due to the memory demands of the textures used exceeding the size of the 4M fast-multipotted texture memory, requiring paging of textures from main RAM (SGI released a no-cost upgrade to 16M of texture memory in the fall, too late for our effort).

We suffered greatly from not designing while immersed in the medium itself. One notable exception to this occurred near the end of the process when we did do a small piece of world layout from inside the virtual environment. This was the placement of the uninhabited Critter icons. We placed a set of Voiceholders randomly in the worlds, then Brenda Laurel donned a helmet and moved the Voiceholders to where she wanted the various Critters to be, and we replaced the Voiceholders with Critters. This was a small presage of what it might be like to fluidly design from within an immersive environment, as opposed to painfully and explicitly calculating coordinates at a desk.

Another painful part of the construction was the process of capturing the environments and turning them into data structures. A tremendous amount of imprecise handwork was involved, from camera positioning to wireframe design. Automating this process is clearly possible, using computer-controlled cameras and techniques such as deriving information about depth from stereo imagery.

Spatialized Audio

Fully spatialized audio was produced by using Crystal River Engineering (CRE) Convolvotrons. These are DSP subsystems that are integrated into an IBM PC clone, which acts as an audio-processing server. With these, sounds are input into a Convolvotron, along with a virtual location and an orientation of the user, and processed to correspond to how a sound would be perceived at such a distance—producing inverse square attenuation, atmospheric coloration (differential frequency attenuation), and the effects of the reflections and absorbtions of a modeled upper body and shoulders, head, and the pinnae of the ears. The Convolvotrons were indirectly controlled by the main computer used to produce the visual VR—an SGI Onyx Reality Engine—through a connection to a NeXT computer that directly controlled both their input sound sources and the location data.

Several sound sources were fed through the Convolvotrons. The first kind included the voices of the two participants from small Sony microphones we added to the Virtual Research VR helmets. This was done so that although the participants occupied differing *physical* spaces, we could map them into the same *virtual* space in a way that was coherent with their body movements within the "magic circles." A third voice, the "voice of the Goddess" (VOG), was spatialized so as to always appear to emanate within the user's own head.[4]

A second class of sounds was environmental sounds such as waterfalls, water drips, river, and wind. Some of these were recorded in the field, and some

---

4. Actually, we positioned VOG at a point 6 virtual inches *above* the head, as an annoying clipping occurred when the position was *within* the head and the participant *moved*. This was apparently a limit of the Convolvotrons' model, which does not account for sounds *inside* a head's volume.

were drawn from standard sound effects libraries. These were digitized and stored in a Macintosh equipped with a SampleCell audio card. These sounds were produced on command from the NeXT—which, in turn, was commanded by the Onyx—and fed into the Convolvotrons.

The most challenging environmental sound was that of a waterfall, which we recorded at four positions—two stereo pairs, one at the base of the falls, and one near the top. This was done so as to emulate a *field* of sound, as opposed to the usual *point* source like a voice or a drip.

Several waterfalls were recorded using a Sony D-7 DAT recorder and a variety of microphones. We compared conventional directional microphones, carefully shielded against spray,[5] and a pair of Sonic Studios head-mounted microphones. The latter proved to have superior frequency response[6] and much greater convenience and utility than the conventional shotgun microphones.[7]

The four waterfall sound sources were positioned at the four corners of the virtual waterfall. This world was composed of 30 temporally successive video fields, warped in 3-space to correspond to the actual topography of the place (with a 2× vertical exaggeration)—this world did not attempt a complete englobement in *space*, but rather it presented a dynamic loop through *time* of the flow field of the moving water.

Although the Convolvotrons are able to spatialize sounds with a reflective model, with up to six walls of differing sound reflection qualities, we used only the anechoic model for all of the sounds—although we had initially planned to use the reflective model for the cave world, a fully enclosed space in which echoes would have been evocative of "caveness." There were two reasons for this choice: First, the reflective model used much more of the computing power of the Convolvotrons, reducing the number of channels; second, it was not completely supported in the existing client on the SGI and would have required work to complete its interface. We used Yamaha sound processors to add reverb to sounds within the Cave world. This proved evocative to most participants but severely annoyed two professional musicians who objected to the sounds presented in the Cave world in an interview following their session.

There were onerous difficulties in integrating and debugging the sounds (and everything else!) within the overall system. There were entirely too many computers involved (the Onyx, a VGX to control the Onyx because its video

---

5. We used nonlubricated condoms to shield the microphones, accomplishing *safe audio recording* in very slippery and wet environs.

6. As measured by a frequency spectrum analyzer program running on one of the Convolvotron systems, they were flat from 40 Hz to 18 kHz, with a mild dip from 18 kHz to 22 kHz.

7. At Brenda's direction that I record the sound of putting one's head *into* a waterfall, I wore these into a 4°C 20-meter high waterfall under a rain poncho—*twice* since the first time I did it, I fell and accidentally turned the recorder off.

output went to the helmets, the NeXT, the two Convolvotron systems, two Macintoshes—one running Grippee server code, the other with the SampleCell audio card—and the Yamaha sound processors), with three major software subsystems held by three programmers and two minor secondary systems. Running the system took a minimum of three people in realtime to manage the various controls. Debugging the spatialized sound, especially achieving coherence with the visual VR, was extremely challenging—errors sometimes went unnoticed for days. It was striking that a visual cue would often apparently "pin" the apparent sound location but that the sound would become startlingly *more* lifelike when it *really* came from the correct location. I remember the first time that the "enticement" critter sounds were properly spatialized—and I was severely startled while "in" the Cave world by Crow's voice speaking just over and behind my left shoulder at a very close distance—I jumped, turned, and looked up, all quite involuntarily.

Ultimately, we achieved good spatialization for all of the sound sources. For example, the Hoodoo world had as one of its continuous environmental sounds a river, positioned in the far distance, corresponding to a real river in the actual place. When we asked users to close their eyes, turn around several times, and point at the river, they were able to point accurately at the apparent location.

In conclusion, I think that the use of multiple channels of spatialized sound in an environment that was integrated with the kinesthetics of participants' bodies in space was powerfully *evocative* and *pleasant*. It provided affordances both for navigation in space and for locating things that had action in the world beyond visual boundaries, it directed attention, and it enhanced conversation.

Some Notes on Perceptual Issues

The Principle of Action

The movement of the body in space creates changes in the information impinging on the ears and the eyes. These changes are very important in building the awareness of what is out "there." The psychologist James Gibson elucidated this idea for vision in his 1979 book *The Ecological Approach to Vision*. We were informed by this principle in the construction of PLACEHOLDER, both in vision and in audition.

Sound is difficult to perceive as being located at a particular place in three-dimensional space when the head and body are immobilized relative to the sound source or when there is no correlation between body movements and changes in the sound. In the real world, when the head and the body are allowed to move and change position relative to an object that makes sound, quite accurate judgments as to the direction and distance of sound sources may be made. Ordinary stereo heard through headphones does not take into account the differences in sound caused by the movements of the body in space.

Remarkably, a white noise source, which consists of random sounds of all frequencies and all phases, may be localized in space by a person—but only if he or she is able to move the head. Body movements help, too. The movement causes changes in the frequency mix; some frequencies are attenuated or diffracted by the head, the pinnae of the ears, and the torso more than others. This relative change in the mix allows the perceiver to deduce where the sound source is located despite the pure randomness of its content.

In PLACEHOLDER, we made use of technologies that track the position and orientation of the head and body and that produce synthetic changes in vision and sound that correlate with the movement of the body. Visually, this was done with the SGI Onyx Reality Engine, which computed what each eye would see from its separate position in space. Auditorially, this was accomplished with CRE Convolvotrons, which process sounds to produce the effects of the reflections, attenuations, and diffractions caused by the head, torso, and pinnae of the ears and the delays between sound arriving at the two ears separated in space. These disparate systems were tightly coupled in PLACEHOLDER to produce a high degree of coherence between vision and audition.

Achieving a sense of place requires a degree of sensitivity to sensory cues and combinatorics. For example, salient verticals and horizontals—such as trees, falling objects, and horizons—must be coherent with one another. Lack of coordination of such cues rapidly produces disorientation, sometimes results in "simulator sickness," and may even make people fall down if they are in a walking VR environment. We devoted considerable attention in PLACE-HOLDER to these issues; some world constructions were discarded because of such difficulties in achieving coherence. Each of the three final worlds had strong cues of this nature—the falling water and the flat, sharp-edged canyon floor in the waterfall world (Figure 11.5); the horizon line and visible trees in the Hoodoo world (Figure 11.6) and the flat floor in the cave world. Additionally, the orientation of the petroglyphs provided information about verticality.

We provided a strong sense of the body in a place via the spatialized sound sources. When a person stood in the center of the circle, there were sound sources in all surrounding directions that could be accurately localized. Sound sources varied in distance from zero in the case of someone putting his or her head in the waterfall near a corner; to two to ten feet for a Critter icon, Voiceholder, or Placemark; to hundreds of feet for the wandering wind sound and the distant river. For this reason, walking about quickly provided a robust feeling of spatial extent. The other participant's voice and correlated movement with the movement of the embodied Critter icon provided cues for distance and size of the space. This space could be quite extensive in the case of watching and listening to Crow fly away above the waterfall to an apparent distance

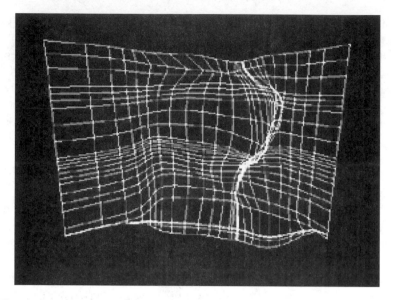

Figure 11.5   The waterfall wireframe defines a virtual relief-projection surface.

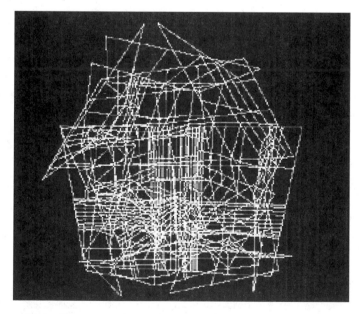

Figure 11.6   The virtual environment of the Hoodoos took the form of camera-originated images arranged in a tiled sphere.

of hundreds of feet. In the Waterfall world, the four-point sample grid that modeled the sound field of the falling water was powerfully felt to be coextensive with the moving visual flow field of the water—into which participants invariably tried to put their heads. The Voiceholders were small objects that could be walked around, peered at from more than one direction, and manipulated (albeit clumsily) and that emitted sounds that were coherent in apparent locality and temporality with visual location and appearance—in this regard, they had the greatest degree of multisensory physicality as objects.

These results of the action of the body in space and correlations with changes in the sensorium—the "Principle of Action"—mark the major defining characteristic of immersive VR as a medium. It is fundamentally different from the older technologies of television, cinema, or stereophonic music in exactly this regard. High resolution is less important than tightly coupled coherent action in the sensorium resulting from the participant's action. Adding low- or medium-resolution affordances in different senses or modalities that are coherent in their combinatorics and that follow the Principle of Action—like adding spatialized sound to stereo video—results in a greater sense of "immersion" than does ultrahigh-resolution, high-frame-rate cinema passively viewed by mass audiences. These latter expressions of the same basic technologies of wide-angle stereo visual display and multichannel sound, which do not present to individual participants the results of their bodies acting in the synthetic world, are more similar to movies than to our goals in PLACEHOLDER and have subtle political implications for the social constructions of body and self.

Reconstructing the Body

An intent in the design of PLACEHOLDER is to cause participants to become more aware of what it is to be an embodied human.

We sought to problematize issues around body and gender *in the realm of the senses* in studied contrast to the usual literary postmodern deconstructionism, which denigrates the visual sense and insists on the primacy of text and which results in a profound disembodiment of cognition and feeling.

Our approach was to remove direct visual evidence of participants' primate bodies and substitute iconic nonmammalian representations that moved through space in accordance with their actions and by a series of sensory transformations. Auditorially, we achieved this by distorting participants' voices in ways that were artistically inspired by the various Critters. One result of this was to render them difficult to identify according to gender. A series of visual mappings was designed, each loosely based on the actual psychophysics of each animal. However, only one of the planned sensory transformations was implemented (Snake's "infrared" vision) due to time constraints. For Crow, these would have included double foveation in each eye, increased specularity of reflections, and the fading from vision of stationary elements of the visual field. For Spider, we intended to emulate the vision of the jumping spider, with its multiple eyes of differing resolutions and spatial extents, merged into the single extent of the VR helmet's presentation. For Fish, we wished to provide sharper vision underwater contrasted with blurry vision out of water, combined with a gradual fading to black when out of water, countered by a "reviving" when returned to water. For Snake, we had hoped to emulate the low-resolution infrared sense that pit vipers such as rattlesnakes enjoy by virtue of the IR-sensing pits located on their snouts; this would have provided a spatially low-resolution but bright image in the Cave world. We implemented a quick hack of this, which was underwhelming.

This effort was incomplete and highly tentative; many questions remain.

Bibliography

Anderson, Sherry Ruth, and Hopkins, Patricia. *The Feminine Face of God*. New York: Bantam Books, 1991.

Baring, Anne, and Cashford, Juleps. *The Myth of the Goddess*. London: Viking Arkana, 1991.

Blauert, Jens. *Spatial Hearing*. Cambridge, Mass.: MIT Press, 1983.

Bogert, Charles Mitchell. *Sensory Cues Used by Rattlesnakes in Their Recognition of Ophidian Enemies*. New York Academy of Sciences, 1941: 329–344.

Brown, Joseph Epes. *The Spiritual Legacy of the American Indian*. New York: Crossroad, 1982.

Buser, Pierre, and Imbert, Michel. *Audition*. Cambridge, Mass.: MIT Press, 1992.

Buser, Pierre, and Imbert, Michel. *Vision*. Cambridge, Mass.: MIT Press, 1992.

Campbell, Joseph. *Historical Atlas of World Mythology, Volume I: The Way of the Animal Powers*. New York: Harper & Row, 1988.

Chatwin, Bruce. *The Songlines*. London: Cape, 1987.

Cowan, James. *Mysteries of the Dreaming: The Spiritual Life of Australian Aborigines*. Bridport, Dorset, UK: Prism Press, 1989.

Darwin, Charles. *The Expression of the Emotions in Man and Animals*. St. Martin, 1980.

de Angulo, Jaime. *Indian Tales*. New York: Hill & Wang, 1953.

Fisher, S. S., et al. "Virtual Interface Environment Workstations." Paper presented at Human Factors Society 32nd Annual Meeting. Anaheim, Calif., October 24–28, 1993.

Gibson, James. *The Ecological Approach to Vision*. Boston: Houghton Mifflin, 1979.

Gimbutas, Marija. *The Goddesses and Gods of Old Europe: Myths and Cult Images*. Berkeley, Calif.: University of California Press, 1974.

Gimbutas, Marija. *The Language of the Goddess*. San Francisco: Harper & Row, 1989.

Gombrich, E. H. "Art and Illusion: A Study in the Psychology of Pictorial Representation." *The A. W. Mellon Lectures in the Fine Arts*. National Gallery of Art, 1956. Princeton, N.J.: Princeton University Press, second edition, 1961.

Highwater, Jamake. *The Primal Mind: Vision and Reality in Indian America*. New York: Harper & Row, 1981.

Higuchi, Tadahiko. *The Visual and Spatial Structure of Landscapes*. Translated by Charles Terry. Cambridge, Mass.: MIT Press, 1983.

Klauber, Laurence Monroe. *Rattlesnakes, Their Habits, Life Histories, and Influence on Mankind*. Berkeley Calif.: University of California Press, 1982.

Land, Michael. "Vision in Other Animals." In *Images and Understanding*. Edited by Horace Barlow, Colin Blakemore, and Miranda Weston-Smith. Cambridge, England: Cambridge University Press, 1990.

Laurel, Brenda. *Computers as Theatre*. Reading, Mass.: Addison-Wesley, 1991; paperbound edition, 1993.

Lopez, Barry. *Crossing Open Ground*. New York: Charles Scribner's Sons, 1988.

Lopez, Barry. *Giving Birth to Thunder, Sleeping with His Daughter: Coyote Builds North America*. Kansas City, Mo.: Andrews & McMeel, 1977.

Marshak, Alexander. "An Ice Age Ancestor?" *National Geographic* (October 1988): 478–481.

McKenna, Terence. *The Archaic Revival*. New York: HarperCollins, 1991.

McLuhan, Marshall and Parker, Harley. *Through the Vanishing Point*. New York: Harper & Row, 1968.

Montessori, Maria. *The Discovery of the Child*. New York: Ballantine Books, 1972. ©1948.

Naimark, Michael. "Elements of Realspace Imaging: A Proposed Taxonomy." *SPIE/SPSE Electronic Imaging Proceedings*, vol. 1457. San Jose, Calif., 1991.

Naimark, Michael. "Presence at the Interface, or Sense of Place, Essence of Place." *Wide Angle*, vol. 15, no. 4. Ohio University School of Film, 1994.

Norberg-Schulz, Christian. *Genius Loci: Towards a Phenomenology of Architecture.* New York: Rizzoli, 1980.

Putman, John. "The Search for Modern Humans." *National Geographic* (October 1988): 438–476.

Rigaud, Jean. "Treasures of Lascaux Cave." *National Geographic* (October 1988): 482–497.

Sams, Jamie, and Carson, David. *Medicine Cards: The Discovery of Power Through the Ways of Animals.* Santa Fe, N.Mex.: Bear & Company, 1988.

Taylor, Rogan. *The Death and Resurrection Show.* London: Anthony Blond, 1985.

von Uexküll, Jakob. *A Stroll Through the World of Animals and Men: A Picture Book of Invisible Worlds.*

Walls, G. L. *The Vertebrate Eye and Its Adaptive Radiation.* New York: Hafner, 1963.

Wise, David H. *Spiders in Ecological Webs.* Cambridge, N.Y.: Cambridge University Press, 1993.

Biographies

Brenda Laurel is a researcher and writer whose work focuses on human-computer interaction and cultural aspects of technology. She is a Member of the research staff at Interval Research Corporation in Palo Alto, California. She is the editor of the book, *The Art of Human-Computer Interface Design* (Addison-Wesley, 1990) and author of *Computers as Theatre* (Addison-Wesley, 1991; second edition, 1993).

Rachel Strickland is an architect, videographer, and interaction designer. Her work of the past 20 years has focused on cinematic dimensions of places in people's everyday experience. She has taught film and video production at MIT and UC Santa Cruz. Before joining Interval Research Corporation, she directed interactive video projects for Apple Computer's Vivarium Program and other research labs.

Rob Tow is a researcher who has two granted and three pending patents in the realm of applied visual psychophysics and perception. He is a Member of the research staff at Interval Research Corporation in Palo Alto, California. He has worked at various research and engineering labs including Xerox PARC, Schlumberger Palo Alto Research, Compression Labs, Inc., Fairchild Camera & Instrument, and Northrop Aviation.

Chapter 12

Beyond Shoot Your Friends: A Call to Arms in the Battle Against Violence

Celia Pearce
Momentum Media Group

Violence in Games: The Dirty Family Secret

Violence in games has become the proverbial "elephant in the living room" of the entertainment industry. Not unlike incest, alcoholism, or wife beating, it's the dirty family secret we see but choose to ignore. Occasionally, we stop to ask ourselves, "Why is this so?" only to resume as if the thought had never crossed our minds. Somehow, we excuse ourselves with rationalizations that allow us to walk away with the delusion that everything is "just fine."

So the question is, What are we going to do about it? Because the problem is, even if we acknowledge that there's something horribly wrong here, we seem baffled as to how to change things. This chapter is an attempt to shine some light so that we may understand exactly why we do what we do. My hope is that this leads us to make more conscious choices about our actions in this industry, rather than feeling strapped into a runaway roller coaster, repeating the same path. This world of simulated death and mayhem is, in fact, a world we've all made, and if we want it to change, we in the game industry are the ones who must change it.

Why Are Video Games So Violent?

At the SIGGRAPH '94 course "Digital Illusion," a woman who was written off as a hot-headed "feminist" (and probably rightly so—I can say that because I'm one myself) stood up during the Q & A period and posed the query, "Why are video games so violent?"

Three different individuals, presumably game designers, stood up to speak in their own defense. Not surprisingly, they were all male. The first responded with the classic argument, "It's what the market wants." Another responded with the couch potato's lament, "We don't know why, we just do it." And the final statement, addressing the gender gap issue, was, "We all know that Tetris is the most popular game among women, but nobody knows why." Together, these three statements amount to the platform upon which the entire violence-in-games tradition is erected.

I begin by taking these questions head-on, followed by a study of some of the social, historical, and psychological issues that conspire to maintain the prevalence of violence in gaming, with an emphasis on multiplayer games. I will also attempt to offer some alternative scenarios for better, more productive approaches to multiuser interactivity.

"It's what the market wants."

In the computer gaming industry, the term "market" is a euphemism. When someone talks about the video game "market," we all know what they are talking about. The image that comes to mind is the classic pimply-faced video gamester who can't get enough of Mortal Kombat and Street Fighter, feeding quarters into an arcade game like a gambler at a slot machine or sitting at home shooting frantically at the television set. I'm speaking of the world's most innocent and maligned victim of demographic opportunism: the ever-vulnerable, ever-receptive, ever-predictable adolescent male.

The adolescent male *is* the computer game market, to the utter exclusion of the entire rest of the human population—including his female counterpart. By way of illustrating my point, let me provide a little anecdote. Some time back, I was asked to pay a visit to the arcade division of a major game company. I had been invited there by a marketing executive who was interested in creating games for girls. We met with the senior manager in the division, who made two statements that I'll never forget. The first was, "Girls? What do I care about girls? They're only 5 percent of my market." The second was, "Our job is to take lunch money away from 14-year-old boys."

The first statement, typical in this testosterone-centered world, is odd considering that females make up about 52 percent of the population. Furthermore, if you visit arcades at all, you'll notice that there *are* actually girls there—accompanying their boyfriends or male friends—but they rarely actually play the games. Even more interesting is the implication of the second statement—that teenage girls are not as stupid and gullible as teenage boys or that perhaps they just have less "lunch money" (disposable income) to waste on developing carpal-tunnel syndrome. I would be hard-pressed to say who these two statements belittle more—the deprived teenage girl forced to spend her lunch money on lunch or the hypnotized teenage boy who prefers to starve for the opportunity to kick someone's face in on a video screen.

What is it about adolescent males that causes tunnel vision in those who determine which concepts will be produced and which tossed in the dustbin? What's at the root of this passionate romance between the game companies and teenage boys? What is it that makes boys tantamount to a flock of "Little Red Riding Hoods" navigating a forest full of wolves with names that end in vowels? You don't have to be Freud to isolate some commonsense answers to these conundrums.

Adolescents, in general, exist in a state of agitated vulnerability and insecurity. This makes them sitting ducks for advertisers, who prey on their sense of inadequacy and their acute fear of social and sexual failure. In fact, video games fulfill some strong, almost overpowering, needs in the adolescent male.

A primary motivation among this group is the need for sexual sublimation. I don't think I'm shocking anyone when I say that video games provide teenage boys with a form of electronic masturbation, a high-tech outlet for otherwise out-of-control hormonal oscillations. The second motivation is to offer them an escape from the ever-frightening female, the object of both attraction and fear (assuming we're talking about heterosexual teenage boys).

A secondary concern for the teenage boy is the "cult of masculinity." Most video games, like comic books and action figures, provide an exaggerated caricature of the male form. Bulging, rippling muscles have grown to mutant proportions, and the women featured in such games and comic books are generally a strange hybrid of hyperfeminine and fe-masculine—preternaturally alert breasts, combat lingerie, big biceps, and a penchant for kicking men in the face, thereby giving a better view of their crotches. (What is this female paradigm teaching boys about women?) One wonders how much the appeal of this exaggerated maleness for the teenage boy has to do with his pubescent state in which he is neither man nor boy.

Perhaps the hypermasculine is a role model, something to aspire to, a pure form of masculinity that is totally distinct and unrelated to anything feminine. For the teenage male, this hypermasculinity seems to give him an anchor during the period when he's unsure where he falls on the boy/man scale. At the same time, he's acquiring a limited repertoire of confrontational skills from characters who speak mostly with their fists.

Once these boys are seduced, which isn't difficult, they quickly become addicted. In fact, my first response to the argument "It's what the market wants" is always, "The market wants crack, but that doesn't mean we should make more of it."

"What the market wants" is a self-fulfilling prophecy. We, "the industry," decide what goes to market, we watch how it sells, and if it sells well, we just make more of the same. Like drug pushers, the marketing people recognize that once you get someone hooked, you have a customer for life, until, of course, they die—or, in the case of video games, grow up.

In spite of the arguments by the "bottom-line" people that violence sells, let's look at the facts. It's true that Doom and Mortal Kombat are among the top-selling games. But so are Myst and Seventh Guest, two games totally unsellable by conventional marketing wisdom. The market for these games happens to include a few other demographics besides teenage boys. Take Myst, a game lacking all the elements deemed necessary for a game to be popular: It has no violence, no action—in fact, it has barely any motion at all. Instead, players encounter a series of beautifully rendered still frames that present a story, a mystery to be solved. There's no thumb candy here. Furthermore, Myst is no less addictive than a martial arts game and appeals to a much wider audience. As a result, it's one of the best-selling CD-ROM games of all time.

"We don't know why, we just do it."

At first blush, this argument appears even thinner than "It's what the market wants." Don't be deceived. It may turn out to be the more honest and accurate response.

It's a sad state of affairs, one I've been observing for some years now. I have friends who work at companies that primarily produce violent games. Most of these individuals are pacifists—pro gun control, against capital punishment. In time, some develop that shadow over their brows—the result of being stuck in a job they can't really put their hearts and souls into but they're doing because there's money to be made. Some don't have a problem (and even enjoy) creating content that contradicts their sociopolitical views. But I've also seen former multimedia visionaries who literally "sold out"—people who once advocated content, story, and character but now speak only of stock options and corporate perks. They love to talk about the technology, the cool effects, the quality of the realtime 3D animation, blue-screen compositing, motion capture, spatialized sound, and, lately, high-end multiuser VR capabilities. "Isn't this cool?" they say, as another body is blown to digital bits in hi-rez 3D.

Why do we push the envelope only to simulate Neolithic behavior? Why are we using some of the most advanced technologies to do little more than blow each other away? It's as if, as our tools evolve, our content and sensibilities devolve. We live in a violent and dangerous world. Why is it that the people who develop ever more advanced methods for recreating reality are creating realities that, in the real world, we are trying to escape? Why not, instead, create from our imaginations better, more positive realities that might help us envision a better world or learn new and more productive ways of interacting?

These questions are rhetorical, but they also have answers. One of them is that the *real* reason why video game designers create violent games is not because the market wants it, but because it's *easier*. It's the same reason we say we hate television but watch it anyway—because it's easier to watch it and hate it than to turn the damn thing off or, better yet, create things for it that we can love.

Imagine yourself trying to figure out a compelling goal for a game, something that will really get people excited and involved, something that will make them forget everything and be totally drawn in. The most visceral and essential instinct in the world is "kill or be killed." There is no more compelling motivation known to humanity. In multiplayer games today, if you look closely, you'll discover they're really all the same game. With few exceptions, there are actually only four multiplayer games: shoot, kick, race, and play ball (also a form of combat). Within each category, they have the same goal. All that distinguishes one from the next are game details, successively higher levels of resolution, speed, and three-dimensionality. From a game design point of view, what's the difference between Street Fighter and Mortal Kombat? The only discernible difference is the level of detail of the blood and guts, which are, ironically, the reward. Doom and Terminator are high-tech shooting galleries; the only advantage Doom has is that it's 3D. BattleTech, the location-based VR game, is just a shooting gallery with "live" moving targets—controlled by other people. You could as easily be shooting wooden ducks at Coney Island.

Racing and sports games suffer equally from a lack of original content. I once met with game designers from one of the largest CD-ROM game companies, who told me soccer was their best-selling game. I congratulated them and pointed out that they hadn't invented soccer but merely ported one of the most popular sports in the world to a computer.

My point is this: It comes down to a matter of pure and simple laziness. If designers put as much energy into coming up with unique content and game structure as they do into high-tech gizmos and special effects, we might find ourselves with a much broader array of options on the game shelf of our local Blockbuster.

Good games that are not violent can sell just fine. In the CD-ROM arena, nonviolent games have actually been the standard for a long time. This has to do, in part, with available resources. With such an abundance of storage and an I/O bottleneck, there's good reason to emphasize story, lush graphics, and personality development. We've seen many fine games, some of which, such as SimCity, have maintained popularity for many years. Children's games, such as Indiana Jones and Putt Putt, have also done well and have demonstrated a clear market for strong content. In the past couple of years, however, CD-ROMs have begun to adapt to the "game machine" market with "Doom" and hybrid content/violence games like "Phantasmagoria."

But, in the consumer game arena, we're just seeing more of the same. Designers are not really designing new games, and publishers aren't supporting them. There was a time when game companies were willing to go out on a limb with new ideas like Pac-Man or Centipede. But, like the movie industry they now outgross, the game industry has become increasingly risk-averse. Remember, though, it's the design that drives the games. Game designers are the ones who ultimately start the process of change—not publishers. Myst wasn't developed by a publisher and was only taken on by a major one after it had built a reputation on its own. Violent games are also design driven. There will always be a push-pull between designers who want to design quality and risk-averse publishers who will point to the "market" for more likely profits. The latter strategy is rarely valid in the long term. Both parties must work together to make an impact, which they certainly have the power to do, and that power will only increase as other forms of interactive media enter the mainstream.

"Tetris is the most popular game among women, but nobody knows why."

If that notion ever crossed your mind, consider this deep thought: Just because you don't know something yourself doesn't mean nobody else does.

When I started working for Edwin Schlossberg, Inc. in 1983, I spent a lot of time at Playland Arcade in Times Square watching people (mostly the "market") playing video games. One game stood out because it was the only one that seemed to attract girls. It was Atari's Pac-Man—and the companion game, Ms. Pac-Man. (Why they didn't call it "Pac-Woman" remains a mystery.) Girls loved the original version, and I suppose Ms. Pac-Man was an attempt to take more lunch money from the female teen contingent.

At that time, I did a lot of playtesting of the games we designed, and I studied numerous articles and papers on the subject. One of the reasons cited for Pac-Man's popularity was the fact that girls preferred collection to shooting as an activity. Pac-Man was about picking things up rather than blowing them away. It also had friendly, appealing characters—even the "bad guy" creatures were cute.

The reason "nobody knows why" Tetris is so popular is that so few game designers take the time to study girls. On the other hand, most arcade and cartridge companies employ armies of young men to spend hours playing and reviewing their games. I doubt very much that Tetris was designed as a girl's game any more than Pac-Man, but the reasons for its female appeal are clear. It possesses two highly appealing attributes to women—puzzle solving and assembling.

One myth that ought to be dispelled at once and for which there is no factual basis is the strange notion that women do not own or use computers.

Women are in the majority of computer users in the workplace. And according to a March 1995 survey in *Marketing to Women* magazine, 24.4 percent of American women own computers versus 28.9 percent of men. This isn't a wide enough gap to imply that women don't have access to hardware. What differs is how they use them. According to the study, women use computers more for writing, drawing, and sending e-mail but less for recreation. In my own informal surveys, I hear time and again, "There's no recreational software that interests me" (with exceptions like Tetris). In addition, if you look at technology in general, you'll find that women are historically quite at ease and skilled with devices such as typewriters, word processors, and telephones—all gadgets whose aim is communication.

The other myth that warrants correction is that men buy more media overall than women. Several studies I've read state that, in fact, women consume more books, videos, and films than men. The only entertainment medium in which men outpurchase women is computer software.

So, let's get down to basics. What follows are rules of thumb I've picked up from research and my own testing. The best way to view it is via comparison, and these are by no means hard and fast rules. There are girls who love to play "twitch" games (emphasizing reflexes over strategy). These are generalizations that can be used as a toolkit for broadening the appeal of computer games.

Two major issues in appealing to women are value and aesthetics. Women like things they feel will add some value to their life rather than things they feel are "time wasters." They also want their entertainment experience to be aesthetically appealing in both sight and sound. Studies of children also show that, even on the playground or in the nursery, games in which winning is the goal are about half as appealing to girls as to boys. Girls enjoy play activities and, when winning is the object, don't emphasize the winner.

In the computer world, where hand-eye games are concerned, men prefer games with a clear and finite goal, such as "kill or be killed," "shoot at this," or "eliminate these." Women prefer activities that involve assembling, collecting, creating, or constructing. Women are not as interested in the idea of beating a machine; they prefer open-ended activities with cumulative results. Women prefer a reward structure to one based on penalty, becoming frustrated by games in which they must repeatedly die or begin a game again. Men, on the other hand, find strong motivation in being penalized and even killed, which they see as a challenge. Women like to solve puzzles and mysteries. In narrative games, women like emphasis on character and story and on psychology and relationships, while men prefer the more goal-oriented story in which you have to do a series of things to avoid dying or to save someone else.

Even if you tackle these issues and begin to address these variances in play styles, there's another fundamental issue that is, I believe, the real heart of the problem. Although I have yet to see any studies done, my own research and testing have led me to the following conclusion: I believe that most women are fundamentally disinterested in a one-on-one interaction with the computer as a form of recreation. Women just plain don't get off on electronic masturbation.

Many psychological and social studies of girls in all stages of development, as well as grown women, have demonstrated the female orientation toward community and communication. This is why women derive less enjoyment from games oriented toward winning. Because their priority is building community rather than competing on an individual level, women tend to prefer collaboration to solitary activities, cooperation to competition, and communication to isolation. Bonding with others is a primary goal in the female value system.

This tells us that there is something inherently unfemale about the entire concept of a single-player game. And, if you watch patterns of play in girls and women, you'll find many women play single-player games in pairs. Even in out-of-home multiplayer games, the isolation of being in a pod doesn't satisfy the female desire for social contact.

As Creative Director of the multiplayer VR game Virtual Adventures, I saw this hypothesis played out again and again. Women liked being able to see and hear other people *within* the vehicle, and they felt completely at home with the teamwork required to accomplish the goal of the game. Because it's family oriented, women can play with their children or spouses, and it gives them a different kind of bonding experience, one based on productive collaboration. The more female-friendly player positions, such as a commander whose role is to verbally coordinate the activities of the team, or a claw operator for collection of eggs, add to the appeal. In observing women playing Battletech, I've seen most of them find the game frustrating and unsatisfying since the entire emphasis is on the relationship with a machine and the destruction of other players—two activities that go against the female grain. Isolation and lack of available cooperation from others add to the aggravation.

This fundamental issue must be addressed in order to really expand the games market to women. Even if a woman is in relative isolation, the minute you introduce experiences that are about communication, empathy, and bonding, she's right at home. You begin to see this when you visit online chat rooms or multiuser text-based games. Realtime text communication is a natural for the female, and women are flourishing on the Internet. We can use this as a role model if we're to expand the game market to include the other 53 percent of the population.

I'm biased toward multiplayer games since that's my experience base. But I also think it's no accident that I have little interest in designing single-player games, let alone playing them. After testing and watching literally hundreds of people, both male and female, playing a wide range of different multiplayer games, I'm convinced that multiuser interactivity is the answer to the "female problem." Games with cooperation and team play invariably win women over, especially if the content is oriented toward their values and priorities.

A History of Recreational Violence

Looking to the Past for Answers About the Future

Due to our almost pathological preoccupation with the future, as well as a national bias toward memory loss, many in the computer industry tend to be myopic when it comes to the history of our craft. The moment I'm called upon to think about the future, I invariably start by looking for answers in the past. I have to ask myself, How did we get where we are? Only then can I get a realistic fix on what can be done to change things.

If looked at in historical context, it turns out that the question "Why are video games so violent?" is not as much of a riddle as it seems. It relates to the answer "We don't know why, we just do it." In fact, much of the reason "we just do it" is that that's the primary way it's been done for as long as anyone can remember—or, in this case, forget. I can think of no better way to formulate a strategy for the future than to look at the path that led us here.

The Uphill Battle Against Violence

I mentioned earlier that the promulgation of violent games can be boiled down to laziness on the part of designers and that it can be compared to complaining about television but watching it anyway. It's important to realize that the history of gaming, in virtually every aspect, is riddled with violence—and so, for that matter, is the history of media. Therefore, the task of creating new paradigms is an uphill battle (and, no—the irony of that metaphor hasn't escaped me). Take it from someone who was once asked if she would be interested in making a theme park ride based on a game like Doom. No thanks. I'll forego the lunch money.

Though I may seem critical of my colleagues in this industry, I provide the following historical overview by way of acknowledging that this snowball has been rolling downhill for a very long time. To stop it or change its direction will require a concerted effort. We know how difficult it is to swim against the tide of history—and yet how necessary at times. So, here's some history of that tide.

Games as War Simulations

If you've spent any time studying games—and I mean the 5,000 years of gaming that preceded the invention of the computer—you're probably already aware of the fact that virtually all classic board games are actually war simulations. Although it evolved into a form of recreation, the game board began as a metaphor for the battlefield. Chess, checkers, backgammon, go, even playing cards, all of these are war games. Long before we had computers, we were making violent games. It's just that the violence was metaphorical, less literal, and more strategically oriented than the visceral forms we're able to create today.

The ancients of both hemispheres also had their own version of Mortal Kombat featuring real avatars in the form of gladiators, jousters, and boxers. These, combined with military training maneuvers, evolved into team sports that used the playing field as the metaphor for the battlefield. Thus, the majority of competitive team sports we have now, and many we've had in the past, also had their origins as war simulations.

Violence in the Media

Aside from violence in gaming, let's look at media for a moment. The modern notion that there's more violence in media today than ever before is another demonstration of historical myopia. There is no more violence in the media today—there's just more media.

Consider Homer—the *Odyssey* is incredibly violent. (Thank Goddess, Homer was blind.) The Old Testament is just one big epic war story. Half of Shakespeare's plays end in a bloodbath, as is the romance of *Romeo and Juliet*. Everyone's dead by the end of the play.

In addition, *actual violence* was a popular form of entertainment in ancient times, much more so than today. I mentioned gladiators and jousters; in Roman times, Christians were thrown to the lions. In the Middle Ages, beheadings and mutilations were a popular spectator activity, not to mention burnings at the stake. And let's not forget about the entertaining crucifixions two millennia ago.

All told, there simply isn't more violence, though it may be more explicit—which leads us to the conclusion that there's a deep human need to express violence in some way. Whether this is something we're capable of evolving beyond remains to be seen. And perhaps we have, at least, evolved to the point where more of our violence is vicarious than actual, although there are several new studies being done to chart the relationship between the two.

"Boys like to shoot."

My comeback to the Tetris question these days is, "We all know boys like to shoot, but nobody knows why."

Perhaps Freud would be better qualified to discuss this than I, but it's a universal axiom. Whether due to nature or nurture, boys begin to shoot from a very early age, turning everything from a mailing tube to a finger into a gun in order to partake in this pastime. Shooting for the sake of mere amusement has always been popular, from archery to skeet to the shooting galleries at every American carnival and boardwalk.

I've always been of the opinion that this deep love of shooting is at the root of the obsession with warfare, from the cold war to the gang war. It's not so much that men like to kill or even that they really crave power or territory. They're merely looking for an excuse to shoot. Regardless of the mode, whether analog or digital, whether lethal, recreational, or both, I think most males find inherent psychophysical enjoyment in the act of shooting, a raw unadulterated pleasure that the majority of females do not share.

Interactive Television—Shoot the TV

Bearing in mind this love of shooting, we shouldn't be surprised that the first indication we had of interaction with our television was to go from passively watching to actually shooting at it. The remote control is a laser gun, of course, and shooting at the screen is also a popular modality of many home video games: "Hey everybody, let's shoot the TV." (I could get into a tangent here about trying to assert power over the object that has, in the past, held us in hypnotic tyranny, or I could present my theory that there's so much shooting on TV that game players have become jealous. But I won't.)

We've covered a lot of ground thus far. We've talked about the roots of war simulation in precomputer games, we've talked about violence in the media, recreational violence, and the love of shooting. With all these critical elements in place, enter the computer . . .

A Brief History of Computer Games

Spacewar!

As a starting point, it's helpful to recall that virtually everything being done today in electronic media has roots in the military. Many of us computer nerds are quintessential peaceniks, but the computer itself was developed primarily as a military tool. When looked at in this light, it becomes clear how we got where we are and why it's so hard to go elsewhere.

It's time for a history lesson. The first record we have of computer gaming was the attempt by MIT's John McCarthy, inventor of the term "artificial intelligence," to write a program that would enable the IBM 704 computer (known as the Hulking Giant) to play chess, roundabout 1959. A few of McCarthy's grad students were even able to hack out a Ping-Pong type of game using the blinking lights on the 704. Two other early gamelike programs were Bouncing Ball and Mouse in the Maze. Bouncing Ball was a simple program on the Whirlwind computer that bounced a dot around on the screen. Mouse in the Maze, perhaps a precursor to Pac-Man, ran on a TX-O and allowed you to draw a maze with a light pen, place some cheese wedges in it, and then watch a styl-ized mouse move through and gobble up the cheese. A VIP version featured martinis, with the mouse growing increasingly more inebriated from one drink to the next, an early and ingenious example of adjusting skill curve. A few other activities were devised during that time, including Marvin Minsky's Minskytron, which drew designs based on points positioned by the user. All computer games at that time involved iterations of an individual doing some-thing to which the computer would respond.

Then, in 1961, Spacewar!, acknowledged as the first multiplayer, realtime computer game, was created (Figure 12.1). It was developed by a group calling themselves the "Hingham Institute Study Group on Space Warfare"—actually a bunch of MIT hackers obsessed with cheesy sci-fi movies who lived in a tene-ment on Hingham Street. Over a period of several months in 1961, they de-vised a wild scenario for a sci-fi game, but it wasn't until the fall that they met the machine of their dreams—the PDP-1. It had everything they wanted: speed, power, and a CRT screen! (The screen, incidentally, was circular.)

Spearheaded by Stephen R. Russel (aka "Slug"), Spacewar! was a multi-player game based on various vector codes. At that time, pretty much all you could do on a computer screen was create vectors, but the game included rock-

Figure 12.1 Spacewar! being played on a PDP-1 on March 27, 1983, by Alan Kotok, Steve Russel, and Shag Gratz. Reprinted with permission of The Computer Museum, Boston.

ets, missiles, and a totally accurate starscape. It evolved strategic elements and, in the end, was quite complex. It was the first game that had realtime *and* multiplayer interaction using input devices hacked from model-railroad switching hardware—and it revolved around shooting.

Pong and the Birth of the Consumer Computer Game

Computer games, though often simple, were not always as violent as they are today. Pong, invented by Atari's Nolan Bushnell in 1972, was similar to MIT's Bouncing Ball and revolutionized the arcade industry. Prior to Pong, arcades were full of pinball, Foosball, and air hockey machines. A tabletop game, it appeared not only in arcades but also in pizza parlors and bars; you could actually sit and eat while playing it with friends. Using a flat paddle controlled with a knob, you knocked a "ball" back and forth, creating a sound something like "pong" with each impact. Fun and simple, it hit home systems in 1974 when cheap microchips became available. Pong, incidentally, appealed to both genders and all ages—part of its inherent charm.

After Pong, virtually all subsequent computer games developed in the 1970s and 1980s were single-player or turn-based games. Akin to Spacewar! were Asteroids, in which you shot at meteorites, and Space Invaders, in which you shot at alien spaceships. Space Invaders was one of the first games that employed the computer's unique ability to adjust the skill level of a game to meet a player's own changing skills during play, speeding up as he or she got better at protecting cities from the onslaught of oncoming invaders. In Centipede, the centipede would try to eat you. Each time you shot it, it split, until there were dozens of centipedes, thereby creating an increase in game challenge. An early arcade game I recall from the late 1970s was Death Race 2000, based on a film of the same name. In it, you drove around in a formula car trying to run down pedestrians. Whenever you hit one, the pedestrian turned into a tombstone, thereby becoming an obstacle in the game. The more tombstones, the harder it was to run down pedestrians—another elegant example of an inherent skill curve built into a game structure.

Pac-Man, the hit game of 1981, eventually became the most popular arcade game of all time. It's probably the only arcade game in history that had a solid female audience, so much so that it spawned a game that was actually targeted *to* women. In the days before "feminist" was a dirty word, the Ms. Pac-Man game developed a strong following. The goal of both games was to move through a series of mazes, eating fruit along the way and shooting at little creatures who would try to eat *you*. For some reason, the overwhelming commercial success of this game never translated into an awareness that women could be a market for arcade games, and so it goes.

Throughout the 1970s and 1980s, single-player games for both arcades and the home flourished and were fairly equally divided between violent and non-violent content. Donkey Kong, Pitfall, and Marble Madness stood shoulder to shoulder with Gauntlet, Lode Runner, and Combat. It wasn't until the late 1980s and early 1990s, coincidentally, after the video game market crashed in 1984, that we started seeing multiplayer games in arcades again—and this time, they were all about fighting and combat.

Virtual Violence

We all know the earliest virtual reality systems were developed for training military personnel. Ivan Sutherland first conceived a workable immersive head-mounted display (HMD) way back in 1968 and actually built it in 1971 (although Mort Heilig had patented an HMD for 3D television display in 1960). His company, Evans and Sutherland, also developed the cockpit display for flight simulators. The early systems started out simple and rough but have evolved to the level where we can create incredibly compelling three-dimensional experiences. The advantage of using this kind of system in military training is that you can model various military situations and "play them out" in a variety of ways, making your mistakes in the safety of your head-mounted display or simulated cockpit. This element of "safe danger" allows for elaborate training techniques in which you can crash a plane while learning to fly without actually dying—or, worse yet, destroying expensive equipment. These techniques were also employed in commercial pilot and NASA training.

I would love to know how much money has been spent by the military on VR since Ivan Sutherland coined the term some 20 years ago. Virtual reality is the ultimate manifestation of what the military research side of computer technology hoped to create—the ability to practice killing without killing, to be killed without dying, to experience the reality of war without entering the battlefield. The dream of creating brilliant military machines has been realized.

It's therefore no wonder that the inclination when creating VR experiences for entertainment has been to create simulations of battle or combat. There are a few artists and eccentrics who have been creating other types of virtual reality for years, but most of the entertainment applications have been derived from military paradigms. Only recently, in fact, has realtime 3D graphics been used in racing simulator games: The result is now a strong presence in arcades.

Battletech was the first location-based, multiuser VR product developed for recreational purposes. First opened in Chicago in August 1990, it can handle up to 16 players. Each player gets inside a small, enclosed pod stuffed to the girders with rocker switches and displays laid out in an elaborate control panel with realtime maps. The action takes place on a monitor/viewport in front of them.

The players take on the roles of high-tech robots in a postapocalyptic cyber-space desert devoid of signs of human activity. The goal is to enter this environment and blow away everyone else on the playing field, repeatedly. The sheer quantity of ways to do this is mind-boggling. You can use dozens of different combinations of guns. Before starting a game, you can select from a menu of six different robot models, each configured in five different combinations of weaponry and armor.

Whenever you get hit, of course, you lose some capability. If hit enough times, you blow up, in which case the "capsule" you are riding in spins up into the air and reenters the home base to be mounted on another body and create further mayhem. This interpretation of Hindu reincarnation is a common element in computer games. One of the things we love about computers is that they allow you to die repeatedly and come back to life—unless you run out of time or money.

A nice feature of the game is that when you get a target in your viewer, the name of your victim (generally a computer "handle") appears on your screen. I like this personal touch. I like to know precisely who I'm killing.

The most interesting thing about the Battletech experience is what happens afterward. When you are done fighting in this high-tech free-for-all, you go out to watch a bird's-eye reenactment of your battle and get a statistic sheet showing exactly who you hit and how many times and who hit you and how effectively. The conversations sound something like this: "Oh, that was you who shot my arm off. Oh, God, I killed you like five times! This is when we all ganged up on you."

It was to Battletech that I first attached the moniker "Shoot Your Friends," which I've been using to describe violent VR games ever since.

The designers went to great lengths to develop and describe the "Battle-mechs," which you select at the start of each game. Once inside the pod, it's almost impossible to figure out what's going on. In fact, the real enjoyment of the game comes only after a few plays, when you finally get used to the hypersensitive-yet-klunky controls. Behind the success of Battletech is a strong following of hardcore repeat players.

There is ostensibly a storyline to the game, but it's mainly delivered in the form of books. Correct me if I'm wrong, but doesn't it seem unlikely that denizens of this cybergladiator game are avid readers? This audience consists of what I call "arcade graduates," guys who are now old enough to date but would still rather play with computers. They tend to be college boys and twentysomethings. It's certainly not a game for women, though it has always had a handful of female followers.

Much to its credit, however, Battletech managed to build quite a cult following at the flagship site in Chicago. Since then, they have repositioned themselves and created a themed environment called Virtual World, a mall-based center where you can play Battletech and their newer game, Red Planet, a race through the canals of Mars. They've seen a slight increase in female attendance as a result of this.

In spite of the elaborate redesign, the real beauty of the game is its primal appeal. The designers have gone to great effort to decorate the game; they have an exhibit, a story line, all sorts of books and ancillary products, and a highly themed lounge environment. None of this is reflected in the content or aesthetics of the game itself. Battletech is a shooting gallery where you are both shooter and target, a high-tech Neanderthal dressed up in fancy clothes. If one is going to all this trouble, why not apply some effort to making a *game* that is a little more sophisticated?

The Military Entertainment Complex

Remember the Cold War? (It was another case of "We don't know why, we just do it.") For those of you old enough to remember, you'll recall the rejoicing when the thing we most dreamed of but dared not hope for actually happened. The nuclear standoff was over, and the cold war ended. This was a time of rejoicing—or was it? In the United States, the celebration was tainted by a harsh reality—that, since the 1950s, we had developed a market system based on operating a wartime economy in peacetime. We spent billions on the military without actually being in a full-scale war.

The end of the cold war resulted in "military downsizing," which left a whole lot of military contractors in the lurch. So, they looked around and they asked themselves, What can we do to maintain our business? What are we going to do with these fancy gizmos we've been developing? And the most important question of all, *Who but the military can afford us?*

The answer was, of course, the entertainment industry. And thus, the Military Entertainment Complex was born.

Toward a New Model:
Creating a New Paradigm for Multiuser Interactivity

In 1993, I had the pleasure to serve as Creative Director for a VR project called "Virtual Adventures," a codevelopment of Iwerks Entertainment and Evans and Sutherland. One reason this was such an amazing opportunity was that, as a young game designer in the early 1980s, one of my assignments was to research military simulation. In my research, I found out that the military was hoarding a treasure trove of cool computer gewgaws. I also found out we would never have access to them, let alone even know what they were. At that time, everything was top secret.

When I came to work on Virtual Adventures, I felt like a kind of nerd-fairy princess. I had developed a couple of VR concepts in the past but never saw one through to completion. Here I was, asked to take one of the most powerful military simulation systems in the world and make it into a game. Not only that, but it had to be a nonviolent, story-based game, a game that women would want to play.

It was a pleasure to work with the E&S crew, who made a nice transition from thousand-page military specifications to my less concrete world of entertainment. I would say things like "We need to make the water look buoyant" and they would look at me and shake their heads. They also gave me a two-hour crash course in virtual reality during a Mecklermedia VR World conference in San Jose. It's to their credit, particularly Joyce Mellus and Kellan Hatch, that this clueless technophobe became an instant expert on the finer points of designing realtime 3D graphics, polygon budgets, and texture mapping.

An interesting aspect of this project was that the entire Iwerks/E&S alliance was violently opposed to violence in the game. This opinion was particularly strong from the E&S team, who I think were looking for a change of scenery and were therefore pretty hard-core about making a politically correct, nonviolent VR game that would be family oriented.

I liken this entire process to hammering swords into plowshares. Virtual Adventures handles up to 24 players in up to four teams of six in vehicles where each person has a control device. There are two robot arms for picking up objects, two periscopes (up and down), an interactive map, and so on. The game is competitive between teams and cooperative within teams. As far as I'm aware, there has been no other VR game developed to date with such a combination of features. The idea was to create a story in which you do something positive—in this case, rescue the Loch Ness Monster's eggs from bounty hunters. To each team, their own ship looks like a "good guy" yellow rescue vehicle and the other ships look like rusty "bad guy" hunters' ships ("just like real life," one of my students recently pointed out).

There is, of course, shooting in the game. This could not be avoided. In order to address this issue, I developed what I called "nonlethal immobilizing gel," or "gloop." The colorful gel has two purposes in the game. One, you can splat it on your opponents' windshield to obscure their view. (A windshield wiper allows them to remove it.) Two, you can use it to shoot at sea creatures that might be attacking either you or Nessie's eggs. The week I wrote the twelve-page "gloop spec" for Evans and Sutherland, all I could say was, "I love this job!"

A few other explosive features were added later because there was a perceived need for more "excitement" in the game—underwater mines that blow you to the surface of the water and gloop torpedoes that let you do the same to another ship if things get really ugly.

What's special about the game is that the players become characters within a story. I remember watching sections of the movie *The Abyss* when we were working on the game, and I wanted the players inside the vehicle to feel like the characters in the film, particularly the dynamic that happens when a group is pulling together toward a common urgent goal.

The underlying premise is that there are six people sharing a vehicle. The motivation for this was primarily economic. Image generators are very expensive, too expensive to allow one per person. This way, six people can share a single piece of equipment, thereby bringing down the cost per seat. The by-product of this is a design that has significant advantages from an experiential and game-play point of view. This was the first shared-vehicle VR game. Now, other VR developers are beginning to devise two-person pods, but none have a group as big as six. I also think it's the reason that, in early tests of the product prototype, women actually rated the product slightly higher than men. So much for 5 percent of the market!

There are many different ways to interact in this game. You can pick a more or less aggressive position. You can take a position that requires hand-eye coordination or one that's more about navigation or communication. You can drive or observe. It's fun to watch how people rise to the occasion—how perfect strangers pull together and sometimes spontaneously develop characters around their selected game roles. You can pick different ways to interact with the system but, much more importantly, different ways to interact with one another. Unlike games where the complexity lies in how you kill, the complexity here involves both a group goal and an individual goal for each player.

Team-to-team interactivity also differs significantly from one-on-one interactivity. In a one-on-one situation, there is a sense of "every man for himself." In a team, the odds become more balanced; you can help one another; your lack of skills can be compensated for by your teammates, and you can quickly help newer players learn the game. You also have voice communication with the opposing teams, which serves to personalize even the competitive interaction.

All of this is by way of presenting some viable alternatives to "shoot your friends." It's quite possible to develop good interactive games that aren't violent. It just takes a little ingenuity and the willingness to try something different. It also doesn't mean the annihilation of old techniques. As we learned with Virtual Adventures, shooting is still one of the easiest things you can do with a computer. It has innate appeal that can't be denied. But there are other reasons to hit a target than "search and destroy." Since working on Virtual Adventures, I've put together a list I call "101 Non-Lethal Uses for a Projectile." There are many other targeting activities that can be integrated into games, and there's a growing group of designers committed to developing new paradigms. Although I enjoy the lack of competition, I would be happier if there were more. I can only hope this inspires a few.

Now That We've Surveyed the Past, Let's Return to the Future . . .

My mantra lately has been "The best way to predict the future is to create it." Not original, I know, but it works.

There are many unpleasant things in our culture that we, as mere computer nerds, don't have the power to change. However, there are a handful of things we *can* do. And one of them is to expand the repertoire of gaming to include activities other than shooting, killing, and beating each other to a pulp. There are enough nonviolent human activities to model from to keep us busy for a long, long time.

We talk a lot about what we can do, about neat tricks we've invented, about ingenious designs and our amazing capabilities as we continue to build smaller, faster machines with more efficient and flexible software. What's discussed on the sidelines but rarely addressed in formal discourse are the social ramifications.

In 1995, I spoke at the Cyberdesigners conference in Denmark. At this small conference, the emphasis was on creative rather than technical aspects of interactive design. Integrated into nearly every discussion was the matter of social impact. At one of the discussion periods, someone asked the question, "What are computers doing to us?" I said, "Computers aren't doing anything to us. Computers are machines. Whatever is being done to us is being done not by the machines but by the people who create content for them." And that would be us.

It's time we stopped skirting these issues. The people creating these new interactive platforms are some of the most brilliant, innovative people in the world. They represent the cutting edge of new technologies and applications. Surely they can devise a more intelligent solution than this. And surely they're capable of transcending the obvious and developing not only new technologies, software engines, and platforms but also new and more expansive stories to tell on those platforms. Why keep telling the same old story of "kill or be killed"? Hasn't it been told to death?

References

Dangelmaier, Heidi, and Goldman, Vivien, "Gender and the Art of Designing Interactive Media," CGDA Report, Volume 1, Issue 5, August 1995.

Graetz, J. M., "The Origin of Spacewar!," The Computer Museum Report, Boston, Fall 1983.

Levy, Steven, *Hackers,* Delta Books/Bantam Doubleday, New York, 1984.

Acknowledgments

I would like to thank David Zeltzer and Professor Fernando J. Corbato of MIT for their gracious assistance in tracking down historical information on Spacewar! and Kelli Auernig and her associates at Evans and Sutherland for historical information. Special thanks to Clark Dodsworth for his support in this and all my work.

Biography

Celia Pearce is recognized as a pioneer in interactive attractions and location-based entertainment. She has been producing, writing, and designing interactives since 1983, when she got her start at the offices of Edwin Schlossberg, Inc., the seminal New York City-based interactive design company. From 1989 to 1996, she was a freelance consultant, providing conceptual and interactive design services to such clients as Universal Parks, Walt Disney Imagineering, and Iwerks Entertainment. She served as Creative Director for the award-winning Iwerks/Evans and Sutherland VR project "Virtual Adventures: The Loch-Ness Expedition," the first story-based, family-oriented VR game with a noncombat goal. She is currently Creative Director of Momentum Media Group in Los Angeles. She teaches at the American Film Institute; Westminster University, London; and Space Invaders Multimedia Program, Denmark; she has spoken at numerous conferences including SIGGRAPH, Mecklermedia VR World, Fun Expo, and the Entertainment Real Estate Forum. She has written for *ACM/Computer Graphics* and London-based *MUTE* Magazine and is currently working on her first book.

Chapter 13

Applying Game Design to Virtual Environments

Stephen Clarke-Willson, Ph.D.
Above the Garage Productions

Introduction

Virtual reality technology—3D navigation plus novel interfaces—is being used to bring improved entertainment experiences to greater and greater numbers of people. This chapter examines how principles of good game design dating back to the best 2D sprite-based games can enhance the design of newer, 3D entertainment environments. In addition, some problems found exclusively in 3D are described and solved. Everything described here has been implemented and tested in products under development.

The current excitement over creating 3D virtual environments has, for the most part, overemphasized the technology and lacked focus on the quality of the actual experience. The original Super Mario Bros. and Zelda series of games developed over the last ten years and published by Nintendo provide a greater virtual experience than 95 percent of the 3D games being published today. Virtual environment designers must carefully consider what made those early games so appealing and apply the same principles today, albeit in a different presentation style. This chapter examines the following list of key game design principles:

- Third-person presentation
- Discovery and exploration
- Movement versus animation
- Player control
- The use of maps
- The use of "weenies"
- Closed environments

- Constant positive feedback with sporadic negative feedback
- Complexity management and slow bullets

Then, the chapter addresses three problems inherent in 3D environments that must be solved in any good entertainment application:

- Lack of depth perception (even with stereographic glasses)
- Management of player viewpoint
- Navigation and targeting support

Game Design Principles

Third-Person Presentation

The classic games (except some driving games) all have an amazing attribute in common—that of third-person point of view (POV). Many driving games, even today, that strive for a straight-through-the-windshield view still allow a third-person POV. By contrast, the vast majority of 3D VR games or experiences adopt a first-person point-of-view wherein your own character is not visible.

There are two good reasons for adopting the first-person POV:

1. It's easier to implement.
2. It's easier to sell.

The first-person POV is easier to implement in a 3D world (and nearly impossible in a 2D world) because several issues, as detailed shortly, are instantly sidestepped. Most importantly, management of depth perception is extremely easy: Game players or viewers simply draw straight lines from their view to anything they see: If it's big, it's close; if it's small, it's far away.

The first-person POV is easier to sell (in other words, to get someone excited about funding) because it provides a more visceral experience, and that's what the majority of game and interactive development today is about. Each game tries to top the previous top game's "rush" of graphics, which is easiest to do with first-person POV. However, this places enormous limitations on the depth of the experience that is possible.

First-person POV is a good first step for the industry, but it must evolve to support third-person POV in order to grow and to attract an audience beyond those looking for a rush. Admittedly, a VR skiing attraction might not be as much fun in third person, where one can see the skier one is controlling, because most of the fun of skiing is in the rush. Skiing (downhill skiing at established resorts) is not about exploring, learning, and discovering.

By contrast, the best 2D games are about these very things. While nearly all popular games, it seems, have an action component, the enduring games also create an environment—even in two dimensions—that invites the player to explore, learn, and discover.

Imagine we want to develop a 3D VR Web site for some commercial purpose. Our first thought will be to provide some kind of visceral experience to attract people. A 3D environment where the world whirls about will attract a certain number of people—mostly males, ages 18 to 35. But now that we have people visiting our Web site, it's probably more important that we encourage them to explore, learn, and discover. We want them to explore so that they'll stay active in our site. We want them to learn our product; otherwise, there's probably no commercial reason to create the site. We want them to discover because it's the internal feeling of "Aha!" that gives intense pleasure and rewards our visitors for coming to our site. This critically important Aha! experience can only be created through careful design; it's not something that comes via a purely visceral experience.

In a Mario Bros. game, the first thing you have to do is jump on a Koopa (that's an enemy sprite for the Mario-impaired). But the second thing you have to do is to navigate a series of blocks; this forces you to explore how your character moves and how the environment reacts to your character.

In a first-person POV game, your character's movement is very limited. In fact, your character doesn't move at all; instead, the world swirls around it. But there is a linear relationship between you, your character, and the world (Figure 13.1).

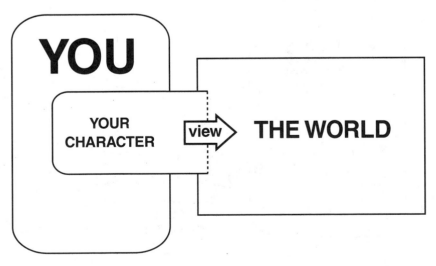

Figure 13.1 Relationship of user to character in first-person POV.

In a third-person POV game, the experience is more complex (Figure 13.2). This triangular relationship between you, your character, and the world provides much greater opportunities for interaction.

Why? Because of your ability to see your character in the world, your mind can see more complex relationships. Instead of a more intense "in-body" experience as with first-person POV, you have a transcendent "out-of-body" experience. That is the real potential of VR—to give you experiences not available in normal life—and third-person POV provides an increased context in which to act and react.

Discovery and Exploration

The act of discovery is what creates the Aha! experience and can be something as simple as realizing that a certain shape in the landscape means you can get help there. Discovery is what cruising the Web is about. Discovering new information is fine, but, in the design of a 3D environment, it's also important that visitors learn to discover "how to" and not just "what." In a Mario game, with a little experience, you learn that you can double-jump and whack two Koopas in one motion. In a 3D VR Web site, for example, where you've created an online store, you would want visitors to learn "how to" by exploring and discovering.

You may need to manipulate your visitors into having this Aha! experience. For instance, you might program your store-clerk character to purposefully get in the way of a new visitor so that your visitor learns to ask the clerk questions.

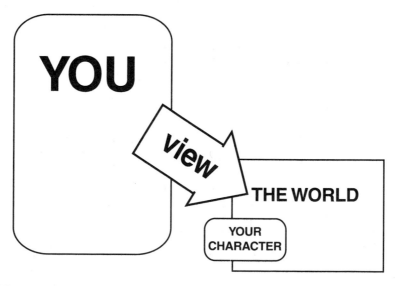

Figure 13.22   Relationship of user to character in third-person POV.

One final note on third-person presentation: Very few movies are made in the first-person mode, yet moviemakers obviously want you to identify with the main character to develop an empathetic link. If you watch a young child (6 to 12 years old) play Mario Bros., you'll see that the child identifies so completely with Mario that the child "projects" into the 2D environment. You can create this same sense of identification in 3D without resorting to a first-person through-the-helmet view.

Movement Versus Animation

In a substantial VR world where objects may be extremely distant, the movement of an object in the world is more important than any fancy animated details. Up close and personal, animated nuances can provide all sorts of visual clues about the character you are interacting with. But more attention must be paid to how these characters or objects move within the environment than is currently being spent because, in a truly rich 3D VR world, there will be a huge number of objects but only a few that the viewer is attending to actively at any one time.

These objects may exist in the environment to attract the viewer's attention and encourage him or her to explore in a particular direction. Extremely detailed, complex character animation is wasted at such a time, when the object may be only a few pixels on the screen. But an amazing thing about people is that we can tell whether that's a person or a robot off in the distance by the motion of the object in the environment. If it bobs up and down like a person walks, then it's probably a person. If it glides a little too smoothly, it's probably not a person, at least as we know them. The simple motion of a few pixels bobbing up and down is enough to clue the viewer that "Hey, there's another person over there!" Particularly if the motion is oversampled and the motion is displayed in a subpixel, anti-aliased environment, very few pixels can express a great deal.

Player Control

Ask any player what he or she likes about Mario Bros. games, and the answer is always the same: control. It's certainly not the graphics. My early experience with VR Web browsers is that they leave me feeling horribly out-of-control of my experience. I'm never quite sure where I'm going to end up or why. There are a lot of technical reasons for this, including latency problems and erratic frame rates, but the problem can be solved even under these conditions by switching to a third-person POV. If I can see myself in the scene, and how I move in relationship to other objects in the scene, then I feel much more in control. If something is bumping me from behind, I can see it. I'm not left in a semiparanoid state where I have no idea what's affecting my character and therefore me.

Even if your user interface is dedicated to first-person POV, you can still increase the sense of player control in complex environments by allowing your viewer to move an icon, perhaps shaped like a camera, through the scene, position it in a safe place, and then switch to that view. I know from personal experience setting up architectural walk-through animations that it's easier to create an animation by manipulating a camera icon in the scene than by trying to animate by looking through the camera. The final goal is the same—a first-person experience of walking through a building—but the control necessary to navigate the environment is first provided through the third-person interface.

The Use of Maps

One way to overcome limitations of first-person presentation is by providing a map mode. Maps, in general, are pretty handy things to have when you have a goal but you don't know how to get there. Maps are also handy to create when you're exploring and want to remember what you've seen so that you can get back to it (again, the map is necessary to achieve a goal).

An incorrect use of maps, in my opinion, is to compensate for the lack of a sense of context that first-person presentation omits. If your game player or 3D VR user is constantly switching to the map to figure out what's going on, then you've failed in the design of your environment. So, when you want to encourage exploration, you want to make sure that maps are unnecessary, and that's done through the use of "wieners."

"Weenies"

This somewhat bizarre term was coined by Walt Disney, who suggested that when designing massive 3D environments (theme parks), it was necessary to lead visitors through the environment the same way one trains a dog—by holding a wiener and leading the dog by the nose.

Obvious weenies at Disneyland are Sleeping Beauty's Castle, which encourages guests to travel from the main entrance to the central hub; the former Rocket Jets, which encourage guests to explore Tomorrowland; the Mark Twain Steamship and dock, which encourage guests to explore Frontierland; and the King Arthur Carousel, which encourages guests to walk over the castle moat and into Fantasyland.

One of the biggest failures in weenie design ever is The Space Place. The Space Place is, in my opinion, an extremely cool, high-tech environment filled with plants and huge cathedral ceilings. It's a restaurant, and it's only open on days that Disneyland is very full. The reason is that nobody knows it's there. It's hidden between Space Mountain and the site of the former Mission to Mars. Even if you walk right up to it, you're hesitant to go inside because the lighting does not invite you in. It's so poorly placed that it's not clear how to improve it, without putting big arrows out in front that say "Come in here!"

Your 3D VR environment needs to have standout landmarks so that it's easy to navigate without a map. The best games, which have typically been designed with very limited graphics, always save a few graphics to denote special and interesting things that should be investigated.

Closed Environments

The best games take place within a limited constrained space. In Myst, you're stuck on a series of islands. In The Seventh Guest, you're trapped in a mansion. In Clue, you're limited to the locations of the house. In chess, checkers, go, and Monopoly,—in fact, in every board game—you are limited to the board. In Dungeons and Dragons, where you sometimes create your own environments, the Dungeon Master sets the limits.

One of the biggest problems in most flight simulators is the sense that you can fly anywhere. The trouble is, in most of "anywhere," there's nothing to look at. If you are creating a virtual environment, you should be sure that anywhere you can go is interesting and that the places you shouldn't go are off limits.

It's also best to disguise the edges of your virtual world. Your viewer shouldn't simply run out of data while cruising your environment; he or she should come to the end of it and want to turn around and go back. At the least, put a fence around the legal area for cruising. Or a force field. Or anything. But don't let your poor viewer walk out into the void. It's not polite.

Constant Positive Feedback with Sporadic Negative Feedback

If you want to exercise editorial control over the way viewers explore your VR environment, you'll want to use weenies to attract them to specific places. Once they arrive, you'll always want to reward them with a treat of some kind. It can be something as simple as a sound bite ("Great!"), or a quick, fun animation, or increasing the score counter, or anything that's special and easily associated with success (perhaps a flashing blue light). For this to work properly, *you must always reward progress toward the goal you desire your visitor to achieve.*

Now, from time to time, you'll want to dissuade your visitor from heading in a specific direction. You might decide to always display a discouraging sign or play a sound like a game show buzzer when someone goes the wrong way. Unfortunately, it's far easier to identify the good things you want someone to focus on than to enumerate every bad or irrelevant thing to avoid. So, it's best to provide sporadic, almost random negative feedback. The idea behind this is that your visitors will become slightly paranoid about straying off the beaten path. Combined with positive feedback, your visitors will learn to always search for those positive vibes that encourage them to go where you want. They'll be a little paranoid if they don't get some positive feedback soon, and they'll start looking for it because it's the only reliable way to avoid negative feedback.

This technique is really helpful when you're creating your own world for someone to explore because, in spite of all the technology, it's simply impossible to delineate every possible path or option. Since your site, if it's on a network, will likely be constantly under construction, you'll never have time to make sure every possible location and approach from every possible angle is complete and bug-free. So, you want your visitors to explore the places that are known to be safe and avoid the places where you might not have completed the job. To get them really paranoid, if they stray way off the beaten track, just terminate their connection from time to time. That'll get them to behave.

If you provide constant negative feedback that is reliably produced, then you'll find a lot of people will spend a lot of time exploring the edges of your universe, looking for this negative feedback. So, keep it sporadic so that they never know if it's coming or not.

Complexity Management and Slow Bullets

In well-designed, seemingly fast arcade games, where player reaction time is very important, the action is carefully orchestrated and, in fact, not really happening as fast as it seems.

One huge and common error in game design is to create a game where the moment you see something appear on the screen you have to react and shoot it. This is OK once in a while but overall provides for boring game play.

At first glance, you might think that all games are made this way: You see it, you shoot it. But, in fact, going all the way back to Space Invaders, the objects actually tend to move quite slowly; the difficulty comes from the *number* of objects marching toward you. If you look at the bombs that get dropped by the aliens at the top of the screen, you'll see they travel quite slowly. If those bombs were the only thing you had to deal with, the game would be pretty simple. But, in the context of all the other action, even one more slow-moving bullet can be overwhelming.

The majority of VR Web sites for the next few years will be fairly static environments where you mostly just wander around. But, as the ability of computers to download and manipulate individual objects increases, the amount of activity within sites, including seeing other visitors, will increase. It's at this point in time where careful attention to the complexity of the scene will become important.

You might think that a site where there are a lot of slow-moving objects (people) milling about talking to one another can't get too complicated. Not so. Just imagine the last overcrowded party you went to. Notice that most chat rooms available on the online services carefully limit the number of visitors per chat room.

Many computer and video games limit the number of active objects on the screen for technical reasons, but as these technical limitations are removed by fast hardware, it will be smart to limit the number of objects on the screen for psychological reasons. If you put too many active objects on the screen at once, no matter how slow and innocent they seem, you can quickly overwhelm your viewer.

Problems Inherent in 3D Environments

Lack of Depth Perception (Even with Stereographic Glasses)

Stereo glasses seem like the next great thing. Stereo glasses that connect to your PC are now available for less than $100, making them a mass consumer item. But here's the problem: People only use their binocular capability for close-in work (say, up to 15 feet or less). After that, they depend on other visual cues, like atmospheric haze, to compute the distance to something.

Perhaps the most important visual clue is differential scrolling of the environment, used most notably and effectively in animated backgrounds (formerly created with multiple-plane camera animation stands). For instance, where I live in Washington state, there are forests on top of rolling hills. If I stand still, I really can't tell how far away one tree or another is, but if I am walking and bobbing up and down slightly, then I quickly get a sense of the distance to different trees.

In the game Doom, the player character bobs up and down while walking, and this does magnificent things in terms of providing a sense of depth. It's too bad there isn't an option to turn it off so that you could compare the effect both with and without.

A company called Vision III in Virginia has developed a 3D effect that doesn't require any special glasses. In their technique, the lens rotates around the axis of view at about 4.5 to 5 cycles per second. The amount of motion is small enough that you don't notice it directly, but the increased information transmitted to your brain from the subtle differential scrolling that occurs gives everything you see much more depth. The effect is subtle, and some people are more attuned to it than others. But it's a more sophisticated version of the bobbing up and down in Doom.

Management of Player Viewpoint

When you develop your 3D environment, you will be faced with a problem that moviemakers never have to face, namely, that your visitor might be able to see the backside of your sets. In the movies, the camera location is strictly controlled, so it's easy to paint only the front side of your sets. At Disneyland, where you can roam at will, everything needs to be painted, including parts of the backstage area that you might come across accidentally from time to time. The same will be true of your VR environment.

If you adopt a third-person presentation, you might consider locking down the camera, but visitors will quickly want to move it. Still, by constructing your "sets" so that it only makes sense to place the camera in friendly places and adding a small restriction (say, the camera can only be placed on the ground), you can avoid a lot of extra work dressing up the back sides of your buildings and walls.

In one VR viewer currently available on the Net, there is a Walk mode and a Fly mode for moving about in the environment. Some environment builders may want to disable flying in order to constrain the range of movement in their environment to something reasonable. A typical techweenie approach is to respond, "But this is VR! You should be able to do anything!" Not true. It's also wrong from a show business standpoint. You don't want a visitor to your VR site to do "just anything" anymore than Disneyland wants you poking around backstage.

Navigation and Targeting Support

Navigating in a 3D environment is tricky, from either a first-person or a third-person POV. In Doom, it's pretty easy because there are actually several constraints on what you can do—the designers know that you're spending most of your time in buildings and that you're not going to turn things upside down. In many VR viewers, there are not any restrictions, and you can turn yourself upside down very quickly.

Even if you can't turn yourself upside down, how do you specify "I want to go there"? If you point at an object and say, "Go there," should it take you there and leave you facing the thing? Most of the time you'll be staring at a wall. Should you have to walk everywhere as in Doom? That could be quite tedious if you're not busy blowing people away.

One approach I've been using is a targeting system for navigating. You point at an object, and your player character points at it. Then, as long as you only move forward or backward, slide right or left, or fly up or down, your player character stays pointed at this object. If you turn left or right, then the targeting lock is lost. This has the benefit of eliminating some of the degrees of freedom available, making it easier to move through the environment, without permanently restricting your movement. You can still see the sights as you cruise, but you're not constantly worried about getting lost because your player character is locked on the goal. If you come across something interesting on your way to your goal, you can break the target lock and look around.

If this targeting approach is part of your navigation system, then you can provide "way-points" for visitors. Just put up signs at interesting places; if your visitors click on the sign, that becomes their destination and they can quickly navigate there.

Summary

The best research investment you can make for virtual environment interface design is to buy a game machine and to sit down and play it for several hours a week. In discussing look-and-feel, it's always easier to discuss look because we have terminology (developed over many centuries). But for now, while interactive design is emerging from the garage into the mainstream of culture, it is still best to "feel" the interface directly, and the best way to do that is to play games.

Biography

Stephen Clarke-Willson received his Ph.D. in Information and Computer Science from the University of California, Irvine, in 1986. As a research scientist at the Northrop Corporation, he developed computer graphics algorithms for the biggest (certainly the most expensive) video game ever created, the B-2 Stealth bomber. He was chief architect of the Patran 3 MCAE system from PDA Engineering. From 1990 until 1994, he was vice president of worldwide product development for Virgin Interactive Entertainment, where he supervised the development of all computer and video games released by the company. Today he is the owner and creative director of Above the Garage Productions, where he is developing a series of 3D games.

Chapter 14

Live: What a Concept!
. . . Networked Games

Chris Crawford
Erasmatazz, LLC

Introduction

In the last few years, interest in interactive entertainment has risen dramatically. As we might expect, many early efforts in this direction have been seriously flawed. The same technologies that made them—and the few significant successes—possible also enable humans to enter the elaborate figments of our imagination called computer games. In fact, a viable and immensely powerful general-purpose way to make games more exciting is simple: *Use real people.* Exactly; there's no opponent like a live opponent—no matter where they might be.

Perhaps the most compelling aspect of networked multiplayer games is their ability to provide interpersonal interaction. As I have often complained, traditional computer games are always about "things, not people"—and this shortcoming has held back the development of the medium. The difficulty, of course, lies in the problems of artificial personality and personal expression. Sure, you could come up with a parser capable of understanding "I love you," but how about "Who was that man I saw you with last night?"—especially with its manifold interpersonal implications?

The problem of automating interpersonal interaction, of coming up with artificial characters that really work, has been attracting attention for some time now, but the sad fact is that it's a very difficult problem. People in the networked games biz toss their heads and laugh, "So what? Who needs artificial personalities when we can have the real thing? And no computer model will ever rival the richness of human interaction!"

They're right on all counts. Moreover, they have another advantage: When you use the computer to connect humans rather than to simulate them, you save lots of resources. My software uses gobs of RAM and zillions of machine cycles to simulate the most rudimentary of human behaviors. The network people don't have to write monster software to handle these problems; all they have to do is ship bits between players. What could be simpler?

But, there are some drawbacks that have so far crippled the network designers, preventing them from realizing the potential of this medium. In this chapter, I will address some of these killer problems and discuss strategies for solving them.

Dropout

This is the worst of the problems. Imagine yourself in the middle of a hot game. Derek has just made a move on your girlfriend; your kid sister has just informed you that she's pregnant but will not reveal the father; and Vanessa has just announced an attempted hostile takeover of your oil company. Things are really cooking when, suddenly, Derek announces that his wife is calling him to dinner, and he drops out of the game for the night. Because he's playing a crucial part in the drama, the whole game is frozen. The problem is compounded by the number of players. The more players there are, the greater the chance that a single-player dropout will shut everything down.

This problem, of course, is not limited to interpersonal games; it's been around for a long time. I recall a story from a U.S. Department of Defense computer simulation that illustrates its severity. The simulation linked up commands from all over the country in joint wargames. I saw a videotape of one such operation, an amphibious invasion. A helicopter had just ferried some troops ashore and had returned to the troopship to make another pickup. It settled down on the landing deck of the troopship and cut its engines. A moment later, a line defect caused the loss of connection with the naval base controlling the troopship. Because the network used distributed computing, the loss of the connection triggered the loss of all units controlled from that station. The troopship suddenly disappeared from the simulation. The helicopter was now hanging in the air, with no power to its engines. It fell into the sea and was treated as a casualty.

The truth is, there is no way to ensure that players will remain in a game they have begun. Some of them will certainly drop out before the game is completed, and if the role they played was crucial, then the game will collapse. What can be done about this?

Dropout Compensation

I know of four basic approaches to the problem: player replacement, noncrucial players, reduced probability of dropout, and "bridge artificial personality."

The first strategy is to immediately replace the missing player with another human. Presumably, there will always be a steady supply of players. All the network need do is hold incoming players for a moment to see whether any existing slots have opened up; if so, then the incoming player is plunked down into the existing game. The problem with this approach is that it drops the new player into a slot he or she knows nothing about. Without knowing the interpersonal history, how can the player appreciate the subtleties of the interpersonal situation? How can he or she know that the character has been, for example, a two-timing, double-dealing, low-down skunk for the last few hours, and that's why everybody hates that character? And consider the experience from the point of view of the other characters. Here's a character who for three hours has followed a consistent course of action—he's a snake! Then, suddenly, the character is transformed into a teddy bear who wants nothing more than to be loved. This isn't a plot twist; it's a plot disjunction. Lastly, there will still be times when there just isn't anybody available—in which case, the game has to shut down. Thus, player replacement doesn't provide us with a satisfying or reliable solution to the problem of dropout.

Another approach attempts to reduce the impact of any single player on the overall game. One such case involved a trading game in which characters engage in bidding for commodities. If one player drops out, the market isn't much affected. A variation on this strategy makes the player a voter in crucial decisions. This strategy eliminates the problem by eliminating the significance of the player. It no longer matters what you do because the game can chug along just fine without you. I don't see much value in this approach: Who would care to play a game in which your action (or even your very existence) doesn't really matter?

A third approach is to reduce the probability of dropout either by reducing the duration of the game or by making the experience turn-sequenced with long intervals between turns so that players can be certain to get their moves in. In the former case, the game is kept to a 30-minute duration or less, reducing the likelihood of player dropout. This works well for adrenaline games. Moreover, it ensures that, should somebody drop out, little is lost. The players can simply start over with a new game. The difficulty is that it limits the richness of play. Short games just can't get into interesting territory. A great many human relationships derive their impact from the context in which they take place. You need to build up some interpersonal history before your interactions with others can become deeply interesting.

The turn-sequenced approach often breaks the game down into daily turns. All players read their news of the day and then enter their moves for the next day. At 5:00 A.M., the central computer processes all the moves and posts the results. Because players need only check in once per day, the likelihood of their missing a move is much reduced. While it works reasonably well with certain types of strategy games that require lots of thought with few moves, it cannot deal with the more intense interaction of interpersonal relationships.

The fourth approach to player dropout problems involves the use of what I call "bridge artificial personality." The idea is to use an artificial personality to bridge gaps created by player dropouts. By noting a player's moves, the computer can build up a model of the player's personality; should the player later drop out, the computer can turn on the artificial personality to take over. While the artificial personality would never be as rich or interesting as the real thing, it might be good enough to cover the gap temporarily.

The downside for bridge artificial personality is that this technology requires considerable work to create. However, such technology, once created, could be adopted to a wide variety of commercial network products, and there is now an extraordinary amount of effort devoted to developing several species of such code. It would also give us a new twist on the Turing test.

Timing

Another difficulty with networked interpersonal games comes from time zone differences. Most people are going to play games during their off hours, typically 7:00 to 10:00 P.M. on weeknights. Unfortunately, this window is too narrow to readily permit people from widely different areas to play at the same time. Indeed, even within the continental United States, this presents a problem: The people on the East Coast are logging off just as the people on the West Coast are getting on. When we start throwing in players from Japan and Europe, the problem becomes insuperable. There is simply no way to bring large numbers of players together from all over the globe at the same time.

Of course, if the game is designed for offline interaction using delayed response or turn sequencing, then this problem vanishes, but human interaction doesn't work like chess. Mood is just as important as strategy, and it's really hard to maintain a mood over a 12-hour time gap. It's my belief that there is no really good solution to this problem. However, partial solutions can work. The trick is to have most of the players from one time zone meeting at a convenient hour, and a few adventurous players from other time zones showing up at an inconvenient hour. In fact, time zones are not a problem, but rather a solution for those who want to play at what most of their neighbors consider an inconvenient hour.

Dramatics

This is not so great a problem, but it still deserves consideration: How do we ensure that the game retains sufficient dramatic content? The problem here arises from the possibility that the players will fail to do interesting things and the game will dissolve into boredom. Or perhaps they'll engage in overdramatic nonsense—dashing from murder to seduction to dragons to space aliens. I see no decent solution to this problem.

Nazis and Dorks

Since the players provide so much of the game's content, quality control of players is crucial to the overall entertainment value of the game. But how do we exercise quality control over the people who are paying the bill? If a particular player prefers to play as a Nazi, constantly shouting "Heil Hitler!," what can be done to protect the more normal players from this person's bad taste? In the same fashion, if one of the players is simply a stupid dork, how can other players be asked to cope with this player?

This is a delicate problem because it involves evaluations of the personal merit of individuals, but it is not a new problem. We all try to organize our social lives to maximize the probability of running into interesting people and minimize the probability of running into unpleasant people. When was the last time you stopped by a bowling alley, a square dance hall, or a Grateful Dead concert? In each of these social gathering places, you have a pretty good idea of the kind of people you're likely to encounter. It would be crass to say that all square dancers are older people with conservative values, but if I wanted to socialize with such people, a square dance would be a great place to start. We all know lots of rules of thumb about where to encounter what kind of people, but such information is not yet available about network sites. Indeed, if there's any generalization you can make about those who frequent networks, it's that they're probably undersocialized male nerds. Not very promising, eh?

Fortunately, there are some things we can do about this problem. The best way is to come up with a "player profile" that rates players in a variety of dimensions such as imagination, consistency, romanticism, team-playing, antisocial attitudes, rudeness, and so on. Every time players complete a game, their coplayers are asked to rate them in each of the dimensions. Once a reasonable set of player profiles have been worked out, specialized games can be set up that have certain personality profile requirements associated with them—for example, "To be allowed to enter this game, you must have a romance rating of at least 6 and a rudeness rating of less than 2." Even this scheme is vulnerable: A group of anarchists could play a series of games with themselves, altering their personality profiles so that they could gain entry into whatever game they chose, where they could wreak havoc. My guess is that, until network environments provide the majority with the power to easily enforce sanctions against individuals, social groups won't be able to prevent troublemakers from intruding on their fun.

Group Size

Another issue in network interpersonal games is the problem of establishing the ideal group size. Social interaction is tricky business: If too few people are involved, the interaction becomes inflexible; if too many are thrown together, the group becomes socially unmanageable. Unfortunately, the ideal size depends largely on the people involved. Some groups will function quite well with one or even two dozen members; others will fall apart with more than five members. There's no way to tell in advance. My guess is that we'll have to start out with the classic seven-person interaction and then figure out ways to modify it.

Free Text or Regulated Inputs?

This is a crucial and difficult decision. Should the players be allowed to interact via freeform text, or should their interactions be regulated through a standard interface language? The former approach gives them the freedom to pursue any options whatsoever to interact in a wide variety of ways, but it suffers from the ability of troublemakers to mess things up for others. In general, I see this problem as minor. However, the regulated input approach has the additional strength that it can allow the computer to regulate some form of reality. That is, regulated inputs can permit the computer to keep track of variables and ensure that actions are in accord with some game-specific notion of reality.

Of course, free text and regulated inputs are not mutually exclusive; it's easy to include both in the same product. The issue is more a matter of how much of the interpersonal interaction takes place through free text and how much goes through regulated inputs. A good example is provided by Habitat, which mixed some free text with some regulated input. The reassuring result from Habitat is that social groups formed and began to establish higher rules of social behavior.

Egalitarianism

This is a particularly thorny problem. The audience expects to be treated as equals, yet much of the richest social interaction arises from the inequalities of the human condition. Some people are richer, some are smarter, some are prettier. These inequalities play on human foibles to generate social conflict. Yet who would want the role of the ugly, poor kid without a high school diploma? How do we reconcile the natural egalitarianism of the customer ("My money is just as green as yours") with the dramatic necessity of inequality?

I think this problem can be resolved through a kind of karma. The very first game you play, you have no karma at all, so you enter the game with a weakling character. However, your overall goal is to improve your karma. Thus, even though you play as an ugly, dumb, poor nobody, if you play well (whatever that means), your karma increases. The next time you play, you'll be given a character who's not quite so ugly, so dumb, or so poor. If you play long enough and well enough, you'll play as one of the Beautiful People. Perhaps you'll be a fabulously wealthy, ravishingly beautiful, young CEO of a major software company. Perhaps you'll get to be a really nasty bad guy with all sorts of exciting opportunities for villainy, and, if you're a truly fine villain, why, your karma increases!

What this suggests is that players should be rated, not by any absolute scale of direct personal achievement, but rather by a scale of dramatic success. In other words, we don't measure a player's performance by how much money is acquired, how many "Fame Points" are picked up, or how many "Cute Chicks" are bedded. Rather, each character should be assigned a set of dramatic goals and evaluated on how well he or she met those goals. Thus, Lovely Nell might be rated on how well she met and married Mr. Right, while Snidely Whiplash will be judged on how many girls he tied to the railroad tracks. Lassie will be judged on how many times she pulls little Timmy out of the well, and Captain Kirk will get points for every time he disables a rampaging computer by making it think a logical impossibility. In other words, you get karma points for being true to your character.

This has the additional merit that it encourages players to spend more time on your network, building up their karma so that they too can play as Scarlett O'Hara, or J. R. Ewing, or Spock. What a delightfully commercial concept!

Biography

Chris Crawford taught physics before joining Atari in 1979. He designed games for the Atari Video Computer System and the Atari Home Computer System, including two educational simulation games: Energy Czar and Scram (a nuclear power plant simulation). He also created Eastern Front (1941), a game that became a best-seller, and Legionnaire. While managing the Games Research Group, he wrote *The Art of Computer Game Design* and created Excalibur, a game about the Arthurian legends. After the general collapse of Atari, he became a freelance game designer and created Balance of Power, his most successful game, having sold about 250,000 units.

From 1986 to 1991, he wrote *Patton Versus Rommel*, *Trust & Betrayal*, *Guns & Butter* (about macroeconomics), *Balance of the Planet* (about environmental problems), and *Patton Strikes Back*. His current project, now five years in the making, is the Erazmatron, a technology for interactive storytelling and a development environment that permits nontechnical artists to control the technology. Along the way he created, edited, and wrote most of *The Journal of Computer Game Design* and founded and ran the Computer Game Developers' Conference during its first seven years. He has lectured on game design in eight countries and many universities.

John Whitney, Sr., circa 1965 in his studio in Pacific Palisades, California. The patented "cam machine," built from military surplus analog gun control devices, was the precursor to the digital computer he used from 1965 to 1995. The cam machine, which followed his pantograph device used to create a title sequence for Hitchcock's *Vertigo* in the late 1950s, became the basis for the "motion graphics" era in Hollywood advertising graphics and the "slit scan" sequence for Kubrick's *2001*. The motion control system included third-axis control of the image with the zoom lens tied to the x-y and rotary movement of art work via servo-controlled stepper motors. In 1963, Whitney wrote, "All my research effort is oriented in anticipation of a fuller employment of modern computer systems dispensing with the camera altogether." He ended his film, *Experiments in Motion Graphics,* in 1968 with the thought that "some day computers would be as small as a desktop TV." In the program notes for *Moondrum,* Whitney writes, "Only in the last decade of this century a new music, a new symbolism—a new kind of abstract expressionist action painting with light and sound is becoming accessible to a solitary individual artist/composer in his own studio." (See frame from *Moondrum* below.) Copyright 1965–1997, Estate of John H. Whitney, Sr.

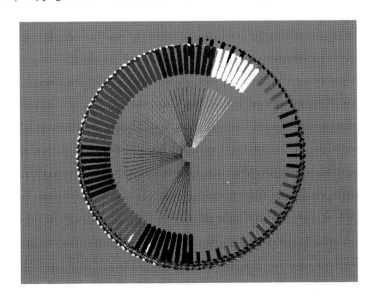

The Walt Disney Company's *Aladdin* HMD attraction. A guest's view of the virtual environment—the city of Agrabah—from a flying carpet. The user's virtual hands can be seen in the lower foreground. Walt Disney Imagineering Research and Development, Inc. Reproduced with permission.

The world's largest computer graphics display system is part of the Fremont Street Experience in downtown Las Vegas, Nevada. It has an image area of 175,700 square feet (more than four acres), and is four blocks long. The barrel-vault space frame structure, designed by Peter Pearce for The Jerde Partnership, is surfaced with almost 2.1 million lights grouped in pixels with four lamps each: red, green, blue, and white. Each light of each pixel can be varied over 8 levels of brightness. It can display live or recorded video and digital animation. Plans for interactive features are being developed.

Chapter 15

Entertainment-Driven Collaboration

Michael Harris
NCR Human Interface Technology Lab

Introduction

Location-Based Entertainment (LBE) attractions, in several guises, are becoming the most publicly visible applications of interactive digital graphics, visualization, and other disciplines. In the amusement industry, convincing sensory illusions and natural interactivity can translate directly into fascination for players and profit for owners.

The focus today is often on the details: 70 mm, simulation, full motion, high-definition television (HDTV), networking, cyberspace, virtual reality, and so on. But these are all "adjectives." What will the "nouns" be? What will players *do* with the technology? Where is the true value? Are these entertainments useful for something besides improving hand-eye coordination and encouraging aggressive behavior?

LBEs are pure human interfaces. They can be networked simulations. Here, at the beginning of an era of awesomely capable technologies, there is a remarkable opportunity to create new frameworks, scenarios, situations, and mythologies.

Most schools have taught that collaboration is the equivalent of cheating. But now, it is becoming obvious that, although some individuals may win by themselves, more certain wins for more people are likely through collaboration. LBEs can help people learn cooperation through play. LBEs can be groupware and may be uniquely supportive of collaboration.

Nolan Bushnell, the founder of Atari, has pointed out, "Never forget: The engineers run the boat." The vessel here is a pleasure cruiser: Traditional amusements, after decades of gradual decline, are being replaced and augmented by LBEs—amusement attractions in theme parks and elsewhere where the engineers are developing and combining advanced interactive technologies and high-resolution visualizations into their most visible and accessible applications. To extend the analogy, this boat is fueled by profit. LBE owners and operators will risk significant investment in technology if there is a reasonable probability of substantial returns. Measures of success include capacity, repeat factor, and buzz (personal testimonials). Investors seek to attract and delight more customers, from more diverse groups, more often.

In the early 1980s, an Atari arcade game called Battlezone caught the attention of Defense Advanced Research Projects Agency (DARPA) planners who saw in it the basis for a simulation and training tool. The concept became SIM-NET, a large-scale tactical training environment in which vehicle simulators, each incorporating realtime simulation and high-resolution image generation systems, interact over local and long-haul networks. SIMNET was perhaps the first fully operational virtual reality system (Sterling 1993) and became the basis for today's Distributed Interactive Simulation (DIS) technology. It supports a wide variety of air and ground vehicles, both human-directed and autonomous, and has permitted the development of fundamental DIS techniques like "selective fidelity" and "remote vehicle approximation" (Figure 15.1).

The purpose of SIMNET is clear and compelling—to train military person-

Figure 15.1   SIMNET tank simulator systems and trainees at Ft. Knox, Kentucky.

Figure 15.2   A "horsey ride."

nel to cooperate effectively in tactical situations. In LBEs, the purpose (for the user) is often far less clear. The technologies in today's LBEs are equally sophisticated, sometimes even more so, but usually the scenario is silly and the experience is not satisfying for most potential customers. In front of many American stores are simple coin-operated ride machines intended to amuse children (Figure 15.2). Current LBEs are far more sophisticated in form but equally juvenile in content—merely high-tech "horsey rides."

Parts of Speech

Discussions of LBEs are usually technology focused, often appearing to consist of unbroken streams of highly specialized buzzwords like DOFs (degrees of freedom), perfs (film frame sizes), HDTV (high-definition television), VR (virtual reality), cybermation, pneumatics, mechatronics, and so on. Conceptually, these can be viewed as adjectives; they may explicate the parameters and dimensions of an LBE, but not its point. The content and the themes are the nouns and verbs. The adjectives define an open-ended "potential for limitless visual experience" (Kamberg 1993). But what unifies the experience, and what determines the boat's destination? "It's the *content*, stupid" (Rundgren 1994).

More "Adjectives"

Given this richer view of the LBE landscape, several additional "adjectives" become essential, such as HI (human interface), PS (performance support), automatic translation, CSCW (computer-supported cooperative work), and groupware.

- Human Interface (HI). To users of most systems, the interface *is* the system. In a goal-oriented structure, the interface may not (and often should not) reflect the underlying functionality it supports. The modern automobile's basic control interface is go faster/go slower/stop/reverse; manual choke, spark advance, and mixture adjustment are irrelevant distractions. An LBE *is* an HI and, in fact, is an extremely pure example, having practically no underlying functionality. HI is the essence of an LBE.

  The ideal LBE interface is lightweight—extremely easy to learn and use, with rapid feedback and no irrelevant complexity. For input, keyboards and mice are clearly inappropriate; fortunately, rich modalities are increasingly practical (gaze, gesture, position, voice, touch). "Blackboarding" and other associative techniques support combining several input modalities to derive complex meanings.

- Performance Support (PS). Simply put, PS lets you use high-tech stuff to help you do something, even though you don't understand high-tech stuff and don't know how to do the thing. More formally, PS is task-oriented, context-sensitive help, ideally presented through multimedia interaction. For LBEs, PS has the power to make interesting scenarios possible even in high-turnover situations. And, PS can be made to adapt to individuals; for example, each player might wear a transponder badge that informs the attraction system about his or her preferred language, so playing instructions can be presented understandably (Hettema 1993).

- Automatic Translation. This is not spirit writing, but rather a possible way to conform to different players' styles of communication. International signs and symbols are useful but assume a shared reality that may not exist. The universal symbol shown (Figure 15.3) cannot prevent harm to those who fail to understand it. Increasingly, translation problems are being acknowledged as, not just English-to-French-to-Japanese, but rather speech-to-text-to-visualization. In LBEs, transponder badges would also help to address this issue.

- Computer-Supported Cooperative Work (CSCW). This focuses on organizational activity—on the impact of technology on groups and organizations: "How is technology *used by* groups?" Groupware focuses on technology itself: "How is technology *designed for* groups?" These terms are relatively new, and their definitions are subject to some debate, but "CSCW is the *game* (nouns, verbs) and groupware is the *gear* (adjectives)" seems workable. In any event, the importance of group activity is increasingly obvious: Most (80 percent or more) human work is cooperative work. In LBEs, group scenarios might well offer increased capacity in addition to richer human interactions. Networked simulations are groupware.

Figure 15.3 The universal symbol for radiation.

Where's the "E"?

At present, entertainment in typical LBEs is simplistic at best. Participants (perhaps "experiencers" is more appropriate since few LBEs are truly interactive) get quick action and high tension: They slash, kick, throw, race, duel, slam, chase, and most of all *compete*. Such parameters favor a demographically narrow audience: male, ages 14 to 24, highly individualistic. These are boy toys: "Women need a *reason* for conflict, men only need a *place*" (Weisman 1993). It is difficult to derive pleasure from simply observing these LBEs; watching is performed only to learn how to win. And, because the focus is on competition, there must inevitably be an eventual winning or losing, after which the experience becomes dull. "None of this is as fun as Coney Island in its heyday" (Nasaw 1993).

What Do People Want?

The author has informally surveyed hundreds of people (including several LBE producers) to gain a sense of the LBEs, amusements, and games they like and dislike. What "nouns" and "verbs" do people want? Some subjective conclusions are:

- Mental and social stimulation—"I want to interact safely with people I don't know."

- Ability for family and friends to play together—"I want to do things unlike work."

- Adventure Travel (ski trekking, mountain climbing, tropical surfing, Class 5 rapids, Alpine luge)—"I want the relaxation of continuous push-ups with the comfort of falling down the stairs in a shopping cart."

- Soft Adventure (thrilling but safe) (Class 3 rapids, visiting haunted castles, Bali, Oz). This seems to involve experiencing hardships to feel entitlement to luxuries—"I want wildness, but with servants and the correct wines."

- Mysteries (Clue), political thrillers (Robert Ludlum), role playing (Supreme Court justice, Barbra Streisand).

- Relationship-centered situations and explorations (participatory soap operas).

- Balance of respectability and titillation; the evocation of sensuality with unpredictability; perhaps a hint of danger, but absolutely no real risk.

- Sensual, symbolic, soft, poetic, *curved*, experiences.

Few respondents expressed personal preferences for today's often violent and competitive experiences. It is clearly time to go "back to the basics: great ideas" (Kamberg 1993).

The Collaboration-Learning Opportunity

Most purposeful human activity requires collaboration. But, in most educational settings, individual performance is the pedagogical emphasis and the basis for evaluation; collaboration is usually treated as cheating. This is slowly changing, however. Cooperative learning is becoming legitimate as people realize that collaboration is often more effective than competition. LBEs could be used to help promote cooperative learning by exploiting "the strong web of connections joining commercial play and cultural cohesion" (Nasaw 1993)—many traditional amusements are cooperative in structure. Another network of connections joins education and entertainment. High-fidelity interactive simulation is known to be of great value in supporting training and learning and is more prominent in successful LBEs. Although SIMNET and other simulation-based training environments have been in use for some time, few LBEs have taken advantage of simulation. Similar situations exist regarding computer image generation and other technologies: They are in use in other fields but are new to LBE.

So, as advanced technologies are integrated into LBEs, we have the opportunity to influence what players will learn from their experiences. LBEs can teach cooperation skills.

Some examples of LBE nouns that would require cooperation and so help impart the necessary skills might be trapeze flying and other circus stunts, tug o' war, team sports, and high finance. Some verbs might be dance, join, play (music), create, and invent.

The public is increasingly concerned about the negative influence of violent and competitive games, and the industry is responding with proposals to institute a game rating system. Surely a sensible and cost-effective response is to develop games that exert positive influence and teach valuable skills.

Collaboration Support Components

To create LBE environments amenable to cooperative behavior, some new structural components may be helpful. They would permit players to define themselves and interact on their own terms while operating within relatively fixed structures. Most of these components would necessarily incorporate built-in performance support facilities and other adjectives discussed earlier.

Players might assume new characteristics or other identities. An LBE could include an assortment of predefined characters (as in SIMNET and Battletech, a commercial networked vehicle simulation where roles are limited to vehicle crew assignments); this gives an illusion of choice while requiring little creative effort. Alternatively, there could be a Personality Construction Kit for building customized identities that players can elaborate between play sessions, as in the Internet-hosted MUD (Multi-User Dungeons-and-Dragons) games. Younger players are often comfortable with personality construction, while many adults prefer choosing among predefined options.

Each player could have a different custom view of the same LBE: One player might be piloting a futuristic racing spaceship, while another might be riding a wild pteranodon. A common specification and operating language would make this possible. Because dissimilar players could play together, many more players would be able to participate; players who "see" differently could nevertheless pool resources and collaborate.

Players could build and modify the games themselves. With sufficiently flexible simulation engines and a common specification language, LBEs could profitably include tools to build and modify the flow of play; play time (and operator income) might markedly increase.

Radical simulation-based LBE scenarios become realizable, widening the range of possible play scenarios. Some examples are business visualizations connected to players' bank accounts (winning earns genuine money) and blood-free war (SIMNET connected to Swiss bank accounts).

Author Larry Niven has written several stories and novels featuring Dream Parks, public places in which group fantasy play is carried out. LBE support components such as those described here could enable Dream Parks to exist in reality, or at least in virtual reality, as "powerful dramatic immersive experiences" (Trumbull 1994).

Summary

Our urban society has devolved from an exciting metropolitan culture filled with amusement parks, picture palaces, dance crazes, and other vital public group spaces and activities into a sterile suburban landscape. The older urban entertainments nurtured a sense of community (however fleeting). Ethnic and regional differences dissolved as diverse groups discovered a common identity as a "republic of pleasure seekers" (Nasaw 1993). This middle-class melding survived the Great Depression and World War II, but not white flight and the spread of commercial television. The mass audience was carved up into innumerable market segments based on age, sex, income . . . People no longer had a coherent culture or a sense of belonging as a unified public. Now, the opportunity exists to develop a new unification based on collaboration-focused activities supported by advanced technology. Some encouraging trends are apparent:

- The infrastructure is being assembled. Worldwide Internet, wideband networks, and distributed simulation protocol standards enable collaborative LBEs today.

- Set-top systems will make "SIMNET in the living room" possible in the near future.

- Game producers and other entertainment companies are creating large development organizations.

- LBEs are being installed in more accessible locations. Sega, Sony, GameWorks, and several other firms are producing mini theme parks in North America and elsewhere.

- The focus of LBE content is evolving toward a broader audience.

The English Channel Tunnel (Chunnel), the North American Free Trade Agreement (NAFTA), and the General Agreement on Tariffs and Trade (GATT) exemplify a worldwide social movement toward collaboration and unification. LBEs and other amusements can support this motion while delivering terrific entertainment, thus providing players with more satisfying experiences, investors with greater profits, and society with better prepared contributors.

References

Hettema, Phil, Senior Vice President for Attraction Development, Universal Creative, Universal Studios Recreation Group, panel discussion remarks at SIGGRAPH '93.

Kamberg, Mario, Director/Designer, Kamberg Design, remarks in panel discussion at SIGGRAPH '93.

Machrone, Bill, "What's Wrong with Multimedia," *PC Magazine*, November 9, 1993.

Nasaw, David, *Going Out: The Rise and Fall of Public Amusements*, Basic Books, New York, 1993.

Parkes, Walter, "Random Access: The Evolution of Storytelling," *Omni Magazine*, December 1993.

Rundgren, Todd, remarks in live performance in Atlanta, Ga., 1994.

Sterling, Bruce, "War is Virtual Hell," *Wired*, premier issue, 1993.

Trumbull, Douglas, LBE designer and film maker, article in the *New York Times*, January 31, 1994.

Weisman, Jordan, founder of Virtual World Entertainment, *Wired* premier issue, 1993.

Acknowledgment

The author wishes to thank haila darcy for unflagging encouragement and support.

Biography

Michael Harris is a video and interactive producer, LBE and game developer, system architect, and theatrical designer. He contributed to the original SIMNET distributed simulation environment, the TRIO adaptive training platform, and many other projects. He is fascinated by risky theatrical lighting, innovative input modalities, group support systems, and innovative aircraft. He is currently developing corporate themed attractions, adaptive dynamic interfaces, and group support systems.

PART 4

Hardware: Beyond Shadow Puppets

In skilled hands, anything can be a puppet: a red clown nose, two forks stuck in dinner rolls, a sock. But some puppets can do more tricks or the same tricks better. Recent puppets can generate a serial stream of motion and gesture data to drive elaborate 3D characters in realtime. Here we look at some developments that make new illusions possible or improve the old ones and, incidentally, at how some of the inventors think.

Shadow puppet theater was a big step forward in character entertainment when it emerged in China, India, and elsewhere more than 1,000 years ago. It added several new classes of illusion to the existing repertoire of storytelling techniques. It enabled marvelous magical transformations, flying, feats of strength, composting, crowd scenes, and evocative clouds and landscapes. Set design benefited greatly. The technologies described here provide similar expanded opportunities for today's storytellers and experience designers.

Turner Whitted's Adventures in Toyland led to his description of the Personal Image Generator; Christopher Hasser and Thomas Massie do the same for haptic and tactile systems. Joanna Alexander and Mark Long of Zombie explain the system and content design requirements for head-mounted displays, which will eventually see a market in the home. Lawrence Leske has been involved in video compression since it began; now, every entertainment developer wants either more bandwidth, better compression, or both, for online ventures. Roy Latham tells us which hardware needs the most development effort and why, followed by Warren Robinett's discussion of the benefits of different immersive systems. Finally, Mort Heilig has supplied patent drawings for the Sensorama Simulator and the Telesphere Mask HMD from the late 1950s. No entertainment ideas are new; only the effectiveness of the implementations improves.

More than set design will benefit this time.

Chapter 16

Personal Image Generators

Turner Whitted
Numerical Design Limited

Introduction

Distributed entertainment calls for delivery of content to the end user on a personal scale. This rather obvious requirement is only now beginning to influence the design of image generation devices. While there is great excitement about the migration of high-performance graphics hardware from the restricted realm of a few hundred thousand engineering workstations to the wide-open spaces of tens of millions of desktop PCs, this falls short of the ultimate goal. In spite of the adjective "personal" in PC, neither desktop nor even laptop computers are truly personal in scale. To gain some perspective on what it means to provide a personal entertainment system, consider audio devices (Figure 16.1).

In almost every respect, audio entertainment is more mature than video. In the days before recording was possible, audio was only available in a centralized form at a concert hall. Recording and broadcasting, which came about within 40 years of each other in the late nineteenth and early twentieth centuries, were the keys to distributed audio. Even in these two forms, distributed audio has undergone radical transformation since then. Some of my earliest memories are of listening to the single large radio in my parents' house and listening to an old Victrola in my grandfather's barn. To my childish imagination, the radio really was large enough to house all of the little people whose voices emanated from the speaker. The Victrola was easier to comprehend since the connection between grooves in the disk, the playback needle, and the horn from which sounds came was graphically depicted in the device's construction. Placing such mechanisms in an automobile to be carried with the listener was a logical intermediate step on the road to placing the delivery terminal on the listener's belt as a complement to the speakers on the listener's head and calling the whole assembly a Walkman.

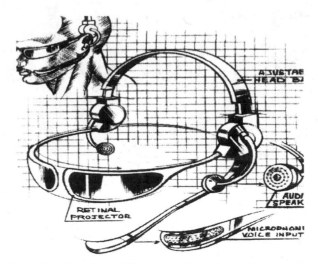

Figure 16.1   Head-mounted display with audio and video sources.

Just as headphones preceded Walkmen by decades, head-mounted displays (HMDs) are quickly being reduced to a personal scale well in advance of belt-mounted image generators. The idealized Walkman-inspired HMD shown in Figure 16.1 represents a nicely proportioned combination of audio and visual sources. Optical considerations aside, it is not terribly far ahead of the current commercial offerings of HMDs.

What, then, can we say about the state of image generators? The notion of a personal image generator (PIG) is almost completely unknown. Today's idea of reduction to personal scale is to make image generation part of personal computers. It seems natural to assume that this technology will then make the jump to laptop computers and perhaps from there the final leap to a RealityEngine in a coat pocket. However, we still measure image generation performance in terms of polygons or pixels per second and not in terms of frames per Watt-hour.

That a change to our way of thinking about graphics systems is needed goes without saying. I suggest that this change is more radical than simply imposing an altered set of design criteria and proceeding down the same path we have taken before. Our current model of a graphics system utilizes digital circuitry to produce geometric descriptions of the world about us and to then convert that geometry to regularly spaced image samples that are presented to us on a televisionlike display. In order to provide high-performance graphics on a truly personal scale, we may be forced to alter every aspect of the current model. However, even radical shifts can be evolutionary, and we must consider the intermediate steps as well as the endpoint.

PIGs are entirely different beasts from laboratory graphics terminals and have entirely different sets of design constraints. The purpose of this chapter is to identify these constraints and redirect thinking away from raw performance toward effectiveness on a personal scale.

Configurations

If workstation graphics is the starting point in the quest for personal display systems and if coat-pocket systems are the ultimate goal, then there are going to be several steps along the way. One would anticipate that these will be successful products in their own right.

To discuss the evolution of configurations without considering applications would be foolish. There are three obvious application areas for immersive display systems:

1. Games—a class of entertainment application in which the user actively steers, controls, and effectively contributes content.

2. Passive entertainment—a class of application in which the user does not control or contribute content even though head-tracked viewing is employed.

3. Communications—enhanced telephony in which the user interacts visually and audibly face-to-face with other participants.

The distinctions among these classes of application are stated much too sharply. For example, a good virtual reality game is likely to be networked and to have player-to-player voice communications as well as the expected visual confrontations. Less obviously, business applications such as videoconferencing have many of the attributes of games. The effectiveness of current videoconferencing is severely limited by "turn-taking" etiquette. An immersive videoconferencing application with spatialized audio and the ability to wander around in "meeting space" eliminates the need for a turn-taking protocol and provides the mechanisms for a rapid, free-for-all style of interaction that includes simultaneous talking, private conversations off to the side, and the general freedom to act as if the conference were physical rather than virtual. The technology to accomplish immersive teleconferencing is roughly the same as that needed for networked games. However, one would expect a business application to cost more and to take place in a different physical setting. Consequently, the configurations may be quite different. Since the entertainment applications intuitively seem to call for more portability, the discussion that follows is directed mainly at them.

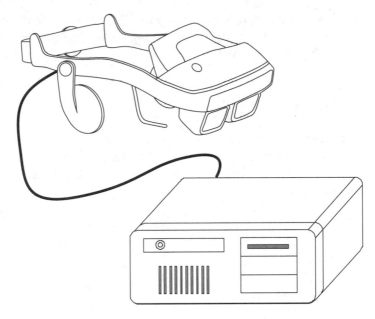

Figure 16.2   Head-mounted display as an add-on to a desktop PC.

We are in the midst of step one along the path to these applications as 3D graphics capability is on the verge of becoming a standard feature of *all* new personal computers. Beyond this transition, the configuration diagrammed in Figure 16.2 is attracting much attention. Here, the HMD is an add-on peripheral to a desktop PC. HMD developers hope to capitalize on the successful penetration of 3D-capable PCs into the home market to provide a platform for immersive applications, primarily games.

There are two analogous configurations that are popular with consumers today. The most physically obvious is the use of headphones in conjunction with hi-fi receivers and amplifiers. This arrangement became popular in the late 1960s and remains common today. Both the PC/HMD and receiver/headphone combinations share the same drawback—users are tethered to the console. As noted earlier, this drawback has been overcome in audio products by making the console itself portable.

A less obvious analog is the telephone. In those cases where the telephone handset is tethered to a base, the umbilical is long and stretchy. More and more, however, cordless phones are finding their way into places where any tether is awkward. The idea of an HMD as a cordless peripheral has great appeal.

Neither of these analogs is perfect. In the case of portable stereos, the application is not interactive and the content, entirely audio, has low bandwidth. As for the telephone, the content also has even lower bandwidth even though it is an interactive medium. With the addition of imagery, an immersive display system has bandwidth requirements that are orders of magnitude greater than audio systems and is interactive even when the content is passive (for example, the head tracker is likely to be enabled even when watching a movie). This requirement suggests that we should not contemplate severing the HMD from the display generator even in a cordless configuration. However, we know that a portable display generator with the storage capacity, network connections, and processing power of a PC console is not reasonable in the near term. (Wearable computer systems, available now for industrial applications, are basically repackaged PCs and are not really in the same category as the entertainment and communications devices described in this chapter.)

Everything we know about applications and most of what we can observe about today's technology seem to lead us to a cordless configuration in which the display generator is a satellite of the console. (To call the console a PC is a bit limiting, but the term "information appliance" sounds so contrived.) We can anticipate a wireless arrangement as shown in Figure 16.3.

This cordless configuration poses problems of its own, including limits on bandwidth to the host. While current infrared links can run as fast as 4 megabits per second, the rate is not high enough to simply transmit video through the link. What can reasonably be placed in such a package is subject to the design requirements and constraints listed in later sections. Because of the limited bandwidth available across the wireless link, one would certainly anticipate that the graphics processor is part of the remote package.

Finally, there is the totally self-contained unit that is the goal toward which these intermediate steps progress. Of recent developments, the system that came closest to commercial reality is the Hasbro VR home entertainment product whose components are diagrammed in Figure 16.4.

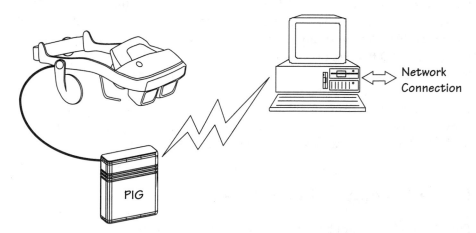

Figure 16.3 Cordless display generator as a satellite of the console.

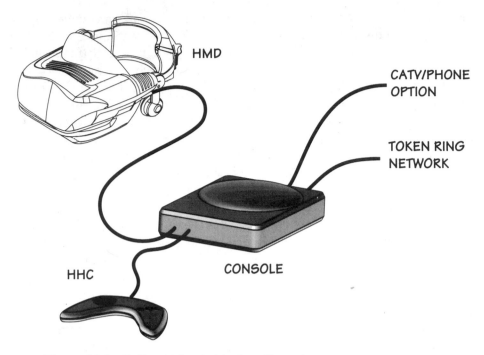

Figure 16.4   Self-contained virtual reality system.

Hasbro's VR system was never completed and brought to market because the cost to the end user would have put it out of the reach of the average consumer. The experience of designing the product left all who participated in the design with convictions of what can or cannot work in a personal display console. Although there is no means of building a wearable consumer product with today's technology, the designers decided to keep the console in close proximity to the user. The inevitable umbilicals were the power cable and the network cables. As physically restrictive as this sounds, it is a far cry from tethering the HMD to a PC or wiring a conventional game console to a television set. The size of the console was intentionally kept small to imply portability.

While extrapolation to a pocket-sized apparatus seems modest, the experience of attempting to build a commercial product with today's technology shows us that there are significant obstacles to get past. The next three sections deal with these technical obstacles and consider potential solutions.

Image Generation Requirements

From a purely academic point of view, head-tracked immersive graphics systems are wonderful to study because they combine a requirement for lightweight, wide field of view (FOV) with high resolution, and the need for high frame rates with low latency. In other words, these systems are devilishly difficult to build. Here are some of the more important considerations and trade-offs.

- **Weight, Cost, and Optics.** Much of the cost of an HMD is in LCD displays. In the Hasbro HMD, a single LCD was combined with very clever optical design. The result had a much lower cost but was also heavier than a design of equivalent quality using two LCDs.

- **FOV and Resolution.** LCD resolution remains a limiting factor. Because a wide field of view is required for effective immersion, the size of any individual pixel of a low-resolution LCD viewed at a wide angle will be noticeable to the viewer. Some manufacturers have opted to restrict the FOV to preserve the density of pixels, but the displays cannot be truly called immersive.

  As HMDs evolve toward higher resolution, the load on the image generator grows proportionally. Stated more pessimistically, load on the image generator increases as the square of the linear density of cells in the LCD. This assumes, of course, that the pixels are presented to the viewer in a uniformly spaced array. Since visual acuity is not uniform over the field of view, it makes sense to distribute the pixel array nonuniformly with greater density in the center and less in the periphery. Even though such a distribution may be accomplished optically, it forces the image generator to adopt a viewing transformation in which straight lines map to curves.

- **Scene Management.** A wider field of view admits more of a scene into the visible image, raising the geometric complexity of the scene. However, the complexity is mainly required in the center of the view. This suggests that the geometric complexity can be managed at the expense of more level of detail preprocessing.

- **Frame Rate and Latency.** These two factors go hand in hand, but in a head-tracked display latency is intolerable. The brute-force approach to reducing latency is to increase the frame rate. However, the head tracking process also contributes to lag, so the benefits of a higher frame rate are limited.

- **Visual Quality.** Convincing immersion requires effective shading and anti-aliasing. While "effective" is not synonymous with "realistic," each feature adds to the burden of the display generator.

LCDs available for low-cost head-mounted displays today are limited to resolutions of 320×200 or less. A modest fill rate of 10-million pixels per second would cover the image area to a depth of 5 at a 30-Hz frame rate but would only cover to a depth of 1 at 640×480 resolution. Geometric throughput requirements are a much squishier set of numbers. On the one hand, it is impossible to discern the details of highly complex scenes on a low-resolution display without anti-aliasing. On the other hand, graphics systems are never exercised at full efficiency, and it is advisable to provide excess capacity at the front end of the graphics pipeline. Again referring to experience from Hasbro's project, we settled on a design with a geometric throughput of approximately 350,000 triangles per second and a good balance of data rates internally in the graphics processor. Ruthlessly simplifying the control logic produced a design that some would consider brute force but whose projected cost was less than $20 when combined with all of the system I/O functions on a single integrated circuit. In the long run, the need for high resolution will defeat such a straightforward design.

Physical Design Constraints

A personal entertainment system, including audio and networking as well as image generation, has overall design constraints that trickle down to constraints imposed on the hardware and software of the PIG subsystem. (Yes, software consumes space, drains the battery, and generates heat, too.) A discussion of these constraints follows.

- **Size.** The minimum configuration of an SGI Reality Engine 1 is a pair of 14"×14" circuit boards. All circuitry for a Sony PlayStation fits within a 7"×10" area. Yet the typical Walkman is no bigger than 3"×4.5" and is only that large because it must accommodate a large and obsolete storage medium, a tape cassette, within its case. There is a large need to further shrink the circuitry to bring image generation to a truly personal level.

- **Power.** The latest advances in nickel-metal-hydride battery design provide as much as 3.5 Watt-hours of energy in a 2-ounce package. Eight ounces of this type of battery could power a 3-Watt display system for up to 3 hours. However, 3 Watts is not very much power at all considering that the power requirements of the HMD itself must be included in this energy budget.

- **Heat.** Personal means wearable. My cellular phone is sometimes uncomfortably hot in my coat pocket. In addition to reducing the size and power consumption of the PIG, reducing its temperature is vital as well.

- **Bandwidth.** This is a can of worms for any number of reasons. Graphics applications have a voracious appetite for bandwidth. Laboratory and high-end commercial systems attack this need with heavy-duty parallelism. Figure 16.5 outlines data flow in a typical graphics application in which only a single memory block is common to the entire graphics system.

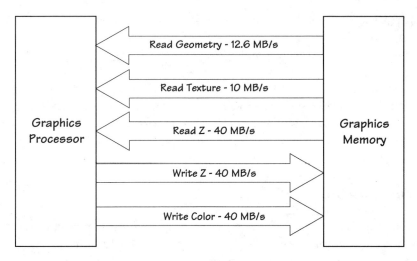

Figure 16.5 Data flow in a typical graphics application.

- **Performance.** It isn't fair to say that performance is what you're left with after all other constraints are satisfied. Resolutions below a certain level are useless. Scene complexity below a certain level makes for an uninteresting product. Lag greater than some amount may make the user ill. Taken together, these considerations define a threshold of acceptable performance. Products whose performance falls below the threshold ought not to be considered. Based on observations of VR games, one can assume that 320×200 is the absolute minimum acceptable resolution, 30 Hz is the minimum frame rate, and the commonly accepted permissible lag of 0.1 second is probably too high. This level of performance provides a comfortable experience and, for entertainment, comfort is as much an issue as effectiveness.

- **Cost.** Cost is the wild card of constraints. Using the history of audio products, we can quickly do some back-of-the-envelope calculations to figure cost targets. When first introduced in 1979, the Sony Walkman Professional sold for $400. Today, a smaller unit of similar quality can be found for less than $100. This reduction in cost is not nearly as dramatic as the real drop in costs of integrated circuitry. Consequently, although it may provide a good example of a target cost for a completed personal entertainment subsystem, it is far too conservative as a guide to the cost of the component circuitry. Nevertheless, let's blindly assume that integrated circuitry, including memory, makes up 25 percent of the cost of the finished product and the manufacturing cost is one-half the suggested retail price. Then, we should work toward a budget of $50 for all circuitry. As a point of comparison, note that the lowest-quality laptop computers hover around $1,000 suggested retail price. If we eliminated all of the disk drives and applied the same rough assumptions, then the circuitry in the laptop computer should have a cost of roughly $100. In other words, this target is not at all far-fetched.

One might be tempted to take a wait-and-see approach to meeting these constraints. After all, the cost of electronic components will surely drop and speed will surely rise. However, there is an opportunity to jump ahead of the device technology with clever architecture.

Architectures

The conventional way of thinking about any display generation system is summarized in Figure 16.6. This model comprises a geometric processor followed by a raster processor. The geometric processing makes heavy use of multiplication and performs a series of operations on each parcel of data. For this reason, off-the-shelf DSPs are popular for geometric processing in high-end graphics systems.

For low-end systems, there is an almost universal assumption that geometric processing is performed in a general-purpose processor. The raster engine, on the other hand, is highly specialized with tight coupling to one or more dedicated display memories and almost always implemented as a special-purpose circuit.

The relevance of this description is that it provides a basis for determining how much performance can be crammed into a small package and powered by batteries for a usable interval. As we can see, the prospects are not encouraging. Even a tiny display system with 4 megabytes of DRAM and a single display generator ASIC will dissipate at least 4 Watts.

If the prospects for achieving a cordless image generator with conventional architectures are so dim, then we should consider such alternatives as the following:

• Cutting the power consumption of digital circuitry.

• Increasing the energy density of batteries.

Figure 16.6 Summary of display generation system.

- Finding more efficient algorithms for image generation.

- Defining a low-power architecture.

The first two alternatives are someone else's battle. That is to say, these advances are part of the general trend in hardware. In spite of steady advances, the energy density of batteries does have physical limits imposed by the chemistry of the battery materials. The most significant gains in battery life are due to the lower operating voltages of digital circuits.

As to progress on the last two items, they are purely the responsibility of those of us who devote our work to graphics. The fact that our overall model of image generation hasn't changed in 25 years makes me think that our ranks are filled with reactionaries. However, there are glimmers of radical thinking that may prove worthy of pursuit. For example, here are three new ideas that may provide a path to a truly untethered immersive apparatus:

1. **Image-Based Rendering.** Image-based rendering, such as that popularized by QuickTime VR (Chen 1995), is a form of display processing that warps an existing image to produce a different view of the scene that appeared in the original image. Because the processing cost for image-based rendering is proportional to the resolution of the display rather than the geometric complexity of the scene, the power requirements should be constant.

   A variant of image-based rendering is postrendering warping (Regan and Pose 1994). This technique opens the possibility of rendering images at a low frame rate while using the postrendering warps to update intermediate frames. If one accepts that warping consumes less power than rendering, then there is economy in this approach.

2. **Difference Rendering.** By rendering both crude and accurate images of the same scene, the difference between the two can be used to restore the crude rendering to full quality. If both accurate and crude rendering as well as differencing are performed on a server, then crude rendering on a client can be restored by transmitting the difference from the server to the client (Levoy 1995). Initially envisioned as a method of producing high-quality imagery on inexpensive set-top boxes, this approach may also offer promise for satellite rendering processors.

3. **Analog Processing.** It is an article of faith that only digital processing provides the accuracy needed for geometric operations. However, analog circuits can perform many of the graphics operations with high accuracy and much lower power (Kirk and Barr 1993). In fact, some

graphics terminals from as late as the 1970s incorporated analog transformation units.

Note that these ideas did not evolve from the need for portability. Given an explicit goal of portability and the clear target of an image generator on a personal scale, other effective approaches will undoubtedly emerge. One can reasonably bet that the PIG architectures will not be merely scaled-down versions of today's architectures.

Applications and Progress

In the past, we would have expected military applications to provide much of the impetus for accelerating the development of PIGs. Engineers preparing for the "digital battlefield" already imagine the dialogue between soldiers and their commander: "Sir, we've plenty of food, water, fuel, and ammunition, but we're running perilously low on batteries." While this is worlds away from an indignant teenager yelling, "Mom, stop at the next convenience store! My ImmerseMan is dead!," it's technically the same problem. A soldier desperate to distinguish friend from foe in a helmet-mounted look-through display depends on the same technology as an adolescent attending an interactive virtual rock concert. It may still be true that war is a bigger enterprise than entertainment, but entertainment executives are seldom accused of preparing for the previous movie, or concert, or television series. In the current age, the demands of commercial applications may well push technology harder and faster than those of military applications. This is not necessarily good since cost becomes the overwhelmingly dominant constraint from the very beginning. We may find ourselves saddled with inferior technology in the first generation and then plagued by backward compatibility woes in subsequent generations.

On the bright side, commercial acceptance demands elegant designs. In 1961, I was the only kid in my neighborhood who rode around wearing military surplus headphones on a bicycle equipped with a long whip antenna, batteries taped under the seat, and a handmade transistor radio strapped to the handlebars. It was clunky, dangerous, and of low quality, but that was the price of mobile rock 'n' roll. The cheap and commercially successful versions of the same product that followed only a few years later were *much* smaller and provided *much* better performance. In the arena of personal entertainment, the primary barrier between awkward experiments and phenomenal commercial success seems to be the hurdle of designing and building to a personal scale at an affordable price.

References

Chen, Shenchang Eric, "QuickTime VR—An Image-Based Approach to Virtual Environment Navigation," in *Proceedings of SIGGRAPH '95* pp. 29–38, Los Angeles, Calif., August 6-11, 1995.

Hasbro, Inc., Press release, July 19, 1995.

Kirk, David B., and Barr, Alan H., "Implementing Rotation Matrix Constraints in Analog VLSI," in *Proceedings of SIGGRAPH '93* pp. 45–52, Anaheim, Calif., August 1-6, 1993.

Levoy, Marc, "Polygon-Assisted JPEG and MPEG Compression of Synthetic Images," *Proceedings of SIGGRAPH '95* pp. 21–28, Los Angeles, Calif., August 6–11, 1995.

Regan, Matthew, and Pose, Ronald, "Priority Rendering with a Virtual Reality Address Recalculation Pipeline," in *Proceedings of SIGGRAPH '94* pp. 155–162, Orlando, Fla., July 24–29, 1994.

Biography

Turner Whitted began his engineering career designing and programming automatic test equipment for the Western Electric Company. He continued as a development engineer, working with Bell Laboratories to design computer interfaces to signal processing and display equipment for the U.S. Navy.

Following that he moved to research, first as a graduate student and later as a member of the technical staff at Bell Laboratories. During this period, he introduced a method of simulating global illumination using ray tracing that continues to be a widely used computer graphics technique.

Returning to software development in 1983, Dr. Whitted cofounded Numerical Design Limited, where he serves as technical director. He is also a research professor of computer science at the University of North Carolina at Chapel Hill and works as an independent consultant on graphics hardware and software.

He earned B.S.E. and M.S. degrees from Duke University and a Ph.D. from North Carolina State University, all in electrical engineering. He is an adjunct research professor at Duke University, papers chair for SIGGRAPH '97, an *IEEE Computer Graphics and Applications* editorial board member, a member of IEEE, and an ACM Fellow.

Chapter 17

Designing and Developing for Head-Mounted Displays

Joanna Alexander and Mark Long
Zombie, LLC

Introduction

Virtual reality is on the verge of becoming a consumer electronic product. Several entertainment systems are now available—both multimedia computers with 3D accelerators and 32/64-bit game consoles—that are capable of real-time virtual reality performance. In addition, several companies have released PC-based head-mounted displays (HMDs) at price points intended to make virtual reality entertainment affordable to the consumer. Soon we'll see low-cost HMDs designed for portable DVD players that will also be compatible with the home 3D platforms. The DVD HMDs will then generate demand for cheaper, higher-resolution displays that can deliver the high-quality experience that consumers are anticipating in VR entertainment.

In order to design and develop for HMDs, software developers must acquire new skills. They must be able to optimize C code for realtime graphics generation, create 3D models for a computationally constrained polygonal environment, integrate 3D audio, and understand the psychophysics of head-mounted displays at a fundamental level. While we don't attempt to cover all these issues in this chapter, we describe the enabling technologies of VR and their respective limitations, the psychophysics of HMDs, stereoscopic versus monoscopic image generation decisions, graphical user interface (GUI) issues, 3D audio, and headtracking for HMDs.

Enabling Technologies of Virtual Reality

Although the term "virtual reality" is relatively new to our vocabulary, the enabling technologies have actually been around for a while. Their origins are found in computer-aided design (CAD) and flight simulation. It's only recently, however, that VR systems and VR-related technologies have descended to a price point that puts them in reach of computer game players. For example, three head-mounted displays have been introduced as peripherals for 32/64-bit multimedia computers and game consoles: the VFX from Forte, the i•glasses from Virtual I/O, and the Virtuality2000 from Virtuality UK. Each uses the same set of enabling components to create the illusion that the player is "inside the game." In each case, the displays are color LCDs, the headtracker is a combination of magnetometers and tilt sensors, the earphones are low-cost stereo speakers, and the optics are injection-molded acrylic.

Image quality is the largest design issue for HMD games. The spatial resolution of consumer market HMDs is less than SVGA, making text unreadable and certain texture maps unresolvable. Spatial resolution has several attributes in an HMD; the two most important are the resolution of the display and the resolution of the optics. HMD manufacturers currently adapt and use displays designed for camcorders and pocket TVs. Those are the only LCDs currently available in mass market quantities (and prices) that meet the form-factor requirements of HMDs. This is a problem because camcorder viewfinders have very low spatial resolutions—usually 640×400 pixels or less. The spatial resolution of these LCDs is currently so low that a player may have difficulty recognizing objects and characters.

An HMD that uses a 320×240 LCD with a 60-degree instantaneous field of view produces a viewed resolution of 5.3 pixels per degree. By way of comparison, the human eye can perceive ~60 pixels per degree (Figure 17.1). When the HMD optics enlarge these small displays, the effect is like looking at a brick wall at a very close distance. The individual color triads are immediately apparent because pixel fill space is low and the layout of the underlying thin film transistor (TFT) structure creates the brick effect. Most HMD designers add a diffusing filter to soften the brick effect, but this exacerbates the already low resolution by further blurring the image. Limited color capability is also a problem of these displays. Currently, even the best active matrix technologies are capable of only 8- or 16-bit depth, while 24-, 32-, and 64-bit color is becoming the norm supported by most workstation displays.

Surprisingly, all of these spatial limitations come about because HMD manufacturers are using LCDs designed for other purposes. While current technology could produce better LCD displays, the existing commercial market doesn't require the investment necessary to manufacture such displays. Better resolution displays are on the way, and they're likely to be half as expensive as the current versions. Portable DVD players will soon create a larger demand for small megapixel LCDs that HMD manufacturers will integrate into their next-generation designs. These small LCDs will also be used in home theater projection systems, which are likely to be quite popular because the image and sound quality of HDTV are so much better than the current television standards.

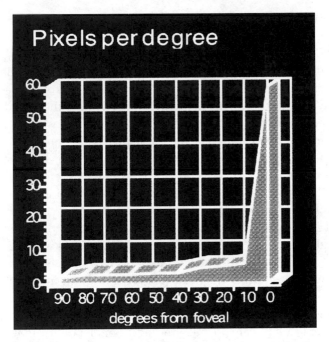

Figure 17.1 Foveal acuity; about 60 pixels per degree or .77 arc-minute per pixel. Acuity drops an order of magnitude at 10° off the foveal axis.

One of the most promising of these new display technologies is ferroelectric liquid crystal (FLC). FLC layers can be made very thin, enabling extremely small pixels, which translates into smaller displays that can be manufactured at lower costs. FLC displays also have larger viewing angles than LCDs, allowing for more compact optical designs that require less power for illumination. Displaytech, Inc., in Boulder, Colorado, has recently integrated FLC technology with a CMOS active matrix mirror backplane to create a display package smaller than a postage stamp with SVGA resolution.

In the longer term, radically different display technologies will make truly compelling VR possible. One of the most promising of these new displays is the retinal scanning laser developed at the University of Washington's Human Interface Technology Laboratory. The retinal laser has no optical lens train, but rather scans the image directly onto the back of the viewer's eye. This means there is no inherent limitation in image resolution. A retinal-scanning laser-based HMD would be able to meet or exceed the foveal acuity of the eye—generating an image that equals the spatial resolution of the real world!

Until the HMD market takes off and creates a demand for megapixel-density LCDs, image quality will continue to be a major issue for developers.

Our own strategy is to straddle the market—to produce games that are HMD "compatible" until a sufficient installed base is developed to support the production of HMD-only games.

All commercial HMDs use molded spherical or aspherical lenses. These lenses have aberrations that a designer must minimize through tradeoffs in the system. How well the designer/manufacturers engineer these tradeoffs largely determines how good the HMD is. Achieving greater precision in objective lens design requires complex lens systems set at precise tolerances. These requirements increase weight and mass, which can make the HMD prohibitively expensive, unwieldy, and delicate. We've found large differences in the optical quality of HMDs and advise designers/developers to carefully evaluate each before deciding which to support.

The real magic of virtual reality is created by the headtracker. Headtrackers can calculate a player's head position and orientation with up to 6 degrees of freedom: 3 rotational degrees (orientation of the head) and 3 translational degrees (position of the head relative to a point in space). All current PC-grade HMDs track only rotational positions because current methods of implementing translational tracking require expensive emissive sensor technology. Players don't seem to miss the additional fidelity that translational tracking provides, however. Our theory is that players adapted to translating their POV by mouse/keyboard/joystick input long ago, and this adaptation carries over.

The headtracker communicates with the CPU via an RS232 3-wire serial interface on most HMDs. When the headtracker is initialized by the application, the CPU puts the headtracker in either a streaming or a polling mode. The default mode for most HMDs is streamed ASCII II packets. In the polled mode, the headtracker awaits a request from the CPU before sending a packet. When position data is relayed, the headtracking component sends a bit stream with information describing the player's rotational head position at rates of ~8 Hz to 60 Hz. The HMD manufacturers' software development kits (SDKs) all include a driver that interprets these packets. Some manufacturers include an ASIC that converts the bit stream to driver instructions. Others send raw data to the CPU for conversion. HMDs with conversion in ASICs are much faster and reduce the computational burden on a CPU already overloaded with the computational requirements of performing 3D graphics calculations and writing to the screen.

Up to now, tracking updates of about 12 MHz to 20 MHz are sufficient; this is driven by the need to match or exceed the frame rate of the average game. As 3D graphics APIs become further optimized for faster CPUs, the frame rates will increase and headtrackers will also need to speed up. Games that go into production for release next year should anticipate these accelerations in performance.

HMD Psychophysics

HMDs can have an effect on a player's vestibular system. Motion sickness is still common even in high-end research VR systems. The main cause of motion sickness is frame latency, which occurs when a player turns the head and the game view lags behind that physical head position. Players overcompensate and their world view becomes like a bucket of water, sloshing back and forth as they attempt to control the latency. Humans can turn their heads at rates approaching 1,700 degrees per second, so all VR systems have some degree of latency. The question for developers is, What is the acceptable range of latency?

The generally acceptable range of frame rates to combat latency seems to be 12 Hz and up. Frame rates in the 8 Hz to 12 Hz range are what VR researchers have called the "barfogenic zone"—a rate too slow for the brain's ability to fuse images into perceived motion and too fast for the eye's ability to secade. (Secading is the rapid movement of the eye's focus point—your eye secades when it reaches the end of a line in this paragraph and jumps to the beginning of the next line.) Anything faster than 20 Hz is going to be perceived by the player as much better quality. At ~30 Hz most players are satisfied with the frame rate. At frame rates above ~45 Hz the increase becomes imperceptible to most players.

Controlling frame rate is a very complex development task. It involves much more than the speed of the headtracker. Frame rate is actually more dependent on scene complexity, which is related to the number and quality of the polygons that make up the world image. Obviously, more detail is desirable, but the state of the art currently requires several compromises to keep the frame rate high enough to be perceived as realtime.

Players generally accommodate to lower frame rates by simply turning their heads more slowly. This is OK for an adventure game, but it's probably not OK for a racing or flying experience, and certainly not for "twitch" games. In anecdotal analysis, we have observed that players actually prefer a slower deterministic frame rate over a periodically fast one. When players can anticipate how rapidly the HMD responds to their head motions, accommodation seems much easier.

HMDs can also temporarily affect the player's vision. In order to create the illusion that the displays (which are actually only 2 inches away from your eyes) are a game world focused somewhere between 30 feet and infinity, a synergistic response of the eye muscles and pupils must be uncoupled. (See Figures 17.2 and 17.3.)

Normally, when we look at an object that's 2 inches away, our eyes actually converge inward and focus at that distance. The human visual system synergistically converges/diverges (eyes rotate in/out) as the pupil focuses. However, when images are viewed on a binocular or biocular HMD, these two

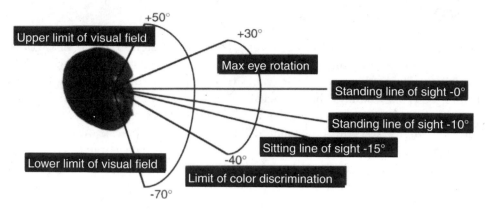

Figure 17.2   Vertical measurements of the human visual field.

ocular responses are uncoupled. The user experiences this as eye strain, which can make the HMD fatiguing to wear for extended periods. Depending on the quality of the HMD's optics, this strain can be either nominal or uncomfortable. Accommodative changes brought about by this convergence are problematic because they reduce retinal image sharpness and cause the eyes to over-accommodate. Developers currently lessen the effect by accurately matching the stereo projection angles of the game environment to an average person's interpupillary distance (the distance between your eyes, ~62 mm) or simply by designing the game to be monoscopic.

Color also has an important psychophysical effect on the player. Because the HMD fills the player's field of view, essentially blocking out the rest of the world, color choice has a greater impact than it would on a monitor. The ANSI standards for workstations and software provide some guidance for color use. For example, magenta can make some players feel uncomfortable if

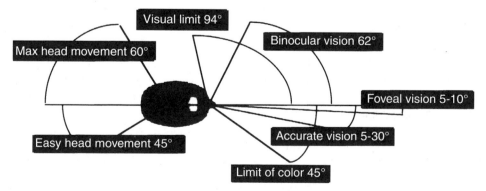

Figure 17.3   Horizontal ranges of the human visual field.

used predominately in a scene, and, since 6 percent of males and 2 percent of females are color-blind, pure blues should be avoided on black backgrounds.

Color can also be used to a designer's advantage. It's possible to select color palettes that create a greater sense of depth. A phenomenon known as chromostereopsis creates the illusion of depth when colors at the far ends of the spectrum are combined in a scene. Deep blues and purples will appear to recede into the background, while red and yellow objects appear to advance into the foreground. This effect can be used quite effectively in shaded environments.

Stereoscopic Versus Monoscopic Designs

All the current PC and game console HMDs are capable of stereoscopic display. Stereoscopic means that there are two images, right and left, generated for the two displays; monoscopic means there is one image generated for the two displays.

Stereoscopic displays can greatly enhance the feeling of immersion or sense of presence in virtual environments. Stereo gives the player important depth cues and perspective. But stereoscopic image generation requires some design trade-offs that a developer should consider before concluding that stereo is the way to go.

The default mode for all of the first generation of consumer HMDs is 320×200×256. In 640×480 mode, there is enough video memory to generate two or four 320×240 buffers. The application can then treat these buffers as one or two pages of paired stereo images. The first 320 pixels on a scan line is then displayed on the left-eye LCD, and the next 320 pixels is displayed on the right-eye LCD. Every other scan line is used to create two separate 320×240 buffers that form the stereo image. The remaining scan lines are not displayed; they can be used as buffers.

Our visual system uses other clues besides left- and right-eye parallax to assimilate depth perspective. Some virtual reality research has concluded that shadows and textures may be more important than parallax (Air Force Super Cockpit Program, DeFanti et al.). So, developers should consider these effects as well. A great example of a virtual reality game that best utilizes this concept is Flight Unlimited by Origin, a biplane flight simulator that uses detailed terrain maps to create highly realistic altitude and speed effects without resorting to stereoscopic display.

The major factor in deciding between a stereoscopic or monoscopic display may ultimately be the type of game you are designing. Stereo vision occurs in a limited range—approximately 2 inches to 200 feet from the eye, with the effect falling off exponentially after just 30 feet. If you are designing a flight simulator where most of the objects and environment are beyond this range, there will be almost no enhancement from stereo; the CPU cycles required to generate the second image are mostly wasted. Driving simulators fall on the edge of stereo vision, with vehicles and environments occurring both inside and outside these parameters. First-person action-adventure games will be enhanced the most—with plenty of opportunities for motion parallax, texture mapping, and shadow/lighting effects.

GUI for HMD-Based Games

Since players are not able to see their hands while wearing an HMD, the GUI must be well integrated into the game environment. This can be difficult due to the limitations imposed by the current generation of HMDs. The display resolution is so low that a player will not be able to read text that appears as anything smaller than 36-point font size. He or she will be unable to resolve certain texture maps or rotate the eyes comfortably off-axis. We recommend as an alternative that game setup be conducted on the monitor. The action then transitions to the HMD in a video sequence that allows the player time to don and adjust the device. Once inside the game, the controls and player status should be part of the environment. Virtuality, Ltd. did a great job with this in Exorex, their Battle-mech arcade game. Audio was used to reinforce the visual cues: WAV files played back alerts and status like "proximity warning!" or "shields 20 percent!" Exorex also had a clever environmental map that could be toggled to overlay onto the out-the-window scene—combining two perspectives simultaneously. This map overlay technique is also successfully employed as a navigation aid in id Software's Doom and Parallax, Inc.'s Descent.

In spite of the inherent visual barrier, it's possible to use the keyboard with HMDs, and many players prefer keyboard control. Nonetheless, control input will be provided more successfully by joysticks and mice. Both can be manipulated by feel and allow the player a greater range of physical motion. As HMDs become more popular, new types of virtual reality input devices that are tracked in 3-space will reach mass-market price points. The Cricket from DIDI is a good example of an input controller with 6 degrees of freedom (DOF). These devices will give designers greater freedom to implement actions like pointing, shooting, and picking up objects. The Forte HMD already ships with a Cyber Puck, a rotational tracking device with 12 programmable keys. These devices further enhance a player's sense of presence by including a physical representation of themselves in their first-person views. The VPL Data Glove and Mattel Power Glove are great examples of this. Seeing one's hand in the virtual space—even if the space is displayed on a television—extends the player's sense of presence into the game space and enhances the illusion of immersion.

3D Audio

Early research in VR indicated that when subjects were shown identical graphical environments, but incrementally superior audio, they thought that the environments accompanied by better sound actually had better graphics. Research pioneers like Scott Foster and Bo Gehring (NASA and Dartmouth, respectively) realized early on that spatialized and localized audio sources contributed greatly to a subject's sense of presence.

Foster illustrates just how powerful human audio-processing power is with an example he calls the "cocktail party effect." "If you think about your ability to follow a conversation at a cocktail party, while at the same time selectively tuning your hearing attention to also listen for the doorbell or to follow a second conversation, you realize that we have the ability to multiprocess incredible amounts of audio data simultaneously," says Foster, "yet we hardly take advantage of this ability in virtual environmental design."

The only current limitation in generating 3D audio is the processing power of the computer or game console. 3D audio can be considered the sonic equivalent of ray tracing—generating sound effects that seem to be reflected, absorbed, radiated, and Doppler shifted. Unfortunately, doing this in realtime for more than one source is computationally intensive and has, until very recently, required an expensive, separate 3D audio card. The addition of programmable digital signal processors and powerful new CPUs in multimedia PCs and game consoles has made it possible to integrate 3D audio; there are several vendors of 3D or spatialized sound drivers. 3D audio APIs currently available on the commercial market include AudioReality from Aureal/Crystal River Engineering and Focal Point from Focal Point Audio.

3D audio adds a new texture to game design. Players are able to localize the source of sounds and search for their point of origin. Designers can enhance the sensations of scale and distance. 3D audio enriches the feel of an environment by accurately characterizing its materials. The reflection and absorption characteristics of wooden walls, metal corridors, and wet floors change the quality of a sound and enhance the user's experience in a synthetic environment.

Consumer-Grade Head-Mounted Displays

The first group of head-mounted displays for the consumer market (the other significant markets being high-end research and simulation) all came from brand-new companies dedicated to consumer VR. Sony and other consumer electronics manufacturers have passed on early entry (Sony has shown but never released an HMD for video viewing called the "Visotron"). The exception is Nintendo, which introduced VirtualBoy—a head-mounted display and computer image generator combined. VirtualBoy appeared to be more of a novelty entertainment device, however, with no ability to head-track or to adapt to anything other than its underpowered image generator. It did, however, have a novel display made up of red LEDs and a vibrating mirror that generates a 320×200 resolution image at eight levels of brightness.

Currently, of the three consumer electronic HMDs available for developers to target, the i•glasses provide the best image and the VFX is the most immersive. The difference in emphasis stems from the fact that the products address different market niches.

Virtual I/O i•glasses

The i•glasses HMD is the current top end of image quality for consumer systems. The virtual image is completely flat with no barrel distortion or chromatic aberration. The improvement was achieved at the expense of the field of view, however, so they are the least immersive of the commercial HMDs. Ergonomically, they are lightweight and unobtrusive. The field of view is sufficiently small that one can simply look down without moving the head and see the space where a keyboard is normally positioned. The i•glasses have two displays— each one has 138,000 color pixels in an active matrix aSi LCD. They can display 256 colors in VGA mode over a 30-degree horizontal field of view (100 percent overlap of left and right images). Rotational head tracking is streamed or polled at selectable rates of 1,200, 2,400, 4,800, 9,600, or 19,200 bps and is sensed at

± 45° pitch in 0.1° steps

± 45° roll in 0.1° steps

0–259.9° yaw in 0.1° steps

Audio input to the i•glasses is via left and right RCA-style connections to the PC sound card. Video input is via an NTSC scan converter (included with the HMD) that takes the VGA out by RS232, converts it to one field-sequential NTSC channel, and inputs it via a single 10-foot cable to the HMD.

Forte VFX

The VFX is a mid-priced consumer HMD designed exclusively for the PC game market, emphasizing maximum immersion and durability. Ergonomic features include a flip-up optical assembly that allows players to pause and make keyboard adjustments without taking the HMD completely off. The VFX displays are 120,000 color pixels active matrix aSi LCDs. They can display 256 colors in VGA mode over an 80-degree horizontal field. Rotational headtracking is streamed or polled at selectable rates of 10 Hz to 60 Hz and is sensed at

± 30° pitch in 0.1° steps

± 30° roll in 0.1° steps

0–360° yaw in 0.1° steps

Audio input to the VFX HMD is via left and right RCA-style connections to the PC sound card. We expect to see their next-generation unit double its spatial resolution at two-thirds the current retail price.

Summary

Unfortunately, no developer can yet manufacture a high-resolution, highly immersive HMD that is lightweight, ergonomically terrific, and within the financial reach of the target market. The reason for this is only partly the technological limitations inherent in manufacturing high-resolution LCDs. The principal reason is the high cost of retooling required to begin production of the higher-resolution product—at this time, the user base is not able to support the upgrade.

As soon as these roadblocks are eliminated, we'll see a rush by developers and game publishers alike to port existing games and write new ones, optimized to take advantage of the unique advantages of immersion in a 3D world. Simultaneously, but with a bit less urgency, we'll see new classes of immersive applications emerge. Some will be for education and training. Others will be primarily social in nature, with no traditional game orientation, like PLACE-HOLDER by Brenda Laurel, Rachel Strickland, and Rob Tow. Others will follow in the path of chat rooms and text-based MUDs. And some of the best will be things we haven't thought of yet.

Biographies

Joanna Alexander and Mark Long are the founders of Zombie, LLC, a virtual reality entertainment company based in Seattle. Formerly with the David Sarnoff Research Center, they have 14 years of combined experience in research and development of virtual reality systems and software. Zombie has designed and developed three games that are engineered for PCs and head-mounted displays: Locus, Ice & Fire, and US Army Rangers. The authors can be reached at joanna@zombie.com and mark@zombie.com and http://www.zombie.com

Chapter 18

The Haptic Illusion

Christopher J. Hasser
Immersion Corporation

Thomas H. Massie
SensAble Devices, Inc.

Introduction

haptic: of or pertaining to the sense of touch, especially the perception of force or tactile sensations caused by interaction with one's environment.
Webster's Ninth New Collegiate Dictionary

In the early days of computing, it seemed either a waste of time or pure genius to use anything other than text to interface with a computer. Events have proven that genius was at work, as we now stare slack-jawed at visual extravaganzas such as the special effects in the movie *Terminator 2* or the entirely computer-animated feature film *Toy Story*. Sound effects have become so ubiquitous that each computer in the "multimedia PC" wave has a host of electronics and speakers dedicated solely to impressive audio displays. Our sense of touch has come in a distant third, with users limited to providing input via a mouse, joystick, or keyboard. People don't interact with the real world this way. We use our hands to perceive as well as to act on our environment, like an artist molding clay, a jeweler fixing a watch, or a surgeon searching for a bullet through a small incision. These activities involve such an immediate level of manual interaction that they aren't easily described in terms of "input" and "output" but clearly contain aspects of both.

Interfaces impoverished by a lack of touch sensation create a dualistic sense of "here, where I am" and "there, behind the glass, in that imaginary world." Today's computer users don't have the ability to touch the imaginary world inside their computer any more than they can feel a football hitting the hand of their hometown receiver in a televised Super Bowl and force his hand to successfully grasp the ball. Imagine being able to reach behind the glass and touch that reality! Head-mounted displays can do a credible job of placing you beyond the glass into a visually immersive environment, but the tease becomes apparent when you reach for something and can't feel it. Haptic interface machines display reality to the sense of touch, turning mirages that disappear when the user grasps for them into palpable illusions. Figure 18.1 shows two motorized haptic interfaces presenting a physical image of a virtual object to the thumb and forefinger of a user's hand.

Webster's defines "haptic" as an adjective meaning "of or pertaining to the sense of touch." In recent use, the term "haptic" has taken on a more developed meaning. The sense of touch includes not only the surface skin sensations normally associated with the touch sense but also kinesthetic sensations of movement, limb position, and muscle tension. (Actually, our sense of forces and object weight relies less on kinesthetic muscle tension receptors and more on our sense of effort as indicated by the central nervous system's output to the muscle spindles.) The terms "proprioceptive" and "proprioception" refer to stimuli originating within an organism and are generally used interchangeably with the terms "kinesthetic" and "kinesthesia." With the inclusion of all these senses, it might seem intuitive to regard haptic sensations as "active" tactile, force, and motion sensations that change as a result of a person's movements through an environment and contact with objects in that environment. With this definition, sensations experienced by a passive user (tactile feedback on a stationary finger) wouldn't be considered "haptic." Some researchers view this as too restrictive and prefer to regard haptic feedback as stimulation of limb force and cutaneous skin sensations regardless of whether a person is actively moving or is a passive recipient of stimuli (Srinivasan 1995).

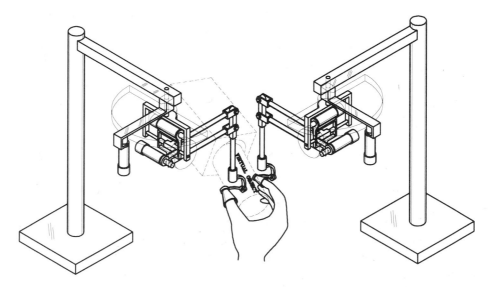

Figure 18.1   Force-reflecting haptic interfaces simulating a virtual object. (Artist: Dave Brock)

The addition of haptic feedback to a virtual reality system can have important benefits. In one study, virtual force-feedback reduced learning time by 50 percent and increased dexterity by 50 percent (Richard et al. 1996). Even with poor-quality force-feedback, another study showed error reduction to a quarter of the level achieved with visual cues alone (Howe and Kontarinis 1992). In addition to giving information about surface details, curvature, texture, and temperature, the tactile sense produces a perception of contact location that can be crucial in the manipulation of objects.

The idea of haptic interfaces isn't new. Some of the first haptic interfaces to virtual environments originated as master controllers for telerobotics. The virtual "hands-on" molecular docking applications at UNC Chapel Hill and at the Air Force's Wright Laboratory are examples of early virtual reality systems using master controllers originally designed to control remote robot arms. Even though haptic interfaces designed specifically for human-computer interaction have only begun to enter widespread use, the idea was presented at least as early as 1965 by Ivan Sutherland:

> *We live in a physical world whose properties we have come to know well through long familiarity. We sense an involvement with this physical world which gives us the ability to predict . . . where objects will fall, how well-known shapes look from other angles, and how much force is required to push objects against friction. We lack corresponding familiarity with the forces on charged particles, forces in nonuniform fields, the effects of nonprojective geometric transformations, and high-inertia, low-friction motion. A display connected to a digital computer gives us a chance to gain familiarity with concepts not realizable in the physical world. It is a looking glass into a mathematical wonderland.*
>
> *If the task of the display is to serve as a looking glass into the mathematical wonderland constructed in a computer memory, it should serve as many senses as possible. So far as I know, no one seriously proposes computer displays of smell or taste. Excellent audio displays exist, but unfortunately we have little ability to have the computer produce meaningful sounds. I want to describe for you a kinesthetic display. The force required to move a joystick could be computer controlled, just as the actuation force on the controls of a Link Trainer are changed to give the feel of a real airplane. With such a display, a computer model of particles in an electric field could combine manual control of the position of a moving charge, replete with the sensation of forces on the charge, with a visual presentation of the charge's position. By use of such an input/output device, we can add a force display to our sight and sound capability.*

Sutherland 1965

Types of Haptic Feedback Devices

Haptic devices can have two types of feedback: force-feedback and tactile feedback. Force-feedback devices act much like robots, with links in series or parallel, powered by electric motors or other actuators to exert forces on the user. The term "force reflection" is used interchangeably with "force-feedback." Tactile feedback devices usually have pin arrays, vibrators, or rotating surfaces to stimulate the cutaneous tactile sense.

Force-Feedback

Force-feedback devices can provide feedback to the user on two levels: coarse (arm) motion and fine (finger) motion. Some systems integrate both fine and coarse force-feedback. Coarse force-feedback devices without fine force-feedback typically have a joystick or other simple hand grip; the user's hand and fingers remain stationary relative to this grip. Fine force-feedback devices without coarse force-feedback must at least have wrist position and orientation sensing to determine the user's hand position or must restrict the user's fingers to a limited workspace.

Both coarse and fine force-feedback systems can take one of two approaches: an exoskeletal construction or an earth-grounded off-the-body construction. Users actually wear exoskeletal devices, which follow the movements of the body joint-for-joint and apply torques to each joint (Figure 18.2). Exoskeletons may be anchored to the ground or to a body part closer to the point of force application (the hips, the shoulder, or even the forearm for a hand exoskeleton). Earth-grounded off-the-body devices provide feedback forces to one or more points on the body without following the body joint-for-joint. As a result, they often have fewer degrees of freedom (DOF) and usually cost less than exoskeletal designs.

One near-term development may involve hybrid systems with exoskeletal and off-the-body components. An application requiring a dextrous finger interface might employ an exoskeletal handmaster such as that in Figure 18.2 mounted to an earth-grounded device to interface with the wrist and arm. Exoskeletal devices become more necessary when more degrees of freedom or more force contact points must be actuated, particularly on the hand (Hasser, Technical Report, 1995). Anthropomorphic arm exoskeletons with 7 DOF can follow a user's elbow and allow the user to achieve the same hand position in more than one way (for example, over or under an obstacle); 6-DOF off-the-body systems can't.

The simplest common earth-grounded device is a joystick. The addition of force-feedback to a joystick can enhance realism in gaming environments, and

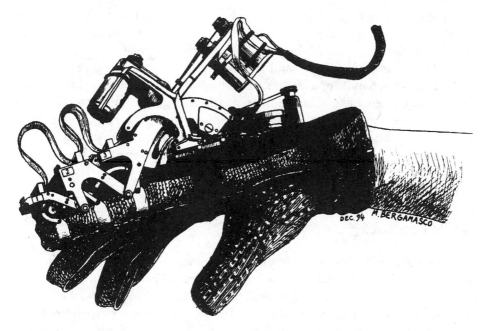

Figure 18.2 A force-reflecting exoskeletal hand master. (Courtesy M. Bergamasco)

recent research has shown that it can improve performance in tasks such as steering wheelchairs and flying airplanes. Some of the more complicated earth-grounded devices include 6-DOF force-reflecting sticks such as those made by JPL/MIT and Cybernet. A new class of interfaces has emerged recently. Members of this class are usually more complicated than joysticks but have fewer than 6 DOF. The new generation of haptic interfaces can be divided into those designed for general use and those designed for a specific task such as medical simulation.

Massie and Salisbury constructed the general-purpose PHANToM, a miniature 3-DOF manipulator shown in Figure 18.1, with a finger thimble on a gimbal for free orientation movement (Massie and Salisbury 1994). More than one PHANToM can be used, one for each finger to allow multifinger grasping and exploration. A system like this could accommodate up to four fingers and would be restricted to desktop use, but may be superior for many applications. General-purpose devices make haptic feedback technology accessible to many disciplines otherwise lacking a "critical mass" that would justify creation of special hardware. They also have begun to build a user base with common hardware experiences that allow users to support one another and create synergy.

Some applications, particularly medical simulation, can justify the development of special-purpose hardware. This approach has numerous advantages.

Often, the device designed within the constraints of a particular task (such as needle insertion) can be designed with fewer DOFs or other features necessary to satisfy general-purpose customers. Also, general-purpose connections to the user's hands such as thimbles and styluses can be replaced by specific hardware such as the handle of a laparoscopic surgical instrument. Special-purpose devices can often be constructed by modifying general-purpose or other special-purpose devices. As a result, commercial hardware manufacturers have developed "portfolios" of user solutions. Users willing to work with off-the-shelf hardware (at least initially) will receive faster delivery at greatly reduced cost.

Tactile Feedback

Tactile feedback devices most often apply stimuli to the fingertip but have also been used on other areas of the hand and body. They typically deliver energy to the skin by applying perpendicular forces, sliding forces, vibrations, heating, or electrical currents. Methods of applying forces perpendicular to the skin have included mechanical pins actuated by solenoids, pneumatics, piezoelectric crystals, and shape-memory alloy wires. Other prototypes have used air jets or pneumatic bladders of various sizes. Perpendicular-force stimulators may be used as single elements or ganged in arrays to give a tactual image of local object shape and texture. Sliding forces may be generated using a rotating cylinder. Voice coils and piezoelectric crystals are the most popular ways of displaying vibration. The Logitech Cyberman mouse had a motor that rotated an eccentric weight to produce vibrations at the user's palm. Thermal stimulation (either hot or cold) can be used to indicate the operating temperature of virtual machinery and to differentiate materials in a virtual world by how cool they feel to the touch. Electrocutaneous stimulators can be used as rings around the fingers or in arrays. Electrocutaneous arrays can successfully present tactile patterns to the user's finger but can be difficult to use.

Why Force-Feedback?

Force-feedback has numerous advantages:

- Reduces training time.
- Reduces dependence on vision for some tasks.
- Reduces task completion time.

• Reduces errors.

• Increases sense of immersion in virtual environments.

In normal manipulation tasks, people rely more on the senses of touch and force than on hand position. Training time will likely be reduced due to the intuitive nature of force reflection. The addition of force-feedback reduces the user's dependence on visual feedback (Massimino and Sheridan 1989), allowing haptic exploration or groping when vision fails to give sufficient understanding or becomes obscured.

Hannaford et al. (1991) showed that the addition of force-feedback to their tasks reduced completion time by 30 percent, forces of contact by 86 percent, and errors by 63 percent. Even with very low bandwidth feedback in another study, errors were reduced to one-quarter the rate with position control alone (Howe and Kontarinis 1992). Patrick et al. (1991) compared simple position control to control with either force-feedback or simplified feedback via a piezo-electric vibrator. Task completion time with the addition of tactile contact (vibration) feedback alone compared favorably to completion time with force-feedback alone. Both were significantly better than no feedback at all. As task difficulty increases, the gap between force-only and tactile-only completion times widens. A key weakness of tactile feedback without force-feedback is that the master can't physically force the user to stop a motion when encountering an immovable virtual object; position correspondence between the human and avatar may be lost.

Richard et al. (1996) used a Rutgers Portable Dextrous Master with Force-Feedback to manipulate three virtual objects in a computer simulation: a ball, a spring, and a soda can. The authors showed that, for the tasks studied, the presence of virtual force-feedback reduced learning time by 50 percent and increased dexterity (as measured by reduction in plastic deformation of the soda can) by 50 percent. In another study with 64 subjects, Richard et al. (1994) showed that, after training, force-feedback to the hand decreased plastic deformation of a hard virtual ball by 65 percent from trials with no force.

Why Tactile Feedback?

Tactile feedback devices use blunt moving pins or other methods to generate touch sensations by stimulating nerve endings near the surface of the skin. Force reflection alone can't provide sufficient sensory feedback to complete many tasks. One powerful feature of the tactile sense is its ability to trigger reflexive changes in grip force when an object is about to slip through the fingers (Westling and Johansson 1984). This results in the use of just enough force to avoid dropping the object, avoids higher forces that might damage a fragile object, and allows a person's grip to adapt to unexpected changes faster than conscious muscle movements would allow. In addition to giving information about slip, the tactile sense produces a perception of contact location (such as the placement of a tool in the hand) that can be crucial in manipulation. In trials with one of the most advanced telerobotic force-reflecting hand systems yet fielded, Jau, Lewis, and Bejczy (1994) found that the lack of tactile feedback significantly hampered object manipulation. Other uses for tactile feedback include the representation of surface details such as curvature and texture. Tactile arrays can be especially useful for the presentation of complex surface features such as Braille or parts of the human body that the user is palpating (Howe et al. 1995). Arrays can be used to present texture information, but so can single-element tactile feedback actuators (Hasser, Master's Thesis, 1995; Minsky 1995).

Only a few force-reflecting projects have included complex tactile feedback (Hasser, Technical Report, 1995; Master's Thesis, 1995; Kontarinis et al. 1995). The challenge of creating hardware to provide adequate tactile feedback equals or exceeds the force-feedback challenge. Adding tactile feedback to a force-feedback device adds mass and complexity to a class of systems that already exists near the boundary of feasibility. The fact that both research areas can be cost- and labor-intensive also helps to explain why few efforts have attempted to add tactile feedback to force-reflecting systems.

Applications

Entertainment

When one talks of haptic interfaces enhancing the sense of "presence," "being there," "immersion," and "suspension of disbelief," the relevance of the technology to entertainment becomes obvious. While "professional" applications of haptic feedback place a primary emphasis on objective performance enhancement and a secondary emphasis on subjective feel, entertainment applications will likely reverse these priorities. The game player should finish the game exclaiming, "Wow, that felt real!"

Another significant difference between entertainment and other applications is price point. Interfaces designed for home use will have to cost more than an order of magnitude less than "professional" devices, perhaps in the $50 to $200 range. The location-based entertainment market will tolerate higher prices, but the need to maintain profit margins, the need for durability, and the fact that the haptic interface will be viewed as a secondary feature in an already expensive system will maintain the pressure to keep prices down.

Entertainment interfaces will have fewer degrees of freedom than many medium-cost professional systems. Systems with 1 and 2 DOF will dominate entertainment applications, with 3-DOF interfaces unlikely to make an appearance in the near future, except perhaps in high-end location-based systems. A steering wheel provides an excellent opportunity for force reflection with a single degree of freedom. Several arcade video games allow drivers to receive vehicle-handling information through motor-induced steering wheel vibrations and turning forces. Joysticks with 2 DOF are perhaps the most ubiquitous user interfaces for home and arcade entertainment, and a handful of force-feedback joysticks exist. Several companies intend to release force-feedback joysticks targeted at the PC game market for under $150. In late 1996, Immersion Corporation began shipping the Impulse Stick as an OEM product to serve the arcade market. Haptic feedback developers must usually rely on cooperation with software vendors. Aura Systems avoided this requirement by marketing the Interactor, a tactile feedback vest that costs less than $90 and uses a subwoofer-like actuator mounted above the user's sternum that is driven by the audio signal from a video game or VCR.

Opportunities also exist in non-game recreational pursuits. Exoskeletons or other intricate hand interfaces might be used to control avatars as hand puppets, either for social interaction or as a tool for animators. Such an interface might prove more economical than full bodysuits. Virtual reality exercise experiences such as cross-country skiing and bicycle riding would provide sensations to the legs and arms that might be considered as haptic feedback, though others restrict the definition of "haptic" to include hand and arm interfaces for exploration and manipulation.

Education

Science education curricula strive to impart an intuitive understanding of physical principles. This can be difficult when the phenomena being studied lie outside the student's experience or cannot be seen by the naked eye. Electrostatic and magnetic fields, elementary aerodynamics, planetary dynamics and gravity fields, molecular attraction, and mechanisms are good examples. If students could feel real forces generated by computer simulations of these phenomena, inaccessible abstractions could be transformed into tangible reality.

Haptic feedback devices give users an impression of a physical reality that can be generated from models of varying complexity and can represent (among other things) Newtonian physics and atomic interactions. Students can interact with haptic feedback devices programmed to demonstrate properties of mass, damping, and compliance. Researchers at the Laboratory for Intelligent Mechanical Systems at Northwestern University built a 1-DOF force-reflecting interface that applies back-and-forth forces to the user's hand. With the haptic interface connected to a virtual model of a cart with a suspended pendulum, a student can "grasp" the cart and move it back and forth, experiencing the mass of the cart and the swinging pendulum. This exposes the student to a classic physics problem, and he or she can even jerk the cart quickly to swing the pendulum up so that it can be balanced like an inverted broomstick.

As with any application of new technology, the question is, What can be done with this technology that couldn't be done without it? Instead of a virtual pendulum, why can't a physics teacher bring a broomstick to class and balance it on his or her hand? Because haptic feedback offers

- The involvement of multiple senses to capture the student's attention and to enhance retention of concepts.

- The ability of the student to work with "what if" scenarios.

- Self-paced semi-autonomous learning.

- Flexibility of several experiments using a single haptic interface.

- Pooled resources and applications that can be distributed in software.

- Automatic data collection from a virtual physical model and a human's input.

Physics students using a virtual pendulum can easily change the mass, shorten the suspending rod, and place the device in a virtual damping fluid. Their teacher can plug in educational applications developed by vendors or the pooled efforts of other teachers. A teacher using a haptic feedback device can develop a *physical* learning experience and send it to colleagues across the country over the Internet.

Aids for the Disabled

Haptic feedback devices use the human touch and motor senses to create a two-way communications link with the computer world and have obvious relevance for anyone who is visually impaired. Because haptic devices can condition human motor inputs by applying damping fields and other algorithms, they are also relevant to persons with motor disabilities.

Researchers for the Phantomate Project at Lund University, Sweden, are currently using a force-reflecting interface to explore applications such as a texture painting system that the blind can use to create and view paintings, an interactive display system for mathematical surface plots, and an interactive battleship game for blind children.

One device, developed as a spinoff of research at the USAF Armstrong Laboratory, creates a virtual tactile surface that allows blind persons to view plotted computer data. TacGraph uses an array of pins attached to the back of a device similar to a computer mouse. As the user moves the device, with his or her finger placed upon the array of pins, the computer keeps track of where the finger is on the desk. The desk surface becomes a "touchable computer screen." As the user's finger moves over a feature such as a plotted line or a Braille label, the pins rise and allow the user to sense the feature. One drawback to this interface is that the pins of the tactile feedback array only move up and down. This crude but state-of-the-art system can't reproduce sliding sensations that are a significant part of Braille and other tactile perception tasks. As a result, users lose track of the plots on the virtual surface when a line curves unexpectedly. One way to solve this problem would be to add two-dimensional force-feedback to the mouse so that the user's finger could be attracted to the plotted line by a virtual rubber band. Force, tactile sensations, or both could be used to display icons, window borders, and textures in a haptic version of a graphical user interface. O'Modhrain and Gillespie (1995) have created just this sort of force-feedback interface, called the MOOSE, and are considering improving it to include tactile feedback.

Another device can help persons with motor disabilities. The Smart Stick, developed at the USAF Armstrong Laboratory with support from the Department of Veterans Affairs, is a special joystick with two motors on it (Repperger, Phillips, and Chelette 1995). The technology can improve the performance of fighter pilots and persons with spastic disorders who drive motorized wheelchairs. It can be difficult for these persons to drive wheelchairs because the spastic motions interfere with intentional control movements of their hands. The stick with motors on it allows the computer to apply forces to the user's hand and measure the motion of the stick. The system can both reduce the spastic motions and use some intelligence to tell the difference between a spasm and an intentional motion. Force-reflecting sticks might also be useful to assist motor-disabled persons interfacing with a computer by providing damping or attractive fields around buttons or icons.

Medicine

Just as with aircraft piloting, medical procedures require much practice, errors are potentially disastrous, and the ability to train using "what if" scenarios can be invaluable. This makes simulation attractive for the field of medicine. Medicine requires the training and performing of complex manual procedures that, in turn, require conceptualization of unseen anatomical structures. This makes haptic feedback attractive (if not required) for medical simulation. Add to this intuitive marriage the fact that medical hardware usually costs much more than entertainment hardware but much less than space program hardware; you may conclude that haptic feedback has found a viable niche in a middle-cost application. Boston Dynamics, High-Techsplanations, Inc., Immersion Corporation, the University of Colorado, and others are developing surgical rehearsal systems with force-reflecting interfaces.

Medical applications may be broken down into four areas, discussed here in the order in which they will likely enter mainstream medical practice:

1. Virtual reality training for manual medical procedures.

2. Preoperative rehearsal for complicated surgical procedures will grow naturally out of the simulation engines and haptic feedback hardware developed for training. Data from practicing physicians' rehearsals might later be recycled to generate training scenarios for students and interns.

3. Teleoperation of local surgical tools, useful for scaling motions and forces or reaching inaccessible operative sites may be aided by "augmented reality," where virtual images created during preoperative planning or diagnostic medical imagery can be overlaid on the "real" environment. Such augmented reality tools are currently being investigated for use in applications like brain surgery, but without haptic feedback to date.

4. Haptic feedback can be used in the teleoperation of surgical tools at a remote site to allow a surgeon to operate on a patient a few hundred kilometers away, for example. These applications are speculative and potentially very costly, but much interest exists in organizations such as the Defense Advanced Research Projects Agency (DARPA).

Procedures involving needles and endoscopic instruments are appealing test cases for virtual haptic training. Both require interaction with anatomical structures that can't be directly visualized (this makes haptic feedback a requirement), and both involve limited degrees of freedom (this makes haptic environment simulation and hardware construction more feasible). Needle simulation projects currently include epidural needle insertion (where a needle is inserted into the spinal column) and intravenous (IV) insertion training. Many other needle procedures are candidates for simulation.

Laparoscopic procedures require the insertion of medical instruments through small incisions in the abdominal wall. The term "endoscopic" describes the more general class of procedures that use small viewing scopes and medical instruments inserted into various locations. Tactile feedback might eventually be useful for these types of applications (Howe et al. 1995).

Science/Industry

The ability of haptic feedback to give the user an intuitive sense of how objects would feel or interact makes the technology applicable to both scientific visualization and industrial design. Molecular docking work begun at the University of North Carolina (UNC) at Chapel Hill and continued by the Air Force's Wright Laboratory serves as an excellent example of scientific visualization. UNC researchers connected a surplus force-reflecting telerobotic control arm to a computer simulation of a drug molecule attempting to "dock" onto a protein molecule. A biochemist using the device can actually feel simulated forces of molecular interaction, with the idea that "hands-on" intuition will augment brute-force computer searches for successful solutions. In another application that bridges the gap between telerobotics and scientific visualization, UNC researchers have connected a PHANToM haptic interface to control the probe of an atomic force microscope (AFM). Using the PHANToM and the surface-following features of the AFM probe, the user can push a nano-scale particle along the surface and feel when the probe slips off the particle.

The premise of scientific visualization applications is that they can provide researchers with insight not easily available using other techniques. Ideally, these advantages should translate into quantitative improvements in research capability. Scientific visualization applications are in a demonstration stage at this point, with few or no "wage-earning" applications fielded to date.

Industrial haptic feedback will allow product design engineers using haptic simulations to feel parts in CAD databases and so on. These interfaces might be extended to allow consumer testing of products that haven't even been constructed. Haptic feedback would be particularly useful to evaluate the feel of switches, knobs, and buttons (MacLean 1996). Users in focus groups could try out potential new car stereo or microwave oven interface panels, perhaps even rearranging the buttons to their own liking. Every one of us probably owns a product that desperately needs this sort of consumer input. As a bonus, the ability to virtually prototype a "touchable" product would be a boon to the early presentation of product proposals. A digital rendition of a physical prototype would also make it easier for geographically dispersed design groups to interact on a realtime basis.

Haptic Software

Software algorithms for rendering haptic environments will borrow many techniques from the arenas of computer graphics and servo control. Figure 18.3 depicts a high-level concept of the inner software loop that uses the following steps:

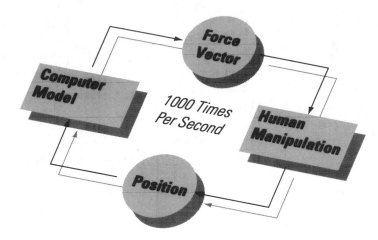

Figure 18.3   A simplified representation of a haptic feedback algorithm.

1. Locate the user's finger position with respect to the virtual environment.

2. Detect collisions between the user's finger and the geometry of virtual objects.

3. Calculate a reaction force vector based on physical laws of the virtual environment.

4. Apply that force vector to the user's finger.

5. Go to A.

There are several parallels between haptic rendering and realtime graphics rendering; haptic rendering requires calculating surface normals across the geometry of an object. Typical computer graphic algorithms, such as Phong shading, can be used for haptic rendering. Just as Phong shading smooths the visual appearance of a faceted object, Phong shading applied to haptic geometries has the effect of making a faceted virtual object feel smoother and therefore more realistic (Morgenbesser 1995). In addition to storing geometric properties of a haptic scene, software has to store uniquely haptic properties of objects such as surface hardness, slipperiness, and texture. As graphics images progressed from simple cartoon-like creations to the rich representations of reality available today, so will haptic images. Most early haptic demonstration programs use simple shapes like cubes and spheres that may move but don't change shape (other than yielding to pressure from a finger or hand). Complex objects or those that can be changed (cut or warped) demand much higher levels of sophistication.

A few basic differences exist between computer graphics and haptics software. Haptic applications are more time-sensitive. For instance, conventional wisdom asserts that 30 to 60 Hz is sufficient for "realtime" virtual graphical environments. This rate is only sufficient because our eyes generally can't detect motion quicker than this. As it turns out, our hands are quite sensitive to vibrations even at 200 to 300 Hz and higher. To create convincing sensations of touch, the loop must occur at an extremely high rate—typically, 300 to 3,000 Hz. The hand *is* quicker than the eye. Time delays from distributed simulations disturb haptic feedback more than visual feedback, just as time delays in teleoperating distant robots cause more trouble when the master controller has force reflection.

Haptic Hardware

There are three primary design criteria necessary for any effective force-reflecting haptic interface. Independent psychophysical testing could establish specifications for each of the three criteria; however, available actuator, sensor, material, and computer technology will ultimately determine the degree to which each of the criteria can be met. The three criteria must be considered simultaneously, as improving the specification for one will inevitably degrade the specifications for the other two. Haptic hardware designers attempt to balance these three to achieve an effective, affordable, haptic interface with existing technologies:

1. Free space must feel free. Users must not be encumbered by the device. That is, the device should exert no external forces on a user moving through free virtual space. Translated into engineering requirements, this means that there should be little back-drive friction, low inertia at the human-machine interface, and no unbalanced weight.

2. Virtual constraints must not be easily saturated. There's nothing more disturbing than leaning against a wall and falling through it. In the virtual world, walls should be solid. The maximum exertable force for the human finger is on the order of 40 to 50 N (newtons), but during precise manipulation people rarely exert peak forces larger than 10 N. In fact, the time-averaged force exerted during normal operation is closer to 1 N.

3. Solid virtual objects must feel stiff. One metric of a force-reflecting interface is the maximum stiffness of the virtual surfaces that it is capable of representing. Because no structure or control loop is infinitely stiff, each virtual object represented through the interface must have some associated compliance. Stiffnesses up to 35 N/cm can be useful, though most users can be convinced that a virtual surface with a stiffness of only 20 N/cm represents a solid, immovable wall. The maximum obtainable stiff-

ness depends not only on the natural frequencies of the device but also on the resolution of the sensors and actuators and the servo rate.

The following sections consider factors relevant to the preceding three criteria in more detail.

Dynamic Range

Dynamic range, the maximum attainable force divided by the back-driven friction, is one of the more important measures of haptic interface performance. A device that can attain a wide range of forces as untainted as possible by friction will offer the highest fidelity interface. Good commercial desktop interfaces achieve very high dynamic ranges between 100:1 and 170:1 (40.0 to 44.6 dB). They appear to the user to be almost friction-free, with low back-driven friction at the fingertip of less than 0.1 N. The maximum force must be high enough to easily stop the human's finger, but friction must be low enough that obtaining the required dynamic range doesn't mean raising the maximum force to fatiguing levels. Every effort should be made to avoid selecting inherently high-friction mechanisms or transmissions.

Force and Fatigue

Reflected forces should be within a comfortable, low-fatigue range, large enough to allow the operator to feel an adequate sense of "presence." Rarely in manipulation will people use their maximum attainable force. A system designed to exceed maximum human forces may be unsafe, fatiguing, and so overdesigned as to be impractical. Force-reflecting haptic interfaces should be capable of peak forces 20 to 30 percent of the human maximum and continuous forces 3 to 15 percent of the human maximum (Hasser, Technical Report, 1995; ASME Session, 1995).

Desktop interfaces with a maximum exertable force of 10 N, roughly 20 percent of the maximum human fingertip force, can represent a believable virtual environment in which a conscious effort is required to drive through virtual obstacles. One reason for their success with relatively low forces is their low friction and low apparent mass. The range between 25 percent and 50 percent of the human maximum is an area of diminishing returns, where fatigue becomes more likely and the apparatus heavier and more cumbersome. Judicious application of peak feedback forces in this range will be appropriate only if these forces can be obtained without overencumbering the operator. Actuators with high torque-mass ratios and power densities will have a significant advantage in this area. The selection of a continuous force capability will depend on the specifics of the task, particularly the percentage of time spent actually applying forces to the user. Anecdotal experience shows that desktop systems can perform well as virtual reality interfaces with a continuous force rating of 1.5 N, 3 percent of the human maximum.

Stiffness and Bandwidth

Stiffness greatly affects the "feel" of a force-reflecting device. Any force-reflecting device designed to represent interactions with rigid objects must be stiff. Since many objects will be rigid in a realistic scenario, the designer can't neglect this requirement. Both the stiffness of the mechanical structure and the servo stiffness combine to contribute to the overall system stiffness. It may be more appropriate to say that each of these factors contributes to degrade overall system stiffness, and, if either factor is significantly worse than the other, its effects will dominate. Structural stiffness, the stiffness in the mechanical components, has often been easier to achieve than servo stiffness, which is limited by the loop rate of the control system. Stiffness is expressed in units of force per unit length. In a stiff system, forces must be increased very rapidly as the device moves only a short distance. A slow control system won't be able to keep up with these changes, and the resulting percept will be sluggish and compliant. Inadequate resolution or response delay in position sensor systems will also contribute to degradation in overall system stiffness.

How stiff is stiff enough? Both structural stiffness and servo system stiffness have costs associated with them (increased weight, computational requirements), providing motivation to design systems for the minimum acceptable stiffness. Current force-reflecting haptic interfaces seem to succeed with stiffnesses ranging from 17.5 N/cm to 80 N/cm (Hasser, Technical Report, 1995; Massie and Salisbury 1994; Rosenberg 1994). During some demonstrations, users can slide easily in the directions tangential to a virtual wall; this additional cue may have aided users in their "suspension of disbelief" when perceiving a rigid wall with less-than-perfectly-rigid devices.

Bandwidth is an indicator of potential information content. Just as a high-bandwidth Internet connection allows a user to acquire information more quickly, a high-bandwidth haptic interface allows the user to both acquire information about and manipulate the virtual environment faster. A low-bandwidth haptic interface performs like a poor-quality audio tape, losing the crisp high-frequency information that makes the difference between experiencing a cheap facsimile and "being there." Bandwidth relates directly to servo stiffness; in many cases, increasing control system bandwidth (decreasing computation time) results in immediate and marked increases in stiffness, improving the realism of the feedback forces. Reductions in mechanism stiffness, such as that due to cable compliance, can also impact bandwidth.

How much bandwidth is enough? Bandwidths exceeding those of the relevant sensory systems won't be appreciated by the users. Two sensory systems contribute predominantly to the user's experience of force reflection. The most obvious is the proprioceptive/kinesthetic sense. Reliable values for kinesthetic/proprioceptive bandwidth are difficult to obtain, but estimates from 20 to 30 Hz have been made (Hasser, Technical Report, 1995; ASME Session, 1995; Brooks 1990). The literature seems to suggest increasing usefulness of force reflection bandwidths from 2 to 30 Hz, with diminishing gains as 30 Hz is approached and surpassed. The second contributor is the tactile sense. Humans can detect tactile vibrations up to 10,000 Hz, according to one source (Geldard 1972). However, the ability to discriminate between stimuli frequencies diminishes above 320 Hz (Brooks 1990). Evidence from studies of the tactile nerves supports the contention that humans can't discriminate between frequencies over 1,000 Hz (Srinivasan 1995).

It can be difficult to design force-feedback systems with bandwidths high enough to be useful to the tactile sense as well as the proprioceptive/kinesthetic sense. One laboratory has had success with the addition of voice coil actuators to an existing force-reflecting haptic interface to improve the presentation of high-frequency vibration information to the tactile sense (Wellman and Howe 1995). The voice coil actuators vibrate the structure of the haptic interface (not touching the skin themselves) and complement the lower-frequency motorized force reflection to produce a blend of low- and high-frequency haptic sensations that appears seamless to the user. Even though the voice coils produced signals up to 4,000 Hz, the researchers found that frequencies beyond 1,000 Hz weren't useful for their task (distinguishing virtual objects of different hardness by tapping them). This approach might enable the use of less expensive force-reflecting hardware in some applications where lighter force-feedback equipment with smaller actuators and slower computation could be complemented with vibration feedback.

The Future of Haptic Feedback

The continuing explosion in computational power and microchip technology has conditioned us to expect exponential growth in all technology areas. This isn't true in many cases, including the design of mechanical systems, where the fundamental laws of physics limit progress as often as manufacturing technology does. Progress will appear rapid for a short while, as the reserve of existing technology is brought to bear on haptic feedback applications. Later advances will be more subject to the relatively slow evolution of materials and actuator technology. Novel actuator developments based upon magnetostrictive, piezoelectric, shape memory metal, and other technologies may provide some long-term options, but traditional actuators such as electric motors and pneumatics will remain dominant for the foreseeable future.

Each degree of freedom added to a haptic device adds the cost of another actuator and controller and makes the mechanical structure more complex. The Maxon motors used in SensAble Devices' PHANToM and in Immersion's Impulse Engines cost over $400 each. SensAble Devices uses motor controllers that cost over $300 for each axis. Entertainment applications are perhaps the only case where cheap motors and plastic gears would result in systems with acceptable performance. Off-the-shelf force-reflecting interfaces currently cost between $2,500 (for a one-axis device) to $430,000 (for a ten-axis device). Figure 18.4 shows that as axes are added, costs increase disproportionately; cost per axis is not merely additive. In addition to mechanical complexity, the fact that few tasks require very complex devices keeps the number of systems with many axes small and their prices large.

A haptic hardware and software application package competitive for a job like medical procedure training would have to be priced in a range comparable

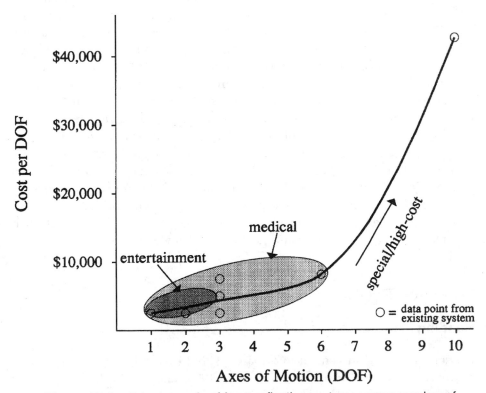

Figure 18.4. Price per axis of force-reflecting systems versus number of axes of motion.

to a personal computer system (currently, $2,000 to $6,000) in order to be commercially feasible. More expensive systems would constitute major systems purchases unsuitable for multiple installations at a single site or wide distribution to cost-sensitive institutions. These price ranges seem realistic in the immediate future. Less complex 1- or 2-DOF systems for arcade-style entertainment are a current fact. Joysticks with 2 DOF that are cost-competitive for home use and that have enough fidelity for gameplay were available at the end of 1996. Simpler systems with vibration feedback such as the Aura Interactor vest may remain viable in the $60 to $100 price range.

Haptic feedback devices have already found commercial success as research and development tools; however, most sales have been to organizations interested in research and development of haptic feedback technology itself! For haptic feedback to become a sustainable technology area, these organizations will have to find applications for haptic feedback with paying customers who return with follow-on orders and new product demands. Force-feedback joysticks of home computer gaming are nearing reality; some experimental site-based systems will incorporate force-feedback in 1997. There are no technical barriers to large-scale adoption for arcade and site-based markets. Penetration into medical applications and scientific visualization will be slow, in part because these applications require sophisticated software with specialized content. The first paying customers will likely be in the area of medical simulation. Penetration into site-based entertainment and scientific visualization will come later, and the most speculative area is the use of haptic feedback devices for home entertainment. The need for hardware to control and deliver mechanical energy to the user makes it difficult to squeeze this technology into the extreme price constraints of the home entertainment market sector. Extensive software development must occur for all application areas, from basic work in haptic rendering algorithms to more focused work for specific products. Both force reflection and tactile feedback offer helpful capabilities, though force reflection will lead in early commercialization. Simple tactile feedback of sensations such as vibration has offered sufficient capability at a low enough price to gain a toehold in the market, but implementation of more complex tactile feedback such as arrays will require more capable hardware at a lower cost.

To Probe Further

Reading

Readers interested in general information should consult chapters on haptic feedback for virtual reality by Srinivasan (1995) and by Burdea and Coiffet (1994). Both appear in books providing general overviews of virtual reality technology. Barfield and Furness (1995) have edited another broad-coverage virtual reality interface book with three chapters relevant to haptic interfaces, including an exhaustive chapter on tactile feedback by Kaczmarek and Bach y Rita. Burdea (1996) has written another book exclusively on haptic feedback technology. It contains extensive coverage of human haptic sensing and control, actuators, existing force and tactile feedback devices, software for physical modeling, hardware/software control issues, and haptic feedback applications. A conference paper by Shimoga (1992) also contains a good review of force and tactile feedback capabilities. Hasser (Technical Report, 1995) and Minsky (1995) have both written more specialized works that include extensive references to the haptic literature.

The expanding research effort in haptic feedback has begun to produce numerous conference papers and journal articles. Many articles relevant to haptics have appeared in the MIT Press journal *Presence—Teleoperators and Virtual Environments*. One particularly relevant conference session is the annual Symposium on Haptic Interfaces for Virtual Environment and Teleoperator Systems at the American Society of Mechanical Engineers (ASME) Winter Annual Meeting. The Virtual Reality Annual International Symposium (VRAIS), sponsored by the Institute of Electrical and Electronics Engineers (IEEE), has had significant haptics content, as has the Telemanipulator Technology Conference sponsored by the Society of Photo-Optical Instrumentation Engineers (SPIE).

World Wide Web

Since the majority of haptics groups seem to have home pages, the World Wide Web offers an excellent jumping-off point for further investigation. Numerous haptics groups are cooperating in an effort to set up a haptics community home page at http://haptic.mech.nwu.edu. Christopher Hasser, one author of this chapter, has a Human Sensory Feedback for Telepresence Project site at http://www.force-feedback.com. Thomas Massie, the other author of this chapter, has a site at http://www.sensable.com.

References

Barfield, W., and Furness, T., editors, *Advanced Interface Design and Virtual Environments*, Oxford University Press, 1995.

Brooks, T. L., "Telerobotic Response Requirements," in *Proceedings of the IEEE International Conference on Systems, Man, and Cybernetics*, pp. 113–120, Los Angeles, Calif., 1990.

Burdea, G. C., *Force and Touch Feedback for Virtual Reality*. John Wiley & Sons, New York, 1996.

Burdea G., and Coiffet, P., *Virtual Reality Technology*, John Wiley & Sons, New York, 1994.

Geldard, F. A., *The Human Senses*, John Wiley & Sons, New York, 1972.

Hannaford, B., Wood, L., McAffee, D., and Zak, H., "Performance Evaluation of a Six-Axis Generalized Force-Reflecting Teleoperator," *IEEE Transactions on Systems, Man, and Cybernetics*, 21(3):620–633, 1991.

Hasser, C. J., *Force-Reflecting Anthropomorphic Hand Masters*, Technical Report AL/CF-TR-1995-0110, USAF Armstrong Laboratory, Wright-Patterson AFB Ohio, 1995.

Hasser, C. J., "Force-Reflecting Anthropomorphic Hand Master Requirements," in *ASME Int. Mech. Eng. Cong. and Exp., Session on Haptic Interfaces for Virtual Environments and Teleoperator Systems*, DSC-Vol. 57-2, San Francisco Calif., November 1995.

Hasser, C. J., "Tactile Feedback for a Force-Reflecting Haptic Display," Master's Thesis, University of Dayton, Dayton, Ohio, 1995.

Howe, R. D., and Kontarinis, D. A., "Task Performance with a Dextrous Tele-operated Hand System," in *Telemanipulator Technology '92*, SPIE, Boston, November 1992.

Howe, R. D., Peine, W. J., Kontarinis, D. A., and Son, J. S., "Remote Palpation Technology," *IEEE Engineering in Medical and Biology Magazine*, May–June 1995.

Jau, B. M., Lewis, M. A., and Bejczy, A. K., "Anthropomorphic Telemanipulation System in Terminus Control Mode," in *Proceedings of RoManSy '94: The Tenth CISM-IFToMM Symposium on Theory and Practice of Robots and Manipulators*, 1994.

Kontarinis, D. A., Son, J. S., Peine, W. J., and Howe, R. D., "A Tactile Shape Sensing and Display System for Teleoperated Manipulation," in *IEEE Conference on Robotics and Automation*, 1995.

MacLean, K. E., "Emulation of Haptic Feedback for Manual Interfaces," Ph.D. Thesis, Massachusetts Institute of Technology, Cambridge, Mass., 1996.

Massie, T. H., and Salisbury, J. K., "Probing Virtual Objects with the PHANToM Haptic Interface," in *ASME Winter Annual Meeting—Session on Haptic Interfaces for Virtual Environment and Teleoperator Systems*, Chicago, November 1994.

Massimino, M., and Sheridan, T. B., "Variable Force and Visual Feedback Effects on Teleoperator Man-Machine Performance," in *NASA Conference on Space Telerobotics*, Pasadena, Calif., 31 January–2 February 1989.

Minsky, M. D. R., "Computational Haptics: The Sandpaper System for Synthesizing Texture with a Force-Feedback Haptic Display," Ph.D. Thesis, Massachusetts Institute of Technology, Cambridge, Mass., 1995.

Morgenbesser, H. B., "Force Shading for Shape Perception in Haptic Virtual Environments," M. Eng. Thesis, Massachusetts Institute of Technology, Cambridge, Mass., 1995.

O'Modhrain, S., and Gillespie, B., *A Haptic Interface for the Digital Sound Studio*, Technical Report, Center for Computer Research in Music and Acoustics, Stanford University, Stanford, Calif., May 1995.

Patrick, N. J. M., Sheridan, T. B., Massimino, M. J., and Marcus, B. A., "Design and Testing of a Nonreactive, Fingertip Tactile Display for Interaction with Remote Environments." Source: Beth Marcus at EXOS, 1991.

Repperger, D. W., Phillips, C. A., and Chelette, T. L., "A Study on Spatially Induced Virtual Force with an Information Theoretic Investigation of Human Performance," *IEEE Transactions on Systems, Man, and Cybernetics*, 25(10):1392–1404, 1995.

Richard, P., Burdea, G., Gomez, D., and Coiffet, P., "A Comparison of Haptic, Visual, and Auditive Force Feedback for Deformable Virtual Objects," in *The Fourth International Conference on Artificial Reality and Tele-Existence (ICAT '94)*, Tokyo, Japan, July 1994.

Richard, P., Birebent, G., Coiffet, P., Burdea, G., Gomez, D., and Langrana, N., "Effect of Frame Rate and Force Feedback on Virtual Object Manipulation," *Presence—Teleoperators and Virtual Environments*, 5(1):1–14, MIT Press, 1996.

Rosenberg, L. B., "Virtual Fixtures: Perceptual Overlays Enhance Operator Performance in Telepresence Tasks," Ph.D. Thesis, Stanford University, Stanford, Calif., 1994.

Shimoga, K.B., "Force and Touch Feedback Devices for Dexterous Telemanipulation," in *NASA-CIRSSE Conference on Intelligent Robotics for Space Exploration*, pp. 158–176, September/October 1992.

Srinivasan, M. A., "Haptic Interfaces," in *Virtual Reality: Scientific and Technological Challenges*, edited by N. I. Durlach and A. S. Mavor, The National Research Council, National Academy Press, Washington, D.C., 1995.

Sutherland, I., "The Ultimate Display," in *Proceedings of the IFIP Congress*, pp. 506–508, 1965.

Wellman, P., and Howe, R. D., "Towards Realistic Vibrotactile Display in Virtual Environments," in *ASME Int. Mech. Eng. Cong. and Exp., Session on Haptic*

Interfaces for Virtual Environments and Teleoperator Systems, DSC-Vol. 57-2, San Francisco Calif., November 1995.

Westling, G., and Johansson, R. S., "Factors Influencing the Force Control During Precision Grip," *Experimental Brain Research*, 53:227–284, 1984.

Acknowledgments

The following people deserve thanks for providing information, reviewing the manuscript, or both: Massimo Bergamasco, Dave Brock, Grigore Burdea, Ed Colgate, Michael Duggan, Brent Gillespie, Gerry Higgins, Heidi Jacobus, John Latta, Marty Luka, Karon MacLean, Beth Marcus, Angie McCavitt, Dwight Meglan, Ted Milner, Charles Nixon, Tom Peurach, Louis Rosenberg, Ken Salisbury, and Mandayam Srinivasan. This chapter was written while Christopher Hasser was serving at the USAF Armstrong Laboratory, with support from the Human Sensory Feedback for Telepresence Project.

Biographies

Christopher Hasser received his M.S. degree in electrical engineering from the University of Dayton while at the USAF Armstrong Laboratory. He has over six years of experience with force and tactile feedback devices as a researcher and research manager. During that time, he managed SBIR contracts, headed the Human Sensory Feedback for Telepresence Project, and became recognized as the Air Force expert on haptic feedback issues. His recent work included the study of force-reflecting control sticks to enhance the performance of airplane and remotely piloted aerial vehicle pilots. He has published extensively and has one patent pending. In June 1996, he joined Immersion Corporation as chief research engineer.

Thomas Massie is currently the chairman and chief technical officer of SensAble Devices, Inc. He received a B.S. degree in electrical engineering and an M.S. degree in mechanical engineering from the Massachusetts Institute of Technology and worked at the MIT Artificial Intelligence Lab, where he coinvented the PHANToM haptic interface. He subsequently founded SensAble Devices to innovate, manufacture, and market the device. Mr. Massie continues to conduct advanced and applied research on both the hardware and software aspects of haptic interfaces. He provides technical assistance to several institutions throughout the world that are incorporating haptic interfaces. His goal is to fundamentally change the way humans and computers interact via the inclusion of touch.

Chapter 19

First Person, Multiple: Images, Video, and the New Realities

Lawrence A. Leske
Silicon Reality, Inc.

Introduction

The first generation of personalized virtual realities has begun. It's now adding familiar images—still and video—to one's choice of personal entertainment universes. Telephone and radio have vastly expanded our aural world, while television, theater, movies, and computer graphics systems extend the visual realm. Though these extensions have progressed from third-person voyeuristic to first-person multiple, they have largely not been individualized. The confluence of 3D, imaging, and video now enables our possible worlds to include real images of familiar people and places and ultimately will include comprehensive individual personalization.

After the easy steps, such as user-defined names and user-selected icons, individualization continues with the personalization of a player's game image, at first, simply by placing his or her face onto his or her character's head. Later, the participant's avatar image may be warped or morphed with archetypes appropriate for his or her new world space—a jungle cat for a jungle world or a mutant for an X-Men world. The player's image will evolve with the adventure to reflect effects of the events happening to the player. These images, part human, part archetype, will be seen by players in virtual mirrors, reflected by health icons on the control panel, and seen by their companions or competitors in networked environments. And, at the nearly inevitable moment of avatar death, they'll see themselves, fallen, in that brief moment of truth before the cycle renews and they are reborn.

Seeing familiar faces in reflection and on others is only part of the development of high-personal-involvement virtual worlds. Much of Earth has been imaged for military flight simulators; these data and the technology will soon be available to all. Satellite and high-altitude reconnaissance photos are being incorporated into databases for large-scale nonmilitary simulations in applications like T_Vision by ART+COM in Berlin and in flight-sim games such as Jetfighter III by Mission Studios in the United States. With these applications, we're building another level of familiar personal reality. The inclusion of city skylines, geographically accurate 3D databases, and, within a few years, the means for you to include home and neighborhood images will complete the first wave of virtual world personalization.

Entertainment often depends on the suspension of disbelief. The visually familiar will heighten one's personal identification with these new worlds. In the vernacular of current video games, what could be more frightening than an attack by aliens against your own home that must be dealt with swiftly and decisively by you?! What can be more vivid than seeing your neighborhood being overrun and transformed by the unknown or more compelling than defending your friends and family?

The Next Generation Has Begun

The next generation of 2D and 3D graphics hardware—accelerator cards—enables the mixing of real with synthetic images. The tools position a scanned photo either in the scene or texture-mapped as an appliqué onto a 3D surface. You can place digitized photos in the virtual environment—the familiar faces of companions, their homes and cities for scene elements, and terrain maps for vehicular simulation. With compression, live or recorded video may also be used within these environments for backgrounds, story development, or, using chromakey techniques, as real images for a 3D scene. Within a few years, this functionality will be on the motherboard.

How does it work? It's conceptually simple, though currently more than a little bit of work. For 2D, static images are simply scanned in and used as parts of 2D objects, such as the side of a rectangular building. The realtime renderer for 2D may simply BitBlt the object to the current screen location. The process is similar in 3D but applied to all the sides of any 3D object. The display program determines the 3D location and orientation of the object, translates this to the current screen view, and then, as required, dynamically resizes, rotates, and filters the image. The image is then applied to some portion of the 3D screen object—it's more work—but now there is true 3D perspective.

For video texture mapping, the process is essentially the same, except that the image is decompressed in real time, a frame at a time, and updated very frequently. This places far greater demands on the imaging process and adds the burden of simultaneous decompression to the rendering engines. While current software decompressors provide reasonable-quality images, the coming generation of MPEG1 video compression and, soon, MPEG2 provide VHS quality or much better. This, combined with chromakey-type matting techniques, will provide a high degree of realism—video-realistic.

Most of these techniques are fairly old and time tested. Texture mapping was introduced by Ed Catmull (now president of Pixar) in 1974 as part of his doctoral thesis at the University of Utah. It was refined by Jim Blinn (now at Microsoft) and Martin Newell in 1976. Ed Catmull and Alvy Ray Smith (a Microsoft Fellow) further refined the art at SIGGRAPH '80 with "3-D Transformations of Images in Scanline Order." In order to more efficiently use these techniques in hardware, T. Porter and T. McDuff introduced the alpha buffer at SIGGRAPH '84 in "Compositing Digital Images."

One basic technique of morphing began in film as "dissolves"—in which one scene fades out while simultaneously the next fades in. The digital version is easily handled by the 3D-ubiquitous alpha buffer. Another morph technique began in classic hand-drawn animation with "inbetweening," wherein key frames are first drawn, every half-second or so, and then the in-between cells are interpolated. For computers, this was first noted by Ronald Baecker in "Picture Driven Animation" in 1969.

Geometric morphing is still fairly difficult and is far more successful in 3D than 2D since 2D polygonal animation mainly consists of 3D projections with insufficient information in individual 2D key frames. Imagine two key frames of a person walking across a stage; the first shows one leg, the other obscured by the visible leg, while the next key frame shows both. How can the second leg be interpolated from the first key frame? A 3D representation is required. This leads directly to inverse kinematics and 3D animation (not covered here) and to 3D morphing, in which two structures and their associated texture maps are "blended" by warping the structures from one to the other and blending their associated textures in the manner of a dissolve. The formal beginning of geometric morphs can be traced to the 1980 paper "Representations for Rigid Solids: Theory, Methods, and Systems" by A. A. G. Requicha.

How Will You Be Morphed to Your Avatar?

At first, you'll assist by hand. First, you take a few photographs of your head (at least front and back views, though more is better). Then, you scan these images and make them available to a 3D modeling program. The basic task is pointing out to the program which parts of your face, head, and body correspond to parts on the avatar. Because of rendering limitations, only a few dozen points (for a few dozen polygons) will be used for a head in the next couple of years, such as the nose, eyes, jaw, and hairline. Those areas will then be mapped to and blended (to adjustable degrees) with your scanned body parts.

As more CPU power and polygons become available, more points will be used for better-looking avatars. By then, the procedure will be a bit more automated. For example, it now takes four or more hours to manually enter all the data needed for a fairly photo-realistic head (200 to 300 polygons), based on two to five scanned photographs. Keyframe morphing (3D modeling) tools in the $500 to $1,000 range include 3D Builder by 3D Construction Company and PhotoModeler by Eos Systems, Inc. For an initial low-polygon avatar, the procedure should take only about an hour, depending on experience.

For ubiquitous higher-quality avatars, improvements are required. Few people want to spend half a day building their avatar image. Improvements include automatic image analysis to determine likely points of correspondence, automated image filters to minimize photo scan problems, and cost reductions to broaden the audience. These are all within the state of the art and are only a matter of time and considerable effort, at which point most of the work to get a good-looking you onto your avatar will be making the photos to scan. By then, you're likely to have video input from your camcorder, eliminating another step in the process. After the mostly-automatic mapping, you'll be able to edit—correcting any subtle errors or enhancing the avatar as you wish. This includes geometric, color, or image changes. Let your imagination be your guide. Who do you want to be today?

Deeper into Technology—Past, Present, and Future

Computer graphics has been around for over 30 years, though not in the home until Atari, Bally, and others started the arcade and home videogame industry in the early 1970s. Although various hardware drawing techniques were devised to speed up the animation, the basics of image creation and display are still the same today.

Digital bits that correspond to the x–y grid positions on the screen (pixels) are the basis of most computer graphics. Like pointillistic images for artists, they determine the intensity of the red, green, and blue phosphors of the chosen display (full-color TFT-LCD when this was written). Even though it's easier to simply assign, for example, the digital numbers 0 through 255 directly to each color so that 8 bits correspond to the intensity or brightness of each red, green, and blue color at every point in the image, it had long been too expensive. Why? Because 24 bits per pixel of DRAM cost far too much to sell to us ordinary folk. Although that's now rapidly changing, we'll take a look at some ways of storing and generating these colors that require far less memory.

In addition, note that cost is not the only problem. Moving 32 bits of image data takes twice as much internal bandwidth as moving 16 bits of data. This is a very big issue for animation because the screen refresh would take twice as long, too, causing a somewhat jerky animation.

Perhaps the first way to reduce the amount of DRAM needed—and still the most common—was indexed colors, at least for those of us who wanted to produce the best-quality pixelated images within the hardware cost limitation. With only, say, 4 bits per pixel, indexing will provide up to 16 different colors without other hardware tricks. Each index can control a color of 4, 6, or 8 bits of red, green, and blue (rgb). With 4 bits each, 4,096 color/intensities can be produced, allowing a decent color palette for the image artist.

Indeed, way back then the only way to make good-looking images was by hand. Each color had to be picked, changed, and changed again in order to overcome the limitations of the 2 to 64 colors then available. Good artists were able to overcome these limitations, with a large added cost in time (they were cheaper then, as were we all). Handiwork was still required when we could afford 8-bit color pixels (indexed). With 8 bits, you can select 256 colors out of an available 4,096 (using a 4, 4, 4 rgb index) or 262,144 (using an 8, 8, 8 rgb index), which made it easier to pick the best colors since there were more to pick from. Then, along came Paul Heckbert with his SIGGRAPH '82 paper "Color Image Quantization for Frame Buffer Display," first showing us how to pick the best (at least then) 256 colors with which to store your full-color (16 million+) original art.

Paul made it much easier to put scanned images into your 8-bit frame buffer. You drew it any way you wanted, and the Heckbert algorithm selected nearly the best ones, automating most of the tedious color selection work. It wasn't quite perfect, but it did better than a pretty good job. Later improvements enabled a really good selection of colors, and variations of this method are now used for many, if not most, images stored/displayed with 8-bit buffers.

At that time, however, you had only maybe 32 Kbytes of ROM for your whole game (or even 128K), and you naturally wanted a lot of images, so this wasn't good enough as a primitive sort of color compression. So, in 1982, a group I was working with for Bally/Midway Games in Chicago, Dave Nutting Associates, began working on compression. Until Heckbert, you were able to get excellent images at 6 bits per pixel (bpp), pretty good ones at 4 bpp, and fairly good ones at 3 bpp. After I heard Heckbert present his paper, I saw the light on how to get good-to-pretty-good images at only 2 bpp. Fairly soon (early 1983), this became the C^3 (Color Cell Compression) algorithm, thanks to the team credited shortly. Soon thereafter, John Pasierb and his group at Bally/Midway produced several arcade video games using this technique, including Journey, licensed from the rock group. Prodded and led by Tom De-Fanti, we reported this technique (mostly written by Tom, after the patent was awarded) at the SIGGRAPH '86 conference with the paper "Two Bit/Pixel Full

Color Encoding" by Graham Campbell, Thomas DeFanti, Jeff Frederiksen, Stephen Joyce, Lawrence Leske, John Lindberg, and Daniel Sandin. This was the team that produced the codec.

Compression for Expansion's Sake

After the paper was published, there was a brief flurry of excitement until everyone discovered it wasn't the holy grail of image compression. Even though it wasn't even close to perfect, it had one purposefully strong feature: It was very easy to decompress (even in software). So, a few years later, Apple produced an improved version for their QuickTime 1.0 Road Pizza Video Compression, developed by Eric Hoffert, Gavin Miller, Lee Mighdoll, and Stephanie Winner. Soon thereafter, Microsoft released the Video for Windows MS1 AVI (audio/video interface), which also derived from the SIGGRAPH '86 paper. Each did, in the best of cases, OK-to-pretty-good imagery.

Both have since been superseded by VQ-based (vector quantization) codecs. The Intel Indeo and the Radius Cinepac (from the mind of Peter Barrett, formerly of SuperMac, and a founder of Rocket Science) are now the primary video codecs for multimedia on personal computers. These are being superseded by MPEG1 software codecs on 100-MHz+ Pentiums, to be followed by MPEG2 on 200-MHz+ MMX Pentiums with DVD support.

So why am I bringing this up for 3D? Two words—texture maps. Even though we can now afford 24-bit buffers, images for textures still take up too many bytes, take too long to transmit on the Net, and use too much system bandwidth. Compressing textures becomes critical. Most texture compression techniques in use are the old standbys just noted, which are satisfactory when your POV is moving quickly, dodging bullets, or if you need only a few brick walls and road surfaces. But compression certainly can't stop there.

The Joint Photographic Experts Group (JPEG) standard for still image compression provides excellent-quality images at 2 bpp. Even down to about 3/4 bpp, it provides very-good-to-good imagery. Consequently, it's now the standard for still images and for textures used in high-end/3D systems. It will move to the 200-MHz+ home 3D-PC in one to two years. Closely following it are two other DCT-based (discrete cosine transform) compression technologies developed by the ISO Moving Pictures Experts Group (MPEG): the MPEG1 and MPEG2 toolkits.

These toolkits are intended for video and film compression, taking advantage of the temporal coherence of image sequences to provide excellent-to-good images at 1.5 bpp to 0.25 bpp. Part of their technique is based on the fact that each frame in a particular sequence is quite similar to those nearest it. So, instead of coding each frame independently, as JPEG does, MPEG uses pointers to very similar looking image blocks from nearby reference frames, either backward or forward in time sequence. Such pointers use far fewer bits than even quantized DCT compression. If that's still not good enough, the compressor can add a compressed error-correction block (the difference between the desired image and the block being pointed to) to further minimize pixel errors, at a slightly higher cost in bits.

MPEG and 3D Don't Mix Well

Since most companies in today's PC-game production business are mixing MPEG-compressed video cut-scenes with uncompressed animation and environments, a word of caution is in order. The MPEG standard practice is to compress a pre-gamma–corrected image, so no further gamma correction is required in order to display correctly. However, most 3D applications generate un-gamma–corrected images. If the PC displays only one or the other at a time, you can simply turn on gamma correction for the 2D and 3D imagery and keep it off for MPEG movies, else they will be double-gamma corrected and wash out, lose contrast, and often become more blocky looking. If the system must display MPEG in a 3D PC environment, then either the MPEG source should not be pre-gamma corrected or there must be a dynamic method to switch between the computer imagery and the MPEG video, else one or the other will definitely not look as good as it should.

Because these techniques are even more computationally expensive than JPEG, they'll be implemented a year or two later in home 3D PCs, when the Pentium MMX technology or equivalent becomes dominant in that market.

Other Compression Methods

What about wavelets and fractals? In general, they're not on the mainstream image compression bandwagon; thus, there is little competitive support to broadly apply them and reduce costs through mass competition. To put this in perspective, I recently saw an experimental version of HDTV that runs at a resolution of 2,048×1,024, at 72 progressive frames per second (fps), using about 18 Mbps, and that delivers excellent-quality video. It's as good as or better than any other HDTV I've seen, which is usually at best only 1,920×1,080, interlaced, at 30 fps—same bandwidth. This technique, developed at Gary Demos' DemoGraFX, appears about 4.7 times more efficient than standard MPEG2 video compression tools. It uses a modified version of the MPEG2 toolkit, with some wavelet-like techniques to provide both standard TV video and HDTV from the same signal. This is an HDTV that I would unhesitatingly buy, while the present proposed standard is at best only slightly better than the new DVD MPEG2 video disk standard now entering mass production. More importantly, the DemoGraFX technique is much more in tune with next-generation 2D/3D PC displays.

As we consider video compression algorithms, it's important to remember that they're just one facet in the overall digital video communication process. The original production of the video is at least as important; high-quality compressed imagery can be made only from high-quality source material.

Your CPU (by Itself) Won't Soon Render Your Personalized VR

It takes over 125 giga-ops of rendering power in order to update a 640 × 480 full-color frame, using anti-aliasing, Gouraud shading, z-buffering, fog, transparency, and perspective-corrected, tri-linear, MIP-mapped, textured triangles, at a depth complexity of 5, at 72 frames per second. Even if your next personal CPU were able to perform six simultaneous, independent operations per clock cycle, at 1-GHz clock frequency, it would have only one-twentieth the power needed for good rendering. And, it would still have to handle audio, music, and geometric 3D-to-2D calculations, as well as the input ports and 2D screen ops. Not likely. So, for the foreseeable future, an auxiliary 3D rendering engine will be needed for good imagery of a character you can easily recognize as a neighbor, friend, or yourself, suitably morphed.

Enough of the soapbox—back to surreality. These compression techniques will all be used to enhance the familiar, at reasonable costs. Soon, the images in your virtual reality will not only look more real but also more than familiar— individually personalized to your preferred Zeitgeist. When is this all going to happen? And what else is expected?

Real Soon Now

The first-generation 3D graphics processors for PCs are able to fully texture-map with at least good-quality bilinear filtering. Soon, the game companies will provide a service to morph the player's image with the prototype chosen by the player. Soon thereafter will appear simpler morphing programs so that the more adventurous can do their own. Later, highly automated morphers will allow the nonprogrammer to control their avatar image and also allow them to bring in other familiar scenes. Images such as their house, room, and local streets will then be easily inserted into the game database for battle in an all-too-recognizable locale.

While all that is unfolding, much larger databases will become available in various virtual environments: San Francisco Bay, New York City, Tokyo, Chicago, London, Istanbul, and Moscow. These databases will then undergo refinements to major sections of cities or areas and, finally, in five to seven years, will allow the integration of video street scenes shot by eager participants. To accomplish all this, a great deal of software will be built to automate each step of the process of image capture, database build and match, and, finally, morph or texture-map into place.

Each stage is an opportunity for game and VR tools developers to bring participants closer to their individual universe—an opportunity to heighten the familiar and move toward the intimate. Each stage is an opportunity for the participant to become the avatar—to work, play, and battle in the avatar's world, their shared world.

Further in the Future

Retailing

Net shopping will progress from the non-avatared POV float-through in the distinctly artificial simulated mall, to the fully textured, photo-real mall, and then to multi-user avatar shopping. In effect, both the shoppers and the shops will be avatars, assuming the identity/configuration most useful at the moment. The principal leverage of a store on the Net will be communication costs, while one of the greatest advantages will be the visual spectacle.

VR shopping will heighten the experience for many, especially the store owners. Net cataloging will increase in effectiveness as the imagery approaches photo-realism. It will be easier to sell virtually anything when the buyer can clearly see it from all angles in realistic contexts. It will be cheaper, easier, and fun to shop in a fantastically grand virtual mall, as long as you're not interested in having other humans actually near you. But don't short those anchor-store stocks yet; some are joining the fray.

With such retailing comes another opportunity: Changes may be made to a product's 3D representation that don't quite reflect reality. Caveat emptor—let the buyer be aware. What you see may not be what you get.

Second- and third-generation virtual malls will evolve far more rapidly than a real mall, with special effects galore and room for literally everyone. Shoppers will evolve their avatars faster than most viruses, from subtle enhancements like makeup to fantastic fashion statements and blends of their visage with those of their favorite celebrities (animal, vegetable, or mineral). Kids will likely shop as their favorite game avatar while continuing that game; their parents will shop nearby (the joys of shared experiences?).

Education

Mass education will be able to progress from the group to the individual and will include group VR activities. The military, along with the airline and super-tanker industry, were for a long time the only ones able to afford accurate simulation. They've been using actual battlefield imagery for years—recently, some sim planes and tanks have been personalized for easy identification and for personal and group morale.

Similarly, police forces have simulators for weapons-handling training in tactical situations. While these are currently limited to fast-switching laserdisc video (FATS, Inc., of Atlanta, Georgia), they will soon use fully 3D virtual environments with photo-real textures. Related systems are being developed by the military for electronic wargame training. However, the cost of personal VR units for general wargaming is likely to be too great even for the Army for many years. Besides, even when they're cheap enough, it will be tough to simulate an invigorating bivouac in a cold, wet swamp.

VR mass education will first occur in the home. Driver's education is now severely hampered by budget problems in many high schools. Consequently, it will begin in the relative safety of the home with simulators. Since fear of crashing contributes to driver failure, high-quality VR imaging coupled with the low cost of crashing should improve success rates for this cohort of new drivers. Note the use of VR to reduce acrophobia by gradual acclimation to greater heights. Student drivers can acclimate to greater speeds and more traffic—and can even experience the terror of New York City driving. Artificial scenes will initially dominate, with large cities' main streets available as texture maps next. Eventually, a driver's own familiar neighborhood will be available for the first crash course.

Personal VR for Socialization

Though there are few other places in mass education for personalized imagery (sports being a phys-ed–unacceptable exception), the VR literature of adventure stories and action games will eventually evolve to the point of socially acceptable intellectual activity. And, unlike the singular participation modes of linear literature, VR environments permit mass participation in games, adventures, and other forms of (r)evolutionary creative expression.

Many uses of this new toolset will demand personalization of each of the many participants, else how can you tell friend from foe? Or can you? One clear effect of this capability is ubiquitous realtime theater, improvisational and otherwise. Actors everywhere will have immeasurably more opportunity to appear in front of online audiences and to play "first-person, multiple" roles, species, and/or genders simultaneously.

Shyness and more serious related socialization problems may also be addressed with hybrid video pipe/polygonal VR systems. A VR environment could introduce the socially impaired safely in the armor of their chosen avatars. They might then gradually progress through less threatening situations with more realistic imagery and live video texture maps, while shedding armor, eventually, for amour. The goal is to be able to meet other "real" avatars in order to ultimately be functional in normal reality, free of fear.

That is the point of VR personalization—to be free to be yourself or whatever you wish to be at that time, to be free to learn in your own style or express yourself as you see fit.

Biography

Lawrence A. (Larry) Leske, has been involved in multimedia for over 20 years—from 2D and 3D video arcade and home console product design and development as chief engineer at Bally/Midway to director of marketing for MPEG2 video compression at C^3 Microsystems—and also involved in strategic analysis. He consults for many semiconductor companies involved in the grand convergence of entertainment, video, computers, and communication systems (satellite, cable, and telephone). Mr. Leske spent four years as the MPEG2 system architect for TV/Com International during the development of their DVB-based satellite and cable transmission system. He is a member of ISO WG11/29 MPEG2 Systems and EBU's Digital Video for Broadcast (DVB) committees. He is also a founder and an advisor to Silicon Reality, Inc., a very high-performance 3D rendering IP company serving the semiconductor market.

Chapter 20

If VR Is So Great, Why Are VR Entertainment Systems So Poor?

Roy W. Latham
CGSD Corporation

Introduction

The concept of three-dimensional graphics in interactive entertainment systems is powerfully attractive. Could anything be more fascinating than exploring an artificial world, reacting to, and—these are entertainment systems—shooting things therein? Yet many people are not impressed by today's interactive entertainment systems. To be sure, there are enthusiasts for today's systems, and, undeniably, some systems are more interesting than others. In fact, today there are a few systems that are quite good, while most remain poor. Enthusiasts overlook limitations that others cannot. There were, for example, enthusiasts for the very first home computers despite the limitation of being programmed through panel switches. Today's VR attractions usually require a similar forgiving attitude: "The wonder is not that it is done well, it is that it is done at all."

Complex Systems

A root cause for the inadequacies of entertainment systems is that these are inherently difficult systems to make work well, quite independently of any limitations imposed by technology or by practical economics. They are difficult because they involve many different disciplines, ranging from the game design and the artistic appearance of the graphics database to the technical specialties of displays, graphics, sound, and human factors. Complex systems are nothing new, of course, but complex systems have traditionally been taken on by large organizations with many types of specialists on staff. The few entertainment systems put together by aerospace firms have ended up as technical successes, but business failures; the way aerospace firms use their teams of specialists apparently does not scale well to projects that are small by aerospace standards.

Quality interactive entertainment systems are difficult enough to produce with an aerospace budget, but the problems are compounded by economic realities. Consumers will pay a lot for entertainment, but not more for interactive electronic entertainment than for other experiences that they perceive as equally pleasurable. Interactive entertainment system developers often judge their products in comparison to others of the same ilk, and developers worry that too many systems are currently on their way to market and that this will result in market saturation. When worrying about impending market saturation, developers are realizing that the number of enthusiasts who will overlook many limitations is limited. However, for products that can meet general standards, the real competition is with other forms of entertainment—everything from golf and bowling to chess and fine dining. Developers who cannot overcome the limitations of the technology well enough to appeal to the general public will indeed encounter trouble ahead.

Many Specialties

Developers who try to do all the design work themselves seem to usually come up short in several aspects of their design. The current novelty of interactive entertainment systems and the small number of systems relative to the number of enthusiasts lead to the possibility of financial success despite serious flaws. Since there are more enthusiasts with low budgets than high budgets, poor-quality low-cost systems have a better chance of survival than high-quality high-cost systems. Over time, however, the notion of "selective quality" will not stand up, and developers who do what they know—and ignore the rest—will ultimately suffer. We are in a transition phase of the market where quality is starting to count.

While some developers continue to attack every aspect of the design without help, more commonly developers now put together a team to build a system. The team approach is potentially a good solution to obtaining needed specialties, but too often the team consists mainly of component manufacturers. System design and integration skills tend to be poorly covered. Manufacturers of image generators, displays, and motion systems participate on a team as a way of promoting the use of their products. Manufacturers may invest up front in the hope of a return in production. However, systems integrators, human factors specialists, market analysts, graphics database designers, and others who sell services do not fit the manufacturing investment model and are less likely to be included in a team. The consequence of excluding the nonmanufacturing skills are poor component selection, systems that are difficult to use, ineffective databases, and system problems such as objectionable lags or lack of synchronization between motion cues and visual imagery. A few examples of typical systems problems illustrate the situation.

Example 1: Lags

Possibly the most annoying design faults are those that lead to long lags between user control actions and the results of those actions in the system. For example, the user pushes the joystick to the right, and some time later the simulated vehicle responds by moving to the right. Or worse, the headtracker display is turned to the right, and some time later the image swivels around to catch up with the new position. Enthusiasts can accept lags as part of the challenge of the game, whereas most people feel frustration, to the point of quickly judging the system unusable.

In a good design, lags are treated with a succession of techniques. Most fundamental is to make the control loops as tight as possible by synchronizing events so that indeterminate waiting periods are eliminated. This includes getting the image generator running at a known update rate and synchronizing control measurements to occur as close to the start of frame computation as possible. This may require hardware modifications to bring out or inject synchronizing signals, but such modifications are typically straightforward. Tightening the control loops also may require direct memory access data transfers or, at least, parallel transfers in response to an interrupt. A completely wrong approach to a design is to have, for example, a headtracker that is unsynchronized with the image generator communicate data over a serial interface and leave the data in a buffer for an indeterminate period.

Once as much of the lag as possible has been squeezed out through synchronization, the rest of the lag must be compensated for as efficiently as possible by extrapolation. There is always, for example, some time delay from the moment the image generator is given a new viewpoint until the scene corresponding to that viewpoint is created and displayed. The viewpoint requested ought to correspond to the viewpoint expected when the image appears. If the user is turning to the right, the viewpoint ought to be slightly to the right of the viewpoint at the time the image generation process is started in order to compensate for the turning motion. Extrapolation can be tricky and will only compensate for short lags, but it is an important part of the whole solution.

For games, the game design can help the accuracy of extrapolation. For example, if the viewpoint is tied to a vehicle, rather than to head position, there is an opportunity to model the vehicle dynamics so that extrapolation will be easier. Events and objects that appear entirely under control of the game software ought to be perfectly predictable for short (roughly 100-millisecond) intervals. Game system designers also can follow the workstation practice of updating cursor position more frequently than the rest of the graphics and design the game so that the cursor is the primary factor in the apparent responsiveness.

Example 2: Ease of Use

Another systems design problem that increases the challenge of a game is to make the controls nonintuitive or counterintuitive. One entertainment system was designed with a requirement that the manually operated throttle had to be returned to its zero setting at game reset points, then advanced to the desired point. Novice players, thinking they were commanding full throttle because the throttle was physically advanced, were, in fact, not moving. The same game had a reverse button on the throttle and an accelerate button on the otherwise-directional joystick control, crossing the control functions. Human factors specialists sometimes claim their design principles to be no more than common sense. If so, it is common sense that is commonly avoided. Everything that makes interactive entertainment more difficult to learn raises the barrier to participation by ordinary people and keeps it in the hands of enthusiasts.

Example 3: Databases

The last example of a characteristic design shortcoming is the database design. Graphics systems, even expensive ones, are severely limited in their ability to create images with much three-dimensional complexity. Entertainment systems provide only a few hundred to a few thousand polygons per image at realtime rates (15 to 30 Hz, or more). Good database design has much to do with making scenes that appear interesting and complex while living within the bounds of system capacity.

A standard technique used in flight simulators for many years is to change the amount of detail in objects depending upon how close each object is to the viewpoint. An object like a tree or a house is modeled in several different versions with widely varying numbers of polygons. A tree viewed close-up will be portrayed using a version with many polygons, whereas the same tree in the distance may be portrayed by a single polygon with a texture pattern. In effect, the succession of models compensates for the effects of perspective in rapidly decreasing the projected size of objects and for the resulting tendency for all the image-generating capacity to be used on small polygons in the distance. Gracefully switching from one version of an object model to the next poses a number of difficulties, but the payoff is significant. Fighting the inverse-squared effects of perspective may provide a factor of a hundred or more increase in apparent complexity.

Despite the technique being standard practice in flight simulation, it is rarely practiced in virtual reality systems or entertainment systems. Popular VR-associated database formats do not even provide structures necessary to support the technique.

These examples of systems design considerations hint at the difficulty of the overall problem. Working against practical cost constraints makes the concerns all the more acute. For example, inexpensive system components are likely to inject more lag than expensive components, so synchronization and compensation techniques bear a greater burden of providing an overall solution. Similarly, limited polygon capacity presses the ability to make databases that appear complex. To date, few entertainment systems have met the design challenges.

Limitations in Technology

While clever design often helps, not every problem can be solved by clever design. For some things, the technology is unavailable at prices that users will support. With today's technology, for example, affordable head-mounted displays are unacceptable to nonenthusiasts. There is little chance that clever design can make dim, fuzzy, low-contrast displays acceptable to the average person, especially when significant lags are thrown in to boot. Producers of head-mounted displays are working diligently to advance the technology, and there is little doubt that much-improved technology is forthcoming. Until the technology improves, systems with head-mounted displays will remain the province of enthusiasts who marvel that it can be done at all.

The good news is that image generator costs are dropping dramatically as accelerated three-dimensional graphics moves into personal computers. Currently, no fewer than 35 companies are in the process of developing chip sets for 3D graphics. Several products have been demonstrated, with many more to come. The best of the low-cost products offer high polygon capacities and good implementations of anti-aliased texture. Common weak points are lack of anti-aliasing of polygon edges and limitation on the resolution of the output imagery. The weaknesses will prove troublesome to location-based entertainment systems; the generation of designs two years hence should treat these problems.

More good news is that we now have an example or two of excellent entertainment systems. The most interesting is The Walt Disney Corporation's

Aladdin attraction. The system features a large, high-quality CRT-based head-mounted display that is cleverly suspended by cables. The databases and graphic image quality are first rate, and the experience includes animated characters that engage the participant.

The Disney example is a triumph of technology, and it is in the landmark position of showing what is possible. It is not, alas, a triumph of low-cost technology. Very good systems from Magic Edge, Inc., and Virtual Worlds Entertainment succeed in attracting other than pure enthusiasts and are steps in the progression of the business. Now that the point has been made that good systems can be built, we should expect to see money flowing into the industry from more tradition-bound large companies.

The greatest untapped area in interactive entertainment development is the development of new game storylines and wholly new types of interactive experiences. High-end interactive systems are expensive, and developers feel obliged to prove an adrenaline rush through classic arcade-style shooting and driving themes; those themes are also most likely to appeal to arcade-bred young enthusiasts, the core audience needed for new ventures. Untapped is the potential for appealing to the much larger demographic of more mature patrons who potentially might devote even more disposable income to such entertainment. It may be some time before anyone is willing to risk putting forth experiences centered on exploration and discovery, art and contemplation, or even strategic problem solving.

Summary

The concept of interactive entertainment is so powerful that the future of the industry is unquestionably bright. Technology exists today to make exciting systems that work well and to do so at a price that nonenthusiasts will pay. The key is to develop systems with a team that covers all the diverse skills required and to develop concepts that can live within the bounds of present technology.

The motion picture industry offers a good model for interactive entertainment projects. Creative and technical talents are assembled for a particular project. No one expects the script writers to invent camera equipment for a motion picture, but VR entertainment developers often attempt equally unlikely crossovers of specialties. That's why interactive products don't live up to the capabilities of the technology.

VR entertainment is emerging from its infancy. We are beginning to see exciting examples of what can be done. Maturity, competition, improved technology, and more investment dollars will ultimately lead to products that reach well beyond enthusiasts to the general public.

Biography

Roy W. Latham is founder and president of CGSD Corporation, Mountain View, California, and publisher of *Real Time Graphics* newsletter. He has over 15 years of experience in graphics and simulation. Prior to founding CGSD, he led major graphics-related R & D projects at Sun Microsystems, Kaiser Electronics, and Link Flight Simulation Division. He holds patents in the field of computer graphics and has authored several published papers as well as the recent Springer-Verlag book *The Dictionary of Computer Graphics Technology and Applications*.

Chapter 21

Interactivity and Individual Viewpoint in Shared Virtual Worlds: The Big Screen Versus Networked Personal Displays

Warren Robinett
Virtual Reality Games, Inc.

Introduction

Most current motion-base rides and other types of location-based entertainment (LBE) are not interactive at this time—these rides provide a canned experience to a passive audience. The experience is essentially a movie, with some tilting and jerking provided by the motion base. To increase the involvement of the audience, and hence the appeal and popularity of these rides, there is interest in making them "interactive."

However, there are problems with the idea of integrating interactive control by audience members into an experience conveyed in a theaterlike setting with a seated audience attending to a single large display screen and speakers. Only a limited and inferior sort of interactivity is feasible under these conditions. The reason that this type of interaction is inferior has to do with the nature of interactivity—the normal human experience of interacting with the world includes not only the ability to make observable changes to the world but also the ability to move oneself through the world and, consequently to be able to observe it from different viewpoints.

This chapter argues that, for many people to have an interactive experience that is shared with the other people inhabiting the same virtual world, it is most effective for each participant to have his or her own personal display device. This allows a unique viewpoint within the virtual world for each participant, and independent viewpoints permit independent self-motion within the virtual world by each participant.

The technical feasibility of creating shared virtual worlds with large numbers of participants, where each participant has an individual viewpoint, has been demonstrated by the U.S. Army SIMNET military training system and by the commercial Habitat project and recent derivatives.

Being interactive means that when you do something, it changes what happens next. An interactive experience mimics the responsive nature of real-world experience—namely, that your actions produce results. You can change the world (a little part of it, at least) by reaching out and manipulating something. In a videogame, the world that is changed by your actions is a virtual world—a simulated world maintained in the memory of a computer. You act through an input device such as a joystick, and you see the results of your actions in the simulated world through the game's display screen. In contrast with videogames, movies are not interactive because the sequence of events is fixed and cannot be changed. No actions are permitted by the viewer. The viewer of a film is a passive observer, an invisible voyeur traveling along a path in space and time chosen by the film's creators.

Current motion-base rides and other location-based entertainment (LBE) attractions are more like movies than videogames, at least at present. The viewers sit in a small theater built atop a motion base that can tilt and jerk the whole theater structure, while the audience inside sees and hears a movie presented on the screen in front of them. The viewers have no interactive control; they are simply passive observers. Thus, these rides could fairly be called movies with a motion base.

But why not add interaction to these rides? Give some sort of input devices to the audience, create a multi-player videogame to generate the graphics (and drive the motion base), and then let the audience enjoy an engaging interactive experience shared and controlled by all. Maybe interactive LBE rides could become as addictive (and profitable) as videogames are in the home market. There is considerable interest in this at present. For example, Amelia Thompson, a vice president at Sequoia Creative, Sun Valley, California, is quoted (Gordon 1993) as saying, "What designers and producers of themed entertainment attractions do is use film and video as a tool to tell the story and create a complete experience. We need to create group experiences that depend on—and invite—the participation of members of the audience to become part of the experience as individuals and as groups. In a traditional movie theater, the film is the experience, and that's no longer enough." Unfortunately, making motion-base rides or movie theaters interactive has some basic problems for audiences of more than, say, a dozen people.

Interactivity Using a Display Shared by Many People

There is an inherent problem with giving a large number of people simultaneous interactive control of anything. In particular, it's not practical for many people to simultaneously control the entire image on the screen. This rules out image changes such as zooms, pans, or dollies (translation of the viewpoint) for control by multiple audience members. However, it's possible for individual audience members to control individual elements within the scene being viewed—for example, in a two-player videogame—but this is effective only for a small number of participants.

Videogames with two players controlling the action on a single screen are common, popular, and effective. Usually, each player controls a single character or vehicle on the screen. Some games, such as car racing games, allow up to four players to control their own icons on a single shared screen. A problem with games of this sort is that the players can lose track of "themselves." That is, they can become confused about which character or vehicle they are controlling on the screen and have to resort to experimentation to establish which icon on the screen responds to their control actions. When this multi-player, shared-screen setup works well, each player focuses on the part of the screen containing his or her own character and what is happening to it.

However, as more players are added, the problem of losing your "self" gets worse, and this multi-player, shared-screen format has rarely been used with more than eight players. When the number of participants gets into the dozens or hundreds, this method of providing multi-player interaction breaks down.

There are other ways for groups of people to interact with on-going events besides controlling little characters on the screen. For example, they can vote. Voting can be livelier than a visit to a voting booth if everyone can vote simultaneously via manual controls and if the audience is allowed hoorays and hisses as the choices unfold. Nevertheless, the interaction by each participant with the virtual world is still pretty limited in such an arrangement.

Another interaction method suited to large groups is shooting. Each audience member can have a simulated gun and can fire away at will at whatever appears on the screen. It would make sense to show the location of all the "bullets" hitting the screen so that the audience members could see what everyone else was shooting at.

It would be foolish to say that none of these kinds of single-screen, group interactive experiences could be fun; they can. But the kind of interactivity available to each audience member is limited to participating in group decisions. (Perhaps there's an opportunity here to study mob psychology.)

What is the fundamental conflict between the shared display and interactivity? Using a single display screen, it's difficult to allow for independent interaction for each participant with the virtual world and to allow for pairwise interaction among the participants. It seems that independent interaction among a large group of people cannot be achieved while they all see and hear the same thing.

To understand the reasons for this, we need to explore the nature of the human experience of interaction.

The Nature of Interactivity

All forms of media attempt to mimic certain aspects of real-world human experience, and this is true, in particular, for interactive media. Just as visual media such as painting and film are bound up with the human experience of seeing the world, interactive media try to mimic the human experience of interacting with things in the world. People pick up, manipulate, and examine objects. People look around in different directions and search for things. People walk and travel around through the world and thus enter into new surroundings with new objects to manipulate. People communicate face-to-face with other people.

Some of the important types of normal human interaction with the things and people in the world may be summed up by saying that people can look, move, act, and talk:

- Look—A person can look around at his or her surroundings.

- Move—A person can move through the world and see it from different viewpoints.

- Act—A person can perform actions that modify the world.

- Talk—A person can communicate with other people.

It is not accidental that we have one-syllable Anglo-Saxon words for each of these things; each one is fundamental to our experience of interacting with the world.

Few would argue that performing actions that modify the world is part of the experience of interaction with the world. Likewise, in a world that contains other people, communicating with those others is surely a form of interaction. However, looking around and moving through the world might be questioned by some as being essential components of the interactive experience.

There is a tendency to focus on the changing of the world as the definition of interactivity and to ignore the necessity of seeing what one is changing. But interaction is not shooting in the dark—it is shooting at specific, perceived targets. Even literal shooting in the dark doesn't make any sense unless one heard an enemy's footsteps or somehow perceived an antagonistic presence. Human manipulations quite frequently are attempts to achieve certain goal states—for example, to get the jug into the refrigerator—that could not be performed blindfolded with thick bandages on the hands. Seeing, hearing, and feeling the world are necessary for successful interaction.

Similarly, moving through the world is an essential aspect of normal human interaction with the world. Everything in the world is not at arm's length, and many things are out of sight. The combination of being able to freely move through a large world and being able to change things in different parts of it is a much more powerful kind of interactivity than being stuck in one place, like a Venus fly-trap, and being able to interact only with that which comes to you.

The importance of voluntary self-motion in the experience of interaction becomes even more obvious when we consider a group of people interacting with one another and with the world. Note that, in any real-world group experience, the people involved do not see and hear the same thing. Each person has a different physical location at any one time, can move around and look closely at specific things, and thus has a different experience than the other people. A group of people may scatter into different rooms or travel to different places and then examine and interact with the objects in those experiences.

Furthermore, communication among people is frequently conversational, with two people talking face-to-face. You can't get your face in front of someone else's face without the ability to move. Enormous numbers of human conversations occur simultaneously throughout the real world, but two people in conversation can hear and understand each other's words because their physical proximity makes their voices rise above the myriad other conversations going on. Thus, the ability to move through the world to change one's "earpoint" is important for enabling communication with other people in the world.

The Problem with Interactivity on the Big Screen

The central problem with trying to make motion-base rides interactive is that, because everyone in the audience views the same display—the big screen—everyone has essentially the same viewpoint into the virtual world. Also, everyone in the audience hears the same thing—the sound coming out of the speakers behind the screen.

The individual audience members cannot move themselves independently through such a virtual world because there is only one viewpoint into the virtual world, shared by all. Audience members cannot focus independently on objects of interest in the virtual world because anything seen by anyone must be seen by all, and the screen becomes cluttered.

Simultaneous conversations between pairs of people in the virtual world is impossible because everyone must hear what anyone hears. Of course, you can still turn around and converse with the person in the seat behind you without electronic mediation. But this limits the kind of group experiences that can be portrayed to those real-world experiences in which the participants sit in rows of chairs during the entire experience. A ride in a rocketship matches this criterion, and so perhaps it is not surprising that the first big success among motion-base rides, Tour of the Universe at the CN Tower in Toronto, was a pretend rocket ride. The same theme was successfully used again at Disneyland in the Star Tours ride.

A rocket ride or a plane ride could be made somewhat interactive by allowing one person in the audience to be the pilot of the craft. This might be much more exciting for all than experiencing a canned ride. But it would be an interactive experience primarily for the person at the controls, and the rest of the audience would be in a passive role.

Creating exciting interactive group experiences in which all the participants stay seated in rows and in which they all see and hear the same thing seems to suffer from major limitations in comparison to the overall breadth of interactive human experience. Perhaps there is a better way to convey multiperson, interactive experience.

Networked Personal Displays

The solution is networked personal displays. When all of the participants have their own display devices, with each person seeing the shared virtual world from an individual viewpoint, then a better mimicking of real-world shared experience becomes feasible. A group of individual display devices can be networked together to mimic the ordinary experience of people moving around and seeing the real world from different and changing vantage points. In such a system, the user has the ability to look around, to move through the world, to perform actions that change the world, and to talk with other people who are also inhabiting the virtual world.

The U.S. Army's SIMNET system has implemented this idea in a spectacular way (Thorpe 1987). The SIMNET system takes individual aircraft flight simulators and tank training simulators and networks them together over telephone lines. This allows several hundred aircraft and tank crews, with each group of three or four soldiers in their own simulator, to fight war games in a shared virtual world. If their simulated vehicles enter the same part of the virtual world, then they can see (and shoot at) one another. Simulated battles involving over a thousand human participants and lasting many hours have taken place using SIMNET. The fidelity of the simulators to the real experience of flying planes and driving tanks was good enough that SIMNET was used for tactical rehearsals by some of the flight crews before their real missions in the 1992 war in Iraq.

Thus, SIMNET has demonstrated the technical feasibility of highly interactive shared experience in a virtual world with a large number of people. It was not done, and could not be done, with a large number of people watching a single, large, shared display device. Individual display devices for each simulator crew were needed to permit the simulated vehicles to move through the virtual world and to see it from their individual viewpoints.

A less expensive project that provided another proof of principle for networked personal displays was the Habitat project, done at Lucasfilm Games (Morningstar and Farmer 1991). Habitat allowed thousands of people to simultaneously inhabit a shared virtual world and to interact with one another when they came into the same part of it. Habitat users saw an image of a character representing themselves on the screen of their personal computers, controlled the movement and actions of their "avatar" using a joystick, and "talked" to other users (when they were nearby) by typing on the keyboard. A user could move through the Habitat world, pick up and carry objects, and communicate with other human users logged on to Habitat.

It's clear from SIMNET, from Habitat, and from other similar projects that have followed, such as NPSNet (Zyda et al. 1993), that networked personal displays are an effective way to create interactive virtual worlds that can be shared by a large number of participants.

Economic Factors

The entertainment-consuming public is sensitive to cost. People routinely pay a few dollars to see a two-hour movie. Yet only rarely will they spend $50 for an individual entertainment experience, and they dislike paying movie prices for entertainment experiences that last only a few minutes, such as current arcade VR games.

The public seems to be willing to pay somewhat more for personal copies of experiences that can be replayed again and again on demand. This includes recorded music, movies on videotape, and home videogames.

Showing the same image to many people simultaneously in a multiperson entertainment experience allows a lower cost per person than providing each user with personal equipment. The current high cost of personal displays provides economic motivation to search for ways to improve the big screen experience.

However, the costs are dropping fast for personal displays. A few years ago, it cost around $250,000 to buy a VR system consisting of head-mounted display (HMD), manual input device, and graphics engine (for example, the RB2 system from VPL). Today, $20,000 will get you a PC-based VR system (for example, a PC, graphics boards, Sense8 software, and Virtual Research HMD). Coming soon are cost-effective VR goggles that will work with home video-games (Johnson-Williams 1993).

This radical change in the cost of personal head-mounted displays should trigger some rethinking of the economic motivations in the tug-of-war between the big screen and personal displays. Personal displays are no longer absurdly expensive. They will be used in interactive home VR experiences and will perhaps be considered a natural development in the videogame entertainment genre.

Whether HMDs will work well in public entertainment facilities remains to be seen. There are several problems in using HMDs in public venues. Hygiene is an issue because an HMD wearer could get lice or catch a disease from an earlier wearer. One type of VR display that does not have this problem is the CAVE, a large box you step inside of with display screens on each surface (Cruz-Neira, Sandin, and DeFanti 1993).

Individual differences, such as the variation in interpupillary distance (IPD) among people, means that a one-size-fits-all HMD will not be adequate for high-fidelity VR experiences. Individual adjustment will be required for each user if an HMD is shared by many people. Note that binoculars have separate focus knobs for the two eyes and can swivel in and out to allow for varying IPD. In the case of eyeglasses or contact lenses, each person has an individually tailored apparatus.

Public entertainment facilities, from videogame parlors to carnivals, have traditionally attracted people with unique equipment that was too expensive for individual purchase. This is what allows videogame arcades to survive, in competition with home videogames. Likewise, movie theaters provide a higher-resolution, wider-angle experience than movies viewed at home on the television. If there was not something better about seeing a movie in a theater, no one would go to them. By the same token, LBE attractions must provide something that is not available at home.

Reproduction of Experience

Perhaps the LBE industry should direct its energies to providing high-fidelity, multisensory recorded experiences (Robinett 1992). This chapter has argued that showing the same thing to many people at once is incompatible with inter-activity, but, for most senses, broadening the sensory coverage works fine with a large audience. Note, in particular, that adding a motion base to a movie did exactly this—it added vestibular stimulation to the movie.

Looking at the history of media is instructive. Photographs provided a kind of re-experiencing of past places, but the silent motion picture was the first to provide an effective reproduction of experience. Adding sound to the motion picture (creating the "talkies") quickly made the silent films obsolete. Likewise, color replaced black-and-white. Stereophonic sound replaced monophonic sound. The high fidelity of CD-sound overwhelmed its competitors. There seems to be an innate desire in people for high-fidelity, broad sensory stimulation.

Sensory coverage is incomplete in current media, and thus there is an opportunity for media innovators. Film and television do not completely fill the visual field; in VR terms, the viewer in not "immersed" in the image. Spatial sound fields of real places cannot be reproduced through two speakers sitting in front of an audience; there is room for improvement in spatialization of sound. In the VR world, sound spatialization has been more fully explored (Wenzel 1992).

The sense of touch is entirely neglected by current media. What is commonly called the "sense of touch" encompasses the ability to sense pressure on the skin, contact, vibration, and temperature. Displays to each of these tactile modes could enhance the reproduction of experience. Tactile displays offer new possibilities for erotic experiences—the "feelies" as foreseen by Aldous Huxley in *Brave New World* (1932).

Force displays are related to tactile displays but affect primarily the muscles, joints, and tendons and can induce joint and body motions in the user. Force-feedback displays are important in flight simulation and teleoperation (for feeling what the remote robot feels). A few car racing videogames (probably the first was Hard Drivin' by Atari Games) have provided force displays, usually in the steering wheel. Both the mechanisms and algorithms have improved steadily, and recent deluxe, sit-down driving games like San Francisco Rush (also by Atari Games) are quite convincing.

Smell displays are another relatively unexplored area; smells can be quite evocative and tend to trigger memories that are more personally significant and less broadly shared than those from other display modes. A good example of smell displays can be found at the T2-3D attraction at Universal Studios, Florida. The sharp tang of burnt gunpowder seems to float directly from the futuristic battlefield into the audience, providing a vivid boost to the illusion. A simple and effective tactile display occurs a few minutes later; when the most dangerous Terminator explodes into a shower of liquid metal, a few cool drops of water fall through the darkness onto each member of the audience!

Gustatory displays would have to dispense stimulants into the user's mouth, with many attendant problems, but such displays would broaden the sensory coverage. Since smell covers a closely related and much more nuanced range of stimuli at lesser difficulty, this is not considered a useful area of research.

The Sensorama

This direction for the development of movie technology—full coverage of the senses—was foreseen by visionary Morton Heilig in the 1950s. After stating his vision for multisensory films in his paper "The Cinema of the Future" (Heilig 1955), he proceeded to work out a detailed design for an "experience theater" that gave, to viewers in a large audience, an illusion of reality by providing a very broad palette of sensory stimulation.

The sensory palette included full-peripheral (wide-field) color images in 3D, directional sound, aromas, wind, vibration, body tilting, and temperature variations. He then built and patented a one-person version of the experience theater, which he called the "Sensorama Simulator." This machine played stereoscopic films, augmented with not only stereophonic sound tracks but also tracks for wind, vibrations, and aromas. The person receiving the recorded experience sat in a special booth to see the wide-angle stereoscopic visuals, hear the binaural sounds, feel the wind and vibrations, and smell the aromas.

Heilig was not able to convince the movie moguls of the 1950s and 1960s to invest in building a full-scale experience theater. However, the Sensorama still works and can display any of the five short multisensory films that Heilig made. He was in his twenties when he wrote his 1955 paper and has not lost interest in his original vision. In his own words, "Most people think I should be dead by now, but I feel very young and I'm planning to build an all-electronic version of my Sensorama machine. Then I want to build a portable small-group entertainment simulator, and ultimately, my experience theater."

If you believe that multisensory, high-fidelity reproduction of experience is the future of entertainment, maybe you should help Mort Heilig make his vision real. (Mort Heilig can be reached at (805) 255-6635/6248. His address is 23870 Pine Street, #1, Newhall, California 91321.)

Summary

Being required to show the same images and sounds to a group of seated people is not a design requirement that makes it easy to design an effective and engaging interactive experience. The individual audience members will have little independent control in such a situation.

A better way to give a large group of people a fully interactive experience in a shared virtual world is by giving each participant a personal display device, thus allowing each person an independent viewpoint into the virtual world. Using networked personal displays, the participants can move through the virtual world independently of one another, can manipulate the objects in the virtual world, and can have many simultaneous conversations going on among themselves within the virtual world.

Adding interactivity is not the only way to enhance the experience provided to people in LBE attractions. Recorded experiences can be conveyed more powerfully by broadening the sensory coverage to more and more of the human senses and by improving the fidelity of sensory reproduction.

References

Cruz-Neira, C., Sandin, D., and DeFanti, T., "Surround-Screen Projection-Based Virtual Reality: Design and Implementation of the CAVE," *Computer Graphics: Proceedings of SIGGRAPH,* pp. 135–142, 1993.

Gordon, C., "Special-Venue Entertainment Is Coming to a Theatre Near You," *Millimeter Magazine,* pp. 58–60, March 1993.

Heilig, M., "El Cine del Futuro" ("The Cinema of the Future"), *Espacios,* Mexico City, 1955, reprinted in *Presence* 1(3), 1992.

Johnson-Williams, M., Presentation at Meckler New York VR Expo, New York City, December 1993.

Morningstar, C., and Farmer, R., "The Lessons of Lucasfilm's Habitat," in *Cyberspace: First Steps,* edited by Michael Benedikt, MIT Press, Cambridge, Mass., pp. 273–301, 1991.

Robinett, W., "Synthetic Experience: A Proposed Taxonomy," *Presence* 1(2), 1992.

Thorpe, J., "The New Technology of Large-Scale Simulator Networking: Implications for Mastering the Art of Warfighting," in *Proceedings of the Ninth Interservice Industry Training Systems Conference,* 1987.

Wenzel, E. M., "Localization and Virtual Acoustic Displays," *Presence* 1(1), 1992.

Zyda, M. J., Pratt, D. R., Falby, J. S., Lombardo, C., and Kelleher, K. M., "The Software Required for the Computer Generation of Virtual Environments," *Presence* 2(2): 130–140, 1993.

Biography

Warren Robinett is a designer of interactive computer graphics software and hardware. In 1978, he designed the Atari videogame Adventure, the first graphical adventure game. In 1980, he was co-founder and chief software engineer at The Learning Company, a publisher of educational software. There, he designed Rocky's Boots, a computer game that teaches digital logic to 11-year-old children. Rocky's Boots won software-of-the-year awards from three magazines in 1983. In 1986, Mr. Robinett worked as a research scientist at NASA Ames Research Center, where he designed the software for the Virtual Environment Workstation, NASA's pioneering virtual reality project. From 1989 to 1992 at the University of North Carolina, he directed the Head-Mounted Display and Nanomanipulator Projects. Mr. Robinett currently serves on the National Academy of Sciences Committee for Virtual Reality Research and Development, and he is associate editor for the journal *Presence*.

Chapter 22

Beginnings: Sensorama and the Telesphere Mask

Mort Heilig[†]
Supercruiser, Inc.

Introduction

It was 1947; I had just mustered out of the medical corps and decided to become a filmmaker. Working in film seemed the best way of combining my interests in art, technology, and education. I returned to Europe, graduated from the Centro di Cinematografia in Rome, under Vittorio De Sica in 1950, and began producing/directing short documentary films. Since Italy is drenched in painting and sculpture, it's easy to understand why I soon came to think of the screen image as a painting that moved and the characters on-screen as dynamic sculptures that one could observe from different angles. To me, a film was a work of art—something an audience surrounded and looked at—and a motion picture theater seemed to me a kind of museum where audiences gathered to observe the film.

My perspective reversed in 1952 when I returned to New York and rushed to Broadway to see the latest sensation, "This Is Cinerama." When the curtain swept up to reveal the now-legendary wide-screen roller coaster ride, I realized that the film's creators were no longer content to have me look *at* the roller coaster but were trying to put me physically *on* the ride. The audience no longer surrounded the work of art; the work of art surrounded the audience—just as reality surrounds us. The spectator was invited to plunge into another world. We no longer needed the device of identifying with a character on the other side of the "window." We could step through it and be a part of the action!

Cinerama was a technological success, but to me it was only a good start, not a burgeoning conclusion. If the new goal of film was to create a convincing illusion of reality, then why not toss tradition to the winds? Why not say

[†]Deceased.

good-bye to the rectangular picture frame, two-dimensional images, horizontal audiences, and the limited senses of sight and hearing, and reach out for everything and anything that would enhance the illusion of reality? Since nobody, including the folks at Cinerama, seemed interested in doing this, I took the plunge myself in spite of limited resources.

Cinema of the Future

To clarify my thoughts, I wrote an article called "The Cinema of the Future," which gathered dust in a drawer for years but finally was published in the Mexican architectural magazine *Espacios* in 1955 (and recently was reprinted in the journal *Presence* by MIT Press). Some of the work embodied in this article, plus my Italian films, got me a job at NBC.

I realized that to achieve the "cinema of the future," two things were necessary. First, I had to carefully study the human nervous system—how it perceives reality (as distinguished from other animals). Second, I could no longer consider a theater to be a piece of architecture; it was a part of a large machine designed to psychologically transport people as effectively as a jet transports them physically.

As I worked out the details of this "machine," I used every technology available in the 1950s: optics, screen surfaces, loudspeakers, precision electric motors, pumps, and analog switchers. My "Experience Theater" created an illusion of reality for a mass audience by filling all of every spectator's senses (just as they're filled in normal life) with color, visual motion, 3D, peripheral imagery, directional sound, aromas, and tactile sensations. The cumulative effect of this goes considerably beyond the 3D IMAX theaters of today.

When I completed my theater design in the late 1950s, I went to Mexico to shoot a film on bullfighting. A presentation that I made at the home of Alfaro Siqueiros, the muralist, led to the financial support of several Mexican architects and the Ministry of Communications. I built a 180-degree fisheye lens and a semispherical screen. Using the lens, I shot a series of extremely wide angle 4"×5" stills and projected them onto/into the semisphere. The effect was riveting. My next step was to build a portable screen and present this effect in New York City to the leaders of the film industry, sure that they would fund the development of a movie camera and reliable projection system. I was wrong. Not one of them could imagine the impact of a fully peripheral image when it moved. We eventually agreed to sell one unit to International Harvester as a combine simulator. Somehow I had to devise a way to make an immersive image move—even if for only one person.

From 1958 to 1961, I designed and, with the financial support of John Miller and Donald Werby, built three working models of a machine I called the "Sensorama Simulator." We did this in a tiny, dilapidated, extraordinary machine shop in the Bronx called Richmark, which evolved into Oxberry, the premiere animation stand manufacturer. Initially, my mission was just to demonstrate to investors the kind of excitement my Experience Theater could generate. As the work progressed, I realized that Sensorama was viable on its own. It could present exciting experiences to one person at thousands of locations where a theater wouldn't fit: hotel lobbies, airports, arcades, ballparks, and restaurants. I charged 25 cents for a two-minute "ride," and the machine played one of four rides in rotation. About this time, someone agreed with my idea; a French machine called the "Scopitone" was introduced in the United States. It was my only direct competition and was probably the first audiovisual jukebox. For the same 25 cents, up to 20 people could gather around a monoscopic film screen; it typically grossed about half my revenues.

To complete my project, it was necessary to build an original 35mm 3D camera, a new kind of closed-loop projector, and wind, aroma, and vibration systems. In addition, the 1,200-pound machine had to be completely automatic, self-explanatory, easy to transport and service, and (as I soon learned) vandal proof. Over several years, the Sensorama Simulators presented a motorcycle ride, a helicopter ride, a dune buggy ride, a date with a teenage girl, and an exotic belly dance to over 200,000 enthusiastic viewers. I also did one film from the point of view of a Coca-Cola bottle going through the bottling plant, in an attempt to pursue commercial accounts.

While designing the Experience Theater and subsequently building the Sensorama Simulator, I determined that a small stereographic video mask placed on the head could provide you with color 3D peripheral imagery, binaural sound, and aromas, with about an 80 percent illusion of reality. I presented my "Telesphere Mask" patent design to the directors of RCA's David Sarnoff Research Center in 1960, but they said they couldn't see any future in it.

Summary

In retrospect, it's clear that I designed three different systems in pursuit of the same goal—to transport people to another reality, realistic or fantastic. The Experience Theater was for large audiences, the Sensorama Simulator was for one to four people, and the Telesphere Mask was for the individual. Each system had its particular set of problems requiring unique solutions. When I examine the multitude of reality-transfer systems today, I recognize many of the same problems, some of whose solutions aren't as effective as ones I discovered 30 years ago. Over the past 40 years, as film, video, and computer technology have matured, I've filled many notebooks with designs, ideas, applications, and dreams that may yet see the light of day.

Biography

Mort Heilig studied at Cornell and received a B.A. degree in philosophy from the University of Chicago. While in the U.S. Army after 1945, he ran audiovisual services at military hospitals in France, then studied painting in Paris, and later received two consecutive Fulbright scholarships and the NBC President's award. He also got a degree in film direction at the Centro Sperimentale di Cinematographica in Rome. For the next 25 years, he produced, wrote, directed, and photographed over 100 documentary films for Communication Design, Inc., NBC, CBS, the U.S. Information Agency, and Mexican Movie Theaters, winning several national and international awards. He also photographed several low-budget features and coproduced and directed the feature *Once*, which was honored at the 1974 Cannes Film Fesitival.

In 1959, he designed and patented the Experience Theater and, in 1960, the Sensorama Simulator and Telesphere Mask, possibly the first head-mounted display. For this early work in experiential simulation, Mr. Heilig has been honored by some with the title "Father of Virtual Reality." He has consulted for Walt Disney Imagineering, Landmark Productions, Wrather Entertainment, Teenage World's Fair, and the Sony Corporation. For the past several years, he has been the CEO of Supercruiser, Inc., of Newhall, California, a developer and manufacturer of innovative sports products, and he is pursuing the realization of several VR projects.

Mort Heilig died on May 14, 1997, after competing in the L.A. Marathon on roller blades of his own design.

N°   3,050,870

THE UNITED STATES OF AMERICA

TO ALL TO WHOM THESE PRESENTS SHALL COME:

Whereas   Morton L. Heilig,

of

Long Beach,   New York,

PRESENTED TO THE **Commissioner of Patents** A PETITION PRAYING FOR
THE GRANT OF LETTERS PATENT FOR AN ALLEGED NEW AND USEFUL INVENTION THE TITLE
AND A DESCRIPTION OF WHICH ARE CONTAINED IN THE SPECIFICATION OF WHICH
A COPY IS HEREUNTO ANNEXED AND MADE A PART HEREOF, AND COMPLIED WITH THE
VARIOUS REQUIREMENTS OF LAW IN SUCH CASES MADE AND PROVIDED, AND

Whereas UPON DUE EXAMINATION MADE THE SAID CLAIMANT   IS
ADJUDGED TO BE JUSTLY ENTITLED TO A PATENT UNDER THE LAW.

NOW THEREFORE THESE **Letters Patent** ARE TO GRANT UNTO THE SAID

Morton L. Heilig, his heirs

OR ASSIGNS

FOR THE TERM OF **SEVENTEEN** YEARS FROM THE DATE OF THIS GRANT

RIGHT TO EXCLUDE OTHERS FROM MAKING, USING OR SELLING THE SAID INVEN-
THROUGHOUT THE UNITED STATES.

*In testimony whereof I have hereunto set my
hand and caused the seal of the Patent Office
to be affixed at the City of Washington
this* twenty-eighth *day of* August,
*in the year of our Lord, one thousand nine
hundred and* sixty-two, *and of the
Independence of the United States of America
the one hundred and* eighty-seventh.

Attest:

Eston G. Johnson
Attesting Officer.

David L. Ladd
Commissioner of Patents.

1

3,050,870
SENSORAMA SIMULATOR
Morton L. Heilig, Long Beach, N.Y.
(10 Sheridan Square, New York 14, N.Y.)
Filed Jan. 10, 1961, Ser. No. 81,864
13 Claims. (Cl. 35—1)

The present invention, generally, relates to simulator apparatus and, more particularly, to apparatus to stimulate the senses of an individual to simulate an actual experience realistically.

There are increasing demands today for ways and means to teach and train individuals without actually subjecting the individuals to possible hazards of particular situations. For example, the armed services must instruct men in the operation and maintenance of extremely complicated and potentially dangerous equipment, and it is desirable to educate the men with the least possible danger to their lives and to possible damage to costly equipment.

Industry, on the other hand, is faced with a similar problem due to present day rapid rate of development of automatic machines. Here, too, it is desired to train a labor force without the accompanying risks.

The above outlined problem has arisen also in educational institutions due to such factors as increasingly complex subject matter being taught, larger groups of students and an inadequate number of teachers. As a result of this situation, there has developed an increased demand for teaching devices which will relieve, if not supplant, the teachers' burden.

Accordingly, it is an object of the present invention to provide an apparatus to simulate a desired experience by developing sensations in a plurality of the senses.

It is also an object of the invention to provide an apparatus for simulating an actual, predetermined experience in the senses of an individual.

A further object of the invention is to provide an apparatus for use by one or more persons to experience a simulated situation.

Another object of the invention is to provide a new and improved apparatus to develop realism in a simulated situation.

Briefly, an apparatus constructed in accordance with the principles of the invention embodies a housing having a hood means mounted thereon to fit about the head of an observer. A visual image projection means is supported by the housing, and an optical means is included to direct images from the projection means to the hood. In addition to the above, means is provided to direct a breeze toward this hood, and at least one odor-sense stimulating substance is positioned to be releasable into the breeze in response to a signal from a suitable coordinating means. It is the cooperative effects of the breeze, the odor, the visual images and binaural sound that stimulate a desired sensation in the senses of an observer. For those instances where a sense of motion is desired, means is provided to induce small vibrations or jolts to simulate movement and, also, to simulate actual impacts.

Other objects of the invention will be pointed out in the following description and claims and illustrated in the accompanying drawings, which disclose, by way of example, the principle of the invention and the best mode which has been contemplated of applying that principle.

In the drawings:

FIG. 1 is a top plan view of a hood arrangement for four viewers in accordance with the invention;

FIG. 2 is an enlarged plan view of only one of the hoods shown in FIG. 1;

FIG. 3 is a front elevational view of the panel inside the hood as taken along the line 3—3 in FIG. 4;

FIG. 4 is a side view in elevation taken along the line 4—4 in FIG. 3;

2

FIG. 5 is a side view in elevation similar to that shown in FIG. 4 but showing a seat, arm rest and controls;

FIG. 6 shows a plan view of a plurality of films in position for selective viewing by one or more persons;

FIG. 7 is a perspective view of one film container in accordance with the invention;

FIG. 7A is a view along the line 7A—7A in FIG. 7;

FIG. 8 is a perspective view of one end for the film container shown in FIG. 7;

FIG. 9 is a view in elevation and in section showing a clasp for the structure of FIG. 8;

FIG. 10 is a view of the optical arrangement in accordance with the invention;

FIG. 11 is a side view partly in section showing one arrangement for enclosing an odor-stimulating substance for release into the hood;

FIG. 12 is a view in perspective showing an arrangement for a plurality of odor-stimulating substance containers for use with an arrangement as shown in FIG. 11;

FIG. 13 is a side view in elevation of a breeze developing arrangement;

FIG. 14 is a plan view of the breeze developing arrangement shown in FIG. 13;

FIG. 15 is a side view in elevation of one film container as shown in FIG. 7 illustrating a rewind mechanism;

FIG. 16 is a gear system for use in the mechanism as shown in FIG. 15;

FIG. 17 is a view of a control linkage for operating the rewind mechanism automatically; and

FIG. 18 is a view of one frame of a film for use in the apparatus of the invention.

Before proceeding with a detailed description of the present invention, a somewhat detailed discussion of the setting in which the invention is cast is believed to be in order.

It is recognized generally that teaching by machine has at least two distinct advantages; (1) enables articulate, talened teachers to reach a greater audience, and (2) enables a subject to be clarified and dramatized to a greater extent than an unaided teacher is capable of doing. It is the great potential afforded by this second point that the present invention is adapted to be directed.

A basic concept in teaching is that a person will have a greater efficiency of learning if he can actually experience a situation as compared with merely reading about it or listening to a lecture. For example, more can be learned about flying a supersonic jet airplane by actually flying one, or a student would understand the structure of an atom better through visual aids than mere word descriptions. Therefore, if a student can experience a situation or an idea in about the same way that he experiences everyday life, it has been shown that he understands better and quicker, and if a student understands better and quicker, he is drawn to the subject matter with greater pleasure and enthusiasm. What the student learns in this manner he retains for a longer period of time.

Since it is either impossible or dangerous to give students life-like experiences, attempts have been made to bring them as close as possible to this ideal by utilizing, for example, photographs, records and motion picture films. However, even the motion picture films, the most realistic of these media, fall far short of conveying to the student the illusion of reality.

The training films which have been used at an early date provided visual movement that was confined to a small rectangle that fills only one-twelfth of the students' normal visual field. Its image is flat and two dimensional, whereas the normal student sees in three dimensions (including depth). Also, such prior training films presented no scents, tactile sensations or directional sound, which are an important part of one's perception of reality.

sensorama

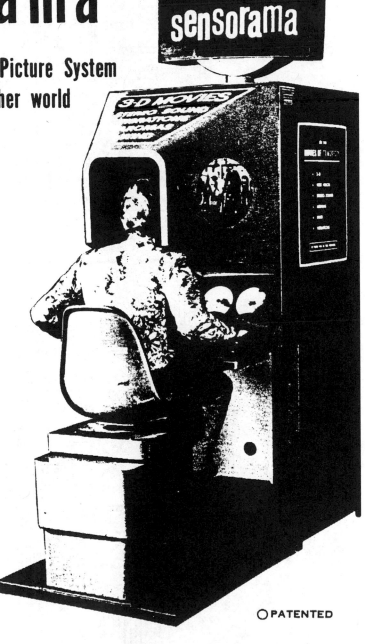

The Revolutionary Motion Picture System that takes you into another world with

- 3–D

- WIDE VISION

- MOTION

- COLOR

- STEREO-SOUND

- AROMAS

- WIND

- VIBRATIONS

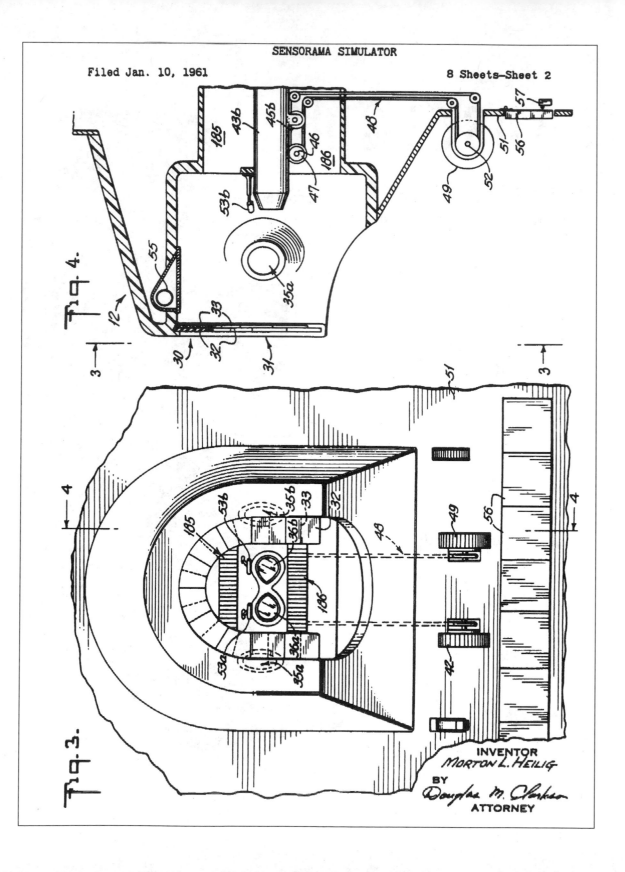

Fig. 4.

Fig. 3.

INVENTOR
MORTON L. HEILIG

BY
Douglas M. Clarkson
ATTORNEY

Fig. 1.

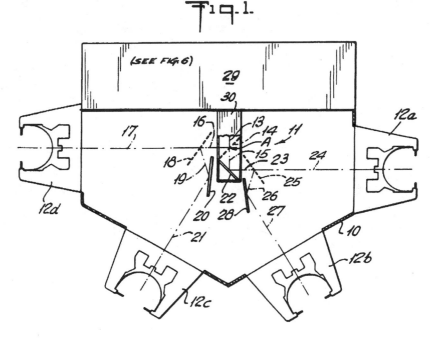

Fig. 2.

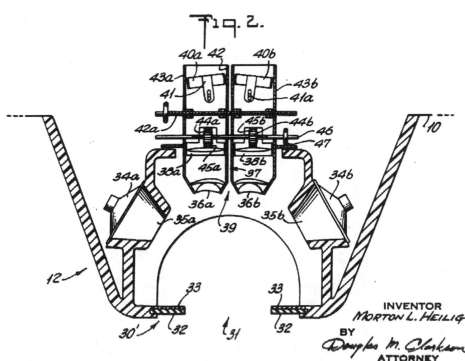

INVENTOR
MORTON L. HEILIG
BY
Douglas M. Clarkson
ATTORNEY

PART 5

Serious Fun

Adrenaline is the quickest revenue-generating response we can evoke. Theme parks and amusement parks have been refining myriad ways to do this for 150 years, providing temporary escape from the day-to-day world. Our most effective escape occurs when we induce emotional involvement by somehow incorporating a story along with the thrills. We've mastered the art of emotionally immersing people in books and movies, but the theme park industry has the difficult task of defining the ultimate in extreme immersive experiences. That problem is also an expensive one because attraction designers have to transport guests bodily into the illusions, then ensure that physical considerations don't dampen the effects. Compressing a plot with fascinating characters into a few minutes of ride, or ride film, requires unusual ingenuity and draws heavily on original properties from other media. There's also sophisticated competition from special-venue films, location-based entertainment centers, and diverse interactive options in the home.

Parks are applying their ingenuity in two directions: inwardly, by increasing the technical sophistication of each attraction; and outwardly, by designing a broader range of concepts and attractions in order to appeal to every possible demographic. Both efforts enhance a rich experience and require plenty of digital expertise, seen and unseen.

The outdoor environment of a major theme park is as carefully designed as the attractions. Nothing is left to chance; we're paying for a subtly cosseted, carefree day. The unseen digital expertise in parks will include guest IDs and a network of intelligent show control systems throughout the environment. That network is part of a watchful sensory and central nervous system that continuously adjusts to safeguard and accentuate the experience of every meandering clump of guests—and follows them home. Their small children will be tracked, their rides and purchases will be noted, and overlooked opportunities to linger and spend more money will be made a bit more obvious. The entire physical environment will get more interesting as they walk by, with microevents tailored to their demographic profile; they're not paying for normalcy. The result is mass customization of the entertainment experience, more revenue, and better-satisfied customers—and invaluable data mining later on.

There are ways an attraction can customize the guests' experience without knowing so much about who and where they are. The Indiana Jones Adventure at Disneyland has enough variable features to maintain the element of surprise for several repeat visits. Attraction designers will eventually be able to play with the guests' real and virtual surroundings simultaneously, using augmented-reality techniques that are costly and relatively fragile now. Beyond that, however, lies largely uncharted territory: how to make an attraction genuinely participatory or meaningfully interactive for large groups of people. Effective solutions to this puzzle could be gold mines.

Another way parks will use interactive technology is to extend elements of the park experience offsite in tiered multiplayer simulator attractions. The first tier is an elaborately themed $40-million site in major theme parks. It uses powerful image generators and a big virtual world database server.

The second tier is in regional parks, malls, and LBE sites, consisting of themed installations (points of presence), with less expensive simulators networked locally and to the first tier's servers.

The customer at home is the third tier, logging into the same virtual environment and using realtime voice links. The aggregate is part of a market imperative to make the park experience—and the experience of its licensed properties—available to as many customers as possible, in as many profitable forms as possible, wherever the customer may be. A Star Trek multiplayer product of this sort is desirable for Paramount as soon as image generators become cost-effective at satisfactory image quality. Then, as interfaces become smarter, other genres and demographics open up. The effort to design and manage experiences in these worlds—and the worlds themselves—is an additional huge task beyond the physical installations, but it amortizes across all those customers at home and can be incrementally updated. In addition, Internet attractions are a powerful cross-marketing tool for a park and for the brand extensions of its film licenses.

Online park offerings don't have to be linked to an attraction. Distributed on hybrid CD-ROM and DVD, the familiar costumed strolling characters will exist in 3D on a park's Web site with enough synthetic personality to greet and play with visitors, incidentally passing along news about the park. This promotional and brand identity function will evolve into significant separate revenue streams, both episodic and social/exploratory.

Those and other digital attractions will grow partly from the movie studios' competitive need for their parks to provide a strong supportive role in the film distribution system and to adapt rapidly to consumer tastes. Location-based entertainment centers and special-venue film sites have an advantage here— their content can be updated more readily.

Parks are early adopters of high technology—they invest in new configurations to maintain their unique appeal. The first chapter in "Serious Fun" is an example of this intent. The Walt Disney Company designed the best civilian VR experience in the world as applied research; the authors report on their experience. Christopher Stapleton of Universal Creative draws upon his university research and work in the New York theater to explain how parks can revitalize the market and the industry by actively engaging the audience in the process of creation. Allen Yamashita and Mario Kamberg, extraordinary film designer/directors, discuss the theory and practice, present and future, of ride films and special-venue films. Sherry McKenna of Oddworld Inhabitants and Richard Edlund of Boss Film have been leaders in producing high-end special filmic effects for their entire careers. They write about the "how" from the human and technical perspectives, respectively. Phil Hettema is Senior Vice President for Universal Creative and directs the development of all their future attractions. He is responsible for applying the new technology used to create the most effective entertainment illusions on Earth and for deciding when that technology is ready.

Chapter 23

Disney's *Aladdin:*
First Steps Toward Storytelling in Virtual Reality

Randy Pausch
University of Virginia

Jon Snoddy, Robert Taylor, Scott Watson, and Eric Haseltine
Walt Disney Imagineering Research and Development

Abstract

Disney Imagineering has developed a high-fidelity virtual reality (VR) attraction where guests fly a magic carpet through a virtual world based on the animated film *Aladdin.* Unlike most existing work on VR, which has focused on hardware and systems software, we assumed high fidelity and focused on using VR as a new medium to tell stories. We fielded our system at EPCOT Center for a period of fourteen months and conducted controlled experiments, observing the reactions of over 45,000 guests.

Our major finding is that in a high fidelity VR experience, men and women of all ages suspend disbelief and accept the illusion that they are in a different place. We have found that in VR, as in all media, content matters. Novices are unimpressed with the technology for its own sake; they care about what there is to do in the virtual world. We can improve the experience by telling a pre-immersion "background story" and by giving the guest a concrete goal to perform in the virtual environment. Our eventual goal is to develop the lexicon for this new storytelling medium: the set of communication techniques shared between directors and the audience. We conclude with a discussion of our second version of the *Aladdin* project, which contains a large number of synthetic characters and a narrative story line.

Introduction

Most existing work on virtual reality (VR) has focused on hardware and system software [1, 3, 5, 6, 7, 10, 12, 23, 24]. The price of a high quality system has placed it out of reach for most people interested in content. Building high quality, low cost VR systems is important, but we believe the exciting challenge in VR is learning what to do with the medium. We believe that the content questions are the really hard ones.

The goal of this project has been to allow the content producers, or authors, to assume the existence of satisfactory technology and to focus directly on authoring in the new medium of VR. We produced high-quality content based on flying a magic carpet in the animated film *Aladdin* [2]. The *Aladdin* HMD attraction figure (on the top of the last page of the color insert) shows a screen shot from the system.

We field-tested the system on over 45,000 guests at EPCOT Center. In this chapter, we report our detailed observations, the guests' exit surveys, and data we recorded during guest experiences. This is not a systems implementation chapter; we describe the hardware and software only as context for describing the guest experience. In addition to guest experiences, we also describe industrial design solutions to the problems of high volume usage. In early 1996, we deployed a second version with a narrative story line and a large number of reactive characters. We conclude with lessons learned from creating virtual environments and characters for our second version, especially controlling the narrative in an interactive medium.

Our underlying premise is that VR is a new medium, as film, radio, and television once were. As motion pictures matured, directors and audiences developed a lexicon including close ups, cross cuts, flash backs, etc. Over time a common language, or lexicon, will evolve for VR; this project is our first step towards that goal.

System Description

In each of our field trials, four guests donned head-mounted displays and piloted a flying carpet. Because they were running on separate systems, the pilots could neither see nor interact with each other.

We designed the system for robustness, high volume usage, and high accessibility. Unlike research setups, theme park equipment is used extensively, continuously, and abusively. Failures with a one-in-a-million chance of happening can occur once a week in a typical theme park attraction.

The Head-Mounted Display

The system used an internally developed head-mounted display (HMD). The two main design constraints were to provide high image quality and to make it easy to put the HMD on quickly, to support the high throughput of guests in a theme park attraction. In early trials we learned that having adjustments such as a focus knob on the HMD confused guests, since they had no baseline to distinguish between high and low image quality. Therefore, we designed a system that would accommodate a large variation in where a guest's eyes sit with respect to the optics.

Image quality considerations drove us to use CRTs instead of LCDs, a tradeoff that increased the HMD's weight and extended its center of mass. We partially compensated for this by providing spring-suspension of the HMD from the ceiling. Major design challenges in the HMD included avoiding visible pixel boundaries, obtaining high contrast, minimizing inter-ocular rivalry, and addressing the weight balance and packaging issues. For head-tracking, we used a magnetic position/orientation tracker.

Unlike many other VR systems, our HMD display was bi-ocular, not stereo. We rendered a single, horizontally wide graphics window and fed partially overlapping view windows to each of the CRTs in the HMD. For applications such as ours, stereoscopy is surprisingly unimportant as a depth cue [8]. We addressed hygiene issues by having the HMD snap onto a per-guest inner "cap" that can be cleaned separately. The inner liner also allowed us to adjust tightness to each guest's head before monopolizing the more expensive HMD and image generator. The HMD fit comfortably over eyeglasses; the only notable issue was guests with hair tied in buns.

Sound

The HMD contained two speakers that rested close to, but not in physical contact with, the guest's ears. We used a combination of stereo ambient sound, binaural recorded sound, and eight channels of localized sound. We recorded the binaural sound track via a high quality binaural head (essentially, microphones placed in a mannequin head). The binaural soundtrack included background voices, animals, and other "clutter" sounds. We recorded multiple binaural tracks, and then mixed those layers to form a composite recording.

When the binaural recording was played during the VR experience, even though those sounds "moved with the head," they established a believable background sound field. It is in this context that the eight special channels were convolved to localize in real-time based on head tracking [26]. The localized channels provided main characters and large sound effects. The stereo sound (primarily music) established emotional context, the binaural sound established the believable three-dimensional space, and the localized sounds gave strong, specific cues for orientation. The three levels increasingly traded recording quality for localization, and the binaural and localized sounds worked well together because they employed the same head-related transfer functions [4].

Seating, Controls, and Motion Base

Guests were seated straddling a motorcycle-style seat. A benefit of this design is that the guests were firmly grounded, with weight on their buttocks, knees, and feet. Additionally, this design accommodated a wide range of heights. Guests gripped a steering mechanism representing the front of a magic carpet. Turning left or right controlled yaw of the carpet, and tilting controlled the pitch of the carpet. Imagine a car's steering wheel; pulling the top of the wheel toward the driver pitched the carpet up, pushing it pitched the carpet down. Pushing the entire mechanism forward controlled velocity.

We mounted the seat on a movable base that pitched up and down in response to the steering control. Originally, the motion base also tilted side-to-side, but this caused discomfort during early testing so we removed the side-to-side tilt. Surprisingly, the presence or absence of a motion base had no substantial effect on guest satisfaction, or anything else we measured with exit surveys. An early version of the system simulated wind with a rate-controlled fan blowing air over the guests. Much to our disappointment, most guests wearing the HMD did not notice it.

Model Management and Show Programming

A custom software system, called the player, provided scene management and character animation playback. The player provided a Scheme interface on top of a C/C++ layer, all on top of SGI Performer [19]. The player used Performer's support for multiple levels of detail. Unlike a flight simulator, most of our scene was close, so we used only two levels of detail per object. Artists created both models for each object because degrading a model "by hand" still produces better results than automatic means [20]. We sometimes used large texture "flats" for distant objects, and switched to three dimensional models as the guest approached.

Programming of various show elements, such as an object's reaction when hit by the carpet, was performed in the topmost layer of the player, a locally developed "Story Animation Language." This SAL layer implemented cooperative lightweight threads on top of Chez Scheme [9], an incrementally compiled Scheme.

In our second version, the database is much larger, and is partitioned into distinct scenes. The player software pre-fetches geometry and texture maps as guests fly from one scene to another [11]. Between scenes, we include explicit "transition areas," such as hallways and caverns. Transition areas have a smaller number of polygons, which buys us time to pre-fetch textures. Transitions bend and twist, thus ensuring that at no point can the guest quickly look back to the previous scene.

Guest Selection

We deployed the system at EPCOT Center in Orlando, Florida, from July 1, 1994 until September 8, 1995. Every twenty minutes a group of up to 120 guests was given a brief technical lecture about VR followed by a demonstration where four guests were selected to "fly a magic carpet."

The attraction was intentionally hidden in a remote area of the park. Most guests entered not because they had a strong interest in VR, but because our attraction was "the next thing" to do. Guests could not volunteer to fly; they were selected by the ride operators. The operators maintained a strict policy of avoiding guests who showed an active interest in VR. Therefore, rather than pertaining to a small subset of VR enthusiasts, we believe that our results are essentially a fair cross section of the theme park population. Some guests did decline the invitation to fly. Interviews revealed this was primarily due to stage fright, not an aversion to trying VR.

The selected pilots did not hear the technical lecture about VR. We gave them a background story that they would be stepping into the feature film *Aladdin*. We instructed them that the main goal was to have fun, but that they were also searching for a character from the film. The marketplace scene was chosen because it 1) contains familiar objects such as doors which establish scale, 2) is a brightly lit daytime scene, and 3) contains wide variety, encouraging exploration. There was typically time for a one-to-three minute practice flight followed by a few minutes of rest before the audience entered and the four minute flight began.

Novices' Experiences

We exposed a large, non-self selected population of guests to a high-fidelity virtual experience in a controlled environment. At least one other system has exposed large numbers of novices to VR [25]. However, Virtuality's users were self-selected. Their users wanted to try VR, and paid for the experience. Our sample is much more diverse.

Our findings are drawn from a variety of sources, including written post-flight guest surveys, logged flight data, extensive conversations with the day-to-day attraction operators, observations of guests' flights, and interviews of guests before, during, and after their flights.

Technologists should be aware that most guests were not impressed by the technology itself; guests assumed VR was possible and had an expectation of extremely high quality. Many had seen the "holodeck" on Star Trek, and expected that level of quality. Once in a virtual environment, guests focused on what there was to do in the virtual world—content matters!

General Observations

We were able to sustain the illusion that the guests were in another place. Men and women of all ages suspended disbelief and a large number reported the sensation that they were "in" the scene. This is hard to conclude from exit surveys, but guests also provided unsolicited cues, such as panicking or ducking their heads as they approached obstacles.

Guests cared about the experience, not the technology. Most guests had no concept of how VR works, nor did they care. They focused on the sensation, which was exhilarating for most guests. Many guests shouted "Wow!" or "Whee!" in their first thirty seconds.

The experience was overwhelming. Between sensory overload and the task of trying to control the carpet's flight, many guests were so cognitively taxed that they had trouble answering questions early in their flights.

Guests needed a goal. If not given a specific goal, guests would ask "What should I be doing?"

Guests needed a background story. We found that giving as much context as possible about the scene helped reduce the severity of the transition from the real to the virtual environment. *Background story* is the set of expectations, goals, major characters, and set of rules that apply to the virtual world. Ironically, in lower fidelity, less believable VR systems, this need for background story may not be as evident. We believe it is the abrupt transition into a *believable* virtual world that is problematic. Performing a good transition from the real to the virtual world is an open challenge.

Guests liked exploring and seeing new spaces. Most guests did not spend much time studying detail in a given place; they tended to move on quickly to new vistas.

Guests did not turn their heads very much. This could be because they were piloting a vehicle or because they were not accustomed to being able to turn their heads when looking at displayed images. For many, we believe the latter. Guests often watched characters "walk out of frame," as would happen with television or movies. Our strongest indication came from many pilots where we waited 90 seconds into their flight, then explicitly told them to turn their heads. At that point, they clearly had the "aha" of the head-tracking experience. While we suspect that different content would be more conducive to head turning, head tracking is far enough from most guests' experiences with film and television that we suspect this will be a problem for many systems.

Controlling the carpet was a problem for many guests. This prompted the addition of test flights before the show began. Many guests flew out into the desert or up above the city to find a space where there were fewer obstacles, making flight easier. Although we could have had the magic carpet fly itself, our surveys indicated that the control and freedom are important parts of the experience. Six-axis control is a very difficult problem and an important design challenge is finding appropriate control constraints.

VR must be personally experienced. In addition to the 45,000 guests who piloted carpets, we had over one million audience members who observed the pilots' progress on display monitors. The audience members enjoyed the show and understood that *something* fascinating was going on with the pilots, but it was clear that VR is foreign enough that most people can not fully comprehend it without direct personal experience. Audience members often asked if the pilots could see or interact with each other.

Presence and Immersion

Although it is difficult to formally measure, we believe that most guests suspended disbelief and had the experience of being in a new place. Our choice of an animated world underscored that believability is different from photo-realism. In fact, we reject the term "simulation," as we provide an experience not possible in reality. Our virtual environment was not realistic, but it was consistent with the large number of animated worlds that guests had seen before. Guests flew but had no fear of heights; guests reacted to the characters but were not afraid of a guard who brandished a sword. In many ways, this environment was compelling without being disturbing.

A common sight in a 3D theater is to see large numbers of guests reaching out to grab the projected image. We speculate that they are compelled to conduct this test because their perceptual and cognitive systems are in conflict;

their eyes tell them the object is within arm's length, but their brain tells them it is just a projection. In our system, we saw no evidence of the need to test. Guests did not intentionally run into objects to see if the objects really existed. In fact, guests did the opposite, often involuntarily ducking when they felt they could not avoid a collision.

In general, we believe that the need for high fidelity can be reduced by engaging the user in a complex, real-time task. For example, the desktop Doom game [14] and the SIMNET tank simulator [18] both get users to the point where the interface becomes transparent and the user focuses on task performance, which requires a sense of presence. Our system did so with the mildest of tasks, that of searching for a character. At first, we suspected that the difficult task of piloting the carpet might lower our fidelity requirements. Therefore, we ran experiments where the carpet flew itself. During those tests, guests achieved the same suspension of disbelief, with the only task being to look around. Our metric for suspension of disbelief was their reactions to the environment, such as ducking when flying near objects.

What produced the effect of immersion is difficult to know. Even for guests who did not turn their heads much, the HMD physically blocked out the real world. Sound was also very important, as many guests remarked that the sound of wind when they flew high, or the crashing noises when they ran into walls strongly reinforced their sense of being there. In post flight interviews, guests told us that their illusion of presence was destroyed when characters did not react.

Reaction to Virtual Characters

It is more difficult to build a believable character than a believable scene. Although our major focus was on building the environments, we were pleased that a few of our guests did respond to characters. The show began with instructions from a parrot who told the pilots to nod their heads. Some guests actually heeded his command. Another character covered his head and shouted "Don't you have a horn on that thing?!" when guests flew near him. Many guests shouted back at this character. One young girl finished the attraction in tears because she had spent several minutes attempting to apologize to him, but instead continually triggered hostile responses whenever she approached him. (All the characters had a small set of dialogue sequences that could be triggered.)

We suspect that the limited believability of our first system's characters is due to low fidelity. All characters in the first show were animated with motion capture, where sensors recorded an actor's body motions in real time and those values were used to drive the animation. Our second version uses higher quality key frame animation. While testing of the second version is not yet complete, early indications are that we will cross a fidelity threshold in character animation much as this project crossed one in environment fidelity.

Men vs. Women

One of our original objectives was to discover whether VR appealed only to the narrow (primarily young male) video game market, or was more like feature films, appealing to males and females of all ages. While *content* will still matter, the technology itself did not turn away any guests. On post flight surveys, the reaction of both genders and all age groups was almost identical on all questions. One major difference was that many women are afraid that they would not be able to operate the equipment properly. This surfaced both as a pre-flight concern and as a post-flight comparison. They often asked how they performed relative to the other pilots. Also, during in-flight interviewing men were more likely to talk about the technology, whereas women were more likely to talk about the experience and emotional impact. Neither men nor women complained about having to wear the HMD.

VR for the Disabled

Everyone involved with the project noted the impact on both the pilots and the audience when motion-impaired guests flew. Accessibility is a fundamental design constraint at Disney parks, and we have a substantial wheelchair population. One of our four stations could be converted for wheelchair access in about ten seconds, and we had several wheelchair fliers per day. The sense of mobility and the joy it brought them was overwhelming.

Motion Sickness

We did not find motion sickness to be as significant an issue as we had feared. During selection, we asked guests if they were prone to motion sickness, and warned that they might feel motion sick during the experience. We also told them they could stop at any time and remove the HMD. Post flight surveys indicated that, as with many theme park attractions, some guests reported discomfort or dizziness, but they mostly described it as a mild sensation. We do not know if guests who felt discomfort or dizziness self-limited their head motion; our logged data showed no such correlation. Reports of discomfort went up when the room was warmer, which is consistent with discomfort reports from platform-based simulator rides. We were careful to limit the duration of the experience. As with any "thrill" experience, discomfort increases with ride length.

Telling Stories in VR

Given that VR can present a compelling illusion, researchers can and should pursue its uses for education, training, medical applications, games, and many other purposes. As a storytelling company, we are focusing on using VR as a story-telling medium.

Sound

In films, the sound track, particularly the musical score, tends to carry the emotional tone for most scenes. Because we no longer control timing we must choose sound tracks that work with wide variation in duration, and we must be able to make the transition smoothly from one ambient sound to the next based on guest actions.

Many VR system architects are concerned with the underlying technology for localizing sound. In our experience, the careful selection/creation of ambient sounds and music, i.e.; the content, is much more important than the specific details, or even the use of, sound localization.

Research Challenges

Based on our experiences, we present the following as open challenges to the research community:

1) Finding mechanisms that allow guests to self-calibrate the intensity of the experience. Currently, we must keep the experience tame enough to be enjoyable for our more sensitive guests.

2) Developing constraints to solve the six-degree-of-freedom problems in controlling flight; for example, navigation and motion through virtual spaces.

3) Development of software to better support animators, especially in the sketching phase. Animators use onion skin paper to superimpose views from multiple frames; this ability is lacking in most software tools.

4) The automatic generation of mouth animation from sound source. This is currently labor intensive and not particularly creative work.

Conclusions

This project gave over 45,000 people a first exposure to virtual reality (VR). While we have made what we consider to be substantial advances in HMD and rendering technology, our major advances have been in learning how to create and present compelling virtual environments. We stress that this is an exercise that requires both artistic and engineering talent and creativity.

Our guests completed written surveys, and with subsets we logged head and carpet motions. Based on that data and interviews before, during and after guest flights, we conclude that:

Guests suspend disbelief. The illusion is compelling enough that most guests accept being in a synthetically generated environment and focus on the environment, not the technology.

VR appeals to everyone. Both genders and all ages had similar responses to our attraction. This leads us to conclude that VR is like feature films in that different content may segment the market, but the basic technology does not. We also note that wheelchair guests find mobility within VR extremely exciting.

VR must be personally experienced. VR is foreign enough that most people cannot comprehend it without direct personal experience.

Fidelity matters. To get most guests to suspend disbelief requires extremely high fidelity. We provide 60 frames per second (at the expense of stereo) for polygonal models with hand-painted texture maps, and we do not use hardware lighting. Texture quality matters much more than polygon count.

Content matters. People love the experience of VR, but even at high fidelity VR by itself is not enough. The public, unlike the developers, is not impressed with the technology. In fact, the public *assumes* that high fidelity VR exists and immediately focuses on what there is to do in the synthetic environment.

The illusion of presence is fragile. Although guests suspend disbelief, inconsistencies can *instantly* shatter the illusion. For example, objects interpenetrating or characters not responding to the guest's presence completely shatter the sense of presence.

Guests need a background story. VR is an overwhelming experience of being thrust into a new environment. A good way to soften this transition is to provide a background story that familiarizes the guest with the new environment before the immersion. This is a standard technique in theme park attractions, typically provided in a pre-show.

Guests need a goal. Guests need to know why they are in the virtual world and what they are supposed to do.

Guests do not turn their heads much. We were surprised at how little people turned their heads in this flight-based experience. We attribute this to the mass of the HMD, the need to look where one is flying, and guests' inexperience with a head-tracked medium.

Input controls are hard. We developed a novel input mechanism for controlling flight. Since no one flies magic carpets in the real world we could not transfer everyday skills. After many design iterations we believe that six axis control is a phenomenally difficult problem and conclude that designers must limit degrees of freedom.

Tell a straightforward story. As we have learned with other intensive media, such as effects laden stereoscopic films and motion-base simulators, when the guest is perceptually overwhelmed it helps to keep the story short and clear. *Aladdin* is a beginning, not an end. Our original goal was to move past the technology. Our first system produces a compelling illusion and our next efforts are to examine whether we can tell stories in this new medium. Our second version of the project, scheduled for release in early 1996, contains a large number of characters and a narrative story line.

References

[1] Jon Airey, John Rohlf, Frederick Brooks, Towards Image Realism with Interactive Update Rates in Complex Virtual Building Environments, ACM SIGGRAPH Special Issue on 1990 Symposium on Interactive 3D Graphics 24:2, 1990, pages 41–50.

[2] Walt Disney Home Video. Distributed by Buena Vista Home Video, Dept. CS, Burbank, CA, 91521. ISBN 1-55890-663-0. Originally released in 1992 as a motion picture.

[3] Chuck Blanchard, Scott Burgess, Young Harvill, Jaron Lanier, Ann Lasko, Reality Built for Two: A Virtual Reality Tool, ACM SIGGRAPH 1990 Symposium on Interactive 3D Graphics, March 1990.

[4] J. P. Blauert, Spatial Hearing, MIT Press, Cambridge, MA, 1983.

[5] Frederick Brooks, Walkthrough—A Dynamic Graphics System for Simulating Virtual Buildings, Proceedings of the 1986 Workshop on 3D Graphics, Chapel Hill, NC, October 23-24, 1986, ACM, pages 9–21.

[6] Steve Bryson, Creon Levit, The Virtual Wind Tunnel, IEEE Computer Graphics and Applications, July 1992, pages 25–34.

[7] Christopher Codella et al., Interactive Simulation in a Multi-Person Virtual World, Proceedings of the ACM SIGCHI Human Factors in Computer Systems Conference, May 1992, pages 329–334.

[8] James Cutting and Peter Vishton, Perceiving Layout and Knowing Distances: The Integration, Relative Potency, and Contextual Use of Different Information About Depth, Handbook of Perception and Cognition: Perception of Space and Motion, Vol. 5, Academic Press (to appear).

[9] R. Kent Dybvig. The Scheme Programming Language. Prentice-Hall, 1987.

[10] S. S. Fisher, A M. McGreevy, J. Humphries, W. Robinett, Virtual Environment Display System, Proceedings of the 1986 Workshop on Interactive 3D Graphics, pages 77–87, October 23–24, 1986.

[11] Thomas Funkhouser, Carlo Sequin, Seth Teller, Management of Large Amounts of Data in Interactive Building Walkthroughs, Proceedings of the 1992 ACM Symposium on Interactive Three-Dimensional Graphics, April, 1992, pages 11–20.

[12] Thomas Furness, The Super Cockpit and Human Factors Challenges, Human Interface Technology (HIT) Laboratory of the Washington Technology Center, Tech Report HITL-M-886-1, October, 1986.

[13] Tinsley A. Galyean, Guided Navigation of Virtual Environments, 1995 ACM Symposium on Interactive 3D Graphics, April 1995, pages 103–104, Monterey, CA.

[14] Id Software, Inc.; information available via http://www.idsoftware.com/

[15] John Lasseter, Principles of Traditional Animation Applied to 3D Computer Animation, Computer Graphics (SIGGRAPH '87 Proceedings) Volume 21, number 4, pages 35–44, July 1987.

[16] Randy Pausch, et al, A Brief Architectural Overview of Alice, a Rapid Prototyping System for Virtual Reality, IEEE Computer Graphics and Applications, May 1995.

[17] Ken Perlin, Real Time Responsive Animation with Personality, IEEE Transactions on Visualization and Computer Graphics, Vol. 1, No. 1.

[18] A. Pope, BBN Report No 7102. The SIMNET Network and Protocols. BBN Systems and Technologies, Cambridge, Massachusetts, 1989.

[19] John Rohlf and James Helman, IRIS Performer: A High Performance Multiprocessing Toolkit for Real-Time 3D Graphics, SIGGRAPH '94 Conference Proceedings, Computer Graphics, July, 1994.

[20] William J. Schroeder, Jonathan A. Zarge, William E. Lorensen, Decimation of Triangle Meshes, Computer Graphics (SIGGRAPH '92 Proceedings) Volume 26, pages 65–70, July 1992.

[21] Sense8 Corporation, 100 Shoreline Highway, Suite 282, Mill Valley, CA 94941, 415/331–6318, http://www.sense8.com/ or info@sense8.com.

[22] Chris Shaw, Mark Green, Jiandong Liang, Yunqi Sun, Decoupled Simulation in Virtual Reality with the MR Toolkit, ACM Transactions on Information Systems, 11:3, pages 287–317, July 1993.

[23] Ivan Sutherland, The Ultimate Display, Proceedings of IFIP (International Federation of Information Processing) '65, Vol. 2, pages 506–508.

[24] Ivan Sutherland, A Head-mounted Three-dimensional Display, Proceedings of the Fall Joint Computer Conference, AFIPS, Vol. 33, pages 757–764.

[25] Virtuality, http://www.virtuality.com; UK office: Virtuality House, 3 Oswin Road, Brailsford Industrial Park, Leicester LE3 1HR, United Kingdom, Tel: +44(0) 116 233 7000, enquiries@virtuality.com; USA office: 7801-7805 Mesquite End Drive, Suite 105, Irving, Texas 75063, USA 001-214-556-1800, 1-800-ILLUSION, enquiries@tx.viruality.com.

[26] E. Wenzel, F. Wightman, S. Fisher, A Virtual Display System for Conveying Three-dimensional Acoustic Information, Proceedings of the Human Factors Society, 32nd Annual Meeting, 1988, pages 86–90.

Acknowledgments

This work is the effort of many talented people over several years; we mention here only a subset but express our gratitude to all involved. Special thanks, in alphabetical order, to Daniele Colajacomo, for managing the character modeling in the EPCOT show; Dave Fink, for helping start the project; Philip Freer and Gary Daines, for their art direction and world design; Andy Ogden, for his industrial design on the steering and HMD; George Scribner, for his work on story and character in the EPCOT show; and Dave Spencer, for his management of the EPCOT show installation.

We thank all the other artists and engineers who worked on this project, and we would especially like to express our deepest gratitude to the families and significant others who supported these individuals in their efforts. We would also like to thank Evans and Sutherland, Silicon Graphics, NASA Ames Research Center, the staff who ran the attraction at EPCOT Center, and Matt Conway.

Biographies

Randy Pausch is an Associate Professor of Computer Science, Human-Computer Interaction, and Design at Carnegie Mellon University. He received a B.S. degree in Computer Science from Brown University in 1982 and a Ph.D.

degree in Computer Science from Carnegie Mellon in 1988. He is a National Science Foundation Presidential Young Investigator and a Lilly Foundation Teaching Fellow, and he has authored or co-authored over 50 technical publications. Randy Pausch can be reached at randy.pausch@cs.cmu.edu.

Jon Snoddy, a 20-year industry veteran, joined GameWorks in March 1996 as Vice President, Design, from the Walt Disney Company, bringing with him an invaluable background in theme park ride and attraction development. He honed his craft developing attractions for Walt Disney Imagineering that combined cutting-edge technology with a high level of artistry. In 1993, Snoddy founded the Walt Disney Virtual Reality Studio which is currently producing the *Aladdin* Virtual Reality ride. He also led the conceptual development and design of the ride system for the wildly popular Indiana Jones attraction. While at Disney, Snoddy developed a number of interactive attraction games and worked on night club concepts for Pleasure Island. Prior to joining Disney, Snoddy was with Lucasfilm's THX division where he was instrumental in transitioning the THX sound system from an industry studio mix product to a worldwide consumer product. He began his career as a technical director working for National Public Radio in Washington, DC with the program "All Things Considered." Snoddy has degrees in journalism and electronics from the University of South Carolina.

Robert Taylor is currently Supervising Producer/Director for Walt Disney TV Animation. He began working with The Walt Disney Corporation in 1988, as a producer, director, or supervising producer on numerous animation projects, including theatrical releases and multiple syndicated TV series packages. Projects include Goof Troop, Bonkers, Duck Tails, and Rescue Rangers. Prior to Disney, Mr. Taylor worked as producer, director, designer, writer, storyboard director, or animator on dozens of internationally-known animation projects, features, and commercials for Hanna Barbera Productions, TMS Animation, Bagdasarian Productions, Melendez Productions, Ralph Bakshi Productions, Depatie-Freleng, Marvel Productions, and Chuck Jones Productions. Projects included: "Grinch that Stole Christmas;" five of Ralph Bakshi's features; Pink Panther short subjects; "Space Ghost;" "Harlem Shuffle" for the Rolling Stones; Garfield; Peanuts; Little Nemo; Spiderman; Gobots; a Billy Joel music video; "Smurfs;" and "Flintstone Kids," to name a few.

Scott Watson is Walt Disney Imagineering's Chief Computer Scientist. He started programming at 9 years of age and wrote demos for IBM's first portable computer when he was in the fifth grade. At Walt Disney Imagineering R&D, he wrote the control software for the "Indiana Jones" Ride Vehicle. He has also created audio and image technology for theme park films and co-designed a computer keyboard for dolphins. For several years, DISNEY.COM was the machine on his desk. Scott holds several patents and has been involved in all of Disney's VR development. He is principal designer of the "Disney*Vision Player," part of an interactive VR story development system that supports realtime Disney-quality character animation and the SAL scripting language. His current interests include enhanced television; the convergence of telecommunications, computers, and consumer electronics; high-fidelity VR applications; and scripting languages.

Eric C. Haseltine is Vice President, Research and Development, for Walt Disney Imagineering, where he has been since 1992, when he began as a Principal Researcher and Technical Director on large-scale virtual reality projects. He is currently responsible for setting technology objectives and for oversight of key technology initiatives and projects, as well as day-to-day management of the Virtual Reality Studio. Prior to that, he was with Hughes Aircraft Co. since 1979, first as head of the Human Factors Group, then senior project engineer, followed by positions as program manager and deputy general manager of Hughes Aircraft Simulator Programs. Projects included design of dome simulator systems, managing $10M to $50M flight simulator programs, and graphics supercomputer systems, as well as managing all new business and R&D projects in the division. Before leaving Hughes, Mr. Haseltine became Director of Engineering for the 7,000-person Training and Support Group, and Chairman, Display Technology Management Council. Mr. Haseltine has a Ph.D. degree in Physiological Psychology from Indiana University and a B.A. degree in Economics and Psychology from the University of California, Berkeley. He has several patents in the fields of laser video projection, optics, and head-mounted displays.

Chapter 24

Adrenaline by Design

Phil Hettema
Universal Creative, Universal Studios Recreation Group

Introduction

I begin with a disclaimer: This chapter addresses only the theme park industry and location-based entertainment facilities—it may have little bearing on other areas of entertainment, digital or otherwise. Key aspects of a theme park experience simply don't exist for other genres but require enormous amounts of our time and attention. I'll review the state of the art of theme park attraction development and discuss what the theme park of the future might be like . . . and what it might not be like.

I spend a fair amount of time thinking about what makes theme parks tick. My responsibilities, besides producing attractions, shows, and rides, include looking for new technologies and new applications of existing technologies that might be used in our Universal theme park projects. What I know about the specifics of digital technology and computer graphics is negligible but, as a producer, I know something about what can and can't be done . . . and my criteria for reviewing potential technologies have little to do with technology. I look at any new technology from the point of view of the audience, then decide whether it might provide a more entertaining experience.

History

I wound up at Universal by pure accident, doing exactly what I always wanted to do. As a kid, I was a Disneyland groupie. I practically memorized the guide book—took it home and pored over it and tried to know every detail about every character, ride, and attraction. But I never really set out to do entertainment, even though I passionately loved it. After high school, I worked for Disney for eight years, at first part-time in the costume department. Simultaneously, a curiosity about puppetry led me to Virginia Austin Curtis, an old vaudevillian puppeteer who had literally played the Palace with her act; she sculpted Mortimer Snerd for Edgar Bergen. I had always had a fascination for animating inanimate objects and making things come to life, and it was through her that I met people like Frank Oz's parents and Tony Urbano. Tony is probably one of the best marionettists ever, in the great tradition of Bill Baird. I worked weekends building puppets for the commercials he did, like dancing drops of milk, talking heads of lettuce, and singing cows. Eventually Tony aligned himself with Sid and Marty Kroft; he convinced them to start a puppet shop and invited me to come and run it.

My point in recounting this piece of history is that my experience in thoroughly low-tech puppetry is indispensable to my work today. The obvious aspect of puppetry is the kinetic sensibility. You have to be able to associate where parts of your body are and how they're moving relative to other things, in ways that you normally don't do. From the kinetics, you develop a good understanding of the essence of movement in order to express character; from those skills, you learn much about the essence of expression. By "essence," I mean minimizing—knowing what to put in and leaving out all but the essentials. That rule always applies.

Designing an Attraction

There are literally dozens of criteria that determine the design of a new attraction. It's never just "Gee, what's the coolest thing we could do with this property?" There are usually some preexisting conditions; we're placing the new property into an environment that is in need of a certain kind of experience. For example, "Let's push the design in this direction because the park needs an action ride" or "We've got too many live shows; we need a thrill ride" or "We need something small and intimate over there." So, the first thing we look at is not the intellectual property or the attraction, but the context into which we will place it.

Then, we analyze the property. It usually has a successful history in society, or we wouldn't have chosen it. Any successful property is pre-sold; people will always come to it with expectations. My first step is to ask, What is the list of expectations I have to fulfill in some form—what is the baseline I must provide or else I haven't delivered that experience? If it's the "Wizard of Oz," I had better not tell that story without Dorothy or, more importantly, without the Tin Woodsman, the Lion, and the Scarecrow. I could design it so that the audience will *be* Dorothy in the story, but those other expected elements had better be there; otherwise, it's some other story. So, we build that list of all the elements until finally we can say, "These are the things we must do."

Then, given those criteria, we can decide what kind of attraction is needed. In the very early stages, we'll often take multiple passes at something, looking at two or three different ideas. We'll take a property and do some development work on it as a live show, as an animated show, and as a ride. We go to a great deal of trouble deciding what works best because the scale of these projects doesn't allow changing our minds once everyone involved has signed off on a design.

The decision process is guided in part by the fact that different properties have different affinities. Some are verbally oriented—those are the toughest because we're a visual and experiential business. Themed experiences are rarely cerebral, and, generally, since we have to tell our story quickly, we can't use dialogue to tell much of it. Some properties are visual; they work well as a dark ride wherein you're basically experiencing a storyboard—a series of scenes in sequence. Some properties are quite situation-based so that if you could put people in the situation of the property, that pretty much *is* the story. In our hypothetical example, maybe we decide on an inverted rollercoaster designed around the "Wizard of Oz" property—there's little room for a story, and we must have those three characters. How can we put that all together? If that "cut-and-paste" method sounds oversimplified, it is. Just combining those elements will not create a great experience. On the contrary, it could be dreadful. This is where creativity, taste, and judgment come in.

In putting it together, the final stage of the concept design is to ask, What is the big idea—what is the one thing we can do that will take the guests to a place they don't expect to go or that will exceed their expectations? We could just retell the story; we need to do at least some piece of the story to make sure we fulfill expectations, but that's not enough. Can we also take them further into the story than they expected—make them interact with the story in a way they didn't anticipate? Can we extend the story beyond where it went the first time? Can we reveal something that makes sense within the context of the story but wasn't part of the original? Because ultimately, the audience comes with those expectations that I must meet, and, if I'm good at what I do, I'll exceed them. So, it's a question of how to tell that story.

The answer to our question is the art of this business: how to visually and then experientially lead someone through an experience so that he or she gets the essence of the story that you're trying to tell. It can be very difficult, whether in a two-minute thrill ride or a six-minute ride experience. Just as in animation or puppetry, the task involves distilling the message, giving visual and audio cues, and understanding how to manipulate focus. In a dimensional experience, you can't cut like an editor, changing from one close-up perspective to another, to tell a story sequentially. You literally have to lead the guest's eye through an experience, and you do that by carefully positioning everything—the guests, the displays, the vehicle they're riding in, and the things they perceive, whether it be visual media, software, dimensional stage sets, or the tableaus of a dark ride. Your tools include sound from all directions and the nuance of lighting; both can draw focus. A sequence of effects can draw focus; the audience might all be looking to the left, and the next moment I can make every one of them look to the right. That's one of the things a magician does. The best magicians can absolutely make you look anywhere they want, whether you think you are willing to or not.

Manipulation of focus is one of the growing areas of applications for digital sensor/actuator systems; they can be used to customize or adapt parts of the show more closely to the guests' moment-to-moment experience. We can build in more surprises to a given ride—maintaining the unexpected for many repeat visits. Timing is critical to much of what we do, so adaptive sensors and actuators can provide more precision in the delivery of cues to the audience—in some unusual cases, maybe even to each individual.

Theme Parks Today

The major technical development of the last decade has been the growth of the simulator attraction—combining film or video software with a synchronized motion platform. Simulators have been developed that range from single-person arcade experiences to multimillion-dollar "megarides" that can accommodate thousands of persons per hour. This trend has brought software ("content") producers running to our industry—and the libraries of software have grown geometrically.

The second major phenomenon has been the advent of the new Holy Grail of theme parks: interactivity. Never has a word been so inflated or misused as "interactivity" has been used by the theme park industry. Ninety percent of the theme park product with the word attached is hardly that; in fact, the word is used almost interchangeably—and incorrectly—with "simulation" or "participatory." Ride-film simulators typically have no interactive elements, while audience participation, a powerful element when properly used in an attraction, goes farther back than medieval puppet shows. Just because a ride moves you through an environment—real or virtual—or because it has a visceral impact, it's not interactive. True interactivity requires an interface, input sensors, and response capability.

The first "GameWorks" experiences are just now making their debut, with a whole new level of interactive experiences. There are also a few location-based centers, like Virtual Worlds or the Virtuality games, that have had interactive attractions for some time. But none of these have taken off on a wide basis so far, and the major theme parks have yet to produce a truly spectacular interactive show. Why is that? It comes down to two things: capacity and demographics.

In the theme park world, you live and die by your attraction capacity—the number of persons who can experience an attraction in a given period of time. And the simple fact is that no one has figured out a ride concept with an interactive interface that can provide an audience capacity of 2,000 to 3,000 persons per hour with a meaningful interactive experience. The location-based entertainment systems that exist now are relatively low-capacity, but, more importantly, have very narrow demographics. Most of the games are target-oriented shooting experiences that tend to appeal to young adult males, leaving out 80 percent of the theme park audience.

So, are there any truly interactive experiences out there today? Well, there aren't many significant ones in this country that I am aware of, other than those I've already mentioned. One notable example I've personally seen is a small park in Tokyo created by the Namco arcade game group, called "Wonder Egg." While most of its attractions fall short of U.S. expectations of show production, effects, and storyline, the creative application of technology to create interactive ride experiences is really clever. Interestingly, though, much of the interactivity is created with rather basic technology, not more sophisticated current components. As is often the case, technology is an important tool, but the *ideas* are the driver in creating a compelling experience. However, while virtual reality, simulation, and special-format films will be important elements of the theme park of the future—such applications will definitely continue to expand—the concept of a 100-percent high-technology theme park misses the point of why people go to theme parks and recreation centers.

People go to spend time with one another, to react and relate to one another in a relaxed, stimulating, and safe environment. They want to find that stimulation in a variety of ways, from the rides and shows to the landscaping and environments—the smells, the visceral responses. This is what recreation is about; this is what theme parks will continue to be about. In an increasingly media-saturated world, coupled with the fact that good interactive digital technology will be available in all our homes within the next decade through TV/cable/phone systems, the "specialness" of digital media-based experiences will diminish.

If you believe that you can get the required wide variety of theme park experiences in an exclusively high-tech entertainment center, I challenge you to visit the annual IAAPA (International Association of Amusement Parks and Attractions) convention and try out ten simulator/ride-film experiences in a row:

1. I bet you will be green after riding three simulator rides.

2. You'll find that all the experiences produce similar visceral responses, regardless of significantly different subject matter.

3. It won't compare to the sensory input you can get by simply walking through a real theme park for 20 minutes.

Digital Extrapolations of the Parks

To me, the compelling new challenge is multiuser interfaces that allow for social interaction in a very direct and human way, which is not the same thing as linking through a network to people I can't see (although that's another key component). From the theme park's perspective, there's not much difference between sitting at home, engrossed, in front of my screen, and sitting at home reading a book; it's still a solitary experience. But there's a world of difference between either of those and broadband recreational interaction. People seek that kind of interaction; the solution to pursue is, How can multiple people in a room share an experience with people elsewhere, either working jointly or as several individual entities?

I hear more talk about online worlds all the time. Almost by definition, it's a different experience than the live group interaction just discussed—but it does start to bridge the gap between solitary and group interaction. Here's another situation where the early implementations of the technology distract us from what's important. If you have a virtual environment in which you can see other people somehow—personas or avatars—the most important thing you can provide to make a rich environment is not typed chat or 3D, but the ability to visibly express oneself. That includes the ability to build a custom representation of who you wish to be, but such an ability is only a start. When technology allows it, I think movement and gesture will be equally if not more important than name and likeness.

You will probably want to use facial expressions, of course, but that's where the experience of history comes in. If you ever try to do puppetry, you'll find a couple of things: that much of the personality of the character is expressed by the body and that it's much easier to get the hang of communicating with that body than with the puppet's facial expressions. There's a subtlety to understanding how and when to make a face express what you want that most people don't readily grasp. That's part of the art of puppetry. We all instinctively understand gesture to a much larger degree. Even a Virtua Fighter arcade game is all about gesture, not about expression, and we not only understand it but also have made that style of game highly successful.

I think the first really successful multiuser (social) attraction will likely have one other feature: live voice communication. Another lesson from puppetry is that users will want to modify their voices. That will be an absolute requirement. If you put people in a room, pass around a puppet, and shield each novice operator behind a screen, when they put that puppet on and start to talk, not one will use their own voice, ever. Usually, they'll come up with a high squeaky voice the first time out. They immediately assume a different persona at the first opportunity, something that virtual entertainment environments can easily provide.

What I've just described isn't around the corner; it's going to take a lot of hard work, some false starts, faster hardware, and far more knowledge of entertainment and experience design than what I've seen demonstrated so far. And it won't make anything you can see in the parks today obsolete; the industry constantly does that already. We've got plenty of technique and more tools and systems than there is time available to master. The crux is to use exactly the right technique at just the right moment.

Summary

My point is not to be a curmudgeon hanging on to the past, but to try and focus on some areas where we really need to challenge ourselves to be more creative. We need to find new interfaces and concepts that can accommodate large numbers of people, while still giving each guest a feeling of real individual interaction. Loren Carpenter's Cinematrix is one technology capable of doing that; each member of the audience feels they are contributing to the group experience and, just as important, is able to share that pleasure with their companions. I'm sure there will eventually be other inventions with that capability.

One truth about the progression of entertainment technology gets clearer and clearer: Nothing old goes away. New devices and tools are developed, but they all just get integrated. The more sophisticated everything gets, the more critical the fundamentals become. The corollary is that no matter what anybody tells you about how some new technology will save you money because of efficiencies, it's probably not true; it just makes the product better. You may be saving time because some tool works faster, but you'll just work on the idea longer.

A goal that we're all pursuing is to create experiences that are attractive to a much broader demographic range, not just "shoot your neighbor" scenarios. Another key area of R&D for us is finding new and creative ways to use image displays, combining them seamlessly with dimensional environments that are aware of their occupants.

One of the most exciting digital developments will be in identifying guests—allowing the guest to interact passively with the environment. Imagine that your theme park admission ticket is a button you wear on your lapel or put in your pocket, which is actually a tiny radio device allowing each guest to be individually recognized as he or she walks past sensors. Walking up to some part of the aware environment—a video display—or through the gate of an attraction, you not only could be greeted by name but also, as you go through the attraction, your image might be captured and stored. It could then reappear as a character in another attraction you're visiting three hours later because a sensor at the second ride's turnstile identified you and called up that image from a central data bank. Or, everything you buy might be put on your account, with a bill at the end of the day. And again, sensors within an attraction can custom-tailor fairly subtle differences in the experience, depending on the size of a group of guests, their movements, or positions.

The market for themed entertainment will continue to grow, and the future is exciting. But success will come to those who have enough vision to look beyond the technology and create fun and exciting experiences in ways that will increase capacity and appeal to all sorts of people.

Biography

Phil Hettema is an expert in the production of spectacular exhibits, live shows, and attractions. As Senior Vice President of Attraction Development for Universal Creative, Universal Studios Recreation Group, he has been responsible for the creation and production of some of their most popular attractions, including *Jurassic Park:* The Ride, *Back to the Future:* The Ride, the Miami Vice Action Spectacular, the *Star Trek* Adventure, the Riot Act Western Stunt Show, the American Tail show and interactive playground, and the World of Cinemagic at Universal Studios Hollywood. He is currently working on Islands of Adventure, Universal Studios' second gated attraction in Orlando. In addition to his theme park credits, Mr. Hettema has an extensive background in the special events field, notably his association with David Wolper as Production Supervisor for the opening and closing ceremonies of the 1986 Statue of Liberty Centennial "Liberty Weekend" celebration, the most ambitious live/TV event ever staged. As a creative consultant, he has considerable experience in art direction, costuming, stage design, and puppetry. He is a guest lecturer on the subject of exhibit and show production at universities and national conferences.

Chapter 25

Beyond Fear and Exhilaration: Hopes and Dreams for Specialty Venue Entertainment

Allen Yamashita
SimEx Digital Studios

Introduction

When I followed Douglas Trumbull out of the theatrical motion picture business to produce films for his start-up Showscan in the early 1980s, "specialty venue entertainment" was a cottage industry. There were a handful of firms in a hand-to-mouth existence making unique shows and technology for world expositions, museums, and the large American theme parks. In the ensuing ten years, the business has mushroomed with new companies and products emerging annually, and industry pioneers IMAX, Iwerks, and Showscan are now publicly traded companies.

This micro-industry's growth is the result of several factors. In no particular order, they include the advance of the microprocessor; the increasing cost-effectiveness of digital imaging; the 1980s bubble economy; the emergence of the Asian leisure market; and, in the mid-1990s, a bullish stock market and the aggressive worldwide deployment of location-based entertainment centers by real estate developers intent on making their retail destinations a complete experience.

Another factor in the momentum is the successful public reception of big-budget simulator rides, 3D large-format film attractions, and illusionary multimedia theatrical shows at Disney and MCA/Universal's theme parks. In fact, it is the values contained in these big-budget programs that specialty venue products are designed to incorporate and emulate. By distilling the essence of a big theme park attraction into smaller physical packages, specialty venue attractions are designed for installation in small areas of real estate at a reasonable cost per seat. Considering the relatively high experience intensity these products deliver, they are, according to marketing claims made by industry prophets, cost-effective enough to be franchised into hundreds of regional and local locations worldwide.

However, before the world is covered in themed entertainment, current products must traverse a few speed bumps. Unlike the attractions of a big theme park, which are visited maybe once every several years, the success of local and regional specialty-entertainment attractions depends on repeat consumption. For these franchised products to succeed, they must have richly compelling content, in a format that can be reprogrammed economically.

What follows are observations on the continuing evolution of two major forms in specialty entertainment today—the large-format theater and the simulation theater—and some thoughts about the future of specialty venue.

Immersion Theaters

Industry pioneer IMAX has been joined by Showscan, Iwerks, Goto, and others in marketing theater technology designed to engulf audiences within a high-resolution movie whose image field of view dominates peripheral vision. Until recently, producers of films for these immersion theaters have concentrated on using the large field of view as windows on the world, leading to the collective development of a spectacular "library" of documentary films.

After 25 years of this largely educational fare, the medium finds itself at an evolutionary crossroads. Two factors are responsible. First, audiences have a growing familiarity with the medium; it's no longer adequate to simply be big and immersive. Audiences become comfortable with the high levels of stimulus and the medium's cues and "language," so compelling content is ever more critical.

In addition, many "obvious" natural subjects that are reasonably cost-effective to film have been exhausted; more adventurous nature material will prove more difficult to produce. Since larger budgets require more paying bums on seats, producers must develop programs, whatever the content, capable of finding a larger audience. This is a difficult conundrum in that most immersion theater venues are museum- and science-center-based—venues that have traditionally cultivated primarily daytime audiences.

Looking around and into the near future, the large-format film is evolving in two significant directions beyond the documentary. One of these applications is as environmental scenography within large theme park entertainment attractions. These film-based attractions use projected 2D and 3D large-format motion pictures in conjunction with big screens, transforming the architecture and scenery context for live actors, simulation motion bases, physical special effects, and action props. Examples include MCA's *Back to the Future: The Ride,* and *T2-3D,* and Disney's *Honey I Shrunk The Audience* and *Muppet Vision 3D.* Because of the huge costs involved, both in terms of the projection/theater technology and of the cost per minute of image production, this type of application will be limited to the large theme parks for the foreseeable future.

The other evolutionary path for large format is the development of material with more "commercial potential"—material capable of drawing an evening audience bent on diversionary fare. IMAX, Sony, and Iwerks have begun funding the production of narrative subjects created directly for the medium and building 3D theaters dedicated to showing them. Judging from the initial enthusiastic public acceptance in Times Square, New York, and Irvine, California, of the first several films, it seems that these special kinds of motion pictures, if entertaining, provocative, and compelling, *will* get people out of the house.

The question is whether enough of these films can be generated economically enough to justify an expanding network of special theaters and the films themselves. Any production in large-format 70 mm is difficult because of the logistics involved in moving a large camera and rig around (read: slowly), not to mention all that 70-mm (actually 65-mm) film racing through the camera (it costs about $18 to purchase, develop, and print a single second of blank film in IMAX). Add to this the cost of actors, wardrobe, and sets required by a dramatic narrative production, and it is easy to see why a simple documentary *without* a theatrical story can easily cost from $2 million to $4 million. It takes little imagination to see how a high-quality 40-minute large-format narrative could start at $4 million to $6 million and escalate quickly into eight figures depending upon the filmmaker's story and design ambition. At these prices, the minimum percentage of existing large-format theaters needed to rent the film to make it financially viable is very high.

In the near future, advancing digital technology may present a partial solution to the large-format cost dilemma. Today's digital techniques allow unprecedented image manipulation possibilities, though it's still economically impractical to work in large formats due to the high costs of data manipulation and storage and to the large amounts of data involved. As microprocessor speeds climb and memory costs fall, the cost/data curve improves. Soon it will be economical to devise and apply image degraining, artifact removal, and missing data interpolation algorithms to small-format film negative for blowup to larger formats.

In the near term, origination negative might be 8-perforation 35mm, which, while not the industry standard 4-perf 35mm format, is still relatively economical compared to shooting in 15-perf 65/70mm. This smaller, less expensive negative will be digitally scanned, degrained, enhanced, repaired, reformatted, and output to 15-perf (or 8- or 10-perf) 65/70mm stock. As the algorithms become more sophisticated and the costs-to-data curve improves, standard fine-grain 4-perf origination negative may be all that's needed.

With such technology available, the necessity to originate in a 15-perf 65/70mm format may only be necessary for special shots and setups, reducing the cost and risk of creating movie product specifically for the large-format medium. These digital blowup and repair techniques will not come cheaply, but today it *is* economical to synthesize and manipulate images that even three years ago would have been astronomically prohibitive.

In addition to made-for-specialty-venue-theater films, this technology might convert selected blockbuster feature films. By using large-format theaters as a premiere showcase, Hollywood distributors could create a buzz for the wider 35mm theatrical release. Though it's arguable that the currently popular in-the-audience's-face style of filmmaking is too extreme in composition and pacing for a large-format image, by the time the economics make sense, audiences will have emerged that crave the gigantic, relentless, cinematic roller coasters that these conversions could create. After all, sensory brutality is a growing trend in all forms of entertainment. It is also relative.

If large-format theaters are adopted as a premiere long-form medium by the major studios, the economics of expanding the network of large-format theaters dedicated for entertainment programs will improve. This development will also positively benefit the existing network of museum-based theaters. The extra "found" museum revenue earned from a Stallone or Bond spectacle at the evening box office might even help to fund regular daytime programs.

Simulation Films: More Than a Gag?

Since the first major simulation installations in the mid-1980s, the content trend in motion simulator theaters has been to present the audience with dangerous situations and then try to convince them they are active participants. This "interaction" through role playing usually involves placing the audience inside a vehicle—train, plane, automobile, bobsled, dune buggy, or airboat—then sending them off on a relentless, four-minute vomit comet.

In the past five years, spurred by the success of big park rides like Back to the Future and Star Tours, the industry has discovered more elaborate "stories." These scenarios involve thrill rides set inside extreme environments like asteroids in space, sunken ships underwater, volcanoes, the center of the earth, and alien planets.

Despite the relative gain in thematic sophistication, the majority of simulator programs are still designed like porn films in that the premise under which the action takes place is always less important than the action itself. The "story" is really just an environment in which to have a quick thrill. This thrill consists of having a succession of visual "pies" thrown in your face while the motion base bumps you around in a series of avoidance maneuvers.

Though unquestionably effective, as a formula, it makes for interchangeable adrenaline experiences. A roller coaster is a roller coaster, no matter what dress it wears. After experiencing three or four, it's tough to differentiate between them. If passive simulation is to be a lasting medium, this dilemma needs consideration. Since a simulation theater is a theater, changing the film and motion program can renew the entire experience. If, however, the marketing premise guiding the movie concepts continues to make the experiences feel similar (even though the films look different), audiences will eventually become ambivalent.

There are other product design hurdles facing simulation. In a large theme park, any one attraction constitutes but one thrill within an all-day succession of experiences. In a small LBE center, a simulator must stand alone with only the "support" of maybe two to four other entertainment attractions. In this setting, an attraction must work harder, provide a more complete experience, and give higher perceived value. If it is to be repeated by local users, there must be more *to* it as a stand-alone experience, or possibly more plot, in a revival of the episodic style of Saturday matinees.

One way LBE or regional locations can face these challenges is to push the development of rides toward more complete experiences, the ride being at the center. This, too, follows the lead of the big theme park attractions, but at lower cost. In a larger show structure, the audience can be presented with a story in multiple sections or acts. A themed and programmed queue line provides atmosphere; a video or film theater introduces the premise, protagonist, antagonist, and dramatic conflict; and the simulator ride plays out the dramatic conflict to a resolution. Within this structure there is potential for the audience to carry into the ride a fragment of an idea or emotional empathy for some aspect of the situation. If the total experience has an emotive component in addition to the visceral one, audiences might remember the experience a little longer than the time it takes to walk to the yogurt shop after leaving the attraction.

Other opportunities to develop the medium in this direction lie in nontraditional market applications—museums, science centers, zoos, and aquariums. These august institutions, especially museums and science centers, are desperately in need of information delivery systems that do more than showcase dead exhibits in glass cases. Kids today are multidimensional in the way they acquire information. If these institutions are to continue to be socially important, they must communicate in ways beyond signage, text, and a TV monitor.

Simulation is a particularly dynamic medium, good for exploring environments and discovering things within them. The worlds of scientific process, inner and outer space, the oceans, and animals are all treasure troves of material. Free of constricting theme park design conventions and allowed to explore new styles and subject matter, simulation might flower into a substantive medium—one more than the sum of its parts.

Our Immediate Future: Business as Usual

The big forms of specialty entertainment—large-screen immersion and simulation theaters—are essentially movie theaters with a twist: bigger and more visceral, but still passive, linear, noninteractive experiences. In the near term, passive media will continue to dominate the specialty venue marketplace for several reasons.

First, most of today's audience still wants to be told a linear narrative story. People want to be in the grip of a good yarn that allows them to sit back and be manipulated. The passive cultural heritage of storytelling in theater, movies, and broadcast has conditioned the general marketplace of consumers. Current specialty movies still tell stories in the traditional way.

Secondly, for most of today's audience, out-of-home entertainment is a social activity. This society can be a couple, a family, or a gathering of friends. It's the reason activities as banal as miniature golf and bowling are still popular in North America. Though we go to movies and sit in the dark, we sit in the dark together. When a movie theater is so crowded as to split the group up, it causes great consternation. Today's audiences want *shared* experiences, and the current products allow them to do it.

Third, the projected motion picture image still packs more information bandwidth at a better cost-per-minute ratio than any other technology around. And, in the next ten years, there isn't anything that looks ready to get close.

Lastly, true group interactivity is still too hard to do, both technically and programmatically. Other than Loren Carpenter's Cinematrix Interactive Entertainment System, no compelling group interactive technology has been convincingly demonstrated. Until today, most other attempts at interactive specialty entertainment can be described as "dumb" interactivity. These include movie products in which the audience gets an A/B choice at plot turns and at the ending; guests "interact" with a couple of buttons hardwired into the backs of seats. As group experiences, such products seem doomed to disappoint the half of the audience that didn't want to go "left" at the fork in the story and to bore those who simply didn't care and wanted the storyteller to get on with it.

New Forms for New Consumers

Squinting into the new century, Boomer notions about what constitutes compelling specialty out-of-home entertainment will be challenged. These new sensibilities and aesthetic values will come from emerging generations of audiences whose world is replete with home and work computers fiber linked to the Web and to each other. For them (and us), information will be less static. They will have in-home access to information and entertainment products consisting not of today's Stone Age scrollable text and still pictures, but dimensional animations that can be touched, manipulated, and changed. Information will be cross-linked and referenced; linearity will be a path that you choose through multiple dimensions of data.

Consumers who use this technology will also be shaped by it. As media content, form, and access become increasingly instantaneous, hybridized, and omnidimensional, the audiences exposed to it tend to become less linear and homogenized in their tastes and consumption habits. New media users will probably be more exposed to the world beyond their village at an earlier age, more urbanized, less nuclear-family oriented, and more politically fractionalized. They will be globally aware but locally, tribally preoccupied.

Currently, there are several specialty-entertainment products with qualities relevant to these future consumers. They include the interactive networked games such as Virtual World, and group-environment games such as Laser-tag, Ultra Zone, and other variants. As in passive simulation ride theaters, these attractions ask audiences to role-play. The networked games provide robotic avatars for the participants, who run around virtual playing fields attempting to destroy each other for points and glory. The environmental tag games pit players against each other in dimly lit themed spaces, attempting to shoot each other or objects in the environment for points and glory. Though both experiences have limited appeal to anyone but young males, they're interesting in several respects.

Realtime Persistence

Unlike a canned movie experience, the individual user's actions affect the course of the program and the program's ultimate outcome in realtime. This repeatedly acknowledges that the participant is *inside* the experience, and that feeling is significant. As Web products, video games, and home computer products increase the amount of "live" animation that can be streamed down the wire and manipulated, people will become more accustomed to teleinteracting. Future consumers will understand how to play inside a program—something relatively few people now over 40 (maybe even 30) can relate to.

Dimensionality

Some of the current interactive networked experiences are truly three-dimensional, realtime, and nonlinear. Though data-crunching rates are still too slow for current imagery to offer the pictorial resolution, detail, and clarity of a contemporary high-quality 2D film experience, cost/performance is evolving rapidly. Soon we'll see the cost of image generators fall to ratios of cost-per-minute-per-guest that make enough economic sense to allow use of projected, higher-than-NTSC video resolution computer graphics that are interactive in realtime. Only ten years ago, the idea of a commercially viable low-rez realtime networked 3D game was laughable. Also, because current and near-future Internet-accessed home game experiences are encumbered by other network traffic, specialty venue sites with dedicated broadband networks, low latency, and high data-refresh rates will be where the best networked experience flourishes.

Personalization

Interactive attractions have the capability of emphasizing an aspect of personalization. By having an in-world identity, real or assumed, temporary or permanent, user integration into the experience is significantly heightened. As time goes on, we'll see interactive systems with advanced sensors and wearable devices tracking guests in the environment. In addition to monitoring guest traffic and gathering marketing information, this capability will extend so that programs can recognize different guests and shape aspects of their experience at critical points, based on behavior. This will support the illusion that guests' time in an experience is theirs to control.

Personalization will also include the ability to represent ourselves within the experience with much more realistic subtlety—whether it's a representation of our faces, our bodies, or a totally fabricated avatar of our own design. All these features will contribute to making people feel that they are together in the same place—even though that place is partially or entirely virtual.

Common design criticism of current interactive experiences is that, until they become group oriented, they won't be significant forms in the specialty out-of-home industry. Though certainly true from today's vantage point, technology does change social perceptions about itself and its interface. As the techniques of interacting become more nuanced and culturally embedded, the demographic group at ease with and interested in the option of playing alone together will mushroom.

The Hybrid Future: Form and Content

Generally, entertainment content will continue to capitalize on marketing opportunities, though it will travel not only vertically downward from the movie or television program but also increasingly laterally, following the CD-ROM,

Web game, music video, daytime talk show, or anything else where a marketable icon can be extracted. The emphasis will continue to involve building upon mythologies that everyone recognizes, as well as ones that are easy to *make* everyone recognize.

In general, form and content will grow in two basic directions: goal-oriented entertainment and experiences that emphasize the journey rather than an objective. The goal-oriented games will be networked experiences on an elaborate scale—scenarios in which the audience plays within a database shared between different facilities. Like the current Virtual World, they'll be skill-oriented and create a draw by being compelling to play over and over again. These products will differ from home-accessed Net games in their level of intensity and visceral impact, as well as their immediate social dimension. They'll employ visual, motion, and auditory technology that no individual will be able to afford to own or download at home.

Not everyone will consider goal-scoring to be entertainment. For these audiences, we will develop experiential environments where the core of the experience is in exploring or unwrapping a story hidden beneath, behind, and within a richly detailed environment. The amusement will be in navigating through the piece at a pace and on a path dictated by the individual or group. They'll be gentle "places," structured so that players come together to assume personas that have a vested interest in helping others instead of killing or maiming them—nuanced social contact.

Finally, we will see an expanding market for experiences that cater to an aging population—experiences that have content aimed at enhancing or showing audiences something concerning their health, well-being, or growth and actualization. Dreaming ahead, I wonder whether one distant day some of these experiences might transcend mere distraction and offer guests something truly valuable, be it an orgasmic exhilaration, a cathartic purging of primal fear, or singularly luscious dreams of utter, if temporary, well-being.

Biography

Allen Yamashita is President and Creative Director of SimEx Digital Studios, a digital animation company in Los Angeles that produces specialty venue film projects and supplies computer graphics to the television commercial and feature film industries.

Chapter 26

Seafari: An Expedition into Motion Base Ride Filmmaking

Mario Kamberg
Mario Kamberg Design

Introduction

When you enter a good ride-film in a theme park, the preshow is carefully designed to set your expectations for a thrilling experience—and to set *you* up for the unexpected. The people who design these attractions encounter plenty of the unexpected, too. We go to great lengths, inadvertently creating unique problems for ourselves as we devise the rides; then, we have to invent our way out of the problems. This chapter is about that sort of designing and inventing: what it takes to produce an attraction that will handle 10,000 people a day. I use examples from two projects: the Funtastic World of Hanna-Barbera at Universal Studios Florida and Seafari at Porto Europa in Wakayama, Japan.

Producing a motion-base ride-film involves different processes and a different approach than producing a traditional film. Conventional storytelling techniques don't work; complex stories and too much dialogue will get buried in the mix. Traditional film-editing techniques that work well in a feature film can be disastrous in terms of the ride; cuts, pans, and zooms do not apply to this medium. Add these issues to the fact that no one wants to build an attraction that's too similar to a previous one, and you're in for an exciting exploration of uncharted territory.

The overriding goal in designing a ride-film attraction is to make the guests feel as if they are *in* the experience, not just watching it. I want them to go places they've never been, see things they've never seen, and feel things they've never felt before. I want to completely inundate their senses with explosive sights, sounds, and feelings. And I want them to come back to do it again. Most importantly, every simulator experience I design and direct is another chance to get closer to creating that ultimate believable reality.

The "I" Word

Ride-films aren't "interactive" in terms of allowing meaningful user control—not yet, anyway. My kind of entertainment design is more accurately called "immersive environments with stories." To some, motion-base rides can seem interactive in that they more broadly engage the guests' sensorium, one characteristic of any true interactive experience. They get the guests *into* the big screen and make them part of the ride, surrounding and immersing them in an environment that they're going to relate to immediately, emotionally, and viscerally.

I would be happy to use some truly interactive technologies to produce my illusions, but the actual visual experience required is orders of magnitude higher in resolution than any realtime image generator can currently handle. With interactivity comes individual control, which tends to smithereen any well-designed plot. Since it's so hard to do a story well with just one plot, it's difficult to imagine the effort needed to devise an attraction with nontrivial user control of plot development by a room full of people. What I've just described will in fact happen, but not on our existing models, and the road to get there will be littered by some spectacular crashes. I believe that two kinds of models are going to emerge in high-tech attractions: ones for guests that want maximum control (maximum imaginary power) and more traditional ones for guests that want their experience maximally orchestrated.

The new model has a downside; it can attract people who desire solo personal escapism, an isolation that abandons the intrinsically wholesome aspect of the group entertainment experience in theme parks. The more realistic that a genuinely interactive virtual experience design becomes, the more dangerous, in a sense, it can become. Such entertainment scenarios are extremely compelling and profitable but will continue to be economically prohibitive in theme parks for quite a while.

Definition

There are some basic rules that usually apply. To achieve the desired first-person POV experience, a ride film needs to be one continuous movement through the environment, with cuts disguised as impacts or obstacles. Conventional intercuts distract from the illusion, making the viewers feel as if they're observing events rather than being part of the experience. Dialogue should be minimal: Trying to tell too much story through dialogue will leave the audience confused and frustrated. The audience will not care or pay attention to complex dialogue, so we rely heavily on visual story cues.

The theme of the attraction must be carried from the preshow to the film to the postshow and the merchandising areas. This is not as easy as it may sound: Everyone on the production team must work together to achieve it. Once you've got the storyline resolved, the main challenge of every ride film is programming the motion base. Every motion-base system has its own nuances and characteristics (and I've rarely had the luxury of working on two projects that use the same base).

Seafari is considered by many to be one of the best ride-film attractions to date, as well as one of the best CGI pieces in any genre. It's still running at Porto Europa, the MCA-built theme park in Wakayama, which opened in 1994. Although we were lucky to have a luxurious budget, the basics of how Seafari was designed and produced—and the snags we ran into—can be applied to all ride films. You're telling a simple story, and you need seven basic things:

1. A clear storyline.

2. A preshow that readies (educates) the audience.

3. Consistent themeing.

4. Great visual design.

5. A seamless film experience.

6. Effective motion design.

7. Synchronous motion-base experience.

An Historical Aside

I got into the ride-film business by a fluke, a right-place-at-the-right-time scenario. I was creative director for special-effects commercials at Digital Pictures and in Los Angeles when I was hired by MCA/Universal for their Funtastic World of Hanna-Barbera at Universal Studios Florida. I was supposed to be the interface between the traditional 2D character animation work and the digitally generated 3D environments—Sherry McKenna's idea and an innovative combination at that time—and to do the motion choreography. Then, both the director and the show designer left, and I wound up doing practically the whole project. I had to adapt the traditional cartoon animation "gags" to happen in less time and in the context of motion; they aren't designed to be flown past at 35 miles per hour. Many, in fact, weren't applicable at all. I believe that one of the reasons it turned out well was its low priority compared to other attractions at the park, like the Spielberg attractions *Jaws* and *ET.* Upper management left my executive producer, Sherry McKenna, and me with considerable relative autonomy to do the job as best we could. The other reason it worked was Bill Hanna and Joe Barbera; they were deeply involved and adapted their brainstorming to both the fast pace and limited dialogue. These extraordinary gagmasters *got it* immediately.

The Hanna-Barbera attraction appeals to all ages; it deals with a fantasy world and fantasy characters rather than hard-edged science fiction or realism, which are more common in this film genre. The situation and plot are fantastical—the characters are from several different cartoon shows set in different eras, and the plot culminates in a simple chase without any really violent behavior. Though this is unusual, I feel there are plenty of good stories to be told that don't rely on violence. In the entertainment business, violence is a shortcut, although an incredibly lucrative one. We need more fantasy and more *passive interactivity* in games and films that we see now, and I don't think the entertainment needs to be as aggressive as it is.

The Process

Preproduction and Story Development

Preproduction design starts with a general concept: What is it we are trying to do? I usually come up with the story concept and do the first treatment; it sets the pace, controls the plot complexity, and begins the character development. Then, a good writer fleshes it out and writes the dialogue, including the preshow dialogue. There are several iterations in refining both the treatment and the script; in Seafari, the final script happened about halfway through the production. The story needs simplicity and clarity. You have four minutes to take the audience somewhere they've never been before, let them experience things they couldn't experience at home, and enable them to share that experience with a group.

The show treatment is now used to start development of preliminary encapsulating motion-base choreography and storyboard design. The Seafari storyboard was probably 100 frames in length and went through perhaps ten revisions over six months, while I was also designing the scenic elements of the preshow and theater space. I received input from many people, including MCA Planning & Development's Vice President and Creative Director, Phil Hettema; Art Director Dale Mason; Jay Stein, President of MCA Recreation Group; and John Leisner, MCA Recreation Services' Vice President of Planning & Development. The show concept, in this case, came from Phil and Dale: "a Jules Verneian undersea ride." They gave me a lot of creative freedom in developing the show treatment and film design. After the storyboards have been approved, you really don't know their adaptability until you experience the vehicle for the first time during choreography. That's when you need to scramble, making the adjustments necessary to the package that has been sold to your management and, in some cases, their client.

Motion base programming and the details of story development best happen in parallel. The ride experience is affected by the mechanical limitations inherent in the motion base. When developing the storyline and programming the base to the ride-film, I'm constantly reminded of the limitations of each. Determining how the software will interact with the base's hardware must occur during the early stages of production.

The ride experience is sensorially rich; it's a very active, physical thing and very visual. When properly done, it's, by definition, unlike anything the guests have ever experienced. And, in four minutes, that experience is not going to have an elaborate plot. Dialogue is always used to help carry the plot, but in small doses; with all the action going on, the guests aren't interested in listening to much detail. Other tools used to reinforce the story and the motion effects include, foremost, the sound effects and music—multitrack surround sound. We also use lighting and sometimes temperature control, wind, or scent cannons. We're trying to involve as many senses as possible in the four minutes we have to entertain guests. With the recently completed Star Trek: The Experience (8-perf 70mm film projected on a dome), we had 167 tracks of sound effects, 45 tracks of orchestral music, and 25 synthesizer tracks, mixed to 16 discrete channels in the theater.

The Preshow

What to Do

Guests standing in the queue line of an attraction are willing participants, with the time and desire to be entertained. In most U.S. theme parks, you're likely to be shuffling along underneath a canopy, perhaps watching a video on overhead monitors. In a fully developed attraction, we turn this queue time into a preshow, where we introduce our characters, begin the plot, set the stage for the entire experience, and welcome the guests as participants. Briefly, the preshow accomplishes the following:

- It sets the premise for the ride.

- It explains to the guests where they're headed.

- It introduces our guides, pilots, and other characters.

- It answers questions—the why, where, when, and how.

• It explains what the ride vehicle looks like and how the guests are expected to board the motion base, often providing diagrams for seating and the like.

MCA built the same high quality into the Seafari attraction that is found in the Universal Studios parks. The entire experience takes place in the fictional French Oceanographic Institute, a big, old, ornate chateau, and the audience is placed in the role of VIP guests. They're supposed to be joining the maiden voyage of a whale-submarine, a research vessel that swims instead of using propellers. (See Figure 26.1.)

Partway through the preshow, the audience learns that something is amiss—the first plot twist (quite common in motion base ride plots). They encounter a 28-foot steel shark-submarine being pulled out of the water with a big bite out of one side. We also discover—on the video monitors—that a larger whale-submarine out there is missing and believed to be in danger. So, instead of going on a VIP cruise, the audience winds up as unintentional guests on a

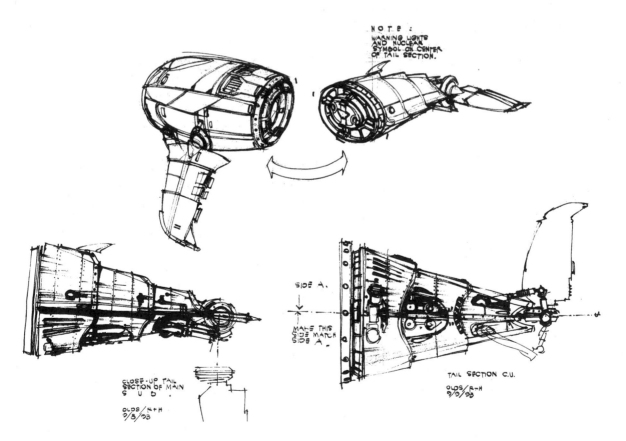

rescue mission. That's the plot: We go find the people who are in danger. Some vivid dramatic plot mechanism like this is almost always invoked.

I suspect that this is the longest and most elaborate ride preshow ever done. Whatever the size and length, the preshow should prepare the audience so that they can immediately jump into the experience when they get on the ride. However, there should be still more unexpected twists in the ride-film itself.

How We Did It

Every room of the preshow entertains people and prepares them for the ride ahead. All the announcements are in Japanese, English, and French, largely for verisimilitude.

Visitors first enter a large, long reception room with exquisite decor in keeping with the look of the chateau exterior—no high-tech intrusions yet. The next room is different. It's the security entrance of the Institute, with a giant steel bank-vault door, held open with hydraulic rams, where visitors are told they will next pass through a "bio scan" to remove bacteria and contaminants from their bodies. The bio scan effect is dramatic—with pulsing lights and sound effects—and ensures that the guests are prepared to see the impossible happen in the next room.

The single-passenger shark-submarine hangs from a gantry from the ceiling. The visitors queue around the central moon pool, where the smoking submarine has apparently just been pulled from the water. This is where the Institute supposedly works on their submarines. The pool is 5 feet deep with constantly bubbling water, environmental sounds, and splashing. The effects create enough water turbulence to obscure the floor and provide the illusion that it connects to the sea. There's a platform to one side with monitors and diagnostic equipment, and announcements come over the strategically placed communication system monitors. Soon a special announcement begins; several characters' dialogue indicates something's amiss to give the guests a feeling of foreboding and urgency.

Guests then enter a tunnel that simulates an underwater passageway between parts of the Institute. While waiting to go into the next room, they can hear what sounds like giant submarines swimming overhead—little pings and noises and whale sounds. From that passageway, guests enter a dispatch area, where they meet the pilot (who briefs them on Institute procedures via video), get their first view of the submarine they'll ride, and see several other doors leading to different places. After the video, the doors at the far end of the dispatch room open. There, the guests are going to wait for their submarine. It hasn't arrived yet, so they are diverted to the Institute's Bio Lab, where they meet the central character of the ride-film. Each stage draws them further into the story. (See Figure 26.2.)

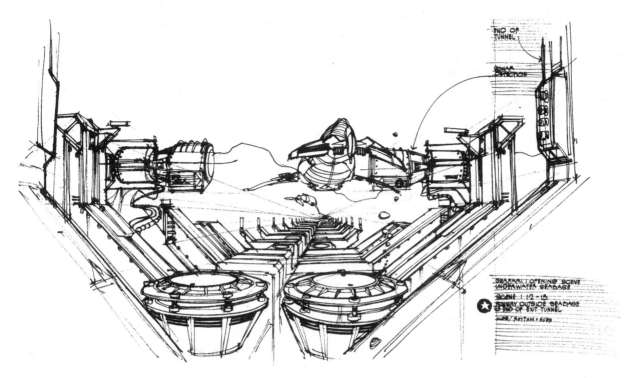

Figure 26.2 Docking ports and exterior runway for subs entering and exiting the seabase.

The Bio Lab is a pleasant, dark, quiet, moody room, carpeted and soft—a very different atmosphere from the metallic noisiness of previous rooms. The guests hear bubbles rising and see a big vertical glass water tank at the far end. It contains Sammy the dolphin—our main character; he wears a computer backpack that allows him to speak. His tank is a fake; it's 8 feet high but only about 1 foot deep, with real bubbles, water, and lighting. Its rear wall is a rear-projection screen, with a VistaVision projector behind the thin layer of water. We combined a computer-generated dolphin, bubbles, and an appropriate murky background, then integrated that with the real lighting of the tank and real bubbles in the foreground. You seem to see a real live dolphin approach, blast up into this tank, introduce himself in a panic, and then swim off to save the day. Sammy's appearance brings an essential note of surprise and irony to the preshow. The audience doesn't yet know that Sammy is the central character; they think the pilot probably is. But, with this new and unexpected character, we've heightened their expectations.

The final room of the preshow is the loading area where guests are loaded into the motion base. The vehicle is suspended over another huge moon pool with sloshing wave machines, sound effects to mimic a busy loading dock, complex equipment, and, again, overhead video monitors. This time, though, you get the safety instructions required for all rides, but from a sort of flight attendant. We queue once again and wait for the doors of the whale-sub to open. The inside and outside design of the submarine is reminiscent of the sub in *20,000 Leagues Under the Sea.* You can see several metal fins on the sides, where whale fins and flukes would be.

By now you may be surprised by the apparent budget for this preshow. It *was* unusual to be afforded the luxury of such a large themed indoor queue line. A more common situation occurred with the space for the Hanna-Barbera attraction's preshow. It was severely reduced late in the development process, when we got a budget cut, and resulted in a lot of redesign and a weirdly proportioned room, but the show still had to properly prepare the same number of people per hour.

The Film

Visual Design

The visual design of the film relies on the vision of the designer and director and partly on the budget. If you were to make Seafari in 1997, it might cost from $5 million to $7 million just for the film. With current tools, that's a good ballpark for this level of production design. The Rhythm & Hues, Inc. team who executed that budget included over 60 people, with Ellen Coss as line producer, Larry Weinberg as senior animator, Lorne Lanning as art director, and Kathy White as technical director.

All through the development of the film, we are constantly reviewing different aspects of different scenes. I spend a great deal of time at the studio, checking key lighting frames, effects and character animation, textures, motion choreography, and modeling. This is all done on studio monitors; the final lighting tests and technical effects are checked on 35mm film or the final format, usually 70mm.

Seafari pushed the envelope in terms of lighting and animation. The style could be described as "high-design, but using the materials and techniques of the 1860s." We did about 80 percent of it with computer graphics. Most of the active image elements, like the tiny columns of air bubbles and the swimming dolphin, were done with physically based modeling software and lit in great detail. The only models and miniatures in this film were the 10-foot high by 30-foot-long sea base (at the beginning) and some of the underwater landscapes.

Set design plays a vital role in conveying our message not only in the preshow but also throughout the ride theater, in the postshow, and into merchandising areas. As production designer, my responsibility is to assure visual continuity throughout the entire show. Once the guests enter the main theater, they should understand what they are there to experience and why. If they don't, we haven't done our job.

Motion Design: Programming and Problem-Solving

Programming the motion base—motion matching—is the main challenge of every ride-film. I test all choreography and keyframe animation sequences on the actual base. Because a base is mechanical, it's limited in how far and how fast it can move. The film production company provides me with video test sequences. These use wireframe or low-detail, solid-shaded objects, choreographing the camera around and through these objects and recording to tape. I then test the tape with the base at the choreography facility, usually an old warehouse in an undesirable part of town. If the base is incapable of moving to coincide with the camera motion, a revised test needs to be shot. I employ this technique with the entire film until I attain the required continuous fluid movement.

The typical problems associated with a simulator attraction involve the motion base. I set up a temporary video projection system on the actual Hughes motion base, and it was like riding a chuck wagon instead of a submarine. You never know how difficult those problems are until you get behind the wheel and start flying. The fix involved converting from 8-bit to 16-bit for smoother motion—a lot of work—but we got what we needed. It was ideal—like flying a glider.

One of the biggest challenges is the surprises that occur once all the elements (film, sound, scenic environment) are in place: the on-site installation of the entire system. In ride-films, the illusion is most effective when you fill the viewers' field of view. If the screen is less enveloping, then their local environment becomes more critical—so does the emotional element of the storyline. Seafari's screen was definitely small—only 35 feet wide and 20 feet high. It's elliptical and rear-projected, so it seems like the front viewing port of the 75-foot-long whale-sub. Because it's not rectangular, it suggests less to the audience about their horizon, supporting the illusion of being underwater. When the experience begins, the seats rise up slightly from the floor and then move independently of the floor and the room. (See Figure 26.3.)

We started the motion programming in Los Angeles. I didn't use the ride's special elliptical rear-projection screen, and just a bare-bones motion platform was bolted to the floor in a dark warehouse near the Burbank Airport. We hung a video projector and a 13-foot screen from the ceiling to test all of our moves. If I had a 30-second move that was questionable, I would drive there with Trey

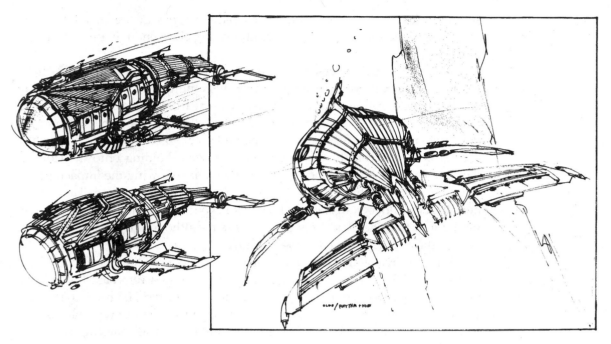

Figure 26.3 Design evolution of the whale sub with large front viewport for the ride-film's screen.

Stokes, the programmer, at a moment's notice and we would sit there and modify it for a few hours. Every day during choreography we would test individual tiny segments of the film. It worked fine; the demos were exciting until upper management signed off on the choreography.

Back to the problem. I arrived in Japan, hung the video projector in the actual darkened room, did some final changes to the motion programming, and it felt great. Then, upper management came by to see the 70mm film for the first time in proper context. They're all sitting next to me, we run the film, and . . . my God, there's no magic; it doesn't work! I was sitting there, panicked, in the middle of an uninteresting filmic experience, with the motion bases incongruously acting as if nothing was wrong. So I did what anyone would do in a situation like that—I lied. I said there was no problem, it just needs a few minor adjustments, so go away and come back in two days, and it'll be perfect. Management walked out the door, and I was ready to jump into the Moon Pool because I had no idea what the problem was. The problem was that I had done all the motion programming with a front-projected video screen, which is far dimmer than a rear-projected VistaVision system, so it didn't light up the sub interior. The minute the film projector came on, it lit up the whole interior of the submarine! The audience, myself included, was too aware of all the neat themeing of the room and was not really paying close enough attention to the film.

So, I ran an older version of the program and suddenly realized that I needed to shock the audience right in the beginning. I needed to get them to grab onto their seats and never even glance away from the screen. In the beginning of the film, you dive down and bump a stone spire on the seafloor; the next time management came in, I crashed into that spire *really* hard and totally surprised them. From that moment on, they were holding onto the sides of their seats with their eyes focused on that screen. Following the impact, I gave the rest of the film slightly more aggressive motion programming. Their attention didn't wander at all because they were expecting that jolt to happen again throughout the ride. And I never did it again—although it got a little violent toward the end. They loved it. (See Figure 26.4.)

You never really know; you just have to interact with the developing show on a daily basis. I've changed the story and action of a film based on a fluke move—it happened while reviewing a video test in the Hanna-Barbera ride. There was a moment where we simply swooped up and down that just felt wonderful. It had nothing to do with the film, but it was magical, like flying dreams when you were a kid. So, I decided to stick an elephant in there as a reason to swoop up, over the elephant, and down again. We redid the boards and added a pink elephant running through the streets; it worked perfectly. Magical things happen that way.

Motion-base choreography, in general, is an arduous process, but precise programming of the base to the film is simply critical to a superior ride. If the motion is even slightly out of sync with the picture, the viewer will not feel a part of the experience, but rather that he or she is simply "watching a film." If it is just a little more out of sync, some guests will get sick.

Where Is This Going?

What will the future unfold for immersive entertainment? Well, pick up Gibson or Stephenson and read for yourself. Retuning reality by plugging a sliver of electronics into the base of your skull doesn't seem so far-fetched when you look at how technology has advanced in the last decade. *Brainstorm* and, more recently, *Strange Days* are feature films that use the idea of projecting multisensorial experiences directly into the brain, creating an illusion that becomes addictive far beyond chemical substances. In that context, our current motion simulators could be compared to manual typewriters; there's plenty of room for improvement.

Figure 26.4 Final version of the Enrol creature, a pivotal character in Seafari.

For me, the future has one main goal, which I hope will be realized soon: to make people fly. Out of all the motion experiences I know of, this is the ultimate thrill. If you've ever had a lucid flying dream, you know what I'm talking about.

There are compromises on every project; it's the nature of a collaborative endeavor. Intentions are spelled out, breaking old boundaries and charting bold new territories. Then, all the hype, show biz pitches, and authentic intentions are forwarded by the creative and technical team to the money men. Promises are made, and innovative technologies are sold. But whatever the pitch, you can rest assured that a 30-percent contingency is the *least* you'll need. You're charting new territory—how can your projected budgets be right on!? Maybe I'm being a bit cynical, but we always pitch a bit on the optimistic side. Ultimately, compromises happen; I have yet to fulfill my Dream of Flying.

All the technology is available right now. No new inventions, new film format, new digital sound system, or new Smell-O-Rama effects are needed. Give me the tools to make my people fly! I'm sounding a bit like Moses, but that's what it boils down to. I get frustrated when I know we have the tools to part the Red Sea, but we're always inches away from the optimum combination of projection system, theater design, seating configuration, and theatrical and ride-vehicle themeing to make the illusion of flight a believable reality.

The closest I came to it was a ride-film for MCA based on the second *Jurassic Park* movie. Phil Hettema brought me in to collaborate with him and Dale Mason to develop the ultimate motion-base experience. I did about six months of design development, but the attraction was unfortunately shelved. This project would have set a new standard for simulated attractions.

What I do for a living is put people into flying machines, yank them out of reality, and immerse them in a fantasy sensory experience, a feeling that we are more familiar with as children, when we fantasize about the future and our dreams are more lucid. Star Trek: The Experience, for Paramount Parks and the Las Vegas Hilton, is another step toward fulfilling my goal. Maybe I'm just one of those impossible-to-satisfy artists, or maybe I'm waiting to take that trode and plug into my cerebral implant. Then, I would no longer have to worry about archaic technology that always seems to cut the illusion short; I would be free to design the wildest fantasy I can conjure up.

Biography

Mario Kamberg has been a director of computer graphics and effects for most of his career. He recently completed work on Paramount Parks' Star Trek: The Experience ride-film attraction at the Las Vegas Hilton. He was director and production designer and directed the motion-base programming. Prior to that, he has worked as the creative director, director, director of motion-base programming, production designer, set designer, and show designer on motion-base ride-films and their themed attractions, television commercials, and television series for the following companies: Robert Abel and Associates, Midocean Motion Pictures, Silvercloud Productions, Digital Productions, Universal Studios Florida (Hanna-Barbera attraction and others), MCA Porto Europa, Japan, and others.

Chapter 27

McKenna on Digital Production

Sherry McKenna
Oddworld Inhabitants

Introduction

People often ask me how producing digital effects differs from producing traditional special effects (which involves models, miniatures, and motion control). They also ask how digital production for movies is different from that of commercials, ride-films, or videogames. In both cases, the two are becoming more similar in some ways and less so in others; recent work seamlessly blends them. But before addressing the differences, the question to answer is, What is producing? The basic process applies to any production project, regardless of method or format, and an understanding of that process is critical to anyone in the field.

The Process

The Bid and the Schedule

For a four-minute motion-based ride-film, a year-and-a-half production schedule is reasonable. Of that, there are three months of preproduction and three months of postproduction, which leaves a year for the actual production. That makes it sound easy—it's not like it has to be done in three days on a live-action set like a commercial. But a year is actually an aggressive schedule because of client approvals. For the most part, any other kind of digital production but a game takes less time.

First, somebody shows up with a rough storyboard. This person might be from a game company, movie studio, theme park, or TV network. Because the client doesn't know what's possible or affordable, the storyboard is not detailed; in some cases, there's only a concept and a deadline. For an action-adventure film, the client might say, "We want to have a plane fly between some mountains, then it meets another plane, then there's a chase, and one plane crashes." For a game the client might say, "We want a world that looks like illustrator X's style, we want this sort of protagonist, and here's the plot concept."

As a producer, I ask questions to help flesh out clients' ideas: "Can you say exactly what the plane is going to look like? What exactly is the character going to do?" At this initial stage, clients' conceptions of the effects they want are usually incomplete. They want a futuristic look, but they're not sure what kind of futuristic. They want two planes in a chase, but they don't know where. Every situation is unique; every client wants to create something that has never been done. And it's not unusual for a client to ask for two things that are mutually exclusive, like "perfect human motion of things that don't flex." It's not feasible to engage in a detailed design process before bidding a job; clients are in a hurry, and few production organizations can invest that much effort in a bid they may not ultimately be awarded.

Early on, I discovered that this situation refines an unusual ability in the producer. I was at Bob Abel's in 1977 when we did a complex animated Levi's commercial of a guy walking a dog. I spent two days figuring out how to figure out how much it should cost, analyzing every little part of each scene; it was a bear. Then, Bob Abel came in, took one look at the storyboard, and named the exact dollar amount that I had determined. I said, "How did you do that? I just spent two days working out each shot and setup." And he said, "It comes from a gut feel, from knowing how difficult things are." It's more about what you *think* something is going to take because you don't really know. You only know what you've done before, but clients ask for things they've never seen before. Bob just looked at it and thought, "Yup, that's difficult; it'll probably be done this way." Nothing can replace the gut reaction of experience—the same experience that won a Clio for that commercial.

In addition to estimating the style, number, and kind of objects to be created and the level of realism expected, a bid must anticipate extensive client involvement and revisions. It's impossible to predict how many iterations it will take before an item wins client approval, so accurate schedules are impossible. But clients expect to approve every aspect of the work—every object, scene, and motion. They want the opportunity to make their opinions known, and they expect you to revise—and continue revising—until the work satisfies their vision. I was computer graphics producer on the feature film *2010*, and we were doing the Jupiter shot. Peter Heinz, the director, said, "I want the surface of Jupiter to move the exact same way it does in real life, including the physics." And we said, "Well, nobody's ever moved the surface of any kind of a planet before, and we have absolutely no idea how to do it."

But he insisted. We hired Craig Upson from JPL and got the real data from NASA for the surface of Jupiter. It soon became clear that the clouds moved much too fast to look realistic, even though they were accurate. This is when you take some artistic license. Unfortunately, Peter could not be convinced, so we animated it accurately using a very difficult particle system at the time. And, of course, when he saw it, he said, "That was way too fast." And we said, "Uh-huh." That's the beauty and difference of digital tools; we could change it without torturously reanimating all those little particles and say very nicely, "OK, how would you like it to move?" To which he answered, "Well, I want it to move the way people would think it would move." Good idea.

To return to the bid issues, which become production issues, a three-day live shoot is going to take three days, even if you go into serious overtime. But the process of digitally designing and developing what ends up on the screen is completely different; what's hard and what's easy does not correspond. As you shoot live action, you're looking at whole scenes; in a digital production, you're combining individual elements to form scenes—much finer granularity. We create the objects, then we put them in motion, light them, and texture them to look like the real (or unreal) thing. There can be issues at any of these additional stages of the process.

Producing is about solving these problems; getting your work and the client's intentions to agree as soon as possible, without eliminating the client from the process and without getting dragged over budget. Sometimes it's about deciding to develop new software tools to do a trick nobody has ever done before. Sometimes, such decisions win you an award, but they always come at a price.

Preproduction

Once the budget has been established, it's time to work with the client to nail down the details. This is preproduction. We spend six weeks to three months to storyboard the entire production. Preproduction rarely involves much computer work; most of the work is colored pencils and airbrushes, creating fully rendered stills that show what each scene will look like. The stills should establish the mood and show the lighting and objects.

We, as producers, can exploit our technology more efficiently than can even the most sophisticated client, so it's good, when clients come to us, that they don't have the scenes worked out to the last detail. This allows the production house to get involved in the design—a situation that results in better production value. Were a client to storyboard everything beforehand, any good production company could still point out improvements that would save time and money. The more design work we do up front, the smoother things go in production. During production, we'll want to concentrate on choreography—design changes at that point would be very expensive and time-consuming.

Once we've completed preproduction, we know essentially what the film is going to be. As we move into production, the two primary concerns are communicating with the client and keeping the project on schedule and budget.

Now is when the folks at the production house are thinking "Oh, my God! I can never get this done in a year" while the client is thinking "A year? I can make as many changes as I want."

The Production

The review-revise-accept cycle is a major difference between live-action special effects and digital work. When you plan a live-action project, you know how many principals and crew members there will be and what can be accomplished in a day's work. Even if the client completely misunderstands your bid, live action has advantages over computer graphics. When you're shooting, clients can see the scenes you set up through the camera or the video assist. They can say, "Have him walk slower," and you do another take. The greatest advantage is that everyone knows that in a day there's time for a limited number of setups and a limited number of takes within those setups.

Somehow this falls apart when we move to digital production. It helps that, instead of a prop construction shop, we can depend on a constantly growing library of 3D objects to select, modify, and morph and on another library of textures to put on them. And we can always use a 3D scanner to replicate objects when necessary. We've created fictional worlds in which we are the masters—no longer held hostage by the laws of physics. But now that we have this creative freedom, clients also have the luxury of being able to change it, and change it, and change it.

That luxury has become the bane of our existence. Somehow, perhaps because digital production schedules are much longer than schedules using either live action or models and miniatures, clients forget that time is money. At what point does a production house say "enough"? If we were exploding a live plane, we would explode it once and live with it—no budget on earth would have room for two takes. If it's a model or miniature, you might have the budget to redo it a few times, but probably not more than that.

A digital client might say, "You know, I think it should be just a little faster." However, neither the client nor we can quantify how much faster. So we make it a little faster, and then the client thinks it's too fast or still too slow. Or worse, the client asks for a very specific change, then, when we show it, we discover that the client's visualization and the actual result of the specific change order are two different things. So, we redo it until the client finally approves—and everyone wonders why digital technology costs so much. Saul Bass, the graphic designer, did his very first digital animation on the Cray at Digital Productions—the AT&T logo—and took literally weeks to explore every possible minute variation before returning to his original idea.

It's still an expensive medium. The computers now cost less but aren't cheap, the salaries are higher, and the process is lengthy. There are many cases where it's more economical to use models and miniatures. But flexibility is a compelling reason to choose digital production even when it's not the least expensive approach. Sometimes, we'll change just one element in a digital effect, and the whole thing will seem new.

Ironically, it's at this stage, when both the client and the production house are in the dark about the precise nature of the job, that we have to create a schedule and budget. Projects are typically bid out to three or four production houses simultaneously, all of whom are in the same position. How do we go about submitting bids honestly? We don't—we guess. We don't know exactly what the objects are supposed to look like, how long they will take to create, or how much detail the client has in mind. So, we guess. Production houses have been guessing for a long time, but they are guesses nonetheless.

Managing the Process

I use a "brick wall" system for managing the review-revise-accept cycle. We give clients a detailed schedule that explains exactly how much time we intend to spend on each scene or transition. Within the time frame allotted for each scene, we'll make as many changes as the client wants. But, when the schedule says that we have to move on to the next scene, we move on. For example, say we have a twelve-scene film and we've determined that each scene should take a month to do. We've already agreed what the scene should look like during preproduction, so now we're primarily concerned with choreography, with nuance. We'll show clients what we intend to do every day. We'll offer them every possible opportunity to provide feedback, and we'll do everything we can to implement their requests. But, when the month is up, we start working on the next scene, except in cases where we've made a technical error. If it's our error, we'll spend all night and all weekend to correct it.

Even though we're clear about this procedure at the outset, some clients ask for creative changes after the cutoff date. Sometimes the people who work with us directly have several layers of management above them, and, even if they like it, their boss's boss might not. We leave this responsibility firmly in the hands of the client—it's the client's job to communicate within his or her organization. Internal disputes within the client's organization are extremely common and are a big part of the reason production houses are accused of running over budget. We try to develop schedules that allow time for these internal review cycles. But, once a schedule is agreed upon, it's my responsibility to stand firm; if the client wants changes after the cutoff date for any reason, I have to call it an overage and attach a dollar figure to it. All overages require two things: solid justification and a client's signature.

Another thing I do to manage the review-revise-accept cycle is ask clients to sign off on their comments and suggestions. I write down everything they say, and, once they're sure that what I've written down is really what they mean, I ask them to sign the piece of paper. For some reason, clients don't particularly like this idea. They're uncomfortable with the thought that we're holding them to something, but I'm actually trying to establish what requirements *we're* willing to be held to—something very different, indeed.

Some Solutions

Solving such problems more effectively requires two changes to the typical model currently used for digital production. To begin with, we need to tie time to money. Second, we can't continue to begin every project with a vague guess about budget and schedule. We need to rationalize the bidding process.

The best way to address the bid problem is for the client to say how much money they have for the computer graphics part of the production. This suggestion causes much anxiety; most clients flat out refuse to tell me and often remind me that they're getting bids from our competition. I'm not sure why clients are so unwilling to divulge the budget—especially since most top production houses deliver more than they're paid for. Their reputations are at stake.

Another means of addressing the bid problem is for the customer to do research up front and find out the going rates. For example, a ride-film along the lines of Seafari costs about $1 million a minute if it's a 35mm, 30-frames-per-second film. If a client intends to do more than that, such as 3D stereoscopic, 70mm, 60-frames-per-second or IMAX (the most unforgiving film format on the planet), it's going to cost more. To combine these in a stereoscopic IMAX or IMAX *Dome,* with underwater action, costs still more. By then, you're somewhere between $1.5 million to $2 million a minute. That doesn't mean you can't do a ride-film for $500,000 a minute. You can; you'll just get one of lesser quality, resolution, frame size, or some other variable.

If a digital production company knows the budget, they can design around it. We can tell the client if part of the storyboard is going to cost big bucks and recommend changes accordingly. If the client has $3 million, we might suggest a two-minute, 35-mm, stereoscopic piece that's only partially underwater, rather than 30 seconds of stereoscopic IMAX from a deep-water submersible.

A formal RFP (request for proposal) is how some larger companies like MCA handle this situation. These typically describe exactly what the client is looking for: all the components, the budget, and maybe even a basic treatment. Production houses have the opportunity to put as much effort into this proposal as they want. (Sometimes the client will even pay something toward the cost of developing proposals.) Because an RFP provides a lot of information up front, including the budget, the bids garnered are more likely to be accurate than traditional bids.

Some Harsh Reality

All this work requires artists, designers, and animators—good ones. When I started in the business, it was impossible to just hire staff; few people in the late 1970s had any experience, and no schools taught computer animation. So, we were resourceful. For modelers, we found architecture students; they had a sense of 3D space and understood blueprints. For coders, we hired engineering grads with strong math backgrounds. We went to the art schools for animators and technical directors; we needed folks who understood story, lighting, color, and perspective—we could teach them the software that our engineers wrote. Environmental Design grads from the Art Center in Pasadena could think in 3D and understood the issues of design. Photography and illustration majors were good candidates because they learned what light and shadow *do*, and they understand composition. Traditional 2D animators could be trained for 3D; they at least understood the art of motion, if not the art of emotion. Notice the term "art"; motion by itself is not enough.

Today, many schools offer degrees in computer animation; it's a terrible problem. Their graduates seem to have bypassed the fundamental courses in art. They know the software and the buzzwords, but do they understand what makes a great story, a great edit, or what makes a character come alive? Not at all. They have no concept of what storytelling is. They didn't learn *why* objects have transparency, reflections, and shadows. They can't paint with light; they don't even understand what it is. After being criticized for so long about hard-edged, unrealistic objects, we finally have a medium that can exercise both sides of the brain but have plenty of computer graphics majors who create emotionless characters, lifeless trees, and mundane backgrounds while the real art majors avoid the computer. So, we get folks with a little right-brain capability and a lot of left-brain thinking; you can see it in their passionless work. There is no love of nature, no motion caused by emotion. Schools are teaching what's easy and profitable to teach, not the grounding for artists' professional careers.

Summary

The differences between live action and digital production are narrowing as digital tools improve and the rendering engines get faster. The two are merging, and the fundamental process is the same—a process that has to do with human skills, not software features. Inventing new effects and never-before-seen tricks isn't the hard part of the job. Making sure clients feel they're part of the process is the hardest part. Production companies want customers to love not only the product but also the experience of working with us; we want them to come back. Producing is about managing the vendor-client relationship and providing a product that meets the customer's expectations on time and on budget. It's just communication—communication about unique illusions that even the artists at the keyboard may have trouble describing.

Biography

Sherry McKenna is president and co-founder (with Lorne Lanning) of the videogame company Oddworld Inhabitants. Their first game, Oddworld: Abe's Odysee, will be released in September 1997. She began her career working for Bob Abel, doing traditional special-effects during the period when he put special effects commercials on the map. She was involved in the 7-Up "Bubbles" commercial with the flying butterfly woman—one of the landmark commercials in the field of special effects—and in campaigns for Levi Strauss, Revlon, and Max Factor. From there, she went into digital production at Digital Productions, doing *The Last Starfighter, 2010,* and many high-end commercials. After that, she was show producer at Universal Studios for the Funtastic World of Hanna-Barbera, a motion-base ride-film, which opened in 1990. On this project, she accomplished the first substantive integration of 3D backgrounds and 2D character animation. From there, she went to Rhythm & Hues, Inc. as Vice President of their Special Projects Division, where they did Seafari and several other projects.

Chapter 28

Seamlessness

Richard Edlund, ASC
Boss Film Studios

Introduction

When I walked onto the set of *Multiplicity,* we had storyboarded the movie, we had discussed it, and we had blocked the scenes. But we also knew that Michael Keaton was an improvisational actor. The director, Harold Ramis, appreciates that. So we knew—or I knew, anyway—that I was going to have to be able to roll with the punches and think on my feet when a new idea came up on the set. Fortunately, the digital realm is flexible enough to handle that. Working digitally gives me great fulfillment and a greater sense of spontaneity and creative freedom than I've ever had.

The language of image-making is being reinvented, and digital is its grammar. Since we know we can digitally integrate all the elements in a film, whether they were filmed traditionally or rendered digitally, we are free to choose whatever technique will produce the best look for each individual shot. That freedom is undoubtedly the biggest blessing that digital technology has bestowed.

There's that word: "freedom." In filmmaking, we're now less tied than ever to the apron strings of technology. Not only do we have far fewer restrictions during the process of filming, but also computers provide surgical ability to manipulate any image already filmed. We have pixel-by-pixel control. In the days of analog technology, being able to break time down into frames per second made the effects possible. Now we can break down each one of those frames into 1,500×2,000 pixels (for a 35mm release print). "Seamless integration" has long been the Holy Grail of the visual-effects world, but now it's within our grasp.

With special effects, I always say you have to invent yourself out of a corner. The script paints you into the corner, then you have to invent a way to pogo out of it. And, we have a digital pogo stick, which is a much more fun tool than those analog-effects tools of the past. With every film we complete, we refine some new digital pogo stick for the toolbox, and it can be applied to any other piece of filmmaking—whether it's a major motion picture, a ride-film or a big-budget commercial.

At Boss, our tools are based on the script and modified for the script because scripts are like the weather—you can't ever predict them. The one thing you can predict is that scriptwriters are all going to the movies and seeing that virtually anything is possible. The result is that now they write virtually anything into the script. Form follows function. As I read it, the script dictates to me some idea of how, technologically, to achieve it.

On *Multiplicity*, our challenge was to film Michael Keaton performing with three clones of himself. In order to get out of those corners into which we would be inevitably painted, we had a trailer full of SGI equipment and technicians, and they were literally writing code on the fly. We would have one shot that required one approach, followed by a different shot that required a different approach, and the software had to be modified on the set to handle it, whether it was matting, split screen, lightning to be synchronized, or whatever.

Multiplicity's House of Mirrors

I had known *Multiplicity* director Harold Ramis since *Ghostbusters*, and I loved the new script; it's funny. The cloning idea was brilliant; I certainly needed a clone, and I knew a lot of other people who did.

While reading the script, I tried to think about the problems that would come up and their solutions. It was important to keep in mind that the film was a comedy—we wouldn't want to put restrictions on the actor to the point where it would suppress the creativity and spontaneity of his performance.

We needed a technology that would be relatively unnoticeable to the director and to the actors—one with which we could shoot various performances, one after the other, that we could composite on set so that we could immediately see the relationship from one performance to the next character, then those two characters in relation to the next character, and then those three in relation to the fourth. It needed to be done in a way that would give the director the confidence to move forward once he had seen the first performance.

There are directors—Robert Zemeckis comes to mind—who will design fantastic effects scenes as part of the movie, but Ramis has a different approach. There are few fancy effects scenes in *Multiplicity*, although there was plenty of clonal body contact and crossovers (hands or fingers of one character crossing in front of another)—all the natural things that would happen if you had four different actors playing the Keaton roles (especially since Michael Keaton acts with his hands and body a lot).

There were shots done with digital motion-control moves—all the shots in the movie had at least a motion-control follow-focus, even the locked-off shots. But the lock-offs were not used because they were effects scenes; that was just the way to play the scene. Ramis would have shot the film much the same way had he actually had four actors working. One of the most elaborate scenes shows three of the clones shaving in a bathroom that has two mirrors. You see nine Michael Keatons (three characters and six reflections), and it's a very complicated composite. But it's played for humor, not for awe.

I suggested using a corner mirror so that you get a reflection and a reflection of the reflection, and then you're on to another mirror so that you get double reflection. When this shot comes on the screen, the audience just cracks up without the script doing anything. They see all these Michael Keatons in there shaving—and each of the three characters has a different attitude and a different shaving approach. It's a very funny shot.

Our motion-control system enabled us to track and shoot partial green screens and achieve absolutely imperceptible moving splits. (The ability to extract perfect green-screen mattes allows freedom to be even bolder in the shots we design.)

The entire system depended upon "eye-line" cameras, in which Keaton would play the first scene to a stand-in with a Sony HandiCam from the position of Keaton's next performance. Keaton would play to the stand-in's video camera. Keaton's moves were tracked by a crew member off-camera with a spotting scope. The scope connected to a motion-controlled laser beam that followed Keaton's feet around. When he came to do his next performance for that take, the stand-in would hold a monitor positioned where his head had been in the previous performance, centered over the moving laser dot on the floor. If the laser moved, the actor followed it. This method worked to keep Michael's eye line always right on the button, which is extremely important. If your eye line doesn't match, the audience doesn't buy the shot because it doesn't look like the actors are playing to each other.

High *Technopia:* A New Film *Species*

Adding motion to filmed entertainment is a development as dramatic as adding sound to the silent movie. Whether you call them ride-films or motion-simulator films or motion-base films, this new genre is emblematic of the digital age. Creating the dynamic visuals that characterize a ride-film and then blending them together believably are tasks that are tailor-made for the digital studios of today. Today's ride-films call into play all the varied techniques of the modern film studio—from models, miniatures, and pyrotechnics to motion-control photography and 3D computer animation.

Among the many choices we make in doing a film, one of the most interesting is deciding which types of shots lend themselves to traditional models and which are better built in the computer. Sometimes, the real thing is better than its digital counterpart. While recent advances in particle system software are moving us closer to simulating explosions, for example, if you want a truly realistic pyrotechnic effect, there's no substitute for blowing things up.

Digital compositing enables us to mix and match effects. When Boss created the visual effects for the feature film *Outbreak* in 1995, we took a shot from a helicopter flying above a forest and digitally matted in fires, smoke, and explosions that had been shot elsewhere. This was possible because we were able to track the motion of the helicopter shot with impunity. The result looked so real that many people believed we had actually set a forest on fire. We did the same thing with the ride-film *Journey to Technopia* when it came time to add pyrotechnics. They look just like the real thing because they are.

Journey to Technopia, which we made for Taejon's Expo '93 in Korea, showed that traditional and computer graphics (CG) models can be integrated in elegant and economical ways. We used a full palette—we combined live-action sets with miniatures, with digital spaceships, with real-world explosions, with motion blur, and with digitally mirrored surfaces. We tracked the explosions, and, when a spaceship took a hit in the dogfight scene, it was replaced within a few frames by an explosion; then, the explosion would fly out of frame because we were dynamically moving through the scene. Using digital compositing techniques to incorporate the explosions and digital spaceships to give a more realistic looking fight, the *Technopia* dogfight scene, brief as it was, exhibited shots far superior to *Star Wars* or any other movie's digital dogfights.

In spite of the mix-and-match advantages I've described here, traditional models will soon be more expensive to use than computer modeling. Once you have a digital landscape modeled in your computer, you can reconfigure it or fly through it at other angles and speeds to create new sequences. We're already seeing increasingly complex elements, such as three-dimensional CG creatures that behave in believably astounding ways. The technology goes back and forth between different types of films and shows up other forms of digital display such as computer games. For example, the technology we developed to create the digital star of *Species* could be readily applied to a ride-film, and Boss has already reused it for computer game characters.

The *Species* technology, an instrumented, motion-capture system, takes a physical puppet and transforms it into a digital character. Four puppeteers manipulate the electric puppet, which has about 60 articulated joints. Positional data is transmitted from the joints to a dozen analog-to-digital (A-to-D) converters, each 3/8-inch thick and about the size of a postage stamp. The converters, located onboard the puppet, send this digital stream of information via a couple of ribbon cables to the main computer that records the movements. The computer does massive computation to generate a version from the chosen point of view and composites that in realtime on the background plate, which is in digital video. There's only a one-fifteenth-second computational delay (owing to the speed of light) between moving the puppet and seeing its actions displayed on a TV monitor as a 3D computer-generated creature. That's like Captain Crunch talking to himself around the world on the phone and listening to his echo.

This kind of realtime feedback is an effective way to give us directable, digital characters whose performances can be shaped on a set just like any actors'. Once such a character is modeled in CG, you can save money and potentially amortize the cost by having it recur in ongoing stories. Perhaps popular digital characters will emerge in the ride-film genre—the modern equivalent of old serials such as *The Purple Phantom Creeps!*

Rendering: *Batman Returns* with Penguins

A purely digital landscape allows filmmakers to easily choreograph every imaginable movement. The laws of gravity, scale, and inertia simply don't apply. Traditional techniques, such as filming models and miniatures using motion-control cameras, have more constraints. When you consider that a ride-film is a dynamic, forward-moving experience, if you're building it all in miniatures, you're burning up (flying over) miniatures at tens of thousands of dollars per second, and you can't create the kind of endless camera move that you can within a 3D computer space. Back when we were filming *Star Wars*, for example, we had to film a race through miles of the Death Star's trench using a model that was only about 60 feet long. Moving the camera at a high rate of speed, we could get only about a 12- to 14-frame shot. So, I wound up using the same trench—and the same three- to four-second piece—over and over, doing blends between shots. With today's fully digital models, this wouldn't even be an issue. Although our work remains as painstaking as ever, we no longer need a whole warehouse and thousands of plastic parts from hundreds of model Ferraris, P-51 Mustangs, submarines, garbage can covers, and so forth. The digital backlot has everything.

But against the improvements of camera choreography, you must weigh the actual appearance of the models. The cityscape required for *Technopia* was so large that to model it in the computer in sufficient detail would have been extremely time-consuming and thus costly. Creating believable surface textures and mapping them onto complex models is a big task; adding dents, scratches, and oil spots in CGI is expensively tedious work. If the goal is realism, there is always a temptation to add more detail simply because you can. Then another form of hard "reality" sets in—the rendering nightmare.

Typically, in the rendering nightmare, just when you think you've reached a solution, somebody pulls out a calculator and says, "Yeah, that's fine, but we need X number of machines and we've only got X minus Y machines." In the case of *Batman Forever*, for instance, somebody discovered that they had better scale their digital model back or they wouldn't be able to render all the needed frames by the year 2000!

Experienced filmmakers, whether they work with polygons, polymers, or props, know that the economics of illusion lie in building exactly as much as the camera needs to see, and no more. Given the complexity of the *Technopia* cityscape, it was clear that adding painted textures to real foam-core models was preferable to building an enormous database. The finished "miniature" city covered about one-third of our stage—some 70 feet by 40 feet. Another third of the stage was taken up by the camera system.

Even though our digital production capacity has increased tenfold since then, if faced with the same task, we would still seriously consider filming a traditional model. At the same time, while it made sense to fly the motion-control camera through the miniature city, the flying ships that filled the air were unquestionably better designed in 3D CGI. Our modelers created space-ships with mirror surfaces that reflected their environment better than anything we could have done with photographed miniatures.

Even as we amass a digital library of 3D props and models from which to draw, we'll continue to make decisions on a case-by-case basis. There's no single best way to do a thing because you'll never encounter quite the same situation and problem again.

When we were doing *Batman Returns*, there was a lot of expectation that it was going to be possible to put hundreds of real penguins wearing rocket packs on their backs into a shot that would be split-screened and composited. This was something we had reservations about. "Oh, yeah, they're trained," we were assured. But you put that kind of stuff on an animal and the animal basically spends a lot of time trying to get it off. So, we decided to try to digitize a penguin.

We brought a penguin in the studio, put it on a grid, and walked it around; we chilled the room to keep it comfortable. We digitized a penguin and then did a test of several penguins walking to camera, and they looked fantastic. They walked accurately, in the eyes of the camera, because penguins are fairly simple creatures—at least in terms of articulation. This was pre-*Jurassic Park*, so it was one of the first solid uses of digital creatures. Then, we realized that the penguin model was far too complex to render 500 of them in a couple of scenes. So, we had to rebuild it with many fewer polygons.

Another dilemma was in animating the penguins—directing the models. Penguins don't want to invade one another's space. So, we used a program written to enable several different penguin walk cycles and to assign each penguin a certain radius of activity. We set them off at different speeds and from different starting points, and they avoided one another automatically.

In Space, There's No One to Provide Fill Light

The look of *Star Wars* was shaped by the limitations of the filmmaking process at that time. Many people had seen actual space images by then because of footage sent back from Apollo and the moon landing. And, in fact, when something is out in space, it's lit by the sun and only the sun—single-source key light with no fill. Any secondary light source that might supply fill light, such as stars, is too far away and too dim to affect the shadow area. The effect is shiny and harsh; metallic equipment reflects jet black.

In *Star Wars*, there's plenty of fill light in space. We tried to keep the amount of fill as low as possible, but we had to deal with blue-screen spill, so we needed some fill light. Since it was a fantasy space movie, that wasn't a problem. Then, when we shot *2010* in 1984, we used a front-projected blue system, which didn't cause any spill. I had had to devise a no-spill, no-fill technique for the outer space scenes. Consequently, either it was shot front-and-back-light as a technique, or it was the front-projected blue on the actors.

In the early digital productions days, it was really a problem not being able to deal with this vast amount of picture information in the computer. Until it was possible to manage the information and be able to scan and record at high enough resolution to intercut with film, every time you pushed a button to output something, it was something like $30,000. You had to be really careful, and, if you wanted a test, you would be allowed just 16 frames. You had to be miserly with every step you made.

On *2010*, working in 65mm, we got about 14 film elements that were not to exceed something like 20 seconds each. We had a total of about 300 shots to do. We economized by having the shots done without a terminator on Jupiter and by having shots done in certain compositions that we could then flop, flip, mirror-image, crop, reposition, and so on, spinning many shots out of these generic elements. It must have cost at least half a million dollars just for the Jupiter element—with and without the Red Spot. And yet, these were important elements because space is so basically boring; it's hard work to make the shots interesting and breathtaking. To give animation to the surface of Jupiter was really important to the movie, so it was worth spending a lot of money. Those elements wouldn't cost anywhere near that today.

Today, even with digital techniques, it's still a nightmare to deal with all that data, and you still have to be miserly about things because we are still—and will always be—faced with directors wanting more than the budget offers.

That situation is permanent, no matter how cheap the technology becomes. Budgets stay about the same but more is expected for the same money, and the fact is, we can deliver it.

Flexibility on the Set

Economy is always part of the challenge. Besides affecting what you do in terms of computer modeling, it affects what you do on the live set, and thinking in budgetary terms is part of being a good effects supervisor.

In *Multiplicity*, there were a few instances where Harold Ramis wanted to do something and it just didn't seem to be worth the effort for that particular shot. But he would quickly understand that and say, "Let's save it for such-and-such a scene instead." If we had five effects shots earmarked for a certain scene or sequence, we would keep it to five shots; if we shot an extra one, we would subtract one elsewhere.

Doing my job well on such a movie includes not only thinking about finances but also being able to understand how everybody is feeling. It might happen that Ramis wanted to revise a shot fairly dramatically, or I would want to redo a live shot because otherwise it would take someone two weeks to fix it in CGI. But at the same time, I might see that Michael Keaton was reaching a boiling point or on the verge of a great performance. So, I would have been remiss in my duty to the director if I had said or done something that would hurt the quality of the live performance, the key to the film—computers or no computers, effects or no effects.

Everybody on the crew rose to the occasion, and Keaton was just great. He really picked up on the situation and understood its limitations, but he also understood the freedom that he had. It was an ultimate actor's opportunity for him; being able to play four different parts in the same movie.

Audiences, Nuance, and Pixels

In any new medium, once audiences get over the initial novelty, they begin to demand quality content. Those who succeed in the film genre, as in other forms of entertainment, will always be those who consistently tell the best tales. There are film directors who present amazing and dynamic stories, and there are people who depend on those directors to come up with the stories. Ride-films have yet to consistently meet this challenge, but we're now at a point in their development where they can and should join the ranks of real storytelling media.

The audience's expectation of effects has become more refined, so whenever we do something that's great, that's brand new—and I've said this ever since *Star Wars*—the audience will appreciate it, but two or three years later, it will be like looking at the original *King Kong*. The original *Star Wars* looks pretty rudimentary now, though it's great, dynamic filmmaking.

To compare today to the Paleotechnic era of photochemical effects, we used to say we could do just about anything, just as we're saying now in the digital age. And year after year, we would hear the suggestion that the technology had already gone as far as it could go. It dumbfounded me because, even within the hideous restrictions that the photochemical process put on us, there were still enormous possibilities. The unique position I was in, as I worked to solve the effects problems for each film, gave me tantalizing glimpses of the myriad other tricks we could try, effects we could do with just the tools at hand, not to mention all the ideas for *new* tools.

What we have now is not only an order-of-magnitude difference in the cost per frame but also an order-of-magnitude difference in creative freedom. For one thing, we have a different brand of technician to work with. The computer people that we were dealing with in those early digital days were primarily math- or science-oriented types such as Gary Demos and others who worked at Digital Productions. The new grads are more art-oriented. Finding a graphics programmer who could understand creative problems and filmmaking dynamics used to be practically impossible; now, we can even look for people with a sense of filmmaking.

We could work magic in special effects before, but only up to a limit. We had to trick and cajole and fight with the analog photochemical process in order to get our results. We could break the film down to each of its 24 frames per second and deal with each frame separately, but now we're able to break each frame down into individually addressable pixels. Not that we've mastered it by any means, but it's comparable to the transition from black-and-white to color film.

Pixels aren't everything. We did some tests to try to maximize the number of pixels because our camera was capable of delivering more pixel information. The standard resolution for computer graphics filmmaking right now is 1,500 by 2,000. We compared increasing the pixel resolution by 25 percent with increasing the bit depth from 8 to 12 and found that the increased bit depth was much more effective in apparent sharpness.

On *Multiplicity*, where we intercut all the time between effects shots and live-action shots, we were pretty satisfied with the level of resolution we were able to get from this system—and that was using anamorphic. (Anamorphic wide-screen or Panavision movies are shot with lenses that squeeze, so on the film it's about 1.2 to 1; you double that when you put on the anamorphic lens, so you wind up with about a 2.4 to 1 projection.) We did a movie called *Turbulence* in super 35 and actually achieved the element quality we need—plus we got some pretty outrageous composites.

Kicking the Soda Machine

A question I hear these days is, can the digital film, especially the ride-film, morph into an interactive attraction? I think that these are two distinct areas of entertainment and likely to stay that way. The so-called passive ride-film can be compared to a roller coaster ride. It gives the audience access to an experience that they couldn't otherwise have. It also preimagines a course of action in all of the things that go along with a ride-film, just as movies do. The director figures out the most dynamic way of presenting a particular scene, and I think he or she is better able to do that than the person who just walks in with a ticket. Today we live with television, where *everything* is pre-imagined; that creates a considerable market for the pre-imagined experience. So, I don't think the ride-film competes with the interactive ride experience. I think realtime, digital interactive attractions are primarily destined for home use because of economics.

A common design hazard, both in ride-films and interactive attractions, is that they can concentrate too much hardware in too few hands—too much expensive equipment and not enough rider throughput to cover the costs. The riders spend X minutes on the ride, and it takes Y more to get them on and off. There's a lot of complex hardware to maintain, and it's being used by people who aren't going to be careful with it. You've also got VR simulators generating CGI images on the fly (a fleet of Reality Engines in a back room kept cool by a 5-million-BTU air-conditioning system) and the headsets and other accessories the players use, which can create hygiene problems.

But, in the home, a person or a family will eventually have their own headsets, bodysuits, and accessories, all hooked up to the PC. There won't be the throughput or hygiene problems. We may someday get to the point where we can cookie-cut these things and crank them out for $9.95, but right now the technology seems too complex, too expensive, and too difficult to maintain in order to get the mass-market buck.

Film-effects production is by its very nature obsessive, involving long hours; with computers, it's more important than ever to know how to set limits. There are still only 24 hours in a day, and you have to leave yourself and the crew time enough to do the job. Rather than driving each other—rather than becoming computer-driven ourselves—how do we drive the technology to make things comfortable for us? Digital technology can be grease for the wheels; it makes possible the combination of all the elements, tools, and techniques.

I was frankly getting bored with photochemistry because we had run up against the same limitations time after time. I got into doing commercials when video-effects commercials became popular. And, after working with devices such as the Harry, with all those bells and whistles, it was really hard to go back to analog.

Look at William Wilder's *Ben Hur.* In order to create the epic chariot race, the stands had to be filled with many extras. The effects depended primarily on optical split screens and matte paintings. Other than that, it was pretty much physical effects with the exception of a few ingenious photographic touches. That movie would be much more readily doable today. You could multiply a crowd and add animation to it in a way that would appear thoroughly convincing, as if it consisted of 100,000 people.

The future of digital technology seems limitless, and that means we still have a long way to go. For extended film sequences and ones with a static camera, cost-effective CGI shots don't yet look realistic enough. In most current productions, the shots that look real are the quick ones, just a little too short to scrutinize.

But now, we control the magic as never before. Unlike the days of photo/chemical/optical technology, we no longer have to know where to kick the soda machine to get a bottle out of it. As digital equipment becomes more facile, we're able to do more in less time. Whether or not the creatives and the folks who write the checks will be satisfied is another question. What always keeps rising is the level of expectations.

Biography

Richard Edlund, ASC, founder of Boss Film Studios, is a four-time Academy Award winner for the visual effects in the *Star Wars* trilogy and *Raiders of the Lost Ark.* Mr. Edlund's work has been honored by Oscar nominations for six other motion pictures, including *2010, Ghostbusters, Poltergeist, Die Hard,* and *Alien 3,* as well as by three Academy Science-Technical Class Two awards. In addition to ride-films and many commercials, his company's feature film credits include *Batman Returns, Ghost, Cliffhanger, Outbreak, Species, Multiplicity, Turbulence, Desperate Measures, Air Force One,* and *Starship Troopers.*

Chapter 29

Theme Parks: Laboratories for Digital Entertainment

Christopher Stapleton
Universal Creative, Universal Studios Recreation Group

Introduction

As a child, my theme park was the Smithsonian Institution, the leading innovator in interactive learning environments. I felt like an adventurer, able to transcend time and space—to actually live the greatest events in history as an ancient warrior, an astronaut, or a dinosaur. Worlds and centuries were vividly encapsulated within a few buildings on the Mall. Unlike in most museums of the time, the exhibits didn't spoon-feed facts with static displays. I was immersed in an interactive environment where I discovered every detail on my own, as if I were Marco Polo, Jules Verne, and Neil Armstrong all at once.

In the 1970s, when an IMAX theater first opened at the National Air and Space Museum, I even fulfilled my lifelong dream of flight. With the technology of large-format 70mm film, the movie *To Fly* (on a screen five stories high) made me feel weightless in body and spirit. I became Icarus, exploring clouds on my wings. My only disappointment was that I couldn't leap into the screen.

It wasn't until *Scientific American* put a data glove and its cyber-reflection on the cover that I realized the technology of virtual reality could take me through the looking glass of the screen. Potentially, I could wrap myself in technology and be immersed in the worlds I explored as a child. Ever since then, I've pursued ways to set the public's imagination afire with digital technology; theme parks are a most natural environment for this work.

Reaching the Audience

Unfortunately, in entertainment, digital technologists encounter a dilemma. The technology is moving forward while the audience seems to be devolving into numb "couch-" or "ride-potatoes." Could it be, as Michael Schrage of the *Los Angeles Times* says, that technology has done too much for us?

When reading a book or listening to a story, we use our imaginations to flesh out details, characters, backgrounds, and story. Audio media give us voices and music; cinema floods us with visual details without demanding anything in return; television even laughs and applauds for us. As exciting and interactive as the new digital media are, can we reach an audience unaccustomed to participating?

The future of digital entertainment depends on new inventions that will reintroduce audiences to interactivity. New concepts need not only to interact with an individual's imagination but also to stimulate social interaction. Theme parks are an ideal environment in which to solve this problem, but few in the industry realize the potential. Consumed with an obsession to satisfy demand, the industry keeps repeating yesterday's blockbusters—ones born in passive media. To lead the industry into the next generation, we must constantly test the market for the undiscovered potential within the technology and the audience.

Creators of revolutionary entertainment concepts in the past have all had live arenas in which to experiment and refine their new ideas: the Romans had the Coliseum, Shakespeare had the Globe, P. T. Barnum had the Big Top, and Walt Disney had his theme park. (Even television had its studio audience, before the laugh track.) Each was dependent on a live audience for immediate feedback to their risk-taking accomplishments. Theme parks can employ this same opportunity by becoming laboratories in which to experiment with the new digital media.

How Can We Inspire the Industry to Experiment?

> *You don't satisfy need, you create need.*
> Peter Brook

Audiences ask for what they know; they don't know how to ask for something that hasn't been invented. Currently, parks imitate the competition instead of exploring innovative concepts. To follow this pattern will further saturate the market—not stimulate it. The concept of "doing the same but better" resists change and stunts our potential growth.

It typically takes several years to bring an attraction from concept to completion, which doesn't allow new technology to take the fast track to a public audience. As a consequence, hardware-based attractions like Jurassic Park, The Ride and the Indiana Jones Adventure are designed as "instant classics" frozen in time. They don't change from the original concept until an eventual upgrade, usually a decade or so later. An assembly plant in Detroit has more flexibility to change with the times than does a theme park. Theme park attractions must be able to take better advantage of technology as it develops.

Theme parks attract a rich demographic cross section of patrons ready to physically immerse themselves with total trust and abandon. They look forward to letting down their guard and enjoying concepts that seem to involve risk. Audiences at Nickelodeon Game Lab (which experiments with new ideas for game shows) are thrilled to think that they become partners in the creative process. They love being the first on their block to experience something new (which starts an ever-widening circle of promotion when they return home and brag to their friends).

Since experimentation does take risks, theme parks are an ideal place to take some careful risks; audiences have plenty of other opportunities within the park to compensate for the occasional disappointment. This provides the greatest asset to innovation—the ability to afford the risk of failure.

Experimentation as Entertainment

Fueled by audiences' constant demand for new attractions that push the envelope of their experience, theme parks must aggressively seek new forms of fantasy that will attract audiences already living in a technically savvy home entertainment environment. Guests, especially in destination parks (those that require travel and overnight accommodations like Universal and Disney), want new experiences that are worth more than the price of admission, hotel, and airfare.

The best way to push the envelope is to design an actual open laboratory where research and entertainment come together to test bold concepts on the public—not to exhibit new tricks, but to evoke discovery on the part of participants; not to imagine the future, but to make them actual participants in its creation. Theme parks have a decided advantage over other entertainment purveyors; our products don't have to be mass-produced, broadcast, or distributed. One-of-a-kind installations are independent of standardization and compatibility issues. Attractions can evolve as insights occur. Cultivating a new mindset would release us from tradition, encourage participants' natural feelings and impulses, and activate a free flow of ideas.

The Future: Vision Versus Illusion

The only problem with anything of tomorrow is that at the pace we're going right now, tomorrow would catch up with us before we got it built.
Walt Disney

Before I became involved in the theme park industry, I visited the newly opened EPCOT Center (Experimental Prototype Community of Tomorrow) at Walt Disney World. Rather than being amazed by futuristic ideas, I discovered that theme parks have not changed much since the old ride-through dioramas of nineteenth-century Coney Island. They're bigger and better, but guests still sit passively in pods as their bodies are fed assembly-line style through elaborately animated sets. The EPCOT experience wasn't truly experimental; it didn't require participation, and the results were predetermined. At the Horizons pavilion, attendants wearing bell-bottoms in the Mod-style decor made it look more like a trip to yesteryear than to tomorrow. The flaw in the design was that it tried to predict the future instead of create the future.

The only way to predict the future is to invent it.
Thomas Edison

Thomas Edison had the right idea. It's only through the innovation derived from experimentation that we can discover the future. This potential has remained dormant because most theme park attractions are hardware-based and dependent on a linear, mechanical process to deliver the experience to the audience. The experience is reproduced for every participant every time. Before beginning an experiment, we cannot know the results; we can only select the elements to combine. Two of the best elements for real experiments are the essence of digital technology: interaction and change. EPCOT's latest attempt at the cutting edge, Innoventions, alludes to this concept, but the attraction was designed in the same old paradigm—a glorified display-window/video arcade.

Inventing the Future

The hybrid or the meeting of two media is a moment of truth and revelation from which new form is born. For the parallel between two media holds us on the frontiers between forms that snap us out of the Narcissus-narcosis. The moment of the meeting of media is a moment of freedom and release from the ordinary trance and numbness imposed by them on our senses.
Marshall McLuhan

When I arrived in Los Angeles in the 1980s to work for Universal Studios, I wanted to pursue what I believe is the potential of theme parks: to combine media within a live forum. In New York City, I had been working with the immediacy of the theater, the power of film, the reach of television, and the dynamics of interactive computer graphics. There was no opportunity to combine them because each branch of entertainment had its own style and attitude and often looked askance at the others.

During my interview at Universal, I saw the model of the Back to the Future, The Ride prototype and knew this was the place to be. Within its hybrid of media, I saw a new medium being born. It not only used the IMAX theater of my youth but also combined it with a hemispherical screen and a motion-base simulator . . . talk about *flying*! I was compelled to leave the more traditional forms of entertainment behind. Even though theme parks tended to be viewed as the bastard child of art and entertainment, they had what was needed—diverse audiences, rich resources, expansive reach, and a playful nature.

After helping to create five multimillion-dollar theme park attractions on three different continents (Universal Studios Florida; Sanrio's Puroland, Japan; Gardaland, Italy), I felt that the industry's process for creating attractions was stuck in a rut of formula, standards, and tradition. I decided to look outside the industry for innovation. And I found that the burgeoning community of Orlando, Florida was teeming with research institutes and corporations focused on advanced R&D for military and aerospace industries.

Operation Entertainment: Inspiring an Industry to Experiment

> *We have learned that beneath the surface of an ordinary everyday normal casual conscious existence there lies a vast dynamic world of impulse and dream, a hinterland of energy which has an independent existence of its own and laws of its own: laws which motivate all our thoughts and our actions.*
>
> Robert Edmund Jones

Many of today's fascinating technological advancements originated in the defense and aerospace industries, where government and academic laboratories accelerated the discovery process through aggressive research initiatives. The cold war left us with a war-chest-turned-toy-chest of exciting tools and solutions in need of new applications. Until now, the entertainment industry has enjoyed the use of these toys without having to pay for their development.

These tools created innovative attractions that took theme parks by storm. Attractions like Universal's *Back to the Future:* The Ride, Disney's Star Tours,

John Waldron's Virtuality, Iwerks' Loch Ness Adventure, and Virtual World's BattleTech were new to entertainment, but they merely mimic government research that had cost taxpayers millions of dollars to develop. When defense money dwindled, entertainment seemed the ideal new customer.

My interest in virtual reality led me to Jacquelyn (Jacki) Ford Morie, an innovative artist and scientist who worked with the University of Central Florida's Institute for Simulation and Training (IST), an academic laboratory doing government research. Together, we laid the groundwork for a research initiative called Operation Entertainment. This project combined IST's mission of transferring military technology to the private sector with the insatiable appetite of the entertainment industry for new ideas.

> *The great discovery of the nineteenth century was the discovery of the technique of discovery.*
> Alfred North Whitehead

Our goal was to create a nurturing environment for experimentation and discovery. This would bring the curiosity of scientists together with the energy and drive for product from entertainment professionals. We invited creatives in entertainment to join us in the laboratory environment to discuss challenges in the industry. We demonstrated state-of-the-art technology to industry professionals, and, in return, they advised us on its application to entertainment. We then developed research proposals that explored solutions for entertainment and new commercial outlets for the developing technology.

The largest obstacle was bridging the mindset of academics (accustomed to open-ended research contracts) with that of entertainment leaders who wanted to buy products off-the-shelf as if they were at an IAAPA (International Association of Amusement Parks and Attractions) convention. The prejudices on both sides were equally extreme. Laboratories saw entertainment groups as a source of loose, fast money, and entertainment leaders viewed academic research as a never-ending drain of funds.

Toy Scouts: Innovation in Fun

> *The most important sense is the sense of wonder.*
> Jacquelyn Ford Morie

The most exciting results came from our work with the Toy Scouts, where we invented new virtual reality and telepresence games. The scouts were students mentored by IST researchers who worked after regular lab hours with entertainment professionals from major studios. We helped the students expand their raw ideas into real-world entertainment solutions.

Inspired by Nickelodeon Studios (MTV Networks), we took an irreverent look at arcade-style games to overcome the typical push-button interfaces. Our goal was to develop full-bodied, physically challenging games using innovative interfaces like trampolines, surfboards, and bungie jumping. The Toy Scouts developed ways to put a participant's entire body into a physical VR experience. Through their input, sweat and energy replaced a single cramped digit.

The 1940s concept of push-button-ease had no place in the "Just Do It"–"No Fear" generation of the Toy Scouts. Their game concepts quickly went beyond shoot-'em-up violence to games of athletic skill and creative imagination. In one, the player would "pump-jump" (jump up and down on an elastic device) to gain altitude in a virtual environment in order to glide down through a 3D obstacle course on a surfboard. In another, the player had to jump, crawl, twist, and turn to find the way out of a virtual three-dimensional maze created by a sweep of his or her own gloved hand. Nose Ball required the players to use their own noses as paddles (not as strange as it sounds for a stereographic simulation).

The greatest revelation was social, not technical. An electrifying environment was created by the free flow of ideas that yielded tremendous results in spite of limited time and money. Teenagers and adults gave up their Friday nights for a new kind of fun. There was a heightened level of serendipity and spontaneity between seasoned professionals learning how to use entirely new sets of tools and students who gained experience with real-life problems. It was the most creative group I had the pleasure of working with since leaving New York City—maybe because most of the scientists saw themselves as artists.

> *The artist picks up the message of cultural and technological challenge decades before its transforming impact occurs. He, then, builds models or Noah's arks for facing the change that is at hand.*
>
> Marshall McLuhan

Universities, from computer science to the art department, provide a rich, under-utilized resource for the industry to explore the future of high-technology entertainment. The Toy Scouts proved that such collaboration can help create a new breed of talent and product and foster a new approach to the creative process. The ever-tightening constraints of production that have stifled both talent and product can be relieved by a university/industry collaboration that would jump-start the long-awaited "revolution" in digital entertainment.

The Pasadena Art Center College of Design, which has historically looked to industry for support, currently demonstrates this potential. Design instructor Norman Schrueman brings in the likes of Universal Studios, Warner Brothers, and Sony to expose students to real-world scenarios. His program has ignited an almost giddy enthusiasm in entertainment leaders unaccustomed to a forum of unrestrained imagination. The next step is to develop a permanent symbiosis that continuously brings fresh ideas to market and stimulates new approaches to the educational process.

Technological Playground of Ideas and Dreams

We saw that, through uninhibited play, new avenues of discovery could be found and that, through uninhibited exploration, new avenues of play were discovered. An open laboratory was the ideal model for an attraction that could help develop both the product and the audience. We wanted to bring the model into a public venue, where a realtime feedback loop could be created that would accelerate the pace of bringing inventions to market. A cross between MIT's Media Lab, MTV, and the local playground, it would be exciting to a broad range of participants (both genders, not just young males).

This idea led Jacki and me to create "The Edge." The challenge was to create a public venue that could successfully entertain while producing useful research results and that, most of all, would make the audience a part of the discovery process.

SIGGRAPH's The Edge

The International SIGGRAPH conference has been a leading showcase of technology for over 20 years and has increasingly influenced the look of modern entertainment. As part of the 1994 conference in Orlando, we created The Edge as a forum to introduce new discoveries to the public and to use experimentation both as entertainment and as a catalyst for change.

The Edge was designed to spark collaboration between inventor and audience. It allowed the exhibits to change every day based on input and feedback from the previous day's interaction with the audience. Over the course of the week, spontaneous collaborations formed new exhibits on the floor and in cyberspace. The audience itself also changed by discovering new avenues of interaction. They became more involved by having hands-on influence on the development of new ideas. The Edge broke new ground by removing established boundaries of technology, culture, age, and preconceived ideas of both the inventor and the audience.

Levels of Play

The environment of The Edge was designed so that technology could break out of the confines of its box (monitors, CPUs, kiosks). With the use of projections, lighting effects, and telepresence, we created an ever-changing "architecture of light" that expanded each player's experience to include a larger audience. The environment engulfed all of the attendees so that everyone became a part of the experience.

We directed each exhibit to have three levels of simultaneous participation: browser, spectator, and active participant. We tried to make each level of participation rewarding so that attendees felt satisfied at any chosen level. The Browser could skim the content and decide if, what, or when to explore further; his or her enjoyment comes from sparking the imagination and the social aspects of the event. A Spectator could observe active participants' experience, either in anticipation of his or her own play or as vicarious entertainment. The Active Participant could interact directly with the exhibit and often with other participants or the inventor. The few active participants, on display to the others and aware of being observed, were crucial parts to the theatrics of the event. If there's enough payoff on the other two levels of participation, this level is not burdened with over-extended queues.

The Arena of Play: The Importance of Location

A key aspect of entertainment venues is their location. From destination theme parks to local malls, audiences are drawn out of their homes by the lure of entertainment and social interaction. Having left the secure surroundings of home, being in the public arena heightens the sense of energy and adventure of the experience.

Their suspension of disbelief is intensified by being immersed in a specially themed physical world, as well as the imaginary destination of the game or ride. The lure of danger combines with a guarantee of safety, letting us experience things we wouldn't attempt in real life. Our guard is down; we trust the creators of the entertainment.

Prior to the creation of Virtual World's Battletech, digital entertainment venues consisted of video arcades with rows of play units in a store front, lit only by neon and fluorescent light. No matter how good the game, the environment had the appeal of a pool hall or peep show. Kids had a better chance of getting permission to go to the tattoo parlor, where at least they would have something to show for the money spent.

Today's competition for larger audiences is driving more design emphasis on the physical environment of arcades. They're growing more like amusement parks and working to improve their image and demographics. DreamWorks and SEGA are venturing with MCA to create the next generation of sites, and there are efforts like SEGA's seven-story "futuractive" mega-arcade, SEGAWORLD, in London.

But the look of digital entertainment hasn't broken out of the cold metallic/neon image that, in time, will be as "period" as old episodes of Star Trek. Designing for change is as important to the physical environment as it is with the technology. Within our experiment, The Edge, the design was not about decor or themeing; it was how to make people more comfortable with both the technology and with one another.

> *Contrary to popular belief, The Edge is not cutting. It is, in fact, rather warm and fuzzy. So warm that it melts the boundaries between art and science, between academia and entertainment, between the artificial and the actual.*
>
> Linda Jacobson

Digital entertainment in the future will break out of its stereotype and have diverse styles such as hi-touch environments, retro-mechanical interfaces, or soft, graceful ride experiences. The environments need to be as diverse as the audience; the "digital" experience should not be segregated to hi-tech arcades.

Capacity

> *So I began two days of what I came to think of as voluntary imprisonment slogging back and forth along endless roped lanes.*
>
> James Yenckel, *Washington Post;* reviewing a theme park visit.

Theme park attractions have been synonymous with queues. They're slaves to capacity because poor capacity either prices an attraction beyond what guests will pay or makes it unprofitable to operate. The faster you can funnel people through gates, fit them into vehicles, and slide them down tracks, the better.

Capacity is the single greatest obstacle to incorporating interactive technology in parks. When adding three seconds to the typical dispatch time can decrease the THC (theoretical hourly capacity) by 10 percent, operators cannot afford to have guests waste time making decisions, learning the technology, getting in and out of equipment, or adjusting helmets. Attractions can fail, not because of low quality, but because of low capacity.

The Cultural Phenomenon of the Sports Arena

Digital games need the ability to play to a larger audience in order to increase capacity and produce more opportunity for revenue (in food and merchandise concessions) to offset the cost of technology. Sports arenas provide an excellent example. The success of out-of-home digital entertainment will depend upon creating public environments that appeal to the entire family on many different levels at once. This potential could easily evolve within collegiate competition, where university science, art, and performance programs can collaborate with the athletic department.

The Spectator: Vicarious Experience

Being a spectator isn't necessarily passive. The advantage of being a spectator is that you can be a participant with anonymity in a crowd. Even though not participating directly, fans play an active role in influencing the outcome of the game. This allows people to express themselves in a nonthreatening forum. It also provides the entertainment experience at higher volume and lower cost. The online spectator market is a huge potential extension of this involvement. The fact that 99 percent of the people who enjoy football do not play hasn't hurt the popularity of the game. Theme parks can capitalize on online access to parks in ways that hype and enhance the actual attraction without diluting the firsthand experience.

The Spectator: Active Experience

Allowing spectators to actually have a controlling influence on the experience is far more direct than cheering on a team as a fan. Perhaps the best example of this is the interactive audience participation system that Loren Carpenter debuted at the 1991 and 1994 SIGGRAPH conferences. It not only allowed for 3,000 to 5,000 simultaneous players but also did so while building a level of excitement that had the audience shouting and cheering with total involvement just moments after it began.

For this game, each member of the audience was given a small two-sided wand as a controlling device. The wand could be turned front or back toward a video camera that read (and showed) it as a red or green pixel in the overall floor plan projected on a screen. The more pixels of one color that were "on," the greater the value fed to the game. The audience, divided into two sides, democratically controlled a pong-style game or a flight simulator. So, if the left side of the audience was showing 50 percent of each color, the plane would go straight; if 60 percent were red, the plane would roll slightly to the right; if 90 percent red, it would bank sharply to the right; and so on.

One surprising outcome of Carpenter's game was that the audience did not perform at an average level, as might be expected, but performed better than average. One Pong game could not be stopped because neither side missed. Another outcome was that the collective did not play conservatively, but played quite boldly. The first large audience to try the experiment immediately performed a perfect loop with an almost perfect landing. In addition, each individual audience member could immediately register his or her influence on the outcome, which heightened the collective fervor. A relatively simple concept on a large scale proved to be quite a revelation. It was equal to transforming a single-viewer nickelodeon to a projection theater serving a massive audience. The implications of these results are both social and financial.

The Player: Teamwork

Another way to bring about more complex social interaction in digital entertainment is to construct scenarios for people to interact with one another. The sense of team play along with competition is something for which we have an innate affinity and desire.

The forerunner of digital team play environments is the U.S. military's SIMNET (SIMulation NETwork). This set of large-scale networked Abrams M1 tank simulators proved to be an effective training device, not in how to handle a specific vehicle, but in team communication. Nonmilitary users who get to try SIMNET tend to have a great time, even though they aren't usually put into a goal-driven scenario but instead are given a free arena in which to play. The fun comes from communicating with other players in the simulator (a gunner, the commander, a radio officer, and a driver) and other simulators.

Attempts to date to recreate these team player environments in location-based entertainment systems (Loch Ness Adventure and BattleTech) have met some success but still don't reach the complexity or dynamic level that the decade-old SIMNET achieved. Recently, however, the expertise has begun to flow the other way, from entertainment to the military. Late in 1996, the most successful multiuser game ever designed, Doom II by id Software, was adapted by the Marine Corps Modeling and Simulation Management Office— a branch of the training and education division at Quantico, Virginia—to provide further development of a fireteam-level (4-person) tactical decision-making simulation. "Marine Doom" is certain to be only the first example of putting the online entertainment industry's content design to work in the military.

Off the Beaten Track

Leave the beaten track occasionally and dive into the woods. You will be certain to find something you have never seen before. Of course, it will be a little thing, but do not ignore it. Follow it up, explore around it; one discovery will lead to another, and before you know it you will have something worth thinking about.

Alexander Graham Bell

When Alexander Graham Bell invented the telephone, he had no idea how his invention would affect the world economy. It happened in small increments—one step at a time. The big advances, the explosion of the inevitable, happened when it fell into the hands of the people. The entertainment industry could learn from this example.

Unleashing the dormant potential of digital entertainment depends on the free flow of ideas, with an emphasis on process over product. This challenges the golden carrot of exclusive ownership of intellectual property rights, which limits much product development. All the ingredients are in place for a revolution in the entertainment industry. Only our mindset needs to change for a transformation to occur. Technology is the easy part; the difficult part is changing mindsets. The audience wants to do more than just experience a theme park: It wants to interact, to give full rein to the imagination and emotions. It wants to *play!*

With play, interaction comes naturally; you need neither a refined nor an educated audience, nor do you have to train or motivate participants. Play is intuitive, self-motivated, and enthusiastic. Most of all, play is imaginative, filled with the fantasies and dreams of the individuals involved—the ideal frame of mind in which to experiment interactively.

Biography

Christopher Stapleton is from Universal Creative at Universal Studios Recreation Services and is a Producer for Universal's Islands of Adventure, opening in 1999 in Orlando, Florida. He has spent the last 20 years as a creative principal developing experiences and environments for entertainment, marketing, and education. His positions have included producer, creative director, design director, and production designer. His work includes projects for film, television, theater, theme parks, museums, computer graphics, retail, restaurants, corporate marketing, and communications from Tokyo, Japan, to Milan, Italy. He has created projects for Walt Disney World, Nickelodeon Studios, Paramount Parks, MTV Networks, Dollywood, and Sanrio.

Mr. Stapleton pioneered the use of interactive computer graphics for marketing with IBM and served as Entertainment Consultant for the Institute for Simulation and Technology, Visual Systems Laboratory, in Orlando. He has been especially active within the ACM/SIGGRAPH organization, where he is chair of the 1998 Outreach Program; was Co-Chair of The Edge (1994), an emerging technology showcase; and was founding Chair of the Orlando chapter. His M.F.A. degree is in design for film and his B.F.A. degree is in design for theater at New York University, Tisch School for the Arts.

PART 6

Trends in the Business of Entertainment Technology

The evolution of high-tech entertainment began outside the home in festivals, fairs, museums, and later, amusement parks and arcades. Our first chapter covers the evolution of the arcade industry and what makes videogames successful. Then, theme parks came into existence in mid-century and became an indispensable marketing vehicle for the Hollywood studios. They've since expanded to include profitable offerings that have nothing to do with the rides. The next step was to move out of the parks. Disney's touring themed ice shows are evergreen, and the recent hit Broadway show of *Beauty and the Beast* quickly spread to three continents. Warner Brothers and Disney built profitable chains of retail outposts in key shopping locations, enhancing brand presence at the same time.

In the meantime, interactive home entertainment mushroomed in quality, variety, and volume—to about $8 billion annual gross revenue. The new technologies have accelerated the rates of change, raised the stakes, created new market niches, and redefined the competitive landscape. This competition triggered several responses by the out-of-home entertainment industries. Most seek to combine shopping, entertainment, socialization, and food. Themed restaurant chains make dinner more exciting, and Location-Based Entertainment centers (LBEs) are becoming more cost-effective. Malls lease space to entertainment tenants and study Universal Studios' CityWalk. Multiplex theaters add new film formats. Video arcades are going upscale, and theme parks are poised to take even the attractions outside the gates. Categorizing becomes useless; the competition is Darwinian. At least part of the recreational offerings at these sites can be changed out as fast as the retail stock, which is good news for all creators of digital entertainment.

Modern LBEs began about 1990 as an outgrowth of video arcades and military simulator concepts. The first generation had hardware and cost hurdles to overcome, and relatively low image quality. In Part 6, two pioneers in the field recount their efforts to come up with a winning formula. Such simulators are a next step for major entertainment companies as they pursue new revenue streams for their top properties in every reasonable market niche. In feature films, that concept is embodied in the phrase "print to plush," meaning that a successful film's negative is "printed" into every viable medium—even, where appropriate, stuffed animals. Computer hardware is approaching the quality threshold for theme parks' broad demographics, so ideas that have kicked around for 30 years are being dusted off. It's time to test the water with several digital offerings. GameWorks, a joint venture by Universal Studios, Dream-Works, and SEGA, began rolling out locations in the spring of 1997. Sony's large, well-thought-out San Francisco site and others will follow.

Later, themed multiplayer simulator sites in major malls will be linked to a theme park attraction's virtual world server—physical outposts of the park. Their virtual worlds will be embedded with adventures, populated by the park's licensed characters, and accessible from home via the Web. At that point, the parks will have ensured that their characters and properties are maximally available to as many customers as possible at all times. All the escalating efforts described here are essentially ways of enhancing *distribution*, perhaps the area of greatest innovation for the next five years.

Meanwhile, back at home, the entertainment conglomerates will soon encounter a new, fast-growing category of decentralized competition: small (and very small) low-cost producers of original, media-rich episodic and live content delivered at low cost on the Web. The result will be more styles of rapidly evolving pop culture for the public to consume. This situation is already established in the music industry. Most of the independent music business—genres like acid house and ambient dub—is a result of synthesizers, digital recording, sampling, and collage techniques used by individual artists on easily affordable equipment.

Affordable tools for similarly sophisticated, independently produced visual entertainment forms are not far behind; the techniques are already well known. In the late 1970s, (Colossal) Pictures of San Francisco began developing them for the groundbreaking Blendo style at great expense and effort, using juxtaposition, layering, and sampling all of media history. Now that the hardware contortions and high cost are disappearing, those techniques are more a matter of talent, or the lack thereof. Some extraordinary new genres of media-rich Web entertainment will emerge from the hubbub: linear, nonlinear, and multiuser. One chapter here addresses preconditions for successful multiuser virtual worlds, the likely site for several new genres.

Online applications will blur the distinction between in-home and out-of-home entertainment. All that matters is that the customer develop a relationship with the licensed property, whether by becoming a character, participant, or audience.

Our first author, Mark Stephen Pierce of Atari, has spent most of his professional career in the video arcade business. His chapter explains the "how" and "why" of that industry and the ways it's connected to other entertainment channels. Jordan Weisman and David Kinney are key pioneers in the business of networked LBE simulators. I asked them to describe how they founded and developed Virtual Worlds and Fightertown and what does and doesn't work in that business model. Museums were once a vital out-of-home entertainment choice; they face market forces that redefine their future as they compete with Hollywood and home entertainment. Hugh Spencer of LORD Cultural Resources takes us on a tour of the innovative presentation technologies in museums of the last century and delineates the competitive measures they're now taking. Then, John Latta of 4th Wave, Inc., defines the requirements for success in online virtual communities, no matter what kind of experience they sell. Finally, Michael Limber, Executive Producer of Angel Studios in Carlsbad, California, describes the teams and tasks required to do high-end digital production efficiently, a difficult task in any medium.

Chapter 30

Coin-Op: The Life (Arcade Videogames)

Mark Stephen Pierce
Atari Games Corporation

Introduction

Dollar volume is the yardstick by which I measure success in pop culture. My focus is the Coin-Operated Arcade videogame—"Coin-ops" for short—and the entertainment that addicts its core audience, 14-year-old males. It is an unusual profession in quest of an evasive product: the "kick-ass hit." The challenge is matched by the reward when success visits. Coin-op regularly allows a relatively small group of people with a strange array of talents to create content that can change pop culture.

Coin-op and its larger consumer shadow have a considerable economic effect. Over the last five years, annual coin-op equipment sales in the United States averaged around $150 million. The estimated U.S. cashbox (money collected from players) stands at about $2.5 billion per year. Domestic sales of consumer interactive entertainment software—videogames—is about $2.5 billion. When you add Japan, Asia, Europe, and all home ("console") videogames, people worldwide spend close to $20 billion annually on videogame entertainment. Videogames in all their guises are a major contender for our leisure time and money.

The industry that concerns itself with the design and manufacture of these devices has been my home since leaving school in the early 1980s. On my first product, I created graphics, animation, and code. I was the lead designer and pixel pusher on half a dozen later games; some met with success. My focus has changed since then—from how to design a great game to how to design an organization that enables designers to design great games. Over a decade of focus groups, field testing, talent hiring, design reviews, and game-selling has led me to some observations on the nature of the business. For the sake of simplicity, this chapter is largely concerned with the U.S. market, which represents about 50 percent of the global market. My intent is to familiarize the reader with an industry that gets little coverage but has had a strong influence on modern entertainment.

Why the Coin-Op Arcade?

Coin-ops and their content—the games themselves—are the source of the lion's share of commercially successful electronic interactive entertainment product. The commercial origin of the videogame industry occurred in 1972 with a game called Pong. The revenue growth curve that ensued and ran unabated until 1982, the year of the video bust, was remarkable. At its peak in 1980–1981, annual coin drop exceeded $6 billion, the operator population hit an all-time high near 13,000 (it's now about 4,000), and Atari's annual revenues alone were pushing $2 billion—passing its parent, Warner Communication's Motion Pictures Group. Since then the consumer entertainment titles that began as arcade hits have historically been the biggest sellers. As measured by market size, the arcade videogame has had the greatest cultural influence of all interactive multimedia formats. Many of the games that originate on home platforms are based on a model that came from the arcade.

Of the $2.5 billion spent in 1996 on home videogame software, about 60 percent is spent on the top ten titles; 25 percent is spent on the top five. From 1990 to 1995, the majority of the five top-selling consumer titles were ports of arcade videogames. Original titles for the PC, like Duke Nukem, Warcraft 2, Doom, Civilization 2, SimCity 2000, and Myst, are making inroads, but the market volume isn't there. When it comes to electronic play, Americans and the world still look to the arcades and arcade-style games.

Over the past 25 years, coin-op games have collected over $125 billion in quarters. This is almost identical to the amount motion pictures reaped at the box office during the same period. Assuming each play cost 25¢ and lasted an average of 90 seconds, it represents about 1.4 million hours of actual gameplay. And it represents more development time, attention, and money devoted to this form than any other. Newer interactive media will evolve through many incarnations before they're visited with the same consumer acceptance as hit arcade properties. The craft of arcade videogames—techniques, products, and their effects—can take us far in understanding what many people want to experience in the more recent interactive entertainment offerings.

One reason coin-op titles find great public acceptance is that they're carefully tested before sale. Coin-op provides the most honest and responsive public acceptance test-bed of all interactive entertainment. When a beta version of a coin-op game is placed on location, we get an immediate and clear indication of whether we have a hot property within one weekend. The pay-per-play rule of thumb—25¢ for 90 seconds of game time—means a game can yield $10 an hour if it's in constant play. We know how good our game is by how close we come to that $10 an hour. If it yields well over the weekend, we're probably onto something. If it sustains good earnings over a week, we keep our fingers crossed. If the earnings are sustained over six weeks, we know we have a game.

When players first see the unit, we have to somehow convince them to pay money to touch and interact with a box. Then, without a manual or tutorials, our games have 90 seconds to convince players that they want to reenlist for another 90 seconds. Imagine how many conversations would be cut short if this were a requirement. We have a tremendous incentive to create an easy, effective human interface design in every coin-op game.

In other forms of interactive entertainment, this is not the case. With consumer software, customers, hyped by word of mouth and reviews in magazines in which game publishers advertise, pay their $50 up front for the box of entertainment. No one really knows how many hours the game is played, if at all, once it leaves the store. The meter is always on for coin-op; we know the state of our appeal at any given time. This is why properties that have been successful in coin-op do well in the home. They're play-tested with a paying public.

How the Industry Works

The Manufacturer

The cycle begins with an unholy marriage of publisher and author. Hardware manufacturers like Atari, Capcom, Konami, Namco, Midway, SNK, and SEGA hire creative people to design games for them to build in their factories. These games take four months to four years to develop, at a cost of $500,000 to $5 million. The design teams' work is a melding of creativity, craft, and cost-effective technology.

After plenty of meetings, hallway conversations, focus groups, and field testing of a new game design, the manufacturer risks millions of dollars on parts and sets out to build the game. A typical upright game costs the manufacturer about $2,000 to build. When it goes into production, the manufacturer's sales team starts booking orders with the scores of distributors that serve as a combination of sales force, parts and service, and operator financing. Distributors commit to purchasing games by the shipping-container full (20 to 40 games per container) and buy them for $3,200 to $13,000 each. Manufacturers make all of their profit in the margin between the gross cost to develop and build the game and the price at which the distributor purchases it.

The Distributor

There are about 40 distributors in North America. Each maintains a sales force, a showroom, a financing department, a maintenance department, and a keen sense of what constitutes a good game. They sell the games to local operators. The average price to them is "out the door" on the operator's pickup truck at just under $4,000, tax and licensing included. The distributor profits from a combination of the markup on the price of the game, financing, and maintenance fees. As the business stands today, financing is a key element in this equation.

The Operator

Most operators have been in the business between 10 and 20 years. Each typically has a route that includes both arcades and street locations. Most also operate pool tables, jukeboxes and cigarette machines. A new game starts out at the operator's highest-grossing locations. Operators gradually rotate a new game between all of their locations in order to most quickly earn back, one quarter at a time, the money they spent on the game. There are three classes of operator locations: Family Entertainment Centers (FECs), arcades, and the "street."

At the operator's best location, one of his or her three arcades, a hot new game will earn $400 to $700 a week. After 8 to 12 weeks, its earnings rate will have tapered to $250, at which point the operator might move the game to one of 10 to 20 street locations. The owner of the street location supplies the floor space, electricity, and customer traffic, while the operator supplies the game and maintenance. They split the weekly cashbox. Games in these locations don't earn as much, but since the operator has already recouped the outlay in the arcade, any additional revenue is profit. Besides, the operator needs places to store all of the old "wood."

. . . Meanwhile, Back at the Manufacturer

The manufacturer, owner of a now-proven hot property, will have begun work on the home versions by paying outside developers about half a million bucks to squeeze the graphics and code of the original design into a Nintendo or SEGA cart or a Sony or PC CD-ROM. This is where the real money is made. A hot design that sells 10,000 arcade units in the United States will gross about $30 million for the manufacturer. And it's almost guaranteed to then sell one to four million units of the home version at $25 to $40 wholesale, for a gross of $25 to $100 million per title.

The bucks don't stop there, either. The best games will trigger action figures, comic books, trading cards, pajamas, Saturday morning cartoons, and even a movie. But, don't quit your day job yet. Fewer than one in three of the games that start development see even an average production run of 4,000 units, and a game with an average production run is barely a break-even proposition for the manufacturer. Like a gambler, the manufacturer only remembers the big wins that carry them through the down cycles—make no mistake; it's a hit-driven business.

The Locations (and Their Customers)

The "Street"

The Street consists of locations where the primary business is something other than arcade entertainment. Convenience stores, pizza parlors, bowling alleys, and bars are typical. There are between 60,000 and 80,000 street locations operating videogames, each with fewer than ten units. Customers at these locations are a combination of whatever spill-over happens from normal traffic, coupled with the locals who hang out by the games. To the site owners, it's an opportunistic use of a few square feet and just a part of their product mix—one that doesn't need much attention. Average weekly take on machines at these locations is about half of what the same games could make at an arcade or FEC. Street locations constitute over 60 percent of the market of standard upright releases. The manufacturer has to penetrate sales of new units to the Street to have enough volume for a true hit.

The Arcades

This is the home of our target demographic, 14-year-old boys. The second ring of the bull's-eye includes males, ages 12 to 22; currently, nobody else matters. Neighborhood arcades contain 20 to 50 machines, with most of the newest, coolest, expensive ones often positioned near the back. Operators provide several game types—for variety to the core users and to provide something for casual customers to explore. There is also typically an array of prizes for players of the children's redemption games (the ones that emit tickets). Across the United States, there are now 10,000 to 13,000 arcades in operation; the total ebbs and flows with industry profitability. Weekly income ranges from $5,000 to $12,000 per site. Because of their greater traffic, these locations can afford the higher-priced ($5,000 to $15,000) pieces. Weekly cashbox collections run $95 to $200 per game, with the top ten games earning between $300 and $1,000.

The average American teenager who visits an arcade will go once or twice a week with a small group of friends. He spends $5 to 10 per week, half on new hot games. The rest is spent on his favorites—he can win longer playtimes. The extreme version of this demographic, the game addict, puts as much as $50 per week into his favorite games. Hard-core gamers constitute about 5 percent of the clientele at an arcade. Because of their skill, they get longer gametimes, and, in the case of fighting games (winner stays/loser pays), they can play quite a while for "free"—though they spent plenty to become that good. These are the trendsetters in the arcades, determining what's hot and what's not. The other players part with coin to beat them and their scores. Arcades themselves are now differentiating; many will continue to match the description just given, while a new, high-end arcade experience is beginning to show up in the choicest sites.

The Family Entertainment Centers

FECs attract the typical arcade crowd but add to it young families (casual players). Arcade devices are just a part of these large sites, which have a wide range of diversions, plus food and beverage. Laser tag, miniature golf, and go-karts were some of the elements used to form early FECs; sites are now designed from the ground up and provide a carefully tuned array of leisure activities. These locations must be located within easy access of large populations. Within this group are the "national accounts," owned by larger companies like Dave and Buster's, Discovery Zone and Wonder Park. Some sites are owned by the manufacturers, which is a way for them to make revenue beyond equipment sales.

A well-managed center in a top location can justify outlays for the most expensive, deluxe, sit-down arcade systems, and is a step toward the fabled LBE. These typically include motion-base simulator systems, often thought of by the public as "VR." VR pieces almost never make back the initial investment; they're used as attractions to lure the casual player in much the same fashion as the carny barker on the circus midway. FECs also have linked multiplayer games like the eight-seat Daytona USA and San Francisco Rush driving games. Some of the top sites like SEGA City at the Irvine Spectrum Entertainment Center in California, the Trocadero in London, Fort Lauderdale's Grand Prix, and Wonder Egg in Tokyo, with their rows of big-screen games, indoor bumper cars, and real Mazda Miatas, are entertainment spectacles in themselves. There were about 2,700 FECs in operation in 1996.

Where Those Boxes Came From

The birth of arcade videogames can be traced to 1962. At that time, there were only four places on the entire planet that had a CRT hooked up to a computer: Stanford, MIT, Carnegie-Mellon, and the University of Utah. The first videogame was designed by an MIT student, Steve Russell, who created "Space War!" as "a personal project for his own entertainment." A kid named Nolan Bushnell was attending the University of Utah about then.

Fast-forward a few years. In 1970, two Ampex employees, Nolan Bushnell and Ted Dabny (who chipped in $500), were joined by Ted's brother John and formed a game development company called Syzygy. This group created a game called "Computer Space," a scaled-down version of Russell's 1963 game Space War!, on what amounted to a discrete logic PC. The California coin-op firm Nutting Associates marketed it; it debuted at the MOA show in the fall of 1971 and reportedly sold 3,000 units. This game—created in Bushnell's daughter Britta's bedroom, which he had converted into a lab—was the first commercially available Coin-Op.

Syzygy continued to develop other games. Nutting retained Syzygy to produce a two-player version of Computer Space. At the same time, Bally retained the company with a $25,000-a-month contract. It was then that Bushnell approached Al Alcorn and asked him to create a game based on his new concept based on two paddles and a ball; Pong was born. Debate still rages over who invented Pong. Magnavox publicly showed the first home videogame console, the Odyssey, on May 3, 1972, in Phoenix, Arizona; it played a game with two "paddles" and a "ball." Though Bushnell claims he didn't attend that event, Atari later did settle out of court and ended up paying royalties to Magnavox. Bushnell created two prototypes of Pong: one with a coin mechanism and one for a demo at Bally in Chicago, where Bushnell intended to convince Bally (and the recently acquired Midway) to take Pong instead of the driving game he had been contracted to deliver. The other unit went into a bar called Andy Capp's on El Camino Real in Sunnyvale, California, and four hours later the bread loaf tin they had rigged as a cashbox was overflowing. People were waiting to get in when the bar opened the next morning. Al Alcorn immediately called Nolan with the news, and Nolan called off the Bally deal. Within a few weeks, Syzygy built the first ten units with orange cabinets. The rest is history.

Very Early Games

The roots of videogames, however, reach much further back. The electronic interactive entertainment market is based on competitive games that predate the harnessing of electricity. Games involved territory, dominance, and hand-eye coordination: aboriginal hunting games, board games, target games, and bowling games. The fundamental compelling features remain in arcade games of today. As a result, the market of electronic interactive entertainment is male-dominated; I leave questions related to this phenomenon and whether it was, is, and always will be mostly a "guy thing" to others. Technology itself, for a variety of reasons, is mostly a male thing. What needs to change before this changes? Will it ever change? Perhaps only guys are stupid enough to care who wins such games (let alone spend countless hours getting good at them).

Games in early cultures served valuable purposes beyond entertainment. As children, we learn through playing games; simulating battle against other creatures or humans was a vehicle for practicing hunting and survival skills. Satisfying basic human yearnings for an arena in which to act out competitiveness and violence has much to do with the content themes of today's arcades.

As things became more civilized, games evolved into parlor room versions—simulations—of the aboriginal games. Go, chess, Parcheesi, and backgammon simulated battles over territory. Aiming games like bocci ball, Pataank, marbles, and darts have roots in spear and arrow hunting games. Games became a leisure activity instead of practice of survival skills for later in life; mastering a game could be an end in itself.

Games are an excuse for people to spend time together. Within that social setting, there is often a desire for establishing dominance over another individual or group. Dominance is established within a defined set of rules, via mastery of the skills that best address the rules. Each player's territory (resources of some kind) is defined at the start; winning is about establishing dominance through laying waste to the other player's territory. If this sounds too aggressive, consider your favorite game. Even a crossword puzzle involves claiming the territory of all of the open spaces that the puzzle's design "possesses." Arcades have become a major contemporary theater for adolescent males to act out the same impulses that caused aboriginal gaming to exist.

Publicly demonstrating that one possesses the skills necessary to deal with violence (real, fantastic, simulated, or implied) is still important in the socialization process. While children no longer need to learn hunting skills, it seems their hind brains have an unquenchable desire to define individual accomplishment. Successful arcade games play into this need for a clear definition of dominance.

Roots of the Arcades: Pageants, Festivals, Carnivals, Fairs, and Circus Midways

In Western culture, the religious festivals associated with Spring, like Osiris in Egypt, the sixth-century B.C. celebrations in Athens honoring Dionysus, and the Roman festivals of the Bacchanalia, Saturnalia, and Lupercalia, were large gatherings of ribald merrymaking, masquerades, and pageants. In northern Europe, pagan carnivals reached their peak in the 14th and 15th centuries. Unable to stamp them out, the church had to accept many of them. Under Catholicism, the original carnival landed on Shrove or Fat Tuesday, the day before Ash Wednesday and the beginning of the season of penance known as Lent.

In the 1800s, the term "carnival" became more associated with local festivals and traveling circuses. With its roots in the circuses of ancient Rome, where chariot races and other events took a toll on Christian participants, the modern circus was born in the closing years of the 18th century. By 1830, traveling circuses with equestrian shows were common in Europe and the United States. After 1869, the three-ring circus emerged with its wide variety of entertainment. Since crowds with leisure time and cash in their pockets were drawn to these events, sideshows and the games that became known as the Midway sprouted around the main tent. Then, clever entrepreneurs added other skill-based attractions and ride devices like swings (flight simulators) and merry-go-rounds (simulators of the equestrian events in the main tent, which were simulating the equestrian events of the Romans). Even the advanced simulation products in arcades are descended from ancient Rome.

Midways became the haunt of the quick-play, cheat-you-fair games of "skill" and chance that taunt players to prove themselves in front of others. All these leisure playgrounds encourage individuals to publicly display gaming prowess. Carnival midways are interactive challenges presented in a way that makes one internally comment, "Oh, I can do that!"—precisely what an arcade game's attract mode must do. Important in these carnival roots is the concept of the owner charging a fee per play, renting time on an experience.

Nickelodeons and Slot Machines: The Automation of Diversions

Turn-of-the-century boardwalks and main streets were the birthplace of automated devices selling entertainment and/or prizes in pocket-change portions. Though the Greek scientist Hero created what may be the first coin-operated vending machine (it dispensed holy water in return for a five-drachma coin), the slot machine, kinescope, and nickelodeon of the late 1800s comprised the first widespread exploitation of the concept of automated pay-per-play entertainment. The term "nickelodeon" derives from the nickel or coin that triggers the event and the Greek root "odeon," or play—play for a coin. It came to be used as the name for the public venue that held the machines. The Slot Machine, as we know it, first appeared in San Francisco in the 1890s as a poker machine, which usually paid out in cigars or bar drinks. Other mechanical devices activated actual instruments that played popular songs of the day, the forerunners of the jukebox. Coin-op arcades are the direct progeny of nickelodeons.

The Pinball Game

Pinball was the final link; the pinball machine triggered the entree of automated devices selling entertainment in pocket-change portions to the street. Unlike slot machines, the only prize with pinball was more game time (though many locations made under-the-table payoffs). While slot machines were relegated to unsavory locations like bars and pool halls, now more wholesome venues with wider audiences, like restaurants, dry goods stores, and soda fountains, could operate these stand-alone units. Early pinball games like Bagatelle (1871) and Log Cabin (1902) led to the unprecedented success of Ballyhoo in the 1920s and other silver-ball games that loaded the cannon for the introduction of videogames. Finally, technologies like the microprocessor, light-emitting diodes, core memory, and affordable CRTs in the late 1960s triggered the videogame explosion in the early 1970s.

Content = The Game

The game is perceived through the player's visual, audio, and tactile senses and takes shape in the player's mind. The more sensory inputs that are (expertly) stimulated in the player, the more an enveloping game state is reinforced. Games that achieve The State within the player are the games whose effect approaches that of good music or, in Mihaly Csikszentmihalyi's term, "flow." Successful game design controls the player's blood pressure. It causes the player to spend small quantities of cash per minute in an intense exchange with a noisy object. To a game designer, it's the coolest thing on earth to achieve.

The range of themes is quite limited. They've evolved through simple public demand and acceptance. I believe they tap into the hind brain of the player. I believe the themes are linked and are a reflection of basic evolutionary survival drives. Adolescents, by definition, are just beginning to understand power in society yet are denied real access to it. videogames simulate the accessing of that power; they are cathartic power play. Representation of self as a small character against the larger on-screen environment that's out to kill the player resonates in the teen mind. Implications of the social context of the arcade are testosterone drenched. The arcade is a place to meet strangers and beat them up.

While development of new themes in interactive entertainment has heated up in the mid-1990s, none of the results have yet achieved broad commercial acceptance. Smaller companies with less overhead tend to experiment with new themes because they require less return on investment, at least initially. If markets for these new themes are established, they will be pursued and refined by larger companies.

The craft of creating the games is largely an oral tradition. There are a few commercial schools that address all the skills necessary for this medium. It takes skilled workers, not just programmers or artists, to create a great piece. For the most part, the manufacturers' employees possess the core competencies necessary to create successful videogames. These companies must attract, educate, and provide technology for scores of designers before the true artists rise to the top. A designer capable of multiple successes is rare indeed, and the target of every development house. Having that talent at the right time with the right technology is even harder. It takes a confluence of individual skill, technology, market timing, and luck to create a successful arcade videogame.

History of Content Creation

The Early 1970s

The first games were just discrete logic hardware. The only designer was the person who laid out the printed circuit board. Graphics consisted of matrices of diodes laid out on big printed circuit boards in the shape of the graphic as it appeared on the screen. Development teams consisted of a hardware guy and a technician, and development time for games took anywhere from one week to three months.

The Late 1970s

With the advent of the microprocessor and its increasing complexity, it became necessary to have a software guy. At first, much of the software guy's role was to blame the bugs on the hardware guy and vice versa. Graphics were created in hexadecimal machine code translated from blocky drawings on graph paper. As things progressed, it became more of a software effort—the programmer/ designer became more powerful. In addition to the programmer, there was usually a dedicated technician and about half a hardware guy. Development times crept up to six months.

The Early 1980s

Artists step to the fore. Somewhere around 1980, as EPROM (electronically programmable read-only memory) storage capacities went up and prices went down, graphics became important. You still needed great moment-to-moment play, but now you also needed great graphics. Color monitor displays increased the need for artists. At the same time, game companies began creating their own custom chips. The graphics that were once diodes on circuit boards, then hex digits, now were being created with software paint tools that clumsily simulated paintbrushes and erasers. Teams included hardware, software, and graphics experts. With the first audio synthesis chips, it became necessary to hire musicians, but then, as now, a project didn't require a full-time audio person. By this time, there was also strong motivation to outdo the home systems; they had begun to seriously hurt arcade attendance. Many games took up to a year to complete.

The Late 1980s

Things only got more complex. Teams still had a hardware person, but now, because of complexities in creating custom chips, there were families of hardware that would be used for more than one game. There was still one programmer per project, but, due mostly to larger storage capacity and higher bit depth, game teams needed two to four artists to create a competitive title. Videogame manufacturers' R&D groups were creating the world's most powerful low-cost graphics chips.

The 1990s

With the rush to invest in multimedia, companies like Sony, SGI, and start-ups like 3Dfx began creating custom graphics chips for the promising future. With tens of millions of dollars being spent on new chip designs, arcade manufacturers found it difficult to compete. Alliances were formed: Sony with Namco, SEGA with Martin Marietta, SGI with Nintendo. Faster processors, more RAM, bigger EPROMs, and hard disks created a voracious appetite for code and graphics. Teams of two or more programmers became common (Japanese teams can have eight or more). Four to six dedicated artists have become the norm, with additional graphics folks handling video processing, stop motion, and motion capture. Budgets now run between $2 million and $4 million in development costs.

Rules of Game Design: Pierce's Top Eleven Gameplay Attributes

In nearly 20 years of experience playing, creating, and managing the creation of videogames, I've identified the following critical attributes. It is essential for a coin-op videogame to possess each of them. Don't leave the lab without them:

1. The game must be visually compelling; it must serve as an automated carny barker in a box. Its presentation—the attract mode—must be aurally and visually compelling—and clear enough to attract passersby (read: suckers). Because it's an element of pop culture, it must look and sound cooler than what has come before. The game must instantly inject the thought "I can do that!" in the player's head.

2. The game must involve the idea of death—of the player's proxy. It must present the most basic goal-oriented activity: Stay alive. Be immortal. Win free plays.

3. The game must contain some representation of violence that is portioned out as playtime progresses and constantly strives for the player's imminent symbolic death. This does not have to be actual violence—it can be anything that eliminates the player's sprite on the video screen, no matter how absurd or impossible.

4. The game must present obstacles to the player that increase the player's exposure to the violence.

5. The game must contain a representation of a self that is placed in an adversarial position against the violence and death of the game. The player should have a representation that instills the belief that there's a shot at victory.

6. The game must offer the ability to control compelling and thrilling actions that the proxy acts out in order to triumph over the violence that prevents them from securing their immortality. This is known in the videogame design world as moment-to-moment gameplay. It's the dialogue between player and machine through its input and output devices.

7. The game's moment-to-moment gameplay must be easy to learn yet hard to master. This is an old chestnut among game designers and players, and it is gospel.

8. Gameplay must contain both random events and learnable patterns. Random elements keep gameplay fresh, while patterns provide the player with the hope that, through mastery, the goal (immortality) will be attained.

9. The game must require an interactive, coordinated physical response by the player to the audiovisual cues of the machine. You don't just watch videogames; you acquire skill and technique to win. You have to feed yourself.

10. The game experience must be portioned into short salable segments. The operator wants the cash collections to exceed the purchase price of the

machine within 6 to 20 weeks of operation. Like a tobacco company deciding the right level of nicotine per cigarette, the designer must give players just enough gameplay per cash unit that they'll return for more.

11. The game must have some novel concept or hook. This can be through either thematic or technological presentation, but, like any fad, it's a disposable pop culture innovation that eventually burns out and is replaced. Effective hooks are developed by keeping one foot in the target demographic subculture.

The Seven Genres

There are seven reliable arcade genres; at any given time, one or two are ascendant. The year 1997 sees fighting games waning and gun games in full dominance. Except for the ever-popular driving games, the half-life of a genre's ascendancy is five to seven years. Here are the seven genres:

1. Classics and Puzzle Games

2. Driving Simulators (both Standard Drivers and Drive and Shooters)

3. Gun Games (on the ground)

4. Sci-Fi shooters (Death From Above, Death From Everywhere, Battle Simulators, Scrollers)

5. Action/Scrollers

6. Fighting Games

7. Sports

Classic Videogames and Puzzle Games

In the "classics" genre are what most baby boomers visualize when they think of arcade videogames. They happened in coin-op's heyday, the mid- 1970s to early 1980s, and enjoyed the broadest base of consumer appeal. These have historically been the largest sellers. Recently, this genre has had little representation in the arcade. Its strong suit is that player status is constantly and unambiguously communicated. One look at the screen and players instantly know they are either outnumbered or making good progress. Since these games were done in much simpler times, they were often largely the work of one or two engineers. The goal is simple: Eliminate all "bad" elements on the screen (claim the territory) and you will live forever . . . or at least until the "Game Over" screen appears.

Within the "Classics" genre is the subset of "Puzzle Games." These share abstract themes, a fixed playfield, and gameplay that both unlocks and plays upon the anal-retentive qualities hidden deep in each of us. The player is presented with a simple, compulsive, addictive task; there is neither plot nor character. The venue for this subgenre has switched from arcades to hand-held and home console devices except in Asia, where modern variations continue to find a loyal player base.

Driving Games

This is the perennial genre, popular with the casual player because of familiarity and with 14-year-old boys desperate for their learner's permits. All offerings have nonintimidating control interfaces: a steering wheel, a gas pedal, and a seat. Content evolution is driven by incremental technology improvements such as force feedback in the steering wheel, subwoofers under the seat, and polygons on the screen. Its cashbox earnings curve is more consistent and long-lived than any other genre, so these offerings can contain more expensive technology. As a manufacturer, you should always have a couple in development.

"Drive and shooters" is a subgroup of the Driver genre. It combines two of the more popular activities in the medium. A real-life version of this style of gameplay is now played on the freeways of Los Angeles. There are few offerings in this category, but almost all have been popular.

Gun Games

"Gun games" are a direct extension of the evergreen shooting galleries on the carnival midway. Stuff comes on the screen, and since you have a gun in your hand and no other way to communicate with the image, you shoot it. These games are immensely popular in today's market.

Sci-Fi Shooters

"Sci-fi shooters" are different from gun games in that they contain a third-person representation of the player that can be manipulated to avoid harm as well as to shoot. The goal is still to survive against all the destruction that is thrown at your little character. Many of these games could also qualify as classics since they enjoyed their highest popularity in the early 1980s. There is still enough demand to support one title per year. The Asian market has much greater acceptance of these titles.

Action/Scrollers

These games are linear in presentation; they rely on a simple goal with obstacles the player must overcome. The player is usually represented as a powerful character, selected from a group of several characters. The genre is dead in the arcade now, mostly because of the glut of similar games on home-game consoles and PCs, where they are known to the trade as platform games. These, too, were most popular in the mid-1980s.

Fighting Games

In 1997, we're past the peak of the reign of the video "fighter," which should be considered violence simulators. This genre began in the late 1980s, but it strikes such a resonant chord in the target age group that it's here to stay. It serves a highly stylized social function for adolescent males. Two players each get to choose one of several hero characters, with unique martial arts skills, costume, physique, secret moves, history, and personality.

Gameplay for the experienced player is related to "rock, scissors, paper." Each player has a health meter superimposed at the top of their side of the screen. Using both defense and attack moves, players try to extinguish opponents by depleting their health meter. In Street Fighter II, the most popular fighting game on earth, each player uses six buttons and a joystick. The joystick changes the position of the character, causing it to walk, jump, duck, and defend. Buttons trigger attack animation sequences, like a punch or kick.

Beneath these simple control inputs lies a complex set of combinations. For example, by rotating the joystick through its lower three positions, then quickly pressing the upper "Fierce" button, the player's character might throw a fireball at the opponent. Timing of these combinations is precise; for the experienced player, the game lies in memorization and the ability to trigger the hidden moves. If a new title catches on, there will inevitably be sequels, with new characters, moves, and situations. Despite what most observers think, all fighting games are not the same.

Sports Games

The sports genre is simply simulations of popular spectator sports, usually themed with a license, like NBA basketball. Players control one or more on-screen characters while the computer controls all the others. As in the sports themselves, the nuance in game design makes for much of the interest in the game. An example is variable wind speed and direction in a golf game.

What the Future Holds for Coin-Ops

The industry has always been something of an idiot savant in the worlds of entertainment and technology. Coin-op created low-cost realtime 3D graphics. Its boom in the 1970s drove down hardware prices, allowing the PC to become a technological and economic reality. Coin-op established basic techniques of interactive entertainment and was the birthplace of pop icons like Mario, Pac-Man, and Mortal Kombat. Despite all this experience, it's a very short-term-focus, close-minded business—only able to see as far as what's necessary for the next hit.

As the American coin-op market continues to stagnate at best, industry leaders wonder where we will be in ten years. Was the wildfire of 1979–1981 an anomaly, or can something new reignite a blaze of equal magnitude, drawing the public from their cocoons replete with VCRs, Web-browsing PCs, and game consoles? Must we be content with marginal profitability on the coin-op side, reaping the true harvest in consumer sales? The scary part is that our domestic business is not growing even at the rate of the population.

There is promise in growing markets like Indonesia, Korea, Brazil, and the sleeping giant, China, but do their cultures find the same games entertaining? Will networked arcades, tournament play, or improved FECs be the spark? I know—if we just could make a really huge mega-hit game . . .

The Manufacturer/Product Development Side

The big corporations lured by the multimedia promise of the early 1990s finally realized, after losing much money drilling dry wells in areas like infotainment, that the only widely successful multimedia are games with arcade roots targeted at adolescent males. They also learned that this industry is a risky and limited market with too few talented authors. All but the most stubborn corporations have gone away, leaving in their wake a few restructured and consolidated companies. Heck, even the Hollywood trade magazine *Variety* no longer runs its short-lived "Multimedia" section. Good riddance.

As the technology trends toward off-the-shelf hardware, coin-op R & D departments will become more focused on software and content. Faster, cheaper technology with higher bandwidth and storage will only raise the quality bar. Within five years we will have worked our way through the "polygon count is paramount" period. Hollywood, videogames, and TV will all use the same digital tools, which will continue to improve the quality of the content and allow game companies to use more external resources in order to create games.

The world will settle on six or seven coin-op companies. Each will have consumer development divisions that will exploit their successful properties. Because of standardized technologies, they'll be able to have more outside development teams, but they will still rely mostly on in-house staff to maintain their core competency.

If the manufacturers are smart, they will figure out a way to get into the cashbox to increase their current share of the overall gross or box office. This is the model that works for the movie industry, which enjoys only a slightly bigger total cashbox but is much bigger on the production side. It will be done through networks that link all games in the country.

The Operations Side

With the banning of cigarette machines in most states and the declining number of bars where pool tables can be operated, the next five to ten years will see more shrinking of the operator base. Every few years a really great game will come along, and operators will forget the bad times for a while. The large national accounts—SEGA, Namco, Nickels and Dimes, Dave and Buster's—will continue to change ownership from time to time, but the number of big FECs and arcades will stabilize in close proximity to the populations that support them.

If operators are smart, they will start sharing the cashbox with the manufacturers, who, in turn, must offer values like higher-end technologies, national advertising, tournaments, networks, and frequent downloaded software updates to extend the earnings curve.

The Player Side

One-stop family fun centers, now nearing or past their peak, will run their course and give way to new formats within five years. Adolescents will be in charge of determining new social gathering spots to be outfitted with interactive play. Arcade games and their consumer ports will continue to be the biggest multimedia market for quite a while. Because of the content, the target market, 14-year-old boys, will basically stay the same. Because of the target market, the content will basically stay the same. If this sounds strange, consider Barbie over the past 30 years. Boys will be boys.

Players will come to enjoy expanded connectivity between games. Intergame, intercity implementations will be toyed with by the manufacturers until the audience decides what they like. Driving games will remain popular.

Summary

Coin-op games are what they are because of what the audience demands. They appeal to the basest of desires—violence, speed, territory, and compulsion—because these are most gratifying to the player base. It's a fashion business that has to quickly respond to customer whims despite a one- to two-year product gestation period. The industry must create the most usable of human interfaces and the most addictive multimedia drug possible in order to exist. It must use many tricks to pull this off in a cost-effective manner. To succeed, it requires a collaboration of artistic, technologic, and literary creativity. All of this makes for an incredibly interesting and challenging industry in which to apply one's craft.

If designers or entrepreneurs involved with interactive entertainment want to go after the big bucks, they shouldn't be surprised if they are constrained to content that doesn't stray far from the Seven Genres. If designers out there prefer to be more innovative by introducing new themes and interactive formats, they shouldn't count on a quick win. Coin-op games and the resulting highest-volume-consumer sellers are what they are from years of natural selection. The Mortal Kombat multi-revenue–stream success story will be hard to repeat with a more politically correct theme. In other words, if you go to Las Vegas looking for the big payoff, you'd better love the tacky architecture. If you want to draw the big crowds, you're gonna need the bright lights, pinkie rings, and plenty of cash to burn.

Biography

In the early Macintosh market, Mark Pierce was the designer/animator of Dark Castle and Beyond Dark Castle. He was also one of the three founders of MacroMind, now MacroMedia, where he drew, animated, and coauthored his way through MusicWorks, ArtGrabber with BodyShop, and, most importantly, VideoWorks (now known as "Director"). Other Mac products for which he designed and/or created artwork were Winter Games and the EASY3D art disk. Prior to these now-forgotten accomplishments, he spent the earlier part of his post-art-school days porting games to crucial platforms like Coleco-Vision and designing/programming and animating Bally's coin-op game Professor Pac-Man. After moving to California in 1985, Mr. Pierce joined Atari, where he was Designer/Animator/Project Leader on the coin-op games Road Riot 4WD, KLAX, Pit-Fighter, and Escape from the Planet of the Robot Monsters. He was also a designer and the animator on RoadBlasters. For the past four years, he has been senior vice president of Coin-Op Product Development and executive producer at Atari Games in Milpitas, California. During his tenure as VP, he has delivered Primal Rage, T-Mek, a novelty game called Hoop It Up, Area 51, Wayne Gretzky 3D Hockey, San Francisco Rush, and Maximum Force.

Chapter 31

The Stories We Played: Building BattleTech and Virtual World

Jordan Weisman
Virtual World Entertainment

Dungeons, Dragons, and Microcomputers

When it opened in August 1990, BattleTech Center—aside from being the embodiment of a lifelong vision—was the first entertainment use of military-type, multiuser networked simulation technology for out-of-home entertainment. We broke new ground in interactive entertainment with BattleTech and made many discoveries about what works and what doesn't in terms of technology, marketing, themeing, attraction design, product longevity, customer orientation, and budget.

My vision of the future of digital games emerged from early interest in microcomputers, the game Dungeons and Dragons, and science-fiction-and-fantasy novels. I had learned how to program on an 8K PET before I was 14, and then I cashed in all my bar mitzvah presents to buy one of the first Apple II's (number 567). Not long after, I dropped out of the Merchant Marine Academy and together with Ross Babcock (a fellow cadet who managed to graduate) formed the Environmental Simulations Project (ESP) in Chicago. After several months of work, we established definitively that no matter how many Apple II's you hook together, you cannot create a simulation that will inspire the masses.

Still, I believed that a series of networked microcomputers could achieve the same goal as an expensive mainframe at a small fraction of the cost, which led to the development of the Tesla VR System and the Multi-User Network Gaming Architecture (MUNGA) software now used at BattleTech centers and Virtual Worlds.

I let my computer gather dust in the summer of 1974 and, as a 14-year-old junior camp counselor in Wisconsin, played my first Dungeons and Dragons

game. Transported suddenly from the North Woods to the dungeon of a medieval castle, I was battling monsters of mythology with only my wits, a sword,
and my comrades-in-arms. My imagination was ignited; I—no, we—were the
stars of a fantasy movie. And we were being challenged to actively think, visualize, and make decisions. We were in control.

Compelled in spite of dyslexia to know everything about the Dungeons
and Dragons game, I became an avid reader of sci-fi/fantasy novels. When I returned to high school and taught my friends to play, I discovered several things
that would later become important to the development of BattleTech Center.
Many of my friends were unwilling to make the mental investment necessary
to get involved in this form of role-playing entertainment. But those who did
generally got in deep, creating an elaborate and evolving culture around the
game. Lesson 1: Furnishing the visuals widens the audience. Lesson 2: What
the players bring to the game is as important as the game itself. Lesson 3: The
social aspect of play is all-important and leads to further socializing, which
leads to more play.

Stimulating Simulation

Ross and I met at the academy's gaming club, then developed a starship bridge
simulator concept in 1978. Our choice was a result of our familiarity with the
academy's $50-million merchant ship bridge simulator, an elaborate replica of
an actual ship's bridge, with video monitors instead of windows. The computer graphics were outstanding for the time. This seemed the ultimate role-
playing device. With computers providing the audio and video in realtime and
an environment that promoted multiplayer interaction, we could bring role-
playing games to a wide entertainment audience. The military shouldn't get all
the toys.

Our five-player design was a sort of "Star Trek and Star Wars meet Aliens"
scenario. It focused on what the players did, how they interacted with each
other, and how, as a team, they interacted with the rest of the universe. A key
concept at this stage was "persistence": The players needed to be able to have a
permanent effect on the simulation world so that, when the players returned,
they could see the results of their prior adventures.

By the time we actually built BattleTech, 12 years later, we had shifted from
a bridge simulator to a networked cockpit simulator. And, as we iterated the
social model of this entertainment concept, we saw that the five-person bridge
was too limited a format. Our target customers were between the ages of 18
and 35; they had the most disposable income and were the most interested in
social activities. But the average social grouping of this demographic contained
two to three people, not five. Forcing strangers to play together in a situation

where every person's actions are dependent on every other person's actions doesn't work. If one player is shooting at an enemy spaceship and the player's pilot suddenly turns in another direction, the shot is blown. This situation becomes intolerable when you have a high percentage of new users, unfamiliar with their game task.

We refined our design to a network of eight one-person cockpit simulators. Strangers would still need to play together to form teams, but each person would control his or her individual cockpit. We kept the group size small because of network load limits but, more importantly, for social reasons—small numbers equal large individual impact. The incentive to work together is there because good teamwork improves individual results.

Do-It-Yourself

I felt the academy's simulator was inefficient—driven by one expensive mainframe computer. It would be cheaper and more failure-proof to do the job with one microcomputer per "station." After determining that our idea was sound but needed more processing power, we set out to raise the money to do it right. Working backward from a ticket price, which could not be higher than the cost of a movie, our business plan derived how much we could spend on the technology. But none of our potential investors believed there was a market for this kind of interactive entertainment or that we could even build the damn things if there were. The road to opening our first site became longer and more twisted than we anticipated.

In 1980, we started a role-playing game (RPG) company that published on paper many of the ideas we had developed for the unbuilt electronic version. We named this publishing company the Freedonian Aeronautics and Space Administration (FASA). Five years after founding, FASA had grown too big for us to manage ourselves, and we brought in my dad, Mort Weisman, as partner and business manager. I figured if he took all the money and ran to the Bahamas (as business managers have been known to do), my mom would yell at him.

A critical and improbable twist in our development path was the sale of a license into the Japanese market, to Dyflex, a company that made roof-sealing products and tennis court materials. They started putting tennis courts on clients' roofs, then began managing the courts, and found themselves in the entertainment business. Their president, Mr. Miura, believed in our vision so completely that he bought the license at a point when all we had was a foam-core model.

One of the biggest jobs we did for them, a new infrared gun and robotics target system for a laser-tag game, was an expensive lesson. In this game, the players competed in teams against robot targets. Dyflex had problems with the system and asked us to build a new one. (The fallacy was that Japanese kids would not like to shoot at each other. This was proven wrong as soon as a facility that allowed them to shoot at each other opened.)

We redesigned the system so that every gun and target had its own microcomputer that communicated via infrared modems. At the end of the game, the guns' computers transmitted details of the game play to a PC that printed out the score sheet and kept a database of high scorers. Because the guns relayed realtime game-play information to the targets, the targets could utter thrilling lines to the players like "You shot my brother in the other room. Prepare to die!" This system could dramatically reduce the cost of both equipment and installation because it eliminated wiring each target to a central computer.

We were half right. Our targets' heads rotated to follow you as you walked across the room, taunted you with pithy Japanese threats, and shot at you. We tested the entire system prior to shipping, but the installation that was scheduled to last three weeks took almost three months.

It seems that many Japanese buildings don't have a common ground to their electrical system, which our system needed in order to establish lock. We had been told that the building's electrical system was grounded, but not that each outlet had its own ground. Each side failed to mention an important piece of information and made a mistaken assumption. The project was beneficial in the long run; it was about professional credibility. Mort went to Japan often during this crisis to meet with our partners and assure them that we would stay with the job. The relationship he built and the fact that we finished the job created a bond between Dyflex and Virtual World that exists to this day.

Real-World Prototyping

Another valuable detour on the road to our first center was the 1990 national auto show circuit. Chrysler hired us to create networked Jeep simulators, in which we discovered key user-experience fundamentals about transferring skills from the real world to a virtual environment.

The simulators were built with real Jeep steering wheels, dashboards, gearshifts, pedals, and seats, so the user-computer interface was about as familiar as you can get. The game was a simple four-minute race across a Baja-desert environment for six drivers. Before the show opened, I demonstrated the system for senior management of Jeep and Chrysler. I will never forget their faces when I parked my Jeep next to a small "hill," then had my staff race their Jeeps up the side of that hill and fly over mine. Although they had paid for it, they didn't understand until that moment what the difference is between a videogame and a virtual world.

VR simulators differ from videogames in two fundamental ways that seem obvious now but comprised at the time a major shift in high-tech game-play dynamics. The first difference is multiple players; your opponents and teammates are human. By 1990, videogame players had learned to win through memorization. Human opponents meant that no two games could ever be played the same way. Each experience would be unique, and the outcome was based on the skill and creativity of the players.

The second difference lay in the plasticity of simulation. A game designer builds in all the possible challenges and solutions ahead of time. Rather than inspire creative problem solving, these codified solutions incite the player to try to recreate the designer's thinking. In simulation, there are no predetermined puzzles or problems. The designers establish a set of limits and physical rules by which the universe works; the rest is all up to the players. We really don't make games; we make sandboxes and give the players some fun tools that they use to create the game.

Back at the auto show, the Jeep simulators were a big hit. Lines averaged a one-and-a-half-hour wait for a four-minute race. It was fascinating to see that although most of these people knew how to drive, many forgot the basics when in the virtual environment. Simple things, such as pressing on the accelerator pedal or shifting into drive, were forgotten. And most of the virtual drivers failed to check behind them and to their right and left; if it wasn't on the screen in front of them, it didn't exist.

As we predicted, players used the Jeep simulators to dare to do what they would not do in real life. They jumped hills, ran over cactus, and, most often, smashed into each other—a demolition derby with no debris to haul away! We left the auto show circuit with plenty of "user-testing" data and confirmation of our ideas. Jeep lesson 1: Even with a familiar interface, user education is required. Jeep lesson 2: People want to use the virtual environment to take risks they would not take in the real world. Jeep lesson 3: Not all players automatically understand the 3D nature of the virtual environment.

Building BattleTech

FASA flourished, and, in 1987, we began R&D on the hardware and software required to build our new form of entertainment. We chose a local group, Incredible Technologies, to help develop our dream. The initial project budget was about $600,000; by the time we opened the first BattleTech Center in downtown Chicago, we had spent just under $3 million.

Our concept of site design revolved around the theatrical concept of the dramatic arc. Simulation is theater and requires the suspension of disbelief; the customer must forget that it's a game. That shapes and colors the entire experience, gets the player's adrenaline flowing, and makes the whole thing worthwhile.

We chose to place our experience in cockpits rather than head-mounted displays (HMDs). HMDs were really cool examples of technology, but because of limited picture resolution and other factors, they weren't and still aren't good tools for the theater of simulation. The physical encumbrance of HMDs would limit our audience, they require more attendants, and they have higher maintenance costs.

Story and Setting

Because we had only enough funds to create one software package, we decided to go with a proven winner; BattleTech was FASA's most popular game and had been for almost five years. To this day, it remains the most popular science-fiction game in the role-playing/strategy gaming market. Each player pilots a 30-foot walking tank from a cockpit in the tank's head. Your futuristic tank-robot is armed with weapons more powerful than those in an entire battalion of modern tanks, and your tank's crushing weight allows you to step on buildings or other "small" things that get in your way. The BattleTech game appeals to the desire to be all-powerful, crush anything in your path, and be the master of all you survey.

We themed the entire center around the game, taking the strong graphic idea of these giant war machines and crafting a detailed, realistic, and sophisticated fictional universe for them. The physical environment carried a clear message. (Unfortunately, it was clear enough to scare off most of the female demographic, something we tried to address with the later design of Virtual World.)

The story and characters of this universe were the long-term strength of BattleTech. You need more than cockpits, good graphics, and good audio to suspend disbelief. You need to put players in the right frame of mind before they get into the cockpit. This makes for willing participants who get swept up by the fantasy. Together, the facility design and staff create the right atmosphere, and the actual graphics and audio execute the job, like warm-up performers and the headline attraction.

Drama in Four Acts

Continuing the metaphor of theater, the BattleTech experience is a three-act drama. Act 1 is exposition (preshow); act 2 is action and climax (main show); act 3 is denouement (postshow wrap-up). We built in an optional-but-encouraged act 4 (after-show socializing).

Act 1, the preshow briefing, introduces the characters, storyline, and equipment. This act creates anticipation. It says that what you are about to do is something special, and, by extension, *you* are something special as well. The preshow teaches players the game objectives and how to operate the vehicles. The better prepared a person is, the better he or she will perform; the better the performance, the more highly rated your product becomes. Thus, the preshow is critical to your customer retention rate. It cannot be skimped on and should be a live demonstration. People learn best from people.

Act 2, the main show, puts each person in a cockpit working with and against the other players. To maintain the essential hook of human interaction, we emphasize in both the preshow and main show that the vehicles one encounters in the game are driven by other humans. The interface they use must be easy to learn for the beginning player but contain endless advanced features to challenge experienced players.

Act 3, the mission-review postshow, is a crucial time of reflection. Here, you and your group examine the story you communally created. Each player receives a printed copy of the story in the form of a pilot's log. These serve as a social conduit to introduce you to the other players, and they validate the events that took place in the virtual environment.

Act 4, the postshow socializing, can't be scripted but is encouraged by the design of the site and by the staff. BattleTech Center attracts a wide range of people within the target demographic and puts them together in interesting combinations, using the bus-crash method. Imagine you ride the bus to work every day, seeing many of the same people. You've probably never talked to them. But then, the bus has an accident, which gives everyone a scare. Instantly, everyone on that bus is your best friend. You're all talking at once, sharing some of your deepest fears and joys. The accident creates a general need that breaks the conversation barrier and makes you into a community. You no longer lack a common subject for conversation.

This happens at Virtual World Entertainment (VWE) every ten minutes, when people come out of their cockpits bursting with adrenaline. The need to share the experience, to retell it from different perspectives with those who also experienced it, breaks down social defenses. In an interview on "Entertainment Tonight," actor Kurt Russell, who became a regular player while he was on location in Chicago for the movie *Backdraft,* called it "electronic bonding."

The Eternal Champions and Local Fame

The winners of our first team championship called themselves the "Eternal Champions." Their story is a testament to the power of VR to make strange bedfellows. It also illustrates the concept of "local fame." One was a law student, one was a maitre d', and the third was a hot-dog vendor. They had the game in common. They respected one another's skills, practiced regularly as a team, and waltzed through the first team championship undefeated. Their names and team logo joined the ranks of the famous fictional units on the wall where they remain to this day.

Reinforcing players' accomplishments through local fame is basic to the themeing of the site. It features images and histories of the backstory's greatest warriors and constantly adds various kinds of recognition of the best local players. Winning a tournament takes on both tangible and intangible benefits. Getting your name on the wall makes you a little famous, but having your name included with the names of the best in the universe makes you a part of (fictional) history. Local fame is the single most important reward that a center can give a customer.

All Virtual World sites constantly reward customers with local fame. Over the years we've added engraved plaques, trophies, and digitally retouched photos that place winners into fictional environments. We've developed lapel pins, custom patches of rank, and custom-embroidered jackets to recognize major victories. We publish a monthly newsletter featuring articles and pictures of winning players. Most important, any regular customer is known to the staff and to most of the other regulars by name, face, and reputation.

On to Virtual World

We hoped to finally attract outside funding for BattleTech Center once we had demonstrated that the technology could be operated profitably. But even then, the investment community wasn't convinced. We had to open a center and prove it. After the first center opened, doing great business and getting enormous publicity, we began to receive hundreds of phone calls from people wanting to open centers, but we could hardly respond to any of them because of lack of resources.

On BattleTech Center's first anniversary, the story began to change. A diverse range of serious investors started approaching us—from biotech executives to David Bowie. Then, Charlie Fink called. He and Tim Disney were researching VR entertainment. Tim and Charlie had worked together at the Disney studio where Charlie was a senior creative executive and Tim was an animated-features writer. They had left the company and developed an idea for an interactive night club called Club Virtual.

BattleTech Center, they thought, was about 70 percent of what they wanted to build. We were on the same wavelength about how interactive fiction and storytelling could evolve.

Tim's creative contributions were important. Along with badly needed capital, he brought a new sensibility to the centers and the games. Charlie brought a brilliant creative mind and great sense of showmanship. He produced new, star-studded preshows that raised the level of the whole product. Together with the creative and technical team already in place, we were ready to create Virtual Worlds.

Broadening the Customer Base

We had a three-part agenda. We wanted to expand the demographics, create a second attraction, and develop a common story from which game universes could spring so that games could be added and modified within an overall theme. This "backstory" is the Virtual Geographic League (VGL), a fictional, hundred-year-old, secret scientific organization founded by Alexander Graham Bell and Nikola Tesla. Along with the story came dramatic changes in the way the centers were designed.

Every Friday and Saturday night, a certain drama plays out at the doors of every BattleTech site. A young couple walks up to the window. The male explains BattleTech to his date and points inside excitedly. The female shakes her head in refusal. Ending A: The male walks away with his date, acting grumpy. Ending B: After a brief argument, the female departs alone and the male goes inside to play.

There were occasional exceptions. About 8 percent of the customers were women, about double the going rate for home video games and arcade games. We wanted to expand our narrow but dedicated audience by creating an environment that welcomes women and couples. To that end, each Virtual World–themed site features a large, elegant bar, often with kitchens for food service. The preshow briefing rooms are private, with projection televisions and good sound systems. The centerpiece of each facility is the Explorers' lounge, a luxurious area for socializing, fitted with overstuffed chairs, couches, and video monitors. Customers gather in the lounge for mission reviews and to watch games in progress. Since our rethemeing, we've seen a doubling of female attendance, to 16 percent, and the number of first-time female visitors increased.

The first two Virtual World sites, opened in 1993 in Walnut Creek (near San Francisco) and San Diego, performed extremely well. Confident that we had evolved the perfect design, we quickly started on four more.

High sales initially obscured how much more it cost to build and operate these centers. We had added additional steps to the customer experience, which, in turn, required additional labor to guide them through. The specialized areas also meant three or more additional employees—at the original center, it took a minimum of only four employees to operate the entire facility. And those specialized areas added to the overall square footage and thus the rent.

At that time we introduced Red Planet, a new attraction that didn't involve shooting. This changed two months later when, due to popular demand, we added three types of weapons. It was mostly a race driving game and seemed likely at first to be less unattractive to women since steering, timing, and acceleration finesse were all useful skills and the biggest vehicle didn't necessarily win. However, it was still a competitive, high-adrenaline experience, so there was little or no improvement in female customers' interest.

Virtual Play Styles and the Military

The way our customers use Red Planet and BattleTech constantly evolves without any changes to the actual product; the design is sufficiently rich to allow an important role for personal style. The Eternal Champions found this out the hard way. After their victory, they figured that they had mastered the game and stopped playing. Six months later, they returned for another competition but didn't win a single game. The strategy and tactics of BattleTech had evolved, and their old style just didn't cut it anymore. Players had developed a three-point turning trick that allowed them to bring their firepower to bear more quickly. The software hadn't changed at all, and the richness of maneuverability that the users discovered is a marker for good game-play design in any adventure world.

Similarly, Red Planet players amazed us by figuring out a way to climb the walls of the Martian canals in their Vectored Thrust Vehicles and then balance them on some narrow monorail tracks. Dave McCoy had added the tracks high on one side of each canal for the day we could run animated trains on them.

By the summer of 1994, there were five centers operating in the United States and eight in Japan, and it was time for the first national and international championships. It was at the national finals in San Diego that we first saw subtle differences in play style around the country. We learned that there were radical differences in play style between the United States and Japan, when the Americans got their butts kicked at the Virtual World Cup competition in Tokyo. BattleTech's first World Grand Master was Hide Kazu, a Japanese professional race car driver. The team champion was team Schike Tai, also Japanese.

A year later, my 1994 Virtual World Cup story was a hit at a roundtable discussion of the Congressional Advisory panel on Technology Assessment (OTA), to which I had been appointed. I was the only one without a heavy-duty rank in front of my name or a long list of degrees after it. As my colleagues began to question me in depth about the event, I discovered that the World Cup had made history. It had been the first multicultural simulation exercise and, as such, had military implications.

It seems that countries don't share their simulations, not even with allies. When a simulation is created, whether for entertainment or training, it's the outgrowth of the creator's perspective and completely interwoven with culture-specific assumptions about fighting. The simulations are then used by people who have the same training and assumptions as the people who created them, so it isn't surprising that the simulations often prove what the creators suspected.

Our experience in taking virtual reality attractions to Japan (and later to Australia, Canada, and England) was unique in that the exact same simulation code was being used by different cultures, allowing unadulterated differences in tactics, weapons systems, and style to be observed and, via the World Cup, put into direct competition with one another.

By the 1996 Virtual World Cup, the American players had studied the Japanese style and evolved a counterstrategy, and so had other teams. The 1996 International Red Planet Grand Master was Linda "Lync" Channon from Australia. The International BattleTech Team Champion was team Combat Committee Knights of Gale, from Tokyo.

Reach Out and Crush Someone

With the opening of the Las Vegas site in September of 1994, we introduced SiteLink, which allows pilots at centers around the country to play against each other via a custom router and ISDN lines. We added Internet terminals for on-line chat between the sites and videophones so that the pilots could talk to one another during mission review. SiteLink has enabled us to transform all our tournaments and competitions into national events. This adds greatly to the events and raises the level of competition.

We also tried hosting regular SiteLink days during which people could come in and play against those in other cities. But, without the trappings of a tournament, these days didn't work, probably because the whole business of location-based entertainment is based on shared, live experience with other people in your physical space. Open, random, SiteLink games were too much like playing a machine—not personal enough, even though your opponents retained that marvelous element of human deviousness.

The organized format of the SiteLink tournaments, on the other hand, provided community building rather than friendship building. People from each site would closely follow the players' progress and reputations so that they would know who they might face in the national finals. It extended each site's community to include the other sites. The lesson relearned with SiteLink is that community is foremost in creating compelling entertainment, whether in a location-based environment, an online environment, or both.

Tesla and MUNGA

In 1987 and again in 1991, we designed our own image-generating computers because there was no hardware even close to our price range that could do what we wanted. By 1994, our System 2/3 was looking pretty long in the tooth (read: old). We determined that we weren't going to design our own again and eventually bought hardware from Division, a small company in England. They had licensed an enormously parallel graphics architecture from the University of North Carolina at Chapel Hill and had brilliantly figured out how to texture-map it and put it on a set of PC cards. Its primary advantage was price/performance, but the deal-closer was that the product actually existed.

The next step was harder: choosing how to spend precious software development resources. We opted to build a game-development and realtime architecture that would allow rapid content delivery and cross-platform development. It was dubbed MUNGA, for Multi-User Network Gaming Architecture. Cross-platform development ability was important because it became apparent that we could not see sufficient return on content through the LBE market alone.

It would take longer to develop the first titles than a quick port would have taken. And, since all our software resources were dedicated to this task, it meant that the 25 existing sites would receive no new games or expansions to existing packages for a while. In retrospect, this decision was the correct one for technical reasons; it may prove to have been the correct one for the long haul. But, in the short term, it hurt; audiences need novelty in entertainment. Ticket sales fell, and the centers' financial performance dropped dramatically.

The Tesla System, introduced in 1995 and named in honor of one of the VGL's founding fathers, was the highest-fidelity experience available to the public at that time. The cockpit featured great graphics and an infinity optics system that created a window feel, plus a specialized audio system designed by Eric Huffman and six auxiliary screens that provide detailed engineering and radar information about your vehicle. The customers' response has been gratifying; we've seen a significant sales rebound in the older retrofitted markets.

Learning Ergonomics (and Other Greek Words)

Designing the cockpits was an iterative learning process. The design must capture the essence of the fantasy, promising that within this cockpit anything is possible, yet it must be practical and maintainable. Our first eight prototypes delivered on the fantasy; they looked great and really felt like a fighting vehicle's cockpit. They featured twin joysticks, one for each hand, a center-mounted throttle, and, best of all, you had to lower yourself down into it. With joysticks on both sides, there could be no side entry, so you had to step onto the seat and into the foot wells. This reinforced the fighter-plane motif, and the sliding canopy worked nicely with it. We played with these cockpits in our testing facility (warehouse) for over a year and thought they were nearly ideal.

Then, we took them to the 1989 Summer Consumer Electronics show in Chicago, where we watched thousands of people try BattleTech, and discovered a few minor details about good cockpit design. First, people didn't exactly *get* into the cockpit. Apparently, only fighter pilots and our design group will actually step onto the seat one is about to occupy. Everyone else tried to step all the way down to the foot wells in one long step, which resulted in what we technically refer to as a "fall" into the seat. I could just see the army of personal injury attorneys forming.

The second flaw was as obvious as the first in retrospect: the center-mounted throttle lever versus the skirt. The throttle's placement worked fine until we saw hundreds of women from the convention fall into the cockpit or decide not to even try. Those determined souls who tried helped us convince guys to work the booth for us during the convention.

The next cockpit design had all the usability and accessibility we needed but retained little of the previous design's fantasy and excitement. We designed hundreds of cockpits and produced five different generations over the years. Each design was an improvement, and, as we grew to understand real-estate costs, each had a smaller footprint. Our current unit is visually effective outside and in yet reasonably easy to enter. It's also the easiest to maintain in the field.

The most recent stage of cockpit development at VWE is entirely personalized: in-home. With good graphic acceleration finally available to the home market, we can now offer networked multiplayer experiences to a much larger market—anyone with an Internet connection. We're using the LBE exposure as a way to differentiate our intellectual property from the competition on store shelves. Users don't get the benefit of cool cockpits and themeing, but they're far more likely to log on and spend some money on a cold winter's night than to drive to our site. When they do visit the site and meet people they've been playing against, it's a special, exciting experience, just as we intended . . . and within a more profitable business model for the operator.

The More Things Change . . .

As of June 1997, there are 24 Virtual World sites of various sizes around the world. Ten thousand new customers come to us every month, and we've sold well over ten million experiences. All this proves one thing: that the most entertaining things on this planet are other people.

So, given this expensively learned obvious piece of information, where are things going both in location-based entertainment and home online entertainment?

I believe the LBE market will grow substantially over the next several years, and much of the direction this growth will take has been influenced by our experiences. The second wave of LBE centers will have a broader integration of entertainment venues so that people can make an entire evening's entertainment of their visit—including food and beverage. Traditional movie theaters are not the ideal partner; the centers need a concentration of interactive entertainment, each probably with different themes and targeted at different age groups. Many of the larger entertainment companies are moving in this direction, which offers opportunities to both technology and content developers. To be successful, the second-generation, larger centers will need to embrace the fact that the social dynamics of the interaction are more important than the technological ones.

The home network phenomenon looks more like the California gold rush all the time. Scores of companies offer multiplayer gaming on private networks and the Internet. Most of the new online game creators do not really understand the differences between local-area network (LAN) and wide-area network (WAN) multiplayer gaming, and some simply do not get what makes "multiplayer" interesting at all.

Many of the Internet gaming networks are based on the idea of reproducing a LAN game in a WAN environment. At first blush, this sounds great; you get to play with people all over the country and can use many games you already know. This strategy is similar to our Site-Link experiences, and I believe that, in the long run, the outcome will be similar, too. SiteLink started strong but quickly faded because people weren't able to establish enough of a relationship with each other. Internet gaming faces the same problems; there must be ways to let people establish relationships before, during, and after the actual playing of the games. The establishment of chat rooms and the like is a good first step, but only a first step.

Persistent-universe games are a better long-term bet for the home networking environment. As opposed to the LAN/WAN short-term, small-number-of-players, multiplayer games, the number of players is theoretically unlimited and the game—or adventure—can be continuous. A player's actions can permanently affect the game environment, which is closely related to the "local fame" I spoke of earlier. As players spend more time in the game, they get to know other players, first from reputation and then from interaction. This provides continuity of social interaction in-world, much better than breaking it up between chat rooms and the game itself.

Both developments depend on the heat derived from pitting one person's skills and creativity against another's. People love to entertain each other; they love to challenge themselves and others. Given the opportunity, most people want to have an active role in creating their own entertainment.

Entertainment has come full circle. The first form of entertainment was community-based cooperative storytelling around the cooking fire. The members of the community entertained themselves, building their stories together, often from common experiences. As the art of storytelling became refined, it fell into the hands of professionals, the minstrels and troubadours who traveled the lands tailoring or creating their stories for each local audience. As these stories became more codified, they turned into plays that were presented to and slightly tailored for the local audiences.

Starting with the introduction of the printing press, the community's ability to interactively create stories diminished. The printed word meant that a storyteller couldn't tailor the story to each audience. The loss of creative control was gradual; there were countless small publishing houses, often local to the community they served. But, when the means of communication switched to movies, radio, and television, local communities could no longer control content.

For the last 50 years, we've lived in a world where very few people create the entertainment for the majority. It has been a one-way street—individuals can do no more than watch. Television shows even laugh and applaud at themselves. The method by which these stories have been created and distributed is very much like digital data processing was only a couple of decades ago.

Twenty years ago, an executive of a progressive company with a data processing department would request a report to be run on some available data. It would often take weeks to receive the report, and if it wasn't what the executive wanted, the cycle started again. Today, the executive is in personal control of the data and its analysis. Such localization represents an enormous empowering of the executive and a building demand for realtime response. It is not a coincidence that many people are now starting to demand the same empowerment and interactivity of their entertainment.

Thus, we return. Social multiplayer network experiences are recreating the entertainment format of our ancestors: collectively told, locally created, interactive storytelling, with the additional requirement of Technicolor fidelity and a wall outlet. It has only taken thousands of years and billions of dollars worth of R&D to bring us back to the fun of telling stories around the cooking fire.

Biography

Jordan Weisman, President and Chief Creative Officer, is the principal creative architect behind Virtual World. In 1980, he, Ross Babcock, and Mort Weisman formed the FASA Corporation, a fantasy role-playing board game publisher. As FASA's president, he codesigned two of the top five best-selling games in the industry, BattleTech and Shadowrun. FASA now publishes multiple lines of science fiction and fantasy novels based on its game universes. It was at FASA that he and Ross Babcock began to develop the principles behind the interactive games now in use at Virtual World. Together, they opened the BattleTech

Center in Chicago in August 1990. This was the first location-based virtual reality center in the world and gave the public a taste of a technology that was formerly the private domain of NASA and the military. Mr. Weisman has received numerous awards for game design and has lectured extensively on VR and game design around the world.

Chapter 32

The Virtual Squadrons of Fightertown

David Kinney
Eagle Interactive

Introduction

There's no question that flight is one of the most common human fantasies. The vehicular version of that fantasy has propelled sales of about 20 million PC-based flight simulator games, production of over 100 feature films, and countless framed photos of airplanes on the walls of corporate senior management. However, short of training to be a jet pilot, you couldn't get a sophisticated flight simulation experience anywhere until Fightertown opened in Irvine, California, in May 1993. It opened with two simulators: an F104 and an F111. Demand drove that quickly to five, and then we outgrew the location and moved in order to double the number of simulators and develop two new entertainment experiences based on different eras in flight history. The experience of flight, in myriad guises, is a revenue generator in many facets of the entertainment industry; mine just happened to be location-based entertainment (LBE).

Fightertown came from an idea I had in 1986 that I later discovered no investor would touch. The project development process I went through and the evolution of the technology may be useful to others as they grope for answers in the complex arena of themed location-based entertainment business.

The year 1986 found me writing requirements for the B2 Stealth bomber's developmental simulator at Northrop. Fresh from the Marine Corps and operational squadrons, I found flight simulation work interesting and challenging. While at Northrop, I became convinced that flight simulators in general and networked interactive simulators in particular would be a big hit with the general public. At that time, the only people with access to this class of flight simulators were test pilots, pilots in the military service, and the engineers working in those areas. The average person—and even some aerospace engineers—didn't have access. I had to develop a way to build high-quality flight simulators while keeping the cost low enough that the public could enjoy them without taking out a loan.

Because of the cost and operational training requirements, modern full-mission flight simulators are primarily stand-alone devices. That is, any interaction with other aircraft or vehicles is from software, not other humans. There are some exceptions to this rule; in tactical aviation, two devices will be networked pitting human against human or flying cooperative missions. This left the art of large groups acting in combined operations to be taught in classrooms and actual flying. It was therefore very important to me that these simulators be voice- and database-linked to enable multiplayer experiences. I had no desire to simulate one pilot's experience in one aircraft; I wanted to create a squadron situation, where a group of people could interact with each other and with other devices at the same time.

Financing with Sticks and Throttles

About 1990, while working on simulation requirements for the Advanced Tactical Fighter (ATF), I decided to devote myself full-time to starting a new company, called Kinney Aero. John Araki, who I had met at Northrop, and Scott Cubbage, who I worked with on the ATF, also believed there was a market for a low-cost flight simulator system for professional applications, not just for entertainment. We knew from our experience in aerospace that there was a need to reduce the cost of such systems.

One of our areas of expertise was the design and implementation of flight-control sticks, throttles, and switches for simulators. So, we developed some low-cost sticks and throttles—relatively low-cost, considering the standards of the day—and managed to sell quite a few. We used that money to continue developing the Fightertown product. We hung in there, just doing contracts for companies like Lockheed and Northrop until we had the funds and the equipment to proceed with our idea.

While continuing to do contract work, John Araki and I did the usual things that people looking for investors do. After we designed the systems, we approached VCs with our ideas on paper and developed numbers for the cost of the hardware, the size of the space, how many turns per hour, the customer's price per turn, equipment depreciation—all the usual stuff. We got responses like "This is a great idea, but I can't invest in it" and "This idea will never work; you can't maintain them" and "People won't come on a regular basis."

Another thing we kept hearing from our potential investors was that they didn't think there were enough pilots out there to support it. They imagined that our primary market must be jet pilots. I tried then, as I continue to try now, to explain that our primary customer was not a jet pilot, but rather somebody who dreamed of flying a jet. As in so many aspects of the entertainment industry, the attraction involves something the customer can't have. Even the experience of flying a civilian aircraft is much different from that of flying a military-type jet.

So, we didn't have much success in raising outside capital. In fact, we had none, which was probably a good thing.

Refining the Concept and Making the Numbers Work

At that time, the visual display systems were extremely expensive. We had to come up with a system that was good enough to do what we needed and yet not drive the price up too much. We couldn't let the cost of a ride exceed what the average person could afford, and we were creating a fairly lengthy experience. The display system for a flight sim consists of one or more realtime 3D image generators, driven by the user's steering, and one or more RGB video projectors. In 1993, a commercial version of such a system—a full-dome, full-mission simulator—cost in the range of $70 million for a single-seat jet. No entertainment business plan could survive such a per-seat cost. We developed a system based on a 486 and a custom graphics generator that used only one video projector and monophonic audio, and we simulated a radio channel for communication between the jets and between them and the tower.

Our first big break was the U.S. Space and Rocket Center in Huntsville, Alabama, and its program called "Aviation Challenge." It's a camp for kids that deals primarily with flying. We designed and sold them some fully integrated cockpits. We took that money and the money from sticks and throttles, built a couple of jet cockpits, wrote a lot more code, and, finally, Fightertown was open for business.

When we opened, the total customer experience during a visit to Fightertown was designed to last upwards of 1 hour and 15 minutes. This included the preshow or briefing, the postshow or debriefing, and the time in the simulator itself. The main experience—the ride in the simulator—lasted 30 minutes. At that time, it seemed like a fairly long experience for that kind of venue. The only high-tech model we had to go on, other than arcades, was Virtual World's BattleTech in Chicago. We knew BattleTech was about a 20-minute-plus experience, with a 10-minute preshow, a 10-minute ride, and an optional postshow review.

We were juggling several factors to determine how long the customer experience should be at Fightertown. How much wear and tear per use was reasonable? The equipment was fairly sophisticated at the time. It was developed and built to be robust, but any time you're getting people in and out of complex cockpits, closing canopies, putting on helmets, checking communications systems, and so forth, there will be cumulative damage and considerable reset (audience turnover) time—best case: 4 minutes. So, I didn't think a 10-minute ride was adequate. The challenge was to determine a time frame that optimized the experience, wasn't long enough to get boring, and gave the customer enough time to really inhabit the role and character assumed (the customers were mostly male). Finally, the price point was critical; customers are comparing what they spent to how much fun they're having. At what price do they think they're getting their money's worth and decide to return for repeat play?

It's easy to look at other venues—movies, go-carts, concerts—and determine what they charge per minute. However, that can be misleading. In certain circumstances, some people will actually pay $1 a minute for a 10-minute experience. But $1 a minute is $60 an hour. Repeat business over the long haul would be hard to get at that price, no matter how good the attraction. We were trying to compete with other out-of-home experiences, and the baseline is a two-hour movie for $7.50.

We came up with the idea of charging only for the 30 minutes the customer spent in the cockpit, but marketing the whole experience at that price. The advertisements would say to the customer, "You're here for 1 hour and 15 minutes at a cost of $30." From the customer's point of view, that was less than 50 cents a minute. From our point of view, looking at the 30 minutes in the cockpit and calculating the maximum customer throughput, it was closer to a buck a minute. All we needed to do was have customers queued and prepped to get in the cockpits the minute they were available. We soon had membership discounts, group rates for corporate events, and league nights, just like bowling, and it turned out to work pretty well. One bit of tuning we did was to shorten the preshow so that the entire experience lasted 1 hour. Another was to improve user comfort. The first customers were really beta testers; they put up with enormous discomfort and inconvenience as we tuned the product. We had to increase the ventilation in the cockpits, for example; some of our largest early customers were able to steam up the whole plastic canopy, which made viewing the video projection screen difficult.

Where's the Audience?

I likened Fightertown more to a bowling alley than an arcade. If you think the concept you're developing will work like a bowling alley, some facts emerge regarding the type of user to expect and where to locate. A bowling alley draws on a user group that's fairly well defined and doesn't generally visit on the spur of the moment. You don't just exclaim while walking down the street, "Hey, let's go bowling!" It's a form of recreation that usually has some planning attached to it, like movies, miniature golf, or go-cart racing. Arcades draw more impulse activity, which is why they work well in shopping malls.

So, Fightertown didn't have to be located in a high-pedestrian-traffic, high-dollar retail area because once our audience was aware it existed, they would find the place and come to it. Bowling alleys aren't often located in malls; the attraction I was designing didn't have to be "downtown." Our demographic had cars, so we could have a lower-cost location, but we would need space for parking. We also needed to be reasonably near a main traffic artery and to have a large population base to draw upon. That population base needed to include plenty of people interested in what we had to offer. In order to serve a market that would enjoy a jet-fighter simulator experience, I selected a site near a major military air base, in a city with a public airport and a second, military one.

At that time, locating in an industrial area allowed us the most square footage for the least amount of money. I wanted the place to be large, impressive, and high-tech looking in order to give the sense of a real flight simulator in a real military base. We wanted to emulate that experience by designing a facility with the same kind of look and feel: big and very technical. We provided realistic zippered jumpsuits with insignia for customers to wear, we used aviation jargon wherever appropriate, and we themed the space as much as possible like an air base. When they left, they took along a photo of themselves in full flight suit and helmet as they sat in the cockpit.

Lots of Wannabes; Few Pilots

In a successful LBE, you must understand your customer. The crucial demographic standard for filling our high-end cockpits at Fightertown, and for flight simulation in general, was a male in his mid-thirties. Did he have to have a college or high school education? Was he a professional or a blue-collar worker? That didn't seem to matter. What mattered was an interest in aviation—primarily jets, of course, but any interest in aviation seemed to do the trick. Earnings went across the board from lawyers and doctors to road builders, construction workers, and Marines at the local air base. They could all afford to repeatedly spend $30 and, occasionally, more for our two-seater motion-base cockpits.

We did many studies, but most proved inconclusive. As predicted, we did not get many actual pilots. One thing became clear; there were two breeds of customer in our core demographic. The casual ones didn't care what type of jet they flew, and the serious ones didn't care very much either but cared a lot about the accuracy of the experience. We also found out that very few of our customers visited by themselves; most came with at least one friend, and three to five in a group was common. This fact maps to our notion that communication and interaction between cockpits is critical. When somebody did show up alone, he quickly got tired of just flying around and needed a friend or opponent in the air. Sometimes, a whole family would visit; the mother and daughter(s) would often just watch while the father and son(s) flew.

A key thing I learned was that the customer wanted an experience as close to an actual jet as possible. The people who came to Fightertown weren't looking for fantasy, except for their fantasy of being a pilot. They wanted to know exactly what it was like to fly in an F-16 or F-15. The flight simulation industry calls this "fidelity," and it's impossible to do that based on the time required to train a customer and the costs for building the device. Besides, if it's too real, novices would spend all their time crashing and wouldn't return. What you *can* do in a public entertainment context is come close to real, concentrating on the elements your audience is going to notice. Those things should be presented in high fidelity, as consistent as possible with the real thing. The way the jet accelerates and turns is important, and so is the way the stick and throttle look and feel, including their switches. We designed the panel switches and the gages and displays to be a little simpler and easier to use than on a real jet, however, and the preflight checkoff list was a lot shorter than a real one.

In the name of fidelity and accuracy, I initially intended to name each simulator model, like our F-16, something different from the actual jet it was patterned on, but we finally settled on "F-16F," meaning a Fightertown F-16, and explained the differences per customer.

Who's the Audience?

Once you know who your market is, the question arises of modifying the venues and the attractions within them to develop a bigger market. In the case of Fightertown, a bigger market means bringing in younger adults, kids (meaning preteens and young teens), and women of all ages. But I don't think Fightertown is a place where kids and adults can coexist very well. It wouldn't be comfortable having adults coming in to do a fantasy role in a fighter plane and kids running around in ill-fitting flight suits and not thinking as much about team play as about blasting one another. Two separate venues might be fine side by side, but I'm not confident about one that consistently mixes adults and kids in one audience, at least not with the type of experience we designed.

Younger men especially and, to some extent, women are not particularly concerned with fidelity in an aviation attraction. They want something that is easy to learn, is reasonably quick, is relatively inexpensive, and has a lot of interactivity. They want to be able to shoot or fly with their friends, and they'll roam in groups. They visit attractions in larger groups, spend typically less time per visit, and the fidelity of the equipment itself is not nearly as important as the social experience. They want to be able to quickly interact with their friends in some sort of competition—racing or shooting each other, achieving some sort of goal. "Capture the Flag" is an old game that this demographic is attracted to.

There are plenty of ways to serve the younger audience, but a big jet simulator is not one of them. You don't need such an expensive device, which is a good thing because you must also charge less than for adults. You want to concentrate on visuals and interactivity, good sound, good communication, and you want to use equipment that holds up well because it's going to get more turns per hour. It is likely to get rougher use, too. We developed a stubby little biplane sim for kids that met these requirements, the "Flying Circus."

I still don't know how to attract women to a Fightertown-style venue, and I'm not sure if at this time it's that important for this sort of product. For one thing, even though the visitors are primarily males, many of the tickets (30 percent) are bought by females in the form of gift certificates for a male friend, father, or brother. So, if you look at who is doing the buying, women already form a large customer base.

Planning for Obsolescence

I think most people in the business world have a good understanding of how to make a profit and what things must be in place to do so. However, I repeatedly observed violations of these rules when it came to competing LBEs. I never really understood it and wasn't privy to the competitions' detailed information, but it seemed to me that developers were spending exorbitant amounts on hardware in comparison to the fees they could realistically charge.

The key to the business of high-tech LBEs is that new hardware is obsolete immediately. You have to invest in equipment in a way that allows you to pay off that equipment in no more than 18 months so that you can afford to make constant hardware enhancements and stay competitive. And, when we're talking about virtual experiences, they're all hardware oriented.

You must also look long and hard at the real costs of software development; it's always very expensive. Since software improvement happens at a relatively slow pace, its cost is sometimes not factored in, but if you employ top-quality people at a good salary and they are working full-time to develop software, that's significant. Along with updating your hardware, the continuous enhancement of software is absolutely critical if you wish to retain customers.

When I started Fightertown, I had a single facility in mind, and I thought I just had to work it out so that the hardware costs plus operations were in keeping with revenue. But I realized that Fightertown should grow quickly to multiple sites, and I found that the key to continued success is constant development of software and its associated cost. That forced me to keep well-paid coders around to continually update and change software. We made the numbers work; it was a profitable endeavor, but there were recurring costs for staff and overhead and for maintenance and updating of both hardware and software, so the equation wasn't particularly straightforward. To cost-effectively open up a single site, you might do well to have an arrangement with an out-of-house software development group for new features and continual updating of the attractions. To justify sufficient staff developers, your business plan probably needs to include several initial sites and a growth scheme, or leverage your game design into other areas of the entertainment business.

Show Business

The people that go to LBEs are social animals; they've left their homes and gone into a public place, so they expect and look forward to meeting people. This is a specific experience they seek out for enjoyment, not something they're required to do. Therefore, location-based entertainment is show business, and the employees are actors who reinforce the theme and the mood. It's crucial to train your employees to engage the customers and help create positive human interaction. You may get this feedback from the customer, "Geez, you know, I was confused by the software, I didn't understand the hardware, and I didn't really learn how to fly. But I really thought the people that work there are great; they're very friendly and helpful and made it a lot of fun!"

Our job is to immerse customers in the experience, entertain them, and make them want to come back for more. That requires skill, legwork, theatrics, and role playing. It extends to the uniforms your employees wear, how they talk to the customers, and how they move around the facility. We redeveloped many of the rules and techniques developed for public-contact employees at Disney years ago. These low-tech, human things will make or break your high-tech attraction.

As a result, you must invest considerably in skills training for your employees, and that investment makes high employee turnover very costly. Theatrics doesn't come easy. Treat your staff well and minimize turnover. Incentives such as stock packages can have a powerful positive effect. Create a worthwhile, motivated working environment for them, a fun environment. You can make sure employees have fun and still be disciplined about it.

Summary

It's important to put this discussion in the proper context: It isn't about the viability of the LBE concept; it's about the merits of relatively low-cost, low-square-footage, high-tech attractions. Currently, the equation for the revenue model leaves little room for error because of cost, a rapidly changing technical base, and a constraining infrastructure. It's similar to the early days of the automobile, when autos were slower than horses: Nobody knew how to maintain them, they cost too much, and the roads were often impassable, but, in retrospect, what an investment!

The high-tech LBE is a tough nut to crack, but the proven key is human contact through interactivity. People desire to get out and socialize, and that can't be done effectively by climbing into individual pods and isolating ourselves. We can isolate ourselves very well at home with our television sets and entertainment centers, and we'll be able to do it more easily next month or next year. So, it should not be news to anyone in this industry that isolated, noninteractive attractions will not work in the long term for out-of-home entertainment.

The individuals visiting these venues want to interact with each other in as many informationally rich ways as possible. The near future will afford plenty of interesting ways to do that in theme parks and LBEs. Soon, online interactivity will enable simultaneous contact with many different people in their homes and allow us to link them to out-of-home, themed environments. It's a short matter of time before we'll see elaborate, high-resolution versions of online entertainment in a themed attraction setting for a reasonable price. With the larger number of players this makes possible, costs can be amortized nicely. It's going to really take off.

Biography

David Kinney received his bachelor's degree in Bio-medical/Mechanical Engineering from the University of New Mexico in 1981, where he went on to become a captain in the Marine Corps working as an aircraft maintenance officer and going through Naval flight officer training. After serving in the Marines, he worked on both the B2 bomber and the Advanced Tactical Fighter before starting his own company and Fightertown. In 1995, he started a new company called Eagle Interactive, in Lake Forest, California, dedicated to bringing flight simulation to the home in the form of PC-based games.

Chapter 33

Supercharging the Cultural Engine: Advanced Media at Heritage and Educational Attractions

Hugh A. D. Spencer
LORD Cultural Resources Planning & Management, Inc.

Introduction

> *I found the Palace of Green Porcelain, when we approached it about noon, deserted and falling into ruin. Only ragged vestiges of glass remained in its windows, and great sheets of the green facing had fallen away from the corroded metallic framework . . . The tiled floor was thick with dust, and a remarkable array of miscellaneous objects was shrouded in dust . . . further in the gallery was the huge skeleton barrel of a Brontosaurus. My museum hypothesis was confirmed.*
>
> The Time Machine 1895

It's appropriate that H. G. Wells places the Time Traveler in a vast museum to discover the fate of human civilization in the far future. Museums are repositories of knowledge where people are able to explore any aspect of science, technology, human history, or the natural world. Museums such as the British Museum of Natural History, the Horniman Free Museum, and the Great Exhibition at the Crystal Palace all influenced Wells' generation, where achievements from the cultures of the worlds, and the vistas of prehistory, were first displayed to popular audiences. Museums are not only storehouses of information, but they can also be places of wonder and entertainment.

When Wells wrote *The Time Machine*, the academic and scientific functions of museums were not widely appreciated; many were the leading-edge attractions of the time. Now, recent trends in tourism, leisure, education, and technology can make cultural institutions like museums and heritage sites among the most dynamic and popular attractions at the end of this century.

Our cultural institutions can be models for understanding by operating a wide range of themed attractions. Further, developments in digital and online media are having profound impact on cultural attractions. These changes will, in turn, impact attractions of all types—and perhaps the very nature of leisure and education in the 21st century.

The Museum as Attraction Model

It may be surprising to consider museums as models for the contemporary attraction, although many techniques and technologies found in today's attractions—roller coasters, animatronics, theme rides, and even cinema—were pioneered at the great museums and expositions of the 19th century. The ways our cultural heritage is communicated to the public now exist in a far more competitive leisure marketplace—much of the reason that museums today employ advanced cinema, multimedia, and simulators. In turn, some themed attractions are now adding more depth to their presentations, providing at least the impression of an "educational" experience.

But, to many, the popular conception of the museum is a large, boring building, obsessed with old, arcane, noninteractive, difficult-to-access information that is devoid of any emotional coefficient. This image is difficult to justify even if we ignore the history of themed attractions and family entertainment centers. Most of us may remember how museum exhibits allowed us to experience the unique, the unusual, and the outright incredible. At a museum, many of us saw our first dinosaurs, witnessed the lifeways of aboriginal peoples, and got to touch the hull of the Apollo 13 command module. The quality and impact of this experience is something that many themed attractions and leisure centers now strive to recreate.

Museum exhibitions and programs are a key model for leisure attractions because they have a common core of programmatic features:

- PLACE—They are special places that you have to go to have a particular experience. You cannot have the actual experience at your home or office.

- EXPERIENCE—This feature is closely related to place. You visit the site to have a unique experience—traveling in space, getting a sense of what it is like to live in a different era or culture, exploring strange new natural environments.

- MEANING—Museums, galleries, heritage sites, and exposition centers are all about meaning. They exist to tell stories, provide context, impart information, encourage understanding, and express feelings. Place and experience are inherently a part of the leisure attraction world. Meaning and messages are elements that many attractions are incorporating into their shows and services.

The Audience: Improvement and Infotainment

In H. G. Wells' time, the Victorians called exhibition visits "edification" or "improvement." Today, we call heritage and educational content in our leisure activities "edutainment" or "infotainment." In the 1990s, as in the 1890s, this is big business. Aging baby boomers are interested in their cultural roots, says David Listokin, at the Center for Urban Policy Research at Rutgers University, and they have greater interest than their parents in things historical and in preservation:

> *Forty-five percent of U.S. adults planning a pleasure trip in spring 1996 said they intended to visit a historic site on vacation . . . an almost equally large share of leisure travelers planned to visit a cultural site . . .*
> American Demographics, 1996

Not only is this a growing audience, but it's also more affluent and educated. Several surveys conducted in the last 15 years indicate that cultural tourists and heritage tourists are willing to spend more time and money at an attraction. The desire to capture this market is one of the reasons for much discussion at IAAPA (theme park) conferences. Many attraction operators are considering ways of adding infotainment elements to their sites.

The Museum as Cultural Engine

Why are museums and heritage sites so valued by key audiences as destination experiences? Answer: Because they have a unique central role in any society as the source of knowledge and authenticity. They're endowed with the voice of credibility to a community—visitors expect to see that which is important and that which is true. These sites contribute to the collective consciousness and memory of society; they help generate values, serving as powerful cultural engines.

The core activities of museums are what make such institutions a unique and pervasive cultural force:

1. Museums collect and preserve artifacts, specimens, and/or works. It's the existence of a collection that distinguishes a museum from related institutions such as science centers, planetariums, and visitor information centers.

2. Museums conduct and/or act as a setting for research and intellectual inquiry. Museums contract research or have curators and associated researchers on staff. And, as with libraries and archives, museums are places where members of the public can come to study and learn new things.

3. Museums carry out public programmes. They do this for several reasons, but the primary goals are to raise public awareness of the institution and attract visitors and to interpret the meaning of the museum's collections and its research.

In the simplest possible terms, museums are places where people can experience the real thing, which is supported by research and made accessible through exhibits and events.

So, if museums are all about the real thing, how then can hypermedia, which is associated with simulation and representation (the fake thing), enhance the function of museums? This isn't a new challenge; museums often lead the way in applying new technology to achieve their mandates. Jeremy Bugler writes of how the Horniman Free Museum in London used new technology at the end of the 19th century:

> *By 1892 Frederick Horniman had established himself as a man who had collected curios and antiquities with passion if not coherence. He had stuffed one large mansion full of objects and artifacts, the whole brilliantly illuminated by an installation of the Electric Light, as one of the local papers said.*
>
> New Society 1978

This was revolutionary; adding electric lighting to the Horniman's galleries increased access to the displays by extending the opening hours of the institution. It also provided a much better view of the exotic ethnographic and biological specimens.

As I discuss the application of new media to core functions of cultural institutions, I will note the historical context wherever possible, using museums to illustrate how these cultural engines have stimulated different information and communication technologies.

Driving the Collecting Engine

Information tools cannot directly handle or physically restore an artifact or scientific specimen. However, information management and database systems are key to the long-term development and care of major collections. Put in the simplest terms, the better able we are to record and retrieve information about artifacts, the better able we are to appreciate the value of, and to care for, these objects.

A milestone in museological history was the development of a flexible, practical system for numbering artifacts and specimens. This was developed early in this century at the Pitt-Rivers Museum in England, which houses a worldwide collection of archaeological and ethnographic items that are diverse but systematically organized. Before the Pitt-Rivers system was adopted, methods of recording information on the location and nature of artifacts in museums were often highly eccentric and inconsistent.

Since the 1970s, many museums have transferred paper files to digital databases. The Canadian Heritage Information Network (CHIN), formed in the 1970s, was one of the first initiatives to standardize collection databases so that they could be accessed by cultural institutions around the world. The digitization and online access of collections and repertoire information is increasingly common through a growing number of institutional Web sites.

Powerful databases that expand the scope of collections records, their new ability to carry audiovisual information, and the ability of researchers to remotely access these records are key recent developments. We can now build flexible and comprehensive data records associated with artifacts, showing how they relate to other artifacts or to a variety of contexts. Collections data can be synthesized and examined at a greatly accelerated rate; an archaeologist can call up data on a specific type of projectile point, compare how it varied geographically, determine how the design may have evolved over time, and then consider how tools made from the same stone were designed. Also, multimedia allows the researcher to see how the tool was manufactured, hear an account by the archaeologist who used it, and access relevant papers. Finally, the data could be called up from the collections of Chicago's Field Museum by a graduate museum studies student in Singapore and, eventually, by the general public.

It is the inclusion of images and sound through multimedia that takes collections management into the realm of research, education, and entertainment. Increasingly, creative and interpretative applications of media challenge the paradigmatic barrier between entertainment and education. New digital tools, as in many other areas, accelerate and enhance this challenge.

Driving the Research and Education Engines

Museums have been slow to apply computers and digital media to enhance their more topic-based and educational engines. In the broadest terms, their applications have roughly paralleled the experience of science centers and children's "museums." However, museums have recently taken several initiatives in the use of digital media and online services to enhance their research and educational services. I will briefly describe some examples.

The Research Center at the U.S. Holocaust Memorial Museum is an advanced electronic archive. Visitors are able to call up information and recollections of Holocaust survivors, as well as different analytical accounts of the events leading up to, during, and after this profound human calamity. The software is intelligent in that it's able to account for linguistic variations in the names of people and events and to track spoken accounts of survivors with maps, graphics, and written text. Museum staff needed much more memory than normal for these multimedia archives because certain conventional means of data compression (fewer frames per second than broadcast television) raised some visitors' suspicion of historical revisionism. The need for an image stream that looks completely untouched is a new form of the demand for authenticity and credibility.

The Thinking Zone at the Museum of Tolerance offers several terminals where social issues are outlined for visitors, their opinions are electronically polled, and the collected results of these polls are then analyzed and displayed. This application allows visitors to participate in the actual programming of the exhibits and to see how their beliefs and attitudes may contribute to social issues.

The Royal Ontario Museum has pioneered several multimedia applications in their galleries since 1991. The Birdsong, Gem Stone, and China Gallery multimedia programmes all offer sound and vision, explore objects and ideas from different perspectives, and show how ideas and objects can morph into one another. What's remarkable is how these digital elements have become increasingly integrated into the overall exhibitry in the galleries. When "Birdsong" was installed in the Birds Gallery, it was a dedicated minitheater space. But, in 1996, the interactive elements in the China Gallery were incorporated directly into the casework of artifact displays. The technology is no longer a media novelty—it's just another tool for education and interpretation.

New interactive techniques and means of communication place severe demands on the gatekeepers and managers of our cultural heritage. We cannot wait while specialists in other fields generate new applications. Those who best know the material must be deeply involved in devising the best ways to communicate it, choosing appropriate technology from *all* that's available. This is equally true for all forms of cultural expression.

Driving the Exhibition and Entertainment Engines

Museums have used exhibitions and entertainment to attract and educate the public for well over a century. While there's a common perception that the use of advanced technology is new to the field, this is not true. It was Charles Babbage, creator of the difference engine, who, as scientific advisor to the Great Exhibition of 1851, noted how many of the modern mass attraction techniques were first devised for that event—a profound influence on future natural history museums, science museums, and theme parks. In his essays to the Academy of Moral Science of the Institute of France, Babbage describes an early form of theme park people mover:

> *Now if the (exhibit) stalls were placed back to back along the centre of the great longitudinal avenues, a railway formed of wooden planks placed edgeways might be raised above the middle of them . . . On this open railway cars mounted on wheels bound with india-rubber, in order to avoid all noise, might travel at the rate of from one to two perhaps three miles an hour. These cars might have luxurious cushions, and hold parties of different numbers . . . (railway) lines should take parties slowly along, so as to allow time to see the crowd below and the wonders of the exhibition, which might be rendered more distinct by means of opera glasses.*
>
> The Exposition of 1851, p. 39

Somewhat later than the world's fairs and theme parks, museums have implemented mass attraction technology since the early 1970s. They're using cinemas, simulators, and virtual realities for two distinct reasons:

- To attract more visitors and thereby generate greater revenues or justify continuing government or corporate support.

- To better interpret the collections and research of the museum. Digital systems are powerful means of making statements about human history, the natural world, and the universe around us. As our knowledge base increases, we naturally want to find better ways of communicating these insights.

There are three working categories in the use of new media and mass attraction technology at museums: advanced cinema, enhanced theater, and voyaging systems.

Advanced Cinema

This includes IMAX, IMAX *Dome*, Showscan, and the range of 8-perf/70mm film formats. Advanced cinema in exhibition environments is a product of the world's fair movement. At Expo '67 in Montreal, a company called Multiscreen Systems was contracted to use a bank of 30 film projectors to create a single giant film image. The difficulty of synchronizing these projectors led the founders of Multiscreen to develop a new system called IMAX, which used a single projector to create an image of comparable size. IMAX premiered at Expo '70 in Osaka, Japan, and was quickly adopted by many museums and science centers around the world. Other systems such as Showscan have opted for high-definition images via fast-frame-rate projectors as an alternative to wide-screen or dome cinema. The film libraries of all these companies reveal a strong commitment to documentaries and science education themes—films that augment the programming of many museums.

Digital technology is mostly applied here to improve the quality of visual and special effects or to make editing and production more efficient. The Miasaur Project at the Royal Ontario Museum features a more direct application; video projectors present a wide-screen programme where visitors select images of different computer-animated examples of dinosaur behavior. This technique is interactive, more flexible than cinema, and considerably less expensive to produce.

Enhanced Theater

This term refers to object theater, interactive theater, and multiscreen presentations. Variations of object theater—sound- and light-animated settings and dioramas—are among the oldest special display techniques. Interactive theater enables visitors to select different programmes and outcomes as the programme emerges. A recent example of this approach is Nauticus in Norfolk, Virginia. Numerous museums and science centres have used multiscreen presentations since the early 1980s; probably the most effective version is the Quadrascope at the Natural History Museum in London, a gigantic video virtual sphere—a living temple of natural processes. Digital technology has been most commonly applied for show control, but it can now be used to generate better images at lower cost.

Voyaging Systems

These are experiences where people are taken from one place to another, either by actual people movers or by simulators (the illusion of transportation). People movers aren't new to the museum world—a Nile trip simulator was created for the Museum of Egyptian Antiquities at the turn of the century, and the New World World's Fair of 1939 featured several examples.

The Time Cars at Jorvik Viking Village in York, England, produced by Heritage Projects, Ltd., in 1985, are a good example of this approach. But while telling the story of this archaeological work in an effective way, this approach has high storage, operational, and real-estate costs. It takes a lot of space, staff, and equipment to operate a people mover.

Ride simulators are one solution to these problems; they're less space-consuming and often require fewer staff. To return to Wells' novel, the first design of a "leisure simulator experience" was an attempt to recreate the journey of his Time Traveler. Inventor Robert Paul's October 24, 1896, British patent application, No. 19984, reads as shown in Figure 33.1.

Paul's proposed prehistoric elements were clearly informed by the then-recent dinosaurs and evolutionary monsters unveiled at 19th-century cultural attractions such as the British Museum of Natural History and the Great Exhibition at the Crystal Palace.

Modern Applications

Museums have lagged in the use of simulators partly because many don't have the same financial and creative resources as do purely entertainment attractions. But the core of this reluctance has been that museums tend to be self-directed experiences—people can choose the path of their visit. Simulators require strict pulsing and sequencing of people, and such visitor processing is antithetical to the traditional museum experience.

IMAX and 8/70 theaters, on the other hand, are acceptable because they run in parallel to the exhibition experience and aren't integral to the visit. Visi-

---

A Novel Form of Exhibition or Entertainment, Means for Presenting the Same

My invention consists of a novel form for exhibition whereby the spectators have presented to their view scenes which are supposed to occur in the future or in the past, while they are given the sensation of voyaging upon a machine through time, and means for presenting the scenes simultaneously and in conjunction with the production of the sensations by the mechanism described below, or its equivalent.

The mechanism I employ consists of a platform, or platforms, each of which contain a suitable number of spectators and which may be enclosed at the sides after the spectators have taken their places, leaving a convenient opening towards which the latter face, and which is directed towards a screen upon which the views are presented.

Figure 33.1 Robert Paul's 1896 time machine ride patent.

tors can decide whether they want to see the film or not—and they can see it before, after, or instead of visiting the galleries. Museums have experimented with sequenced exhibit programming since the 1980s, such as the Museum of the Moving Image in London (1985), which uses a sequenced storyline to describe the history of British film and television. The common audio tours at heritage sites and art galleries also deliver more sequenced exhibitions.

Accepting the challenge of visitor processing has permitted museums to include simulators as integral parts of their exhibition programmes. The Imperial War Museum uses a 4-degree-of-freedom capsule simulator to fly visitors through their collection of archival air-war films. The Evolator at the New Mexico Museum of Natural History is an elevator simulator and special effects gallery that creates a threshold experience into their prehistoric displays. A recent museum simulator, called "Opening the West: The Ride," is at the Canadian Museum of Civilization. This is an open-platform system, supplied by SimEx of Toronto, that allows visitors to take an ever-transforming flight over Canadian landscapes. It's a first in museological history—repurposing a simulator that was designed for a world's fair into a permanent museum context. You can expect more such crossovers of content between industries in the future.

The Promise of the Future: Converging Engines

There is an exciting overlap in the ways that digital and interactive media serve the core functions of cultural institutions. The database software originally used for documentation and management of collections can now supply a wide range of analytical and audiovisual capabilities. This is a great boon to curatorial research and public education. In *Operating Manual for Spaceship Earth*, Buckminster Fuller describes a subsistence black box, a compact, highly portable machine that provides the essentials for human life: water, food, shelter, and communication. Culture and education are also essential to human life; soon, digital access to museums and other culture repositories will serve as a cultural information black box. These boxes will be powerful, personalizable engines of culture and knowledge that provide access to and enhance a museum's administration, research, education, and celebration. They will be wired into wider networks to connect and collaborate with the information "boxes" at other institutions—science centers, libraries, archives, art galleries, performing arts centers, and other museums. And, as the interactive sophistication of these systems grows, they have great potential as a means of public access, interpretation, entertainment, and celebration—becoming the basis of attractions that are more popular, more effective, and even less expensive to operate. We will develop "intelligent" Internet repositories that constantly evolve and personalize their structure with use, to enhance each user's access to the practices, processes, and artifacts of our cultural heritage.

The Risks of Disassembling the Cultural Engine

Today, museums and heritage centers actively provide online and hypermedia services. Many have their own Web sites and multiple hypermedia systems detailing their collections and exhibits. These applications are highly accessible extensions of the experience available at the actual site. As of 1997, there are several projects to collect and distribute digital versions of major art, literature, and historical collections. Some of these projects include 3D scanning of artifacts and fitting them with their own photographic texture maps. Licensing and distribution of such massive databases is likely to become a major revenue stream for some institutions. Concerns regarding these projects usually focus on the possibility that digital reproductions of collections and sites will somehow replace the real ones.

These potential substitutions do entail risks—particularly to the meaning and authenticity of the collections and the heritage they represent. If the representation becomes too removed from reality, its context can be distorted or lost. Perhaps a greater risk is limits to actual access—wherein the majority of people would be offered digital replicas, while only a privileged few can experience the actual objects.

That scenario represents an erosion of the role of museums in our society— a disassembling of the cultural engine—that runs counter to prevailing trends in education and leisure. However, online, remote, and digital services are having an impact on these areas as well, and it's difficult to determine all the social consequences.

In most cases, the online presence of cultural heritage institutions and their collections won't eclipse the actual institutions. The very existence of museums is based on the presence of collections, which occupy physical space, just as the existence of an opera is based on live performances. Further, people will continue to occupy local communities—and our institutions serve as cultural icons and symbols of cultural distinction and integrity. People in a community will still feel proud of their museums, and people who visit a community will still want to visit them. The credibility that many cultural institutions enjoy, and that many purely recreational attractions envy, is likely to continue. And the sheer number and variety of interactive digital applications at cultural institutions will continue to increase.

Much of this process can be viewed as a form of technological Darwinism, where suppliers and creators of new media compete for sales and roles in an important and potentially profitable environment. But, in the long view, it's more of a model for the natural evolution of cultural institutions, where digital and online capacity enable more people to discover more about their own culture and the cultures of others. Digital techniques will enhance the role of our human heritage in the 21st century, supercharging what are already unique, invaluable cultural engines.

References

Baggage, Charles, *The Exposition Of 1851; Or Views of the Industry, the Science, and the Government Of England,* Second Edition, with Additions, John Murray, Albemare Street, London, 1851.

Bugler, Jeremy, "Chamber of Horrors," *New Society,* 1(6): 55–56, 1978.

Listokin, David, "Heritage Tourism Is Hot," *American Demographics,* pp. 13–14, September 1996.

Lord, Barry, and Dexter Lord, Gail, editors, *The Manual of Museum Planning,* Her Majesty's Stationery Office, London, 1991.

Ramsaye, Terry, "Robert Paul and the Time Machine," in *The Definitive Time Machine. A Critical Edition of H. G. Wells Scientific Romance with Introduction and Notes,* edited by Harry M. Geduld, University of Indiana Press, Bloomington and Indianapolis, 1987.

Wells, H. G., 1895, in *The Definitive Time Machine. A Critical Edition of H. G. Wells Scientific Romance with Introduction and Notes,* edited by Harry M. Geduld, University of Indiana Press, Bloomington and Indianapolis, 1987.

Biography

Hugh Spencer was trained in social anthropology and museum studies and has been active in the field of cultural planning and exhibition development since 1977. He has participated in exhibition projects for the Horniman Free Museum, the Hamilton Children's Museum, and the Royal Ontario Museum. Since 1987, Mr. Spencer has been a member of the firm of LORD Cultural Resources Planning & Management, Inc., where he is currently principal-in-charge of exhibition planning. His projects include curating an exhibition on Canadian science fiction for the National Library of Canada, consulting with the National Industrial Centre for Virtual Reality in Salford, England, and scripting the recently opened Singapore Discovery Centre—a $30-million interactive entertainment/education project.

Chapter 34

Virtual Communities: Real or Virtual?

John N. Latta, Ph.D.
4th Wave, Inc.

Introduction

Virtual communities are a cyberspace emulation of society. Avatars run about, behaving in a manner similar to activities in today's hectic society. Most of our shopping is done with ease in 3D virtual malls, while merchants are pleased with the low overhead and shrinkage. Secure transactions of all kinds are transparent and ubiquitous. Even cars can be driven in simulators to distant locations. Students of all ages go to virtual classrooms. Many large virtual worlds exist with endless opportunities for exploration, doing work, having fun, and social interaction.

It all has the ring of a nice chime—or does it? Today, the sound is not a chime but a discordant bong. Why? Viable virtual communities must fulfill three critical criteria: modality quality, social context, and market need.

Modality Quality

Our primary modality is sight, and we're the most visually literate culture in human history, yet today's shared space imagery in virtual communities is silly. Permanent objects like buildings are either easy-to-display but boring monochrome boxes or are nicely texture-mapped but contribute to glacial frame rates. A few thousand polygons per world is far from sufficient. With static photographs of individuals pasted onto avatars' facial texture maps, we can look like old high school photos on stick bodies—hardly compelling.

The second most critical stimulus, and the one that best communicates human emotion and mood, is sound. Here again, 3D, or spatialized, audio is emerging but is hardly mainstream. An effective virtual environment needs the ability to display ambient sounds, voice, and the sound effects caused by one's use of the virtual objects. Currently, audio in some virtual environments gives the impression that we're wearing mufflers while speaking through straws into an echo chamber.

Tactile and force-feedback interfaces can make virtual environments come alive. When properly implemented, they're genuinely intuitive, transparently helping users use and navigate through the environment. Most of today's devices are bulky, crude, inconvenient, and limited in volumetric coverage. When everything has the feel of a machine gun, the virtual context is that of an old gangster movie, and so is the range of social possibilities.

Social Context

Within real life, each culture is a refined set of rules that sets a framework for the norms of the society and all our interactions with others. The protocols for interaction in virtual communities are fragmentary and poorly defined; much of what we can and cannot do is bounded by the limitations of the technology. Network bandwidth and latency constraints place severe restrictions on the quality of interactions we have with others and the number of individuals in a shared space. Thus, the social context is not shaped by our relationships with individuals but by the workarounds, shortcuts, and approximations caused by the limitations of the technology—hardly the substrate for a community.

Market Need

There has long been a tenet that markets meet consumer needs. Needs can be met in many ways, giving consumers many choices—the function of an open, competitive free market. Consider shopping—a very complex social context and market dynamic. Mall shopping can be a shared social experience with a friend or a mad rush to get a specific item in the shortest possible time. Merchants are very effective in both observing and interacting with shoppers, optimizing the shopping environment to gain the greatest purchasing volume. The current shared shopping experience in cyberspace is hardly compelling and mostly frustrating. It's a solution in search of an uncertain market need, given the intense competition for consumer time and money. The "killer use" for shared virtual environments is waiting to be found.

Given these imperfections, how is the bong turned into a chime?

Quality, Sensibility, and Richness

The Quality Imperative

First, there must be a quality imperative. Not that virtual communities must emulate real communities, but the gap in the quality of the experience must be narrowed from where it is today. The most obvious example is in 3D image generation. Today's virtual community systems rely on software rendering on the client. The result is crude, faceted figures and environments that emulate reality only through much reliance on one's imagination. Most adults aren't interested in going from a real environment to an imagined one when they're shopping, meeting friends, or working. Such transitions are acceptable to children, but adults have narrower interests in fantasy.

We see the emergence of an important and relevant trend in entertainment software: how 3D acceleration technology is being used for human characters. That is, in polygon-limited 3D accelerators, the preference in polygon allocation is to individuals in scenes. Rather than making higher-quality environments, the polygon budget is allocated to the various characters or avatars. In early 1997, a high-end PC 3D accelerator could output 5,000 polygons in real time at a good frame rate (30 frames per second minimum) with all the filtering features turned on. Recognizable, personable figures typically take at least 5,000 polygons. Thus, a reasonable scene with one person could easily require 10,000 polygons. When we go shopping with five of our closest friends, assuming that they are near us, this could consume 30,000 polygons before we even see anything to buy. PC technology that achieves this performance may be common at about 2,000. Note how this relates to our earlier assessment—the baseline technology of virtual communities shouldn't need to be subsidized by increased mental effort; you shouldn't have to stretch your imagination to visualize a friend. The person should be recognizable, and his or her avatar must provide a degree of behavior (gestural) emulation, a tall order in terms of current technology. The same level of realism is crucial for another reason: satisfactory product representation, whether the product is an object or a virtual experience.

The quality gap between real and virtual also includes latency. In our interactions with individuals, we seldom experience long delays. An early example of such latency was telephony over synchronous-orbit satellites; the delay was unacceptable. As a result, satellite voice traffic has diminished substantially, moving back to undersea cables and land lines. In networks with unpredictable delay, like the Internet, this only compounds the kinds of compensation that individuals or their software must make as they attempt to interact, which often causes still more lag. The issue is compounded further because delays come from at least two sources: the network and the 3D image generator. In addition, latency disparity between modalities may be especially annoying. For example, the difference in delay between the visual and auditory creates lip-sync problems when watching individuals.

The multifaceted quality gap thus results in a requirement for participant compensation. That is, to what degree must the participant adjust for the limitations in the ability of the system to emulate real with virtual? Rather than the often used term "suspension of disbelief," it might be better to call it "reality disparity." In fantasy, some compensation is always required in terms of sensual perception and interaction with others. Put another way, we make-believe what the tools cannot do. As the virtual environment seeks to emulate normal human events and activities, many of which involve financial transactions, the component of acceptable fantasy must diminish. Thus, in a less-than-ideal virtual environment, such as exists today, it's very difficult to accomplish plausible commercial offerings that participants will agree to use repeatedly and habitually.

Virtual communities require the integration of many components; for them to be useful and functional, a system-level commitment must be made to quality in many forms. Today, quality is sporadic and not well correlated with the end objective, that of the perceived virtual world. A carefully integrated system would allow a less disjointed presentation of the illusion.

Start Making Sense

Second, the applications must make sense. Among other things, successful virtual communities must be shared spaces, whose functions can overlap with other competing technologies. An example of a real shared space is a conference room meeting. A group teleconferencing application that uses video to link multiple locations is a competing technology to a virtual conference, which emulates the conference room and includes individuals from distant locations sitting at a virtual table. What is the value of the latter over a more conventional video teleconference? We suspect little; in most cases, less value is derived because of the abstraction required of the participants and the artifactual distractions introduced by the simulation. The group shopping experience is often cited as an activity in virtual communities, but again, there are many psychological and sociological factors involved—a dynamic that will be hard for virtual shopping to match. What, then, is a good example? We are drawn back to entertainment as the anchor application. Why?

A critical reason is that games have a high degree of fantasy, and, with the current state of the technology, much fantasy is required to bridge the virtual-to-real gap. Yet, in many cases, even games must be compromised. From a male perspective, appealing games involve fast action; this is where latency is already an impediment, though technology is emerging to reduce latency effects in networked game play. Virtual community entertainment might be of greatest interest to women and girls. Feminine preferences in game play include exploration, building things, and social interaction. Each can have an enduring quality over time in situations where experiences and relationships are established and then evolve. With enough rich, transparent social features, such games are likely to be less sensitive to image quality abstractions and latency. In current graphical virtual communities, female participation of 25 percent is not unusual; in some cases, the core users are 50 percent female. Thus, elements of feminine play can favor virtual communities as they might be constructed now and in the near future.

Provide Richness

Third, virtual communities need richly compelling content to be attractive, but the issue is far more complex than the placement of games, avatars, and objects within environments. There are interesting parallels with the Internet. It could be said that the Internet had content when the traffic was dominated by file transfers—the content was programs and data accessed by the ftp. In comparison with the impact of the Web, ftp seems mundane. The user interface changed the utility of the Net, but, more importantly, it brought rich opportunities for content. The Web created the opportunity for a new plateau of design aesthetics for both content and the user interface. We cannot lose sight of the metaphor that the Web is based on—interactive publishing via HTML pages. Yet, the idea of virtual communities goes well beyond a publishing metaphor. Even something as simple as the exploration of 3D spaces has many perceptual elements besides the shapes, sizes, and colors of the space. Just as with HTML, navigation and access can be as important as the data because, without a means to get to content, there *is* no content—hence, the popularity of search engines. Since a major portion of the content in virtual communities is their participants, we must look to and beyond psychology to understand the role of individuals. We must include environmental social psychology, which deals with the totality of people in spaces. It seems we've gone in a circle, having started with content and ending up with psychology of the participants, where the participants are content. Correct—just another measure of the range of issues and level of complexity to be addressed in making virtual communities viable.

Where does this leave us in our assessment of virtual communities? There is only one conclusion: The technology and its implementations are crude and in search of a market need.

What is required to go forward? There are five factors that gate the development of a market.

The Gates

3D Infrastructure

To create a mass market for economically viable virtual communities, there needs to be an installed and active base of at least 10-million 3D accelerators with at least 50M pixel/sec performance. This creates a minimal client target from which a vertical or horizontal market can evolve. The software infrastructure must improve to where 3D functionality is embedded in more applications. It must be much easier than today to use (navigate and interact), model, and modify 3D worlds and the objects in them. In short, 3D technology must become pervasive, with significant commonality of function from world to world, no matter who made and operates them. This massive task of developing effective commonality is currently underestimated, ignored, and/or obscured by even more basic design hurdles.

Better Representations of Humans

People should look like recognizable individuals, and they should have recognizable attributes—"fantasy minimization" properties. Just as we can pick out an individual from some distance without even seeing his or her face, the same should happen in cyberspace. In font technology, "hinting" is used to generate quality characters in limited-resolution situations. Just as inverse kinematics changed the quality of animate body motions, another leap in technology will be required to effectively represent humans behaving in cyberspace with unique personalities and realistic physical attributes.

Social Interactions Mature in Cyberspace

While e-mail has created its own social dynamic on an individual level, companies have also absorbed e-mail in their own business culture. The same can be said of 2D GUIs with HTML home pages on the Web. Yet, the dynamic of social interaction in networked 3D is far from mature. A culture of accepted norms, in the context of the limitations of the technology, must develop. This will initially be shaped within today's crude systems and evolve with time. Just as our culture is shaped by history and today's environments, the same can be said of cyberspace—which is now effectively in B.C. (Before Cyberspace).

Ease of Use

Navigation devices that are as simple to use as walking do not yet exist. No head-mounted displays (HMDs) or other physical barriers to participation should be involved. User interfaces and navigation must be genuinely intuitive and easy to accomplish—travel must feel "natural" or barely be noticed at all. Existing 3-space browsers are confusing and difficult to navigate, and most 6-degree-of-freedom (DOF) navigation devices are unnatural to use and hard to learn, even though we evolved with the ability to move in 3D space. The fundamental task of just getting around must be trivial, not hard to learn or accomplish. The two F's—feel and force—will be a component in making interaction with virtual communities come alive. Voice, though still difficult to deploy at reasonable cost, will eventually play a critical part in simplifying our conceptual and virtual travels, too.

Utility

Cyberspace virtual communities must be able to do something well that is compelling to the participants and difficult or impossible to do in other ways. Of the many useful tools developed for personal computers, none successfully attempt to do more than a couple of functions—a few techniques for enhancing our ability to process one or two data types. The tools and functions for a ubiquitous cyberspace must do at least that much, and probably a great deal more, since it is competing not just with items at hand but our entire environment. Of the five factors, this will likely be the most difficult factor to accomplish.

Illustrations Approaching Market Reality

Our five factors show how difficult it is to accomplish virtual communities, and thus one would surmise that the near-term potential is rather bleak. Let us take a different perspective and ask the question, Are there near-term applications that leverage existing technology and provide credible and enjoyable experiences? We will explore this by considering three examples: My Home, Fantasy Friends, and Play Everywhere.

My Home

The best-selling mass-market category for 3D software is home design programs. These applications go well beyond homes and include not only internal design but also external design, landscaping, and even deck design. These programs are largely used by women to conceptualize a new home or to remodel one. There is already a component of fantasy in designing and visualizing a home, and thus the line between reality and fantasy is easily blurred. The criteria for a successful home representation is that it look credible and be customizable by the user.

The extension of this software family into a virtual community setting is conceptually straightforward. For example, these programs could output to VRML 2.x. By posting your version of My Home on an Internet server, there is a means for others to visit My Home. Two or more individuals could meet in My Home, be it a representation of your actual home or a virtual one, for social interaction just as in real life. Consider having tea during a visit at My Home. When evaluated against the five factors, two have clear shortcomings: human representation and social interaction. In the My Home example, both are closely related. We are assuming that the visitors to the home all have sufficient 3D acceleration performance in the client that the representation of the home is not only credible but recognizable and realistic.

The "visit" experience is what's critical in making this virtual community viable. Ideally, one would like a first-person perspective and to see the other individuals in much the same way as it's done today. Further, body and facial movements should track the individual and be recognizable as that person's. With today's technology, this can hardly be done without considerable body encumbrances. The role of behaviors associated with individuals and the ability of those behaviors to reflect actual mannerisms present a significant challenge. The set of social norms for those behaviors is another underdeveloped factor. Should the visitors be allowed to walk around the home without the host being present? In virtual environments, the social and physical techniques for dealing with such questions in the real world must be augmented and emulated in software. Few development efforts have scratched the surface here. In spite of these limitations, My Home has the potential of building on an already large consumer interest category and extending it to a shared experience. One advantage of this application is that the number of participants would be small. The content of this community, that is, My Home, should already be available using existing or upgraded home design software; this application is a logical extension to an existing social experience.

Fantasy Friends

Given that children find it easy to construct and interact in their own fantasies, why not have a children's virtual community in environments they understand and can relate to? We call this Fantasy Friends, and it combines cartoons, branded characters, and children's interest in participation in what they see.

Saturday morning cartoons deliver branded characters in fantasy situations; the closest children get to this fantasy is to buy toys of the characters or situations. With these items, in their own homes, they construct fantasy situations, or play. The virtual community can be a direct extension, where Fantasy Friends is implemented as an extension of a particular Saturday episode, complete with characters and environment. Children could replay or construct new situations with the characters and play some of the characters themselves. The social situation would be defined by the norms of the particular characters. Here is where some caution would have to be exercised, in a manner that children's programming is already under some criticism for; that is, these virtual environments need to encourage positive behavior. The community environment would not only have the characters in them but also other children or characters being played by children. It is easy to see how this could become quite complex. The critical implication of one of our five points is evident: ease of use. A child who is too young to adequately manipulate the interface is not too young to see that his or her older siblings are having fun; without interface options, frustration will ensue. The worlds and play spaces would also have to be segmented or dynamically cloned to limit the number of participants. This is a systems and scalability issue, not one that limits the enjoyment children derive from the experience.

Of our five points, ease of use is the most important here; the designers need to match the play interaction with the target players. The criterion for success has to be derived satisfaction from play as gauged by the children—a tough standard to meet. Embedded in this is the ability for children to have an avatar that establishes a particular personality with which they can identify over time. Another factor related to the points is the representation of the characters, including their behavior and intelligence. Although there is considerable latitude in what the cartoon characters can do, each should have a recognizable personality. This implies considerable intelligence in the characters, which must be manifested in realtime in the context of multiple users—a formidable task.

In Fantasy Friends, we leverage weaknesses of today's 3D and virtual community technology into strengths. At the same time, there are high expectations for credible interactions, even in a fantasy world, that are highly demanding of the underlying technology in terms of artificial intelligence and social environment simulations.

Play Everywhere

Our Play Everywhere community concept brings seamless continuous entertainment across many locations that provide varied means of play. Although one may conceptualize this as an extension of continuous chat, it is fundamentally richer. Play Everywhere has many components, including in-home and out-of-home. The community or communities would be segmented into locales and functions. Although there is some parallel with the ImagiNation Network, Play Everywhere would have the quality of the imagery and the degree of nuance of the interaction as a function of "where played."

Consider a baseball game where the players can play at home or in an elaborate sports bar. This example has the advantage that the social context is well known—everyone knows what the objectives of the game are. The out-of-home players have the advantage of a richer experience. In our example, this could be a sports bar; in this venue, they would have a centrally located "play stage" where the batting player would wear the team jacket. This jacket—and the bat—would be instrumented for motion tracking. When the batter is up, he or she would wear the jacket and swing at pitched balls. Base running could be done on a treadmill in the high-end sports bars, but, in most cases, this would be confined to controlling the PC as the key play device. Batters and other game roles could also play from home, but a different skill set would be required in that these players would likely not wear the instrumented jacket.

What are the practical implications of this, especially with respect to our five points? One of the more critical is social interaction; in this Play Everywhere example, "social" equates to "game play." Because the play interaction is defined by a set of rules that define baseball, our application has a standard that must be emulated across diverse platforms and playing conditions. If, for example, one player is a laggard because of the platform or the game's implementation on a particular platform, his or her play would disadvantage the whole team. Thus, the integration of disparate play is critical, including the potential for handicapping, in making play both credible and enjoyable. The other essential component is the 3D infrastructure, which supports not only visualization but also the actual play. This includes motion tracking, ball dynamics simulation, and the development of out-of-home venues. Note that this latter could become a franchise business and, in the context of our examples, just another infrastructure component.

These three examples illustrate not only the variety of ways in which virtual communities can be defined but also how difficult it will be to accomplish. We return to a simple premise: If virtual communities are to profitably simulate real community interaction, the criterion for success must be the minimization of the gap between real and virtual. It's a matter of turning bongs into chimes.

Biography

Dr. Latta has B.E.S., M.S., and Ph.D. degrees in electrical engineering. His early research at the University of Michigan, RCA Labs, and Bell Labs was in the computer design of holographic optics systems. He has been involved in computers, systems engineering, and entrepreneurial efforts for the last 25 years. As president of 4th Wave, a firm based in Alexandria, Virginia, Dr. Latta is involved in the technologies of 3D, multimedia, personal computers, and virtual reality. He and the staff consult on emerging markets and the evaluation of how advanced technologies can be applied to products. 4th Wave has as its clients many of the top firms in the computer, semiconductor, and telecommunications industries. Dr. Latta has written and spoken on the developing markets of personal computers, multimedia, and virtual reality in the United States, Europe, and Japan. He is the author of numerous reports and papers and is quoted in the *Wall Street Journal,* the *New York Times,* and *Time* magazine. He is also the editor in chief of the *WAVE Report,* an electronic newsletter that covers 3D, multimedia, and shared environments.

Chapter 35

Surreal Estate Development: Secrets of the Synthetic World Builders

Michael Limber
Angel Studios

Introduction

As the promise of virtual reality begins to come true, new skills are required to take advantage of the emerging interactive technologies. At this point in the evolution of the field, skilled groups of artists and scientists are required to generate compelling virtual experiences. The structure of these groups is unique, and its collaborative success depends on the careful integration of computer technology and creative content. This chapter describes a way to do so.

Language of all kinds requires the systematic use of our conceptual faculties. With written language, a few marks on a page convey complex thoughts and emotions that can completely consume the reader. This ability to transport the mind to another time and context is as unique as the desire itself. All expressive forms enable the recreation of some aspect of reality according to the artist's internal view of the world.

The introductions of photography, film, and recorded sound each allowed greater range of expression. Reality could be recorded, edited, and rearranged to present a synthetic but very believable series of events. Theater and cinema can be considered early forms of virtual reality. The audience sits in a darkened room where, for a while, they're transported to another dimension. The written word hasn't been the same since.

Film and television, however powerful, are generally confined to the bounds of "real" reality. Both require special effects to represent ideas and events that are

Parts of this chapter were published in different form as course notes at SIGGRAPH '94-'96 and TiLE95.

intangible or currently impossible. The advent of three-dimensional computer graphics set a precedent in the ability to portray fantastic yet realistic forms. But traditional computer animation is still a passive experience. Viewers watch and listen while their bodies are motionless. Thoughts and feelings can be evoked this way, but a true VR experience involves full interaction.

With the advent of VR, we're now poised to create experiences that completely immerse the senses. Sight, sound, touch, and smell can be manipulated synthetically to produce a seemingly transcendental effect. Entwined in media hyperbole, enshrined by modern philosophers, and dreaded by technophobes, VR promises to change the way everything from science to art is expressed and perceived. The open question for this new medium is the same for all forms of expression—what content shall it express?

Up to this point, complex computer graphics have required the skills of numerous scientists and programmers. Elaborate scenes involve painstaking communication to the computer at a very low level. For this reason (coupled with the speed of the available hardware), significant synthetic imagery is usually seen only for brief moments of graphic spectacle. The reputation of computer graphics' visual impact and style has overshadowed concerns about its creative content.

This is changing. Computers offer a unique opportunity for the creative and technical sides of human nature to collaborate. Advances in hardware performance and object-oriented programming are giving us a first glimpse at the shores of a new moldable frontier. We can shape our new worlds any way we want, and it will reflect on us and on our values.

This chapter attempts to show the importance of taking a Renaissance approach to the development of realtime interactive experiences, of integrating the skills of not only scientists, technicians, and engineers but also writers, designers, and artists. After establishing a brief historical context, we will examine a model for developing, creating, and producing compelling virtual content.

Historical Background

Most of the initial development of 3D computer graphic science, back in the mid-1960s, was for realtime military flight simulators. The cost of training fighter pilots in real planes far exceeded the cost of developing a synthetic approach. The esoteric new technology gained popularity as the field of Scientific Visualization emerged. Complex intangible phenomena could be made visible to the naked eye. Since the computational cost of realtime simulation was high, computer animation technology developed that enabled high-resolution, frame-by-frame output of lengthy time-dynamic visualizations.

The value of this photo-realistic visual technology was soon apparent to the business community. By the late 1970s, broadcast IDs, corporate logos, and the occasional commercial and film effect debuted a new art form to large audiences. By the late 1980s, computer graphics not only was a familiar workhorse of broadcast television but also was finally embraced by the cinema as a viable tool. Concurrently, millions of people were exposed to interactive experiences through personal computers and cartridge-based videogames.

Since that time, the entertainment market has become a major force in the development of graphics technology, including virtual reality. The gaming industry has already embraced it. The venture capital community, which waited out the initial media storm, is now active. The growth curve of development and interest appears to be exponential.

New Opportunities

Film and Television

These new computer technologies are creating opportunities in film and television. Automated animation techniques will make more long-form computer-generated projects feasible. Faster hardware and increased software control is giving digital effects longer and longer screen times, and more significant characters will soon be digitally generated. There are numerous fully computer-generated films currently in production, and several weekly TV series are using digital scenery and characters. The real revolution will come when these shows are developed and produced in real time.

Video Arcades

Traditional video arcades are going to make a dramatic change in the next few years. New 3D interactive rides and experiences will soon replace some of the popular 2D sprite-based games. Affordable motion-base units, high-resolution head-mounted displays, and a wide range of 3D realtime interactive games will change the small standing-room-only video parlors into large interactive gaming centers. Many owners are teaming up with mall and theater operators to widen the appeal of their locations. The large videogame companies are using these arcades as test-beds for new approaches to 3D gaming.

Consumer Platforms

Current consumer videogame profit surpasses that of feature film box-office intake; it topped $20 billion in 1995. The market for the new realtime 3D products will surpass that. The teenaged gamers of ten years ago have grown up, and they're still playing games—but their tastes have matured. All of the major consumer game companies are currently manufacturing new 32-bit and 64-bit platforms with 3D capability. Some have collaborated with realtime hardware makers to produce these next-generation machines, and developers are rushing to learn the new skills required to exploit them.

Location-Based Entertainment

Dynamic location-based entertainment (LBE) projects are attempting to displace the large amusement park iron rides. Eventually, networked full-immersion simulation centers will fill a market niche between traditional centralized theme parks and arcades. The realtime software experiences can be updated and changed frequently, giving a long-term appeal to the locations. Because most motion-base systems are relatively small compared to roller coasters, simulation centers can be set up almost anywhere; in fact, many portable systems exist. Advanced versions may soon radically change the shape of county fairs and sports events. From Las Vegas casinos to shopping malls and cruise lines, operators are finding that virtual reality is drawing more than just teenage interest. The market's demographic age range is rapidly widening.

Technology Developments

CPUs and I/O Devices

Developments in hardware are raising the standards and expectations for computer-generated images and experiences. Some PCs are approaching the performance of some high-end workstations—at a fraction of the cost. Graphics hardware companies are releasing 32- and 64-bit hardware with 3D capacity of around 500 to 2,000 un-anti-aliased untextured polygons per frame. The cost will be between $200 and $500. The high-end manufacturers are also quickly raising performance. Some realtime image generator hardware is currently capable of generating elaborate realtime interactive scenarios—about 3,000 to 5,000 anti-aliased textured polygons per frame running at 60 Hz. In 1995, these machines cost between $100,000 and $250,000. In 1996, that same power is available in the $25,000 to $50,000 range.

A wide range of new input devices allow for unprecedented data capture. From 3D laser scanners and 3-space digitizing devices to full-body motion capture systems and facial expression sensing units, data from the real world can be captured and used to develop the new digital "unreal" estate.

Like input devices, output devices are multiplying in complexity and interactive function. There are many potential uses of high-resolution head-mounted displays. From training simulators and medical applications to CAD workstations and realtime consumer gaming platforms, these new output devices allow the user full immersion. New designs do away with screens altogether and project images directly onto the retina of the eye. Also, varieties of motion-base units and force-feedback devices are multiplying in number, providing convincing synchronized physical responses to virtual events.

Networks

One of the most significant developments in the advent of realtime interactivity is the establishment of large-scale networks. Governments and private companies are committed to developing a high-bandwidth digital communications infrastructure. The superior speed and bandwidth of fiber optics seem sure to uncork the bottle on sophisticated realtime multiuser interaction and communication.

Applications

Simulation and intelligent-agent applications are maturing rapidly, as are complex physical dynamics and kinematics software libraries. The ability to compute the effects of gravity and wind and the behaviors of fabric and skin is opening the door on elaborate dynamic forms, all running in realtime. Realtime particle systems make commonplace the creation of believable flocks of birds, smoke, dust, and meandering bubbles. Developments in automating distinct human and animal motion and behavior are promising to populate virtual reality with believable counterparts.

The Skills

Successful control of this new medium requires a wide range of specialized skills. Knowledge of content, form, reality, and "virtuality" must be extensive. Creative groups must have experience creating novel concepts and fiction, designing varieties of detailed artwork, building elaborate 3D models and environments, and creating evocative character expression and behavior. Programmers need to be familiar with everything from realtime 3D simulation and complex physical dynamics to intricate multiplayer interactivity, numerous device interfaces, and networks. The learning curve for these skills is long, but, when combined, they can be used to build expansive and unique synthetic worlds and experiences. Within the next few years, nearly everyone will have experienced them firsthand.

Certain companies already possess many of the necessary talents and can take advantage of this window of opportunity. Defense industry simulation companies are exploring the entertainment market and developing entertainment concepts. They're familiar with 3D graphics and realtime simulation but have much to learn about the creative requirements of entertainment. The large videogame companies are also upgrading their technical skills. They're familiar with creating content and 2D artwork for single-player games on small computers, but the tasks involved in dealing with large quantities of dynamic 3D data, behavior, and technology are a new discipline.

There is another type of company well poised to take advantage of this new technology—the traditional high-end computer graphics production facilities. The more experienced studios have always had to rely on strong in-house software development teams to produce work of lasting significance. Their software departments must constantly invent more efficient techniques of dealing with high-resolution data and complex scene descriptions, not to mention new visual tricks. Their creative departments have consistent yet flexible talents, and many are extensive enough to produce intricate, fully digital, long-form projects.

But market pressures are tough; the large capital investment in necessary equipment, along with the expensive staff talent, make the task almost prohibitive. High-resolution computer graphics production is mostly service work. Companies rarely have any equity interest in the projects they produce; a marginal income and a good reputation are signs of success. If these organizations can make the leap to developing their own content, many may enjoy fiscal success as well.

Aside from the necessity of developing proprietary content, it's essential for the software department to make some changes as well. They must build a robust library of diverse simulation software. In general, realtime and physical dynamics programming is a natural progression toward speeding up and automating otherwise painstaking animation production. But it also includes the complexity of generating and keeping track of dynamic interactions between entities in the virtual world. This leap into object-oriented realtime programming and artificial intelligence is essential to be competitive in the new interactive markets.

Realtime Content Production

With few exceptions, the production of realtime content is similar to the production of conventional 3D computer graphics. A fundamental difference at this early stage of the industry is the necessity for in-house development of the creative content as well as the necessary 3D realtime techniques. Companies not only must invent the technology but also, because of its unique nature, must invent creative applications for it. Because of the high expenses, projects tend to be driven by commercial demands. In general, most production companies are hired to solve someone else's creative problems. Initiating an original idea for a virtual experience, a realtime game, or an interactive fiction is a new task for many otherwise experienced production groups.

So, who will develop these creative properties and how will they do it? The following sections outline a production model for realtime virtual environments and interactive content. The background for this information comes from my experience as chief operating officer and head of production for Angel Studios of Carlsbad, California. Best known for its work on *The Lawnmower Man* and Peter Gabriel's "Kiss That Frog" music video, Angel Studios now develops content for 3D realtime interactive entertainment.

Team Breakdown

The most vital asset of any organization is the synergy created by its individuals. Getting the entire team to collaborate effectively is the key to creating content of lasting quality. Following is a list of the major team members involved in interactive content production and their functions.

The Management Team

Producer

The producer is the overseer and integrator of all aspects of a project. From initial bids and final budgets to personnel and resource scheduling, the producer serves as the tip of the production pyramid. The producer is the bridge between the creative, the production, and the software teams. When developing content for an outside client, the producer is also the liaison for all interactions with the customer. When developing content in-house, the producer serves as a link between the content distributor and the production department. The producer also plays a major role in selecting the team members for any given project and in generating a complete and realistic schedule for the allocation of resources and the timely execution of the work. As companies get larger and the projects increase in number and scope, the producer may need several assistant producers to distribute the work load.

Creative Director

Working closely with the producer and other project directors, the creative director manages the creative team and helps define a consistent aesthetic approach for each interactive project. From concept formation and content selection through progressive refinements and final interactive testing, the creative director is the aesthetic cornerstone of the interactive production studio.

Production Director

The production director supervises all in-house production. Responsibilities include deciding which production approach to take, ensuring standards and specifications for each part of a project, and coping with the inevitable unexpected production dilemmas. The production director works closely with the creative and software teams, assuring the smooth progress of each stage. Production directors need to be experienced technical directors themselves to supervise the overlapping production of diverse projects.

Software Director

The software director defines the entire company's programming technology. Realtime applications are pushing the limits of available computer technology, and pioneering virtual experiences require revolutionary software techniques. The software director determines what aspects of an application to emphasize for each project and which programmers should perform what tasks.

The Creative Team

Game Designer

Since most current realtime development revolves around interactive entertainment, another essential team member is the game designer. Serving as the creative team leader, the game designer usually comes up with the initial creative concept. All aspects of game design, from concept and game logic to artwork and gameplay, come under the guiding hand of the game designer. Generally creating the fiction for the experience, the game designer works closely with the art director and production artists to outline and design the project.

Art Director

Once the concept has been outlined, the art director steps in to visualize the idea. Concept sketches are produced, and the creative team uses them to stimulate further dialogue and development. They are responsible for all of the project's aesthetic concerns, from start to finish, and ensure continuity and consistency for all artwork. A talented art director can make an interactive experience both visually exciting and creatively compelling.

Sound Designer

A key aspect of any realtime experience is convincing sound design. The sound designer uses a wide range of tools to create interactive theme music, sampled voice-overs, and holophonically placed sound effects. Otherwise well-done projects may fail because of poor sound design. A good sound designer's work tends to integrate the entire project, completing the intended effect and permitting the audience to truly immerse themselves.

The Production Team

Technical Director

The technical director must integrate all the different aspects of a production team's effort into a cohesive whole ready for the proposed application. From organizing models and setting up precomputed sequences to tuning the application and managing varieties of data, the technical director organizes, produces, and refines the project. The software team members work closely with the technical director to make sure realtime experiences are as engaging and attractive as traditional passive events, like television and film.

3D Artist

All virtual worlds require extensive model building. The 3D artist takes design concept sketches and storyboards and creates digital models using a variety of sophisticated construction tools. Some objects are static and fairly straightforward to make. Others, like detailed dynamic characters and elaborate animated devices, require talents similar to those of an architect or sculptor. Making models for realtime applications requires creating well-proportioned *low-detail* objects. Making a 50,000-polygon human character look good isn't difficult. Making a 500-polygon human look good is.

Production Artist

Once a project is in production, there is generally much artwork to be generated. Included in the production artist's duties are everything from complete maps of virtual worlds and object construction drafts to model sculptures and artwork for texture maps. Supervised by the game designer and the art director, the production artist brings to full life all of the previous conceptual work and provides the production material for the look and feel of the realtime experience.

The Software Team

Application Programmer

Each application tends to build off an existing library of solutions. Since each project is also unique, the application programmer is in charge of developing and maintaining the structure and content of each realtime program. He or she integrates the efforts of the rest of the software and production teams and assembles a single piece of executable code that comprises the entire interactive experience.

Simulation and Dynamics Programmer

Essential for a convincing simulation, the simulation and dynamics programmer is the physics and behavior expert. This person needs strong skills in physics, mathematics, and dynamics and should be able to combine these disciplines effectively. Realtime inverse and forward kinematics, particle dynamics, collision detection, and character automation are all concerns of the simulation programmer.

Interface Programmer

The final success of the project is assured if the human interface is intuitive and effortless. The work of all the other team members can be lost if the interaction interface is clumsy and complex. From on-screen information and selection menus to sequence scheduling and user input processing, the interface programmer is responsible for maintaining the quality of the interaction between human and machine. The style of the interface is inextricably tied to the creative director's vision and the game designer's intent.

Device Programmer

All interactive experiences require interfacing with numerous devices and accessories. From joysticks, data gloves, and digital audio equipment to head-mounted displays, body trackers, and 6-degree-of-freedom (DOF) motion bases, the device programmer integrates physical devices with the interactive application to produce the virtual reality effect. Since interactivity between users is an essential component of VR, the device programmer also handles all networking tasks.

The Application

Equally as important as the development of the creative content is the development of the technical content. The software application executes control over the description and behavior of a virtual scene. Since virtual worlds by their nature need to have autonomous aspects, the software used in building and managing these realtime environments must have a sophistication well beyond that which is currently commercially available. Developing robust in-house software code and libraries is essential for breaking new ground and limits.

For the now-traditional method of producing computer graphics, there are a number of fairly complete third-party software solutions available. Offering a high level of scene management and control with numerous sophisticated effects and procedures, these programs make the creation of high-resolution imagery more accessible than ever before. But many of the computationally expensive software techniques in these packages are not well suited to high-speed realtime software requirements. It will be some time before we see complete and integrated off-the-shelf realtime packages.

The following is a specification outline for advanced realtime simulation software. It is by no means inclusive, but it covers the main features and techniques necessary for the production of realtime interactive content. Its content represents thousands of man-hours of experimentation and exploration. I believe it is a minimum specification for dealing with the complex problems associated with creating realtime interactive content.

Overview

What's required is a collection of high-performance tools for developing state-of-the-art, realtime, 3D interactive experiences for simulation, VR, gaming, and animation. They must run on a highly optimized library of C++ programs, which forms the basis of a complete simulation package. They must support a variety of hardware, from 32-bit home systems and PCs to high-performance graphics engines, with transparent support for commercial rendering packages, as well as a complete complement of general data-processing tools, along with low-level vector, matrix, and math operations.

Scene management would use a hierarchical scene description structure, supporting dynamic load management, multiple cameras and lights, custom and automatic culling, and level of detail (LOD) features. It should take advantage of new multiprocessing technology for simulation, drawing, culling, and custom applications and support multiple viewports and hardware pipelines.

Built-in distributed networking capability is a necessity for gaming scenarios and large production environments.

You also need realtime options for generating radiosity lighting effects, edge-on fading to simulate gaseous objects, and multipass rendering for high-quality shading and special effects like realtime bump maps, as well as optimized display list processing for nonlinear deformations and n-dimensional shape interpolation.

Dynamics Simulation

One of the most important features of any realtime system is how well it deals with physical dynamics of objects and entities in a virtual environment. Some key features for this include optimized forward and inverse kinematics (with integrated motion capture), hierarchical collision detection using surface geometry and/or primitives, and realtime nonlinear spring-mass networks. Also included are multiple dynamic particle systems that can interact with global forces and other objects, efficient height-above-terrain and range finding, and eye-path collision avoidance.

Behavioral Simulation

Populating virtual worlds with intelligent agents and entities is critical in developing compelling interactive experiences. Using an extensible object-oriented approach provides controls for creating varieties of autonomous friends and foes. To support photo-realistic animations, it's useful to allow for imported keyframe data from third-party animation packages, as well as a variety of motion capture systems, like the Polhemus FastTrak and Ascension's Flock-of-Birds.

Database Generation

The construction tools should offer a full-function point, line, polygon, and patch database editor, as well as an interface for objects from third-party products. You should also allow for dynamic integration of newly developed modeling tools, with a generic graphical user interface builder. In this way, new software techniques can be integrated and released to the entire studio in a matter of minutes. Finally, you need an extensive library of floating-point image-processing tools for image manipulation and texture generation and management.

Audio Features

Sound is absolutely critical in a virtual world; full MIDI support is a good starting point. 3D placement of localized sounds, ambient sounds, and virtual microphones all help drive the illusion home. You need an efficient toolkit of digital sound editing and imaging tools, configurable enough to support a variety of hardware/software audio interfaces.

Hardware Interface

It's essential to be able to import and export data from a wide variety of input and output devices. For example, 2-DOF to 6-DOF motion bases, stereoscopic and head-mounted displays, and full-body motion tracking systems need to be supported with a customizable networked input event queue, and that's just part of the list.

Extension Packages

Certainly a library of generic objects and environments is a must for efficient production, as well as a feature-based environment generator. Many applications require extensive vehicle dynamics with elaborate weapons and explosion handling capabilities. Software libraries for synthetic actors and crowds can be added along with feature-based expression editors with automated lip-sync support. All these features can be used for high-resolution photo-realistic animation production systems. Efficient security encryption, production management, and tracking should eventually be integrated into the system.

These specifications and suggestions are an example of what is required to produce truly compelling interactive content. If the user is to get deeply involved in a simulation of a virtual world, that depiction must be complete, consistent, and coherent. Advanced programming techniques must be used if one is to achieve a willing suspension of disbelief using a reasonable amount of production time and money.

Summary

A dynamic balance between strong creative and technical teams, a thriving research and development effort, and a genuine enthusiasm for the work are the ingredients most likely to produce an engaging product. For now, the task is still fairly complicated. As these techniques and procedures become more refined, the depiction of more lush and detailed worlds will be possible. Not until the look and feel of the interactive experience is as good as the product's cover art and not until the content has the depth and appeal of some of our best art forms will true realtime interactive experiences fulfill the promise of virtual reality.

One day it may be possible for a creative designer, writer, and director to sit together in a special room and develop interactive experiences merely by discussing and describing the content to a sophisticated computer. Their ideas would be interpreted and turned into representations in realtime, as well as any modifications they might have. A "black box" of this kind would let the human designer operate at a high level, much like a film director currently directs actors. However, there are plenty of useful incremental technology steps between here and there.

Most of the opportunities we've discussed pertain to leisure and entertainment; that's temporary. High costs have limited these technologies' wide application to areas of high visibility and profit. As the price/performance ratio of the equipment and techniques improves, we'll see more educational, medical, and industrial uses. This is just one part of the beginning in a new era of expression and communication.

No matter what the application, the development of realtime interactive technology will always require the combined efforts of artists and scientists. During the Renaissance, a driving curiosity about nature and a benevolent respect for the human mind created a fertile environment for new inventions and creative ideas. Many of those artistic developments and technological innovations are still admired today because of their universal appeal and their timeless qualities. Today, the field of realtime interactive entertainment may be the catalyst to once again make both the arts and sciences accessible, exciting, and meaningful to everyone.

Biography

Michael Limber joined Angel Studios in 1989, where he is Executive Producer, overseeing the 3D production of all projects. He has over ten years of experience in producing 3D computer animation for films, commercials, and music videos. At Angel Studios, he has been responsible for producing animation sequences in the feature film *The Lawnmower Man;* Peter Gabriel's music video, Mindblender, and ECCO: The Tides of Time, SEGA's sequel to the original game, Ecco the Dolphin. He is also lead 3D artist for Buggie-Boogie, a video game for the Nintendo 64. Prior to Angel Studios, he was head animator at Post Perfect and technical director at Digital Productions. He holds a B.S. degree in architecture from UC Berkeley and a Master's degree in industrial design from Pratt Institute.

Index

A

Abel, Bob, 406, 412
Above the Garage Productions, 239
Abrams M1 tank simulators, 436
Abstractions, 40
Academy of Moral Science of Institute of
    France, 495
Accelerator cards, 312
Acoustic cues, 138
Acoustic environment, sound in, 138
Action-adventure film, storyboard for,
    405–406
Actions
    buffer, 163
    definition of, 162
    within group, 163
Action/scrollers, 458
Actors, 162–166
    attributes, 168–170
    combining actions of, 163
Adventure, 341
Adventures in Toyland, 259
Aero, Kinney, 480
Agents, 79
    autonomy for autonomous, 166–168
    decision making in autonomous, 170–174
    definition of, 161
    interaction between avatars and, 161–162
    personality definition for, 168–170
Aha! experience, 232
Aids for disabled, 296–297
Aiming games, 450
Air Force One, 423
Air Traffic Control Training system, 123
Aladdin, 328, 357–372
Alcorn, Al, 449
Alexander, Joanna, 259, 285
Algorithms
    color cell compression, 315
    games based on, 156–157
    Heckbert, 315
    Lee's, 156–157
    software, for rendering, 299–301
America On-Line (AOL), 62
Amusement parks. *See also* Theme parks
    interactive technology at, 353–355

as model for interactive entertainment,
    154–155
Analog models, 100
Analog processing, 271–272
Analytical Sciences Corporation, The (TASC),
    123–124
Anamorphic wide-screen movies, 421–422
Anasazi petroglyphs, 186
Angels Flight, 187
Angel Studios, 519, 526
Animation
    3D, 313
    automated techniques, 515
    frame-by-frame, 5
    inverse causality in, 174–176
    procedural, 162–166
    read-time, 80
    versus movement, 233
Anti-aliasing, 318
Anti-aliasing, 107
Apple Computer, 133
    Vivarium Program of, 208
Application-layer interactivity, 78
Application programmer, 522
Applications programming interface (API), 80
Araki, John, 480
Aramaic, 130
Arcades, 446, 447–448
Arcade video games, 443–461
    content creation, 453–454
    distributor, 446
    economics in, 443–444
    future of, 459–460
    genres, 456–459
    history of, 449–452
    locations, 447–449
    manufacturer, 445, 446–447
    operator, 446
    reasons for, 444–445
    rules of game design, 454–456
    themes in, 452–453
Area 51, 461
ARPANET, 85
ART+COM, 312
Art director, 520
ArtGrabber, 461
Artificial experiences, 33, 44

This book is published as part of the SIGGRAPH Books Series with ACM Press Books, a collaborative effort among ACM SIGGRAPH, ACM Press, and Addison-Wesley Publishing Company. The SIGGRAPH Books Series publishes books on theory, practice, applications, and imaging in computer graphics and interactive techniques, some developed from courses, papers, or panels presented at the annual ACM SIGGRAPH conference.

Editor: Stephen Spencer, The Ohio State University

Editorial Board:
Mike Bailey, San Diego Supercomputer Center
Wayne Carlson, The Ohio State University
George S. Carson, GSC Associates
Ed Catmull, Pixar
Tom DeFanti, University of Illinois, Chicago
Richard L. Phillips, Los Alamos National Laboratory
Andries van Dam, Brown University

MEMBERSHIP INFORMATION

Founded in 1947, ACM is the oldest and largest educational scientific society in the information technology field. Through its high-quality publications and its services, ACM is a major force in advancing the skills and knowledge of IT professionals throughout the world. From a dedicated group of 78, ACM is now 85,000 strong, with 34 special interest groups, including SIGGRAPH, and more than 60 chapters and student chapters.

For more than 25 years, SIGGRAPH and its conferences have provided the world's forum for the interchange of information on computer graphics and interactive techniques. SIGGRAPH members come from many disciplines and include researchers, hardware and software systems designers, algorithm and applications developers, visualization scientists, educators, technology developers for interactive visual communications, animators and special-effects artists, graphic designers, and fine artists.

For further information about ACM and ACM SIGGRAPH, contact:

ACM Member Services
1515 Broadway, 17th floor
New York, NY 10036-5701
Phone: 1-212-626-0500
Fax: 1-212-944-1318
E-mail: acmhelp @ acm.org

ACM European Service Center
108 Cowley Road
Oxford , OX4 1JF, United Kingdom
Phone: +44-1865-382388
Fax: +44-1865-381388
E-mail: acm_europe @ acm.org

URL: http://www.acm.org